# From Different Shores

# From Different Shores

*Perspectives on Race and Ethnicity in America*

SECOND EDITION

Edited by

# Ronald Takaki

New York   Oxford
OXFORD UNIVERSITY PRESS
1994

Oxford University Press

Oxford   New York   Toronto
Delhi   Bombay   Calcutta   Madras   Karachi
Petaling Jaya   Singapore   Hong Kong   Tokyo
Nairobi   Dar es Salaam   Cape Town
Melbourne   Auckland   Madrid

and associated companies in
Berlin   Ibadan

Library of Congress Cataloging-in-Publication Data
From different shores : perspectives on race and ethnicity in America
edited by Ronald Takaki.—2nd ed.
p. cm.  Includes bibliographical references.
ISBN 0-19-508368-7
1. United States—Race relations.  2. United States—Ethnic
relations.  I. Takaki, Ronald T., 1939–
E184.A1F745      1994
305.8′00973—dc20   93-25535

9 8 7 6 5 4 3 2 1

Printed in the United States of America
on acid-free paper

# Contents

# From Different Shores

# Introduction: Different Shores

In the community where I lived as a child, my neighbors were Japanese, Chinese, Hawaiian, and Portuguese. Nearby there were Filipinos and Puerto Ricans. As I grew up, I sometimes wondered why—why were we from so many "different shores," from Asia and Europe as well as Hawaii itself, living together in Palolo Valley on the island of Oahu? My teachers and my textbooks did not explain the reasons why we were there.

After graduation from high school, I attended a college on the mainland where I found myself invited to dinners for "foreign students." I politely tried to explain to my kind hosts that I was not a foreign student; still they insisted that I accept their invitations. My fellow students (and even my professors) would ask me where I had learned to speak English. "In this country," I would reply. And sometimes I would add, "I was born in America, and my family has been here for three generations." Like myself, they had been taught little or nothing about America's ethnic diversity, and they thought I looked like a foreigner.

The college curriculum itself contributed to their perception of me. Courses in American literature and history, by not including knowledge about racial minorities, had rendered them outsiders. "American," in effect, meant "white." All of the readings assigned in my course on American literature, for example, were written by white authors. We did not read works by Zora Neale Hurston (*Their Eyes Were Watching God*), Carlos Bulosan (*America Is in the Heart*), and Toshio Mori (*Yokohama, California*). Here was a course on the literature of America, but it did not teach the literature of all Americans.

For graduate study, I entered a Ph.D. program in American history. And there I studied the history of America as if there had been no racial minorities in this country's past, certainly no Chicanos and no Asians. The war against Mexico was studied, and the Chinese were given a brief reference in discussions of the transcontinental railroad. Blacks were there, in the antebellum South, as slaves. And Indians were present, too, as obstacles to progress or as an ill-fated race. I was in an American history Ph.D. program, but I was not studying the history of all the peoples of America.

But I felt the stirrings of protest and agitation happening outside the university as the civil rights movement of the sixties awakened America to the presence of blacks and the problem of racial inequality. I found myself deeply involved in the study of race relations in the Old South. After completing a dissertation on the Southern defense of slavery, I began teaching black history but soon realized the need to study also the experiences of Native Americans, Chicanos, and Asian Americans. This awareness led me to broaden my focus and to write *Iron Cages: Race and Culture in 19th-Century America,* a comparative study of the experiences of the different racial groups (and also white workers and women) within the context of the culture and economy of the United States.

While writing this book, I returned on a sabbatical to the place where I had grown up. There, on hot afternoons, I often visited an old retired uncle, and the two of us would sit in the backyard and "talk story." During one of these discussions, my uncle exclaimed, "Hey, why you no go write a book about us, huh? After all, your grandfather came over here as a contract laborer. He worked on the plantation. And your mother was born on the plantation, and also all of your aunts and uncles." And I replied, "Why not?"

Some time after making this casual remark, I found myself examining old documents in archives and came across scores of business memoranda. One of them, dated August 22, 1890, from Theo. H. Davies and Company to C. McClennan, manager of the Laupahoehoe plantation, acknowledged receipt of an order for:

> tobacco
> portuguese laborers. We have ordered 20 men for you.
> lumber
> 7 ft. iron bar
> wool mattress
> olive oil

In another memorandum on July 2, 1890, the Davies Company wrote McClennan regarding an order for bone meal, canvas, "Japanese laborers," macaroni, and a "Chinaman." A letter of May 5, 1908, from H. Hackfield and Company (now American Factors) to George Wilcox of the Grove Farm plantation listed alphabetically orders for "Fertilizer" and "Filipinos." As I read these fading documents, I finally began to understand why peoples from all over the world lived in my neighborhood.

Recently, America's racial and ethnic diversity has been the focus of much attention. In 1990, for example, *Time* magazine published a cover story on "America's Changing Colors." "Someday soon," it announced, white Americans will become a "minority group." How soon? "By 2056, when someone born today will be 66 years old, the 'average' U.S. resident . . . will trace his or her descent to Africa, Asia, the Hispanic world, the Pacific Islands, Arabia—almost anywhere but white Europe." Leading this change in ethnic composition is California. "Whites of all ages account for just 58% of California's population. In San Jose bearers of the Vietnamese surname Nguyen outnumber the Joneses in the telephone directory 14 columns to eight." *Time* wondered what our society would be like when whites are no longer the majority. "The deeper significance of America's becoming a majority nonwhite society is what it means to the national psyche, to individuals' sense of what it is to be American. People of color have often felt that whites treated equality as a benevolence granted to minorities rather than as an inherent natural right. Surely that condescension will wither."

But is such a future so sure, or is *Time* overly optimistic? What does it mean for American society to be so diverse, and can racial inequality be overcome?

In *Ethnic America: A History* (1981), Thomas Sowell offers some answers. His scope is comprehensive. Though he overlooks Native Americans, he has chapters on the Irish, Germans, Jews, Italians, Chinese, Japanese, blacks, Puerto Ricans, and Mexicans. His report on ethnic America is cheerful and optimistic. "There are wide variations in the rates of progress among Americans," he states sanguinely, "but progress itself is pervasive." As Sowell notes, examples to support such a contention not only abound, they are also dramatic. Descendants of slaves today sit in Congress and on the Supreme Court, and

O. J. Simpson is hailed as an American phenomenon. Ethnic groups have made it or are making it into middle-class society. Many of them, especially Jews and Asian Americans, have family incomes above the national average. And even Puerto Ricans, Mexican Americans, and blacks are on the road to progress.

This new assessment has led Sowell to dismiss or deemphasize the importance of prejudice or group discrimination: "If bigotry alone was a sufficient causal explanation [for inequality], Jews and Japanese would not be among the most prosperous American ethnic groups." "Color," Sowell acknowledges, did play a "major role" in determining the fate of many Americans. But it was not an all-powerful determinant, he counters, and it has and can be overcome. How? Sowell examines different ethnic groups, one by one, in order to explain why ethnic Americans have been able to improve their lives.

Politics could not have been an important factor, Sowell contends, pointing out that "the Japanese, like the Chinese, studiously avoided political agitation for their rights." Neither was education the key to ethnic mobility and success: "The educational panacea is undermined by the history of groups like the Jews, the Chinese, and the Japanese, who first rose by their labor and their business sense and only later on could afford to send their children to college."

More important than their labor, Sowell argues, was their "middle class" orientation and values of discipline, obedience, politeness, hard work, thrift, industry, diligence, and self-reliance. Sowell sings high praises to the Chinese laundryman, the Japanese gardener, and the Jewish shopkeeper: "What made these humble occupations avenues to affluence was the effort, thrift, dependability, and foresight that built businesses out of 'menial' tasks and turned sweat into capital."

Sowell applauds the most successful ethnic groups—Jews and Japanese—as paragons of middle-class virtues. Jews, whose family incomes are the highest of any large ethnic group—72 percent above the national average—have a "very low rate of alcoholism" and a "traditional concern for cleanliness." The most important area of restraint, for Sowell, involves family size. Jewish families are among the smallest, and the average Japanese American woman in the thirty-five to forty-four age bracket has only 2.2 children compared to 3 children for the average American woman in the same age category. On the other hand, women of the less successful groups—blacks, Puerto Ricans, and Mexican Americans—have the "highest fertility rates." Thus, they have less financial and human resources to invest in individual children, enabling them to seize educational opportunities to advance themselves.

Sowell's historical study is mainly a prescription for the present. *Ethnic America* seeks to describe the successful ethnic groups in order to offer instruction to groups still in poverty. Sowell advises discontented racial minorities to avoid the "confrontationist" methods of "militant" blacks. They should shun reliance on government intervention and welfare. They should instead follow the example of the Japanese, whose "quiet persistence" and hard work have enabled them to rise from the internment camps of World War II to a family-income status 32 percent above the national average. Sowell's "history" contains a conservative message: accommodation and self-help should be the strategy for racial minorities.

But how seriously we consider Sowell's prescription should depend on our assessment of his scholarship. Sowell reports ethnic "progress," but how should progress be measured? In *Ethnic America,* we may have a case where the means of measurement may be the message. *How* we calculate success may determine our conclusions. For example, in his discussion of Puerto Ricans, Sowell compares the incomes of Puerto Rican families headed by males in the twenty-five to thirty-four age bracket with the incomes of "families of other Americans of the same description," demonstrating that the income of such Puerto Rican families is 96 percent of the other families and that Puerto Rican "progress" has occurred. But we need to know what proportion of all Puerto Rican families are headed by males; otherwise, we would be making conclusions based on families that do not represent the group itself. Furthermore, two-thirds of the Puerto Rican population on the mainland lives in New York, where both family incomes and the cost of living are higher than the national average.

Similarly, Sowell calls the high family income of Japanese Americans remarkable. But he fails to underscore two crucial characteristics of this group. First, more Japanese American families have two income earners than the average family. In 1970, both husbands and wives worked in over half of all Japanese American families, compared to 39 percent of all families in the country. Hence the fact that Japanese American families have higher earnings than the average family indicates that there are more members of each Japanese American family working. Second, Japanese Americans are concentrated in urban areas and also in Hawaii and California, states that have considerably higher average incomes and higher costs of living than the nation as a whole.

Even where Sowell's statistical analysis is accurate, his interpretation is sometimes open to question. According to Sowell, women of the less successful groups—blacks, Puerto Ricans, and Mexican Americans—have more children than women of the groups that have advanced themselves socially and economically. What does this finding mean? Here Sowell quips, "The rich get richer, and the poor have children." He views the high fertility rate of the women in these groups as a cause of their poverty: it "directly lowers the standard of living of a group by spreading a given income more thinly among family members." But, we need to ask, is a high fertility rate an effect or a cause of poverty?

In *Ethnic America,* Sowell assumes that the experiences of white ethnic groups and racial minorities have been different in degree rather than in kind. They were all "ethnic." But only blacks were enslaved, only Native Americans were removed to reservations, only Chinese were singled out for exclusion, and only Japanese Americans (not Italian Americans or German Americans) were placed in concentration camps. This difference between "ethnic" and "racial" experiences can be seen in the Naturalization Law of 1790. Sowell does not even mention this law, which remained in effect until 1952 and which reserved naturalized citizenship for whites only.

Finally, what does Sowell's analysis of ethnic America mean in terms of public policy? Whereas Sowell does not explicitly relate his historical thesis to public policy, he questions the need for and the political wisdom of affirmative action. If Japanese Americans can succeed through their own efforts and without government intervention, then so can blacks and other racial minorities. "Controversial" affirmative action programs, Sowell contends, have had "little or no effect beyond what had already been achieved under 'equal opportunity' policies in the 1960s." Moreover, the "public perception" of affirmative action has engendered "strong resentment" among whites generally. Thus, what we have in Sowell's celebration of the "progress" of ethnic America is a criticism of affirmative action.

Curiously, Sowell seems to have found some support or tacit agreement in radical or left circles, recently from Christopher Jencks in the *New York Review of Books.* In the conclusion of his review of Sowell's *Ethnic America,* Jencks observes: "In today's political environment the only argument that will persuade minorities not to seek protection from competition is prudential: certain short-term benefits, especially those that derive from reverse discrimination, may cost blacks more than the benefits are worth."

This statement is extraordinarily provocative, for Jencks considers himself a "radical" as opposed to a "conservative." Jencks identifies Sowell as the latter and explains what it means to be a conservative in terms of the affirmative action issue. Essentially, it involves an assessment of affirmative action as "reverse discrimination" and as "harmful" governmental efforts to eliminate discrimination. But what does it mean to be a radical on this issue? Here, as it turns out, Jencks is not a radical.

In his evaluation of Sowell, Jencks assumes the validity of the theory of reverse discrimination. He states, for example, that it is a "fact" that affirmative action policies have sometimes led to discrimination against whites. But he fails to question whether this fact is really a fact—to substantiate the claim of reverse discrimination. More important, Jencks does not provide a definition of racial discrimination. The term, Jencks should have made clear, describes the historical and official, government-sanctioned categorization of a group based on race for the purpose of social subordination and economic exploitation. An attempt at a definition might have clarified the difference between the racial experience and the white "ethnic" experience, and offered a way to assess the prospects for racial minorities to overcome inequality without the government acting affirmatively to eliminate it.

To use the term *reverse discrimination* to describe affirmative action is both confusing and incorrect. Affirmative action, contrary to a popular notion, does not impose quotas. Rather, it requires employers to assess the racial composition of their workers and to develop timetables and goals for creating greater opportunities for the employment of racial minorities. Thus, affirmative action is actually designed to address the legacy of past racial discrimination and existing inequality by training and identifying qualified individuals of excluded racial minorities and allowing them greater access to equality of opportunity in education and employment.

What Jencks does instead is to give scholarly legitimacy to the theory and claim of reverse discrimination. He is a "radical," yet he turns out to agree with Sowell, a "conservative." He presents his case in the progressive *New York Review of Books,* and does so as a "radical," advising racial minorities that affirmative action is not "prudential." However, his very analysis, by accepting Sowell's definition of racial discrimination and the validity of reverse discrimination, contributes in effect to the very "political environment" making affirmative action imprudent. Thus, in the end, Jencks, like Sowell, pushes upward the cost of benefits derived from affirmative action even as he asks racial minorities whether the price might not be too high.

"History," Sowell writes, "is what happened, not what we wish had happened. . . .

History can sometimes help us to assess our beliefs about the past or about the present or future." All of this is true. But clearly, as this discussion of Sowell shows, there are different ways to study race and ethnicity in America's past and present.

The collection of essays in this book invites students to participate in this lively discourse. Its title has a double meaning. *From Different Shores* refers to the multiple origins of Americans—how our roots can be traced to Europe, Africa, Latin America, Asia, and North America itself. Who we are and how we are perceived and treated in terms of race and ethnicity are conditioned by where we came from originally. But the title also describes the different and conflicting ways scholars have approached and understood the experiences of racial and ethnic groups—how they have stood on different shores in terms of their viewpoints. Like everyone else, scholars have ideas and beliefs about human nature and society. Their conceptions of what the moral universe is or should be, how people behave and should behave, what America is and what it should be, influence the ways they frame their questions, select and examine their evidence, and draw their conclusions.

In this anthology, essays representing a wide range of shores have been gathered between two covers in order to involve students in the discussion and debate over the nature and meaning of America's social diversity. By reading them side by side, we can discern the different ways scholars have addressed questions of race and ethnicity.

Several essays have been drawn from seminal books such as Winthrop Jordan's *White over Black: American Attitudes toward the Negro, 1550–1812,* John Higham's *Strangers in the Land: Patterns of American Nativism,* and Lester Thurow's *The Zero-Sum Society.* Other selections, such as Edna Bonacich's analysis of "ethnic antagonism" and Robert Blauner's essay on "internal colonialism," have broken new theoretical ground in the study of race relations. Some have been drawn from well-known controversial studies: Nathan Glazer's *Affirmative Discrimination* and Charles Murray's *Losing Ground.* The essays also represent new scholarship by leading minority intellectuals, including William Julius Wilson (*The Declining Significance of Race*), Mario García (*Desert Immigrants: The Mexicans of El Paso*), and Paula Gunn Allen (*The Sacred Hoop: Recovering the Feminine in American Indian Traditions*). Altogether the authors selected reflect the multiracial diversity the anthology seeks to study.

Mostly historical and sociological, the essays together enable us to examine Asian Americans, blacks, Chicanos, Native Americans, and Puerto Ricans as well as European immigrant or white "ethnic" groups. They have been organized into six parts: "Patterns," the historical configurations of race and ethnicity; "Culture," the realm of ideology and perceptions; "Class," the economic and material basis of social divisions; "Gender," the experiences of women and how they have intersected with race and class; "Public Policy," especially the debate over affirmative action and welfare; and "Prospects," with a focus on the "culture wars."

As you read the essays, you will find yourself asking: How have the experiences of racial minorities in the United States been similar to and different from each other? Is "race" the same as "ethnicity"? How has culture shaped race and ethnic relations? What has been the relationship between race and class? How can race and gender be compared? Moreover, how can racial inequality be explained, and what public policies or strategies are needed to address it?

# PART I
# Patterns

In the spring of 1980, two scholars found themselves standing on different shores, engaged in a face-to-face debate over the nature of racial inequality in America's past and present. Nathan Glazer of Harvard University and Ronald Takaki of the University of California at Berkeley had been invited by the University of Wisconsin to give keynote lectures at a conference on "Ethnicity and Public Policy." Their opposing perspectives reflected a dynamic discourse conditioned by nearly twenty years of political and social developments.

Both Glazer and Takaki had been influenced by the civil rights movement of the early sixties. They shared Martin Luther King's vision of an America where people would be judged by the content of their character rather than by the color of their skin. And they supported the Civil Rights Act which prohibited racial discrimination. But, as it turned out, the 1964 law constituted a very different landmark for each of them—the culmination of an American tradition of equality for Glazer and the turning point in the movement for equality for Takaki.

The Civil Rights Act of 1964, for Glazer, represented the view that the function of government should be negative: the state should only outlaw racial discrimination. No longer subjected to discrimination, racial minorities would be able to follow the path of European immigrants and their offspring and advance themselves as individuals into the mainstream of American society. Treated as an individual rather than as a member of a group, everyone would be judged according to merit. The law guaranteed to everyone the promise of America: equality of opportunity.

For Takaki, on the other hand, the 1964 law became a first step toward the realization of equality of condition. He doubted the sufficiency of the prohibition of racial discrimination: equality of opportunity for individuals was unlikely to occur in a society of unequal groups. Structures of inequality such as poverty, inferior education, occupational stratification, and inner-city ghettos required the government to act affirmatively and to promote opportunities for racial minorities based on group rights. The ideas of individualism and meritocracy actually reinforced the reality of racial inequality, for they in effect blamed minorities themselves for their impoverished conditions.

The divergent perspectives of Glazer and Takaki were sharpened by the political polarization occurring in society. The black revolts in Watts, Detroit, and Newark in the sixties exploded the notion that racism was a "Southern problem" and that civil rights was needed only for blacks below the Mason-Dixon line. The cry for black power and assertion of black pride challenged liberal assumptions of integration and assimilation. The development of ethnic studies programs in universities and colleges across the country provided new possibilities for the cultural diversification of the traditional curriculum. Meanwhile, the federal government developed mechanisms to enforce the 1964 Civil Rights Act. In 1965, President Lyndon Johnson issued Executive Order 11246, prohibiting racial discrimination by government contractors and requiring them to take "affirmative action" to remove the barriers of discrimination. Educational institutions also instituted admissions programs to diversify the racial composition of their students and provide educational opportunities to racial minorities.

But, by the early seventies, a white backlash was underway. One of the symbols of this reaction was a suit by Allan Bakke against the University of California, claiming that affirmative action had discriminated against him as a white person. The Bakke case joined the issue of whether the government should emphasize group rights in order to reduce racial inequality, or only prohibit racial discrimination. Bakke's lawyers charged that affirmative action constituted "reverse discrimination." But supporters of affirmative action replied that color-conscious programs to ensure educational and employment opportunities for racial minorities were necessary to overcome the effects of past discrimination. "In order to get beyond racism," Supreme Court Justice Harry Blackmun explained, "we must first take account of race. There is no other way. And in order to treat some persons equally, we must treat them differently."

Within this context of change and controversy, Glazer and Takaki found themselves reflecting on America's past. History, they thought, had to be studied, for beliefs about the past shaped views of the present. Knowing who we have been as a people told us who are and also who we should be. In 1975 Glazer presented his findings in "The Emergence of an American Ethnic Pattern," published as the opening chapter of his book, *Affirmative Discrimination: Ethnic Inequality and Public Policy*. Four years later, Takaki offered a different analysis of American history in *Iron Cages: Race and Culture in 19th-Century America*. The following year, the conference at the University of Wisconsin provided the forum for Glazer and Takaki to discuss their scholarly differences directly.

In this section, we have side by side Glazer's "The Emergence of an American Ethnic Pattern" and Takaki's "Reflections on Racial Patterns in America," originally presented at the University of Wisconsin conference. Read together, they show how differently the two scholars approach and understand America's past. They challenge us to assess how we view race and ethnicity. Are the racial minorities of today like the European immigrants of yesterday? In other words, will blacks and other racial minorities eventually make it into the mainstream of American society without government assistance, as did the Jews, Italians, and other groups originally from Europe? Or are the experiences of Asians, blacks, Chicanos, and Native Americans qualitatively different from the experiences of white "ethnic" groups? Finally, the two essays ask us to become more aware of how we think about history. How do we know what we know about our past?

# The Emergence of an American Ethnic Pattern

NATHAN GLAZER

In the middle of the last decade, we in the United States seemed to have reached a national consensus as to how we should respond to the reality of racial and ethnic-group prejudice and racial and ethnic-group difference. Almost simultaneously, we began to move away from that consensus into new divisions and a new period of conflict and controversy. The consensus was marked by three major pieces of legislation: the Civil Rights Act of 1964, the Voting Rights Act of 1965, and the Immigration Act of 1965. Following the passage of the Civil Rights and Voting Rights acts, the Federal government intervened firmly in the South to end the one-hundred-year resistance of the white South to full political, civil, and social equality for blacks, insofar as this resistance was embodied in law and public practice. The passage of the Immigration Act of 1965 marked the disappearance from Federal law of crucial distinctions on the basis of race and national origin. The nation agreed with this act that there would be no effort to control the future ethnic and racial character of the American population and rejected the claim that some racial and ethnic groups were more suited to be Americans than others.

In the phrase reiterated again and again in the Civil Rights Act of 1964, no distinction was to be made in the right to vote, in the provision of public services, the right to public employment, the right to public education, on the ground of "race, color, religion, or national origin." Paradoxically, we then began an extensive effort to record the race, color, and (some) national origins of just about every student and employee and recipient of government benefits or services in the nation; to require public and private employers to undertake action to benefit given groups; and school systems to assign their children on the basis of their race, color, and (some) national origins. This monumental restructuring of public policy to take into account the race, color, and national origin of individuals, it is argued by Federal administrators and courts, is required to enforce the laws against discrimination on these very grounds. It is a transitional period, they say, to that condition called for in the Constitution and the laws, when no account at all is to be taken of race, color, and national origin. But others see it as a direct contradiction of the Constitution and the laws, and of the consensus that emerged after long struggle in the middle 1960s.

I will examine . . . policies in three areas: employment, school desgregation, and residential location. I will analyze the position of those who support present policies and will argue that the consensus of the middle 1960s has been broken, and that it was and remains the right policy for the United States—right for the groups that had suffered, and in some measure still suffer, from prejudice and discrimination, and right for the nation as a whole.

But the first step is to try to characterize and understand the consensus of the middle 1960s. This is not to be understood as an historically new response to the unprecedented events of those years—the vicious resistance in great parts of the South to the efforts of blacks to practice their political rights, the South's resistance to school desegregation, the shocking assassination of a President identified with the hopes of suppressed minority groups. It is to be understood rather as the culmination of the development of a distinctive American orientation to ethnic difference and diversity with a history of almost 200 years. That orientation was shaped by three decisions. They were not taken all at once, or absolutely, or in full consciousness of their implications, but the major tendencies of American thought and political action have regularly given their assent to them.

From Nathan Glazer, *Affirmative Discrimination: Ethnic Inequality and Public Policy*. Copyright © 1975 by Nathan Glazer. Reprinted by permission of Basic Books, Inc., Publishers.

The three decisions were:

First, the entire world would be allowed to enter the United States. The claim that some nations or races were to be favored in entry over others was, for a while, accepted, but it was eventually rejected. And once having entered into the United States—and whether that entry was by means of forced enslavement, free immigration, or conquest—all citizens would have equal rights. No group would be considered subordinate to another.

Second, no separate ethnic group was to be allowed to establish an independent polity in the United States. This was to be a union of states and a nation of free individuals, not a nation of politically defined ethnic groups.

Third, no group, however, would be required to give up its group character and distinctiveness as the price of full entry into the American society and polity.

There is of course an inevitable breathtaking arrogance in asserting that *this* has been *the* course of American history. It would be almost equally breathtaking to assert that *any* distinctive course can be discerned in the history of the shaping of the American people out of many different stocks. It is in part an act of faith to find any *one* course that the development of American society has in some way been reaching toward: It smacks of the unfashionable effort to give a "purpose," a direction, to history. Certainly this direction is not to be thought of as some unconscious immanent tendency continuing to reveal itself in American history. Direction in history is taken only in the concrete actions of men and of groups of men. Those actions in the United States have included—in direct conflict with the large direction I have described—the enslavement of the Negro, anti-immigrant and anti-Catholic movements that have arisen again and again in American life, the near extermination of the American Indian, the maintenance of blacks in a subordinated and degraded position for a hundred years after the Civil War, the lynching of Chinese, the exclusion of Oriental immigrants, the restriction of immigration from Southern and Eastern Europe, the relocation of the Japanese and the near confiscation of their property, the resistance to school desegregation, and so forth. If we are to seek a "direction" in American history that defines a distinctive approach to the relationship of the various ethnic groups that make up American society, the sequence of events just listed might well be made the central tendency of American history. Many current writers and scholars

would have it so: They argue that racism defines our history—racism directed against blacks, Indians, Mexican Americans, Puerto Ricans, Filipinos, Chinese, Japanese, and some European ethnic groups. Many would have it that even the last ten years should be interpreted as a losing battle against this racism, now evident in the fact that colleges and universities resist goals and targets for minority hiring, that preferential admissions to professional schools are fought in the courts, that the attempt to desegregate the schools in the North and West has now met a resistance extremely difficult to overcome, that housing for poor and minority groups is excluded from many suburbs.

I think this is a selective misreading of American history: that the American polity has instead been defined by a steady expansion of the definition of those who may be included in it to the point where it now includes all humanity; that the United States has become the first great nation that defines itself not in terms of ethnic origin but in terms of adherence to common rules of citizenship; that no one is now excluded from the broadest access to what the society makes possible; and that this access is combined with a considerable concern for whatever is necessary to maintain group identity and loyalty. This has not been an easy course to shape or maintain, or to understand. There have been many threats to this complex and distinctive pattern for the accommodation of group difference that has developed in American society. The chief threats in the past were, on the one hand, the danger of a permanent subordination of certain racial and ethnic groups to others, of the establishment of a caste system in the United States; and on the other hand, the demand that those accepted into American society become Americanized or assimilated, and lose any distinctive group identity. The threat of the last ten years to this distinctive American pattern, however, has been of quite another sort. The new threat that followed the most decisive public actions ever taken to overcome subordination and caste status was that the nation would, under the pressure of those recently subordinated to inferior status, be permanently sectioned on the basis of group membership and identification, and that an experiment in a new way of reconciling a national polity with group distinctiveness would have to be abandoned. Many did not and do not see this latter possibility as any threat at all, but consider it only the guarantee and fulfillment of the commitment of American society to admit all peoples into full citizenship. They see the threat to a decent multigroup society rising from quite another direction: the arrogance and anger of the American people, specifically those who are descended from colonists and earlier immigrants, aroused by the effort to achieve full equality for all individuals and all groups. The prevailing understanding of the present mood is that those who have their share—and more—want to turn their backs on the process that is necessary to dismantle a caste society in which some groups are held in permanent subordination. I think this is a radical misreading of the past few years. . . .

But [my] task [here] is a rather different one: If the history of American society in relationship to many of the groups that make it up is not a history of racism, what is it? How do we define an emergent American attitude toward the problem of the creation of one nation out of many peoples?

I have suggested there were three major decisions—decisions not taken at any single point of time, but taken again and again throughout our history—which defined this American distinctiveness. The first was that all should be welcome and that the definition of America should be a political one, defined by commitment to ideals, and by adherence to a newly created or freshly joined community defined by its ideals, rather than by ethnicity. Inevitably "American" did come to denote an "ethnicity," a "culture," something akin to other nations. A common life did create a common culture, habits, language, a commonness which parallels the commonness of other nations with their more primordial sense of commonness. But whereas all European and many Asian nations have grown out of a primordial group of long history, bound together by culture, religion, language, in the American case there was a continual struggle between the nation understood in these terms—akin to those in which the French, or English, or Germans understood themselves—and the nation understood in very different terms.

Yehoshua Arieli describes a number of ways in which a pattern of national identification has been achieved. In some cases, national identification is imposed by force; in others, it has grown gradually, and ". . . resulted from a long-established community of life, traditions, and institutions. . . ." But ". . . in the United States, national consciousness was shaped by social and political values which claimed universal validity and which were nevertheless the American way of life. Unlike other Western nations, America claimed to possess a 'social

system' fundamentally opposed to and a real alternative to . . ."—and here I edit Arieli, but not against his meaning—". . . [other social systems], with which it competed by claiming to represent the way to ultimate progress and a true social happiness."[1] These different terms in which American nationality defined itself consisted not only of the decisive revolutionary act of separation from England and self-definition as a separate nation. They also included for many of those who founded and helped define the nation the rejection of ethnic exclusivity.

Three writers to my mind have, in recent years, given the best definition of what it meant to found a nation in this way: Seymour Martin Lipset in *The First New Nation;* Hans Kohn in his book *American Nationalism: An Interpretive Essay;* and Yehoshua Arieli in *Individualism and Nationalism in American Ideology.*

Arieli argues forcefully that the American Revolution should *not* be seen as another uprising of an oppressed nation, but as an event whose main shapers presented it as significant for the world and all its peoples:

All the attempts made by Americans to define the meaning of their independence and their Revolution showed an awareness that these signified more than a change in the form of government and nationality. Madison spoke of the American government as one which has "no model on the face of the globe." For Washington, the United States exhibited perhaps the first example of government erected on the simple principles of nature, and its establishment he considered as an era in human history. . . . John Adams was convinced that a greater question than that of American Independence "will never be decided among men." For Jefferson, America was the proof that under a form of government in accordance "with the rights of mankind," self-government would close the circle of human felicity and open a "widespread field for the blessings of freedom and equal laws." Thomas Paine hailed the American Revolution as the beginning of the universal reformation of mankind and its society with the result "that man becomes what he ought." For Emerson, America was ". . . a last effort of the Divine Providence in behalf of the Human race."[2]

We might of course expect a second-generation sociologist, a scholar who found refuge here, and another refuge who has become a scholar in a newly founded democratic nation to respond to these claims, to reverberate to them, so to speak. We might also expect Jewish scholars to respond to these claims, for if the United States was very late in fulfilling its promise to blacks, Indians, Mexican Americans, and others—that is, those of other races—it almost from the beginning offered an open field and freedom to those who practiced another religion. Can a more searching examination, however, sustain these claims? Could it not also be said that American independence and the establishment of a new country was little more than the assertion of the arrogance of British colonists, refusing to accept a moderate overseas government more solicitous of the rights of Indians and blacks than they were, insisting on taking the land from the Indians and on the right to import and hold black men as slaves, and eventually threatening their neighbors with imperial expansion?

Our history, indeed, included all this. Even the appropriation of the name "American" for the citizens of the United States is seen by our neighbors to the north and to the south as a symbol of arrogance. Yet other interpretations of this appropriation are possible. The Americans *did* accept as the name for themselves a name with no ethnic reference, a name even with no limited geographical reference (since the Americas include all the Western Hemisphere). One side of this self-naming may be seen as a threat to the rest of the Americas and as arrogance in ignoring their existence. But another side must also be noted: the rejection by this naming of any reference to English or British or any other ethnic or racial origins, thus emphasizing in the name itself the openness of the society to all, the fact that it was not limited to one ethnic group, on language, one religion.

Lipset argues that the American nation from the beginning established and defined its national identity on the basis of its decisive break, through revolution, with England, and, by extension, with the entire old world. This weakened the ethnic identification with England. Further, two values became dominant in American society and the shaping of American character, equality and achievement, and these values can be seen sharply marked in American society from the beginning of its independent political existence.[3] One point about these two values that I would emphasize is that, by their nature, they cannot remain ethnically exclusive. And the most far-sighted of the early leaders understood this. Thus, to quote Hans Kohn:

Thomas Jefferson, who as a young man had opposed immigration, wished in 1817 to keep the doors of America open, "to consecrate a sanctuary for those whom the misrule of Europe may compel to seek happiness in other climes." . . . This proclamation of an open port for immigrants was in keeping with Jefferson's faith in America's national mission as mankind's vanguard in the fight for individual liberty, the embodiment of the rational and humanitarian ideals of eighteenth century man.

The American nation,

Hans Kohn continues, summarizing Jefferson's point of view,

was to be a universal nation—not only in the sense that the idea which it pursued was believed to be universal and valid for the whole of mankind, but also in the sense that it was a nation composed of many ethnic strains. Such a nation, held together by liberty and diversity, had to be firmly integrated around allegiance to the American idea, an idea to which everyone could be assimilated for the very reason that it was a universal idea. To facilitate the process of integration, Jefferson strongly opposed the settlement of immigrants in compact groups, and advocated their wide distribution among the older settlers for the purpose of "quicker amalgamation."[4]

Of course, to one tradition we can oppose another. If Jefferson was positive about the immigration of other groups, Benjamin Franklin was suspicious. "For many years," Arieli writes, "he strenuously argued against the wisdom of permitting the immigration of non-English settlers, who 'will never adopt our language or customs anymore than they can acquire our complexion.' "[5] Undoubtedly, he was influenced by the substantial number of Germans in Pennsylvania, itself established as an open colony of refuge:

This will in a few years [Franklin wrote] become a German colony: Instead of their Learning our Language, we must learn theirs, or live as in a foreign country. Already the English begin to quit particular Neighborhoods surrounded by Dutch, being made uneasy by the Disagreeableness of dissonant Manners; and in Time, Numbers will probably quit the Province for the same Reason. Besides, the Dutch under-live, and are thereby enabled to under-work and under-sell the English; who are thereby extremely incommoded, and consequently disgusted, so that there can be no cordial Affection or Unity between the two Nations.[6]

The themes are, of course, familiar ones: They were to be repeated for many groups more distant from the Anglo-American stock than the Germans, who were, after all, of related tongue and Protestant religion. And yet this was a private comment, to be set against a public one that, again to quote Kohn, "extolled Anglo-America as a place of refuge."[7]

There were two traditions from the beginning, traditions exemplified by different men and social groups, and carried in tension within the same men. Yet even to say there were two traditions makes the issue somewhat sharper than it could have been during the early history of the United States. After all, the very men who spoke about the equal rights of all men accepted slavery. If they spoke of the United States as a sanctuary for all, they clearly thought of men very like themselves who might be seeking it and were not confronted with the hard realities of men of very different culture, religion, and race taking up their offer. In addition, we must take account of the expansive rhetoric of a moment in which a nation was being founded. Yet stipulating all of these cautions, there was a development implied in the founding documents and ideas which steadily encouraged the more inclusive definitions of who was eligible to become a full participant in American life. In the Revolution and its aftermath, limitations on participation in public life by the propertyless, Catholics, and Jews were lifted. Waiting in the wings, so to speak, were other categories, implied in the founding principles. That some others waited for almost two centuries, and that their equality came not only because of founding principles but because of complex social and political developments is true; but the principles were there, exerting their steady pressure, and indeed even in 1975 much of the argument over how to define full equality for different groups revolves around a Constitution that dates to 1787.[8]

As Arieli puts it: "Whatever the impact of universal concepts on the American historical experience, the conservative and nativistic interprets of American history, no less than their opponents, concede that American nationality has to be defined, at least to some degree, by reference to certain political and social concepts; that it is a way of life and an attitude which somehow represents ultimate social values. . . ."[9]

There is no Supreme Historian, sitting in heaven, who totes up the record and tells us which way the balance of history ran. One picks out a dominant theme, on the basis of one's experience as well as one's knowledge, and our choice is made, in part, on the basis of our hopes for the future as well as our experience. In the 1950s and 1960s men like Kohn and Arieli wanted to emphasize the inclusive tradition; in the later 1960s and in the 1970s, many historians and other scholars want to show us the exclusive tradition. There is enough to choose from on both sides. We can quote Melville, writing in 1849:

There is something in the contemplation of the mode in which America has been settled, that, in a noble breast, should forever extinguish the prejudices of national dislike. Settled by the people of all nations, all nations may claim her for their own. You cannot spill a drop of American blood without spilling the blood of the whole world. . . . We are not a narrow tribe of men with a bigoted Hebrew nationality—whose blood has been debased in the attempt to ennoble it, by maintaining an exclusive succession among ourselves. No; our blood is as the flood of the Amazon, made up of a thousand noble currents all pouring into one. We are not a nation, so much as a world. . . . On this Western Hemisphere all tribes and peoples are forming into one federal whole. . . .[10]

Or James Fenimore Cooper, writing in 1838:

The great immigration of foreigners into the country, and the practice of remaining, or of assembling, in the large towns, renders universal suffrage doubly oppressive to the citizens of the latter. The natives of other countries bring with them the prejudices of another . . . . state of society; . . . and it is a painful and humiliating fact, that several of the principal places of this country are, virtually, under the control of this class, who have few convictions of liberty. . . . Many of them cannot even speak the language of the land, and perhaps a majority of them cannot read the great social compact, by which society is held together.[11]

In certain periods, it seems clear, one voice or another was dominant. The uprising of the white South in the Civil War marked the most determined effort to change the pattern into one in which other races and groups, labeled inferior, were to be held in permanent subjection and subordination. A new justification was to be established for this "heresy," as Arieli dubs it—and in the American context, heresy it was. Justification was to be found in religion, in pragmatic necessity, in political theory, even surprisingly enough in Auguste Comte's new-founded science of sociology, which was drawn upon to show the superiority of slave labor to Northern, immigrant, free labor, and of a society founded on slavery to one founded on free immigration.[12]

It is revealing that one great effort to avoid the conflict consisted of the rapid upsurge of the "American" party [the "Know-Nothings"] which labored to unite discordant political factions by making ethnic and religious loyalties the basis of national identification. It sought to substitute for traditional American values a nationalism of the Old World type based on common descent and religion, and thus to divert against the "foreigners" the antagonisms that existed among the native-born. Similarly, the theory of race which justified Negro slavery also aimed to create an identity between North and South on the basis of a common belief in white superiority and through territorial expansion. Yet the historical situation and the national tradition frustrated these efforts and turned the conflict between free and slave-holding states into a gigantic struggle over the nature of American social ideals.[13]

After early remarkable successes, the Know-Nothings disintegrated before the rise of the new Republican party, thus setting a pattern that other nativist movements were to follow again and again, such as the American Protective Association of the 1890s and the Ku Klux Klan of the 1920s—first a sudden upsurge that seemed to carry all before it, and then, equally suddenly, disintegration. The challenges to the central American pattern, brief and intense, were rapidly overtaken by the major tendency to a greater inclusiveness. The Know-Nothings disintegrated, and the South lost the war. The heresy was, for a while, extirpated.

In the wake of the Civil War, the great Southern heresy that had threatened the idea of American nationality as broadly inclusive seemed crushed. As John Higham writes of those postwar years:

America had developed a fluid, variegated culture by incorporating alien peoples into its midst, and the experience had fixed in American thought a faith in the nation's capacity for assimilation. This faith, carrying with it a sense of the foreigner's essential identification with American life, expressed itself in a type of nationalism that had long offset and outweighed the defensive spirit of nativism. A cosmopolitan and democratic ideal of nationality made assimilation plausible to Americans. . . .

The twin ideals of a common humanity and of equal rights continued in the 1870's and 1880's to foster faith in assimilation. Temporarily the tasks of post-war reconstruction even widened assimilationist ideals; for the Radical Republicans' effort to redeem the southern Negro, to draw him within the pale of the state, and to weld the two races into a homogeneous nationality discouraged emphasis on human differences. To James Russell Lowell, for example, just and equal treatment of black men meant simply an enlargement of the Christian mission which the United States had long performed in bringing together the peoples of all nations in a common manhood. And Elisha Mulford, philosopher of Reconstruction, argued that the nation "is inclusive of the whole people. . . . There is no difference of wealth, or race, or physical condition, that can be made the ground of exclusion from it."[14]

But of course, new threats and new heresies were rising, and the United States was soon to enter a dark age in which the promise of an all-embracing citizenship and nationality, already a hundred years old, was, for a while, quite submerged. Indeed, the very New England elite who had refused to accept slavery and celebrated the open door themselves began to undergo a significant change as the flood of immigration poured into the country after the Civil War, a flood that became increasingly Catholic, increasingly non-English speaking, increasingly Jewish and Central and Eastern European as the century wore on. By the 1890s, a new criticism—which took many forms—of an inclusive idea of American citizenship was arising. The New England intellectuals, now displaced politically and culturally, no longer carried on the tradition of the American revolution. Having attacked the racist ideology of the South before the Civil War, many succumbed to a new, if milder, racism which placed the Anglo-Saxon or "Germanic" element of the American people at the apex of world evolution as the carriers of some special racial commitment to liberty and free government. On quite a different cultural level, waves of anti-Catholicism spread through the masses of white Protestant farmers and workers, peaking in the American Protective Association of the late 1880s and 1890s, which had as rapid a rise—and fall—as Know-Nothingism before the Civil War. Anti-Semitism for the first time appeared in the United States. Some scholars discern it in the Populist movement of the 1890s, some do not. But all recognize it in an increasing exclusivism of wealthy Eastern Americans in the same period. In the West, an anti-Chinese movement became virulent among white workingmen, and led to the first restriction of American immigration in 1882. By the end of the decade, the strongest and darkest thread of this skein of prejudice and discrimination dominated the rest as the modest gains of Reconstruction were swept aside in the South, Jim Crow laws were fastened on the free Negro, the last Negro representatives were swept from Congress, and a rigid caste system was imposed upon the black, by law in the South and custom in the North.[15]

Each thread of this complex pattern deserves full analysis, and in the present mood, in which the American past is being reviewed by scholars representing many oppressed groups, and in a time when many see the United States as the chief force of reaction in the world, each thread is receiving such analysis. For fifty years, between the 1890s and the 1930s, exclusivism was dominant. It affected many groups—blacks and Orientals, Jews and Catholics, Indians and Mexican Americans—in many ways. One can at least explain some of the reasons for the reaction against admitting all people into the country and to full citizenship. People of position felt threatened by the incoming flood of immigrants. Workers and shopkeepers without stable position also felt threatened, by the Chinese, the blacks, the Catholics, the immigrants, with the same fears that Franklin had expressed 150 years before over the Germans "under-living, under-selling, and under-working" the English. Those not in direct competition with the immigrant and the black felt the fears just as strongly, as we see in the case of the farmers, who tried to understand the sudden falls in price which threatened to destroy them by resorting to a belief in dark plots by international financial forces. Fears do not justify prejudice, discrimination, and racism, but they help explain it. And the expansion of American society to include strangers from all over the world was not without its real losses as well as its imaginary fears.

Barbara Solomon has recorded the story of the New England intellectuals at the turn of the century. Earlier, they had supported free immigration as well as abolition. Thus, long before Emma Lazarus, James Russell Lowell delivered some verses quite reminiscent of her poem on the Statue of Liberty, in an ode delivered at Harvard in 1861. He spoke of the American nation as:

> *She that lifts up the mankind of the poor,*
> *She of the open soul and open door,*
> *With room about her hearth for all mankind!*[16]

And in an address delivered in 1878, Emerson wrote: "Opportunity of civil rights, of education, of personal power, and not less of wealth; doors wide open . . . invitation to every nation, to every race and skin, . . . hospitality of fair field and equal laws to all. Let them compete, and success to the strongest, the wisest, and the best."[17] By the end of the century, many had quite given up their faith in democracy and the equality of all peoples and had become enamored of the notion that American liberty sprang from German forests and could not be maintained by the flood of immigrants from Eastern and Southern Europe. (Of course, not all New England intellectuals took this course. Preeminently in opposition were Charles Eliot, President of Harvard—though not, alas, his successor, President Lowell—and William James. Eliot wrote in 1920: "I should

like to be saved from loss of faith in democracy as I grow old and foolish. I should be very sorry to wind up as the three Adamses did. I shall not, unless I lose my mind."[18]) Essentially, what troubled the New England intellectuals who no longer followed the democratic faith of Emerson was the threat to American homogeneity, for a measure of homogeneity had indeed existed before the heavier floods of immigration had begun. In our present-day mood of easy analysis of American racism, we would argue that they were defending their economic, political, and social interests. But their economic interests were not threatened by immigration: Quite the contrary, the immigrants gave New England industry an important source of cheap labor. Their political interests were not threatened, for their local political domination had already been lost to the Irish immigrants when the flood of East Europeans and Italians began seriously to concern them in the 1890s. Indeed, these new immigrants offered them, perhaps, a chance to regain political power. Their social interests were not deeply involved, for there seemed little chance that the new immigrants would join them in polite society.

Where, then, did they feel threatened? They felt they were losing their country, that what they knew of as America was disappearing and becoming something else, and that American culture was going to be radically changed into something they would not recognize. Small-town life, country pleasures, certain forms of education, modes of recreation, characteristic tendencies in religion—this whole complex, they feared, was in danger. As we learn from Solomon's book, no crude or simple prejudice activated them. Many of the old New Englanders who favored immigration restriction were active in social work among the immigrants, and some were patrons of bright immigrant youths. But they did not want to see the American culture they knew go.

As one of them wrote, in a passage quoted by Horace M. Kallen: "We are submerged beneath a conquest so complete that the very name of us means something not ourselves. . . . I feel as I should think an Indian might feel, in the face of ourselves that were."[19] Henry James, returning to this country in 1907 after an absence of twenty-five years—he still considered himself an American—expressed this shock most vividly: "This sense of dispossession . . . haunted me so, I was to feel . . . that the art of beguiling or duping it became an art to be cultivated—though the fond alternative vision was never long to be obscured . . . of the luxury of some such close and sweet and *whole* national consciousness as that of the Switzer and the Scot."[20]

Toward the end of his life, William Dean Howells, who had enjoyed seeing French Canadians and Italians around Boston in the 1870s and had praised the Jewish immigrant writer Abraham Cahan, wrote a novel, *The Vacation of the Kelwyns,* subtitled *An Idyll of the Mid-1870's.* We are introduced to a New England landscape in the year of the centennial celebrations of 1876. Kelwyn, a university lecturer, is spending the summer with his family in a large Shaker family house, now empty. The New England countryside is slightly menacing that year with "tramps"—unemployed workers— and foreigners wander through it: a Frenchman with a trained bear, Italian organ grinders, some gypsies. Kelwyn bears no antipathy to them—quite the contrary, they enliven the scene, and, as he says, they cook better than the natives, and may help make life pleasanter. And yet, one feels an unutterable sadness over the passing of a peculiarly American civilization. The Shaker house is empty, and will never be filled again; the surviving Shakers have misguidedly furnished it for the Kelwyns with new furniture; the New England countryside is different from what it has been; and the year of the centennial—Howells seems to be saying— marks the passing of something simple and sweet in America. Indeed, the centennial itself involves deeper feeling in some of the characters in the book than we can imagine any national celebration since evoking.

In the North, exclusivism expressed itself in resistance to immigration from Eastern and Southern Europe and suspicion of immigrant settlements in the cities—of their habits, their culture, their impact on political life and on urban amenities. The Negroes were present—they always had been—but they were so few and so far down the social scale that they were scarcely seen as a threat to anything. In the South, exclusivism was directed primarily against the Negroes, though Catholics and Jews came in for their share of prejudice and, on occasion, violence. In the West, the Chinese and the Japanese were the main targets of a pervasive racism which included the Mexicans and the Indians.

The dismantling of this system of prejudice and discrimination in law and custom began in the 1930s. In the North, the ethnic groups created by the new immigration began to play a significant role in politics; and blacks, after the disenfranchisement of the 1890s, began again to appear in politics. The last mass anti-Catholic movement was the Klan's in the 1920s. It had a short life, and was in eclipse by the time Al Smith ran for President in 1928. Anti-Semitism had a longer life, but the war against Hitler ended with the surprising discovery that anti-Semitism, so strong in the Thirties, was undergoing a rapid and unexpected deflation. And similarly with anti-Chinese and Japanese prejudice. The immigration restriction law of 1924 was modified to accept at least token numbers of people from all nations and races in 1952, and all elements of national or racial preference were expunged in 1965.

Of course, the major bastion of race discrimination was the South, and the legal subordination of the Negro there remained firm throughout the 1930s and 1940s. But twenty years of liberal domination of national politics, by a coalition in which in Northern cities blacks played an important role, finally made its effects felt in the administration of President Truman. The Armed Forces were desegregated, national demands for the enfranchisement of Southern blacks became stronger and began to receive the support of court decisions, and a major stage in the elimination of discriminatory legislation was reached with the Supreme Court decision of 1954 barring segregation in the public schools. With the Civil Rights Act of 1964 and the Voting Rights Act of 1965, the caste system of the South was dismantled. The thrust for equality now shifted from the legal position of the group to the achievement of concrete advances in economic and political strength.

Thus for the past forty years, the pattern of American political development has been to ever widen the circle of those eligible for inclusion in the American polity with full access to political rights. The circle now embraces—as premature hyperbolic statements made as long as 200 years ago suggested it would—all humanity, without tests of race, color, national origin, religion, or language. . . .

Two other elements describe the American ethnic pattern, and these are not as easily marked by the processes of political decision-making, whether by court, legislature, or war. The first additional element is that the process of inclusion set limits on the extent to which different national polities could be set up on American soil. By "polity" I refer to some degree of political identity, formally recognized by public authority. Many multiethnic societies do recognize different ethnic groups as political entities. In the Soviet Union, each is formally entitled to a separate state or autonomous region (though these distinctive units exercise their powers in a state in which all individuals and subunits are rigidly controlled by a central dictatorship). Even a group dispersed throughout the Soviet Union such as the Jews is recognized as a separate nationality; and at one time, this nationality had rights, such as separate schools, publications, publishing houses. In Eastern Europe, where successor states to the German, Russian, and Austro-Hungarian Empire were set up after World War I, once again national rights were given to groups, even to such groups as the Jews, who were dispersed throughout the national territory. In nations that have been created by migration, such as the United States, we do not have examples of something like "national rights."

But the United States is more strict than others in preventing the possibility that subnational entities will arise. Consider the case of Canada, which is also a multiethnic society. The major minority national group, the French, is a compactly settled group which was conquered in the eighteenth century: It was not created through migration into a preexisting homogeneous or multiethnic nation. There are far more extensive national rights for the French than the United States allows for any group. Bilingualism is recognized not only in the areas of French settlement, but throughout the country. It is required of civil servants.

But what is the position of the "third element," those neither of English nor French origin? Their language has rapidly become English (except in the isolated prairie settlements of Eastern Europe farmers); nevertheless, as French rights have become more and more secured, they, too, have come to demand some special rights. In contrast with the United States, Canadian nationality is made up of *two* distinct founding ethnic groups, the French Canadians and the descendants of settlers from the original conquering power, to which have been added many ethnic groups derived from immigrants. There is a certain resistance among the third element—whether Jews in Montreal and Toronto, or Ukrainians in the West—to identifying fully with or assimilating to one or the other founding group, in part because these founding groups persist in maintaining specific ethnic characteristics of an English or French character. This is understandable: Canada was not founded in a revolutionary break from the fatherland, whether French or English, and while it is true a distinct Canadian personality and character did develop in both the French

and English element, no great emphasis was placed on specifically distinguishing "Canadian" from everything "non-Canadian."[21] This created a problem for new immigrant groups: Were they to maintain their original ethnic characteristics to the same extent that the founding groups did? And it created a problem for the polity. To what extent were the new immigrant groups to be encouraged to do so, or hindered in doing so? Thus, becoming Canadian did not imply, to the same extent that becoming American did, an abandonment of immigrant ethnic traits and a becoming something different. And so, the assimilation of ethnic groups in Canada did not proceed as rapidly as that of their ethnic relatives in the United States.

Among the possibilities for making political accommodation to groups of different ethnic character in a contemporary state, the United States falls near one end of the spectrum in denying formal recognition for any purpose to ethnic entities. In contrast to Canada, we do not ask for "ethnicity" in our census—though some government census sample surveys have recently done so—nor do we demand that each respondent select an ethnic origin.

Our pattern has been to resist the creation of formal political entities with ethnic characteristics. The pattern was set as early as the 1820s, when, as the historian of American immigration, Marcus Hansen, describes it, a number of European groups thought of establishing a New Germany or a New Ireland in the United States. He writes:

> The first step in any of these dreams [to establish branches of other nations on American soil] was the acquisition of land. But the government of the United States, though possessed of millions of acres, proved unwilling to give a single acre for the purpose. It expressed its opinion in unmistakable terms in the year 1818 when the Irish societies of New York and Philadelphia, burdened with a large number of charitable cases, petitioned Congress for a land grant in the West on which to establish their dependents. Congress refused, agreeing with the report of a special committee that it would be undesirable to concentrate alien peoples geographically. If a grant were made to the Irish, the Germans would be the next, and so with other nationalities. The result would be a patchwork nation of foreign settlements. Probably no decision in the history of American immigration policy possesses more profound significance. By its terms the immigrant was to enjoy no special privileges to encourage his coming; also he was to suffer no special restrictions. His opportunities were those of the native, nothing more, nothing less.[22]

No new nations would be established on American soil. We were to be, if a Federal republic, a republic of states, and even the states were not to be the carriers of an ethnic or national pattern. Most divergent from this norm, perhaps, is New Mexico, a state created out of conquered territory with a settled population, or the special rights of the Spanish-origin settlers of the Gadsden Purchase in Arizona; but even in those states, the rights of the Spanish-speaking barely lead to the creation of an ethnic state, although some militant Chicano leaders would perhaps like to see this happen.

Finally, there was a third set of decisions that defined the American ethnic pattern: Any ethnic group could maintain itself, if it so wished, on a *voluntary* basis. It would not be hampered in maintaining its distinctive religion, in publishing newspapers or books in its own language, in establishing its own schools, and, indeed, in maintaining loyalty to its old country.

This was a policy, if one will, of "salutary neglect." If immigrants could not establish new polities, they could do just about anything else. They could establish schools in their own language. They could teach their own religion, whether it was the ancient faith of Rome or the newly founded variants of Judaism and Islam developed by American blacks. When the state of Washington tried, in the early 1920s, to make public education a state monopoly, the Supreme Court said it could not.[23] Immigrants could establish their own churches and, under the doctrine of state-church separation, these would neither be more favored nor less favored than the churches of the original settlers which had once been established churches. They could establish their own hospitals, cemeteries, social service agencies to their own taste. All would be tax exempt: The state, in effect, respected whatever any group more or less wanted to consider education, or health and welfare, or religion, or charity. (Polygamy was one exception.) Indeed, the hospitals and social service agencies of these groups were even eligible for state funds, just as the institutions set up by the churches and groups of the early settlers had been. Immigrants could send money freely to their homelands, they could support the national movements of their various groups, and they could also, relatively easily, get tax exemption for their contributions to anything that smacked of religion, education, health and welfare, or charity.

There was no central public policy organized around the idea that the ethnic groups were a positive good, and therefore should be allowed whatever freedom they needed to maintain themselves. Policymakers generally never thought of the matter. It was, rather, that there was a *general* freedom, greater than in most other countries, to do what one willed. The mere fact that city planning and the controls associated with it were so much weaker than in other countries made it easy to set up churches, schools, and the like. In a society in which land could easily be bought and sold, fortunes easily made (and unmade), and mobility was high, there were, in effect, two sets of forces set loose: One force tended to break up the ethnic communities, for it was easy in American society to distance oneself from family and ethnic group, if one wanted to; but at the same time, and this is what is often forgotten, it was also easy to establish the institutions that one desired. This meant, of course, that every church divided again and again: The state was disinterested, and thus every variant of liberalism and orthodoxy could express itself freely in institutional form. It also meant there was no hindrance to the maintenance of what one wished to maintain.

One of the interesting general findings of ethnic research is that affluence and assimilation have double effects. On the one hand, many individuals become distant from their origins, throw themselves with enthusiasm into becoming full "Americans," and change name, language, and religion to forms that are more typical of earlier settlers. On the other hand, however, many use their increased wealth and competence in English to *strengthen* the ethnic group and its associations. It is hard to draw up a balance as to which tendency is stronger, because different people evaluate different effects differently. Thus undoubtedly, with longer residence in the United States, folk aspects of the culture weaken, and those attached to them feel that the original culture is lost. Yet associational and organizational forms of ethnicity are strengthened. For example, the one-room school, the *heder,* where Jewish children learned their letters, their prayers, and a bit of Bible under the tutelage of an Old World teacher, disappeared; so it become possible to say that the true old East European Jewish culture was gone. But regularly organized religious and Hebrew schools, with classrooms and teachers after the American pattern, increased greatly in number, and more Jewish children had some formal Jewish education under the organized system than under the folk system. Or, to take another example, undoubtedly, in 1975, the more folkish aspects of Ukrainian culture have weakened, both for the pre-World War II and post-World War II immigrants. This weakening is associated with assimilation and higher income. But now there are chairs for Ukrainian studies at Harvard, supported by funds raised by Ukrainian students. It is this kind of tradeoff that makes it so difficult to decide whether there is really, as Marcus Hansen suggested, a third-generation return to ethnic origins and interests. There is a return, but as is true of any return, it is to something quite different from what was there before.

In any case, whatever the character of the return, it is American freedom which makes it possible, as American freedom makes possible the maintenance and continuity and branchings out of whatever part of their ethnic heritage immigrants and their children want to pursue.

When we look now at our three sets of decisions—that all may be included in the nation, that they may not establish new nations here, and that they may, nevertheless, freely maintain whatever aspects of a national existence they are inclined to—we seem to have a classic Hegelian series of thesis, antithesis, and synthesis. The synthesis raises its own new questions, and these become steadily more sharp, to the point where many argue we must begin again with a new thesis. For the three sets of decisions create an ambiguous status for any ethnic group. The combination of first, you may become full citizens; second, you may not establish a national entity; third, you may establish most of the elements of a national entity voluntarily without hindrance, does not create an easily definable status for the ethnic group. The ethnic group is one of the building blocks of American society, politics, and economy, none of which can be fully understood without reference to ethnic group formation and maintenance, but this type of group is not given any political recognition or formal status. No one is "enrolled" in an ethnic group, except American Indians, for whom we still maintain a formally distinct political status defined by birth (but any individual Indian can give up this status). For all public purposes, everyone else is only a citizen. No one may be denied the right to political participation, to education, to jobs because of an ethnic status, nor may anyone be given better access to political appointments or election, or to jobs, or education because of ethnic status. And yet we pore over the statistics and try to estimate relative standings and movements among ethnic groups.

A distinction of great importance to our society is thus given no formal recognition and yet has great meaning in determining the individual's fate. In this sense, ethnicity is akin to "class" in a liberal society. Class does not denote any formal status in law and yet plays a great role in the life of the individual. Ethnicity shares with class—since neither has any formal public status—a vagueness of boundaries and limits and uncertainty as to the degree to which any person is associated with any grouping. No member of the upper, middle, or lower class—or choose what terms you wish—needs to act the way most other members of that class do; nothing but social pressure will hold him to any behavior. Similarly with persons whom we would consider "belonging" to ethnic groups: They may accept that belonging or reject it. Admittedly, there are some groups, marked by race, where belonging is just about imposed by the outside world, as against other less sharply marked groups. Nevertheless, the voluntary character of ethnicity is what makes it so distinctive in the American setting. It is voluntary not only in the sense that no one may be required to be part of a group and share its corporate concerns and activities; no one is impelled *not* to be part of a group, either. Ethnicity in the United States, then, is part of the burden of freedom of all modern men who must choose what they are to be. In the United States, one is required neither to put on ethnicity nor to take it off. Certainly this contributes to our confusion and uncertainty in talking about it.

Undoubtedly, if this nation had chosen—as others have—either one of the two conflicting ideals that have been placed before us at different times, the "melting pot" or "cultural pluralism," the ambiguities of ethnic identity in the United States and the tensions it creates would be less. Under the first circumstance, we would have chosen a full assimilation to a new identity. Many nations have attempted this: some forcefully and unsuccessfully, as did Czarist Russia in relation to certain minority groups; some with a supreme self-confidence, such as France, which took it for granted that the status of the French citizen, *tout court,* should satisfy any civilized man; some, with hardly any great self-consciousness, such as Argentina, which assimilated enormous numbers of European immigrants into a new identity, one in which they seemed quite content to give up an earlier ethnic identity, such as Spanish or Italian. If a nation does choose this path of full assimilation, a clear course is set before the immigrant and his children. Similarly, if the principle is to be that of cultural pluralism, another clear course is set. We have not set either course, neither the one of eliminating all signs of ethnic identity—through force or through the attractions of assimilation—nor the other of providing the facilities for the maintenance of ethnic identity.

But our difficulties do not arise simply because of the ambiguities of personal identity. They arise because of the concrete reality that, even in a time of political equality (or as close to political equality as formal measures can ensure), ever greater attention is paid to social and economic inequality.

If we search earlier discussions of the immigrant and of ethnic groups, we will not find any sharp attention to these inequalities. It was assumed that time alone would reduce them, or that the satisfactions of political equality would be sufficient. It was assumed, perhaps, that social and economic inequalities would be seen as *individual* deprivations, not as *group* deprivations. But there was one great group whose degree of deprivation was so severe that it was clearly to be ascribed to the group's, not the individual's, status. This was the Negro group. As we concentrated our attention in the 1960s on the gaps that separated Negroes from others, other groups of somewhat similar social and economic status began to draw attention to *their* situation. And as these new groups came onto the horizon of public attention, still others which had not been known previously for their self-consciousness or organization in raising forceful demands and drawing attention to their situation entered the process. What began as an effort to redress the inequality of the Negro turned into an effort to redress the inequality of all deprived groups.

But how is this to be done? And does not the effort to redress upset the basic American ethnic pattern? To redress inequalities means, first of all, to define them. It means the recording of ethnic identities, the setting of boundaries separating "affected" groups from "unaffected" groups, arguments among the as yet "unaffected" whether they, too, do not have claims to be considered "affected." It turned out that the effort to make the Negro equal to the *other* Americans raised the question of who *are* the other Americans? How many of them

can define their own group as *also* deprived? The drawing of group definitions increased the possibilities of conflicts between groups and raised the serious question, what is legitimate redress for inequality?

In 1964, we declared that no account should be taken of race, color, national origin, or religion in the spheres of voting, jobs, and education (in 1968, we added housing). Yet no sooner had we made this national assertion than we entered into an unexampled recording of the records of the color, race, and national origin of every individual in every significant sphere of his life. Having placed into law the dissenting opinion of *Plessy* v. *Ferguson* that our Constitution is color-blind, we entered into a period of color- and group-consciousness with a vengeance.

Larger and larger areas of employment came under increasingly stringent controls so that each offer of a job, each promotion, each dismissal had to be considered in the light of its effects on group ratios in employment. Inevitably, this meant the ethnic group of each individual began to affect and, in many cases, to dominate consideration of whether that individual would be hired, promoted, or dismissed. In the public school systems, questions of student and teacher assignment became increasingly dominated by considerations of each individual's ethnic group: Children and teachers of certain races and ethnic groups could be assigned to this school but not to that one. The courts and government agencies were called upon to act with ever greater vigor to assure that, in each housing development and in each community, certain proportions of residents by race would be achieved, and a new body of law and practice began to build up which would, in this field, too, require public action on the basis of an individual's race and ethnic group. In each case, it was argued, positive public action on the basis of race and ethnicity was required to overcome a previous harmful public action on the basis of race and ethnicity.

Was it true that the only way the great national effort to overcome discrimination against groups could be carried out was by recording, fixing, and acting upon the group affiliation of every person in the country? Whether this was or was not the only way, it is the way we have taken. . . .

# NOTES

1. Yehoshua Arieli, *Individualism and Nationalism in American Ideology,* Cambridge, Massachusetts: Harvard University Press, 1964 (Penguin Books edition, 1966, pp. 19–20).

2. Arieli, *op. cit.*, pp. 86–87.

3. Seymour Martin Lipset, *The First New Nation*, New York: Basic Books, 1963, esp. Chap. 2, "Formulating a National Identity," and Chap. 3, "A Changing American Character?"

4. Hans Kohn, *American Nationalism: An Interpretive Essay*, New York: Macmillan, 1957 (Collier Books edition, 1961, p. 144).

5. Arieli, *op. cit.*, p. 44.

6. Kohn, *op. cit.*, pp. 143–144, quoting from Max Savelle, *Seeds of Liberty: The Genesis of the American Mind*, New York: Knopf, 1948, p. 567 f.

7. Kohn, *op. cit.*, p. 143.

8. On the legal position of Jews, see Oscar and Mary F. Handlin, "The Acquisition of Political and Social Rights by the Jews in the United States," *American Jewish Year Book*, Vol. 56, New York: American Jewish Committee, 1955, and Philadelphia: The Jewish Publication Society of America, 1955, pp. 43–98. There is no equally convenient summary for the legal position of Catholics, but see Anson Phelps Stokes, *Church and States in the United States*, New York: Harper and Bros., 1950, Vol. I, Chaps. V and XII.

9. Arieli, *op. cit.*, pp. 27–28.

10. From *Redburn: His First Voyage*, quoted in Kohn, *op. cit.*, pp. 153–154.

11. From *The American Democrat*, New York: Knopf, p. 135, quoted in Kohn, *op. cit.*, p. 162.

12. Arieli, *op. cit.*, pp. 293–305.

13. Arieli, *op. cit.*, p. 292.

14. John Higham, *Strangers in the Land: Patterns of American Nativism, 1860–1925*, New Brunswick, New Jersey: Rutgers University Press, 1955, pp. 20–21.

15. For this period, see Higham, *op. cit.*; Seymour Martin Lipset and Earl Raab, *The Politics of Unreason: Right-Wing Extremism in America, 1790–1970*, Chaps. 3–4, New York: Harper & Row, 1970; C. Vann Woodward, *The Strange Career of Jim Crow*, New York: Oxford University Press, 1955.

16. Kohn, *op. cit.*, p. 161.

17. Kohn, *op. cit.*, p. 143.

18. Barbara Miller Solomon, *Ancestors and Immigrants: A Changing New England Tradition*, Cambridge, Massachusetts: Harvard University Press, 1956, p. 176.

19. Horace M. Kallen, *Culture and Democracy in the United States*, New York: Boni and Liveright, 1924, p. 93. Kallen does not give the writer's name but describes him as "a great American man of letters, who has better than anyone else I know interpreted to the world the spirit of America as New England." The writer was probably his teacher at Harvard, to whom he dedicated this book, Barrett Wendell.

20. Henry James, *American Notes*, New York: Charles Scribner's Sons, 1946 [originally 1907], p. 86.

21. Seymour Martin Lipset analyzes the significance of the difference in the political origins of the United States and Canada in "Revolution and Counterrevolution: The United States and Canada," Chap. 2 in *Revolution and Counterrevolution: Change and Persistence in Social Structures*, New York: Basic Books, 1968.

22. Marcus Hansen, *The Immigrant in American History*, Cambridge, Massachusetts: Harvard University Press, 1940, p. 132.

23. *Pierce v. Society of Sisters*, 268 U.S. 510 (1925). Of course, as public and bureaucratic controls multiply in every part of life, this freedom is restricted, and not only for ethnic groups. It means that the establishment of church or school in a single-family house—a typical pattern—may run into zoning and planning restrictions, and often does; that the establishment of a nursery or an old-age home in less than institutional quarters fulfilling state requirements becomes almost impossible. New groups suffer probably more from these restrictions than old groups. But I note that a magnificent nineteenth-century Richard Morris Hunt-designed home for the aged in New York, maintained by an old Protestant welfare agency, is to be demolished because it cannot meet state standards of "proper" facilities for the aged. All suffer from the ever-widening reach of state controls.

# Reflections on Racial Patterns in America

RONALD TAKAKI

When Allan Bakke filed his suit against the University of California Medical School at Davis in 1974, he surely did not expect his grievance to be elevated into circles of scholarship. Yet scholarly efforts to provide a theoretical justification for Bakke's claim that affirmative action policy discriminated against whites were already well underway. Consequently, four years later, racial minorities found themselves facing a scholarly theory of "reverse discrimination" as well as the Supreme Court's *Bakke* decision itself. During this time, Nathan Glazer of Harvard University has emerged as the leading architect of this new anti-affirmative action scholarship, and his book, *Affirmative Discrimination: Ethnic Inequality and Public Policy,* spearheaded the intellectual assault on affirmative action. Published in 1975 and issued in paperback in 1978, the book has been widely read and has commanded much attention in the conference rooms of public policy makers as well as society at large.[1]

Excerpts from reviews quoted on the back cover of the paperback edition are intended to do more than announce its importance. They warn us not to ignore the book:

> A tempered, factually argued, vigorous polemic against the predominant drift of public policy on racial issues over the past decade. Public issues only infrequently receive serious, sustained arguments of this high order.
> *The New York Times Book Review*

> Glazer writes provocatively, instead of ideologically, about a sensitive subject that needs airing.
> *Business Week*

> His views, based on solid research, deserve the widest debate.
> *The Christian Science Monitor*[2]

As the excerpts suggest, the book has more than a scholarly purpose. Indeed, as Glazer himself makes clear in his 1978 Introduction, he is seeking to influence public policy makers, particularly the justices of the Supreme Court in their deliberations on affirmative action cases such as the Allan Bakke case. "In *Affirmative Discrimination,*" he writes, "I attacked the justice and the wisdom of shifting from individual rights to group rights in devising policies to overcome racial and ethnic-group discrimination and its heritage." While Glazer claims that he has "no intention of 'predicting' the course of the Supreme Court," he describes the courts as the "final battleground" for the issue of affirmative action and encourages Americans who share his "vision to engage in litigation and submit amicus briefs against the new policies." In short, *Affirmative Discrimination* is Glazer's amicus brief.[3]

His book requires our attention. We could, I think, avoid his book if it were only an empirical study of employment, education and housing. But his analysis also advances a theory of an "American ethnic pattern" to interpret American history and to influence present public policy making.[4]

At the heart of Glazer's theory is a hope, a vision of a good society in which "men and women are judged on the basis of their abilities rather than their color, race, or ethnic origin." The "first principle of a liberal society," he insists, is the assertion that "the individual and the individual's interests and good and welfare are the test of a good society." Thus for Glazer, there is only one proper solution to the problem of racial inequality: the heritage of discrimination can and should be overcome by "simply attacking discrimination."[5]

A theoretician of the anti-affirmative action backlash, Glazer gives articulation to an angry popular mood, a widespread resentment against the demands of racial minorities, and a moral outrage felt by the Allan Bakkes of America. He both describes and supports the point of

From Ronald Takaki, "Reflections on Racial Patterns in America: An Historical Perspective," *Ethnicity and Public Policy* I (1982): 1–23. Reprinted by permission of the Board of Regents, University of Wisconsin System.

view of the white ethnics: "They entered a society in which they were scorned; they nevertheless worked hard, they received little or no support from government or public agencies, their children received no special attention in school or special opportunity to attend college. . . . They contrast their situation with that of blacks and other minority groups today and see substantial differences in treatment. They consider themselves patriotic and appreciative of the United States even though they received no special benefit." While Glazer admits the comparison may be "crude and unfair," he essentially agrees with its main contention, that blacks and other racial minorities should not receive "special" opportunities, "special" treatment, and "special" benefits. Instead, they should emulate the example of the white ethnics.[6]

In his opening chapter, "The Emergence of an American Ethnic Pattern," Glazer develops the historical and theoretical underpinnings of his critique of affirmative action policies. He uses this to provide the conceptual framework for the entire book and refers to its main points throughout the study. Viewing affirmative action policies from his historical perspective, Glazer asks at the end of the book: "How have policies which so sharply reverse the consensus developed over two hundred years of American history established themselves so powerfully in a scant ten years?"[7]

But what was that "consensus" which had developed over two hundred years? According to Glazer, the mid-1960s witnessed the emergence of a "national consensus" on solutions to the problems of racial and ethnic prejudice. This consensus was reflected in three laws: the Civil Rights Act of 1964, the Voting Rights Act of 1965, and the Immigration Act of 1965. Essentially these laws prohibited discrimination based on race, color, religion, or national origin. But "paradoxically," Glazer argues, a new policy of affirmative action or "discrimination" was then instituted, and the consensus was "broken." Thus was shattered the "culmination" of the development of a "distinctive American orientation of ethnic difference and diversity with a history of almost 200 years."[8]

Glazer bases his theory of an American ethnic pattern on three historical developments or "decisions":

First, the entire world would be allowed to enter the United States. The claim that some nations or races were to be favored in entry over others was, for a while, accepted, but it was eventually rejected. And once having entered into the United States—and

whether that entry was by means of forced enslavement, free immigration, or conquest—all citizens would have equal rights. No group would be considered subordinate to another.

Second, no separate ethnic group was to be allowed to establish an independent polity in the United States. This was to be a union of states and a nation of free individuals, not a nation of politically defined ethnic groups.

Third, no group, however, would be required to give up its group character and distinctiveness as the price of full entry into the American society and polity.

All three decisions were inclusionist rather than exclusionist. Though a notion favoring the entry of particular immigrants or races was accepted "for a while," American society eventually allowed the inclusion of all racial and ethnic groups. The decisions were also egalitarian: all citizens, regardless of race, ethnicity, or religion, would have equal rights. These decisions also promoted tolerance and acceptance of cultural and ethnic diversity: a group would be allowed to maintain its cultural values and identity. Finally, all three decisions minimized, even denied, differences between the experiences of "racial" and white "ethnic" groups in American history.[9]

While Glazer describes the three decisions as integral parts of the "central" American pattern, he does acknowledge the existence of contrary "actions"—black slavery, anti-immigrant nativism, the "near extermination" of the American Indian, the lynching of Chinese, the relocation of Japanese Americans during World War II, and so forth. He even notes that, "for fifty years, between the 1890s and the 1930s, exclusivism was dominant." Nevertheless, for Glazer all of these contrary developments do not represent the "large direction," the "major tendency to a greater inclusiveness," in American history.[10]

Thus the three decisions are claimed to be major components of historical reality in America, and as a historian I had to ask whether the claim could stand the test of a rigorous and critical examination of the historical evidence. More specifically, I had to ask whether Glazer's theory of an American "ethnic" pattern could explain the history of racial minorities in America.

The first is the most important of all three decisions, for it permitted the "entire" world to enter the United States and extended "equal" rights to all citizens regardless of their means of entry. In order for us to determine whether this decision actually existed historically and whether it represented a major pattern, we need to review the history of citizenship and the right of suffrage in the United States. We also need to develop a more precise chronological measurement of how long "for a while" really was.[11]

The phrase "for a while" could refer to the early national period, when Congress made its first effort to define American citizenship in the Naturalization Law of 1790. This law specified that only free "white" immigrants would be eligible for naturalized citizenship. Clearly, this law did not allow the "entire" world to enter the United States as potential citizens or members of the body politic. Non-"white" immigrants were not permitted to be naturalized until the Walter-McCarran Act of 1952, which stated that "the right of a person to become a naturalized citizen of the United States shall not be denied or abridged because of race. . . ." What is important to note here about the first naturalization law is the fact that it remained in effect for 162 years, or for a very long time.[12]

One of the first laws to be passed by Congress, the Naturalization Law of 1790 acquired special significance in the nineteenth century due to westward expansionism and the entry of Chinese laborers into America. The two developments were closely linked. Shortly after the end of the war against Mexico, which enabled the United States to annex California, Aaron H. Palmer, a "Counsellor of the Supreme Court of the United States," submitted to Congress a plan for the extension of American markets into Asia and the importation of Chinese workers to develop American industries. "The commodious port of San Francisco," he declared, "is destined to become the great emporium of our commerce on the Pacific; and so soon as it is connected by railroad with the Atlantic States, will become the most eligible point of departure for steamers to . . . China." To build the transcontinental railroad as well as to bring the "fertile lands of California" under cultivation, Palmer recommended the immigration of Chinese. Here, in this remarkable report, was a public policy blueprint which explicitly integrated American expansion into Asia with Asiatic immigration to America.[13]

During the next three decades, tens of thousands of Chinese were recruited to work in this country. Between 1850 and 1880, the Chinese population in the United States increased from 7,520 to 105,465, a fifteen-fold increase; in 1870 the Chinese constituted 8.6 percent of the total population of California and an impressive 25 percent of the wage-earning force. But the inclusion of the Chinese in the economic structure was accompanied by their political exclusion. Not "white," they were ineligible for naturalized citizenship. They were, in effect, migrant laborers, forced to be foreigners forever. Unlike white "ethnic" immigrants such as Italians, Poles, and Irish, the Chinese were a politically proscribed labor force. They were a part of America's production process but not her body politic. American businessmen expected them to be here only on a temporary basis and located them in a racially segmented labor market. Central Pacific Railroad employer Charles Crocker, for example, told a legislative committee: "I do not believe they are going to remain here long enough to become good citizens, and I would not admit them to citizenship." Crocker also explained how the presence of Chinese workers could elevate white workers in a stratified racial/occupational structure: "I believe that the effect of Chinese labor upon white labor has an elevating instead of degrading tendency. I think that every white man who is intelligent and able to work, who is more than a digger in a ditch . . . who has the capacity of being something else, can get to be something else by the presence of Chinese labor easier than he could without it. . . . There is proof of that in the fact that after we get the Chinamen to work, we took the more intelligent of the white laborers and made foremen of them." Businessmen "availed" themselves of this "unlimited" supply of "cheap" Chinese labor to build their railroads and operate their factories. After the Chinese migrant workers had completed their service, they were urged to return to their homeland, while others came to replace them. The employers of Chinese labor did not want these workers to remain in this country and become "thick" (to use Crocker's term) in American society.[14]

Enacted long before the entry of Asians into America, the Naturalization Law also had another consequence for immigrants from the east. Where white "ethnic" immigrants were legally entitled to own land in this country, Asian immigrants were subjected to a special form of discrimination. Defined as "aliens ineligible for citizenship," Chinese and other Asian immigrants were also denied, by state legislation, the right to own property in California, Washington, Arizona, Oregon, Idaho, Nebraska, Texas, Kansas, Louisiana, Montana, New Mexico, Minnesota, and Missouri. Thus Asian immigrants were excluded from the very process of land ownership, social mobility, and transformation of immigrants into Americans which Frederick Jackson Turner celebrated in his famous essay on the significance of the frontier in American history.[15]

Ironically, the Naturalization Law also excluded Native Americans from citizenship. Though they were born in the United States, they were regarded as members of tribes, or as domestic subjects or nationals; their status was considered analogous to children of foreign diplomats born here. As "foreigners," they could not seek naturalized citizenship, for they were not "white." Even the Fourteenth Amendment, which defined federal citizenship, did not apply to Native Americans. While Native Americans could become United States citizens through treaties with specific tribes or through allotment programs such as the Dawes Act of 1887, general citizenship for the original American was not granted until 1924.[16]

But what happened to nonwhite citizens? Did they have "equal" rights, particularly the right of suffrage? Citizenship did not necessarily carry this right, for states determined the requirements for voting. A review of this history reveals a basic political inequality between white citizens and nonwhite citizens.

The 1965 Voting Rights Act did not actually culminate a history of political inclusion for blacks. In the North, during the most important period of political inclusion—the era of Jacksonian Democracy—the establishment of universal manhood suffrage was for white men only. In reality, the inclusion of greater numbers of white men, including recent Irish immigrants, was usually accompanied by the exclusion of black citizens from the suffrage. The New York Constitution of 1821, for example, granted the vote to all free "white" male citizens who possessed a freehold, paid taxes, had served in the state militia, or had worked on the highways; it also retained the property requirement for black citizens, increasing it from $100 to $250. The Pennsylvania Constitution of 1838 went even further: it provided for universal "white" manhood suffrage and thus disenfranchised black citizens completely. In the South, except for a brief period during Reconstruction, black citizens were systematically excluded from participation in the political process. Thus the 1965 law, enacted in response to massive black pressure and protest under the leadership of Martin Luther King, was a break from a long history of denial of voting rights to racial as opposed to "ethnic" minority citizens.[17]

This difference between race and ethnicity in terms of suffrage may also be seen in the experiences of Native Americans. While the Treaty of Guadalupe-Hidalgo had offered United States citizenship to Mexicans living within the acquired territories, the 1849 Constitution of California granted the right of suffrage only to every "white" male citizen of the United States and only to every "white" male citizen of Mexico who had elected to become a United States citizen. A color line, in short, had been drawn for the granting of suffrage to American citizens in California. Native Americans were also proscribed politically in other states. The Fifteenth Amendment, which provided that the right to vote shall not be denied or abridged because of race or color, did not apply to noncitizen Indians. Even after Indians were granted citizenship under the 1924 law, however, many of them were designated "Indians not taxed" or "persons under guardianship" and disenfranchised in states like Arizona, New Mexico, Idaho, and Washington.[18]

Study of the history of citizenship and suffrage disclosed a racial and exclusionist pattern. For 162 years, the Naturalization Law, while allowing various European or "white" ethnic groups to enter the United States and acquire citizenship, specifically denied citizenship to other groups on a racial basis. While suffrage was extended to white men, it was withheld from men of color. Thus what actually developed historically in American society was a pattern of citizenship and suffrage which drew a very sharp distinction between "ethnicity" and "race."

Like the first one, the second and third decisions also require our critical examination. According to Glazer, all Americans would be viewed and treated as "free individuals," not members of "politically defined ethnic groups" or "polities." Still, Americans could, if they wished, maintain an ethnic group identity on a voluntary basis. They would be allowed to have their distinctive religion, their own language, their own schools, and even to maintain their "loyalty" to their "old country."[19]

While decisions two and three may have been true for white "ethnic" groups like the Irish and Germans, they certainly do not accurately describe the historical experiences of "racial" groups. This difference was particularly evident during World War II when Japanese Americans, unlike German Americans and Italian Americans, were forcefully interned in relocation camps. They were, in effect, defined and treated as a "polity" by the federal government. Of the 120,000 internees, 70,000 were United States citizens by right of birth. Japanese in America were not regarded as "free individuals" but as members of a polity simply because of their Japanese ancestry. In the camps, draft-age Nisei men were required to fill out and sign a loyalty questionnaire entitled "Statement of United States Citizenship of Japanese Ances-try." At the end of the long list of questions, they were asked:

> No. 27. Are you willing to serve in the armed forces of the United States on combat duty wherever ordered?

> No. 28. Will you swear unqualified allegiance to the United States of America and faithfully defend the United States from any or all attack by foreign or domestic forces, and forswear any form of allegiance or obedience to the Japanese em-peror, to any other foreign government, power or organization?

Young men of Italian or German ancestry were not subjected to such a "loyalty" test.[20]

The Native American experience also does not fit well into decisions two and three. Indians have historically been formally treated as mem-bers of polities, not as "free individuals." The Constitution of the United States recognized Indian tribes as polities: Article I, Section 2, excluded from state representation in Congress "Indians not taxed"; and Article I, Section 4, granted Congress the power to "regulate Com-merce with foreign Nations . . . and with In-dian Tribes." The Indian Trade and Intercourse Act of 1802 provided that no land cessions in Indian territory could be made except by "treaty" between Congress and the Indian tribe. The view of Indian tribes as polities was explicitly expressed in the 1871 case of *McKay* v. *Campbell*. Denying the Fourteenth Amend-ment had extended citizenship to Indians, the court ruled:

> To be a citizen of the United States by reason of his birth, a person must not only be born within its territorial limits, but he must also be born subject to its jurisdiction. . . . But the Indian tribes within the limits of the United States have always been held to be distinct and independent political communities, retaining the right of self-government, though subject to the protecting power of the United States.

The removal of Choctaws, Creeks, and Chero-kees in the 1830s and the relocation of Sioux and Cheyennes on reservations in the 1870s were also based on the conception of Indian tribes as polities.[21]

This policy of defining Indians as members of tribes and as members of culturally distinct groups was used as a means to control them. The strategy can be seen in the actions of two

important policy makers on Indian affairs. President Andrew Jackson, claiming Indians were culturally distinct and could not survive in white civilization, proposed their removal be-yond the Mississippi River. Regarding Indian tribes as polities, Jackson was able to negotiate removal treaties with them and to transfer Indian lands into the "markett," to use the president's spelling. As Commissioner of Indian Affairs in 1872, Francis Amasa Walker saw that he could not continue Jackson's policy of removing Indians beyond the Mississippi River. By then the "markett" had already reached the Pacific Ocean, and a new future for the Indian in the West had to be defined. Walker's proposal was to "consolidate" Indian tribes onto one or two "grand reservations." Accord-ing to his plan, warlike tribes would be relo-cated on extensive tracts in the West, and all Indian "bands" outside of the reservation would be "liable to be struck by the military at any time, without warning, and without any implied hostility to those members of the tribe" living within the reservation. For Walker, it was a policy of military convenience to treat Indian tribes as polities.[22]

Yet, it must be noted, federal Indian policies were not entirely consistent. At times they also reflected an inclusionist pattern. Even Walker's reservation system was designed to "civilize" Indians and prepare them for entry into Ameri-can white society. His proposal would enable the federal government and to extend over Indians what Walker called "a rigid reformatory discipline." The crucial term is *reformatory*. On the reservations Indians would be trained, "required" to learn the arts of industry, and placed on a course of "self-improvement." Not allowed to "escape work," Indians would be helped over the rough places on "the white man's road." Furthermore, some federal poli-cies prohibited the recognition of Indian tribes as independent polities in the United States. The Indian Appropriation Act of 1871, for example, provided that "hereafter no Indian nation or tribe within the territory of the United States shall be acknowledged or recognized as an independent nation, tribe, or power, with whom the United States may contract by treaty." But the aim of this law was not to recognize Indians as "free individuals" but to reduce tribal power and give railroad corpora-tions access to Indian lands and right-of-way through Indian territory.[23]

Federal inclusionist policies also required the Indian to give up his group character and distinctiveness as the "price" of full entry into

Dawes act - Nathan

American society and polity. Nowhere can this be seen more clearly than in the Dawes Act of 1887, also known as the Indian Allotment Act. This law, which white reformers hailed as the "Indian Emancipation Act," promised to bring to a close a "century of dishonor." What it actually did was to grant the president power, at his discretion and without the Indians' consent, to break up reservations and allot lands to individual Indians. The Dawes Act also permitted the federal government to secure tribal consent to sell "surplus" reservation lands—lands which remained after allotment had taken place—to white settlers. The effect of this policy on the Indian land base was predictable. Between 1887 and 1934, when the allotment policy was terminated, 60 percent of the Indian land base had been transferred to whites: 60 million acres had been sold as "surplus" lands to whites by the federal government, and 27 million acres—or two-thirds of the land allotted to individual Indians—had been transferred to whites through private transactions. This tremendous reduction of the Indian land base has had a very destructive impact on Native American cultures—their distinctive religions, languages, and ethnic group identities. The law also conferred citizenship upon the allottees and any other Indians who would abandon their tribes and adopt the "habits of civilized life." Thus the Dawes Act, offering Indians entry, exacted a "price."[24]

Still, Glazer insists that the history of American society in relation to its many groups is "not a history of racism," and he lines up three authorities to back his claim: Yehoshua Arieli, Hans Kohn, and Seymour Martin Lipset.[25]

Arieli's main point in his *Individualism and Nationalism in American Ideology* supports Glazer's inclusionist hypothesis. The American experience, according to Arieli, has emphasized individualism, egalitarianism, and freedom rather than ethnic or racial group characteristics and limitations. He traces these ideas back to the founding fathers, noting that "citizenship was the only criterion which made the individual a member of the national community." As paraphrased by Glazer, Arieli claims that many of those who "founded and helped define the nation" rejected "ethnic exclusivity."[26]

He acknowledges, however, the existence of a tradition of exclusionism, and cites Benjamin Franklin as an example of this. As quoted by Glazer, Arieli points out how Franklin "strenuously argued against the wisdom of permitting the immigration of non-English settlers, who

'will never adopt our language or customs anymore than they can acquire our complexion.' " Glazer then adds, Franklin was "undoubtedly" influenced by the substantial number of Germans in Pennsylvania. If we go to the original source of Franklin's statement as quoted in Arieli, we will find that it was taken from Franklin's essay on "Observations Concerning the Increase of Mankind." A reading of this essay will quickly reveal that Franklin's deeper concern was based on race. He observed that the number of "purely white People" in the world was proportionately very small. "All Africa was black or tawny, Asia chiefly tawny, and America (exclusive of the new comers) wholly so." The English were the "principle Body of white People," and Franklin wished there were more of them in America. "And while we are . . . Scouring our Planet, by clearing America of Woods, and so making this Side of our globe reflect a brighter Light to the Eyes of Inhabitants in Mars or Venus," he declared, "why should we in the Sight of Superior Beings, darken its People? why increase the Sons of Africa, by Planting them in America, where we have so fair an opportunity, by excluding Blacks and Tawneys, of increasing the lovely White . . . ?"[27]

Still, it can be argued, as does Glazer, that Franklin's was a "private" comment to be set against a "public" one which proclaimed America "a place of refuge." Arieli emphasizes this larger American purpose and quotes Alexis de Tocqueville to illustrate this theme of an inclusionist American nationality. Writing to a friend, the perspicacious French visitor exclaimed:

> Picture to yourself . . . if you can, a society which comprises all the nations of the world . . . people differing from one another in language, in beliefs, in opinions; in a word a society possessing no roots, no memories, no prejudices, no routine, no common ideas, no national character, yet with a happiness a hundred times greater than our own. . . . This, then, is our starting point. What is the connecting link between these so different elements? How are they welded into one people?[28]

Curiously, Arieli discusses American citizenship without a single reference to the Naturalization Law of 1790, which limited naturalized citizenship to a particular racial group. Moreover, he quotes Tocqueville very selectively. Actually, what the astute Frenchman found striking in American society was not only the "general equality of condition" but also the fact that this condition was reserved for white men only. As he traveled through America, he noticed how blacks had been reduced to slaves in the South and pariahs in the North and how Indians were the victims of removal and genocide. Describing Northern racial segregation, Tocqueville wrote:

> The same schools do not receive the children of the black and the European. In the theaters gold cannot procure a seat for the servile race beside their former masters; in the hospitals they lie apart; and although they are allowed to invoke the same God as the whites, it must be at a different altar and in their own churches, with their own clergy. The gates of heaven are not closed against them, but their inferiority is continued to the very confines of the other world. When the Negro dies, his bones are cast aside, and the distinction of condition prevails even in the equality of death.

And witnessing a band of Choctaws driven westward by United States soldiers, Tocqueville reported:

> It was then the middle of winter, and the cold was unusually severe; the snow had frozen hard upon the ground, and the river was drifting huge masses of ice. The Indians had their families with them, and they brought in their train the wounded and the sick, with children newly born and old men upon the verge of death.

What awed Tocqueville was the ability of white society to deprive the Indians of their rights and exterminate them "with singular felicity, tranquilly, legally, philanthropically. . . ." As he caught a glimpse of a peculiar horror present in an American racial pattern, he remarked in barbed language: "It is impossible to destroy men with more respect for the laws of humanity."[29]

Tocqueville's observations on racial inequality were neither cursory nor isolated comments in his writings. In fact, they are interspersed throughout his two-volume study *Democracy in America,* and the last chapter of Volume I is a 109-page assessment of "The Present and Probable Future Condition of the Three Races That Inhabit the Territory of the United States." In this chapter Tocqueville offered a grim prognosis of the pattern of race in America: "The European is to the other races of mankind what man himself is to the lower animals: he makes them subservient to his use, and when he cannot subdue he destroys them." Thus Tocqueville predicted that the Indians would perish as whites expanded their civilization westward, and blacks would continue to be kept subordinate and "fastened" to whites "without intermingling."[30]

How do we account for Arieli's glaring oversights—his failure to note the first naturalization law and Tocqueville's critical assessment of racism in America? One reason, I think, is a tendency to meld together ethnicity and race— to use both terms interchangeably as if they were the same. Hans Kohn in *American Nationalism* also seems to make this mistake. Consequently, he asserts that the "first sharp restriction of immigration" occurred in the 1920s. It would have been impossible for Kohn to have written such a statement unless he were ignorant of the 1882 Chinese Exclusion Act, which was the first immigration restriction law, or unless he viewed immigration wholly in relation to European or white "ethnics." In his chapter on "A Nation of Many Nations," Kohn is really studying ethnicity, not race, but he does not differentiate between the two.[31]

The most revealing example of this confusion is Kohn's discussion of Thomas Jefferson and the founding father's conception of America as a "sanctuary" and a "Canaan." Here we have a situation where Glazer draws from Kohn to requote Jefferson and repeats Kohn's claim that Jefferson viewed America as a "universal nation," composed of "many ethnic strains." If we trace the source of the quotation, we will find that Kohn took it from Jefferson's letter to George Flower, written on September 12, 1817, and published in Volume VII of *The Writings of Thomas Jefferson,* edited by H. A. Washington. If we examine the entire letter, we will plainly see that Jefferson was actually referring to white "ethnic" immigrants—Swiss, French, and Germans. Within this context, then, America was a "sanctuary" for white immigrants fleeing from the "misrule of Europe."[32]

If we browse through Volume VII of Jefferson's *Writings,* we will come across uncontestable proof that Jefferson's inclusionism was for white ethnics only. In a letter to D. Thomas Humphreys, dated February 8, 1817, Jefferson supported a proposal for the removal of free blacks to Africa. "Perhaps the proposition now on the carpet at Washington to provide an establishment on the coast of Africa for voluntary emigrations of peoples of color," Jefferson wrote, "may be the corner stone of this future edifice." Thus, when Jefferson discussed in his letter to Flower, written only several months later, the "quicker amalgamation" of new settlers, he was restricting this process to white ethnic groups.[33]

Though Jefferson was the owner of 200 slaves, he advocated the abolition of slavery and the removal of blacks from America. He believed that blacks and whites could never coexist in America because of "the real distinctions" which "nature" had made between the two races. "The first difference which strikes us is that of color," Jefferson explained. "And is this difference of no importance? Is it not the foundation of a greater or less share of beauty in the two races? Are not the fine mixtures of red and white, the expressions of every passion by greater or less suffusions of color in the one, preferable to that eternal monotony, which reigns in the countenances, that immovable veil of black which covers the emotions of the other race?" To Jefferson, white was beautiful. Even blacks themselves admitted so, he thought: "Add to these, flowing hair, a more elegant symmetry of form, their own judgment in favor of whites, declared by their preference of them, as uniformly as is the preference of Oranootan for the black woman over those of his own species." Given these differences, black removal was a way to preserve white qualities. Commenting on the breeding of domestic animals, Jefferson asked: "The circumstance of superior beauty is thought worthy of attention in the propagation of our horses, dogs, and other domestic animals; why not in that of man?" In his published book, *Notes on the State of Virginia,* Jefferson described the black population as a "blot" and insisted that the black, when freed, had to be removed "beyond the reach of mixture."[34]

Jefferson even devised a plan for black removal. To remove all of them at once, he thought, was not "practicable." He estimated that such a project would take twenty-five years, during which time the slave population would have doubled. Furthermore, the value of the slaves would amount to $600 million, and the cost of transportation and provisions would add up to $300 million. Jefferson recommended instead the deportation of the future generation of blacks: black infants would be taken from their mothers and trained in industrious occupations until they reached a proper age for deportation. Since Jefferson calculated a newborn infant was worth only $22.50, the estimated loss of slave property would be reduced from $600 million to only $37.5 million. Jefferson suggested they be transported to the independent black nation of Santo Domingo. "Suppose the whole annual increase to be sixty thousand effective births," he speculated on the future of blacks in America, "fifty vessels, of four hundred tons burthen each, constantly employed in that short run, would carry off the increase of every year, and the old stock would die off in the ordinary course of nature, lessening from the commencement until its final

disappearance." He was confident the effects of his plan would be "blessed." As for the taking of children from their mothers, Jefferson remarked: "The separation of infants from their mothers . . . would produce some scruples of humanity. But this would be straining at a gnat, and swallowing a camel."[35]

In his discussion on Jefferson, Kohn neglects Jefferson's views on race and consequently fails to understand the founding father's ideas on American nationality. Likewise, in his analysis of the role of the educational system in the "integration" of the "products of many lands into a basic sense of 'belonging,' " Kohn refers to Benjamin Rush's educational philosophy and Rush's desire to create a more "homogeneous" people, but ignores the Pennsylvania physician's attitudes toward blacks. To understand fully what Rush meant by a "homogeneous" American people, his essay on "Observations intended to favour a supposition that the black Color (as it is called) of the Negro is derived from the LEPROSY" cannot be overlooked. A signer of the Declaration of Independence, a seminal theoretician of American psychiatry, and one of the nation's leading educators, Dr. Rush read his essay at a meeting of the American Philosophical Society in 1792. In his "observations," he explained that a combination of factors—"unwholesome diet," "greater heat," "more savage manners," and "bilious fevers"—probably produced leprosy in the skin among blacks in Africa. Despite their condition of leprosy, blacks were as healthy and long-lived as whites, he claimed, for local diseases of the skin seldom affected general health or the duration of life. The more visible symptoms of leprosy were the Negro's physical features—the "big lip," "flat nose," "woolly hair," and especially the black color of his skin. A physician, Rush prescribed a "cure" for the sick Negro: "Depletion, whether by bleeding, purging, or abstinence has been often observed to lessen the black color in negroes. The effects of the above remedies in curing the common leprosy, satisfy me that they might be used with advantage in that state of leprosy which I conceive to exist in the skin of negroes." But until they could be "cured," Dr. Rush recommended an interim separation of the two races. "The facts and principles which have been delivered," he warned, "should teach white people the necessity of keeping up that prejudice against such connections with them (Negroes), as would tend to infect posterity with any portion of their disorder." To "cure" Negroes and to whiten the entire society would be, for Rush, to make the people of the new nation "more homogeneous."[36]

The third authority Glazer cites is Seymour Martin Lipset, author of *The First New Nation: The United States in Historical and Comparative Perspective.* According to Glazer, Lipset views the American Revolution as an event which weakened the ethnic identification with England and led to the emergence of equality and achievement as dominant values in American society. My own reading of Lipset suggests that he cannot be grouped with Arieli, Kohn, and Glazer himself. Where they tend to mix together ethnicity and race, Lipset makes a sharp distinction between the two: "American egalitarianism is, of course, for white men only. The treatment of the Negro makes a mockery of this value now as it has in the past."[37]

This perspective on an American "racial" pattern, while it is not developed or documented historically, leads Lipset to a very different conclusion from the one offered in Glazer's *Affirmative Discrimination.* Though both Lipset and Glazer share a similar understanding of American values, they separate on the issue of public policy and racial inequality. Where Glazer, from the perspective of the emergence of an American "ethnic" pattern, insists that all that can and should be done for blacks is to extend the legal status of equality to individuals regardless of race, Lipset contends that "perhaps the most important fact to recognize about the current situation of the American Negro is that *equality is not enough to assure his movement into the larger society.*" Where Glazer asserts that all the federal government should do is to outlaw racial discrimination in employment, Lipset points out the persistence of the enormous differentiation between white and black incomes, the disproportionate rate of unemployment among blacks, and the problems of structural black unemployment—the low level of education among blacks and the elimination of unskilled labor resulting from automation. "Fair employment legislation," Lipset argues, "does little good if there are no decent jobs available for which the bulk of Negroes are qualified. . . . To break this vicious cycle (of black illiteracy and unemployment), it is necessary to treat the Negro more than equally. . . ."[38]

But if Lipset is correct, how do we respond to what Glazer describes as "the remarkably rapid improvement in the black economic and occupational position in the 1960s"? If we look at certain kinds of data, we can find support for Glazer's contention that the "heritage of discrimination" can be eliminated by "simply attacking discrimination." As Glazer shows, in the North and West in 1969, the median income of black husband-wife families with family heads under thirty-five years of age was 91 percent of the median income of white families in the same category. For the nation as a whole, the median income of black husband-wife families rose from 62 percent of the median income of comparable white families in 1959 to 85 percent in 1972. During this period, blacks also made inroads into occupations of greater security and higher status. The percentage of male "Negroes and other races" (Glazer notes that this group as a whole is over 90 percent black) increased in several employment fields. Their percentages jumped from 4.9 percent in 1963 to 8.2 percent in 1973 for professional and technical workers, from 15.3 percent to 22.9 percent for white-collar workers, and from 10.7 percent to 14.9 percent for craft workers.[39]

But these advances, while important, must be analyzed within the total context of the black economic situation. While the black median income rose from 54 percent of the white median income in 1959 to 66 percent in 1969, it dropped back to 58 percent in 1972. Meanwhile, between 1959 and 1973, of all black families in poverty, those with male heads declined from 1,300,000 to 550,000, while families with female heads increased from 550,000 to 970,000. While black female-headed families constituted 23.7 percent of all black families in 1965, they increased to 34 percent in 1974, forming almost two-thirds of all black families in poverty. While blacks made important gains in several occupational fields, they remained behind whites. In 1973, only 8.2 percent of male "Negroes and other races" were professional and technical workers compared to 14.2 percent of whites, only 15.3 percent of them were white-collar workers compared to 41.7 percent of whites, and only 14.9 percent of them were craft workers compared to 21.5 percent of whites. While the unemployment rate for blacks and other races dropped from 12.6 percent (compared to 6.1 percent for whites) in 1958 to 6.7 percent (compared to 3.2 percent for whites) in 1968, it rose again to 9.9 percent (compared to 5.0 percent for whites) in 1974. Furthermore, while the unemployment rate for blacks and other races sixteen to nineteen years old dropped slightly from 27.4 percent (compared to 14.4 percent for whites) in 1958 to 25 percent (compared to 11.0 percent for whites) in 1968, it soared sharply to 32.9 percent (compared to 14.0 percent for whites) in 1974. Since the publication of Glazer's book in 1975, the median income of black families has continued to remain forty or more percentage points behind the median income of white families— 43 percent in 1977 and 41 percent in 1978. The number of black single-parent families headed by women has also continued to rise, from 1.4 million in 1970 to 2.3 million in 1978, and has undercut much of the gains made by black two-spouse families which Glazer highlights. For every black family that made it into the middle class, three other black families joined the bottom of American society. While black families comprised 22 percent of all low-income households in 1970, they accounted for 28 percent in 1978.[40]

The total picture suggests the black economic situation is highly complex. We must acknowledge that some black "progress" has occurred. The number of blacks in the professional, technical, white-collar, and crafts occupations has increased. But we cannot claim this improvement was wholly the result of anti-discrimination legislation. We must also take into account the general expansion of the American economy in the 1960s as well as affirmative action pressures and policies which were in operation during this time of black economic improvement. Still, while recognizing these gains, we must not overlook or diminish the importance of the overriding and persistent reality of economic inequality between blacks and whites. Blacks still lag behind whites in median incomes, still find themselves underrepresented in the higher-status and better-paying occupations, and still constitute a disproportionately large percentage of low-income and impoverished families. Moreover, underclass blacks may be facing a particularly grim future in a cybernated and service-producing economy. The high rate of black unemployment, which has been around twice the unemployment rate among whites, must be viewed within the context of a major structural shift from goods to service production; the proportion of workers in the service-producing sector of the economy has increased from 49 percent in 1947 to 64 percent in 1968. Thus employment expansion has been located largely in clerical, professional, and administrative fields, which have higher educational and training requirements for employment.[41]

What, then, is to be done, and what would constitute responsible and informed public policies regarding the problem of racial inequality in America? How we answer this question will depend on how we perceive the problem—its nature and its history.

America, despite its racial pattern of domination and exclusion, contained a counterpointing perspective. In his resonant musings, a lonely poet—Walt Whitman—celebrated a vision of democratic tolerance and indiscriminate inclusionism. In Whitman's "America," peoples of all colors could come together, mixing in a great democracy yet respecting the rich cultural diversity of a multiracial society. Thus the poet sang:

> Of every hue and caste am I, of every rank and
>   religion,
> A farmer, mechanic, artist, gentleman, sailor,
>   quaker,
> Prisoner, fancy-man, rowdy, lawyer, physician,
>   priest,
> I resist any thing better than my own diversity.

Whitman saluted "all the inhabitants of the earth." For the American poet, "all races and cultures" were to be "accepted, to be saluted, not to be controlled or placed in hierarchy." And in America, all were to be welcomed— "Chinese, Irish, German, pauper or not, criminal or not—all, all, without exceptions." Ours was not to be a society for "special types" but for the "great mass of people—the vast, surging, hopeful army of workers."[42]

But Whitman's was not the vision of America's public policy makers. Where the poet offered a democratic alternative, the representatives to Congress enacted the 1790 Naturalization Law and the 1882 Chinese Exclusion Act. Where the poet joyfully perceived the promise of a culturally diverse America, federal officials removed Indians and relocated Japanese Americans. Where the poet embraced an egalitarianism for all, regardless of race, men in power like Jefferson, Rush, and Walker worked to build a homogeneous society for special types. Where the poet welcomed all immigrants into the "hopeful army of workers," corporate leaders like Crocker constructed racially divided, segmented labor markets which reflected an American racial pattern.

This pattern was discerned long ago by Herman Melville and emblematized in his description of the crew of the *Pequod* and the whaling industry's labor force. "Not one in two of the many thousand men before the mast employed in the American whale fishery, are American born, though pretty nearly all the officers are," reported Melville's Ishmael. "Herein it is the same with the American whale fishery as with the American army and military and merchant navies, and the engineering forces employed in the construction of the American Canals and Railroads. The same, I say, because in all these cases the native American liberally provides the brains, the rest of the world as generally supplying the muscles." A significant supply of the "muscles" on board the *Pequod* had been drawn from workers of color—blacks, Indians, Pacific Islanders, and Asians. The social divisions within the ship's crew represented the occupational/racial structure in American labor and society. While not all whites were officers, all officers or men on deck were white, and all workers of color were below deck.[43]

The American racial pattern which Melville depicted in 1851 still largely exists today in its basic form, and will continue long after the enactment of legislation prohibiting discrimination based on color, race, or ethnic origin, unless public policies act affirmately to overcome racial inequality. Due to racially exclusionist forces and developments in American history, racial inequality and occupational stratification have come to coexist in a mutually reinforcing and dynamic structural relationship which continues to operate more powerfully than direct forms of racial prejudice and discrimination. To diminish the significance of racial oppression in America's past and to define racial inequality as a problem of prejudice and limit the solution as the outlawing of individual acts of discrimination, as does Glazer, is effectively to leave intact the very structures of racial inequality.

## NOTES

1. Nathan Glazer, *Affirmative Discrimination: Ethnic Inequality and Public Policy* (New York: 1978, originally published in 1975).
2. Back cover of 1978 paperback edition.
3. Glazer, *Affirmative Discrimination*, pp. ix, xvi, xvii.
4. See ibid., chapters 2, 3, and 4.
5. Ibid., pp. 220, 197, xi.
6. Ibid., p. 194.
7. Ibid., p. 204.
8. Ibid., pp. 3, 4, 5.
9. Ibid., p. 5.
10. Ibid., pp. 5, 6, 7, 15, 17.
11. Ibid., p. 5.
12. *Debates and Proceedings in the Congress of the United States,* 1789–1791, 2 vols. (Washington, D.C.: 1834), vol. 1: 998, 1284, vol. 2: 1148–56, 1162, 2264. For the Walter-McCarran Act, see Frank Chuman, *The Bamboo People: The Law and Japanese-Americans* (Del Mar, Calif.: 1976) p. 312.
13. Aaron H. Palmer, *Memoir, geographical, political, and commercial, on the present state, productive resources, and capabilities for commerce, of Siberia, Manchuria, and the Asiatic Islands of the Northern Pacific Ocean; and on the importance of opening commercial intercourse with those countries,* March 8, 1848. U.S. Cong., Senate, 30th Cong., 1st sess., Senate misc. no. 80, pp. 1, 52, 60, 61.
14. Charles Crocker, testimony, in *Report of the Joint Special Committee to Investigate Chinese Immigration,* Senate Report No. 689, 44th Cong., 2nd sess., 1876–77, pp. 667, 679, 680.
15. Chuman, *Bamboo People*, pp. 217, 218.
16. Felix S. Cohen, *Handbook of Federal Indian Law* (Albuquerque: 1958, originally published in 1942), pp. 153–59.
17. See Takaki, *Iron Cages: Race and Culture in 19th-Century America* (New York: 1979), p. 111.
18. Francis Newton Thorpe, ed., *The Federal and State Constitutions, Colonial Charters, and Other Organic Laws of the States, Territories, and Colonies now or heretofore forming the United States of America* (Washington: 1909), vol. 1. *Treaty of Guadalupe-Hidalgo,* p. 381, *Constitution of California,* 1849, p. 393; Cohen, *Handbook of Federal Indian Law,* pp. 155–59.
19. Glazer, *Affirmative Discrimination*, pp. 5, 22–29.
20. "Statement of United States Citizenship of Japanese Ancestry," quoted in Michi Weglyn, *Years of Infamy: The Untold Story of America's Concentration Camps* (New York: 1976), p. 155.
21. Cohen, *Handbook of Federal Indian Law,* p. 155.
22. Andrew Jackson, "First Annual Message to Congress," in James D. Richardson, ed., *A Compilation of the Messages and Papers of the Presidents, 1789–1897* (Washington: 1897), 2: 456–58; Jackson to General John Coffee, April 7, 1832, in John Spencer Bassett, ed., *Correspondence of Andrew Jackson,* 6 vols. (Washington: 1926), 4: 430; Francis Amasa Walker, *The Indian Question* (Boston: 1874), pp. 10, 62–67.
23. Francis Amasa Walker, *Annual Report of the Commissioner of Indian Affairs to the Secretary of the*

*Interior for the Year 1872* (Washington: 1872), pp. 11, 63, 64, 77–79, 94, 95; *Indian Appropriation Act,* quoted in Walker, *Indian Question,* p. 5.

24. For a discussion of the Dawes Act, see Takaki, *Iron Cages,* pp. 188–93.

25. Glazer, *Affirmative Discrimination,* p. 8.

26. Yehoshua Arieli, *Individualism and Nationalism in American Ideology* (Baltimore: 1966, originally published in 1964), p. 22; Glazer, *Affirmative Discrimination,* pp. 8–9.

27. Glazer, *Affirmative Discrimination,* p. 12; Arieli, *Individualism and Nationalism,* p. 44; Benjamin Franklin, "Observations Concerning the Increase of Mankind" (1751), in Leonard W. Labaree, ed., *The Papers of Benjamin Franklin* (New Haven: 1959), 4: 234.

28. Glazer, *Affirmative Discrimination,* p. 12; Alexis de Tocqueville, quoted in Arieli, *Individualism and Nationalism,* p. 17.

29. Alexis de Tocqueville, *Democracy in America,* 2 vols. (New York: 1945, originally published in 1835), 1: 373–74, 352–53, 364.

30. Ibid., pp. 370, 343–452.

31. Hans Kohn, *American Nationalism: An Interpretative Essay* (New York: 1961, originally published in 1954), pp. 168, 139–75.

32. Thomas Jefferson, quoted in Kohn, *American Nationalism,* requoted in Glazer, *Affirmative Discrimination,* p. 12; Jefferson to George Flower, September 12, 1817, in H. A. Washington, ed., *The Writings of Thomas Jefferson* (Washington: 1853–54), 7: 84.

33. Jefferson to Doctor Thomas Humphreys, February 8, 1817, ibid., pp. 57–58.

34. Thomas Jefferson, *Notes on the State of Virginia* (New York: 1964, originally published in 1785), pp. 85, 139, 133, 127; Jefferson to Dr. Edward Bancroft, January 16, 1788, in Edwin M. Betts, ed., *Thomas Jefferson's Farm Book* (Princeton: 1953), p. 10.

35. Jefferson to Jared Sparks, February 4, 1824, in Paul L. Ford, ed., *The Works of Thomas Jefferson* (New York: 1892–99), 12: 334–39.

36. Kohn, *American Nationalism,* pp. 173–74; Benjamin Rush, "Observations intended to favour a supposition that the black color (as it is called) of the Negroes is derived from the LEPROSY," *Transactions of the American Philosophical Society,* vol. 4. (1799): 289–97; Benjamin Rush, "Of the Mode of Education Proper in a Republic," in his *Essays, Literary, Moral & Philosophical* (Philadelphia: 1798), p. 19.

37. Glazer, *Affirmative Discrimination,* p. 11; Seymour Martin Lipset, *The First New Nation: The United States in Historical and Comparative Perspective* (New York: 1967, originally published in 1963), pp. 379–80.

38. Lipset, *First New Nation,* pp. 381–82.

39. Glazer, *Affirmative Discrimination,* pp. 197; 41–42.

40. Ibid.; William J. Wilson, *The Declining Significance of Race: Blacks and Changing American Institutions* (Chicago: 1978), pp. 90, 91; *Current Population Reports,* Series P-20, Bureau of the Census, No. 340: "Household and Family Characteristics" (U.S. Government Printing Office: 1979), Table E, cited in Andrew Hacker, "Creating American Inequality," *New York Review of Books,* XXVII, No. 4: 23; see also ibid. for other comparisons. The most detailed study of this issue is Reynolds Farley, "Racial Progress in the Last Two Decades: What Can We Determine about Who Benefitted and Why?" paper presented at the 1979 Annual Meeting of the American Sociological Association.

41. Dorothy K. Newman et. al., *Protest, Politics, and Prosperity: Black Americans and White Institutions, 1940–75* (New York: 1978), p. 64; Wilson, *Declining Significance of Race,* pp. 93–95.

42. Walt Whitman, *Leaves of Grass and Selected Prose* (New York: 1958), pp. 38, 1, 25, 18, 78, 83, 89, 399–400, 340, 121, 343; Walt Whitman, in Horace Traubel, *With Walt Whitman in Canada,* 2 vols. (New York: 1915), 2: 34–35.

43. Herman Melville, *Moby Dick, or the Whale* (Boston: 1956, originally published in 1851), pp. 108.

# PART II
# Culture

The "ethnic" pattern and the "racial" pattern discerned by Glazer and Takaki, respectively, developed within an American cultural context. By culture, I mean a constellation of moral values about how people should think and behave, ideas and beliefs about human nature and society, and images of the past as well as the future. Culture, as Antonio Gramsci has observed, can be hegemonic: "an order in which a certain way of life and thought is dominant, in which one concept of reality is diffused throughout society in all its institutional and private manifestations, informing with its spirit all taste, morality, customs, religious and political principles, and all social relations." As such, culture provides the filters through which men and women view the world around them.

In American culture, one of the fundamental principles is individualism—the belief that individuals are or should be responsible for themselves and should be judged according to their merits or lack of them. Men and women should be allowed to have equality of opportunity, a chance to advance individually, to get as far as possible, regardless of social origin. They should have freedom to fulfill their own purposes and be rewarded by a justly earned place in society. Merit or individual achievement should be the basis for power, place, and privilege in society.

Individualism in our culture embraces the powerful and emotional image of America as a place where men and women would be able to find a new beginning. "In the beginning," wrote John Locke, "all the world was America." The new land offered the possibility of creating a new social order, free from the ancient feudalism of European society. Here, in America, people would be self-governing, free to pursue visions of new and hopeful possibilities for themselves as individuals. Here, as Benjamin Franklin explained to Europeans considering emigration to America two centuries ago, if immigrants "are poor, they begin first as Servants or Journeymen; and if they are sober, industrious, and frugal, they soon become Masters, establish themselves in Business, marry, raise Families, and become respectable Citizens." Here, as Charles Murray has recently recounted the story of the American epic, "immigrants arrive penniless and work their way up. The sharecropper's son becomes an assembly-line worker and his granddaughter goes to college. The immigrant who speaks no English has a son who goes to night school for nine years and finally gets a law degree."

This culture of individualism is deeply rooted in the American past. In the seventeenth century, New England Puritanism located authority in the individual self. Individual men and women had to demonstrate, above all to their individual consciences, the signs of their salvation: work, self-control, and obedience to one's calling. Individualism within Puritan society also involved a sense of social responsibility and connectedness to the community.

During the late eighteenth century, the concept of individualism was transformed into a political principle, forming the basis of a new national cultural consensus, as Americans rebelled against England and established a new independent nation. As American revolutionaries demonstrated and protested in the streets against British rule, they took pieces of the crown and symbolically scattered them among the people. Individually, each American possessed a piece of authority. Power and responsibility, under this new politics, would henceforth be placed within the individual self. Americans would and should be self-governing in the new republic. This culture of individualism derived its vision of society and human nature not only from Puritanism but also from the Enlightenment, particularly from the philosophy of Locke. The purpose of the state, as defined by Locke, would be essentially negative. Men and women, to remove themselves from a state of nature, had agreed to a social contract—the institution of government to protect themselves against violations of their rights to life, liberty, and property. Within this agreement, each individual would be self-governing.

A half-century after the American Revolution, a young Frenchman named Alexis de Tocqueville visited the new republic and found that nothing there struck him more forcibly than "the general condition of equality." This condition exercised a "prodigious influence" on the whole course of society, giving a "peculiar" direction to public opinion, a "peculiar" tenor to the laws, and "peculiar" habits to the governed.

The more Tocqueville reflected on the essence of American culture, the more he perceived this "equality of condition" as "the fundamental fact," "the central point" of American society. Scanning the history of the last seven hundred years, he saw the United States as the culmination of a long process. The Crusades and the English wars had decimated the nobles and divided their property, the invention of firearms had equalized vassal and noble on the battlefield, printing had made knowledge available to all classes, and the discovery of America had opened a thousand new paths to wealth. Finally, in this movement toward equality of condition, occurred the American Revolution. During the war, "the doctrine of the sovereignty of the people came out of the townships and took possession of the state. Every class was enlisted in its cause; battles were fought and victories obtained for it; it became the law of laws." In America, a new man had emerged. He owed nothing to any other and expected nothing; he stood alone, confident he controlled his own destiny, thrown back forever upon himself alone, and confined "entirely within the solitude of his own heart."

But the "equality of condition," Tocqueville also observed, was for whites only. He realized that American culture was complex, even contradictory. As the French visitor traveled around the United States and witnessed the celebration of individualism and equality, he also saw the horrors of Indian removal and the reality of segregation in the North and slavery in the South for blacks. Indians and blacks, Tocqueville reported, were denied the very promise of America.

Some one hundred years later, another European visitor-scholar, Gunnar Myrdal, described this contradiction as an "American Dilemma":

> the ever-raging conflict between, on the one hand, the valuations preserved on the general plane . . . the "American Creed," where the American thinks, talks, and acts under the

influence of high national and Christian precepts, and, on the other hand, valuations on specific planes of individual and group living, where personal and group prejudice against particular persons or types of people . . . dominate his outlook.

But how can we account for this American dilemma?

American culture, according to Myrdal, contained within it not only ideas of democracy and equality but also images of blacks as inferior, lazy, low in intelligence, irresponsible, driven largely by bodily needs. Such negative racial stereotypes developed in relationship to the enslavement of blacks: slavery or the institutionalized exploitation and subordination of blacks led to the stigmatization of their black skin. Their color became a badge of their inferiority, their degraded social status. The stereotypes, in turn, justified slavery and racial discrimination. In the end, a "vicious cycle" emerged as racial imagery reinforced economic conditions for blacks and as economic conditions produced social patterns of black inferiority.

But, in the first essay in this section on culture, Winthrop Jordan argues that racial imagery of black inferiority actually predated slavery in the English colonies. Jordan offers evidence showing that negative impressions of blacks were present in English society before the English colonization of the New World and before slavery became an important institution in English America. But Jordan advances beyond a presentation of the evidence. Utilizing the psychological theory of projection or the theory that repressed sexuality and fears can sometimes be projected onto others, Jordan asks what such racial imagery reveals about English culture and the American culture that sprang from it. Deep within our culture, Jordan suggests, lurk libidinal anxieties shaping racial attitudes and race relations.

While Jordan's study focuses on black-white relations, it does raise questions regarding other out-groups, particularly Native Americans. As Jordan states, it would be "impossible to see clearly what Americans thought of Negroes without ascertaining their almost contrary thoughts concerning Indians: in the settlement of this country the red and black peoples served white men as aids to navigation by which they would find their safe positions as they ventured into America." But what were the "contrary thoughts" about Indians? James Madison, assessing the triracial composition of America, observed: "Next to the case of the black race within our bosom, that of the red on our borders is the problem most baffling to the policy of our country." In "The Metaphysics of Civilization: Indians and the Age of Jackson," Ronald Takaki explores the "contrary thoughts" and the "problem" of the "red race on our borders." Cultural images of Indians, he finds, enabled white society to expand the market; moreover, they helped whites define more clearly and sharply who they were and what America was as a civilized society. As President Andrew Jackson informed Congress, "Our conduct toward these people [Indians] is deeply interesting to our national character."

But did other groups also serve as "aids to navigation"? During the age of American industrialization, most of the immigrant laborers came from Europe, especially from Central, Southern, and Eastern Europe. In "Strangers in the Land: Nativism and Nationalism," John Higham asks us to compare the experiences of racial minorities and certain European immigrant working-class groups. What are the similarities and differences between racism and ethnocentrism?

The dominant culture in America has depicted out-groups differently; in turn, many of them have also responded differently. In "Border Culture," Mario García examines the experiences of Mexican immigrants. Unlike immigrants from Europe and Asia, they remained in close physical proximity to their homeland. What they created in El Paso was a culture that was literally on the border of two countries. Though Asian immigrants were thousands of miles and an ocean away from their homelands, they, too, carried their cultures to America. How important are the cultures of the groups as forces conditioning their responses? Ivan Light attempts to answer this question in his analysis of the reasons why blacks have not realized the promise of America. In his essay, "Ethnic Enterprise in America: Japanese, Chinese, and Blacks," Light compares the success of the Japanese and Chinese in this country with the failure of blacks in business activity. Culture, for Light, is a key determinant. Credit-rotating systems, ascriptive moral communities, and values of work and savings are crucial. But do certain economic conditions—poverty—function more decisively, shaping attitudes, expectations, and ways of looking at the world?

The larger society, Vine Deloria observes in "Identity and Culture," judges racial minorities by its cultural belief in the doctrine of self-help. According to this belief, every minority individual, given time and opportunity, can become successful. The "absence of motivation" rather than the existence of discrimination is cited as the reason why most members of racial minorities do not advance themselves into the middle class. But this very culture of white society has led to reforms based on the premise that the conditions of minorities were due to a "deprivation of white values." Minorities, Deloria insists, must maintain their own cultures and identities; cultural diversity is essential for the realization of the American promise of equality.

American culture defines who Americans are and who they should be. Its idea of individualism and meritocracy assumes we all have equal freedom and equal choice to determine our individual fates. But can we all do so, or do racial and class divisions make some of us more equal than others? As a lens for viewing society, our culture may be actually shrouding much of reality, the structures of racial inequality such as poverty, the ghetto, entrapment in meaningless and low-paying jobs, and deficient schooling. Many Americans, because of structural barriers, do not actually have equality of opportunity; thus, they still find themselves denied the "equality of condition" that Tocqueville thought was "fundamental" and "central" to the meaning of America.

# First Impressions: Libidinous Blacks

WINTHROP JORDAN

When the Atlantic nations of Europe began expanding overseas in the sixteenth century, Portugal led the way to Africa and to the east while Spain founded a great empire in America. It was not until the reign of Queen Elizabeth that Englishmen came to realize that overseas exploration and plantations could bring home wealth, power, glory, and fascinating information. By the early years of the seventeenth century Englishmen had developed a taste for empire and for tales of adventure and discovery. More than is usual in human affairs, one man, the great chronicler Richard Hakluyt, had roused enthusiasm for western planting and had stirred the nation with his monumental compilation, *The Principal Navigations, Voyages, Traffiques and Discoveries of the English Nation.* Here was a work to widen a people's horizons. Its exhilarating accounts of voyages to all quarters of the globe constituted a national hymn, a scientific treatise, a sermon, and an adventure story.

English voyagers did not touch upon the shores of West Africa until after 1550, nearly a century after Prince Henry the Navigator had mounted the sustained Portuguese thrust southward for a water passage to the Orient. Usually Englishmen came to Africa to trade goods *with* the natives. The earliest English descriptions of West Africa were written by adventurous traders, men who had no special interest in converting the natives or, except for the famous Hawkins voyages in the 1560's, in otherwise laying hands on them. Extensive English participation in the slave trade did not develop until well into the seventeenth century. Initially English contact with Africans did not take place primarily in a context which prejudged the Negro as a slave, at least not as a slave of Englishmen. Rather, Englishmen met Africans merely as another sort of men.

Englishmen found the peoples of Africa very different from themselves. "Negroes" looked different to Englishmen; their religion was un-Christian; their manner of living was anything but English; they seemed to be a particularly libidinous sort of people. All these clusters of perceptions were related to each other, though they may be spread apart for inspection, and they were related also to the circumstances of contact in Africa, to previously accumulated traditions concerning that strange and distant continent, and to certain special qualities of English society on the eve of its expansion into the New World.

## THE BLACKNESS WITHOUT

For Englishmen, the most arresting characteristic of the newly discovered African was his color. Travelers rarely failed to comment upon it; indeed when describing Africans they frequently began with complexion and then moved on to dress (or, as they saw, lack of it) and manners. At Cape Verde, "These people are all blacke, and are called Negroes, without any apparell, saving before their privities." Robert Baker's narrative poem recounting his two voyages to the West African coast in 1562 and 1563 introduced the people he saw with these engaging lines:

> And entering in [a river], we see
> a number of black soules,
> Whose likelinesse seem'd men to be,
> but all as blacke as coles.
> Their Captain comes to me
> as naked as my naile,
> Not having witte or honestie
> to cover once his taile.

Englishmen actually described Negroes as *black*—an exaggerated term which in itself

From Winthrop D. Jordan, *White Over Black: American Attitudes Toward the Negro, 1550–1812.* Copyright © 1968 by the University of North Carolina Press. Reprinted by permission of the publisher.

suggests that the Negro's complexion had powerful impact upon their perceptions. Even the peoples of northern Africa seemed so dark that Englishmen tended to call them "black" and let further refinements go by the board. In Shakespeare's day, the Moors, including Othello, were commonly portrayed as pitchy black and the terms *Moor* and *Negro* were used almost interchangeably. With curious inconsistency, however, Englishmen recognized that Africans south of the Sahara were not at all the same people as the much more familiar Moors. Sometimes they referred to West Africans as "black Moors" to distinguish them from the peoples of North Africa.

The powerful impact which the Negro's color made upon Englishmen must have been partly owing to suddenness of contact. Though the Bible as well as the arts and literature of antiquity and the Middle Ages offered some slight introduction to the "Ethiope," England's immediate acquaintance with "black"-skinned peoples came with relative rapidity. People much darker than Englishmen were not entirely unfamiliar, but really "black" men were virtually unknown except as vaguely referred to in the hazy literature about the sub-Sahara which had filtered down from antiquity. Native West Africans probably first appeared in London in 1554: in that year five "Negroes," as one trader reported, were taken to England, "kept till they could speake the language," and then brought back again "to be a helpe to Englishmen" who were engaged in trade with Africans on the coast. Hakluyt's later discussion of these Africans suggests that these "blacke Moores" were a novelty to Englishmen. In this respect the English experience was markedly different from that of the Spanish and Portuguese who for centuries had been in close contact with North Africa and had actually been invaded and subjected by people both darker and more "highly civilized" than themselves. The impact of the Negro's color was the more powerful upon Englishmen, moreover, because England's principal contact with Africans came in West Africa and the Congo, which meant that one of the lightest-skinned of the earth's peoples suddenly came face to face with one of the darkest.

In England perhaps more than in southern Europe, the concept of blackness was loaded with intense meaning. Long before they found that some men were black, Englishmen found in the idea of blackness a way of expressing some of their most ingrained values. No other color except white conveyed so much emotional impact. As described by the *Oxford English Dictionary,* the meaning of *black* before the sixteenth century included, "Deeply stained with dirt; soiled, dirty, foul. . . . Having dark or deadly purposes, malignant; pertaining to or involving death, deadly; baneful, disastrous, sinister. . . . Foul, iniquitous, atrocious, horrible, wicked. . . . Indicating disgrace, censure, liability to punishment, etc." Black was an emotinally partisan color, the handmaid and symbol of baseness and evil, a sign of danger and repulsion.

Embedded in the concept of blackness was its direct opposite—whiteness. No other colors so clearly implied opposition, "beinge coloures utterlye contrary":

> *Everye white will have its blacke,*
> *And everye sweete its sowre.*

White and black connoted purity and filthiness, virginity and sin, virtue and baseness, beauty and ugliness, beneficence and evil, God and the devil. Whiteness, moreover, carried a special significance for Elizabethan Englishmen: it was, particularly when complemented by red, the color of perfect human beauty, especially *female* beauty. This ideal was already centuries old in Elizabeth's time, and their fair Queen was its very embodiment: her cheeks were "roses in a bed of lillies." (Elizabeth was naturally pale but like many ladies then and since she freshened her "lillies" at the cosmetic table.) An adoring nation knew precisely what a beautiful Queen looked like.

> *Her cheeke, her chinne, her neck, her nose,*
> *This was a lillye, that was a rose;*
> *Her bosome, sleeke as Paris plaster,*
> *Held upp twoo bowles of Alabaster.*

By contrast, the Negro was ugly, by reason of his color and also his "horrid Curles" and "disfigured" lips and nose. A century later blackness still required apology: one of the earliest attempts to delineate the West African as a heroic character, the popular story *Oroonoko* (1688), presented Negroes as capable of blushing and turning pale. It was important, if incalculably so, that English discovery of black Africans came at a time when the accepted English standard of ideal beauty was a fair complexion of rose and white. Negroes seemed the very picture of perverse negation.

From the first, however, many English observers displayed a certain sophistication about the Negro's color. Despite an ethnocentric tendency to find blackness repulsive, many writers were fully aware that Africans themselves might have different tastes. As early as 1621 one writer told of the "Jetty coloured" Negroes, "Who in their native beauty most delight, / And in contempt doe paint the Divell white"; this assertion became almost a commonplace. Many accounts of Africa reported explicitly that the Negro's preference in colors were inverse to the European's. Even the Negro's features were conceded to be appealing to Negroes.

## THE CAUSES OF COMPLEXION

Black human beings were not only startling but extremely puzzling. The complexion of Africans posed problems about its nature, especially its permanence and utility, its cause and origin, and its significance. Although these were rather separate questions, there was a pronounced tendency among Englishmen and other Europeans to formulate the problem in terms of causation alone. If the cause of human blackness could be explained, then its nature and significance would follow.

Not that the problem was completely novel. The ancient Greeks had touched upon it. The story of Phaëton's driving the chariot sun wildly through the heavens apparently served as an explanation for the Ethiopian's blackness even before written records, and traces of this ancient fable were still drifting about during the seventeenth century. Ptolemy had made the important suggestion that the Negro's blackness and woolly hair were caused by exposure to the hot sun and had pointed out that people in northern climates were white and those in temperate areas an intermediate color. Before the sixteenth century, though, the question of the Negro's color can hardly be said to have drawn the attention of Englishmen or indeed of Europeans generally.

The discovery of West Africa and the development of Negro slavery made the question far more urgent. The range of possible answers was rigidly restricted, however, by the virtually universal assumption, dictated by church and Scripture, that all mankind stemmed from a single source. Indeed it is impossible fully to understand the various efforts at explaining the Negro's complexion without bearing in mind the strength of the tradition which in 1614 made the chronicler, the Reverend Samuel Purchas,

proclaim vehemently: "the tawney Moore, blacke Negro, duskie Libyan, ash-coloured Indian, olive-coloured American, should with the whiter European become one *sheep-fold,* under *one great Sheepheard . . .* without any more distinction of Colour, Nation, Language, Sexe, Condition, all may bee *One* in him that is One. . . ."

In general, the most satisfactory answer to the problem was some sort of reference to the action of the sun, whether the sun was assumed to have scorched the skin, drawn the bile, or blackened the blood. People living on the [Equator] had obviously been getting too much of it; after all, even Englishmen were darkened by a little exposure. How much more, then, with the Negroes who were "so scorched and vexed with the heat of the sunne, that in many places they curse it when it riseth." This association of the Negro's color with the sun became a commonplace in Elizabethan literature; as Shakespeare's Prince of Morocco apologized, "Mislike me not for my complexion,/ The shadow'd livery of the burnish'd sun,/ To whom I am a neighbour and near bred."

Unfortunately this theory ran headlong into a stubborn fact of nature which simply could not be overriden: if the equatorial inhabitants of Africa were blackened by the sun, why not the people living on the same Line in America? Logic required them to be the same color. Yet by the middle of the sixteenth century it was becoming perfectly apparent that the Indians living in the hottest regions of the New World could by no stretch of the imagination be described as black. They were "olive" or "tawny," and moreover they had long hair rather than the curious "wool" of Negroes. Clearly the method of accounting for human complexion by latitude just did not work. The worst of it was that the formula did not seem altogether wrong, since it was apparent that in general men in hot climates tended to be darker than in cold ones.

Another difficulty with the climatic explanation of skin color arose as lengthening experience provided more knowledge about Negroes. If the heat of the sun caused the Negro's blackness, then his removal to cold northerly countries ought to result in his losing it; even if he did not himself surrender his peculiar color, surely his descendants must. By mid-seventeenth century it was becoming increasingly apparent that this expectation was ill founded: Negroes in Europe and northern America were simply not whitening up very noticeably.

From the beginning, in fact, some Englishmen were certain that the Negro's blackness was permanent and innate and that no amount of cold was going to alter it. There was good authority in Jeremiah 13:23: "Can the Ethiopian change his skin/ or the leopard his spots?" Elizabethan dramatists used the stock expression "to wash in Ethiop white" as indicating sheer impossibility. In 1578 a voyager and speculative geographer, George Best, announced that the blackness of Negroes "proceedeth of some naturall infection of the first inhabitants of that country, and so all the whole progenie of them descended, are still polluted with the same blot of infection." An essayist in 1695 declared firmly, "A negroe will always be a negroe, carry him to Greenland, give him chalk, feed and manage him never so many ways."

There was an alternative to the naturalistic explanations of the Negro's blackness. Some writers felt that God's curse on Ham (Cham), or upon his son Canaan, and all their descendants was entirely sufficient to account for the color of Negroes. This could be an appealing explanation, especially for men like George Best who wished to stress the "natural infection" of blackness and for those who hoped to incorporate the Negro's complexion securely within the accepted history of mankind. The original story in Genesis 9 and 10 was that after the Flood, Ham had looked upon his father's "nakedness" as Noah lay drunk in his tent, but the other two sons, Shem and Japheth, had covered their father without looking upon him; when Noah awoke he cursed Canaan, son of Ham, saying that he would be a "servant of servants" unto his brothers. Given this text, the question becomes why a tale which logically implied slavery but absolutely nothing about skin color should have become a popular explanation of the Negro's blackness. The matter is puzzling, but probably, over the very long run, the story was supported by the ancient association of heat with sensuality and by the fact that some sub-Saharan Africans had been enslaved by Europeans since ancient times. In addition, the extraordinary persistence of the tale in the face of centuries of constant refutation was probably sustained by a feeling that blackness could scarcely be anything *but* a curse and by the common need to confirm the facts of nature by specific reference to Scripture. In contrast to the climatic theory, God's curse provided a satisfying purposiveness which the sun's scorching heat could not match until the eighteenth century.

In the long run, of course, the Negro's color attained greatest significance not as a scientific problem but as a social fact. Englishmen found blackness in human beings a peculiar and important point of difference. The African's color set him radically *apart* from Englishmen. But then, distant Africa had been known to Christians for ages as a land of men radically different in religion.

## DEFECTIVE RELIGION

While distinctive appearance set Africans apart in a novel way, their religious condition distinguished them in a more familiar manner. Englishmen and Christians everywhere were sufficiently acquainted with the concept of heathenism that they confronted its living representatives without puzzlement. Certainly the rather sudden discovery that the world was teeming with heathen people made for heightened vividness and urgency in a long-standing problem; but it was the fact that this problem was already well formulated long before contact with Africa which proved important in shaping English reaction to the Negro's defective religious condition.

In one sense heathenism was less a "problem" for Christians than an exercise in self-definition: the heathen condition defined by negation the proper Christian life. In another sense, the presence of heathenism in the world constituted an imperative to intensification of religious commitment. From its origin Christianity was a universalist, proselytizing religion, and the sacred and secular histories of Christianity made manifest the necessity of bringing non-Christians into the fold. For Englishmen, then, the heathenism of Negroes was at once a counter-image of their own religion and a summons to eradicate an important distinction between the two peoples. Yet the interaction of these two facets of the concept of heathenism made for a peculiar difficulty: On the one hand, to act upon the felt necessity of converting Africans would have been to eradicate the point of distinction which Englishmen found most familiar and most readily comprehensible. Yet if they did not act upon this necessity, continued heathenism among Negroes would remain an unwelcome reminder to Englishmen that they were not meeting their obligations to their own faith—nor to the benighted Negroes. Englishmen resolved this implicit dilemma by doing nothing.

Considering the strength of the Christian tradition, it is almost startling that Englishmen failed to respond to the discovery of heathenism in Africa with at least the rudiments of a campaign for conversion. Although the impulse to spread Christianity seems to have been weaker in Englishmen than, say, in the Catholic Portuguese, it cannot be said that Englishmen were indifferent to the obligation imposed upon them by the overseas discoveries of the sixteenth century. While they were badly out of practice at the business of conversion (again in contrast to the Portuguese) and while they had never before been faced with the practical difficulties involved in Christianizing entire continents, they nonetheless were able to contemplate with equanimity and even eagerness the prospect of converting the heathen. Indeed they went so far as to conclude that converting the natives in America was sufficiently important to demand English settlement there. As it turned out, the well-publicized English program for converting Indians produced very meager results, but the avowed intentions certainly were genuine. It was in marked contrast, therefore, that Englishmen did not avow similar intentions concerning Africans until the late eighteenth century. Fully as much as with skin color, though less consciously, Englishmen distinguished between the heathenisms of Indians and of Negroes.

It is not easy to account for the distinction which Englishmen made. On the basis of the traveler's reports there was no reason for Englishmen to suppose Indians inherently superior to Negroes as candidates for conversion. But America was not Africa. Englishmen contemplated settling in America, where voyagers had established the King's claim and where supposedly the climate was temperate; in contrast, Englishmen did not envision settlement in Africa, which had quickly gained notoriety as a graveyard for Europeans and where the Portuguese had been first on the scene. Certainly these very different circumstances meant that Englishmen confronted Negroes and Indians in radically different social contexts and that Englishmen would find it far easier to contemplate converting Indians than Negroes. Yet it remains difficult to see why Negroes were not included, at least as a secondary target. The fact that English contact with Africans so frequently occurred in a context of slave dealing does not entirely explain the omission of Negroes, since in that same context the Portuguese and Spanish did sometimes attempt to minister to the souls of Africans and since Englishmen in America enslaved Indians when good occasion arose. Given these circumstances, it is hard to escape the conclusion that the distinction which Englishmen made as to conversion was at least in some small measure modeled after the difference they saw in skin color.

The most important aspect of English reaction to African heathenism was that Englishmen evidently did not regard it as separable from the Negro's other attributes. Heathenism was treated not so much as a specifically religious defect but as one manifestation of a general refusal to measure up to proper standards, as a failure to be English or even civilized. There was every reason for Englishmen to fuse the various attributes they found in Africans. During the first century of English contact with Africa, Protestant Christianity was an important element in English patriotism; especially during the struggle against Spain the Elizabethan's special Christianity was interwoven into his conception of his own nationality, and he was therefore inclined to regard the Negroes' lack of true religion as part of theirs. Being a Christian was not merely a matter of subscribing to certain doctrines; it was a quality inherent in oneself and in one's society. It was interconnected with all the other attributes of normal and proper men: as one of the earliest English travelers described Africans, they were "a people of beastly living, without a God, lawe, religion, or common wealth"—which was to say that Negroes were not Englishmen. Far from isolating African heathenism as a separate characteristic, English travelers sometimes linked it explicitly with blackness and savagery.

## SAVAGE BEHAVIOR

The condition of savagery—the failure to be civilized—set Negroes apart from Englishmen in an ill-defined but crucial fashion. Africans were *different* from Englishmen in so many ways: in their clothing, housing, farming, warfare, language, government, morals, and (not least important) in their table manners. To judge from the comments of voyagers, Englishmen had an unquenchable thirst for the details of savage life. Englishmen were, indeed, enormously curious about their rapidly expanding world, and it is scarcely surprising that they should have taken an interest in reports about cosmetic mutilation, polygamy, infanticide, ritual murder, and the like. In addition, reports about "savages" began arriving at a time when

Englishmen very much needed to be able to translate their apprehensive interest in an uncontrollable world out of medieval religious terms. The discovery of savages overseas enabled them to make this translation easily, to move from miracles to verifiable monstrosities, from heaven to earth.

As with skin color, English reporting of African customs was partly an exercise in self-inspection by means of comparison. The necessity of continuously measuring African practices with an English yardstick of course tended to emphasize the differences between the two groups, but it also made for heightened sensitivity to instances of similarity. Thus the Englishman's ethnocentrism tended to distort his perception of African culture in two opposite directions. While it led him to emphasize differences and to condemn deviations from the English norm, it led him also to seek out similarities. Particularly, Englishmen were inclined to see the structures of African societies as analogous to their own, complete with kings, counselors, gentlemen, and the baser sort. Here especially they found Africans like themselves, partly because they knew no other way to describe any society and partly because there was actually good basis for such a view of the social organization of West African communities.

Despite the fascination and self-instruction Englishmen derived from discussing the savage behavior of Africans, they never felt that savagery was as important a quality in Africans as it was in the American Indians. As was the case with heathenism, contrasting social contexts played an important role in shaping the English response to savagery in the two peoples. Inevitably, the savagery of the Indians assumed a special significance in the minds of those actively engaged in a program of planting civilization in the American wilderness. The case with the African was different; the English errand into Africa was not a new or a perfect community but a business trip. No hope was entertained for civilizing the Negro's steaming continent, and Englishmen therefore lacked compelling reason to develop a program for remodeling the African natives.

From the beginning, also, the importance of the Negro's savagery was muted by the Negro's color. Englishmen could go a long way toward expressing their sense of being different from Africans merely by calling them "black." By contrast, the aboriginals in America did not have the appearance of being radically distinct from Europeans except in religion and savage behavior. English voyagers placed much less emphasis upon the Indian's physiognomy to distract their attention from what they regarded as his essential quality, his savagery.

It would be a mistake, however, to slight the importance of what was seen as the African's savagery, since it fascinated Englishmen from the very first. English observers in West Africa were sometimes so profoundly impressed by the Negro's behavior that they resorted to a powerful metaphor with which to express their own sense of difference from him. They knew perfectly well that Negroes were men, yet they frequently described the Africans as "brutish" or "bestial" or "beastly." The supposed hideous tortures, cannibalism, rapacious warfare, revolting diet (and so forth page after page) seemed somehow to place the Negro among the beasts. The eventual circumstances of the Englishman's contact with Africans served to strengthen this feeling. *Slave* traders in Africa necessarily handled Negroes the same way men in England handled beasts, herding and examining and buying, as with any other animals which were products of commerce.

## THE APES OF AFRICA

If Negroes were likened to beasts, there was in Africa a beast which was likened to men. It was a strange and eventually tragic happenstance of nature that Africa was the habitat of the animal which in appearance most resembles man. The animal called "orang-outang" by contemporaries (actually the chimpanzee) was native to those parts of western Africa where the early slave trade was heavily concentrated. Though Englishmen were acquainted (for the most part vicariously) with monkeys and baboons, they were unfamiliar with tail-less apes who walked about like men. Accordingly, it happened that Englishmen were introduced to the anthropoid apes and to Negroes at the same time and in the same place. The startlingly human appearance and movements of the "ape"—a generic term though often used as a synonym for the "orang-outang"—aroused some curious speculations.

In large measure these speculations derived from traditions which had been accumulating in Western culture since ancient times. Medieval books on animals contained rosters of strange creatures who in one way or another seemed disturbingly to resemble men. There were the *simia* and the *cynocephali* and the *satyri* and the others, all variously described and related to one another, all jumbled in a characteristic blend of ancient reports and medieval morality. The confusion was not easily nor rapidly dispelled, and many of the traditions established by this literature were very much alive during the seventeenth century.

The section on apes in Edward Topsell's *Historie of Foure-Footed Beastes* (1607) serves to illustrate how certain seemingly trivial traditions and associations persisted in such form that they were bound to affect the way in which Englishmen would perceive the inhabitants of Africa. Above all, according to Topsell, "apes" were venerous. The red apes were "so venerous that they will ravish their Women." Baboons were "as lustful and venerous as goats"; a baboon which had been "brought to the French king . . . above all loved the companie of women, and young maidens; his genitall member was greater than might match the quantity of his other parts." Pictures of two varieties of apes, a "Satyre" and an "Ægopithecus," graphically emphasized the "virile member."

In addition to stressing the "lustful disposition" of the ape kind, Topsell's compilation contained suggestions concerning the character of simian facial features. "Men that have low and flat nostrils," readers were told in the section on apes, "are Libidinous as Apes that attempt women. . . ." There also seemed to be some connection between apes and devils. In a not altogether successful attempt to distinguish the "Satyre-apes" from the mythical creatures of that name, Topsell straightened everything out by explaining that it was "probable, that Devils take not any dænomination or shape from Satyres, but rather the Apes themselves from Devils whome they resemble, for there are many things common to the Satyre-apes and devilish Satyres." Association of apes and/or satyrs with devils was common in England: the inner logic of this association derived from uneasiness concerning the ape's "indecent likenesse and imitation of man"; it revolved around evil and sexual sin; and, rather tenuously, it connected apes with blackness.

Given this tradition and the coincidence of contact, it was virtually inevitable that Englishmen should discern similarity between the manlike beasts and the beastlike men of Africa. A few commentators went so far as to suggest that Negroes had sprung from the generation of ape-kind or that apes were themselves the offspring of Negroes and some unknown African beast. These contentions were squarely in line with the ancient tradition that Africa was a land "bringing dailie foorth newe monsters"

because, as Aristotle himself had suggested, many different species came into proximity at the scarce watering places. Jean Bodin, the famous sixteenth-century French political theorist, summarized this wisdom of the ages with the categorical remark that "promiscuous coition of men and animals took place, wherefore the regions of Africa produce for us so many monsters." Despite all these monsters out of Africa, the notion that Negroes stemmed from beasts in a literal sense was not widely believed. It simply floated about, available, later, for anyone who wanted it.

Far more common and persistent was the notion that there sometimes occurred "a beastly copulation or conjuncture" between apes and Negroes, and especially that apes were inclined wantonly to attack Negro women. The very explicit idea that apes assaulted female human beings was not new; Africans were merely being asked to demonstrate what Europeans had known for centuries. As late as the 1730's a well-traveled, well-educated, and intelligent naval surgeon, John Atkins, was not at all certain that the stories were false: "At some Places the *Negroes* have been suspected of Bestiality with them [apes and monkeys], and by the Boldness and Affection they are known under some Circumstances to express to our Females; the Ignorance and Stupidity on the other side, to guide or control Lust; but more from the near resemblance [of apes] . . . to the Human Species would tempt one to suspect the Fact."

By the time Atkins addressed himself to this evidently fascinating problem, some of the confusion arising from the resemblance of apes to men had been dispelled. In 1699 the web of legend and unverified fact was disentangled by Edward Tyson, whose comparative study of a young "orang-outang" was a masterwork of critical scientific investigation. Throughout his dissection of the chimpanzee, Tyson meticulously compared the animal with human beings in every anatomical detail, and he established beyond question both the close relationship and the non-identity of ape and man. Here was a step forward; the question of the ape's proper place in nature was now grounded upon much firmer knowledge of the facts. Despite their scientific importance, Tyson's conclusions did nothing to weaken the vigorous tradition which linked the Negro with the ape. The supposed affinity between apes and men had as frequently been expressed in sexual as in anatomical terms, and his findings did not effectively rule out the possibility of unnatural sexual unions. Tyson himself remarked that orangs were especially given to venery.

The sexual association of apes with Negroes had an inner logic which kept it alive: sexual union seemed to prove a certain affinity without going so far as to indicate actual identity—which was what Englishmen really thought was the case. By forging a sexual link between Negroes and apes, furthermore, Englishmen were able to give vent to their feeling that Negroes were a lewd, lascivious, and wanton people.

## LIBIDINOUS MEN

Undertones of sexuality run throughout many English accounts of West Africa. To liken Africans—any human beings—to beasts was to stress the animal within the man. Indeed the sexual connotations embodied in the terms *bestial* and *beastly* were considerably stronger in Elizabethan English than they are today, and when the Elizabethan traveler pinned these epithets upon the behavior of Africans he was more frequently registering a sense of sexual shock than describing swinish manners.

Lecherousness among Africans was at times for Englishmen merely another attribute which one would expect to find among heathen, savage, beastlike men. One commentator's remarks made evident how closely interrelated all these attributes were in the minds of Englishmen: "They have no knowledge of God . . . they are very greedie eaters, and no lesse drinkers, and very lecherous, and theevish, and much addicted to uncleanenesse: one man hath as many wives as hee is able to keepe and maintaine." Sexuality was what one expected of savages.

Clearly, however, the association of Africans with potent sexuality represented more than an incidental appendage to the concept of savagery. Long before first English contact with West Africa, the inhabitants of virtually the entire continent stood confirmed in European literature as lustful and venerous. About 1526 Leo Africanus (a Spanish Moroccan Moor converted to Christianity) supplied an influential description of the little-known lands of "Barbary," "Libya," "Numedia," and "Land of Negroes"; and Leo was as explicit as he was imaginative. In the English translation (1600) readers were informed concerning the "Negroes" that "there is no Nation under Heaven more prone to Venery." Leo disclosed that "the

Negroes . . . leade a beastly kind of life, being utterly destitute of the use of reason, of dexteritie of wit, and of all arts. Yea, they so behave themselves, as if they had continually lived in a Forrest among wild beasts. They have great swarmes of Harlots among them; whereupon a man may easily conjecture their manner of living." Nor was Leo Africanus the only scholar to elaborate upon the ancient classical sources concerning Africa. In a highly eclectic work first published in 1566, Jean Bodin sifted the writings of ancient authorities and concluded that heat and lust went hand in hand and that "in Ethiopia . . . the race of men is very keen and lustful." Bodin announced in a thoroughly characteristic sentence, "Ptolemy reported that on account of southern sensuality Venus chiefly is worshipped in Africa and that the constellation of Scorpion, which pertains to the pudenda, dominates that continent."

Depiction of the Negro as a lustful creature was not radically new, therefore, when Englishmen first met Africans face to face. Seizing upon and reconfirming these long-standing and apparently common notions, Elizabethan travelers and literati dwelt explicitly with ease upon the especial sexuality of Africans. Othello's embraces were "the gross clasps of a lascivious Moor." Francis Bacon's *New Atlantis* (1624) referred to "an holy hermit" who "desired to see the Spirit of Fornication; and there appeared to him a little foul ugly Æthiop." Negro men, reported a seventeenth-century traveler, sported "large Propagators." In 1623 Richard Jobson, a sympathetic observer, reported that Mandingo men were "furnisht with such members as are after a sort burthensome unto them." Another commentator thought Negroes "very lustful and impudent, especially, when they come to hide their nakedness (for a *Negroes* hiding his Members, their extraordinary greatness) is a token of their Lust, and therefore much troubled with the Pox." By the eighteenth century a report on the sexual aggressiveness of African women was virtually required of European commentators. By then, of course, with many Englishmen actively participating in the slave trade, there were pressures making for descriptions of "hot constitution'd Ladies" possessed of a "temper hot and lascivious, making no scruple to prostitute themselves to the *Europeans* for a very slender profit, so great is their inclination to white men."

While the animus underlying these and similar remarks becomes sufficiently obvious once Englishmen began active participation in the slave trade, it is less easy to see why Englishmen should have fastened upon Negroes a pronounced sexuality virtually upon first sight. The ancient notions distilled by Bodin and Leo Africanus must have helped pattern initial English perceptions. Yet clearly there was something in English culture working in this direction. It is certain that the presumption of powerful sexuality in black men was far from being an incidental or casual association in the minds of Englishmen. How very deeply this association operated is obvious in *Othello*, a drama which loses most of its power and several of its central points if it is read with the assumption that because the black man was the hero English audiences were indifferent to his blackness. Shakespeare was writing both *about* and *to* his countrymen's feelings concerning physical distinctions between peoples; the play is shot through with the language of blackness and sex. Iago goes out of his way to talk about his own motives: "I hate the Moor,/ And it is thought abroad that 'twixt my sheets/ He has done my office." Later, he becomes more direct, "For that I do suspect the lusty Moor hath leaped into my seat." It was upon this so obviously absurd suspicion that Iago based his resolve to "turn her virtue into pitch." Such was his success, of course, that Othello finally rushes off "to furnish me with some means of death for the fair devil." With this contorted denomination of Desdemona, Othello unwittingly revealed how deeply Iago's promptings about Desdemona's "own clime, complexion, and degree" had eaten into his consciousness. Othello was driven into accepting the premise that the physical distinction *matters:* "For she had eyes," he has to reassure himself, "and chose me." Then, as his suspicions give way to certainty, he equates her character with his own complexion:

> Her name, that was as fresh,
> As Dian's visage, is now begrim'd and black
> As mine own face.

This important aspect of Iago's triumph over the noble Moor was a subtly inverted reflection of the propositions which Iago, hidden in the darkness, worked upon the fair lady's father. No one knew better than Iago how to play upon hidden strings of emotion. Not content with the straightforward crudity that "your daughter and the Moor are now making the beast with two backs," Iago told the agitated Brabantio that "an old black ram/ Is tupping your white ewe" and alluded politely to "your daughter cover'd

with a Barbary horse." This was not merely the language of (as we say) a "dirty" mind: it was the integrated imagery of blackness and whiteness, of Africa, of the sexuality of beasts and the bestiality of sex. And of course Iago was entirely successful in persuading Brabantio, who had initially welcomed Othello into his house, that the marriage was "against all rules of nature." Eventually Brabantio came to demand of Othello what could have brought a girl "so tender, fair, and happy"

> To incur a general mock
> Run from her guardage to the sooty bosom
> Of such a thing as thou.

Altogether a curious way for a senator to address a successful general.

These and similar remarks in the play *Othello* suggest that Shakespeare and his audiences were not totally indifferent to the sexual union of "black" men and "white" women. Shakespeare did not condemn such union; rather, he played upon an inner theme of black and white sexuality, showing how the poisonous mind of a white man perverted and destroyed the noblest of loves by means of bringing to the surface (from the darkness, whence Iago spoke) the lurking shadows of animal sex to assault the whiteness of chastity. Never did "dirty" words more dramatically "blacken" a "fair" name. At the play's climax, standing stunned by the realization that the wife he has murdered was innocent, Othello groans to Emilia, " 'Twas I that killed her"; and Emilia responds with a torrent of condemnation: "O! the more angel she,/ And you the blacker devil." Of Desdemona: "She was too fond of her filthy bargain." To Othello: "O gull! O dolt!/ As ignorant as dirt!" Shakespeare's genius lay precisely in juxtaposing these two pairs: inner blackness and inner whiteness. The drama meant little if his audiences had felt no response to this cross-inversion and to the deeply turbulent double meaning of black *over* white.

It required a very great dramatist to expose some of the more inward biocultural values which led—or drove—Englishmen to accept readily the notion that Negroes were peculiarly sexual men. Probably these values and the ancient reputation of Africa upon which they built were of primary importance in determining the response of Englishmen to Africans. Whatever the importance of biologic elements in these values—whatever the effects of long northern nights, of living in a cool climate, of possessing light-colored bodies which excreted contrasting lumps of darkness—these values by Shakespeare's time were interlocked with English history and culture and, more immediately, with the circumstances of contact with Africans and the social upheaval of Tudor England.

## THE BLACKNESS WITHIN

The Protestant Reformation in England was a complex development, but certainly it may be said that during the sixteenth and early seventeenth centuries the content and tone of English Christianity were altered in the direction of Biblicism, personal piety, individual judgment, and more intense self-scrutiny and internalized control. Many pious Englishmen, not all of them "Puritans," came to approach life as if conducting an examination and to approach Scripture as if peering in a mirror. As a result, their inner energies were brought into the almost rational world of legend, myth, and literature. The taut Puritan and the bawdy Elizabethan were not so much enemies as partners in this adventure which we usually think of in terms of great literature—of Milton and Shakespeare—and social conflict—of Saints and Cavaliers. The age was driven by the twin spirits of adventure and control, and while "adventurous Elizabethans" embarked upon voyages of discovery overseas, many others embarked upon inward voyages of discovery. Some men, like William Bradford and John Winthrop, were to do both. Given this charged atmosphere of (self-)discovery, it is scarcely surprising that Englishmen should have used peoples overseas as social mirrors and that they were especially inclined to discover attributes in savages which they found first, but could not speak of, in themselves.

Nowhere is the way in which certain of these cultural attributes came to bear upon Negroes more clearly illustrated than in a discourse by George Best, an Elizabethan adventurer who sailed in 1577 in search of the Northwest Passage. In the course of demonstrating the habitability of all parts of the world, George Best veered off to the problem of the color of Negroes. The cause of their blackness, he decided, was explained in Scripture. Noah and his sons and their wives were "white" and "by course of nature should have begotten . . . white children. But the envie of our great and continuall enemie the wicked Spirite is such, that as hee coulde not suffer our olde father Adam to live in the felicitie and Angelike state

wherein he was first created . . . so againe, finding at this flood none but a father and three sons living, hee so caused one of them to disobey his fathers commandment, that after him all his posteritie should bee accursed." The "fact" of this "disobedience," Best continued, was this: Noah "commanded" his sons and their wives to behold God "with reverence and feare," and that

> while they remained in the Arke, they should use continencie, and abstaine from carnall copulation with their wives . . . which good instructions and exhortations notwithstanding his wicked sonne Cham disobeyed, and being perswaded that the first childe borne after the flood . . . should inherite . . . all the dominions of the earth, hee . . . used company with his wife, and craftily went about thereby to dis-inherite the off-spring of his other two brethren.

To punish this "wicked and detestable fact," God willed that "a sonne should bee born whose name was Chus, who not onely it selfe, but all his posteritie after him should bee so blacke and lothsome, that it might remain a spectacle of disobedience to all the worlde. And of this blacke and cursed Chus came all these blacke Moores which are in Africa."

The inner themes running throughout this extraordinary exegesis testify eloquently to the completeness with which English perceptions could integrate sexuality with blackness, the devil, and the judgment of a God who had originally created man not only "Angelike" but "white." These running equations lay embedded at a deep and almost inaccessible level of Elizabethan culture; only occasionally did they appear in complete clarity, as when evil dreams

> . . . hale me from my sleepe like forked Devils,
> Midnight, thou Æthiope, Empresse of Black Soules,
>    Thou general
> Bawde to the whole world.

But what is still more arresting about George Best's discourse is the shaft of light it throws upon the dark mood of strain and control in Elizabethan culture. In an important sense, Best's remarks are not about Negroes; rather they play upon a theme of external discipline exercised upon the man who fails to discipline himself. The linkages he established— "disobedience" with "carnall copulation" with something "black and lothsome"—were not his alone. The term *dirt* first began to acquire its meaning of moral impurity, of smuttiness, at the very end of the sixteenth century. Perhaps the key term, though, is "disobedience"—to

God and parents—and perhaps therefore, the passage echoes one of the central concerns of Englishmen of the sixteenth and early seventeenth centuries. Tudor England was undergoing social ferment, caused in large part by an increasingly commercialized economy and reflected in such legislative monuments as the Statute of Apprentices and the Elizabethan vagrancy and poor laws. Overseas mercantile expansion brought profits and adventure but also a sense, in some men, of disquietude. One commentator declared that the merchants, "whose number if so increased in these our daies," had "in times past" traded chiefly with European countries but "now . . . as men not contented with these journies, they have sought out the east and west Indies, and made now and then suspicious voiages." Literate Englishmen generally (again not merely the Puritans) were concerned with the apparent disintegration of social and moral controls at home; they fretted endlessly over the "masterless men" who had once had a proper place in the social order but who were now wandering about, begging, robbing, raping. They fretted also about the absence of a spirit of due subordination—of children to parents and servants to masters. They assailed what seemed a growing spirit of avariciousness, a spirit which one social critic described revealingly as "a barbarous or slavish desire to turne the [penny]." They denounced the laborers who demanded too high wages, the masters who squeezed their servants, and the landed gentlemen who valued sheep more than men—in short, the spirit of George Best's Cham, who aimed to have his son "inherite and possesse all the dominions of the earth."

It was the case with English confrontation with Africans, then, that a society in a state of rapid flux, undergoing important changes in religious values, and comprised of men who were energetically on the make and acutely and often uncomfortably self-conscious of being so, came upon a people less technologically advanced, markedly different in appearance and culture. From the first, Englishmen tended to set Africans over against themselves, to stress what they conceived to be radically contrasting qualities of color, religion, and style of life, as well as animality and a peculiarly potent sexuality. What Englishmen did not at first fully realize was that Africans were potentially subjects for a special kind of obedience and subordination which was to arise as adventurous Englishmen sought to possess for themselves and their children one of the most bountiful dominions of the earth. When they came to plant themselves in the New World, they were to find that they had not entirely left behind the spirit of avarice and insubordination. Nor does it appear, in light of attitudes that developed during their first two centuries in America, that they left behind all the impressions initially gathered of the *Negro* before he became pre-eminently the *slave*.

# The Metaphysics of Civilization:
# Indians and the Age of Jackson

RONALD TAKAKI

## AN AGE OF CONFIDENCE

Confidence, as Herman Melville observed in his novel *The Confidence-Man,* was one of the buoyant forces in American society during the era of the Market Revolution—"the indispensable basis of all sorts of business transactions" without which "commerce between man and man" would, like "a watch," run down and stop. Confidence in business and also in society generally involved both the need for moral self-assurance and the use of disguises. Like Melville's characters on board the steamboat *Fidèle,* white Americans had to have moral faith in themselves—to be assured they were innocent of brutality and sin even if they had to tell themselves they were so. And like Melville's confidence-man with his myriad of roles and masks, they employed disguises in their social and political relationships. Role-playing and the use of masks, David Brion Davis has noted, was widespread in Jacksonian society, where "individual success depended on effective presentation of self and on convincing definitions of new situations." Nowhere did whites demonstrate the importance of confidence as moral self-assurance and deception, especially self-deception, more than in their conduct toward Indians. In the removal and extermination of Indians, they were able to admire the Indian-killer and elevate hatred for the Indian into a morality—an awesome achievement which Melville analyzed in his chapters on the "metaphysics of Indian-hating."

In this story, Melville described how disguises could be used to uncover rather than shroud reality. His confidence-man poses as a cosmopolitan gentleman in order to expose the contradictions of Indian-hating. On the deck of the *Fidèle,* a symbol of the Market Revolution, he meets a westerner who offers to tell a story about Colonel John Moredock, an Indian-hater. Though the cosmopolitan gentleman appears to be merely an interested listener, he is actually preparing to demolish the westerner's credibility in a brilliant exercise in epistemology. Even the westerner's teeth do not escape his critical scrutiny. "And though his teeth were singularly good," the confidence-man alias cosmopolitan gentleman remarks to himself, "those same ungracious ones might have hinted that they were too good to be true; or rather, were not so good as they might be; since the best false teeth are those made with at least two or three blemishes, the more to look like life." The examination of the westerner's teeth leads the cosmopolitan gentleman to ask implicitly: What is reality? Meanwhile he listens intently as the westerner tells him about Colonel Moredock.

Indian-hating, the westerner says, is "no monopoly" of Colonel Moredock but "a passion, in one form or other, and to a degree, greater or less, largely shared among the class to which he belonged." A backwooodsman, Moredock is "self-willed," "self-reliant," and "lonely," not merely content to be alone but "anxious" to be by himself. He has a "private passion" stemming from an unforgettable outrage: his mother had been slain by Indians. The tragedy has turned him into an avenger and his rage is raised to a religious zeal. He takes a "vow," settles his "temporal affairs," and has the "solemnity" of a "monk." The armed party he leads to punish the Indians are pledged to serve him for "forty days." Moredock, in short, is a pious ascetic, seeking violent revenge, fully aware that Indian-hating requires "the renunciation of ambition, with its objects—the pomps and glories of the world. . . ." Thus, Indian-hating, the westerner explains, is "not wholly without the efficacy of a devout sentiment."

Moredock's "private passion" demands that he hate and kill Indians, not only the ones responsible for his mother's death but all Indians, the westerner continues. His entire body/self is organized to destroy: his nerves are "electric wires—sensitive, but steel," his "finger like a trigger." He seldom stirs without his rifle, almost as if the weapon were a part of his body. A superb athlete and marksman, he is a master of woodland cunning, skilled in the art of tracking Indians, "ever on the noiseless trail; cool, collected, patient; less seen than felt; snuffing, smelling—a Leather-stocking Nemesis."

A killer, Moredock is, nonetheless, an example of "something apparently self-contradicting," the westerner adds. He and "nearly all Indian-haters have at bottom loving hearts." Moredock himself is "not without humane feelings"—"no cold husband or colder father, he." Indeed, with nobody, "Indians excepted," does he conduct himself other than in a courteous manner. Moredock is also greatly respected in white society: "famous" in his time, he is even pressed to become a candidate for governor of Illinois. The high regard Moredock enjoys is well deserved, for he has opened the West for settlement and American white progress, serving selflessly as the "captain in the vanguard of conquering civilization" and as the "Pathfinder, provider of security to those who come after him." After the westerner completes his story, the cosmopolitan gentleman, wondering how a monomaniac killer could be a good father and an esteemed citizen and how hatred for Indians could be a metaphysics for civilization, asks skeptically: "If the man of hate, how could John Moredock be also the man of love?"

What Melville was observing here, through the confidence-man, was the metaphysics of Indian-hating. His westerner is not merely telling an interesting story about Colonel John Moredock: He is also offering a metaphysical justification for the destruction of Indians. While Melville provided a much-needed criticism of Indian-hating, he missed an opportunity to reveal an even more complex dimension to this phenomenon. Separating the westerner from Colonel Moredock, Melville failed to note a perverse possibility—the combination of both the metaphysician and the Indian-hater in the same person. Such an integration occurred in

reality and could be found in the life of Lewis Cass.

A colonel under General William Henry Harrison during the War of 1812, governor of Michigan Territory from 1813 to 1831, and secretary of war under President Andrew Jackson, Cass led troops in battles against Indians, concluded treaties with them, and helped to remove them beyond the Mississippi River. He also articulated a metaphysics for his actions. While he was governor, Cass wrote an essay on "Policy and Practice of the United States and Great Britain in their Treatment of Indians," published in the *North American Review* in 1827; and shortly before he became secretary of war, he wrote another essay, succinctly titled "Removal of the Indians."

The presence of Indians in nineteenth-century America, for Cass, was a "moral phenomenon." They had been in contact with whites and civilization for two centuries, and yet they had not advanced in their "moral qualities." Cass found this condition puzzling. "A principle of progressive improvement seems almost inherent in human nature," he wrote. "Communities of men, as well as individuals, are stimulated by a desire to meliorate their condition." "Meliorate" had a republican and Jacksonian meaning for Cass: to strive "in the career of life to acquire riches, or honor, or power, or some other object. . . ." But there was

> little of all this in the constitution of our savages. Like the bear, and deer, and buffalo of his own forests, an Indian lives as his father lived, and dies as his father died. He never attempts to imitate the arts of his civilized neighbors. His life passes away in a succession of listless indolence, and of vigorous exertion to provide for his animal wants, or to gratify his baleful passions. . . . Efforts . . . have not been wanting to teach and reclaim him. But he is perhaps destined to disappear with the forests. . . .

The forests, Cass continued, could not be abandoned to "hopeless sterility," but must give way to the "march of cultivation and improvement."

Thus, as it turned out, Cass—a one-time Colonel Moredock or Indian-fighter—had become a westerner or metaphysician of Indian-hating. What happened to Cass suggests the complex processes at work in Indian-white relations during the age of the Market Revolution. And like Melville's confidence-man, we realize the need to examine more closely and critically the metaphysics of Indian-hating.

But, as we turn to a scrutiny of Robert Montgomery Bird and Andrew Jackson, we quickly discover how difficult is our task and how puzzling is reality. The problem is an epistemological one. Bird and Jackson were disguise artists; they used the techniques of confidence to cover up rather than to expose the crimes and moral absurdities of the market society. As the author of the popular Indian-hating novel, *Nick of the Woods, or the Jibbenainosay,* published in 1837, Bird presented a moral justification for the extermination of Indians. As the conqueror of the Creeks in the war of 1813–14 and as the president of the United States responsible for Indian removal, Jackson developed a philosophical explanation which transformed Indian deaths into moral inevitability. In their exercise of confidence—the use of disguises in the quest for moral self-assurance—both men had formulated a metaphysics of Indian-hating that sprang from as well as sustained the material base of the Market Revolution.

## JIBBENAINOSAY: INDIAN-HATING IN FANTASY

As a metaphysician of Indian-hating, Bird was more ingenious than Melville's westerner. In *Nick of the Woods,* published during the era of Indian removal and reprinted more than twenty-one times, he justified as well as condemned the violence and hate whites were directing against Indians. How this contradiction developed in Bird is revealed in an examination of his private letters, childhood writings, later unpublished fictional works, and the novel itself. In reality, Bird was hardly the simple anti-Indian writer he appeared to have been and even thought he was. Indeed, in his effort to degrade Indians, Bird used such a multitude of masks and deceptions that he became involved in an exercise in confidence more subtle and bizarre than he himself may have fully realized.

Actually Bird did not grow up on the frontier, and his contact with the wilderness and Indians was extremely limited. He was born in New Castle, Delaware, in 1806, into a family which had lived on the eastern seaboard and in settled society for generations. A Whig, Bird identified with the gentility and order of an established social hierarchy, and felt uncomfortable in the society of the Market Revolution, where the pursuit of money and social mobility seemed to have possessed Americans. Financially unsuccessful as a doctor in Philadelphia and uncertain about medicine as a career, he gave his practice up after one year and decided to become a novelist and playwright—a decision which would lead him to reflect on the meaning of the Market Revolution and its impact on white as well as Indian society.

Writing, for Bird, was a way out of the "distasteful" world of business which prevailed in the new market society. He did not have, his wife later reported, "the American propensity and talent for making money." His "soul full of poetry" and his "brain stored with book-learning," he was "ignorant as a child or a woman of all business matters." Still, as a writer, Bird discovered he had not freed himself from the market, and found himself unhappily dependent on profit-oriented publishers. He was told it was necessary for an author to "sacrifice" his first book and give it to the publisher for "nothing." And he complained: "This seems to be a pretty state of things indeed, that an author should *give* a bookseller one book for the privilege of selling him a second. . . ." Regretting his "misfortune of being unknown," Bird viewed the market as a pernicious influence on literature and American letters in general.

As a novelist in a society of enterprise, Bird believed the American writer had to overcome certain literary problems or "great disadvantages": Americans were a people without "romance," "traditions," and "antique associations," and their history was "short, meager & monotonous." They lacked the feudal ambience of the Old World where a writer could find "the truest & most fruitful gardens of romance" and the inspiration of "lofty feelings and chivalrous sentiments." In the heroes of European literature, he remarked enviously, "the human passions had their fullest sway . . . more romantically than will ever a people engaged in the levelling & unenthusiastic bustle of gain. Where shall the American novelist look for his hero?" Bird wanted America to have her own literature and her own heroes. But, in his view, Americans were in a "state of mental vassalage to foreigners. . . . Our opinions, our sentiments, our tastes, all come to us from abroad. Who, then, is to remind us of the interests and duties of Americans?" Like Ralph Waldo Emerson and Nathaniel Hawthorne, Bird had delineated one of the vexing predicaments of the American writer. He did not think America provided the materials he needed as a novelist, for he did not want to write about American enterprise—the unheroic and crass making of money. Yet he was determined to throw off America's vassalage to Europe and help create a truly national literature.

In his search for a way out of this dilemma, Bird noted the significance of the Indian in the making of an American nationality and a national literature. If Americans were to be original and assert their cultural independence from Europe, he insisted, they must depend on America rather than Europe for the sources of their cultural identity. This independence should be expressed even in the names Americans gave to their villages and towns. "The hankering after the vanities of the old world," Bird wrote, "is in no way so ridiculously manifested, as in the christening of our new villages. What despicable folly it is to steal the names of the remarkable cities of ancient & modern Europe, & apply them to the several clusters of taverns, smithies, & variety stores which compose our infant hamlets." Americans should not "steal" names from Europe; rather they should take them from "the peculiar & sonorous titles which the aborigines were wont to apply to some spot in the neighborhood." Indeed, Bird added, many of the Indian names were "infinitely more beautiful than the sweetest" that could be found in any European gazetteer. The Indian, for Bird, offered white Americans a means to realize their own national identity.

Yet, almost like a plot out of a Hawthorne novel, this creation of a white American nationality had its origins in greed and sin: the very use of Indian names for white villages and towns involved the destruction of Indians and seizure of their lands. Bird himself recognized this reality and felt a sense of guilt. Traveling through the South and Southwest in 1833, he witnessed the injustices whites had committed against Indians. On April 23, he wrote in his diary after visiting Macon, Georgia: "Poor Cherokees your Destiny is known—But Georgia, though she strike ye from the face of the Earth, yet has she permitted your name to rest on a humble flower. But while that flower keeps for your memory the pity & admiration of posterity, what a stench of shame shall be sent up by the foul rank weeds that have overgrown the fields of your oppressor." Bird was referring to the flower named the "Cherokee Rose." Two weeks later, after an encounter with a Creek, Bird wrote to his fiancée, Mary Mayer:

Even the deserts here blossom like the rose; and the sterile woodlands, which the hand of oppression is this moment wresting from the poor Creeks, are all full of beauty. . . . Talking of Creeks, I saw one fellow, one day, stalking near some wigwams, who was really as noble in figure and carriage, and as picturesque in costume, as I have imagined a wild man to be. . . . As this creature approached

me with the strut and port of a god, his head elevated, his eyes neither seeking nor shunning me, but shining now to the right and now to the left, as if he felt himself the guardian spirit of his tribe . . . and had nothing to do with looking after white men—it struck me there was something in his carriage very like such a swagger of self-esteem. . . . I had saluted the gentleman, and received no other return than a most magnificent and impartial grunt. . . . I was so tickled at his vainglory that I burst into a laugh. This insult, for which I was instantly sorry—for his pride was the only possession of which my countrymen had not robbed him—stung him. He halted, wheeled half around, falling into an attitude really majestic and Apollo-like, and gave me a look of such fierce and fiery intensity that I began to wish I had my pistols about me.

Several days later, in a letter to a friend, Bird again lamented: "Then thought I, in the solitude of the pine barrens of Georgia, I shall feel very poetical; and among the Muscogee Groves, I shall see wandering red men, and verify old visions of romance. . . . I saw proud warriors; but they always came to sell green strawberries, and beg tobacco." The very materials Bird needed as a writer and as a maker of a national culture were derived from what he regarded as robbery and murder.

Actually the Indian had existed in Bird's consciousness long before he developed an interest in creating a national literature and before he had met Indians in the South. As a boy, he had fantasized about them in a short story written in his school composition book. In "The White-Washed Cottage of the Susquehanna, an Indian Story," a young white boy named Charley Merton and his family are living in peace and harmony in a cottage on the bank of the Susquehanna River. One day they are forced to flee to the blockhouse in town in order to avoid an Indian attack; but they are ambushed, and all the whites, except Charley and his mother, are killed. Their captor is a "frightful savage" chief who, to their surprise, speaks French. Charley's mother speaks to Wingenund in French and learns that his father was a Frenchman and his mother an Indian. "Oh sir," she asks, "why did you murder my husband then?" And the chief replies: "Oh you forget that I am no Frenchman, I am an Indian. Though my father was a Frenchman, my mother was an Indian, and I am bound to revenge the injuries done upon her countrymen and mine." Charley and his mother are taken to the Indian village, where Wingenund treats them kindly. But they find out from him that a rival chief will soon be returning with his warriors, and that their lives will be in danger. Taking a canoe, Charley and his mother secretly paddle away. Their escape causes great commotion in the village; but Wingenund, discovering his canoe is missing, says nothing, allowing them to escape. They return to their cottage and find Charley's father alive; the blows he had received during the ambush had not been fatal. Thus the family is joyously reunited. Years later, Charley is sitting on his porch, and an Indian approaches him. "Votre nom, n'est ça pas Charley M.?" the Indian asks. Charley and his parents excitedly welcome Wingenund, begging him to "live with them and be a white man." The chief declines their offer, gives Charley a handsome bow and quiver, and departs, loaded with presents they had given him.

In this amazing story, written during Bird's childhood, the Indians are viewed as sources of great terror: they are disrupters of peace and harmony, "frightful savages," and killers of whites. Yet they are also described sympathetically: Wingenund is a kind and considerate person, and the anger he feels springs from the injuries whites had inflicted upon Indians. The final episode of the fantasy indicates the possible choices the young Bird thought the Indian possessed: he could live with whites and become "a white man," or he could remain in the wilderness. Thus Charley and his parents appear to have survived the traumatic experience of Indian violence emotionally unscarred: hate for the Indian and an impulsive rage for revenge do not seem to possess or deform them.

Many years after he had written the story about Charley, Bird returned to the theme of Indian violence and its psychological effect on whites. In "Awossagame," an unpublished story probably drafted after his visit to the South in the 1830s, Bird located Indian-white conflict in New England during colonial times and explicitly acknowledged the wrongs whites had committed against Indians. "Our forefathers of New England were strange people," Bird wrote at the beginning of his narrative. "They came, as homeless and landless exiles, among a rude but not inhospitable people race, whom after a few years they did not scruple to dispossess of their lands homes & possessions." Here, in his description of the initial encounter between whites and Indians in New England, was the language Bird had used to chastise whites in Georgia for their crimes against Indians.

In "Awossagame," Bird focused on John Gilbert, a harsh magistrate and fanatical Indian-hater. A one-time papist, he had been converted to "the true faith" and was now "foremost in the persecution of papists, quakers, and anabaptists." Like Charley's family, Gilbert had been the victim of Indian violence: his wife and two daughters had been slain during an attack on their village. The "misfortune" had frozen the "gentler feelings of his heart. . . . He had no family—he was alone in the world." Interpreting the slaying as God's vengeance against him for his sinful idolatry, Gilbert turned away from Catholicism and developed a fierce hatred for Indians. The fury of his hate is directed against an Indian girl, Awossagame, who is on trial for witchcraft. Magistrate Gilbert pours his venom on her, calling her "a lewd & devilish pagan," a member of an "accursed race," and a "loose savage." Her defender, Elliot Sherwyn, insists she is innocent, and Gilbert replies sharply, "Is she not an Indian?" He then breaks into an uncontrollable "expression of rancorous and malignant hate." During the trial, the girl is ordered to bare her arm in order to reveal an imprint of the "devil's mark." Suddenly Gilbert recognizes the popish symbol he himself had placed upon one of his daughters many years ago and rushes to her, crying aloud, "My child! My child! my Elizabeth! my lost Elizabeth!" Happily reunited with his daughter, Gilbert casts off the gloom and "misanthropy" which had sustained him in his hatred for the Indian.

Bird probably wrote "Awossagame" during the period he was working on *Nick of the Woods,* for both stories have somewhat similar plots involving Indian-haters. But Bird treated Indians and their haters very differently in each story. In "Awossagame," he not only portrayed Indians sympathetically, placing their violence within the context of white possession of Indian "lands homes" and contrasting the malevolent Gilbert with the poor innocent Awossagame, but also pointed out the absurdity of racial stereotyping and the tragic consequences of racial hate. In *Nick of the Woods,* on the other hand, Bird denounced Indians almost as if he were Gilbert of "Awossagame." One of the purposes of the novel, he explained, was to destroy the popular image of noble Indians created by James Fenimore Cooper, and to depict "real Indians."

"The North American savage," Bird declared in his preface, "has never appeared to us the gallant and heroic personage he seems to others. . . . [W]e look into the woods for the mighty warrior . . . and behold him retiring, laden with the scalps of miserable squaws and their babes. Heroical?" Bird insisted he was describing Indians as they actually were in their "natural barbaric state"—"ignorant, violent, debased, brutal"—and as they appeared in war or the scalp hunt, when "all the worst deformities of the savage temperament" received their "strongest and fiercest development." In the novel itself, Bird spoke through a renegade, Braxley, to emphasize Indian brutality, especially in the form of Indian violence to white women. The fair Edith, one of the principal characters, is captured by Indians and taken to their village. There Braxley tells her that her cries for help are in vain: "From whom do you expect it? From wild, murderous, besotted Indians, who, if roused from their drunken slumbers, would be more like to assail you with their hatchets than to weep for your sorrows? Know, fair Edith, . . . that there is not one of them who would not rather see those golden tresses hung blackening in the smoke from the rafters of his wigwam, than floating over the brows they adorn. . . ." Here, unmistakably, was the same hate Gilbert had expressed.

Yet, in *Nick of the Woods,* Bird probed the contradictions of Indian-hating more deeply than he had in "Awossagame" and critically exposed the deformities and agony hate and violence produced. Unlike Gilbert, the Indian-hater of the novel is an unusually complex person. He is a gentle and peaceful man, known as Nathan Quaker, who wanders alone in the woods with his dog; yet he is also Nathan Slaughter, a man of great hate and violence, who roves the forests with his bear, killing Indians and carving huge crosses on the chests of his victims. Among the Indians, he is known as the Jibbenainosay, or the spirit that walks, or the devil. Significantly, Bird's Indian-hater is unable to separate successfully these parts of his personality. Thus, he kills Indians but feels enormous guilt for each bloody deed he commits. As he shoots them he must assure himself again and again that he is a "man of peace." Overwhelmed by the deep remorse his own violence has generated, Nathan Quaker/Slaughter insists he is only protecting fair Edith and her companions against "bloodthirsty savages." And he cries out to his friend Roland: "And thee does not think then . . . thee is not of the opinion . . . thee does not altogether hold it to be as a blood-guiltiness, and a wickedness . . . that I did take to me the weapon of war, and shoot thee wicked oppressors, to the saving of thee life? . . . Truly, friend, thee sees it couldn't be helped; and, truly, I don't think thee conscience can condemn me."

Nathan's torment and guilt distinguish him from Melville's Indian-hater. Yet he is in one sense very much like Colonel Moredock, for Nathan, too, is a man with a tragic past. To Roland, he tells how his wife and children were slain by Indians. As Roland listens to the horrible details of the attack, he notices that Nathan is behaving strangely, resembling "a raging maniac," his mouth foaming and his body convulsing. Suddenly Nathan's cap falls off, revealing a hideous scar. Hiding beneath his cap the grotesque reminder of a scalping, Nathan nurtures a hate and a passion for revenge which shocks Roland. The depth of Nathan's "insanity" is exposed when Nathan Quaker/Slaughter encourages Roland to take the scalps of the dead Indians lying around them. "Truly, friend," he assures him, "if thee is of that mind, truly, I won't oppose thee." The suggestion appalls Roland; regarding himself as civilized, he draws back in revulsion. "Their scalps? *I* scalp them!" Roland exclaims. "I am no butcher. I leave them to the bears and wolves, which the villains in their natures so strongly resembled. I will kill Indians wherever I can; but no scalping, Nathan, no scalping for me!" After they leave the scene of carnage, Roland notices blood dripping from Nathan's knife sheath: scarred, Nathan himself has become a scalper.

Aware of his deformity, Nathan seems to have no choice but to isolate himself from civilization and satisfy his thirst for blood. Thus, he is doomed to a life of loneliness, unable to have human relationships, a wanderer in the wilderness. He is "houseless Nathan." Yet he was very much needed in the society of the Market Revolution, for he was a pathfinder, clearing the way for a civilization of enterprise, busy axes, plowed fields, farmhouses, and towns and cities. He was the advance guard of settlement, where the fair Ediths of America would be safe from "murderous" and "drunken" Indians. Moreover, Nathan was also needed by the Rolands of America, for as long as he existed and embodied insanity and perverse violence, men like Roland could claim they were not "butchers," not madmen.

Still, the novel contains a curious contradiction and a profound irony: the effort to degrade the Indian shades into a condemnation of Indian-hating, the depiction of the barbarity of "real Indians" turns out to be the vivid description of the psychotic cruelty of the Indian-hater, and the literary search for an American hero leads to the creation of an antihero. Unlike "The White-Washed Cottage" and "Awossagame," *Nick of the Woods* disguises the sympathy Bird had for Indians and the guilt he felt for what whites had done to them—the stealing of "lands homes" from "the poor Creeks" and the "striking" of Cherokees from the "face of the Earth." Only four years before the publication of the novel, Bird had called his countrymen "oppressors" and "robbers" in their conduct toward the Indian. Bird's agony—his twisting and turning—reflected the ambivalent emotions of a sensitive and informed man trying to create a national literature and American identity, and to make some moral sense out of the material developments of his time—the expansion of the market and the destruction of the Indian.

*Nick of the Woods* was Bird's way of trying to work out this distressing dilemma. As the shrillness of the novel's attack on the image of the noble Indian would suggest, Bird himself did not believe in his portrait of the "real Indian." But he needed to believe in it. Thus he simplified white-Indian conflict into a fantasized struggle between good and evil—between innocent whites like Nathan and his family, settling in the West in search of a peaceful agrarian life, and wild Indians seeking to butcher and scalp white women and children. This kind of myth-making enabled Bird as well as readers who shared his complicated feelings to relieve their guilt and at the same time justify violence against Indians. Yet, in the novel, the dichotomy between good and evil quickly disintegrates into awesome ambiguity. Nathan Quaker's encounter with Indians deforms him: he is filled with hate, killing and scalping Indians while pathetically reaffirming his innocence. Regardless of what had happened to him in the past, Nathan, in his brutality, is forced to stand condemned, particularly in his own eyes. His bloodthirstiness and the mutilated Indian corpses betray him as a psychotic killer. Thus, Nathan Quaker/Slaughter in effect turns against his own creator, Bird himself, exposing the anti-Indian violence and hate Bird witnessed in his own time and tried to justify in his novel. In this strange way, Bird resembled the Americans aboard Melville's *Fidèle* but was even more complex: he was his own confidence man.

## JACKSON: METAPHYSICIAN
## OF INDIAN-HATING

In his "Eulogy" on the death of Andrew Jackson, Washington McCartney asked, "What *was* Andrew Jackson, and what did he *do,* that he should receive such honors while living, and, when dead, should gather a nation round his tomb?" One answer must have been painfully obvious to Cherokee leader John Ross. Aware that the president had been what McCartney described as the "imbodiment" [*sic*] of the nation's "true spirit" and "ruling passion," the "head of the great movement of the age," Ross had offered a bitter insight into the meaning of this symbol for an age. "I knew," he had declared, "that the perpetrator of a wrong never forgives his victims."

Indeed, during the age of Indian removal, American society needed confidence. Enterprising whites had to find a way to expand the market, "lop off" Indian lands, and destroy Indians without inflicting guilt and moral agony upon themselves. Or else, as they could see in Bird's Nathan Quaker/Slaughter, they were in danger of disintegrating into foaming madness. They already knew what Jackson had declared in his first annual message to Congress: their "conduct toward these people" was "deeply interesting" to the "national character." Aware that the identity of white Americans as a moral people was at stake, they hoped the president would be able to resolve their dilemma. Jackson succeeded: he broke Creek resistance at the battle of Horse Shoe Bend in 1814 and helped to make the Southwest safe for white settlement. He also developed and expressed a metaphysics which provided the disguises whites needed in order to be both Quaker and Slaughter, and to do what Nathan could not—both love and destroy Indians. For this "achievement" as well as for the Bank War, the Maysville Road Veto, and the preservation of the Union during the nullification crisis, Jackson gathered a "nation round his tomb."

Born in 1767, Andrew Jackson was only nine years old when Americans like Rush and Jefferson declared their independence from the king. Yet he came to represent the republican conduct and consciousness for which the Revolution had been fought. Throughout his life, he did not allow himself to forget the "bravery and blood" of his "fore fathers" and the "independent rights" they had secured for him and other Americans; he insisted that Americans be worthy of the name of "freemen." As president, Jackson invoked what historian Marvin Meyers has described as a "persuasion," in order to restore republican faith of the fathers among sons pursuing worldly goods in the society of the Market Revolution.

In life and in legend, Jackson was, in many ways, the archetype of the self-made republican man. "He seems to have been an orphan from the plow to the Presidency," a eulogist exclaimed many years after Jackson's death. "He must, therefore, be regarded as the architect of his own fortunes." Actually, Jackson *had* been an orphan: his father died two months before he was born in the Carolina frontier, and his mother died when he was fourteen years old. But before she left him forever, she gave him some republican advice: "Never tell a lie, nor take what is not your own, nor sue anybody for slander or assault and battery. Always settle them cases yourself!" Self-reliant and self-governing, Jackson virtually had no childhood, or at least no adolescence. To his admirers and to Jackson himself, this assumption of responsibility at an early age prepared him to "rise rapidly with a rapidly rising people." Looking back at his own childhood, Jackson attributed his success to the challenges and difficulties he had to overcome early in his life. "I have been Tossed upon the waves of fortune from youthood," he wrote. "I have experienced prosperity and adversity. It was this that gave me knowledge of human nature, it was this that forced into action, all the energies of my mind, and ultimately caused me to progress through life as I have done. . . ." Even as he referred to the "blood" of the "fore fathers," Jackson knew he could claim responsibility for securing his rights: he had been captured by the British in 1781 and was slashed with a sword by a British officer for refusing to blacken the man's boots. Thus, as it turned out, the "blood" shed had included his own.

The fortune Jackson made was also his own. He squandered his inheritance in gambling houses and brothels; as a young lawyer, he was a "roaring, rollicking, game-cocking, horse-racing, card-playing, mischievous fellow. . . ." His life at this time was hardly one of republican virtue; yet, in a way, this profligacy reinforced Jackson's republican origins. His inheritance, his last remaining family tie destroyed, as Michael Rogin has noted, Jackson would begin "a new life totally alone." Completely responsible for himself and determined to be self-made, he would have no king, no parents even, and certainly no inheritance. In 1787, Jackson moved to Nashville to make his fortune on the frontier. There he practiced law, speculated in land, and opened stores to sell goods from Philadelphia. He also married into one of the leading families of the Cumberland and became a wealthy Tennessee planter with more than a hundred slaves. The key to his success was his involvement in land speculation—land acquired from Indians. In 1796, for example, Jackson paid a speculator $100 for a half-interest in 5,000 acres at the Chickasaw bluffs on the Mississippi, and immediately sold half of his share for $312. He held on to the remaining share until 1818, when he negotiated the Chickasaw treaty and opened the area to white settlement; then he sold it for $5,000.

No shining republican himself, Jackson nevertheless offered republican advice to his nephew and son. He sent Andrew J. Donelson instructions on the need to guard against temptations. Many snares, the uncle warned, would be laid for the "inexperienced youth" to lead him into "dissipation, vice, and folly." While the young man should not deprive himself of "proper relaxation" or "innocent amusement," he should seek out only "virtuous" company and exercise care in his relationships with women: "Among the virtuous females, you ought to cultivate an acquaintance, and shun the intercourse of the others as you would the society of the viper . . . it is intercourse with the latter discription [*sic*] that engenders corruption, and contaminates the morals, and fits the young mind for any act of unguarded baseness. . . ." On another occasion, Jackson warned his son against accumulating debt: "Be always certain, if you wish to be independent, to keep your wants within your means, always when you have money, paying for them when bought." In his own conduct as a ribald young lawyer and a land speculator, Jackson could not claim authority to teach republican lessons even to his nephew and son, much less to society in general. The source of this authority had to be located elsewhere—in the fierce self-discipline and control Jackson had imposed on himself as a soldier and Indian-fighter.

For Jackson, republican virtue was achieved in war. The War of 1812 and the Creek War of 1813–14 gave him the opportunity to overcome what he called the "indolence" which threatened to destroy him, and to seek republican purification and regeneration through violence. A "free born son" of America, Jackson went to war against the British to defend the "only republick now existing in the world," the "fabric cemented by the blood of our fathers." A "brave son of Tennessee," Jackson led troops against Creeks in Mississippi to conquer "the cream of the Creek country" for the expansion of the "republick" and to avenge the deaths of more than 200 people killed by hostile Creeks at Fort Mims. A soldier, separated from his frivolous and bourgeois past, he could now view himself as a worthy republican son. From the battlefield, he wrote to his wife: "I can only say your good understanding, and reflection will reconcile you to our separation, the situation of our country require it for who could brook a British tyranny, who would not prefer dying free, struggling for our liberty and religion, than live a British slave." Jackson believed Americans had to have republican discipline and exercise it in war in order to protect their freedom. They must "never prefer an inglorious sloth, a supine inactivity to the honorable toil of carrying the republican standard to the heights of Abraham," Commander Jackson told his troops. As a soldier, Jackson could lay claim to the republican virtue of respectable work, which he could not do as a land speculator.

As Jackson marched against the Indians, he also waged a private battle against his own body. His "fore fathers" had had to discipline the physical self in order to deny pleasure; Jackson had to discipline his body in order to defy pain. His had been a life of illness and physical agony. He had contracted smallpox as a teenager, and suffered from recurrent malaria, fevers, and rheumatism. Chronically constipated, he was often in extreme discomfort in the field, especially during "a severe attacke of the Bowell complaint." He suffered from attacks of dysentery, which caused painful cramps and diarrhea. His body reflected his sickly condition: over six feet tall, he weighed only 145 pounds. Jackson felt an almost constant pain in his chest, where a bullet received in a duel with Charles Dickinson in 1806 was still lodged close to his heart. Shortly before he departed for the Creek campaign, he had exchanged gunfire with Thomas Hart Benton, and a bullet had fractured his left shoulder. His body broken and feverish, Jackson marched into the field against the Creeks. Called "Old Hickory" by his troops, he was admired for his power to withstand hardship and pain. His victory over the British at New Orleans was interpreted as a personal triumph over his ailing body. There, as one observer described the battle, Jackson barely had the strength to stand erect without support. "His body was sustained alone by the spirit within," and "the disease contracted in the swamps of Alabama still clung to him." Jackson prevailed over both the British and the body: "Reduced to a mere skeleton, unable to digest his food, and unrefreshed by sleep, his life seemed to be preserved by some miraculous agency."

His body disciplined, Jackson used violence to bring Indians under control. His struggle to dominate both his body and the Indians was integrated: military campaigns in the Creek War enabled him to subordinate his physical self and to destroy Indians. Indians, for Jackson, personified the body. He believed they were impulsive and lacked "discipline." He also viewed Indian men as sexual threats to white women; few incidents aroused his wrath as much as the Indian capture of white women. Jackson made the case of Mrs. Crawly his "own." Angrily protesting her capture and confinement to "a mortar, naked, lascerated," he demanded that the "brave sons of Tennessee" wipe away this "blushing shame."

During the campaign against the Creeks in 1813–14, Jackson denounced his Indian enemies as "savage bloodhounds" and "blood thirsty barbarians," and urged his troops to exterminate them. "I know," he told his men, "you will teach the cannibals who reveled in the carnage of our unoffending Citizens at Fort Meems that the thunder of our arms is more terrible than the Earth quakes of their Prophets, and that Heaven Dooms to inevitable destruction the wretch who Smiles at the torture he inflicts and who neither spares female innocence, declining age nor helpless infancy." Shortly before the battle of Horse Shoe Bend in March 1814, Jackson was in a state of rage. "I must distroy [sic] those deluded victims doomed to distruction [sic] by their own restless and savage conduct," he wrote to Major General Thomas Pinckney. The next day, he sent Pinckney another letter, and again he snarled at his enemies. Calling them "savage dogs," he wrote: "It is by the charge I distroy [sic] from eight to ten of them, for one they kill of my men, by charging them I have on all occasions preserved the scalps of my killed." At the battle of Horse Shoe Bend, Jackson and his troops surrounded some 800 Creeks at a bend in the river and killed almost all of them, including women and children. After the battle, he sent cloth worn by the slain warriors to the ladies of Tennessee. His soldiers cut long strips of skin from the bodies of the dead Indians and used them for bridle reins; they also cut the tip of each dead Indian's nose to count the number of enemy bodies.

In the Creek War of 1813–14, Jackson had accomplished more than the conquest of Indian lands, or what he described, in a letter written to Thomas Pinckney after his victory at Horse Shoe Bend, as the "valuable country" west of the Cosee and north of the "allabama." He had also done more than punish Indians for exercising "lawless tyranny" over "helpless and unprotected" white women, for murdering white mothers and their "little prattling infants," and for capturing white women. Most importantly, in the war, Jackson had purified the republican self. He was no longer a high-living lawyer and shady land speculator. In the wilderness, he had disciplined and chastened himself, and triumphed over "indolence," "sloth," pain, and Indians. Jackson was ready to be the leader of a democracy in quest of the restoration of republican virtue; he was also ready to lead the nation in the removal of Indians.

Fourteen years later, Jackson, still remembered as a heroic Indian fighter, was elected to the presidency. During the age of Jackson, some 70,000 Indians were removed from their homes in the South and driven west of the Mississippi River. Due to violence, disease, starvation, dangerous travel conditions, and harsh winter weather, almost one-third of the Southern Indians died. By 1844, the South was, as far as Indians were concerned, a "white man's country." Jackson had extended Jefferson's empire of liberty by removing Indians toward the "Stony mountains."

As president, Jackson played a complex and decisive role in Indian removal. Shortly after his election, he supported the efforts of three Southern states—Georgia, Alabama, and Mississippi—to abolish Indian tribal units and laws and to extend state authority over Indians. Georgia subjected them to militia duty, state taxes, and suits for debts, while it denied them suffrage as well as the right to bring suits and to testify in court. All three states opened Indian territory to white settlement; they also encouraged intruders and allowed whites to take Indian lands, including "improved" or cultivated tracts. As the states imperialistically extended their authority over Indian territory, Jackson told Congress: "If the states chose to extend their laws over them it would not be in the power of the federal government to prevent it." Actually, as Michael Rogin has pointed out, Jackson's assertions of federal impotence in this case made him "the passive spectator of a policy he had actively advocated." Jackson knew what his responsibility in this matter was as the chief executive of the United States. Treaties and federal laws had given Congress, not the states, authority over the Indians. The Indian Trade and Intercourse Act of 1802 had provided that no land cessions could be made except by treaty with a tribe, and that federal law, not state law, would operate in Indian

territory. In 1832 the United States Supreme Court ruled against the extension of state law into Indian territory, but Jackson refused to enforce the Court's decision.

While claiming federal powerlessness, Jackson collaborated and conspired with state officials to usurp tribal lands and remove Indians. In a letter to Jackson dated February 3, 1830, General John Coffee outlined the strategy for this collaboration:

> Deprive the chiefs of the power they now possess, take from their own code of laws, and reduce them to plain citizenship . . . and they will soon determine to move, and then there will be no difficulty in getting the poor Indians to give their consent. All this will be done by the State of Georgia if the United States do not interfere with her law—. . . . This will of course silence those in our country who constantly seek for causes to complain—It may indeed turn them loose upon Georgia, but that matters not, it is Georgia who clamors for the Indian lands, and she alone is entitled to the blame if any there be.

In this strategy to break up tribes, "reduce" Indians to citizenship, and force them to give up their lands and move away, all Jackson had to do, as president, was make certain the federal government did not interfere with the law of the state of Georgia.

But Jackson did not limit himself to noninterference. He also met with Indians to inform them that he had no power to help in their resistance against the states and to advise them to migrate to the West. Jackson even employed "confidential agents" to manipulate the chiefs and persuade them to accept removal. The secret mission of these "confidential agents," as stated in a letter from Secretary of War John Eaton to General William Carroll, was to use bribery to influence "the Chiefs and influential men." "It is believed," wrote Eaton, "that the more careful you are to secure from even the Chiefs the official character you carry with you, the better—Since no circumstance is too slight to excite their suspicion or awaken their jealousy; Presents in your discretion to the amount of not more than $2000 might be made with effect, but attaching to you the poorer Indians, as you pass through their Country, given as their friend; and the same to the Children of the Chiefs, and the Chiefs themselves, in clothes, or otherwise." Jackson did not have to depend heavily on deception and bribery to remove Indians, however. He had available two "legal" methods: indirect removal through the land allotment program and direct removal through treaty.

Used to deprive Creeks, Choctaws, and Chickasaws of their territories, the land allotment program provided for granting land in fee simple title to individual Indians. As a landowner, an Indian could be "reduced" to citizenship, or he could sell and move west of the Mississippi River. In the Treaty of Dancing Rabbit Creek, for example, Choctaw families and individuals were instructed to register with an Indian agent within six months after the ratification of the treaty if they wished to remain in the state of Mississippi and receive a grant of land. Seemingly, the program gave Indians a choice as well as a fair chance to succeed in white society. Under this program, however, thousands of individual Indians were "given," sometimes forced to accept, land grants only to have land speculators take their fee simple titles. Everywhere federal certifying agents cooperated with speculators to defraud Indians or their lands. The Columbus Land Company, for instance, took a group of Creeks from one agent to another to sign contracts for grants. Speculators bribed certifying agents to approve fraudulent contracts; often the agents were the speculators themselves. After they had secured lands for individual Indians, speculators set up stores which extended credit to them in exchange for land titles as collateral, and then took over the deeds as they failed to pay off their debts. Under the program, Mary Young has calculated, speculators acquired 80 to 90 percent of the lands granted to southeastern Indians, or some 25 million acres of land.

The land allotment program enabled white speculators, farmers, and planters to take Indian lands "legally" and to absolve themselves from reponsibility for the Indians' poverty, removal, and destruction. Indians had been "given" land and responsibility for their own welfare; whites could not be blamed if they got into debt, lost their lands, and had to remove beyond the Mississippi. As Secretary of War Lewis Cass explained, "[O]ur citizens were disposed to buy and the Indians to sell. . . . The subsequent disposition which shall be made of these payments seems to be utterly beyond the reach of the Government. . . . The improvident habits of the Indians can not be controlled by regulations. . . . If they waste it, as waste it they too often will, it is deeply to be regretted yet still it is only exercising a right conferred upon them by the treaty." a Lockean contractual framework had been imposed upon the Indian: he was no longer defined as a member of a community or tribe but as an individual.

Entitled to own and sell private property, he was thrust into the market system. Thus, a victim of manipulation and fraud, the Indian was blamed for his own ruin.

In a letter to General John Coffee on April 7, 1832, Jackson bluntly stated the real purpose of the land allotment program: "The object of the government now is, to have all their reservations surveyed and laid off as early as we can." Once Indians had been granted individual land allotments, they would "sell and move to the West." And then Jackson added: "When the reserves are surveyed it will require but a short time to compleat the ballance and have it into markett. . . ." What Jackson wanted in the market was the Indian's land, not the Indian himself as a Lockean farmer.

Where Jackson was not able to buy out and remove Indians individually, he turned to the treaty method to remove the entire tribe directly. This was the strategy used against the Cherokees. In 1834, Jackson failed to secure a treaty for the cession of Cherokee lands and removal of the tribe to the West. The next year he sent the Reverend J. F. Schermerhorn to negotiate a treaty with the pro-removal faction of the Cherokees. The treaty provided that the Cherokees would cede their entire eastern territory and relocate beyond the Mississippi in exchange for $4.5 million from the federal government. Signed in Washington on March 14, the treaty had to be ratified by the tribe in full council to be effective. The council rejected the treaty, however, and Schermerhorn made arrangements for another meeting in December, to be held in New Echota, Georgia, to negotiate a new treaty. To Secretary Cass, he wrote: "We shall make a treaty with those who attend, and rely upon it." Meanwhile, the Georgia militia jailed the anti-removal leader, John Ross, and suppressed the Cherokee newspaper. With the opposition silenced, Schermerhorn proceeded to make a treaty with those in attendance, even though they constituted only a tiny fraction of the entire Cherokee tribe and though none of the principal officers of the tribe was present. The Treaty of New Echota was signed and sent to Washington for ratification by Congress.

Jackson "relied upon it," and successfully urged Congress to ratify the treaty. But the federal government's dishonesty could not be covered up. Appointed to enroll the Cherokees for removal, Major W. M. Davis found out what had actually happened at New Echota and wrote a letter to Secretary Cass to expose Schermerhon's shameful chicanery:

Sir, that paper . . . called a treaty, is not treaty at all, because not sanctioned by the great body of the Cherokee and made without their participation or assent. I solemnly declare to you that upon its reference to the Cherokee people it would be instantly rejected by nine-tenths of them. . . . The most cunning and artful means were resorted to to conceal the paucity of numbers present at the treaty. . . . Mr. Schermerhorn's apparent design was to conceal the real number present and to impose on the public and the government on this point. The delegation taken to Washington by Mr. Schermerhorn had no more authority to make a treaty than any other dozen Cherokee accidentally picked up for the purpose.

The Treaty of New Echota was a known fraud; still, the president responded to it as if it were the voice of the Cherokee people.

Ratification triggered the movement of thousands of white intruders into Cherokee territory. They seized Cherokee farms and cultivated lands, forcing out and often murdering the inhabitants. Still the Cherokees refused to recognize the treaty and leave their territory; finally, in 1838, the federal government ordered the army to round up 15,000 of them. Placed in detention camps and then marched west beyond the Mississippi in the dead of winter, more than 4,000 Cherokees died on the "Trail of Tears."

As the president responsible for Indian removal, Jackson was a philosopher as well as a policy maker. While he negotiated fraudulent treaties and schemed with state leaders to acquire Indian lands, he offered solemn reflections on the destinies of whites and Indians. A leader of his people, he recognized the need to explain the nation's conduct toward Indians, to give it moral meaning. In his writings, messages to Congress, and personal letters, Jackson presented a philosphical justification for the extermination of Native Americans.

Jackson's metaphysics began with a confession: white efforts to civilize the Indian had failed. Whites had purchased lands from Indians and thrust them farther into the wilderness, forcing them to remain in a "wandering state." Some Indians in the South had become civilized and learned the art of farming, Jackson noted; but they had set up an "independent government" within the state of Georgia. Such a "foreign government" could not be tolerated. Thus, civilized Indians had to submit to the state. But, unlike Jefferson, Jackson did not believe the Indian could remain within the state, surrounded by whites in civilized society, and survive. "The fate of the Mohigan, the Narragansett, and the Delaware is fast overtaking the Choctaw, the Cherokee, and the Creek.

That this fate surely awaits them if they remain within the limits of the State does not admit of a doubt." Like the tribes before them, they would disappear. "Humanity and national honor demand that every effort be made to avert so great a calamity." Driven by "feelings of justice," Jackson asked whether something could be done "to preserve this much-injured race." And he offered an answer. He proposed that a district west of the Mississippi be set aside—"to be guaranteed to the Indian tribes as long as they shall occupy it." There they would be free to live in peace and to have their own government "as long as the grass grows, or water runs."

Urging Indians to seek new homes beyond the Mississippi, Jackson encouraged them to follow the example of whites, become a people in motion, restless and expansive. "Doubtless it will be painful [for Indians] to leave the graves of their fathers," Jackson told Congress. "But what do they more than our ancestors did or than our children are now doing? To better their condition in an unknown land our forefathers left all that was dear in earthly objects. Our children by thousands yearly leave the land of their birth to seek new homes in distant regions." Movement, geographical and social, represented progress and a Jacksonian way of life. It enabled white Americans to develop "power and faculties of man in their highest perfection."

Time and again, Jackson insisted he wanted to be "just" and "humane" toward the Indians. He wanted to protect them from the "mercenary influence of white men," and to exercise a "parental" control over them and perpetuate their race. He explained that he wanted them to be happy and that their happiness depended on removal. Jackson regarded himself as a "father," concerned about the welfare of his Indian "children." He instructed Major David Haley to transmit to the chiefs of the Choctaws his advice as their "father." "That the chiefs and warriors may fully understand this talk," wrote Jackson, "you will please go amongst, & read it to, and fully explain to them. Tell them it is from my own mouth you have rec'd it and that I never speak with a forked tongue." His advice to the Indians was to move beyond the Mississippi; and, if they refused to accept this advice, Jackson warned, they must then be responsible for whatever happened to them. "I feel conscious of having done my duty to my red children," he said, "and if any failure of my good intentions arises, it will be attributable to their want of duty to themselves, not to me."

Ultimately, as Jackson revealed in his removal of the Seminoles, white paternalism drew its power from the barrel of a gun. In his letter to the Seminoles in 1835, the president offered paternal advice as he threatened paternal power. Addressing them as "My Children," he said he was sorry to learn that they had been listening to "bad counsel." "You know me," he assured them, "and you know that I would not deceive, nor advise you to do anything that was unjust or injurious." As a "friend," Jackson claimed he offered them "the words of truth." White people were settling around them, and the game had disappeared from their country. "Your people are poor and hungry," he observed. "Even if you had a right to stay, how could you live where you now are?" Then he warned them about the market system as if it were an impersonal force and he were not a part of it. "You have sold all your country. . . . The tract you have ceded will soon be surveyed and sold, and immediately afterwards will be occupied by a white population." Thus, Seminoles should migrate to the West where game was yet abundant and where they would be far away from the market and whites. If they remained, they would starve and be forced to steal from whites. "You will be resisted, punished, perhaps killed," the white father predicted. Again, he urged them to leave, and then added: "But lest some of your rash young men should forcibly oppose your arrangements for removal, I have ordered a large military force to be sent among you."

Seminoles, under the leadership of Osceola, refused to accept Jackson's fatherly advice and took up armed resistance. Enraged, Jackson sent enough troops to Florida "as might eat Powell [Osceola] and his few." But the Seminoles were not so easily crushed. After Jackson left office in 1837, he continued to focus his fury on the insubordinate tribe. In a memorandum on the Florida campaign, he recommended a strategy to bring Seminole defiance to a quick end. American commanders should conduct search-and-destroy missions, and order their troops to find Seminole villages and capture or destroy the women. Unless they knew "where the Indian women were," Jackson wrote, United States soldiers would never be effective. Their effort would be "like a combined operation to encompass a wolf in the hamocks without knowing first where her den and whelps were."

Here was the propensity for violence which Jefferson had fearfully described as the "most boisterous passions," and which Jackson had disguised, giving it moral legitimacy. Many years before Indian removal, commander Jackson had declared to his troops after the bloody victory at Horse Shoe Bend:

> The fiends of the Tallapoosa will no longer murder our women and children, or disturb the quiet of our borders. Their midnight flambeaux will no more illumine their Council house or shine upon the victim of their infernal orgies. They have disappeared from the face of the Earth. In their places a new generation will arise who will know their duties better. The weapons of warfare will be exchanged for the utensils of husbandry; and the wilderness which now withers in sterility and seems to mourn the desolation which overspreads it, will blossom as the rose, and become the nursery of the arts. . . . How lamentable it is that the path to peace should lead through blood, and over the carcases of the slain!! But it is in the dispensation of that providence, which inflicts partial evil to produce general good.

There, on the dark and bloody ground of the West, General Jackson had developed a justification for violence against Indians and a metaphysics for genocide. White violence was a necessary partial evil for the realization of a general good—the extension of white civilization and the transformation of the wilderness into an agrarian society and a nursery of the arts. As president, Jackson took this rationale and incorporated it into the national consciousness. In his second annual message to Congress, he declared:

> Humanity has often wept over the fate of the aborigines of this country, and Philanthropy has been long busily employed in devising means to avert it, but its progress has never for a moment been arrested, and one by one have many powerful tribes disappeared from the earth. To follow to the tomb the last of his race and tread on the graves of extinct nations excite melancholy reflections. But true philanthropy reconciles the mind to these vicissitudes as it does to the extinction of one generation to make room for another.

In all this, the president reassured the nation, as the general had earlier reassured his troops, that nothing was to be "regretted." "Philanthropy could not wish to see this continent restored to the condition in which it was found by our forefathers." And the metaphysician than asked: "What good man would prefer a country covered with forests and ranged by a few thousand savages to our extensive Republic, studded with cities, towns, and prosperous farms . . . filled with all the blessings of liberty, civilization, and religion?" As the president meditated on the disappearance of Indians and the "melancholy reflections" it excited, he claimed for white Americans their moral innocence. What had happened to the Indians was inevitable, even moral.

The metaphysics of Indian-hating, for Jackson, had begun in the Creek War of 1813–14 and was completed in the Bank War of 1832–36. In his war against Indians, Jackson had used them to define savagery. Thus, he described them as "cannibals," "savage dogs," "bloodhounds," and "blood thirsty" slayers of innocent white women and children. His attack on Indians, however, did not enable him to formulate a clear and precise definition of civilization, especially a republican one. His references to the "free born sons" of the "republick" and the republican "fabric" of the revolutionary forefathers were vague and inadequate. Victorious over "savages," Jackson still needed to identify the possessors of republican virtue—the "real people." This he did in his war against the Bank of the United States.

In Jackson's mind, the Bank War was similar to his military campaign against the Creeks: it was a struggle to preserve the virtues of the Old Republic. The privately controlled Second Bank of the United States, chartered in 1816 and the depository for federal funds, was "a system at war" with "the genius" of the institutions the republican fathers had established. Scheduled for a renewal of its charter during Jackson's presidency, the bank encountered his republican wrath. "Our Fathers," he declared, had "perilled their lives" to arrest the "natural instinct to reach after new acquisitions." The "Revolutionary struggle" should not be weakened in "lavish public disbursements"; corporations with "exclusive privileges" should not be allowed to undermine the "original" checks and balances of the Constitution.

The bank represented, to Jackson, an even greater and more insidious threat to republicans than the Creeks. The red enemies were "stupid mortals," relying on "subterfuges" such as their "grim visages" and "hideous yells" rather than on their bravery. By contrast, the bank constituted a consolidation of power: Through its "silent" and "secret" operation and through shrewd manipulation, a few corrupt men were able to acquire control over the "labor and earnings of the great body of the people." In his famous bank veto message, which resulted in the destruction of the bank, Jackson declared:

> It is to be regretted that the rich and powerful too often bend the acts of government to their selfish purposes. Distinctions in society will always exist under every just government. Equality of talents, of education, or of wealth can not be produced by human institution. In the full enjoyment of the gifts of Heaven and the fruits of superior industry, economy, and virtue, every man is equally entitled to protection by law; but when the laws undertake to add to these just advantages artificial distinctions, to grant titles, gratuities, and exclusive privileges, to make the rich richer and the potent more powerful, the humble members of society— the farmers, mechanics, and laborers—who have neither the time nor the means of securing like favors to themselves—have a right to complain of the injustice of their Government.

The bank and its system of paper money engendered a "spirit of speculation injurious to the habits and character of the people," an "eager desire to amass wealth without labor," a "craving desire for luxurious enjoyment," and a "sickly appetite for effeminate indulgence." The republican fathers had located the source of corruption in the king; Jackson located it in the bank. The new "hydra of corruption" drained from the people their power to resist cupidity, idleness, temptation, and extravagance.

Regardless of whether he was struggling against the "moneyed power" or the Indians, Jackson excluded both groups from the "real people"—the farmers, mechanics, and laborers. "The bone and sinew of the country," they depended on their own "honest industry" and economy for success. Self-governing and independent, they cultivated the soil, earned the fruits of their own labor, and possessed the "habits of economy and simplicity" so congenial to the "character of republicans." But the corrupt men of wealth and the Indians were antagonistic to honest labor. While the former exploited the privileges granted to them by the government in order to enrich themselves, the latter lacked the "intelligence, industry, the moral habits," "the desire of improvement," and the capacity for self-government. "Observation proves that the great body of the southern tribes of Indians," Jackson claimed, "are erratic in their habits, and wanting in those endowments which are suited to a people who would direct themselves. . . ." "Children of the forests," they did not cultivate the land. How could they, asked Jackson, make claims on tracts on which they had neither dwelt nor made "improvements," merely because they had "seen them from the mountain or passed them in the chase?" In Jackson's judgment, neither men of "artificial distinctions" nor Indians had a place in a republican society.

The parallel between Jackson's military campaign against Indians and his war against the bank was distressingly evident to Nicholas Biddle. "The worthy President," observed Bank Director Biddle, "thinks because he has scalped Indians . . . he is to have his way with the Bank." Biddle's was a most perspicacious remark. Indeed, in Jackson's fantasy, Indians were "those monsters," while the bank was "the monster." Indians threatened to kill Jackson and other whites in the West and lay waste "the abodes of industry." The bank, too, "waged war upon the people" of the "republick" and appeared to threaten Jackson personally. "The bank, Mr. Van Buren, is trying to kill me, *but* I will kill it," the president exclaimed in fury. "I've got my foot upon it and I'll crush it." A slayer of "monsters," Jackson destroyed the Creeks at Horse Shoe Bend and the Bank of the United States and swept both of them from "the face of the Earth."

Confidence, as Melville suggested in his novel, was a political style which depended on role-playing, and which was widely used in Jacksonian society. Unlike Melville's confidence-man, Jackson employed confidence as a technique to take himself and his society away from rather than toward exposure, critical awareness, and redemption. In Jackson's service, disguises enabled him to give events his own definitions, and to judge his and the nation's actions in a variety of ways and in accordance with their economic interests and psychological needs. His was a "persuasion" which not only allowed him to destroy the bank as he nurtured a nostalgia for an old agrarian republic but also made it possible for him to advance the market as he articulated compassion and regret for the Indians.

In the removal and killing of Indians, the expansion of the market, and the formulation of a metaphysics of Indian-hating, Jackson was in effect the nation's confidence-man. Undeniably, as Jackson himself acknowledged, how whites conducted themselves in relations with Indians was "deeply interesting" to their "national character." They must not be guilty of capitalist corruption, moral absurdity, or mass murders. As president, Jackson told them they were not, and skillfully exercised confidence in his own conduct toward Indians. He excluded them from the "real people" and claimed they were hunters and wanderers as he encouraged intruders to seize cultivated and improved Indian lands. He called himself "father" and Indians "children" as he employed "confiden-

tial agents" to deceive and bribe Indians in order to remove them from their lands; he insisted that the government be kept pure and separated from the corruption of land speculators as he permitted the government to be used in their service. He assured the Indians that his advice to them was based on "feelings of justice" as he moved their lands into the "markett." Indeed, through the use of a multitude of disguises, Jackson protected the moral character of the American people as he served the class interests of the speculators, farmers, and planters seeking to appropriate Indian lands.

But what Jackson *was* and what he *did* involved more than the appropriation of millions of acres of Indian lands. As general and as president, Jackson had built a "pyramid of skulls." Indians lost their lives as well as their lands. A Jibbenainosay in reality, he accomplished what Bird fantasized—Indian deaths. He helped to bring about that "calamity" which he said he was seeking to avoid, and succeeded precisely where Nathan Quaker/Slaughter had failed. He was able to dissociate his acts of violence against Indians from his claims of compassion, and to integrate both into a metaphysics of civilization which allowed whites to destroy the Indian and assure themselves that the Indian's extinction was not to be "regretted." This was an integration Nathan Quaker/ Slaughter could not achieve. Unable to engage in self-deception, despite all of his disguises, Nathan knew he was a killer—knew murder was murder and evil was evil. He possessed a singular sanity Jackson did not have. Both Quaker and Slaughter, Jackson was seemingly able to be what Melville's confidence-man thought was impossible for Colonel John Moredock—a man of love and also of hate, a good father and also an Indian-killer. Soon after the battle of Horse Shoe Bend, Jackson wrote to his wife: "The *carnage* was *dreadful*. . . . I hope shortly to put an end to the war and return to your arms, kiss my little andrew for me, tell him I have a warriors bow and quiver for him." "No cold husband or colder father," Jackson was at the same time like the Jibbenainosay, a "Leather-stocking Nemesis." "And Natty, what sort of a white man is he?" asked D. H. Lawrence. "Why, he is a man with a gun. He is a killer, a slayer. Patient and gentle as he is, he is a slayer. Self-effacing . . . still he is a killer."

# Strangers in the Land: Nativism and Nationalism

## JOHN HIGHAM

Unlike the older Catholic population, the southern and eastern Europeans who had begun to arrive in considerable numbers during the 1880's lived in the American imagination only in the form of a few vague, ethnic stereotypes. They occupied, in other words, no distinctive place, either separately or collectively, in the traditions of American nationalism. In the 1890's, for the first time, they became a significant factor in the growth of nativism. An initial distrust, compounded largely out of their culture and appearance, swelled into a pressing sense of menace, into hatred, and into violence. This process went forward essentially along two lines: first and most commonly, the general anti-foreign feelings touched off by the internal and international shocks of the late nineteenth century were discharged with special force against these new targets so that each of the southeastern European groups appeared as a particularly insidious representative of the whole foreign menace; secondly and more slowly, a campaign got under way against the new immigration as a unique entity, constituting in its difference from other foreign groups the essence of the nation's peril. The first type of attack was midwife to the second. The new immigrants had the very bad luck to arrive in America en masse at a time when nativism was already running at full tilt, and when neither anarchist nor Jesuit afforded a wholly satisfactory victim for it.

The hostilities which southeastern Europeans faced depended partly on their increasing prominence on the American scene. During the early nineties, peasants and Jews poured out of southern and eastern Europe in ever larger numbers, fleeing from poverty and inhumanity to a new promised land. Cutthroat competition among the transatlantic steamship companies eased their flight; steerage rates on first-class boats dropped to $10 or even less. The depression sharply reduced all immigration, but the new current never fell below one hundred thousand persons per year—a level it had first reached in 1887. More exclusively than most older immigrant groups, the new ones swarmed into the slums, the factories, and the mines. Either urbanites or industrial workers, and usually both, they played a role in American life that lent itself to nativist interpretation. In the crowded places where they made their homes, they lived as a class apart, the least assimilated and most impoverished of the immigrants. Hence, they symbolized vividly the social and economic ills with which nativists identified the immigrants generally. Fears of developing class cleavage could easily center on them; and with less perversion of logic than anti-Catholicism required, the problems of depression and unrest could be associated with them. Above all, each of the southern and eastern European nationalities seemed to Americans in some way a disturber of the peace, thereby focalizing the fear of foreign-bred discontent.

On the other hand, the new immigrants, although vulnerable as symbols of a general foreign problem, did not yet stand out readily as a collective entity. Until 1896 the old influx from northern and western Europe surpassed the southern and eastern European current. All in all, at least 80 percent of the European-born population of the United States in the mid-nineties still derived from those accustomed sources—Germany, Great Britain, Scandinavia, France, Switzerland, and the Low Countries. Furthermore, concentration of settlement limited the impact of the new groups. While a few coastal cities and industrial complexes felt their arrival sharply, large parts of the country hardly knew them at all. Two-thirds of the first-generation Italians, for example, settled in the mid-Atlantic and New England states. Most of America was just beginning to learn of their presence, largely at secondhand. Consequently most of the hatred of Italians, Slavs, and Jews consisted of general anti-foreign attitudes refracted through specific national stereotypes.

The Slavic coal miners of Pennsylvania illustrate very well how the new immigration inherited a wider, pre-existing animus. They acquired the immigrant's standard reputation for disorder in an unusually simple, direct form. The American mind contained, apparently, no distinctive "Slavic" stereotype, comparable to Italian and Jewish stereotypes, which might have individualized the hostile response. Consequently Slavic and Magyar laborers impressed public opinion at large simply as foreigners par excellence: uncivilized, unruly, and dangerous.

The impression fed upon the Slavic coal miners' sporadic but increasing involvement in labor unrest. Ironically, while other working-men continued to despise them as cheap and docile competitors, the general public fixed its eyes on their lapses from docility. Already the Slavs had incurred the indignation of employers for participating in the coke strike of 1886; during the greater industrial conflicts of the nineties, they encountered the hostility of the whole middle-class community. By 1891, when Henry Clay Frick precipitated a strike of fourteen thousand coke workers by posting a new wage scale, Slavic and Magyar nationalities well outnumbered the older immigrants and native Americans in the bituminous fields. Although British and Americans led the strike, it was generally interpreted as an uprising of "Huns," who, in the words of the New York *Tribune,* were "the most dangerous of labor-unionists and strikers. They fill up with liquor and cannot be reasoned with." The company brought in nonunion workers, a step which resulted in riots and vandalism on the part of the strikers. In this tense situation, a crowd of "Huns," returning from a mass meeting, passed a frightened detachment of state militia guarding a company store. Someone fired a shot, the strikers fled, and the militia fired two volleys after them. Ten dead and fifty wounded immigrants littered the road. According to the *Tribune,* the militia's action was "upheld by businessmen and all law-abiding people in the entire region."

Frick finally succeeded in breaking the strike, though he was to face a similar walkout three years later. This time an immigrant mob killed Frick's chief engineer, causing the Pittsburgh *Times* to report that the whole region was "trembling on the brink of an insurrection. Never before were the dangerous foreigners so thoroughly aroused." A sheriff's posse, equally aroused, pursued the escaping strikers, shooting several and arresting 138 for murder. No sooner was this strike defeated than a general work stoppage throughout the bituminous coal fields ensued, bringing its quota of violence and police brutalities.

The bloodiest episode occurred in 1897. While the United Mine Workers Union was leading the new immigrants to victory in the bituminous fields, an attempt to launch a strike in the anthracite country provoked disaster. About 150 Polish and Hungarian strikers, entirely unarmed, set out from Hazleton, Pennsylvania, toward a nearby town, intent on urging the men there to join the walkout. The sheriff, persuaded by the coal owners that an organized march was illegal, gathered a posse of 102 deputies to intercept it. As the strikers came in sight, the sheriff ordered them to return. Someone struck him, frightening him into commanding the deputies to fire. They poured volley after volley into the surprised and terror-ized crowd as it stampeded in flight. They killed twenty-one immigrants and wounded forty more. The sheriff, a former mine forman, explained that the crowd consisted of "infuri-ated foreigners . . . like wild beasts." Other mine foremen agreed that if the strikers had been American-born no blood would have flowed.

In the case of the Italians, a rather similar fear of "infuriated foreigners" took a different twist. Anti-foreign sentiment filtered through a specific ethnic stereotype when Italians were involved; for in American eyes they bore the mark of Cain. They suggested the stiletto, the Maffia, the deed of impassioned violence. "The disposition to assassinate in revenge for a fancied wrong," declared the Baltimore *News,* "is a marked trait in the character of this impulsive and inexorable race." Every time a simple Italian laborer resorted to his knife, the newspapers stressed the fact of his nationality; the most trivial fracas in Mulberry Street caused a headline on "Italian Vendetta." The stereotype conditioned every major outburst of anti-Italian sentiment in the 1890's. The distinctive nativism which swarthy *paesani* experienced took the guise of social discipline applied to alleged acts of homicide.

Time and again, lynching parties struck at Italians charged with murder. In 1891 a wild rumor that drunken Italian laborers had cut the throats of a whole American family in West Virginia set off further rumors of a pitched battle between a sheriff's posse and the assassins. In 1895, when the southern Colorado coal fields were gripped by violent labor strife, a group of miners and other residents systematically massacred six Italian workers implicated in the death of an American saloonkeeper. A year later a mob dragged three Italians from jail in a small Louisiana town and hanged them. The biggest incident convulsed New Orleans—and then the whole country—at the beginning of the decade. The city combined southern folkways with all of the social problems of the urban North, and as the most southerly of American ports, it was the haven of a large migration from Sicily. In 1891 the superintendent of police was murdered under conditions which pointed to the local Sicilian population. Wholesale arrests followed in an atmosphere of hysteria. The mayor issued a public appeal: "We must teach these people a lesson that they will not forget for all time." The city council appointed a citizen's committee to suggest ways of preventing the influx of European criminals. But when some of the accused were tried, the jury (which may have been suborned) stunned the city by refusing to convict. While officials stood idly by, a mob proceeded "to remedy the failure of justice" by lynching eleven Italian suspects. With apparent unanimity local newspapers and business leaders blessed the action.

At that point jingoism intruded upon what had begun as a local, internal episode, transforming it into a nation-wide commotion and a diplomatic crisis. Italy sought redress for the victims' families and punishment of the mob that murdered them. Secretary of State James G. Blaine treated the plea cavalierly, whereupon Italy abruptly recalled her minister in Washington. Internal hatred and external conflict now interacted directly, producing an explosion of feeling against Italy and enormously magnifying the fear of Italian-Americans. A belief that the Italian fleet might suddenly descend on the United States gained fairly wide credence, and patriots flexed their muscles in preparation. Italians within the country now appeared as a potential fifth column; obviously these people could not be depended upon in times of national danger. There were reports of Italian immigrants riddling an American flag with bullets; a rumor circulated that several uniformed corps of Italians were drilling in New York. In Wheeling, West Virginia, miners went on strike because their employer refused to discharge two Italians; the strikers vowed they would not work with men "allied to a nation that was trying to bring about a war with the United States." A

patriotic society demanded war if Italy continued shipping criminals to the United States. The *Review of Reviews* saw two lessons in the affair: that America must have a navy to protect itself from "wanton insult," and an immigration policy to keep out "the refuse of the murderbreeds of Southern Europe."

Clearly, as the *Review* pointed out, a revival of Americanism was emerging from the New Orleans incident. Not just Italian immigration but the whole immigration question was dramatized as nothing had dramatized it since the Haymarket Affair. The press, the pulpit, and the magazines rang with demands for stringent restriction. The influential *Nation* concluded that a secure modern state rested on community of language and proposed therefore to limit immigration to English-speaking applicants. This severe idea met considerable favor.

The third major group in the new immigration, the Jews, was also buffeted by the nativism and jingoism of the nineties. They had, of course, their own unique status, fixed by the ancient Shylock stereotype; they stood for chicane rather than crime or revolution. (The American public had heard little as yet about the radical labor movements stirring in the New York ghetto.) But the Jews' supposedly unscrupulous greed now seemed as potentially subversive as the doings of bloodthirsty Italians, "furious Huns," or Irish papists. Hatred, rooted in much the same conditions, lashed them all in rather similar ways.

The Jews felt, too, the violence endemic in that period. Beginning in the late eighties, the first serious anti-Semitic demonstrations in American history occurred in parts of the lower South where Jewish supply merchants were common. In several parishes of Louisiana debt-ridden farmers stormed into town, wrecked Jewish stores, and threatened to kill any Jews who remained in the area. During the worst year, 1893, night-riders burned dozens of farmhouses belonging to Jewish landlords in southern Mississippi, and open threats drove a substantial number of Jewish businessmen from Louisiana. Persecution in northern cities generally took the form of personal taunts and assaults. Russo-Polish Jews had been stoned occasionally in the early eighties, and in the next decade this petty kind of Jew-baiting became much more common. One serious incident broke out in a New Jersey mill town in 1891. Five hundred tending boys employed in the local glass works went on a rampage when the management hired fourteen young Russian Jews. Three days of riotous demonstrations caused most of the Jewish residents to flee from the area. In one sense the Jews came off a little better than the other minorities; apparently no lives were lost in any of these episodes.

A substantial ideological onslaught accompanied the physical assaults, however. In response to the tensions of the 1890's, the Shylock stereotype—which tended to obscure distinctions between the relatively well-to-do German Jews and the newcomers from eastern Europe—assumed a new potency. To some nativists, the Jews were capable of dominating or ruining American business. Tradition connected Jews with gold, which was becoming one of the major touchstones of internal strife. After 1890 the government's determination to maintain the gold standard excited enormous discontent and defined the great political issue of the period. Since greedy, destructive forces seemed somehow at work in the government and economy, suspicion dawned that a Jewish bid for supremacy was wreaking the havoc America could not control. Agrarian radicals, absorbed in a passionate crusade for free silver, sometimes yielded to this conjecture, but the idea was not theirs alone. The patrician Henry Adams concluded that the United States lay at the mercy of the Jews, and a New York workingman vowed: "The Russian Jews and the other Jews will completely control the finances and Government of this country in ten years, or they will all be dead. . . . The hatred with which they are regarded . . . ought to be a warning to them. The people of this country . . . won't be starved and driven to the wall by Jews who are guilty of all the crimes, tricks and wiles that have hitherto been unknown and unthought of by civilized humanity."

Here too jingoism played a part. It was not enough for jingo-inflamed nativists to see the Jews solely as an internal threat. They were a people without single national home or center of power: an *international* people. Since gold was becoming, in fact, a more and more firmly established international standard, millions of Americans associated their country's troubles with an international medium of exchange and felt themselves in the toils of a world-wide money-power. Did the Jews perhaps have an international loyalty above all governments, a quenchless resolve to rule the world themselves? For at least a few nativists, the new tendency to see America's adversaries operating on a world stage inflated the Jewish peril from one of national subversion to one of world domination. An occasional eastern conservative detected a clandestine Jewish league controlling the money markets of the world, or blamed the depression on Jewish bankers who were said to be shipping America's gold to Europe. Western agrarians not infrequently slipped into similar allusions. Minnesota's Ignatius Donnelly wrote a utopian novel, *Caesar's Column,* prophesying a totally degraded society ruled by a Jewish world oligarchy. The greatest of the silverites, William Jennings Bryan, bluntly accused President Cleveland of putting the country in the hands of the English Rothschilds.

In nineteenth-century America, even so, the menace of world Jewry was undoubtedly less important than related fears of Italians and Catholics. Certainly the vision of an Italian fifth column precipitated more immediate consequences, and the expectation of a papal uprising created greater hysteria. The chief significance of the "International Jew" lay far in the future. Denationalized and universal, the symbol curiously mingled jingoism with isolationism. It was less a summons to fight than a command to withdraw, and its full impact would not come until American nationalism reverted from a strategy of belligerent intervention to one of belligerent isolation.

For understanding late nineteenth century nativism, it is not the latent possibilities of the new anti-Semitism which need emphasis, but rather the common qualities in the assaults on the various new immigrant nationalities. No longer scorned simply for "mere habits of life," each of the major groups from southern and eastern Europe stood forth as a challenge to the nation, either endangering American institutions by unruly behavior or threatening through avarice to possess them. In lashing out at each of these ethnic groups, a distraught society secured a whole set of new adversaries.

On the other hand, the discovery that the miscellaneous Slavs, Jews, and Italians constituted a collective type, a "new immigration," dawned more gradually. The concept of a new immigration would seem to have been largely the work of cultivated minds rather than a simple derivative of popular instincts. Certainly mass opinion in the nineties pictured the Italian, the Slav, and the Jew chiefly within the context of a general foreign peril. The fact of a rising influx of southern Europeans with unusually low living standards had been mentioned as early as 1884 in the discussion of the contract labor bill but did not receive much notice. Occasionally in the late eighties and with increasing frequency after 1890, a few keen observers in the East pointed to the proportional decline of northwestern European en-

*nativism < fear of imported discontent with childhood*

trants. After 1890, as the comfortable belief faded that this was a mere, temporary eddy in the migratory system, a handful of nativist intellectuals confronted the problem of defining the general threat which the whole movement from southern and eastern Europe raised to the nation's destiny.

Neither of the major traditions of nativist thought quite fitted the problem. The anti-radical theme, with its fears of imported discontent, applied to Europeans as a whole, and surely the new immigrants presented a more docile appearance than did Irish labor leaders or the German anarchists who hanged for the Haymarket Affair. Anti-Catholic nationalism, aside from failing to account for the new Jewish immigration, reeked of religious fanaticism which literate and cultured people now disavowed. On the eve of the A.P.A.'s rise to national prominence, a typical nativist intellectual rejoiced that the present movement against immigration would be free from attacks on Catholics. There was, however, a third nativist tradition—weaker than the other two but more adaptable to the purpose at hand. The old idea that America belongs peculiarly to the Anglo-Saxon race would define the special danger of the new immigration if one assumed that northern Europeans were at least first cousins to the Anglo-Saxons.

Eastern patrician intellectuals had been the keepers of the Anglo-Saxon tradition since the Civil War, and in the climate of the nineties it was not difficult for some of them to convert a doctrine that defined their own sense of nationality into censure of an immigrant throng that displayed few common traits except the indubitable fact that it was not Anglo-Saxon. Hardly had the new immigration begun to attract attention when race-conscious intellectuals discovered its hereditary taint. In 1890 the Brahmin president of the American Economic Association alerted his fellow scholars to the new tide of "races of . . . the very lowest stage of degradation." About the same time Henry Cabot Lodge noticed the shift away from northwestern Europe and began to bristle at its racial consequences.

When Lodge raised the banner of race against the new immigration, it acquired its most dangerous adversary. As Massachusetts' scholar-in-politics, he dominated both the intellectual and legislative phases of nativism. To this dual role, Lodge's own interests and values imperiously summoned him; he embodied in remarkable degree some of the major forces underlying late nineteenth century xenophobia. From his precise Vandyke beard to his clipped Boston accent, Lodge was the model of a patrician. He was steeped in English culture— English to the last fiber of his thought, said Henry Adams—in pride of ancestry, and in nostalgia for New England's past. During the 1870's he had plunged into a study of the Anglo-Saxons; a thesis on early Anglo-Saxon law brought him the first Ph.D. that Harvard conferred in political science. Secondly, connected with Lodge's race consciousness was a morbid sensitivity to the danger of extensive social change. He had a lively repugnance for both the rising plutocracy and the restive mob, and he felt acutely the general nativist response to class conflict. By 1888, as a fledgling Congressman, he was pointing to the diminishing supply of free land in the West and the growth of unrest in the East as reasons for restricting immigration. Finally, while attacking immigration in domestic affairs, Lodge was adopting a belligerent stance in foreign affairs. His campaign against the new immigration during the 1890's interlaced with a jingoist crusade for expansion. Lodge the jingo hated England as much as Lodge the Anglo-Saxon loved the English; accordingly, his diplomatic belligerence took the form of an assertion of American power, his pleas for restriction a defense of the English race. But these and other inconsistencies in the life of the cold, cultivated little Senator were merely logical. They were resolved at another level—in the emotions of nationalism which shaped and guided his career.

Although the Anglo-Saxon tradition in the mid-nineties still swayed few outside of an eastern elite, through Lodge and others around him that elite occupied a position of strategic influence. Both the ideological instrument and the political leadership necessary to bring into a single focus the chaotic resentments against the new immigrant were therefore at hand.

# Border Culture

MARIO T. GARCÍA

Working among themselves as manual laborers and living in segregated barrios adjacent to their homeland, Mexican immigrants in El Paso and throughout the Southwest, like other new-comers to the United States, maintained native customs that helped provide a sense of community. As one historian has correctly written of the northern movement of Mexicans: "Mexican immigration bore little resemblance to the 'uprooting' experience which Oscar Handlin depicted as characteristic of European immigration. Indeed, continuity rather than alienation, marginality and social disorganization, characterized Mexican immigration." Yet, within El Paso's large Mexican population, cultural differences also existed. Mexican Americans, educated and sophisticated political refugees, and the mass of poor immigrants comprised diverse cultural enclaves although they were linked by a common language and certain Mexican traditions. Moreover, cultural continuity coexisted with some cultural change. The immigrants' adjustment to new working conditions, especially in urban areas, their relationship with more Americanized Mexican Americans, and the impact of certain gringo institutions such as the schools introduced a gradual acculturation. Cultural change among Mexican immigrants, especially children, likewise occurred because, as Ernesto Galarza indicates, working class immigration brought "no formal institutions to perpetuate its culture." Cultural continuity as well as cultural change, the two in time developing a Mexican border culture, can be detected in the family, recreational activities, religion, and voluntary associations.

The family represented the most basic cultural institution transferred by Mexican immigrants and was the most resistant barrier to American assimilation. Besides young single males who entered the United States seeking work, many families also arrived. The Dillingham Commission report of 1911 observed that a high percentage of Mexican laborers in western industries had brought their wives from Mexico. According to the commission, 81.5 percent of Mexican railroad shop workers in the survey reported their wives in the United States. Investigators discovered a similar condition in urban related work. Sixty percent of Mexicans employed as construction workers by street railways stated they had their wives with them. Although no substantial research has been done on the composition and nature of working-class or peasant families in Mexico during the late nineteenth and early twentieth centuries, nevertheless it appears that the family formed a strong social and economic unit. Galarza in his autobiography, *Barrio Boy,* recalls that his family in rural Nayarit included not only his mother (who had divorced his father prior to Galarza's birth) but also his aunt, three uncles, and two cousins. In the Galarza household the men went to labor in the fields during the day while the women and children performed the housework and cooking.

Although some Mexican women in El Paso and throughout the urban Southwest contributed to household incomes by taking in wash or lodgers, no disintegration took place in the traditional pattern of men being the chief wage earners and women doing household work (of course, certain lower-class women in Mexico were wageworkers). The 1900 El Paso census sample shows that no mothers and almost no daughters, most being too young, worked outside the home in an immigrant family headed by the father (although no data exist, some women may have worked part-time). Nevertheless, the necessity of more women having to become wage-workers over the years no doubt affected family patterns. This appears to be true as daughters grew to working

From Mario T. García, *Desert Immigrants. The Mexicans of El Paso, 1880–1920.* New Haven: Yale Univ. Press, 1981. Excerpts from "Border Culture," pp. 197–231. Reprinted by permission of Yale University Press. Footnotes have been deleted.

age throughout the region. According to a Los Angeles survey taken by Paul S. Taylor in 1928, the majority of Mexican women took jobs in industry because "of poverty, due either to the irregular work of the male members of the family, or to the combination of large families, low wages, high rents." However, the entrance of women into the job market constituted, as Taylor put it, a process "contrary to their customs and traditions." Taylor believed that "such radical changes" in the daily lives of Mexican women could not help but produce cultural changes, especially within the family. The University of California scholar observed both older as well as younger women in industrial jobs, but he detected more profound alterations in the habits of younger Mexicans. Not only did they adapt to the work routine better, but what little education they secured in American schools, especially the learning of English, made them more productive and efficient. "They look upon some sort of industrial work" Taylor wrote, "as soon as they have completed the minimum amount of schooling as the natural course of events." Besides acquiring some new material and cultural tastes that they introduced into the home, by the 1920s young Mexican working women appear to have begun to exhibit a desire for greater independence from strict family practices. "Her parents are apt to be ignored," Taylor stressed, "she tends to break away from the old custom of parental authority." Whether Taylor's observations would also pertain to El Paso cannot be determined due to a lack of similar studies in the border city. Certainly, young Mexican women who worked in the laundries and garment factories, and possibly even as domestics, may have displayed parallel characteristics.

The economic necessity for Mexican women to find jobs likewise appears to have challenged to a degree the traditional male-dominated Mexican family structure. Although perhaps Mexican fathers could more easily accept their daughters than their wives working outside the home, a pattern not uncommon in Mexico, still Taylor noticed that Mexican men resented women working or wanting to work. One man stated that women should not work because that was a man's duty, whereas women's consisted of keeping house. Another husband told Taylor that he could not allow his wife to work because his friends would then think he could not adequately provide for his family. Another insisted that his wife could not have a job outside the home since no women in his family

had ever worked; moreover, it was neither necessary nor correct. The pressure of higher living costs north of the border, however, eventually forced many Mexican women into the job market. While more research needs to be conducted into the full impact that this process had on family culture, it seems that traditional patterns slowly changed over the years. One Mexican man who had lived in the United States for over 25 years told anthropologist Manuel Gamio in the 1920s that he disliked the transformation Mexican women underwent in the Southwest. According to Carlos Ibáñez, he disliked American laws that allowed women too many rights and made them less subordinate to men. "Now the Mexican women who come here," Ibáñez emphasized, "also take advantage of the laws and want to be like the American women." Because of the change, Ibáñez concluded that if he ever married it would be in Mexico.

Within the family, Mexicans preserved many native cultural traditions that aided them in their transition to a new American setting by providing a familiar cultural environment. It is difficult to arrive at an accurate picture of family life in El Paso, but anthropologist Manuel Gamio noted certain customs being practiced in the late 1920s by Mexican immigrant families in El Paso and other southwestern locations. Gamio observed that despite the fact that Mexican immigrants accepted American material goods such as housing, clothing, domestic utensils, and machinery, they still retained earlier popular customs. These included folklore, songs and ballads, birthday celebrations, saints' days, baptisms, weddings, and funerals in the traditional style. Owing to poverty, a lack of physicians in the barrios plus traditional customs the Mexican scholar witnessed the continued use of medicinal herbs by both Mexican immigrants and Mexican Americans. "In almost all parts of America where there are Mexicans and Mexican-Americans," he stressed, "there are Mexican drug stores in which there is a great sale of every sort of medicinal plant." Mexicans along the border could also find remedies for their physical and emotional ailments by visiting Mexican healers known as *curanderos*. "I cure by means of herbs" one *curandera* in Tucson informed Gamio, "but I never promise to cure this one or that one because that is something of God. . . . I have cured many Mexicans of syphilis and tuberculosis and other diseases. I have also helped to assist at childbirth many times, when the doctors have let me. The existence of such popular traditions illustrates what scholars have discovered in studies of migration patterns: the persistance of earlier preindustrial cultural practices within an industrializing society—or what one sociologist refers to as an "urban village."

Immigrant families interviewed by Gamio further acknowledged that for the most part they continued to cook Mexican style. "I don't suffer in the matter of food," one woman told him in Los Angeles, "for my mother cooks at home as if we were in Mexico. There are some dishes which are different but we generally eat Mexican style and rice and beans are almost never lacking from our table." According to a report by one of Gamio's associates, however, Mexican families in certain areas purchased items such as canned chile, canned sauces, and canned tomatoes from California. Obtaining food processed in the United States often led to complaints about the inadequacy and poor quality of American products in the cooking of Mexican dishes. "The foodstuffs, besides costing a lot," another woman informed Gamio, "are no good for making good Mexican food . . . so that it might be said that the food is half-Mexican and half-American, being neither the one nor the other." Most Mexican families in El Paso avoided this dietary problem by apparently purchasing much of their food in Juárez.

Outside the home, Mexicans patronized various other forms of entertainment and recreation. Men visited Mexican bars, pool halls, and gambling establishments in both El Paso and Juárez. At the turn of the century, some Mexicans sponsored horse races in Washington Park with attendance from not only the city but the surrounding area as well. On its visits to the border the circus stood out as a special treat for Mexican children and their parents. The *Times* recorded in 1887 that many Mexicans as well as Americans had attended John Robinson's Great Circus in back of the Santa Fe depot. Elephants, camels, and other strange beasts, a reporter observed, captured the attention of the Mexican spectators. Mexicans from the adjacent territory also came in large numbers. They camped next to the circus tents, the *Times* man wrote, and everyone spent their *dinero* freely. Mexicans along with Americans eagerly awaited the arrival of such special attractions as the Ringling Brothers' "Greatest Show on Earth" and Barnum and Bailey's circus. Besides American circuses, small Mexican traveling shows with acrobats and sideshows called *carpas* visited El Paso and performed in Chihuahuita. According to one Mexican American critic, these carpas included

improvised satirical skits. "The brief, topical skits of la carpa," he proposes, "with their focus on physical movement and rapid verbal gymnastics are the progenitors of today's [Chicano] 'actos.' "

Mexicans also spent their limited leisure time at spectator sports that helped distract their minds from homesickness, work, and harsh living conditions. Bullfights in Juárez, for example, were a cultural link with la patria. Boxing matches on both sides of the border enticed many males. Mexican boxers such as Benny Chávez and Mexican Americans like lightweight Aurelio Herrera held special attraction for the Mexican fans. By 1900 Mexicans also began to show an interest in American baseball. In addition to its attraction as a spectator event, some Mexicans, mostly Mexican Americans, organized baseball teams of their own. The Internationals stood out as the earliest and most popular Mexican baseball team in the border city. With an all Mexican lineup and playing against Anglo-American teams, the Internationals proved to be one of the finest clubs in El Paso for several years and played games throughout the Southwest. Sportswriters considered the Mexican American players among the finest athletes. José "Curly" Villarreal, playing for a local team in 1917, was regarded as the best pitcher in the city league. One writer commented that with Curly on the pitching mound "it is a safe bet that a large number of Mexican fans will be out Sunday to see their favorite in action."

The allure of American baseball for Mexicans transcended the border and began to have a cultural impact in Mexico. "Baseball is showing promise," the *Times* proudly reported in 1908, "of becoming the national game of Mexico as well as the United States." Admitting that other foreign sports such as cricket, field hockey, and polo had some following in the neighboring republic, the *Times* believed that those cultural imports could not compare with the "grand old game." The newspaper subjectively concluded that the sport physically suited the Mexicans due to their "natural quickness." Moreover, it recognized the language influence that baseball had on Mexicans with the acceptance of baseball terms such as "You're out." The *Times* further understood the political objective American baseball served in Mexico. Baseball would create a sympathetic link between Americans and Mexicans. Two men cheering for the same team, it emphasized, would find it more difficult to disagree on other matters. At the same time that the United States had become Mexico's principal trade partner and investor, the *Times* boasted that south of the border American baseball had outdistanced British, French, German, and other European sports. The border publication predicted that it would be only a matter of time before the "better classes" in Mexico would stop bullfighting and then baseball would become the national sport. "When the mob can no longer have it [bull-fighting]," the *Times* stressed, "baseball will be the national game from Central America to the Great Lakes."

In spite of strong Mexican cultural influences in El Paso owing to increased Mexican immigration and the city's proximity to the border, Mexicans underwent subtle cultural changes. After 1910, for example, they faced the acculturating influence of American mass culture through the silent movies. Although it does not appear that the early movie houses such as the Crawford, the Grand, the Little Wigwam, and the Bijou specifically excluded Mexicans, the attendance of Mexicans at the movies grew when several Mexican theaters opened by the period of World War I. The International Amusement Company of El Paso, owned and managed by Mexican businessmen including Mexican American politico Frank Alderete, operated seven theaters in the border city. These included the Alcázar, the Eureka, the Hidalgo, the Paris, the Iris, and Rex movie houses on South El Paso Street. By 1917, these theaters showed some films produced in Mexico but for the most part Mexican audiences paid 6 or 11 cents admission, depending on where one sat, to see American movies featuring such stars as Charlie Chaplin, Mary Pickford, and Fatty Arbuckle. "Regardless of what some may say," *La Patria* commented in reviewing a Chaplin film at the Teatro Rex, "Carlos Chaplin is a magnificent artist; he is not a vulgar clown, but rather a refined and competent comic actor, whose every gesture, every graceful pose, brings forth joy not only for children, but for adults."

Besides exposing Mexicans to some American material and cultural values and mores, the movies also may have influenced their ability to understand some English. Mexicans employed by the movie houses translated English subtitles to Spanish ones, which appeared at the bottom of the screen below the original dialogue. American slang was no problem, remarked a *Times* reporter, for the translators of slapstick comedies screened at Mexican theaters. Even Americans studying Spanish took advantage of the process and visited Mexican theaters to improve their Spanish reading ability. The reporter further noted that the technique of imposing the Spanish translation on the films had been invented by a Mexican employee of the International Amusement Company and "is now in use wherever American films are used for Spanish-speaking audiences. Guillermo Balderas recalls that his own brother Eduardo worked as a translator in one of the Mexican movie houses. "These were 'silent movies,' " Balderas remembers, "that were translated into Spanish." By the 1920s American movies were an important acculturating agent, especially on the first generation native born, on both sides of the border. As one Mexican immigrant explained in a corrido, Hollywood films had enticed him to leave Mexico for the "promised land":

> I dreamed in my youth of being a movie star
> And one of these days I came to visit Hollywood.

For Mexican immigrants, Catholicism provided a familiar cultural environment as well as institutional support for their adjustment north of the border. The Catholic Church in El Paso, under the control of Irish Americans, recognized quite early that it would have to establish separate facilities for its Mexican members. Consequently, it organized Mexican parishes in the barrios to serve the particular religious and social needs of the immigrants. Unlike many national churches in the United States, however, those in El Paso were not staffed, for the most part, by Mexican priests, of whom there was an apparent shortage in the Southwest, but by Italian and American clergy. As a result the Church not only took into consideration Mexican cultural traditions but also became an agent of Americanization among its parishioners, especially those families, many of them political refugees, who could afford to send their children to Catholic schools. Still, the mass of Mexican immigrants retained their popular religious beliefs and practices by transferring them across the border. Regardless of economic or political backgrounds, first generation immigrants and political refugees, through their reestablishment of spiritual societies common in Mexico as well as the reenactment of native Mexican religious celebrations, successfully maintained cultural continuity and helped create a sense of community in the barrios.

As an institution, the Catholic Church in El Paso pursued a bicultural approach in its treatment of Mexican immigrants. The southside parochial schools, for example, under the direction of the American Sisters of Loretto emphasized, as one part of their curriculum, the Americanization of their students and attempted to change what they considered to be the Mexicans' bad cultural habits.

In addition to a basic curriculum emphasizing religious and academic subjects with some industrial and domestic training, Sacred Heart School presented performances displaying both the talents of young Mexicans as well as the influences of American middle-class culture. The *Times* reported in 1895 that Sacred Heart School students would offer a musical and dramatic entertainment at the old stone church on North Oregon Street. Mainly performed in English, the school's closing exercise in 1904 took place at Myar's Opera House, where a large audience assembled. According to the *Times* critic, the entertainment not only proved to be interesting but also reflected great credit on the nuns who taught at Sacred Heart. The best acts included the singing of "The Poor Old Tramps" by a male choir and an instrumental performance by the Mandolin Club that "was rendered without a single discord, and gave promise that El Paso will have a number of skillful musicians, who, with light touch, will call forth the music that stirs men's souls." Some of the girls who presented a drama in three acts entitled "The Little Waiters" received "round upon round of applause, and demonstrated the fact that several of the young ladies had real dramatic ability." Impressed, the *Times* gave credit to the students' teachers and praised the Catholic Church for its work among the Mexican children of the city. The performance had demonstrated, the paper concluded, "that there is an efficient and practical movement on foot to educate the Catholic youths and young girls of El Paso and teach them how to become good citizens and dutiable daughters and faithful wives."

Yet English and middle-class American customs at Sacred Heart shared the curriculum with Spanish and Mexican cultural traditions. Cleofas Calleros, who attended Sacred Heart during the first decade of the century, remembered that although there were only two Mexican teachers in a faculty of ten, both English and Spanish were used in instruction along with American and Mexican history. Years later, lecturing to the 1919 graduating girls of Sacred Heart, the Italian pastor of the parish encouraged them to adopt the best of other cultures but to never forget who they were: young Catholic Mexican girls, who were obliged to follow Christ and, as Mexicans, to conserve the beautiful customs and traditions of *la raza*.

Hence, Sacred Heart as well as the other Mexican parochial schools served a two-fold purpose. They helped transmit Mexican ethnicity and, at the same time, provided lessons in English and American culture in order to assist students to adjust and hopefully succeed in the United States.

Next to Sacred Heart, the religious and cultural activities of St. Ignatius Church at Park and Second perhaps best exemplified the Church's interest in the Mexicans' adjustment. For the spiritual needs of its members, St. Ignatius sponsored a variety of religious groups popular in Mexico. In 1905 some women formed the League of the Sacred Heart and the Congregation of the Daughters of Mary (Congregación de las Hijas de María). That same year a group of young people and children organized the Congregation of San Luis Gonzaga as a prayer union for youth. Care of the church sacristy led to the beginning of the Altar Society. Still other parishioners, expecially women, belonged to additional religious associations such as the Society of Good Death (Buena Muerte), the Society of Our Lady of Guadalupe, the Society of Divine Providence, and the Association of Christian Mothers. Besides their specific devotions, many of these organizations assisted in the more popular religious ceremonies among the Mexican working class such as the Feast of Our Lady of Guadalupe and, of course, at Christmas, when parishioners performed the Shepherds' Play (Los Pastores). The Corpus Christi procession held every June, however, was the most impressive popular religious feast day, clearly fostering a communal spirit among the entire Mexican population of El Paso. Although this event centered around Sacred Heart Church, all Mexican parishes participated. In 1919, for example, between 10,000 and 20,000 Mexicans marched in the annual procession with thousands more watching, making the *Revista Católica,* the Spanish-language Jesuit newspaper in the city, declare that the Mexican colony saw Corpus Christi as an ethnic holiday.

St. Ignatius supported various other cultural and recreational activities as well. Shortly after the church opened, it hired Trinidad Concha to assemble a young women's orchestra, which by 1908 appeared in public concerts. Concha further directed the church's well-known choir. In 1912 St. Ignatius obtained the benefit of another musical group when a boys' band at Sacred Heart had to leave that parish because it made too much noise and instead moved to St. Ignatius. This marked the start of the young people's band, which gained much prominence under the direction of Professor Melitón Concha. By 1918 St. Ignatius also had one of the largest Mexican athletic clubs in the city. Founded by the church to counter the success of the Mexican YMCA, the Association of Catholic Youth (Asociación Católica de Jóvenes), better known as the Club Anahuac, sponsored both athletic and cultural events. It possessed the best baseball, football, tennis, and basketball teams in south El Paso and won several city-wide contests. Moreover, its 100 members aided in the building of athletic and playground facilities for the children of the area. And, as part of its expression of loyalty to the United States during World War I, the club held picnics and athletic exhibitions to raise money for the war fund of the Knights of Columbus. "The young members of this club," it appealed to other Mexicans, "moved by a sense of duty and humanitarianism, and not being able to contribute in any other way to relieve the suffering of our own brothers, have decided to help through this exhibition. Won't you help us by attending? *Remember:* It will benefit our brothers who are fighting on the front lines."

Indeed, the war gave St. Ignatius and the Catholic Church of El Paso another opportunity to stress the Americanization of the Mexicans, especially youth. After the United States declared war in 1917, the priests of St. Ignatius explained to their parishioners the alien registration provisions of the draft law and urged them to cooperate with the civil and military authorities. The church also requested Mexicans to buy Liberty Bonds (Bonas de la Libertad). Yet the parish's proudest contribution to the war came when more than 40 young Mexican men, both native born and foreign born, enlisted for military service, despite the fact that most Mexicans in the city claimed draft exemptions owing to their alien status. A few of the Mexican soldiers, moreover, served with distinction. Marcos B. Armijo, who died in battle, received the Distinguished Service Cross, while the French government honored Manuel J. Escajeda with the Croix de Guerre. Marcelino Serna, however, represented not only St. Ignatius' most distinguished soldier but one of the most decorated in El Paso and Texas. Serna received the American Distinguished Service Cross, the French Croix de Guerre and Military Medal, the Italian Cross of Merit, and the British Medal of Bravery. This demonstration of American patriotism on the part of St. Ignatius' youth revealed the conviction of the Catholic Church in El Paso that, regardless of

native sentiments, Mexicans for their own economic benefit should learn the language, customs, and values of the United States as quickly as possible. After the war the Church strongly supported the city's Americanization program, which included night schools for Mexican adults. In an editorial even the sometime anti-American *Revista Católica* encouraged its Mexican readers to avail themselves of this education in order to help them obtain better jobs. "The movement initiated in Washington," the Mexican Catholic paper pointed out, "to 'Americanize' all foreigners in the United States has reached El Paso, and all indicators show that it will prove more fruitful in this city than in other places. The name of this program will scare off many Mexicans and perhaps because of this fear many will not take advantage of this excellent opportunity to improve their conditions."

Hence, by 1920 the Catholic Church in El Paso through its endorsement of postwar Americanization programs as well as its own efforts in the parochial schools served, along with the public schools, as a major American institution of socialization, especially for the children of Mexican immigrants. Based on a viewpoint stressing loyalty to both Church and country, which by the 1920s and 1930s increasingly meant the United States, the Catholic Church in the Southwest assisted Mexicans not only to adjust to border life but, ultimately, to believe in the American Dream. Still, the constant stream of additional immigrants into El Paso and other southwestern areas after 1920, as well as the proximity of Mexico, meant that Mexican immigrant parishes were never completely Americanized. Rather than examples of an earlier past, many of them, due to continued immigration from Mexico, remain viable though poor institutions helping to link Mexican immigrant communities in the United States with the mother country and culture.

As a form of ethnic self-protection as well as an expression of ethnicity, Mexican social organizations in El Paso revealed the Mexicans' accommodation to their new American setting. Forced to organize in a new and sometimes hostile society, some of El Paso's Mexicans, especially more skilled and educated ones, formed several mutual and fraternal associations that helped provide organized leadership in the Mexican settlement. Similar societies, moreover, existed in Mexico and hence were familiar forms of association. As mediating institutions the mutual and fraternal organizations, besides aiding in the preservation and encouragement of

Mexican ethnic consciousness among the immigrants, helped form a more permanent and cohesive Mexican community.

As early as 1893 the Mexican newspapaer *El Hispano-Americano* printed a notice from La Unión Occidental Mexicana (the Mexican Western Union), which was one of the first Mexican mutual aid societies in El Paso. "It is neither more nor less than what its name implies a group of persons of Mexican origin," stated organizer and political exile Víctor L. Ochoa. He went on to explain that the unión had several objectives: to aid and defend its members, to "unalterably" maintain the Spanish language, to protect the morality of its members, and to spread fraternal bonds among Mexican nationals in the United States. In addition, when a member died, his wife and children would receive $2.50 from each unión member. One year later another mutual aid society, Los Caballeros del Progreso (the Gentlemen of Progress), stressed that the poor economic conditions of Mexicans in the United States resulted from a lack of unity and that in order to alleviate this problem Los Caballeros had been organized. *El Defensor* noted that when one of the society's members who had not kept up his dues died, Los Caballeros refused to pay the funeral costs as a lesson to other negligent members.

One Mexican newspaper also urged unity through organizations when it observed in 1899 that despite the large numbers of Mexicans in El Paso, the city's oldest Mexican mutual benefit society (1888), the Sociedad Mutualista Mexicana "La Protectora," had only 40 members. It pointed out the validity of the motto "Unity Makes Force" and informed its readers that only through organization had the United States become a great power. "If it is true then that unity makes force," it added, "then we do not understand why Mexicans do not develop those relationships that will unite us." The Sociedad Mutualista Mexicana "La Protectora," the paper asserted, aimed to unite and protect Mexicans who lived in El Paso. Had it not been for this society, the paper believed that Mexicans in the city would have been deprived of a common meeting place where they "could exchange impressions of our beloved country." *Las Noticas* further reminded Mexicans of their obligation to one another as members of the same race "and sons of the same mother: Mexico." Among its benefits, "La Protectora" assisted members who required hospitalization and paid for funeral costs. *Las Dos Américas,* another Mexican

newspaper in El Paso, expressed its gratitude in 1898 to "La Protectora's" Mexican American president, A. J. Escajeda, and its vice-president, C. Aguirre, for their consideration during the funeral of Antonio G. Gallardo, who had been killed by a Southern Pacific train at Deming, New Mexico. Although it appears that the membership of "La Protectora" remained small, it met regularly every second and fourth Monday of the month. Its leadership seems to have come from Mexican Americans like Escajeda, but the entire composition of its membership cannot be determined.

As more Mexicans arrived in El Paso by the turn of the century, several other benefit and fraternal groups appeared. The *Times* announced in 1907 that seven Mexican societies of El Paso would participate in that year's 16th of September celebrations honoring Mexican independence. These included La Benéfica patriotic society from the smelter, the Sociedad Unión Constructora, La Mutualista, Los Hijos de Hidalgo, and the Sociedad Filarmónica. "Few Americans if any," a Mexican told a *Times reporter,*

> are aware of the wonderful growth and activity to be found in the Mexican fraternal orders now existing in the Southwest.
>
> While the chief element of these orders is made up of the common working class, it must be remembered that there are also affiliated with these societies many Mexicans of culture—among them professional and business men. El Paso has the distinction of having the largest number of these lodges; Tucson ranking next, it being the place where two of the most important orders, the "Sociedad Zaragoza" and the "Sociedad Hispano-Americana" have their home offices.

He further explained that the Hispano-American society paid $1,000 to the family of a deceased member and $200 to a member upon the death of his wife. In addition he declared that although the Sociedad Zaragoza had been operating for a shorter time than other societies, it had a larger membership with 28 branches throughout Arizona, New Mexico, and Texas. In El Paso it was represented by Lodge No. 18, founded that year with 90 members.

The growing numbers of Mexican immigrants and refugees in El Paso after 1910 also influenced the expansion of these societies. "Mexicans in El Paso are interested in lodge work to an extent probably not generally known," member Pedro A. Candelaria stated in an interview in 1915. Candelaria observed that the Sociedad Mutualista Mexicana had a membership of 115 and La Constructora had 300 members. Both represented the two largest societies in the city and intended to protect the widows and orphans of deceased members. Each of these organizations assessed every member $3 whenever a death occurred and turned the amount over to the widow. Candelaria pointed out that still another lodge, La Benéfica, operated in East El Paso. These organizations had developed substantially in recent years, he concluded, owing to the arrival of Mexican refugees.

The sharp rise in the Mexican population of the Southwest during the years of the Mexican Revolution encouraged consolidation among Mexican mutual aid societies and increased their emphasis on insurance practices. The best example of the change can be seen in the activities of La Sociedad Alianza Hispano-Americana. Organized in 1894 in Tucson, it grew from a small number of lodges to 88 in 1919 with more than 4,000 members from California to Texas, and with additional lodges in northern Mexico. It hoped to unite all Mexicans and Latin Americans in the United States into one "family" under the principles of "protection, morality, and education." According to the Alianza's historian, its membership consisted of both lower-middle-class and working-class people. In one of the largest demonstrations of Mexican social organization in the United States, El Paso hosted a national convention of the Alianza in 1910 attended by close to 200 delegates from New Mexico, Arizona, Southern California, and Texas. At their opening session the mayors of both El Paso and Juárez welcomed the delegates and assured them they would not be molested by the police of either border town. One of the main items in the convention's agenda dealt with changes in insurance payments. Every member paid a flat rate of $1 each month for $1,000 insurance without regard to age or other conditions. However, the *Times* reported that the officers were eager to adopt a more scientific plan. The finance committee noted that the supreme lodge had $16,790 on hand of which $14,000 had been put in the reserve fund. Although the convention voted to retain a flat rate for present members, it approved a new classified assessment for future ones but kept the amount of insurance that could be secured at $500 or $1,000, with $100 and $200 funeral benefits.

Nine years later *La Patria* published an advertisement for the Alianza containing both its insurance provisions and a list of its lodges in the Southwest. The notice emphasized that the Alianza had no political or religious qualifications for membership, that it treated every member equally, that each received the same benefits, and that it spent none of its members' funds for amusements. The Alianza also stressed that women could purchase a policy, "for we believe them to be as worthy and as entitled to the same right to protect their children who depend on them." Despite the fact that most of its members were "humble workers," the Alianza proudly announced that since its formation it had paid out a million and a half dollars in benefits. To share in the Alianza's protection, a Mexican had to pay $3.50 admission fee plus $1 to $2 for a medical examination. Monthly payments would then be determined by the amount of the policy and the age of its holder. "We respectfully invite you and your family to join the 'Alianza,'" the ad told the readers of *La Patria*. In 1919 three of its lodges, apparently located in Chihuahuita, functioned in El Paso. *La Patria* observed that members of the different lodges could attend one another's meetings. In addition Jesús M. Ortiz, who had been named Alianza organizer for Texas, believed that a new chapter could be established in East El Paso since many Mexicans there had expressed an interest in the society. Besides El Paso, lodges could be found in nearby New Mexico in Silver City, Hillsboro, Santa Rita, Las Cruces, and Hurley.

Like other immigrant organizations in the United States, the Mexican mutual and fraternal societies of El Paso provided social and cultural activities for their members. Many of these social functions consisted of dances sponsored by different lodges. In 1911, for example, the Mexican secret societies held a grand ball at the Fraternal Brotherhood Hall. "The national colors of Mexico will be flying," the *Times* commented, "and those who cannot have one of the most enjoyable times of their life . . . will be hard to please." In 1919 the Logia Morelos held its Second Grand Ball at Liberty Hall and in 1920 the Sociedad Mutualista Zaragoza Independiente sponsored a literary and dance show to celebrate its twelfth anniversary. That same year the Alianza hosted an artistic presentation to raise funds. Moreover, the lodges sponsored the 16th of September celebrations as well as other Mexican patriotic holidays. When William Howard Taft met Porfirio Díaz in El Paso in 1909, the city's Mexican societies turned out in force to honor both leaders and the nations they represented. "As the president's carriage neared the position occupied by the Mexican societies," a reporter noticed of Taft's parade down El Paso street, "there was a tumult of applause, cheers and cries of "Viva Taft! Viva Taft!' " After Taft had visited Díaz in Juárez, the Mexican organizations joined the parade up El Paso Street to downtown Cleveland Square. "Four different Mexican societies," the *Times* observed, "numbering about 1,000 men and all wearing natty uniforms comprised the divisions."

For Mexican Americans, the social activities of the lodges became quite important because participation in Anglo-Saxon society remained limited. Although the Women's Club, the El Paso Country Club, and other American social organizations had no clear policy on the exclusion of Mexican members, businessman Félix Martínez, who belonged to the Toltec Men's Club, appears to have been one of the few persons of Mexican descent throughout the period who claimed membership in an American social group. Social intercourse between Mexicans and Americans on an organized level seems to have occurred only during special political or patriotic events or the arrival of major Mexican dignitaries such as Díaz. Because of this de facto social separation as well as their own cultural affinity, Mexican Americans either formed their own clubs or joined immigrant organizations. In 1907 the Logia Fraternal No. 30, composed exclusively of Mexican Americans, held a banquet in honor of Mexican Independence Day at the Sheldon Hotel attended by 132 persons including 35 prominent American politicians. The walls of the big dining room had been decorated with a number of Mexican and American flags, "while at the south end of the hall facing the toastmaster was an immense Mexican and a huge American flag leaning so close together that their folds embraced each other." After some of the American guests spoke, lodge officer Agapito Martínez emphasized that it gave him great pride to say that every member of the lodge held American citizenship and yet could also be proud of Mexico's achievements. "Freedom," said editor Lauro Aguirre, "started the fire at Philadelphia, at Paris and in Mexico." Z. M. Oriza ended the speeches by a toast to the menu motto "After All, What is Better than Friendship."

The annual 16th of September celebration proved to be not only the most important Mexican cultural event in El Paso, and throughout the Southwest, but also an indication of the level of social organization and cooperation that could occur among the different Mexican societies. The 1897 ceremonies, for example, stood out as one of the most successful holidays in El Paso and revealed the various cultural activities

that often took place during this community fiesta. As early as July, the Mexican newspaper *El Monitor* announced a meeting of La Junta Patriótica Mexicana (the Mexican Patriotic Council) to select a board of directors and decide on the best format for the 16th of September celebration. One month later the paper criticized some Mexican Americans who did not believe that the 16th of September had any meaning for them and refused to support the festivities: "To these 'Agringados' (Americanized Mexicans) who negate that they are Mexicans because they were born in the United States, we ask: what blood runs through their veins? Do they think they are members of the Anglo-Saxon race who only happen to have dark skins because they were born on the border! What nonsense! (Qué barbaridad!)." *El Monitor* went on to add that this did not mean that Mexican Americans should not be good citizens of the United States and even fight for "Tío Samuel" if it went to war against a European or an Asiatic nation. However, in the event of conflict between the United States and Mexico or a Latin American nation, *El Monitor* believed that every Mexican living north of the border should go to the defense of their "blood brothers" and the country of their parents' birth. The paper concluded by asking: "Why should there be any reason now for us to feel ashamed of being a Mexican?"

Led by the Junta Patrótica, the Mexicans of El Paso prepared to celebrate the independence of Mexico. In its September 12th edition, *El Monitor* dedicated its coverage to the Mexican workers of the city, "to whom we wish all kinds of happiness during these glorious days." It also reminded its readers of the events to be held on both the fifteenth and the sixteenth, and commented that the prepared program left nothing to be desired, thanks to the work of the Junta. Similar festivities would occur in other areas of Texas, as well as in New Mexico, Arizona, and California, but the paper predicted that one of the best 16th of Septembers would be held in El Paso. To stimulate patriotic sentiments, *El Monitor* retold the story of the fathers of Mexican independence, Hidalgo and Morelos, and of the independence struggle against the "tyranny of Spain." "Long live the illustrious Liberator," the article eulogized Hidalgo, "and, 'Viva Mexico!' "

Organized in honor of the Mexican colony, especially the Junta Patriótica and the Mexican consul Francisco Mallén, only rain spotted an otherwise flawless event. The celebration began on the morning of the fifteenth, when Consul

Mallén dedicated the observance to Don Porfirio Díaz. That evening the Junta, the Mexican mutual benefit society "La Protectora," and the Mexican students of Sacred Heart School marched from Fifth Street, bordering the downtown area, to Sacred Heart Church in Chihuahuita preceded by a Mexican band. Throughout the route the homes and businesses of both Mexicans and Americans had been decorated with the Mexican tricolors. At 8:00 P.M. Consul Mallén and the president of the Junta, Dr. Rechy, accompanied by their wives arrived at the platform in front of the church and the program commenced by the playing of the Mexican national anthem. The more than 3,000 people who attended also heard recitations by several young people as well as songs and piano recitals. A speech in English by lawyer T.J. Beall that praised Mexican independence and Hidalgo received much applause. After several songs Don Esteban Gómez del Campo delivered the main speech touching on various Mexican historical themes. The band then played both the Mexican and American anthems followed by two tunes originally composed by Trinidad Concha entitled "On the Shores of the Rio Grande" and "Through El Paso." At last the secretary of the Junta read Hidalgo's act of independence ("El grito de Dolores") and Consul Mallén said a few words. the program concluded with the Mexican national anthem sung by a chorus of young Mexican women. The following morning of the sixteenth, a parade through downtown El Paso containing both Mexican and American units ended the independence day celebrations.

As the 16th of September festivities partly indicated, different cultural influences touched the Mexican population of El Paso. Given diverse cultural levels within the Mexican settlement, these influences also had varied effects and responses. More acculturated than the immigrants, the minority of Mexican Americans felt the pull of both cultures much more strongly. "This civilization is American nominally," Gamio observed of Mexican Americans in the 1920s, "and exhibits the principal material aspects of modern American civilization, but intellectually and emotionally it lives in local Mexican traditions." On the other hand, the recently arrived immigrants retained to a considerable degree their native traditions in the form of language, folklore, superstitions, songs, and religious holidays, which expressed their national origins. However, the impact of American industrialization and urbanization forced the immigrants to adjust to changed conditions. In the process many of El Paso's Mexicans formed relationships with one another through family, recreational, mutual aid, fraternal, and patriotic organizations that, on the one hand, provided a cultural security and continuity and, on the other, revealed new American conditions and influences. Moreover, the schools, both public and parochial, American material goods, and, to a degree, churches represented institutions and attractions within the barrios that affected the subtle and gradual Americanization of the Mexicans.

Although their culture underwent some transformation as they adjusted to immigrant life, Mexicans, as Gamio further recognized, "never became integrally assimilated to American civilization." He believed that the problem retarding the complete Americanization of the Mexicans lay in the large gulf between what he called "purely American culture" and "purely Mexican culture." The economic discrimination and segregation aimed at Mexicans in El Paso also made it difficult to assimilate them as well as Mexican Americans because employers desired to keep them as a source of cheap labor. Furthermore, unlike European immigration, which slowed to a trickle in the 1920s, Mexican immigration persisted and reinforced a distinct Mexican presence in El Paso. Too, most Mexicans believed they would soon return to their homeland and therefore felt no strong motivation to discard their cultural traditions. Mexico, of course, was right next door. Consequently, a dialectical relationship existed between the immigrant's native culture and the attempt by American institutions and reformers to restructure earlier habits and instill a new urban-industrial discipline among the Mexicans. The eventual result: a Mexican border culture, neither completely Mexican nor American, but one revealing contrasting attractions and pressures between both cultures. Yet Mexican border culture was and is by no means monolithic because different experiences are represented. Recent arrivals display what Galarza calls "the most authentic transplant of Mexican working-class culture," whereas middle-class newcomers, such as many of the political refugees during the Revolutionary period, bring with them a more sophisticated bourgeois one of both Mexican and European origins. Finally, Mexican Americans, especially the children and grandchildren of immigrants, have faced an erosion of their Mexican culture as American institutions, including an acculturated family environment, bring them into the fold of American mass culture.

# Ethnic Enterprise in America:
# Japanese, Chinese, and Blacks

IVAN LIGHT

The single most prominent argument advanced to explain the black Americans underrepresentation in small business has fastened on his special difficulty in securing business loans from institutional lenders, especially from banks. This explanation is 200 years old. It asserts that, because of poverty, lack of capital, and inability to borrow, blacks have been unable to finance business ventures. In its most straightforward form, this argument holds that black business failed to develop because prejudiced white bankers were unwilling to make business loans to black applicants at all or were willing to make loans but only on terms very much less favorable than those extended to white borrowers with equivalent business credentials. In a more sophisticated version, the argument maintains that black borrowers were relatively disadvantaged in the capital market simply by virtue of their impoverishment and the marginal status of their businesses. Impecunious blacks opening solo proprietorships were objectively higher risks than were the typically wealthier whites opening larger businesses. Hence, quite apart from discriminatory treatment at the hands of white bankers, blacks did not receive loans at all or received them only at a higher price than did whites. The humble stature of black business implicated borrowers in a vicious cycle of smallness, credit difficulties, smallness.

However, the discrimination-in-lending theory has lately lost the preeminent place it formerly occupied among explanations of Negro business retardation. In the first place, studies of small businessmen have shown that, contrary to expectation, loans from institutions have been relatively insignificant among the financial resources actually employed by proprietors in the capitalization of small firms. Only a small percentage of proprietors have reported seeking or obtaining bank loans in order to open a small business; by far the greater percentage rely entirely on their personal resources, especially their own savings, and loans from kin and friends: "Small new enterprises are financed primarily by owners, their relatives and friends, and by suppliers of materials and equipment. Banking institutions extend only slight accommodation to small new businesses." These findings do not support the familiar argument that institutional discrimination in lending produced black difficulties in small business. On the contrary, these findings suggest that even had racial discrimination been exceptionally severe in commercial lending, it could have had only a minor impact. Since bank credit has been so insignificant a resource for new proprietors in general, even complete denial of bank credit could hardly account for the Negro's singular difficulties in small business.

Reviewing the relevant arguments, Gunnar Myrdal observed that "the credit situation has certainly been one of the major obstacles barring the way for the Negro businessman." Yet Myrdal also complained that the credit theory appeared highly inadequate when the Negro's actual involvement in small business was contrasted with that of foreign-born whites, and especially with that of Americans of Japanese or Chinese descent. If discrimination in lending accounted for black underrepresentation in business, then the Orientals ought also to have been underrepresented relative to more advantaged foreign-born whites. In turn, one would expect the foreign-born whites to have been underrepresented relative to native-born whites. If smallness or poverty accounted for the Negro's difficulties in securing commercial loans, then smallness ought to have interfered with foreign-born whites and Orientals as well.

But, in fact, both foreign-born whites and Orientals were overrepresented in business relative to native whites, who presumably suffered no discrimination in lending. If Orientals and foreign-born whites were able to overcome these handicaps, then why were black Americans not also able to surmount them?

Accounting for these anomalies has necessitated a reconsideration of black business history in which the emphasis has shifted from financial to social causes. E. Franklin Frazier's "tradition-of-enterprise" hypothesis stands out as the general paradigm for research in this area: "Although no systematic study has been undertaken of the social causes of the failure of the Negro to achieve success as a businessman, it appears from what we know of the social and cultural history of the Negro that it is the result largely of the lack of traditions in the field of business enterprise." "Experience in buying and selling" was apparently the tradition Frazier thought relevant, for he explicitly deemphasized the role played by "such economic factors as . . . availability of capital," evidently because of Myrdal's earlier discussion.

In his discussion of Negro business, Eugene Foley has followed Frazier's lead in interpreting Negro business from the perspective of traditions; however, Foley singled out a different tradition: "In the final analysis, the fundamental reason that Negroes have not advanced in business is the lack of business success symbols available to them." Foley's theory has an advantage of concreteness relative to Frazier. However, Foley's view of the relevant traditions is flimsy and probably incorrect, for there is a very old tradition of successful Negro businessmen in the United States. This tradition is, to be sure, one of successful individuals, rather than one based on collective experience. But it is withal a tradition that offers "business success symbols" to Negroes. Around the turn of the century Booker T. Washington undertook an energetic campaign to bring these black entrepreneurs to popular attention. But the subsequent decline of Negro business despite the vigorous turn-of-the-century popularization of business success symbols suggests that the problems of Negro business were independent of popularized success symbols.

## ROTATING CREDIT ASSOCIATIONS

Regarding questions of finance as purely economic and, therefore, beyond the pale of sociological analysis, Frazier failed to follow up lines of inquiry suggested by his own conclusion. That is, Frazier did not inquire into cultural traditions relevant to the capitalization of small business even though he had himself singled out "tradition" as of overriding importance in accounting for Negro underrepresentation in business. Recent anthropological studies of economic development have generated renewed scholarly interest in traditions of informal financial cooperation in many areas of the non-Western world. Although these are practical economic traditions, they are a part of functioning cultures. Hence they are of sociological as well as of economic interest. These informal methods of financial cooperation are of considerable importance in fulfilling Frazier's program of research, because they constitute concrete traditions relevant to the financing of small business enterprises.

Although the details of such financial cooperation differ by region, Clifford Geertz has shown that a basic model can be extracted from the manifest diversity of ethnic customs. This basic model he has appropriately labeled the "rotating credit association." In a comprehensive review of rotating credit associations throughout the world, Shirley Ardener has agreed with Geertz that basic principles of rotating credit can be extracted from the diversity of customs, but she has slightly restated the formula for expressing the essential rotating credit idea. She defines it as "an association formed upon a core of participants who agree to make regular contributions to a fund which is given, in whole or in part, to each contributor in rotation." Within the limits of the rotating credit association as defined, Ardener was also able to specify the axes of variation which distinguish local customs from one another. That is, local rotating credit associations frequently differ with regard to membership size and criteria of membership, organization of the association, types of funds, transferability of funds, deductions from the fund, and sanctions imposed on members. But despite variations in these important respects, the rotating credit association may be taken as a generic type of cooperative financial institution. In many parts of the non-Western world, this type of association serves or has served many of the functions of Western banks. Such associations are, above all, credit institutions which lend lump sums of money to members. In this activity, rotating credit associations are found frequently to "assist in small scale capital formation."

Of especial importance to this discussion are

the rotating credit associations of southern China, Japan, and West Africa. Immigrants to the United States from southern China and Japan employed traditional rotating credit associations as their principal device for capitalizing small business. West Indian blacks brought the West African rotating credit association to the United States; they too used this traditional practice to finance small businesses. American-born Negroes apparently did not employ a similar institution. Hence, the rotating credit association suggests itself as a specific tradition in the field of business which accounts, in some measure, for the differential business success of American-born Negroes, West Indian Negroes, and Orientals.

## HUI IN CHINA AND IN THE UNITED STATES

The generic term for the Cantonese rotating credit association is *hui,* which means simply "association" or "club." Several variants of hui existed in China, but the rotating credit principle was everywhere strongly pronounced. Such associations are thought to be about 800 years old in China.

D. H. Kulp described a simple form of hui used in southern China. Greatly more complex variants of hui also existed, but the simple lottery scheme described by Kulp illustrates the basic principle of the Cantonese hui. A person in need of a lump sum of money would take the initiative in organizing a hui by securing from friends or relatives an agreement to pay a stipulated sum of money—say, $5—every month into a common pool. In a hui of ten members, the organizer himself received the first lump sum created, or $50, which he employed as he pleased. A month later the organizer held a feast in his home for the ten contributors. At the feast the ten members again contributed $5 each to create a fund of $50. A lottery determined which member (excluding the organizer) would receive the lump sum. Since a member could receive the lump sum only once, at each subsequent feast the pool of members still in the lottery narrowed until, finally, at the tenth feast the outstanding member automatically received the lump sum of $50. The organizer never contributed to the money pool; his repayment was exclusively in the form of the ten feasts, each of which was supposed to have cost him $5. At the conclusion of the ten feasts, each member would have dribbled away $55 in cash and would have received one lump sum of $50 and ten 50-cent feasts. Also, the organizer of the hui had received the interest-free use of $50 when he needed it, eight of the ten members had received an advance on their contribution (credit), and all of the participants had enjoyed ten sumptuous feasts in convivial company.

If the membership chose, a hui could be organized on less benevolent lines. Instead of a lottery to determine which member of the club would take the pot, each eligible member might submit a sealed bid indicating how much interest he was prepared to pay to have the use of the money. The high bidder received the pot. This system of hui operation placed a clear premium on not needing the money. Those who wanted the money in the early rounds of the hui would have to compete and pay a high interest. On the other hand, wealthier members who were not in need of money could collect the high interest paid by members who needed the use of their surplus. This form of hui created an investment opportunity for the wealthy and tended to enlist the profit motive in the extension of credit. Of course, even in this more capitalistic form of mutual aid, the interest actually paid by members in need of money tended to be less than what they would have paid for equivalent funds obtained from the town moneylender.

Cantonese in the United States employed the hui as a means of acquiring capital for business purposes. The extent of the practice is impossible to ascertain with precision, but the evidence suggests that the traditional hui was widely used and of first importance in the funding of small business enterprises. An early reference to what was probably a hui is found in Helen Clark's discussion of Chinese in New York City; however, the earliest discovered reference to what was certainly a Cantonese hui appears in Helen Cather's history of the Chinese in San Francisco:

> The Chinese have a peculiar method of obtaining funds without going to commercial banks. If a responsible Chinaman needs an amount of money, he will organize an association, each member of which will promise to pay a certain amount on a specified day of each month for a given length of time. For instance, if the organizer wants $1,300 he may ask 12 others to join with him and each will promise to pay $100 each month for 13 months. The organizer has the use of the $1,300 the first month. When the date of the meeting comes around again, the members assemble and each pays his $100, including the organizer. All but the

organizer, who has had the use of the money, bid for the pool. The man paying the highest bid pays the amount of the bid to each of the others and has the money. This continues for 13 months. Each man makes his payment each month but those who have already used the money cannot bid for it again. By the end of the 13-month period, each will have paid in $1,300 and have had the use of the whole amount.

Cather did not name the institution she described, but it was clearly a Cantonese hui of the bidding type. In regard to the origins of the practice, she learned from informants that "This is a very old Chinese custom and is still [1932] practiced by the Chinese in San Francisco. Since a man may belong to several of these associations at one time, it is not hard for a Chinaman to secure funds on short notice, for he can estimate from past bids about how much he must bid to secure the money."

In his history of San Francisco's Chinatown, Richard Dare mentions the *yueh-woey* custom which was frequently used to secure business capital. Like the institution described by Cather, Dare's yueh-woey was of the bidding and interest-paying type. In New York City's Chinatown, Virginia Heyer also found a bidding type of hui in operation. Memberships were usually limited to persons from the same village in China:

> Sometimes members of small associations form loan societies to provide capital for fellow members who hope to start businesses. Each member contributes a fixed amount of money to a common fund. The one who offers the highest rate of interest in secret bid gets to borrow the whole fund, though first he must repay the full interest. . . . This method of financing business ventures was frequent in the past, but in recent years [1953] it is said to have been less common.

Betty Lee Sung has recently described a hui of the bidding type which was popular among the Chinese in New York before 1950. One hundred members of the hui (all of the same clan) paid $10 a week for 100 weeks. Each week members bid for the $1,000 pot. If there were no bidders, a lottery among the outstanding members determined which one would receive the total fund subscribed at a stipulated low rate of interest. The hui described by Sung did not include conviviality, and the number of members greatly exceeded that characteristic of the hui in South China. In American Chinatowns, the hui had evidently become more commercial and less fraternal: "The *hui* in effect served as a systematic savings method for the thrifty and as a source of credit for those who needed a lump

sum in cash for business or other reasons. Few Chinese utilized American banks." The economic importance of the hui in the Chinese-American small business economy was emphasized by Gor Yun Leong, who observed that, "without such societies, very few businesses could be started."

## KO IN JAPAN AND IN THE UNITED STATES

Variously called *ko, tanomoshi,* or *mujin,* the Japanese form of the rotating credit association was probably adapted in the thirteenth century from the Chinese institution. In Japan, ko clubs among rural villagers included from twenty to fifty persons, whereas, according to Hsiao-tung Fei, the Chinese hui normally included only eight to fourteen persons. Unlike the hui, the Japanese institution sometimes included unrelated persons. Ko clubs met twice yearly, but the hui met monthly. Since the ko typically included more members than the hui, the Japanese clubs sometimes carried on as long as twenty years before each of the participants had received his portion. Ko was an extremely popular financial institution in rural Japan as late as the 1930s. According to John Embree, richer villagers and those in special need of funds belonged to several clubs. More of the villagers' money was tied up in ko than in commercial banks, credit unions, or postal savings.

Both a bidding system and a lottery system of ko were practiced. Only the bidding system provided for the payment of interest by early drawers to late drawers. Under the rules of the bidding system, an organizer would receive the first portion. Meetings were held at the organizer's residence where refreshments were served and business was combined with sociability. At the second meeting, bidders for the combined fund indicated the amount of payment they were willing to receive from the other participants. The lowest bidder received the fund thus created. Having once received the fund, persons were obliged to pay back at the regular meetings the full stipulated contribution. Thus, as the ko wore on, fewer and fewer persons were bidding for the fund and fewer and fewer could be released by a low bid from the necessity of paying back the stipulated rate.

In the United States the memberships of ko associations were usually composed of immigrants from the same prefecture or village in

Japan. Religious organizations, Buddhist and Christian alike, also organized clubs for the benefit of their congregants. But congruent with the Japanese traditions of neighborliness, neighborhood and friendship groups also started clubs. Although the larger ko clubs required each member to furnish guarantors, the meetings of the clubs were social as well as financial occasions. Sake was served before dinner and members entertained one another with friendly conversation. Interest payments were tendered as gifts rather than as payments for the use of money.

In Hawaii, northern California, and the Pacific Northwest, Japanese settlers referred to the rotating credit associations as *tanomoshi*. In southern California the term *mujin* prevailed. Exactly how extensively these clubs were used is difficult to ascertain, but Fumiko Fukuoka referred to the mujin as "a common and popular form of mutual financial aid association among the Japanese in Southern California." She observes that this "ancient form of mutual aid association" had been "brought to America by the Japanese immigrants." Of foreign-born Japanese sampled in California in the course of a 1965–66 survey, almost one-half reported having participated in some form of economic combination involving the pooling of money. Of the participating half, 90 percent had taken part in a tanomoshi. According to Embree, Hawaiian Japanese organized tanomoshi which met monthly rather than biannually as in Japan and in which larger sums were invested.

In 1922 Schichiro Matsui charged that white-owned banks in California discriminated against Japanese businessmen and farmers. Nonetheless, the tanomoshi permitted Japanese to capitalize business enterprises on their own. "Very popular among the Japanese in every line of trade," the tanomoshi was helpful because "a merchant without security may thus obtain credit." Two decades later S. F. Miyamoto also stressed the economic importance of tanomoshi among Japanese in Seattle:

> Few [Japanese] . . . were able to expand their business individually to any great extent. Possibly without a system of cooperative financing the Japanese would not have developed the economic structure that they did. Fortunately, they met their needs through adaptations of Japanese customs, such as the money-pool known as the *tanomoshi*. . . . It is difficult to ascertain the extent to which such pools were used by the Japanese immigrants . . . but from the wide-spread recognition of its use, it was probably no inconsequential part of their financing practices. The largest hotel

ever attempted by the Japanese, a transaction involving some $90,000, . . . was financed on the basis of a *tanomoshi*.

Commentators agreed that the rotating credit associations were more popular with Japanese of the immigrant generation than with their American-born offspring, the nisei, especially those with college degrees. For purposes of financing business operations, the nisei preferred the impersonal credit union or savings and loan association. According to a nisei informant, Japanese in the San Francisco Bay region no longer employ the tanomoshi for purposes of business capitalization. However, the custom survives. Its purposes are now social, and only small sums are invested. This information agrees with the findings of Minako Kurokawa's recent study of Japanese small businessmen in San Francisco. She noted that, as a source of business capitalization, "the traditional institution of mutual aid [tanomoshi] . . . was not mentioned by respondents." On the other hand, a nisei informant in Los Angeles claims to be personally involved in an on-going tanomoshi, the members of which are still principally interested in securing capital for business purposes. According to this informant, the custom remains very widespread among Japanese in Los Angeles and retains its business significance.

## *ESUSU* IN AFRICA, BRITAIN, AND THE AMERICAS

Anthropological research has documented the existence of rotating credit associations in many parts of Africa, including West Africa from which the progenitors of American Negroes were abducted as slaves. Although the details of administration and organization differ substantially among African regions and peoples, the essential rotating credit principle is virtually ubiquitous. However, one such rotating credit institution, the Nigerian *esusu,* is of especial importance here because of its historical influence on Negro business in the Americas. The esusu developed in southeastern Nigeria among the Yoruba people. Among the Yoruba's northern neighbors, the Nupe, the rotating credit institution is known as *dashi,* but the Nupe's custom differs little from the Yoruba's. The antiquity of the esusu has not yet been finally established, but researchers are of the opinion that the custom was indigenously African.

Certainly the Yoruba esusu existed as early as 1843, for it is mentioned in a Yoruba vocabulary of that date. In Sierra Leone, thrift clubs of some sort existed as early as 1794, but they cannot be positively identified as organized on the rotating credit principle.

In his discussion of Yoruba associations, A. K. Ajisafe provides a statement of the esusu institution which summarizes its formal operation:

> There is a certain society called Esusu. This society deals with monetary matters only, and it helps its members to save and raise money thus: Every member shall pay a certain fixed sum of money regularly at a fixed time (say every fifth or ninth day). And one of the subscribing members shall take the total amount thus subscribed for his or her own personal use. The next subscription shall be taken by another member; this shall so continue rotationally until every member has taken.

In the principle of pooling funds and rotating the pot among the membership, the Yoruba esusu does not differ from either of its Oriental counterparts; however, in common practice, it exhibits some idiosyncrasies. As W. R. Bascom observed, "anyone who wishes to do so may found an *esusu* group, provided that others are willing to entrust their money to him." But the organizer or president of the esusu needed only to be known; he did not need to know all of the members personally. Once an organizer had announced his intention to sponsor an esusu, persons willing to entrust their money to him indicated a willingness to join. Such personal acquaintances of the organizer, if accepted, became in turn heads of "roads." There were as many separate roads as there were persons who had directly contacted the organizer and had been scrutinized and accepted by him. As heads of roads, these personal acquaintances of the organizer were entitled to contact their own friends and kin concerning membership in the esusu. Heads of the roads normally were responsible for "collecting the contributions and making the disbursements within their subgroups which consist of members who have applied to them rather than to the founder for admission." In this manner the Yoruba esusu delegated responsibility for the integrity of all members from the original organizer to managers known and appointed by and accountable to him.

The Yoruba esusu was apparently carried to the Americas by African slaves. Indeed Bascom bases his argument for the indigenous African origins of the esusu on the persistence in the West Indies of the same custom among the descendants of slaves. An early reference mentions the practice of *asu* in the British Bahamas in 1910:

> Another method of promoting thrift is apparently of Yoruban origin. Little associations called "Asu" are formed of one or two dozen people who agree to contribute weekly a small sum toward a common fund. Every month (?) the amount thus pooled is handed to a member, in order of seniority of admission, and makes a little nest-egg for investment or relief. These "Asu" have no written statutes or regulations, no regular officers, but carry on their affairs without fraud or miscalculation.

In the Trinidad village studied by M. J. Herskovits, residents referred to their rotating credit association as *susu*. As Herskovits observed, the term is clearly a corruption of the Yoruba word esusu. Trinidadians originally from Barbados and Guiana told Herskovits of the form of the susu in their birthplaces. In Barbados the rotating credit association was commonly known as "the meeting" and in Guiana as "boxi money." According to Herskovits, the Trinidadian susu "takes the form of a cooperative pooling of earnings by those in the group, so that each member may benefit by obtaining in turn, and at one time, all the money paid in by the entire group on a given date. Members may contribute the same amount. The total of the weekly contribution . . . is called 'a hand.' "

Jamaicans refer to their rotating credit association as "partners." The partners in Jamaica is headed by a "banker" and the membership is composed of "throwers." In operation the club is apparently identical to the susu of Trinidad. In the Jamaican setting, however, members apparently used their partnership portions for business capitalization, whereas rural Trinidadians appear to have made use of the fund only for consumption purposes. Many Jamaican petty traders used their partnership "draw" to restock their stalls with imported goods for which they were required to pay cash. The partnership constituted the "most important source of capital for petty traders."

West Indian migration to the United States commenced around 1900 and continued until 1924. In 1920, at the peak of the immigration, foreign-born Negroes, almost exclusively West Indians, numbered 73,803, of whom 36,613 resided in New York City. Most of these migrants came from the British West Indies. West Indians in Harlem distinguished themselves from native-born Negroes by their remarkable propensity to operate small business enterprises. The West Indians, W. A. Domingo observed, "are forever launching out in business, and such retail businesses as are in the hands of Negroes in Harlem are largely in the control of the foreign-born." Moreover, the West Indians were more aggressive than the native-born Negroes in their choice of self-employment enterprises. Whereas native-born Negroes tended only to open noncompetitive service enterprises, the West Indians operated grocery stores, tailor shops, jewelry stores, and fruit vending and real estate operations in which they undertook direct competition with whites doing business in the ghetto. Only the Bajan, it was said, could withstand the competition of the Jew.

The thriftiness of the West Indians provoked resentment on the part of American-born Negroes who regarded the West Indians as stingy and grasping. Some of the West Indians' thrift expressed itself in patronage of orthodox savings institutions, especially the postal savings. However, the West Indians in Harlem also employed the traditional susu credit institution as a savings device. According to Amy Jacques Garvey, higher status West Indian migrants of urban origin "acquired the habit of accumulating capital" through the partners system from enforced contact with lower status West Indians of rural origins. Mrs. Garvey adds that in Harlem, "Women were mostly active in running the [partners] system—being bankers and collectors. Some 'threw a regular hand' for their husbands or brothers to enable them to operate small businesses. Later, the West Indian shopkeepers, barbers, etc. operated bigger 'pools' for setting up or capitalizing existing small business, or buying homes." The partners draw also permitted a West Indian to purchase passage for relatives to the United States and to finance the secondary education of their children in the islands. As to the extensiveness of the practice of partners in Harlem, Mrs. Garvey observes that "the 'partners' system was fairly widespread in the 1920's and 1930's, but the Depression lessened its usage."

The significance of the partners as a factor in West Indian saving is further illustrated by postwar British West Indian migration to Britain. As in Harlem during the first several decades of the century, West Indians in Britain attracted attention because of their extraordinary frugality. Observers noted that West Indian migrants tended to "economize to a much greater extent than comparable English income groups." Investigating the savings habits of London's Jamaicans, Hyndman reported

that the traditional partners played the leading role:

> Methods of saving vary, but the most prevalent is the friendly cooperative effort normally referred to by Jamaicans as "partner." Other names for similar systems in the Eastern group of islands are "Sousou," "chitty," "syndicate." This is a simple method based on mutual trust between friends and relations, and complete confidence in the man or woman who is organizer—fifteen or twenty people pay a weekly sum of between one pound and five pounds to the organizers. Either by drawing lots or by prior arrangement, the total amount at the end of each week goes to one of the twenty. . . . In some instances the weekly payments necessitate a strenuous savings effort, but in most cases the "partners" is carried on time and again with satisfaction on all sides.

R. B. Davison's sample of Jamaican migrants in Britain also disclosed the persistence of the partners custom. At the end of the first year after arrival, 25 percent of Jamaicans sampled reported that they were presently involved in a partners or had recently been so involved. Other Jamaicans reported that they would participate in partners if only they could find an on-going group with a reliable membership and banker. One Jamaican claimed to be still participating by mail in a partners in Jamaica. "The urge to engage in some form of cooperative savings," observed Davison, "is strong among at least a substantial minority of the Jamaican community."

As in the United States, West Indians in Britain evinced a strong interest in real estate investment. In providing financial resources for such investment, the partners played a major role. Hyndman found that, by means of continuous participation in the partners, Jamaicans became able to "command a large sum of ready cash," which often provided "the initial payment on a house" or the passage to Britain of a family member. Racial discrimination in housing rentals apparently influenced the Jamaicans' schedule of priorities. West Indians scrimped in order "to achieve property ownership because of the difficulties experienced in providing adequate accommodation" for themselves and their families. Jamaicans came to own a substantial amount of real property in a relatively short time, especially in view of their impoverished origins. Of Davison's sample of Jamaicans, 75 percent were residing in houses "as tenants of Jamaican landlords." Jamaican-owned housing thus clearly encompassed almost enough units to house the entire Jamaican population. Virtually all of this real estate had, of course, been purchased since 1945.

## ROTATING CREDIT AS A TRADITION OF ENTERPRISE

The employment of the esusu by West Indian migrants in Harlem and again in Britain illustrates the manner in which a traditional economic custom encouraged the business activities of immigrants. The process was much the same thing among Chinese, Japanese, and West Indians. But unlike any of these immigrant groups, American-born Negroes in the United States did not employ any rotating credit institution, apparently because this African economic custom had vanished from their cultural repertoire. Since ethnographic accounts of black life in the United States did not consciously investigate the persistence of the Yoruba esusu or its variants, only negative evidence for this proposition exists. That is, lack of reference to rotating credit associations among Negroes in the United States may be taken as a prima facie evidence that such practices were not, in fact, employed. Students of this question have thus far been unable to locate any instance of rotating credit practices among American-born Negroes. Even Herskovits made no mention of rotating credit associations in the United States, although his own research in Trinidad had awakened him to the persistence of this Africanism.

The persistence of the rotating credit associations among Chinese, Japanese, and West Indians provides tangible support for E. F. Frazier's contention that tradition played a critical role in the business success of "other alien groups" and that a lack of traditions inhibited Negro-owned business in the United States. Moreover, it makes possible an understanding of why racial discrimination in lending affected American-born Negroes more deleteriously than it did Orientals and foreign-born Negroes. Unlike the Chinese, Japanese, and West Indians, American-born Negroes did not have the rotating credit tradition to fall back on as a source of capital for small business enterprises. Hence, they were especially dependent on banks and lending companies for credit; and when such credit was for one reason or another denied, they possessed no traditional resources for making do on their own.

## SLAVERY AND EMANCIPATION IN THE BRITISH WEST INDIES AND IN THE UNITED STATES

The absence of the rotating credit association among American-born Negroes probably involves a cultural disappearance in that the custom was very likely known to blacks brought as slaves to North America. Strongly prevailing scholarly opinion does maintain that Yoruba slaves brought the custom of esusu to the West Indies, but the possibility cannot be ruled out that free African laborers imported the custom after emancipation in 1838. Moreover, in the present state of knowledge, it cannot positively be asserted that rotating credit institutions existed on the western coast of Africa prior to 1834, although they probably did. Since most slave trading was conducted prior to 1834, the supposition that African slaves carried the esusu with them to the New World depends on the existence of the custom in West Africa during the slaving period.

If, however, slaves did carry the esusu with them to the New World, then the nonexistence of the rotating credit institution among blacks in the United States suggests a genuine cultural disappearance. West Indian and American slaves did not differ in the African regions from which they were abducted. Indeed, the West Indies served as a "seasoning" place for slaves ultimately sold in the American South. The West Indian or American destination of abducted blacks was, in effect, random in respect to region of African origin. Whatever the tribal and ethnic mélange of blacks in North America, a similar distribution doubtless characterized the West Indian blacks. Accordingly, social conditions in the British West Indies and in the southern portion of the United States presumably account for the persistence of the esusu only in the islands.

In accounting for the survival of the esusu in the Caribbean and its apparent demise in the United States, the "bedrock" facts are those of demography. Throughout the slavery period the black population of the Caribbean islands dramatically exceeded the white population. "West Indian planters," remarks W. D. Jordan, "were lost not so much in the Caribbean as in a sea of blacks." This demographic situation in the Indies contrasted vividly with that in the United States, where Africans were a numerical minority. To be sure, blacks in the United States occasionally constituted a local majority; yet the numerical preponderance which they everywhere enjoyed in the Indies was rarely matched in the United States. All-black Caribbean islands were hospitable to the perpetuation of African cultural traditions such as the esusu. The outnumbered and subdued blacks in the southern portion of the United States confronted much more formidable barriers to the perpetuation of African culture traits.

Administrative necessity, furthermore, induced the West Indian slaveholders to institutionalize the operation of a slaves' economy. This indulgence reflected the shortage of whites which deprived West Indian slaveholders of the administrators necessary to supervise subsistence farming as an organized function of the plantation. These activities had, in consequence, to be left to the initiative of the blacks. To support themselves, slaves were customarily and typically provided with plots of land on which to grow their own subsistence. Alternate Saturdays and Sundays were made available to permit slaves to attend to their cultivation. Slaves also kept stock and had recognized grazing rights on the plantation grounds. In the British Caribbean, these informal expectations were elevated to the status of statutory law by the Consolidated Slave Acts of 1820 which required owners to provide slaves with "rights" in land and in the free time to cultivate it. Since the sugar estates made little organized provision for their own subsistence, the white plantation overlords were themselves economically dependent on the slaves' economy for their own provisioning. By the mid-eighteenth century, for example, the entire population of Jamaica was completely dependent on the black economy for its subsistence. The economic dependence of the whites and their well-justified fears of insurrection tended, of course, to inhibit them from interfering with the economic activities which the slaves claimed as "rights." Thus, the slave's economy of the West Indies acquired not only a traditional and then statutory legitimacy; it also acquired in the course of time a porcupine coat of protective sanctions.

Although Caribbean slaves were entitled to plots and to time off for cultivating them, not all slaves opted to be cultivators. Some slaves devoted their free time to trade and to crafts. Division of labor encouraged the exchange of commodities and the formation of markets for that purpose. Both blacks and whites attended these weekly markets. Slaves successful in commerce could employ their proceeds for the purchase of manumission. The peculium of the slaves enjoyed recognition in custom and later in law such that slaves were entitled to alienate or to inherit property, and to accumulate without hindrance the wherewithal for their own manumission. Through this participation in the slave-operated subeconomy of the Indies, some few blacks even attained substantial wealth.

The great leeway accorded the slaves in the organization of their subsistence economy reduced the external obstacles to the maintenance of African economic traditions. Such traditions of production had an everyday significance in that, even under slavery, provisioning remained a daily concern of every slave: "The production of a per capita agricultural surplus within the internal economy under slavery facilitated . . . the development of a strong marketing pattern which probably rested on the foundations of the African cultural heritage of the slaves." Part of this heritage, it is reasonable to suppose, was the esusu.

American slaveholders generally preferred to provision their blacks from plantation storehouses, and subsistence farming was organized as a regular function of the plantation. To be sure, many slaveholders in the United States supplied small plots and time off for the slaves as useful incentives. Some masters even permitted slaves thus rewarded to sell their produce in town rather than to the plantation. But even where the small-plot-and-free-time system prevailed, they were only incentives. American slaves never achieved the consensually, not to mention legally, validated rights to self-maintenance that Caribbean blacks enjoyed. Where such activities were tolerated, they depended on the *bon plaisir* of the slaveholders. Since the peculium of the slave did not achieve a consensually or legally validated status in the United States—with rights of alienation, inheritance, and manumission—the legal and moral basis of the slave-operated economy was absent.

Trade among slaves or between slaves and whites was, in the United States, an irregular, sporadic occurrence. The *licet* of the slaveholders intervened between slaves and commerce; and slaveholders in the United States were of divided opinion concerning the desirability of such trade. This situation contrasts rather starkly with the weekly markets in the major towns of the West Indies. Hence, it is inappropriate to speak of a slave-operated subsistence economy in the United States. Since such an economy was clearly relevant to the survival of cooperative African economic customs, the lack of slave self-maintenance and markets in the United States would tend to account for the disappearance of such customs among American blacks.

In the South, nonslaveholders and smaller slave plantations grew food and feed crops for their own maintenance and for local sale. This source of supply was routinely available to any slaveholding plantations that did not make their own provision for subsistence agriculture. In a crisis, such as unruliness among the slaves, even the self-provisioning plantations could purchase supplies from local whites. Such provisioning would tide the owners over the period of discontent, while deprivation would, on the other hand, help to bring insubordinate blacks to their senses. Such relief was unavailable to West Indian cultivators who became, accordingly, more dependent on the private economic activities of their own blacks. The small white freeholders in the southern United States also provided a militia capable of suppressing black insurrection. The support of these armed whites further strengthened the hand of the American slaveowner against his own slaves. Equivalent local military assistance was unavailable to West Indian plantation managers, who found it doubly expedient to refrain from interfering with the slaves' "rightful" economic activities.

The great size of the West Indian sugar plantations and the practice of absentee ownership also contributed to the survival of African customs and culture among the slaves. Immense West Indian sugar plantations employed hundreds of slaves in the cane fields. Hired white administrators oversaw the administration of plantation work. The owners of the plantations typically preferred to reside in the comfort of London where they could most comfortably enjoy the proceeds of the diligent labor of their distant blacks. Overseers were poor whites who viewed their position in the Indies as a temporary exile from which they hoped to return to England as wealthy men. Absentee owners naturally viewed their West Indian enterprises in purely financial terms. "Kindliness and comfort, cruelty and hardship were rated at balance-sheet value."

In the United States, even the larger cotton plantations were small when compared to the norm of Indies sugar plantations. Moreover, many small- and medium-sized southern farms held from one to twenty slaves who were accordingly dispersed in small clusters throughout the region. By 1860, somewhat less than one-half of all slaves in the United States lived on farms which employed no more than twenty slaves. The smaller size of the holdings brought slaves into personal contact with their owners. Indeed, on the smallest farms, owner and slave worked side by side in the fields, although whites resorted to common field work only from necessity. Larger plantations employed poor whites to oversee production. As in the West Indies, overseers were transient and faithless. Absentee ownership, however, was exceptional in the United States. Plantation owners preferred to live on their lands where they occupied the main roost in a collonaded white mansion overlooking the shanties of their blacks. These conditions were propitious for the creation of a patriarchal relationship between a planter and his Negroes. Certainly southern conditions were more conducive to such a development than were West Indian conditions, where blacks in great numbers confronted an absentee owner or corporation only through the written reports of transient administrators. Compared to his West Indian counterpart, the southern Negro was well situated to absorb the culture of the slaveholders. Whatever the other implications of this relationship, it can hardly have induced a conservative attitude in the slaves concerning the desirability of retaining or practicing African customs.

Postemancipation conditions in the West Indies were also more conducive to the survival of African economic customs than were postemancipation conditions in the United States. In the British Caribbean, with the exception of Barbados, the emancipation of the slaves was followed by the widespread withdrawal of the freedmen from wage labor on the sugar plantations. The freedmen retreated to the interior of the islands where there remained extensive tracts of unsettled Crown lands available for squatting. Here the freedmen founded free villages and subsistence farming communities of their own—greatly to the inconvenience of the sugar plantation owners who desired their participation as "free" laborers on the plantations. Subsistence farming in the backwoods was not a profitable way of life, but those who followed it remained free of the domination of the large estates. In the isolated inland communities, African economic customs were readily applicable to the everyday tasks of production.

In contrast, emancipation in the American South did not release the freedmen from the domination of the plantation system. Since unsettled tracts of public lands were unavailable to them, blacks could not retreat from the cotton-dominated plantation economy to subsistence farming on their own account. Hence, the American plantation system resurrected itself upon titulary "free" labor in the form of sharecropping agreements between white owners and freedmen. For political reasons, the "forty acres and a mule" promised the freedmen did not materialize. Yet precisely this land reform would have been necessary to duplicate through political intervention the subsistence farming, freeholding Negro communities which sprang up in the West Indies without political intervention. It may be that by 1856 African economic customs had already disappeared from the cultural repertoire of American blacks. In any event, tenant farming and debt peonage were unfavorable conditions for the operation of cooperative African economic practices. In the West Indies, on the other hand, the postemancipation social situation of Negroes encouraged continued reliance on cooperative economic customs.

In the broad view, these considerations suggest a casual chain ultimately linking the eradication of African economic customs under the North American slavery regime to the subsequent disadvantages of American-born Negroes in the field of business credit in the urban North. On the other hand, pre- and postemancipation social conditions in the British West Indies permitted the intergenerational continuity of African customs. In the hands of the West Indian descendants of slaves in Harlem, the perpetuated African economic customs encouraged and facilitated the business activities of the immigrants. These suppositions are congruent with the accepted scholarly belief that African customs, in particular the esusu,

were part of the cultural heritage of slaves in both the United States and in the West Indies. Insofar as an environmental explanation can account for the manifest lack of the rotating credit association among American-born blacks but not among West Indian blacks, the environmental explanation tends to buttress the supposition that esusu disappeared from the cultural repertoire of American blacks.

Every step of this historic process is not equally in focus at this time. It remains to be documented, for example, that rotating credit was actually employed by slaves in the operation of their separate subsistence economy in the West Indies. Hence, there is only a speculative case for the supposition that social conditions in the United States extirpated the esusu from the cultural repertoire of blacks in this country, whereas social conditions in the West Indies encouraged their persistence. All conjectures as to causality must, naturally, come to grips with the manifest fact that American-born Negroes did not employ esusu in the twentieth century, whereas West Indian Negroes did.

# Identity and Culture

VINE DELORIA, JR.

Contemporary society is often characterized by astute observers as ahistorical and therefore lacking a discernible orientation and direction; it represents, Arthur Miller argued, "generalized, moralistic mush." The roots of this condition can be found in postwar technological and political developments: industrialism on a massive scale; electronic communications; improved transportation facilities; universal, although sometimes superficial, education; and the emergence of America as a world superpower. No single factor is more important than any other; they are all interdependent and play a critical role in how we perceive ourselves and our problems.

Historical dislocation is important to recognize because it speaks directly to the conceptions of progress held by the majority and confuses the standards minorities are measured against. Traditional perceptions of social conditions depend ultimately on sets of data gathered in customary categories and on the ensuing arguments that revolve around the optimistic or pessimistic interpretation of information based, almost always, on an assumed incremental pattern of growth. The first step in any accurate appraisal of arguments on either side is to formulate a context within which the extent of historical dislocation can be determined. Although the Second World War must form the baseline from which we can examine the progress of racial minorities in recent times, the conditions out of which minorities emerged in the postwar decades originated shortly before the beginning of this century.

The 1890s are a critical decade in American history; both the white majority and the racial minorities experienced substantial changes during these years that exert continuing influence today. American society saw the final consolidation of large industries into trust and national corporations, a process that began in the Civil War and was completed with a reduction of the Western lands to their final political, social, and economic institutional expressions. Although many Americans think individual initiative epitomized the 1890s, and some writers see the robber baron as the personification of the age, Christopher Lasch argued, with justification, that "the nineteenth-century cult of success placed surprisingly little emphasis on competition. It measured achievement not against the achievements of others but against an abstract ideal of discipline and self-denial." John D. Rockefeller distributing dimes and moral admonitions is a more accurate picture of those years than Jay Gould frantically fleeing New York City, his bags bulging with railroad bonds. At any rate, white Americans often like to think of the age as one of individual initiative triumphant over competition, and they continue to gauge minority efforts to succeed by this mystical standard.

While white urban Americans were moving rapidly, if unknowingly, into an industrial age that cherished managerial skills over hard work, blacks, Mexican Americans, American Indians, and Puerto Ricans were being subjected to a form of legal exclusion unique in human history. Although given the franchise in 1870 by the Fifteenth Amendment, by the last decade of the nineteenth century blacks saw their political rights destroyed. This was accomplished by a line of reasoning that distinguished state from national citizenship, beginning with the Slaughterhouse Cases, expanded by the Civil Rights Cases, and finally articulated in *Plessy v. Ferguson* in 1896 as "separate but equal" citizenship. In a debate in 1901, Congressman Marlin E. Olmstead of Pennsylvania indicated the magnitude of subsequent black disfranchisement when he introduced a resolution to get

From Vine Deloria, Jr., "Identity and Culture," in *Daedalus,* Journal of the American Academy of Arts and Sciences, *American Indians, Blacks, Chicanos, and Puerto Ricans,* vol. 110, no. 2, Spring 1981. Cambridge, Mass. Reprinted by permission of *Daedalus.* Footnotes have been deleted.

Congress to enforce the provisions of the Fourteenth Amendment:

> In the seven districts of Mississippi the total vote cast for all Congressional candidates in 1890 was 62,652; in 1898, 27,045. In the seven districts of South Carolina the total vote in 1890 was 73,522 and 28,831 in 1898. In the six districts of Louisiana 74,542 in 1890 and 33,161 in 1898.

He further noted that one member of the House representing six counties in South Carolina, with a population in 1890 of 158,851, received only 1,765 votes. The *Plessy* decision only gave legal formality to a social and economic movement that transformed blacks from citizens to subjects.

According to Frederick Jackson Turner, the frontier closed with the 1890 census reports. This announcement, combined with a wave of nostalgia generated by touring Wild West shows that attempted to relive the frontier adventure, permanently accorded Indians a mythical existence. The General Allotment Act of 1887 was the progenitor of nearly a hundred agreements between the U.S. government and the Indian tribes to subdivide tribal land estates into small farming tracts. The act fragmented tribal customs, and enabled Indian Commissioner Francis Leupp to remark a decade later that Indian affairs were now merely a matter of administration. The Indian, now a ward of the massive federal bureaucracy, fell permanently into a subservient status, receiving as income only the pittance that the Bureau of Indian Affairs asked as a price for the lease of his lands.

Mexican Americans were reduced to political impotence following the Mexican War, although some of the well-to-do continued to exercise local influence in parts of Texas, New Mexico, Arizona, and California. Mexican land grants expressed the property rights and political identities of the Mexican settlements, but the Court of Private Claims, established in 1891, by a variety of legal technicalities dispossessed almost all the landowning Mexicans and eliminated the common lands of villages that had been their heritage for centuries. The reduction of the large numbers of incoming Oriental agricultural workers through restrictive legislation boosted the economic value of Mexican American families. Working in the fields of California and Texas, these families became seasonal serfs to the large ranchers and farmers. Use of Mexican laborers on railroad construction completed the task of dispersing the indigenous Mexican community throughout the southwestern United States.

Puerto Rico fell as a prize to the United States in the Spanish-American War in 1898. The island was perceived, as were the Philippine and Hawaiian islands, as destined for perpetual colonial status both because of noncontiguity to the mainland and the large native population that precluded significant white settlement and domination. When the Supreme Court excluded the island from the application of the constitutional Bill of Rights in the Insular Cases, it was evident that Puerto Rico, although culturally distinct from the United States, would remain a colonial possession until it served no useful purpose in American hemispheric plans.

Public attitudes and perceptions do follow statutory enactments, and the legal-political subversion that made these racial minorities less than full citizens served to reinforce racial stereotypes that had formerly suggested their subhuman qualities. Pseudoscientific pronouncements regarding the lesser technical and cultural accomplishments of these groups bolstered the legal prohibitions against them; the discriminatory status seemed a benign step of wardship on a progressive march upward toward eventual civilized status. Separate and unequal educational facilities were justified by majority beliefs in the inherent inferiority of the colored races, and the low level of achievement of pupils produced by substandard schools was cited as further scientific evidence of the reality of the cultural evolutionary incline these groups were attempting to ascend. The educational system, which was then being expanded in order to socialize European peasant immigrants arriving in the United States, became the major public institution for suppressing these groups.

The Depression and the Second World War each brought a measure of equality for racial minorities. National social welfare programs sponsored by the New Deal were generally applied with a minimal amount of discrimination. American Indians and Mexican Americans served in the armed forces with only sporadic incidents of discrimination, Puerto Ricans were generally used in installations on their island, and blacks served in all branches, although they played a strange, subservient role in the navy as ships stewards. The irony of German and Italian prisoners of war having more social status and privileges than American racial minorities was not missed by sensitive observers, and caused acute embarrassment. If one chose to debate theories of racial superiority, similarities between Nazi treatment of the Jews and the status of blacks in the South made justifying the war against Germany difficult.

For the majority, the 1950s were calm, peaceful years, but for the racial minorities, they were a turbulent time when fundamental changes occurred. Two major activities dominated these years: migration and the stabilization of institutions representing these minority communities in the larger society. The industrial needs of the Second World War, even more than the First—which saw immense black migration from the South—required relocating tremendous numbers of workers into the war industries, primarily in the Midwest and the Pacific Coast. Black migration to Northern cities increased dramatically, and American Indians and Mexican Americans moved in large numbers to the West Coast. This pattern continued once the war was over. Puerto Ricans migrated in large numbers to New York and other Eastern cities in the early 1950s. After 1954, under the federal policy of relocation, significant numbers of American Indians were relocated to Midwestern cities to learn new industrial skills. The bracero program, begun in 1942 in partial answer to wartime labor needs in agriculture, became a permanent answer to low-cost labor requirements in the Southwest.

Although life in the urban ghetto exposed racial minorities to new ideas and values, the sense of deprivation, isolation, and vulnerability increased, as obvious economic disparities reminded people of their subservient status. Access to national communications media compensated to some degree for the social liabilities of urban life, because such access enabled members of the different minority groups to establish new working relationships with others similarly situated. The larger national organizations such as the National Association for the Advancement of Colored People, the League of United Latin American Citizens, the G.I. Forum, and the National Congress of American Indians experienced tremendous growth during the fifties, and began to exert a new kind of political leadership previously absent in race relations.

During the postwar years, self-help doctrines permeated American society, and although these doctrines provided no real avenue for expression by any of the communities, they nevertheless formed the standards by which the larger society judged minorities. In the misguided hope that withdrawal of support services to the reservations would create a new wave of individualism among Indians, Congress terminated federal responsibility for them. "Operation Bootstrap," Luis Muñoz Marin's island

version of self-help for Puerto Rico, was seen by acute observers of that island as a modern version of old imperialist and mercantilist practices. Bootstrapping did little to resolve the island's economic problems, and served primarily to link the masses of poor with the consumer society and to show people what they could *not* have rather than provide them with the conveniences and products of modern industrialism.

Education was the primary field in which self-help reigned as the guiding ideology. The John Hay Whitney Foundation Opportunity Fellowships provided financial assistance to minority students for graduate education, while the G.I. Bill, available during most of the fifties, provided subsistence benefits to veterans for undergraduate training. American belief in education as the basis of full citizenship and economic prosperity was underlined in the conflicts over school desegregation. These conflicts reached a crescendo following the *Brown v. Board of Education of Topeka, Kansas,* decision in 1954, which abolished the legal basis for separate educational facilities for minorities. Successful individuals who escaped the poverty and discrimination that were the lot of their group were touted as proof that self-help worked; it was believed that every member of the racial minorities, given the time and opportunity, could become successful. The absence of motivation rather than discrimination was cited as the reason the majority of each group did not progress. That a handful of people escaped the severe handicaps of segregation was advanced as evidence of the ultimate capability of the groups, provided they accepted the tediously slow and incremental changes offered them.

The chief characteristic of minorities during the fifties was their invisibility to the majority. Lulled into believing that America was a land of limitless opportunities, most whites assumed that minorities were either prospering or wanted to remain in poverty and helplessness. Discrimination was explained as the desire of minorities to remain "with their own kind," and only the Montgomery bus boycott and subsequent nonviolent demonstrations by the emerging civil rights movement proved otherwise. With each demonstration, more of the majority began to understand the desperate straits of the minorities in education, housing, employment, and access to public facilities.

Desegregation of educational facilities challenged traditional beliefs about education and raised fundamental questions regarding the nature of American institutions. Desegregation entailed more than equal opportunity; it confronted separatism in every form, and perpetuated the belief that access to Anglo-Saxon beliefs, values, and domestic behavior patterns constituted equality in the larger sense. The problems of inherited advantage—class and not race—lay beneath the surface struggles over desegregation. The Selective Service Act of 1951 was typical of the confused perception of race and class. The act imposed universal military obligation on the young, but nevertheless exempted the offspring of the affluent, who were able to get deferments to attend college, and then to serve as officers—if they were drafted into the armed forces at all. It basically created a military composed of minorities and lower-class whites rather than a democratic citizen army. Equal opportunity, which the minorities eagerly sought, actually meant having access to the informal networks and relationships of the affluent majority rather than the chance to compete in the marketplace.

Until the sixties, identity and culture were inseparable concepts that encompassed the same phenomena and were indistinguishable in their objective reality. Segregation forced minorities to create institutions, similar to those enjoyed by the majority, that could provide a measure of activity to reassure them of their status as Americans. The realization that such measures were necessary because of the exclusionary practices of the majority was a long time in coming. Thus the beauty pageants "Miss Black U.S.A." and "Miss Indian America" were created because of the discriminatory practices of the majority, not because they expressed values transcending all groups in society. Minorities were *identified* by skin color, but the confirmation of this identification depended on the recognition of parallel institutions and community participation. Truly indigenous activities and institutions qualitatively distinct from majority values went unnoticed and unappreciated. The outward expression of minority community life, however, was that of American culture, not one of distinctive variance from majority behavior.

The election of John F. Kennedy as president in 1960 began a period of radical change in American society. "America's leading man," as Norman Mailer aptly described him, recruited "the best and the brightest," as one commentator cynically described the New Frontiersmen who came to Washington with the Democratic visitors. Kennedy was the first truly media-oriented president; he was obsessively concerned with his image. In courting the racial minorities during the campaign, he created a

gap between public perceptions and performance that had to be closed to preserve his fragile electoral coalition. His first inclination was to keep the minorities calm, and hope that negotiated settlements behind the scenes could solve the civil rights problem with minimal disruption of the traditional American lifestyle. In February 1960 the sit-ins began in Greensboro, North Carolina, and in 1961, as Kennedy was getting the New Frontier established, the Freedom Rides began, with a well-integrated group of white and black protestors challenging segregation on public transportation in the South. The liberal community, looking to Kennedy for leadership, forced his hand, and federal involvement in the civil rights struggle became a reluctant reality.

Consider, then, the situation that the four racial minorities confronted as the sixties began. The *de jure* impediments to education were being removed in the South, and in their collapse other legal obstacles were falling. *De facto* discrimination, although obvious, was still excused by the misinformed majority as the result of slothful attitudes of the minorities. Phrasing their demands for legal reform as "freedom," "integration now," and "self-determination," the minorities began to agitate for reform more substantial than merely eliminating institutional barriers. Mistaking image for substance, Americans came to believe that Martin Luther King's call for nonviolence would forever dominate protest tactics. Most white Americans, in fact, believed that even King's peaceful protests were too violent; they convinced themselves that a peaceful and clear articulation of goals would produce instant and reasonable change. The burning question of the day, asked of every minority with complaints about discriminatory treatment, was, "What do you want?"—as if identification of the problem in simple terms was akin to its solution.

The first phase of the civil rights movement succeeded, although in tracing its ideological roots, there seems to be no consistent theory to explain its potency. Perhaps a majority of Americans had so confused their political and economic beliefs that they saw in desegregation a solution to pressing social, educational, and economic problems a century in the making. This is entirely possible; as legal barriers started to collapse and the majority began to accept racial minorities as equals in their access to public institutions and services, there was a discernible backlash when the implications of equality were fully understood. Allowing minorities to purchase any seat in the stadium was permissible; assisting them in earning enough to afford to attend sporting events and dramatic productions was an indication that minorities were pushing too hard and too fast.

Blacks bore the brunt of majority rage and reaction because the primary discriminatory laws were aimed at their exclusion. The other minorities suffered proportionately in relation to their proximity to the black movement as far as *de jure* discrimination was concerned. Mexican Americans living, like Southern blacks, in predominantly rural locations confronted long-standing institutional racism that had become a natural part of the Southwestern environment. But insofar as the other minorities were able to distinguish themselves from blacks, they escaped direct and continual confrontation with majority backlash. The other minorities were at first happy to be dissociated from the suffering and abuse connected with nonviolence, and were able to remain somewhat aloof by reassuring local whites that they truly believed in law and order—which in translation meant they would not protest their conditions until they were certain of success. Indians, in fact, went to considerable trouble in their efforts to remain separate and to preserve their newly acclaimed status as America's most abused, but also most patient and peaceful, minority.

Although we can look back with some disappointment at the hesitancy of the other minorities to engage in civil rights demonstrations, there were pressing reasons for their refusal to become involved that went to the heart of minority identity as the different groups perceived it. The other minorities had not been as consistently oppressed as blacks. In 1945, in *Méndez v. Westminster,* Mexican Americans had won a major victory in getting their culture and language protected by the Fourteenth Amendment. Return migrations to the island relieved the intolerable pressures facing the Puerto Rican community in the United States, and language enabled many Puerto Ricans to distinguish themselves sufficiently from blacks to give them both a measure of status and relief from the oppressive institutions founded in *Plessy.* Indians had long since traded the right of self-government for continuing federal services and supervision. Thus the other groups felt they had as much to lose as gain by becoming identified with a major assault on long-standing institutional racism. The majority had cleverly played them against the blacks, and since most liberals saw the race problem primarily in terms of black/white relations, these groups saw no reason to forfeit this minor leverage for intangible and tenuous benefits.

The March on Washington in 1963 in quest of jobs was applauded for its commitment to nonviolence, but produced no congressional action to help fulfill its avowed goals. Removal of *de jure* prohibitions on full citizenship was not seen as directly related to *de facto* discrimination in the economic arena. But when white civil rights workers were killed in the South, the political leadership began to take civil rights seriously. Following the beating to death of the Reverend James Reeb in Selma, Alabama, President Lyndon Johnson appeared before a joint session of Congress, spurred by thousands of telegrams demanding action. Adopting the civil rights slogan, "We Shall Overcome," Johnson appealed for immediate passage of the Voting Rights Act of 1965.

Three major pieces of legislation mark the first phase of the civil rights movement: the Civil Rights Act of 1964, the Voting Rights Act of 1965, and the Fair Housing Act of 1968. Each was passed only as a memorial to the death of a prominent person after all peaceful efforts to effect change had failed. The majority accepted these statutes not simply because Kennedy, Reeb, and Martin Luther King had been slain in senseless violence, but because they were presented in terms familiar to the people. "Why shouldn't people have these rights?" was the question that undergirded these laws, and few intelligent people could justify excluding minorities from the exercise of the rights articulated by the statutes. Since minority identity had been a function of prohibitions that people recognized as outmoded, a substantial number of Americans believed that racial problems would vanish with passage of corrective legislation.

Elimination of *de jure* discrimination only served to highlight the existing *de facto* patterns of discrimination erected during the long twilight struggle for legal equality. Real participation in American life involved economic independence, and although civil rights laws prohibited discrimination against minorities in their public lives, the reality was that, apart from the few middle-class people of each group, the masses lacked the means to enjoy their newly defined rights. The legal identity established by exclusionary statutes gave way to a new identity of poverty that generated its own mythological roots and drew upon ancient stereotypes for justification. President Johnson, recognizing early that political rights depend on economic independence, initiated a massive war on poverty in 1964 to help alleviate the pressing problems of minority groups. Although a century of oppression was cited as justification for many programs, the thrust of the new social welfare concerns was rooted in the outmoded liberalism of the past that saw education as the key to full citizenship. Thus, most of the Johnson Administration's specific solutions to poverty involved funding early childhood educational services, not a massive transfer of capital to minority communities. A decade and a half later, former liberals such as Nathan Glazer remarked, with some degree of disappointment, "We would have had a right to expect that, with growing desegregation and with greater sums of money being put into education, Black-White achievement gaps would diminish markedly. They haven't changed much." There was, one can conclude, no ready answer available to the majority that had any realistic chance of success absent a recognition that the nation's wealth badly needed redistribution.

Two major ideologies can be identified in the social programs of the sixties that affect us today. Minority participation in the new programs involved an articulation of poverty statistics that presented a negative image of minority groups and phrased their condition as a deprivation of white values and practices. Thus education was seen as an immense problem area and not as a natural part of the community's life. In the rush to give new meaning to equal opportunity, traditional institutions within majority groups suffered from neglect. Many activities were regarded as inadequate and were seen as part of the problem rather than an indigenous expression of concern. The path to educational parity was interpreted as conformity to majority values, which were presumed to be the universal norm. Statistical data assumed Western civilization as the cultural context, and minorities became subgroups that lacked critical attributes. As the ideology of participation evolved, new groups were added to eligibility sections of social welfare programs, so that initial goals became blurred, and a strange kind of pork-barrel agency emerged able to provide funds to almost any group for almost any activity.

The corollary to educational deprivation was the idea that all racial minorities shared a common culture of poverty. Differences among minorities were thought less important than the new description of their status that barred them from full social and economic participation. In some instances, the majority adopted cultural particularities of the different minority groups— black music, Indian attire, Mexican and Puerto Rican food—but these appropriations were quickly regarded as the property of the majority, not the unique heritage of these groups. Manners of dress and dance, ethical values, and introspective concerns now visible in the white majority are traceable to minority influences and the majority's embrace of the external characteristics of a romanticized culture of poverty.

Legal discrimination created in racial minorities a feeling of solidarity and a tendency to rely on community resources. Individuals patronized their own institutions because they were prohibited from using facilities of the majority. *De facto* segregation meant a shift from racial to class discrimination and enabled the middle class of each minority to enter into the majority arena, leaving behind the less fortunate of their community. Group solidarity shattered, and many individuals in the middle class abandoned leadership roles and accepted token status as members of the new affluent society, adopting, in some instances, what Joseph Heller called "America's inhuman callousness." Almost every effort made by minorities to participate naturally in American society seemed thwarted by misplaced concerns of the majority.

Affirmative action was typical of the dilemmas facing minorities. Federal intervention was unquestionably needed to assure equal treatment in employment practices, because in both private and public sectors, the manipulation of job requirements and qualifications eliminated worthy minorities from consideration. Yet even here the heritage of racism worked to blunt efforts to right past wrongs. Federal and state officials charged with integrating programs often filled quotas with pliable minority group members and then refused to take the next step to make significant economic opportunity a reality. Individuals hired under these circumstances were often fearful of losing their jobs and thus failed to develop their individual good fortune for the benefit of their group. In federal programs especially, the four minorities each developed "tracks" on which a selected group of individuals moved up the bureaucratic hierarchy. Lateral movement through the government into agencies not directly connected with the activities of minority groups occurred rarely. Through an ironic twist of fate, these minorities moved from a caste system, where they were subjects of the government, to a social welfare system, where they were its clients, with barely a nod toward citizenship.

Identification by the discontented in the majority with racial minorities during the later sixties created a new image that further confused the public identity of these groups. Linking discontent with the war in Vietnam and environmental concern with protests against racism and discrimination—and putting them all into the general category "counterculture"— the older members of the white majority shifted their attitudes and began to believe that the racial minorities had achieved enough progress. This mood was heightened and accelerated by the power movements within minority groups, which were grounded in access to the national media and which featured a surplus of inflammatory rhetoric about revolution. Forgetting the General Motors strike during the Depression and the farm rebellions against mortgage foreclosures during the New Deal, the majority convinced themselves that energetic protest was not the American way, and stiffened their resistance to any further social changes. The racial minorities found themselves in a poisoned atmosphere created by other protests; their public identity, perceived as part of a counterculture that sought to tear out all roots of American beliefs, became increasingly negative.

Coincident with the power movements, and in part a manifestation of their cultural dimension, were the demands for ethnic studies in colleges and universities. Although higher education was rapidly opening its doors to a much greater number of minority students, many of these students, taken directly from ghettos, barrios, and reservations, were alienated by the rigid curriculum requirements that to them smacked of cultural imperialism.

Protests against university rules and regulations forced many campus administrators to submit to unreasonable demands that completely transformed the programs in ethnic studies from educational to ideological training grounds. Political rhetoric often polarized the development of new courses that could have informed both minority and majority about the role of minority groups in American history. Beneath the political rhetoric, however, lay a deeper and more fundamental issue that attracted minorities and made the subject more explosive than it seemed to be. Robert Bellah, commenting on the literature of Black Power, for example, noted that "it is not economic or political grievances that propel the activists, though they are acute, but rather a profound need for inner worth and authenticity." He observed that the movements were seen as personally redemptive, redemptive for communities, and perhaps universally redemptive,

although it is doubtful that even the minorities were asking these programs to perform this function.

Minority history, in most instances, had not been written from a minority viewpoint; thus the only path open to a discussion of minorities in American history was to emphasize mistreatment of minorities by the majority. The anthologies used in ethnic studies courses reflected bizarre beliefs and callous misconduct on the part of the whites toward minorities, so much so that ethnic studies programs rapidly became centers of discontent, imperiling their acceptance by the academic community they wished to join. Although the majority was prepared to admit minorities into the historical mainstream, it was not prepared for the materials gathered by minority scholars to prove their case. The submergence of racial minorities had produced such a homogenized and sanitized version of American history that the documents cited seemed impossible to believe.

Ethnic studies programs were never able to distinguish between the culture in local communities and the political identity the groups necessarily had to assert in order to qualify for government assistance and protection. Out of this dilemma emerged the recognition that identity and culture were very much different from what had been supposed. Minorities, like other Americans, adopted a materialistic interpretation of culture and concentrated on external and objective features that clearly distinguished them from the majority. Language became as much a political tool as a cultural treasure. "Afros" and long hair marked the black and Indian response to the homogenization the educational institutions demanded, and the variance was defended in the case of Indian religious groups, although growing hair long was in fact a political act. In attempting to resolve the dispute between identity and culture, minority groups became consumers of their own culture, which they objectified, and this consumption was understood as a political act that affirmed a nationalistic identity. The acid test for ethnic studies was, unfortunately, economic. Although the students of the sixties and early seventies flocked to such courses, the downturn in the economy by the mid-seventies made such courses anachronisms: minority students, like others seeking a piece of the American corporate pie, switched to management and business administration courses.

The retrospective view of cultural progress and achievement that confronted the minorities as they tried to distinguish themselves from mainstream Americans called for a reexamination of their historical experiences. Historical review would recapture first the essence of life prior to the encounter with white America, and then the conditions of oppression thereafter that generated the poetry, song, folklore, community institutions, and sardonic commentary that heartened the people in times of severe stress. Much of the postwar literature revolved around the latter period as compounded by this generation's involvement in the events of the age, and as interpreted by them. The few efforts to return to precontact days involved more romanticism than reality, but these efforts provided the significant religious context that made sense of a people buffeted by rapid and often incomprehensible change. Ultimately, most contemporary expressions of minority culture assumed an antiwhite, anti-industrialism posture.

In spite of the promises of equality, the larger society seemed to impinge on minority communities in two basic areas: the displacement of groups by industrial and redevelopment schemes, and intrusions by well-meaning whites seeking to create better conditions for minorities. Disruption of neighborhoods by projects shattered the ability of communities to impose informal local controls on individuals, and meant that each community's service infrastructure was increasingly controlled by outsiders. Working within local communities, well-wishers who had influence with outside forces often sought to become spokespeople for the community, thereby disrupting traditional problem-solving techniques and alienating people. The result was a reduction in local leadership and its replacement by external supervisors beholden to larger agencies and institutions that controlled the resources required to change conditions. That more sporadic violence did not occur is testimony to the patience of the mass of minority group members.

During the 1950s, minority groups were always referred to as problems—the black problem, the Puerto Rican problem—as if their emergence in the social fabric had been accidental, punitive to the majority, but capable of resolution by clever and determined techniques. The disappearance of this term, which relegated minority existence to adjectival status within the homogeneity of American life, marks a major shift in perception by the majority. Although conditions of Indians and Puerto Ricans are sometimes described by the majority as a "plight," which connotes perpetual status, by and large the majority has incorporated the presence of racial minorities in its wider vision of American life.

During the postwar era, the majority of members of the different minorities, like other Americans, generally followed the trends and fashions in life-style brought about by industrialization. The universal hedonistic culture fostered by the entertainment media encompassed the racial minorities, sometimes making their cause fashionable, but more often portraying them as darker imitations of the typical white American. This homogenization of cultural values and world view, while creating a more favorable feeling toward minorities, tended to submerge the root cause of their dilemma— white racism—in a cuddly, if somewhat nebulous, American mythology that ultimately affixes the blame for the minorities' condition on themselves. In this benign milieu, group identity and the particularity of culture become given quantities that are incapable of serving as vehicles to distinguish the unique quality of groups.

The velocity of change during the postwar decades in America might very well have radically altered the status of these groups had there not been a particular objective hurdle— segregation laws—for them to overcome. The postwar baby boom, coincident with the development of nationwide television programming, produced a generation that was capable of intense feelings but that lacked the traditional literary background that had previously characterized white Americans. President John F. Kennedy transformed the intellectual from theoretical maverick to stylish government consultant precisely at the time when hard thinking might have resolved domestic differences. The impact on minority groups was considerable. Apart from Martin Luther King, minority leadership in the postwar decades, and particularly in the 1970s, was largely a matter of personification and symbolic presence rather than realistic representation of groups. As a result, many Americans assumed that the presence of minority leaders in positions of prominence testified to their acceptance of American values on behalf of their constituents.

There is no question that blacks and American Indians have made an impact on the domestic scene, but for entirely different reasons. The introduction of considerable black talent into declining areas of American life sparked a significant renaissance. Sports such as basketball, for example, changed radically with the admission of amazingly agile black athletes. And popular music moved from swing bands and traditional romantic ballads toward the blues-jazz-gospel rhythms of Southern folkways, producing the modern variations of the rock style.

American Indians, traditionally aloof from whites except for ceremonial purposes—such as adopting politicians into their tribes—influenced American society by invoking the romance of their ancestral traditions. The simple technology of pre-Columbian days was heralded as sophisticated ecological knowledge, and their esoteric religious ceremonials became rites of passage for many young white Americans. If there was one overwhelming symbol of the fascination that Indians held for other Americans in the sixties, it was the movie *Billy Jack*. In this film, a half-breed Indian pacifist demonstrates his beliefs by breaking as many red-neck bones as possible, and submits to a sequence of rattlesnake bites to prove his religious sincerity. The message of this dreadful film was traditional American Western lore dressed in buckskins, authenticated by an intense Lutheran belief that justification by faith alone is sufficient. But its immense popularity indicates that it struck a responsive chord in majority hearts and minds.

Puerto Ricans and Mexicans did not seem to make an impact on the popular values of American society. Overshadowed by the "pop" Indian image and the black presence, these groups found neither intense national oppression nor encouragement. The isolated locales in which they were concentrated contained the same kinds of institutional brutality and discrimination, yet the international flavor of the so-called Hispanic communities gave them a blurred, if slightly favorable, image in the eyes of the public. Both Puerto Ricans and Mexicans seem more inclined to make culture-bearing a masculine phenomenon, as distinguished from white Americans, where culture is strictly female, and the black and Indian communities, where culture is a shared responsibility. The protection that Puerto Rican and Mexican folkways offered to their cultural heritage thus may have proved decisive in preserving it from expropriation by the larger society.

The Puerto Rican independence movement, still a minor item in most American newspapers, has enabled Puerto Ricans to project their concerns to an international arena. The continuing presence of Castroism in the Caribbean makes it imperative that a new relationship be developed that is more congenial to the mass of Puerto Ricans. Although rarely articulated, this seems to place Puerto Rican concerns in a category different from those of the other three groups. The Mexicans also have an ultra-domestic dimension to be exploited. Although the government of Mexico shows little concern for its nationals who cross the border to do stoop labor, incisive observers of the domestic scene suggest that any severe oppression of Mexicans may have serious repercussions in the international community. Consequently, the American posture toward "illegals" is confused and nebulous, and depends primarily on political expedients of the moment rather than on an understanding of the nature of the problem. The continuing migration between Manhattan and Puerto Rico and the annual influx of illegals across the U.S.-Mexican border enable these groups to replenish their cultural strength, a condition that blacks and American Indians no longer have.

The international dimension is critically important because both blacks and American Indians have attempted to move into that arena to express their concerns. Stokely Carmichael, the most prominent black spokesman to try to link American domestic problems with the emergence of the African bloc of Third World countries, was considerably disappointed when African leaders failed to respond. In 1977 a delegation of American Indians went to Geneva to present their concerns to a subcommittee of the United Nations. The Indians were popular primarily because of the romantic image they projected with their costumes. Their accusations against the colonial policies of the United States failed to move the European delegates, whose countries shared responsibility for the Indians' traumatic history.

Contemporary conditions suggest that these four minority groups, like the rest of American society, need to grasp a new sense of historical continuity if they wish to make the future intelligible. Although the white majority has lost faith in itself as the bearer of the highest values of Western civilization—and in that sense becomes ahistorical—the racial minorities find it difficult to distinguish the inner essence of their historical experience from their continuing oppressive relationships with the white majority. An insightful commentator of the domestic scene, Tom Wolfe, points out, however, that racial and ethnic minorities continue to have heroes, while the majority finds its national heroes only when there is an external threat to the country, indicating, perhaps, that minorities retain sufficient identity to overcome the ahistorical handicap.

Racial minorities appear in the larger hemispheric history as groups without origins, by-products of a larger process, and therefore peoples without futures, apart from their client status as one of the unsolved problems of industrial America. The fundamental change of the last few decades is a shift from race to class, although some observers such as William Styron argue that the concern with race relations merely spreads to new groups rather than being transformed. Racial discrimination still exists on a group basis, but white society, recognizing the changes of the immediate past, allows a small number from each minority to participate in the benefits of the ruling class. Thus an indelible cultural and emotional servitude has been impressed upon minorities that will not be easy to erase.

The increasing complexity of American society seems to thwart this generation's discernment of a clearly understood national identity. Proliferating institutions and agencies, public and private, discourage meaningful comprehension by ordinary citizens, and vest decision-making in a smaller, select group of experts, whose authority, in most instances, is unquestioned. Bureaucrats have replaced priests as interpreters of social reality, and the racial minorities, linked to government and corporate activities as recipients of economic largess, are placed in a permanent reactive role in society. Since the continuation of economic assistance generally involves behaving in certain socially acceptable ways, cultural conflict can be expected to increase as minorities weigh the price to be paid for the privilege of full participation in social activities. American society is increasingly dominated by a managerial elite, which includes selected members of racial minorities, but which views the mass of citizens with aloof disdain, manipulating images and symbols as a means of continuing its control. It remains to be seen whether the minority members of the new elite can leaven the new social mixture with cultural values distinct from the majority.

Racial minorities will always have a social/political identity because of their obvious presence within a large white majority. It is unlikely that blatant *de jure* discrimination comparable to that of the past can be restored absent a terrible catastrophe and subsequent loss of rationality by a high percentage of Americans. *De facto* discrimination and segregation, however, remain as critical problems because they basically reflect the cumulative product of millions of individual decisions regarding social and economic values, decisions that originate in the unarticulated and sometimes subconscious views of the white majority. Insofar as problems will continue to exist for racial minorities, America is no nearer resolving its most pressing dilemma. Brutal measures have declined with the increase of majority sophistication, but basic attitudes create new forms of oppression, unique to the age but ancient in impact. As the cultural traditions of racial minorities erode and become homogenized by modern communications, the fearful possibility exists that these groups will be sapped of their natural resources for survival and become perpetual wards of the welfare state. Thus, although legal political identity remains a strong interest of the racial minorities, the real task for them is to broaden American perceptions of cultural diversity, both as a measure of protection and as an avenue for eventual realization of the American promise of equality and justice.

# PART III
# Class

American culture, as discussed in the previous section, contained within it a constellation of racial and ethnic images. As a racial ideology, it supported the social subordination of Asians, blacks, Mexicans, and Native Americans. As an ethnocentric ideology, it promoted a nativist nationalism aimed at Central and Southern European immigrants. But culture operated in relationship to the economy: ideas and images interfaced dialectically with particular economic developments and material conditions. In this context, race and ethnicity functioned within an American class structure.

Racial imagery sometimes emerged as class imagery, applied to blacks and other racial minorities as well as white workers. In the North during the nineteenth century, for example, blacks found themselves stereotyped as child-savages. They were viewed as "immature" and "irresponsible," and denounced as "indolent" and "good-for-nothing." They were said to be "naturally lazy, childlike." Depicted as low in intelligence, blacks were used by white parents to discipline their own children, warning them to improve themselves in school or they would be as ignorant as a "nigger." Blacks were also feared as a libidinous race, dominated by their sexual passions.

Racial images were strikingly similar to class images. Newspaper editors, educators, ministers, and industrial capitalists described the white lower and working classes as the "slaves" of their "passions." "Ignorant," "lazy," and "sensual," Irish immigrants were dominated by the "lower" rather than the "higher" pleasures, it was claimed; they possessed a "love for vicious excitement" and sought to satisfy a "gratification merely animal." Irish children were said to be "undisciplined," "inheriting" the "stupidity of centuries of ignorant ancestors." Factory workers were dismissed for gambling, drinking, and "debaucheries." Irish immigrants were blamed for their lack of self-control, particularly in their sexuality. In a society in which restraint was the most widely used method of birth control, large Irish families were viewed as signs of this weakness: "Did wealth consist in children, it is well known, that the Irish would be rich people." Worried about bulging cities and the growing presence of an industrial proletariat, Horace Mann believed education was necessary to save the working masses from "falling back into the conditions of half-barbarous or of savage life." As Irish immigrants crowded into cities and factories in the North, racial and class imagery often blurred together into an ideology that disciplined white workers by defining for them the standards of proper moral behavior and justified factory regimentation and mechanisms for controlling white laborers.

Caste and class intersections also occurred below the Mason-Dixon Line. Southern society in reality was heterogeneous in terms of both race and class. In fact, the overwhelming majority of whites did not own slaves: in 1850, only 6.2 percent of the Southern white population possessed slaves.

The era of sectional conflict that led to the disruption of the Union also witnessed white class tensions within the South. During the slavery debate in the Virginia Legislature of 1831–32, the peculiar institution was denounced as antagonistic to white workers: it "banishes free white labor, exterminates the mechanic, the artisan. . . . It deprives them of occupation. It deprives them of bread." During the next two decades, competition between white workers and slaves became even more intense as planters directed their slaves into the mechanic trades. Protesting against this competition, white workers in Mississippi, Georgia, and South Carolina forced the enactment of laws restricting the hiring of slave laborers. Worried about this escalating conflict between white classes in the South, the editor of a Mississippi newspaper issued a warning to the slaveholding class: "The [slaveholders'] policy of teaching negroes the various trades . . . tends to make the rich richer and the poor poorer, by bringing slave labor into competition with white labor, and thus arraying capital against labor . . . and this will produce a spirit of antagonism between the rich and poor."

In their response to this internal class conflict within Southern white society, many planters and Southern leaders formulated a proslavery argument. Aggressively celebrating the superiority of the slave system of labor, they claimed their black workers were "comfortable," "docile," "submissive," and "happy." More important, they added, in the South, where labor was black and in bondage, capitalists could exercise total power over the working class. Black workers had no right to assemble, vote, or bear arms, and could easily be punished for acts of insubordination. The vision of the proslavery argument was one of a society where white workers would be eliminated, where capitalists would be free from the interference of strikes and unions, and where class divisions would constitute caste divisions.

This was not entirely a Southern vision; neither was it applied only to blacks. During the nineteenth century, Chinese began entering this country and numbered over 100,000 by 1880. Most of them were located in California, where in 1870 they represented 8.6 percent of the state's population and 25 percent of the work force. The Chinese were present everywhere in the economy. The Central Pacific Railroad depended heavily on them: 90 percent of its 10,000 workers were Chinese. The Chinese were also extensively involved in manufacturing, representing 46 percent of the San Francisco work force in four key industries: boot and shoe, woolens, cigar and tobacco, and sewing. The significant role of Chinese labor in the industrial development of California was widely recognized. In his essay, "Chinaman or White Man, Which?" the Reverend O. Gibson observed in 1873: "At the rates of labor which existed in the early days of California, or at the rates which would instantly prevail were the Chinese removed from our midst, not one of the few manufacturing interests which have lately sprung up on these shores, could be maintained a single day." Three years later, R. G. McClellan noted in his book, *The Golden State:* "In mining, farming, in factories and in the labor generally of California the employment of the Chinese has been found most desirable; and much of the labor done by these people if performed by white men at higher wages could not be continued nor made possible."

As businessmen employed Chinese laborers, they developed a caste/class ideology. "If society must have 'mudsills,' " they declared, "it is certainly better to take them from a race which would be benefited by even that position in a civilized community, than subject a portion of our own race to a position which they have outgrown." The Chinese would be a migrant and proscribed work force. An internally colonized working class, Chinese laborers would be inducted into the process of production but excluded from American society.

The employment of Chinese laborers gave businessmen a weapon against white workers, a means to discipline them and break their strikes. In the West, a traveler noted the importance of Chinese workers as strikebreakers: "In the factories of San Francisco they had none but Irish, paying them three dollars a day in gold. They struck, and demanded four dollars. Immediately their places, numbering three hundred, were supplied by Chinamen at one dollar a day." In the East, factory owners imported Chinese laborers for the same purpose. In 1870, Charles Sampson transported Chinese workers across the continent to his shoe factory in North Adams, Massachusetts, in order to break a strike of Irish laborers. Sampson's daring act quickly became the focus of media attention and support. In *Scribner's Monthly,* William Shanks reported that the Chinese "labored regularly and constantly, losing no blue Mondays on account of Sunday's dissipations; nor wasting hours in idle holidays. . . . The quality of the work was found to be fully equal to that of the Crispins." In fact, the employment of the Chinese had enabled Sampson to widen the margin of his profits. The saving in the cost of production for a week's work was $840, which amounted to $40,000 a year. Another writer for *Scribner's Monthly* praised Sampson's strikebreaking tactic: "If for no other purpose than the breaking up of the incipient steps toward labor combinations and 'Trade Unions' . . . the advent of Chinese labor should be hailed with warm welcome." The "heathen Chinee," he concluded, could be the "final solution" to the labor problem in America.

But, in 1882, Congress passed instead the Chinese Exclusion Act, prohibiting the entry of Chinese laborers into the United States. In the discussion on the bill, congressmen and senators anxiously noted how the presence of an "industrial army of Asiatic laborers" was exacerbating the conflict between white labor and capital. Supporters of the bill feared this conflict would lead to social revolution and chaos. They worried about the struggle between labor unions and the industrial "nabobs" and "grandees," the employers of Chinese labor. In the aftermath of the violent Railroad Strike of 1877, they apprehensively witnessed the "disorder, strikes, riot, and bloodshed" sweeping through the industrial cities of America. "The gate," they insisted, "must be closed." Thus, one of the fears lending to the passage of the Chinese Exclusion Act was the prospect that American society would be destroyed between the millstones of a hungry and violent white working class and a yellow proletariat under the control of an American capitalist elite.

What is significant to note about the passage of the Chinese Exclusion Act is the widespread support it received. A majority of congressmen and senators from every section of the country—the West, the Northeast, the Middle Atlantic, the Midwest, and the South—voted for the bill. Support for Chinese exclusion came from states where there were no Chinese and where competition between white workers and Chinese laborers did not exist. This fact suggests that the 1882 act in reality had little relationship to the Chinese themselves. It may have been, to a more important extent, a response to the increasing and violent class conflicts developing within white society. To prohibit Chinese immigration would be to eliminate an issue the labor movement was using to organize white workers.

The discussion here highlights the need for studying the complex relationship of race and class in American society. As we analyze the ways class tensions and conflicts have conditioned and shaped race relations, we need to ask: Who has benefited from racism—white capitalists or white workers? What has been the relationship between racial inequality and the development of white class stratification?

In "The 'Giddy Multitude': Race and Class in Early Virginia," historian T. H. Breen focuses on a turning point in the history of colonial society. During Bacon's Rebellion of 1676, an army drawn from the lower classes—white and black—fought together for a common political purpose. According to Breen, the rebellion was not simply an inter-regional conflict between up-country and low-country Virginia; more important, it was a class struggle transcending racial divisions within the "giddy multitude." But events and developments afterward undermined this unity. Breen's study of this interracial class revolt recovers a moment in our past when subsequent history could have been different. What would have happened had the "giddy multitude" won?

Breen places the history of class and race within the context of the changing economy. Similarly, Clara Rodríguez in "Puerto Ricans and the Political Economy of New York" and Gerald Vizenor in "Wampum to Pictures of Presidents" underscore the importance of economic forces and developments. While Rodriguez examines the experiences of Puerto Ricans as a racially segmented labor force in New York, Vizenor reflects on the problem of Native American unemployment and economic underdevelopment on reservations. Situated in different locations in the capitalist economy, Puerto Ricans in the city need to struggle for integration in a labor market which is racially and occupationally stratified, and Native Americans need to integrate the reservations into the larger economy without undermining their communities and damaging their lands.

Finally, what are the possibilities of class coalitions across racial lines? In "Racial Domination and Class Conflict in Capitalist Agriculture: The Oxnard Sugar Beet Workers' Strike of 1903," Tomás Almaguer shows how Japanese and Mexican laborers came together in a significant moment of class solidarity. Edna Bonacich, however, implicitly doubts whether white workers would join such a coalition. In "A Theory of Ethnic Antagonism: The Split Labor Market," she locates primary responsibility for racism in the white working class. Seeking to protect their interests, white laborers in the nineteenth century pressed for racial exclusion and for occupational stratification based on race. But in "Colonized and Immigrant Minorities," Robert Blauner finds a different reason for ethnic conflict, noting the role of capitalists in the entry, labor exploitation, and social subordination of internally "colonized" minorities. While racial divisions would present problems for building interracial coalitions of workers, Blauner would suggest, the source of such divisions—the capitalist class—could offer them a common ground.

# The "Giddy Multitude":
# Race and Class in Early Virginia

T. H. BREEN

Seventeenth-century Virginians were an unruly lot. While New Englanders lived in relative peace with one another, Virginians rioted and rebelled; even in periods of apparent calm, they were haunted by the specter of social unrest. These men witnessed a series of disorders between 1660 and 1683, most of which were local in character, some were only threats of violence, but a few involved several counties and one escalated into a colony-wide civil war.

Wealthy planters and political officeholders at the time offered a simple explanation for these events. In each case opportunities had played upon the hopes and fears of the "giddy multitude," an amalgam of indentured servants and slaves, of poor whites and blacks, of landless freemen and debtors. Nathaniel Bacon was the most successful and therefore the most notorious of these agitators, but there were others. A gang of desperate *Oliverian* Soldiers" supposedly organized the servant uprising of 1663, and high governing officials believed Robert Beverley, Sr., clerk of the House of Burgesses, had sparked the tobacco cutting riots of 1683. No one will ever know whether the mass of discontented workers fully supported, or even understood, the demands of a Bacon or Beverley. The "giddy multitude" may have taken advantage of divisions within the ruling class to express its anger over economic and social conditions beyond its control. Whatever its goals, control of this group preoccupied the Virginia gentry for nearly a quarter century.

During the 1680s Virginia's time of troubles drew to a close, and by the beginning of the eighteenth century the colony had achieved remarkable social stability. The Glorious Revolution in America which disrupted New York and Massachusetts in 1689 passed almost unnoticed in Virginia. To be sure, the tobacco planters were apprehensive about a band of black Maroons that harassed the settlers of the northern counties, but there was little talk of a general uprising of poor whites, indentured servants and Negro slaves. The "giddy multitude" which a few years earlier had caused Governor William Berkeley to despair of ever controlling "a People wher six parts of seaven at least are Poore Endebted Discontented and Armed" had ceased to threaten the colony's internal peace.

Many elements contributed to the transformation of Virginia society during the last half of the seventeenth century, but none seems more curious than the disappearance of the "giddy multitude." This group of malcontents requires closer investigation, but unfortunately, the judicial records and tax lists from this period are incomplete, making it difficult to determine the precise identity of these people. The sources are rich enough, however, to provide substantial information about the general character of the "giddy multitude." By examining this material one begins to understand why the great planters regarded the lower classes as such a serious threat to Virginia's internal security. This analysis should also suggest how the changing composition of the colony's labor force between 1660 and 1710 affected Virginia's progress from chronic disorder to stability and more, how it fundamentally altered the relationship between blacks and whites.

A pamphleteer writing about Virginia at mid-century observed the colony's earliest years had been marked by failure and disappointment. But those unhappy days, he argued, were gone forever, and Virginians could anticipate a new era of prosperity. Evidence seemed to support his claims. The colonists had recently reduced the once powerful Powhatan Confederacy to

From T. H. Breen, "A Changing Labor Force and Race Relations in Virginia, 1660–1710," *Journal of Social History* VII (Fall 1973): 3–18. Copyright © 1973 by Peter N. Stearns. Reprinted by permission of the publisher. Footnotes have been deleted.

impotence, pushing local Indians to the frontiers of white settlement. Planters rushed to develop the fertile tobacco-producing lands along the rivers north of the James, first the York and then the Rappahannock and Potomac. What Virginia needed—what it had always needed—was a large inexpensive labor force, workers who could perform the tedious tasks necessary to bring tobacco to market.

In the middle of the seventeenth century, the solution to this problem was the importation of white indentured servants. Some historians have claimed that Virginia planters preferred white laborers to Negro slaves, but the argument is not persuasive. Before the mid-1680s, the mainland colonies did not possess a reliable, inexpensive source of blacks. White Englishmen were available, however, in large numbers. Beginning in the 1650s, indentured servants flooded into Virginia at a faster rate than ever before, several thousand arriving annually. Many came voluntarily. They were people who, in Governor Berkeley's words, arrived in America with a "hope of bettering their condition in a Growing Country." Most signed their indentures while still in the mother country, promising to work for a stated number of years in exchange for the costs of transportation, food, clothes and shelter in Virginia. Almost nothing is known about the class of people who found this offer attractive, but many were probably middling sorts.

Other servants found themselves in Virginia even though they had little or no desire to be there. Unscrupulous merchants called "spirits" took advantage of the labor boom, dumping over the years many English laborers onto the colonial market. The "spirits" operated out of England's major port cities, preying upon the poor, young and unsuspecting. Some victims were enticed to the New World with stories of quick riches; others were coerced. One man testified before Parliament in 1660 that he had been sent "against his will to Virginia" by his sister's "cruell contrivance." Once a vessel left England, the "spirited" servants reportedly received just enough food to stay alive. It was even rumored in the mother country that if a storm threatened the ship, the sailors were likely to throw an old person overboard as a suspected witch. That seventeenth-century Englishmen found such stories credible indicates that the servants' voyage to America could often be a terrible ordeal. Since the "spirits" seldom kept records of their dealings, their share of the servant commerce is difficult to estimate. Historians minimize the extent of this

illicit trade, but one author describing the colony in 1649 claimed that the "spirits" were the planters' chief source of indentured servants.

Great Virginia planters expressed disappointment with the quality of their servants regardless of the means by which they had been recruited. The owners of large tobacco plantations wanted hard-working, honest and obedient laborers, but the merchants seemed to be delivering "the very scum and off-scouring" of England. The planters, no doubt, were guilty of hyperbole, combining poor and ignorant persons with a few known criminals into a single category of undesirables. Throughout Berkeley's administration, leaders complained about the "importacon of Newgateers" and "Jaylebirds" whom they regarded as a serious threat to the colony's security. The gentry came to see the servants as a dangerous and untrustworthy group requiring constant surveillance. How much these attitudes affected relations between individual masters and servants is impossible to determine, but the planters' representation of the indentured workers as a bunch of "desperate villans" may have been a self-fulfilling description.

Many servants were as disappointed with their masters as their masters were with them. As early as 1649, rumors circulated in England that "all those servants who are sent to *Virginia* are sold as slaves." Tales of harsh treatment were probably the source of such stories. One man who returned to the mother country reported that he had "served as a slave" in Virginia for nine years and had "endured great hardshipp." But the servants' unhappiness had deeper roots than hard labor and poor food. Many were not psychologically prepared for life in Virginia, and the frustrations they experienced led in time to bitterness and depression. For a majority of servants the colony had represented a new start, an opportunity to achieve wealth and status denied them in England. Propagandists fed these hopes, depicting Virginia as a land of milk and honey. Indeed, one writer observed that servants about to emigrate spoke of the colony as "a place where food shall drop into their mouthes." Many expected free land at the end of their service. The reality never matched the dreams. Virginia at mid-century burst inflated expectations and shocked all but the well-informed. William Bullock, a pamphleteer writing in 1649, understood this problem and warned planters about purchasing servants who "not finding what was promised, their courage abates, & their minds being dejected, their work is according."

The servants' life did not necessarily improve when they reached the end of their contracts. What the new freemen desired most was land, but no one in Virginia seemed willing to furnish it. Successful planters were not eager to establish commercial rivals. Indeed, contemporaries condemned the covetousness of those members of the Virginian gentry who engrossed "great Tracts of land" and deprived others of the means to achieve economic independence. In his account of Bacon's Rebellion, William Sherwood denounced the colony's "Land lopers" who claimed thousands of acres yet "never cultivated any part of itt . . . thereby preventing others seateing, soe that too many rather then to be Tennants, seate upon remote barren Land." Since before 1680 remote lands meant constant danger from the Indians, many ex-servants chose to work for wages or rent land in secure areas rather than to settle on the frontier. It has been estimated that no more than six percent of this group ever became independent planters. Landless laborers more often became overseers on the plantations, supervising servants and slaves whose condition differed little from their own.

Freemen found themselves tied to an economic system over which they had little control. Fluctuations in the price of tobacco could reduce wage earners and small planters to abject poverty. It was not a question of work habits. According to an account in 1667, a man, on the average, could produce 1,200 pounds of tobacco each year, which after taxes left him with approximately 50 shillings. It left so little, in fact, that the colony's secretary marvelled, "I can attribute it to nothing but the great mercy of God . . . that keeps them [the small planters] from mutiny and confusion." In 1672 Governor Berkeley explained to the English Privy Council that single freemen could hardly maintain themselves by their own labor. They fell into debt, unable to purchase necessary imported goods—especially clothing. Whatever hopes they once entertained of becoming prosperous planters gave way to anger. Their numbers swelled, and their disappointment must have discouraged those persons who were still indentured. Certainly, no one seemed surprised when the king's commissioners, investigating in 1677 the causes of Bacon's Rebellion, discovered a major part of the rebel army had been "Free men that had but lately crept out of the condition of Servants."

Another component of the "giddy multitude"

was Virginia's Negroes. Historians knew relatively little about this group. Governor Berkeley thought there were some 2,000 blacks in the colony of 1671, but recent scholarship regards that estimate as high. By the early 1680s, the Negro population had probably risen to three or four thousand. A majority of the blacks in this period appear to have come to Virginia from the West Indies. Around the turn of the century, for example, it was reported on the authority of one planter that before 1680 "what negroes were brought to Virginia were imported generally from Barbados." There is no way of ascertaining how long the blacks had lived on Barbados before transferring to the mainland, but it is doubtful Virginia planters would have invested what little capital they possessed in expensive "unseasoned" laborers who could easily die after a single summer in the tobacco fields. If the blacks had stayed a year or two on Barbados, they probably learned to speak some English. Morgan Godwyn, a minister who had visited the island colony in the 1670s, noted that many Negroes there not only spoke English, but did so "no worse than the natural born subjects of that Kingdom." Their facility with the English language could have played an important part in Virginia's unrest, for it would have enabled blacks to communicate with indentured servants and poor whites.

The status of black men in mid-seventeenth-century Virginia remains obscure; a few were free, some were indentured servants and most were probably slaves. After 1660 the Virginia legislature began to deprive black people of basic civil rights. Although the process of total debasement was not completed until the 1700s, it has generally been assumed that Negroes were a separate and subordinate group within Virginia as early as Governor Berkeley's second administration (1662–1677). The problem with this interpretation is that it relies too heavily upon statute law as opposed to social practice, and dismisses the fact that some whites and blacks cooperated—even conspired together—until the late 1670s.

No one could deny that many whites saw Negroes as property to be exploited, and these men may have been responsible for shaping Virginia legislation. On the lowest levels of colonial society, however, race prejudice may have developed more slowly than it did among the successful planters. Black and white field hands could hardly have overlooked the things they had in common. For the Negroes the original trip from Africa to the West Indies had been a terrible ordeal. Few whites had experienced a psychological shock of this magnitude, but some of them had been forceably abducted and confined in foul quarters until a ship was prepared to sail, and were then transported to the New World under conditions vaguely similar to those endured by Africans. Although little is known about the relative treatment of whites and blacks in Virginia before Bacon's Rebellion, it is doubtful that English servants fared better than Negroes. Evidence from Barbados at this time reveals that planters there regarded white servants as a short-term investment to be exploited ruthlessly and thus, "for the time the servants have the worser lives [than the Negroes], for they are put to very hard labour, ill lodging, and their dyet very sleight." If such conditions prevailed on the mainland, it would help explain why some poor and indentured whites voluntarily joined with black men to challenge the planters' authority. One should understand, of course, that a willingness to cooperate under certain circumstances does not mean white laborers regarded Negroes as their equals. Indeed, such actions only indicate that economic grievances could sometimes outweigh race prejudice.

Between 1660 and 1685, members of the colony's labor force expressed their discontent in a variety of ways, some by isolated, spontaneous acts of violence, others by larger conspiratorial ventures. If an individual became desperate enough, he or she might strike a master. Disaffected servants and slaves also ran away. The problem of fleeing bondsmen became quite serious in Berkeley's Virginia, and numerous colonial statutes tried to curb the practice. People often ran away in groups, fearing perhaps the Indians or the wilderness itself. Servants and slaves, eager for freedom and lured by rumors of a better life somewhere else, slipped away into the forests. Blacks and whites sometimes fled together, conscious that without cooperation their bid for freedom and escape might fail and bring instead immediate physical punishment and probably additional years of drudgery. Whatever the terrors of flight, there were always persons desperate enough to take the chance. Some even plotted escape on shipboard before seeing America. Planters assumed that the desire for freedom was contagious and that unless runaways were quickly suppressed, other men—black and white—would soon imitate them. When a group of fugitive slaves frustrated all attempts to retake them in 1672, the planters' greatest concern was that "other negroes, Indians or servants . . . [might] fly north and joyne with them."

Insurrection offered another means by which discontented workers expressed unhappiness with conditions in Virginia. While such organized disturbances were relatively infrequent, an occasional uprising reinforced the planters' fears and remained a source of uneasiness years after the violence had been quelled. During the early 1660s, servants upset the peace in several counties. The first disorder occurred in York and appears to have been sparked by complaints among indentured workers of "hard usage" and inadequate diet. Several conspirators, weary of "corne & water," demanded meat at least two or three times a week. The leader, an indentured servant named Isaac Friend, suggested that his followers petition the king for redress. This idea was dropped when someone pointed out that even if Charles II would listen, the group could never get a letter out of Virginia. Friend then decided that 40 servants should band together and "get Armes & he would be the first & have them cry as they went along, 'who would be for Liberty, and free from bondage,' & that there would be enough come to them & they would goe through the Countrey and kill those that made any opposition, & that they would either be free or die for it." Someone apparently revealed the plans before Friend and the others began their freedom march through Virginia. When the commissioners of York questioned the leader about his actions, he admitted making seditious speeches, but protested that he never intended to put the scheme into operation. Despite Friend's assurance, York officials refused to regard the episode as a servants' prank. They ordered Friend's master to keep close watch over him and warned the heads of all families in the country to take note of "like dangerous discourses."

Two years later officials in Gloucester County, a fast growing region north of York, discovered another conspiracy. The causes of this disturbance are difficult to reconstruct since most of the Gloucester records have been lost and the surviving testimony is inconsistent. In his history of Virginia published in 1705, Robert Beverley, Jr., claimed that veterans of Cromwell's army who had been transported to the colony as indentured servants stirred up "the poor People . . . [and] form'd a villanous Plot to destroy their Masters, and afterwards to set up for themselves." Presumably Beverley drew his information from old planters and local tradition, but the available contemporary documents do not mention "*Oliverian* Soldiers." A Gloucester court in 1663 accused nine "Laborers" of conspiring to arm 30 persons to over-throw the government of Virginia. While extant depositions reveal nothing about the political ideas of this group, they do suggest that some participants regarded bondage as their primary grievance. For example, one member reported that the conspirators had secretly pledged to seize weapons, march on the colonial capital and "demand our freedome." If the royal governor denied this request, the rebels planned to leave Virginia.

The reaction to the attempted servant upris-ing of 1663 appears excessive unless one consid-ers it in the context of the strained relationship between the major tobacco planters and colo-nial laborers. After the organizers of the plot had been captured and several executed, the servant who had warned the planters received his freedom and £200. The day on which the conspirators were arrested became an annual holiday. Virginia officials notified Charles II of the details of the insurrection in such exagger-ated terms that the king immediately ordered the colonists to construct a fortress to protect the governor and his loyal officials. As late as 1670, the memory of the servant plot could still unnerve the gentry of Gloucester, Middlesex and York. Indeed, when it appeared that the mother country had allowed too many criminals and undesirables to emigrate to Virginia, the leading planters of these counties protested and reminded royal officials of "the horror yet remaining amongst us of the barbarous designe of those villaines in September 1663 who attempted at once the subversion of our Reli-gion, Lawes, libertyes, rights and priviledges."

During the 12 years preceding Bacon's Re-bellion, fear of the labor force increasingly affected the character of Virginian society. Although no organized violence against the planters or the government occurred in this period, the laborers—black and white—constituted a subversive element. They were essential to the colony's economic well-being, but at the same time, no one trusted them. It was a foolish plantation owner who did not recognize the danger, for in a community in which so many men were unhappy, even seemingly contented workers might be potential conspirators. The tobacco gentry tried to regu-late the lives of their bondsmen, and according to colonial statute, any servant who attended an unlawful meeting or travelled about the country-side without a pass risked arrest. But these measures were insufficient to insure domestic tranquillity. Even if the behavior of the slaves and servants could have been closely controlled

(a doubtful proposition at best), the poor freemen remained a threat.

The extent of Virginia's social instability was revealed by events in 1676. Indian raids exacer-bated long-standing grievances, and when a young planter named Nathaniel Bacon came forward as spokesman for the discontented, he sparked a civil war. Because Bacon's Rebellion was the most momentous event in seventeenth-century Virginia, it has been the object of intense investigation. Historians concerned chiefly with the behavior of the colony's elite have offered several interpretations of what motivated the leaders of this insurrection. Such analysis is of little value in understanding the "giddy multitude," however, since whatever the aims of Bacon and his lieutenants, there is little evidence their goals were the same as those of their followers. Contemporaries, in fact, be-lieved Bacon had aroused popular fears and frustrations to achieve his own private ends. The House of Burgesses concluded in 1677 that this rebellion, like others before it, resulted from "false Rumors, Infused by ill affected persons provoking an itching desire" in the common people. Indeed, the loyal planters around Berkeley despised Bacon not so much because he was ambitious or even because he had led an unauthorized march against local Indians, but because he had carried his case to the populace. After Bacon had been captured in June 1676, the governor pardoned him; and even though the rebel leader had defied Berke-ley's orders several times and slaughtered a village of friendly Occaneechee Indians, Berke-ley believed Bacon's submission to be sincere. But Bacon had already stirred forces beyond his control. His followers demanded action. Within two days of receiving his pardon, Bacon "heard what an incredible Number of the meanest of the People were every where Armed to assist him and his cause." He did not disappoint them. Had Bacon somehow confined the dis-pute to the upper class, he might have been forgiven for his erratic behavior, but once the servants, slaves and poor freemen became involved, he had to be crushed.

Participants on both sides of the conflict believed it had pitted the rich against the poor, the privileged against the oppressed or as Berkeley described it, the "Rabble" against "the better sort of people." There is no reason to doubt the validity of this assessment. To many persons, the Rebellion must have seemed the type of class confrontation which Berkeley and his friends had long feared. "The poverty of the Country is such," Bacon declared, "that all the power and sway is got into the hands of the rich, who by extorious advantages, having the common people in their debt, have always curbed and oppressed them in all manner of wayes." Although historians may discover the Virginian gentry was not as selfish as Bacon claimed, the leader's class rhetoric appealed to a large number of colonists.

It would be interesting to identify these people, to know more about their social status, but the rebels have preserved their anonymity. Surviving records have yielded only a few names out of the hundreds who took up arms against the government. Contemporaries, however, insisted Bacon's troops had been recruited from the lowest ranks of Virginia society. They were the rabble, the disaffected, the vulgar, the indigent. In June 1676, loyalist William Sherwood reported, "Now tag, rag, and bobtayle carry a high hand." Philip Ludwell, another prominent colonial official, told an English correspondent that Bacon had raised 500 soldiers "whose fortunes & Inclinations being equally desperate, were fit for the purpose there being not 20 in the whole Route, but what were Idle & will not worke, or such whose Debaucherie or Ill Husbandry has brought in Debt beyond hopes or thought of payment." Another account described the rebel army as a body composed of three parts: "freemen, searvants, and slaves."

The lower-class origins of Bacon's troops receives additional verification from a narrative written by an English sea captain, Thomas Grantham. This rough adventurer arrived in Virginia just as the Rebellion was ending. Bacon had already died, and groups of dispirited rebels throughout the colony were debating whether to surrender or carry on the fight. Grantham volunteered to serve as an intermediary between Berkeley and his enemies. The governor accepted the offer, and the captain set off in his thirty-gun ship, the *Concord,* in search of the rebel bands. At a fortified position called West Point, he persuaded Joseph Ingram and "about 250" soldiers to submit to the governor's authority in exchange for a full pardon. Grantham then travelled three miles more to the plantation of Colonel John West, the rebels' "Chiefe Garrison and Magazine." At West's home he encountered approximately 400 "English and Negroes in Armes." In fact, he confronted the very sort of men that Berkeley's followers had often claimed supported Bacon.

The soldiers complained about Ingram's capitulation, and some urged shooting Grantham on the spot. But the captain knew how to talk himself out of difficult situations and brazenly informed "the negroes and Servants, that they were all pardoned and freed from their Slavery." With other such "faire promises" and a liberal supply of brandy, Grantham won most of the discouraged rebels over to the government, but "eighty Negroes and Twenty English . . . would not deliver their Armes." Perhaps these holdouts realized the captain had no power to grant bondsmen freedom; perhaps they believed fighting in a desperate cause better than returning to their masters. Whatever their reasoning, Grantham was one step ahead of the rebels. He tricked them onto a small boat by promising safe passage across the York River, and when the Negroes and servants were aboard, he threatened to blow them out of the water with the guns of the *Concord* unless they immediately surrendered. His account closes with the return of the captured "Negroes & Servants . . . to their Masters."

The presence of so many black rebels at West's plantation provides evidence that many Virginians in Berkeley's time regarded economic status, not race, as the essential social distinction. Even the gentry seems to have viewed the blacks primarily as a component of the "giddy multitude." If the large tobacco planters could have played the white laborers off against the Negroes, they surely would have. The governor's supporters charged Bacon with many failings: atheism, hypocrisy, pride, avarice; but no one attacked the rebel leader for partiality toward black men. One loyalist account of the Rebellion noted that Richard Lawrence, one of Bacon's advisors, had indulged in "the darke imbraces of a Blackamoore, his slave," but in the narrative literature of this period, such racial comments were rare.

If the colonial gentry had been as worried about the danger of black insurrection in 1676 as they were in the eighteenth century, one would have expected some writer to have condemned Bacon's arming the slaves. The silence on this point is especially strange since it had long been illegal in Virginia for Negroes to bear arms. Englishmen such as Captain Grantham appear to have been more conscious of the mixed racial character of Bacon's army than were the local planters. Possibly the colonists had come to view the entire labor force, not just a part of it, as the threat to their safety. The absence of racial slurs does not indicate that Virginia leaders in 1676 felt no prejudice against Negroes. Rather, the planters may have taken for granted the cooperation of slaves, servants, and poor freemen.

Bacon's Rebellion has often been described as a turning point in Virginia's history. The settlement of the insurrection did bring about important political changes, especially in the colony's relationship to England; but it did almost nothing to allay the gentry's fear of the "giddy multitude." The social and economic conditions that had originally caused the labor force to participate in the disorder persisted after calm supposedly had been restored. In 1677, a small and relatively insignificant disturbance near Albemarle Sound in California revealed the degree of the planters' uneasiness about maintaining order within their own colony. The disruption, known as Culpeper's Rebellion, grew out of several local grievances, the chief being the collection of a Parliamentary tax. What bothered the Virginians was not the rebels' specific demands, but the character of the rebels themselves. Observers in Carolina reported that Culpeper's force included the worst elements in colonial society. One person warned that if this band of impoverished whites and blacks succeeded in Carolina, it might soon "make Inroads and dayly Incursions" on Virginia.

An even graver danger was the temptation which the Albemarle community presented to the poor laborers and bondsmen in other colonies. As one Carolinian explained, Virginia leaders hoped for a quick suppression of the rebels, "Being exceeding sensible of the dangerous consequences of this Rebellion, as that if they be not suddenly subdued hundreds of idle debtors, theeves, Negroes, Indians and English servants will fly unto them." There is no evidence that Virginia workers actually ran to the Albemarle settlements. The fear of a lower-class exodus, however, is more significant than the fact. The colony's elite assumed a coalition of "servants, Slaves & Debtors" would defy established authority if the opportunity arose, and since Virginia's economy had not improved following Bacon's Rebellion, no one knew when a confrontation might occur.

In 1681, five years after Bacon's death, Virginia's leaders were still worried about the possibility of a general servant uprising. At one point they urged the king to allow the foot companies originally sent to Virginia in 1677 to remain so that the Redcoats could "prevent or suppress any Insurrection that may otherwise happen during the necessitous unsettled condition of the Colonie." And Thomas Lord Culpeper, the colony's royal governor (no relation to the leader of the Carolina disorder), regarded the labor force as the chief threat to

internal peace. In 1679 the king had instructed Culpeper to "take care that all Planters and Christian Servants be well and fitly provided with Arms." But after living in Virginia only a short time, the governor realized the crown's order was impractical, if not counter-productive. In 1681 Culpeper scribbled in the margin next to this instruction: "Masters have arms. Servants not trusted with them."

The lower classes once again turned to violence in the spring of 1682. The primary cause of this disturbance was chronic economic depression, although the political ambitions of Robert Beverley, Sr., clerk of the House of Burgesses, probably served as a catalyst for unrest. For several years, over-production of tobacco had brought hard times to everyone. In an effort to raise prices, some Virginians advocated the voluntary cessation of planting. Royal officials, however, discouraged these plans in the belief they would reduce customs revenue (a tax based on the volume of trade). When the colony's governor prorogued the Burgesses preventing any legislation on the issue, people in Gloucester took matters into their own hands. Mobs marched from plantation to plantation, cutting tobacco plants as they went. Each victim immediately became a fervid "cutter," since once his crop had been destroyed, he wanted to insure that his neighbors did not profit by his loss. The panic spread to other counties, and although Deputy Governor Henry Chicheley quickly dispatched cavalry units to apprehend the leading "mutineers" and to frustrate further "Insurrection and outrages," the rioting and "night mischiefs" continued for well over a month.

After 1682 the character of social violence changed in Virginia. Never again would the "giddy multitude"—indentured servants, black slaves and poor freemen—make common cause against the colony's ruling planters. In fact, the plant-cutting riots were the last major disturbance in which white laborers of any sort took part. Over the next two decades, white men came to regard blacks—and blacks alone—as the chief threat to Virginia's tranquility.

The transformation came slowly; for several years colonial leaders were hardly aware of it. Late in the summer of 1682, Secretary Spencer predicted new disorders simply because it was the season when "All plantations [are] flowing with Syder." He even thought he detected a spirit of unrest that "Bacon's Rebellion left itching behind it." But no rebellion occurred. In 1683, Governor Culpeper reported that all was calm in Virginia. "All hands are at worke," he wrote, "none excepted. And yet there is an evil spiritt at Worke, who governed in our Time of Anarchy." Again, no disorder followed. Two years later, Governor Francis Effingham asked William Blathwayt, secretary of the Lords of Trade, for a special force of 20 men "in Case any disorder should accidenteally happen," but the Governor undermined the urgency of his request by admitting "all things here are in a peaceable and Quiett Condition." The lower-class whites, the common people, seemed interested in planting tobacco, settling frontier lands and raising families, and none showed much inclination toward organized violence. Not even the Glorious Revolution or rumors that hordes of Maryland Catholics planned to descend upon the colony could stir the "giddy multitude." In 1697, the governor's council in Virginia reported: "The country is in peace and happiness." By 1700, the general uprisings of whites, sometimes supported by a few Negroes, were no more than an unpleasant memory. The eighteenth-century Virginia gentry feared the blacks and the policies of certain aggressive royal governors, but no one expressed appre-hension about the poor whites, the tenants, the indentured servants or the debtors. The prob-lem is to explain how this change came about.

Many elements contributed to the transforma-tion of Virginia, but none was more important than the rise of tobacco prices after 1684. In Berkeley's time, the tobacco market had gener-ally been poor. Some years were better than others, but prices never regained the level achieved in 1660. During the last two decades of the seventeenth century, economic conditions improved. The demand for Virginia crops ex-panded, and poor yields and natural disasters occurred often enough to prevent market satura-tion. These were not boom years as the 1620s had been, but tobacco prices were high enough to raise the lower classes out of the poverty that had been so widespread before the 1680s. Contemporaries appreciated the relationship between economic improvement and social tran-quillity. Governor Culpeper informed crown officials in 1683 that "peace and quietness" would continue in Virginia "so long as tobacco bears a price." The next year Spencer observed that the people had calmed down since they had begun working for a full harvest.

While rising prices reduced social tensions, they did not in themselves bring about the disappearance of the "giddy multitude." The character of the labor force also changed during this period. Before Bacon's Rebellion, planters imported thousands of indentured servants; and

because the demand for workers exceeded the supply, planters accepted whomever merchants delivered. After 1680, however, commercial developments outside Virginia altered the ser-vant trade. English companies achieved the capacity to ship Negroes directly from Africa to the mainland colonies and, during the last years of the seventeenth century, tobacco planters purchased slaves in increasingly larger num-bers. This new source of labor was not only more economic than the indentured servants had been, but it also allowed planters greater selectivity in the choice of servants. William Fitzhugh, for example, one of the colony's major slaveholders, refused to take "ordinary servants," warning a trader, "I would have a good one or none."

A second element affecting the quality of indentured servants was England's crackdown on the "spirits." In 1682 Charles II issued a proclamation regulating the recruitment of ser-vants. No indenture would be valid unless signed before a magistrate in the mother coun-try, and no person under 14 years old could be shipped to America without parental consent. The king's humanitarian act may in part have been an attempt to protect legitimate merchants from fraudulent suits by individuals claiming to have been abducted. In the early 1680s a group calling itself "the Principall Merchants of En-gland traders to the Plantacions" protested that unnecessary prosecutions had so discouraged traders from carrying servants to the New World that some colonies would soon find themselves with "few white men to Governe & direct the Negroes."

Whatever the causes, the number of inden-tured servants arriving in Virginia dwindled. Those who did immigrate, however, were of a higher social rank than those who flooded the colony at mid-century. Large planters wanted servants with special skills. In 1687 Fitzhugh advised an Englishman how to establish a plantation in Virginia: "the best methods to be pursued therein is, to get a Carpenter & Bricklayer Servants, & send them in here to serve 4 or five years, in which time of their Service they might reasonably build a substan-tial good house . . . & earn money enough besides in their said time, at spare times from your work . . . as will purchase plank, nails & other materials." Of the seven indentured servants mentioned in Fitzhugh's will, one was a carpenter, one a glazier and another the planter's own cousin. Unlike the planters of Berkeley's time, Fitzhugh's contemporaries sel-dom complained that their servants were "desperate villans" recruited from the "very scum" of England. Conditions had changed. The indentured workers who emigrated after the mid-1680s escaped the crushing poverty and frustrations that so embittered the previous generation of servants. For these later arrivals Virginia may well have appeared a land of opportunity.

The poor freemen also became less disruptive in this period. Landless and indebted persons, many of them former servants, had once flocked to Bacon's standard. Yet, by the mid-1680s, no one seems to have regarded them as a serious threat to Virginia's internal security. These people benefited greatly from improved economic conditions. Few at the lowest levels of white society experienced the grinding poverty that a decade earlier had driven desperate men to violence. Food was abundant and clothes easier to obtain. Indeed, by the beginning of the eighteenth century, Virginians boasted of eradicating poverty. The planter-historian, Robert Beverley, Jr., noted in 1705 that the colonists "live in so happy a Climate, and have so fertile a Soil, that no body is poor enough to beg, or want Food, though they have abundance of People that are lazy enough to deserve it." Beverley concluded that compared to European nations, Virginia was "the best poor man's Country in the World." Foreign visitors corroborated Beverley's observation. When a French Protestant, Francis Louis Michel, travelled through Virginia in 1702, he reported finding no poor people and wrote: "It is indeed said truthfully that there is no other country, where it is possible with so few means and so easily to make an honest living and be in easy circumstances." As tobacco prices improved, the less prosperous freemen found wealthier neighbors willing to advance credit. And if a person possessed a special skill or trade, he could command a good wage. "I have seen a common journeyman paid annually 30 lbs. sterling, including his board," one man wrote. "But I have heard of master workmen who receive about a guinea daily."

As always, freemen wanted land. In Berkeley's time, hostile Indians along the frontier and "Land lopers" among the gentry frustrated this desire. After the mid-1680s, however, changes in Virginia reduced these obstructions—the colonists simply removed the Indians. A foreign traveller at the turn of the century discovered that Indians "have not come into the colony to inflict damage, because for one thing they are afraid of the English power, but especially because they are unable to flee from the cavalry." As early as 1687, Virginians counselled prospective colonists that Indians "are not greatly to be feared."

Often the colony's most influential planters, such as William Byrd, William Fitzhugh and Ralph Wormeley, claimed the vacated Indian lands. One means to obtain large tracts in the west was to lead the militia in a successful march against the Indians. "The colonels of these troops," a Frenchman explained, "claimed the plantations of the savages & had them surveyed, so that at the present time [1687] there are large tracts of very good land for sale in Virginia." Some of these men held onto the land, building the vast estates that became an integral part of the Virginia aristocracy in the eighteenth century, but much of the acreage was sold. Several Virginians, in fact, became speculators and showed no desire to discourage small farmers from settling the newly secured territory. Fitzhugh, one of the colony's largest landowners, urged an English associate to promote the planter's Virginia lands, for any transfer "will be doubly advantageous to me first by meeting with an opportunity to serve you through your friends, & secondly, by profitably either selling or tenementing my Land, which till so done, is rather a charge than profit." Easy and flexible terms were offered to interested buyers. Ralph Wormeley, for example, was willing to sell "ten thousand acres of ground he owned . . . for one écu an acre."

If landless freemen could not afford acreage in Virginia, they could move to Carolina or Pennsylvania, areas largely inaccessible before 1680. This practice was fairly common. In 1695, Governor Francis Nicholson complained "many families, but especially young men" were leaving Virginia and Maryland for Pennsylvania where land could be purchased at a lower rate. A visitor to Virginia in 1702 "heard many good reports about Pennsylvania and that some people from Virginia moved there." Whichever option the ex-servant chose—buying land in Virginia or moving—he could anticipate becoming an independent planter. Although relatively few advanced to the highest ranks of society, the freeman's horizons were broader in 1700 than they had been in 1670.

After the 1680s the experience of the blacks in Virginia was increasingly different from that of other colonists. Improved tobacco prices raised white laborers out of poverty, making their servitude endurable and their freemanship secure. But the same economic conditions brought large numbers of Negroes into the colony as slaves. No one knows exactly how rapidly the black population grew after 1680. There seem to have been about 4,000 slaves at the time of the tobacco-cutting riots. Estimates of the size of the Negro population in 1700 range as high as 20,000. Even if this figure is excessive, the number of Africans arriving in Virginia expanded substantially in the last two decades of the seventeenth century.

The leading tobacco planters required no encouragement to make the transition from white to black labor. The wealthiest among them had accumulated enough capital to purchase and maintain large gangs of Negroes. For the first time in the century, English trading companies were able to supply blacks on a reasonably regular basis. The colonists bought all the Negroes the slavers could transport and then demanded more. In 1696, a group of Chesapeake planters and merchants petitioned Parliament to lift restrictions on the African trade, since the company holding the monopoly (the Royal African Company) could not meet the escalating demand for blacks in Maryland and Virginia.

The changes in the slave community were more complex than revealed by population statistics alone. In fact, the sheer growth in numbers only partially explains why whites no longer joined with blacks to threaten planter society. An equally important element in understanding race relations in this period was the Negroes' experience before arriving in Virginia. With each passing year an increasing proportion of slaves came directly from Africa. These immigrants had no stopover in Barbados to learn English or to adjust either physically or mentally to an alien culture. They were simply dumped on the wharves of the river plantations in a state of shock, barely alive after the ocean crossing. Conditions on the slave ships were terrible. One vessel from Guinea unloaded 230 blacks, but reported that a hundred more had died at sea. No white servant in this period, no matter how poor, how bitter or badly treated, could identify with these frightened Africans. The terrors they had so recently faced were beyond comprehension. The sale of the blacks emphasized the difference between races. "The negroes are brought annually in large numbers," a visitor to Virginia recounted at the turn of the century. "They can be selected according to pleasure, young and old, men and women. They are entirely naked when they arrive, having only corals of different colors around their necks and arms." These strange, helpless blacks repulsed the writer who noted that even

the Indians seemed preferable to these "animal-like people." His reactions, no doubt, were shared by many white Virginians. In 1699, members of the House of Burgesses described the blacks in a manner unknown in Berkeley's time, claiming it unnecessary to expose slaves to Christianity, since "the gross barbarity and rudeness of their manners, the variety and strangeness of their languages and the weakness and shallowness of their minds rendered it in a manner impossible to attain to any progress in their conversion."

Language became a major barrier between white laborers and the thousands of new black immigrants. Before the 1690s, no one recorded any problem in communicating with Negroes. Indeed, it is difficult to comprehend how servants and slaves could have conspired to run away or rebel had they been unable to understand one another. The flood of Africans directly into Virginia not only made it difficult for whites to deal with blacks, but also hindered communications between blacks. The colonists apparently regarded the great variety of African tongues as a protection against black insurrection. Early in the eighteenth century, Governor Alexander Spotswood, convinced of the need for stricter controls over the labor force, warned Virginians that the slaves' "Babel of Languages" offered no real security, since "freedom Wears a Cap which can without a Tongue, Call Together all Those who long to Shake off the fetters of Slavery."

The blacks hated their status. They ran away whenever possible, and on at least one occasion, formed a small band that terrorized the colonists of Rappahannock County. Rumors of Negro plots made the planters uneasy, with good reason. A group of slaves could easily have seized a plantation and murdered the master and his family before troops could have been summoned. But there was little chance that the blacks at this time could have overrun the colony; without the support of poorer whites and indentured servants, they were badly outnumbered. The white cavalry that hunted down the Indians could have done the same to the slaves. The changes in Virginia society after the mid-1680s had set whites against blacks, the armed, organized forces of the planters against the small, isolated groups of slaves. In Berkeley's time the militia had been regarded as a means of protecting the elite from the entire labor force, but early in the eighteenth century, historian Hugh Jones reported that "in each county is a great number of disciplined and armed militia, ready in case of any sudden irruption of Indians or insurrection of Negroes." The labor force was still the major threat to internal security in Virginia, but now the laborers were predominantly black.

Like the Barbadians, the seventeenth-century Virginians exchanged white servants for Negro slaves, and in so doing, exchanged a fear of the "giddy multitude" for a fear of slave rebellion. By 1700, whites had achieved a sense of race solidarity at the expense of blacks. Negroes were set apart as objects of contempt and ridicule. The whites, even the meanest among them, always knew there was a class of men permanently below them. But the story of Virginia's labor force between 1660 and 1710 was more than a dreary narrative of suffering and oppression. For a few decades, it had been possible to overlook racial differences, a time when a common experience of desperate poverty and broken dreams brought some whites and blacks together. Such conditions were present in the American South during the 1890s, and it is not unlikely that they will appear again.

# Puerto Ricans and the Political Economy of New York

CLARA E. RODRÍGUEZ

## POST-MIGRATION EFFECTS

Many of the myriad aspects of the Puerto Rican community in New York have been examined, discussed, deplored, or excused without sufficient attention being paid to the effects of the New York economy on Puerto Ricans. Generally, the economy has been superficially analyzed and then only as a push or pull factor in the migration of Puerto Ricans to New York. The role of the economy in determining what happened after Puerto Ricans migrated to New York has yet to be fully examined in the growing body of literature on Puerto Ricans.

It is clear from available data that Puerto Ricans have not been evenly integrated into the New York economy. Comparing the occupational distribution of Puerto Ricans between 1950 and 1970, we see that relative to blacks and whites, Puerto Ricans have been, and are, disproportionately represented in the blue-collar occupations. This disproportionate concentration vis-à-vis other groups held constant between 1950 and 1970—despite a significant decrease (from 61.0 percent to 51.3 percent) in the proportion of Puerto Ricans in the blue-collar jobs between 1960 and 1970. That is, although the proportion of Puerto Rican blue-collar workers decreased, the proportion of black and white blue-collar workers still remains significantly lower.

This decrease in blue-collar workers between 1960 and 1970 seems to be accounted for by an increase in service-sector workers rather than by significant gains in white-collar employment. Thus, with respect to white-collar jobs, Puerto Ricans have the smallest proportion of white-collar workers of all three groups: 27.2 percent compared to 32.5 percent for blacks and 51 percent for the total population. When we look at the figures in more detail, we see that there has been greater mobility of Puerto Rican females into white-collar occupations than of Puerto Rican males. The mere analysis of the proportions of blue-collar and white-collar workers in the labor force is not itself sufficient to indicate what has been the relative success of Puerto Rican economic integration, for some blue-collar workers earn more than many white-collar workers. Thus, it is necessary to look at income differentials by occupation.

Within each occupational group Puerto Rican males and females are paid less than black or white males or females. No data are available by specific occupations—for example, doctors or plumbers—but the figures indicate fairly clearly that Puerto Ricans have only marginally been integrated into the New York economy.

If we look at unemployment rates for Puerto Rican males between 1950 and 1970, we see the same lack of integration. In each year the unemployment rate for Puerto Rican males in New York was about double that of whites and higher than that of blacks. For the years 1950, 1960, and 1970 respectively, unemployment among Puerto Rican males was 10.6, 9.9, and 6.2 percent, while among "nonwhites," it was 8.4, 6.9, and 5.4 percent, and among "others," it was 5.1, 4.3, and 3.9 percent. Had the labor-force participation rates of Puerto Rican males in the New York Standard Metropolitan Statistical Area (SMSA) not declined substantially between 1960 and 1970, the unemployment rate would have been even higher.

Since the labor market is the prime determinant of income in the United States it is not surprising to find that Puerto Ricans are poorer

From Centro de Estudios Puertorriqueños, *Labor Migration Under Capitalism: The Puerto Rican Experience.* Copyright © 1979 by the Research Foundation of the City of New York. Reprinted by permission of Monthly Review Foundation. Footnotes and tables have been deleted.

than either whites or blacks. The proportion of families with incomes below $7,000 (the low-income budget line) is 64 percent for Puerto Ricans, as compared with 29 percent for whites and 49 percent for blacks, while the proportion of families in poverty (under $3,700) was similarly skewed, with 30 percent of Puerto Rican families being thus classified in 1970, compared with 12 percent of all races and 21 percent of blacks. The median family income of Puerto Ricans has also lagged a considerable distance behind that of other groups since 1950: in New York City in 1970 it was $5,575, compared to $10,424 for whites and $7,150 for blacks.

## DETERMINANT FACTORS AFFECTING THE SOCIOECONOMIC POSITION OF PUERTO RICANS

What are the root causes of Puerto Rican high unemployment, skewed occupational distribution, and low income? If we examine the economy and its relation to Puerto Ricans, we find a number of factors that, combined, account for these phenomena. These include automation, sectoral decline, blue-collar structural unemployment, racial and ethnic prejudice, restrictive union policies, inadequate educational opportunities, and the restriction of Puerto Ricans from government employment.

In a nutshell, here is how these factors operate and interact. Automation and the movement of surviving blue-collar jobs to the suburbs, the South, and to other countries have caused a sectoral decline in the number of manufacturing jobs available in New York City. Since these trends occurred more rapidly than out-migration or the retraining of blue-collar workers to fill white-collar jobs, a severe problem of blue-collar structural unemployment arose. Because of racial and ethnic prejudice, restrictive union policies, inadequate educational opportunities, and the restriction of Puerto Ricans from government employment, Puerto Ricans bore the brunt of this blue-collar structural unemployment. The indices cited above are but manifestations of the problems of the economy vis-à-vis Puerto Ricans.

### Automation

Automation is one of the more significant changes the economy was undergoing during the Puerto Rican migration. The effects of automation upon the black labor force have already been discussed and examined fairly closely. Given the similarities of the black and Puerto Rican labor forces, the same line of analysis is applicable to Puerto Ricans. Thus, it is argued that the effects of automation are and were very dramatically felt in the blue-collar workforce, and since a large proportion of black (and an even larger proportion of Puerto Rican) workers are blue collar, the black labor force has been more affected by automation than the white labor force.

Since Puerto Ricans have the highest proportion of blue-collar laborers in New York City, they have been the most affected.

### Suburbanization

Paralleling automation was a trend toward increased suburbanization of industry which placed many blue-collar jobs in the suburbs. If Puerto Ricans came to know about suburban job openings, transportation to the jobs, if present, was expensive in terms of money and time—adding one or two hours to each workday. In addition, the industries in the suburbs already had a substantial pool of labor among the suburbanites who had moved nearby or would soon flee the city to get those jobs. Thus the jobs in the suburbs were fairly unattainable to Puerto Ricans, while the attainable jobs in the city were few. Moreover, the numbers of city jobs held by suburbanites who commute into the city is very high. Although many of the jobs held by commuters are white collar and thus may not be immediately open to many Puerto Ricans, they do further delimit the opportunity structure for Puerto Ricans.

The effect that suburbanization of industry and people had on Puerto Ricans was not just limited to employment. It depleted the tax base of the cities. With a shrinking middle class, the revenues collected proved insufficient to cover the services usually provided. At the same time, the city, with its younger, poorer population, had greater demands put on its services. Thus, while the Puerto Ricans had greater needs, the city had less money.

### Sectoral Decline

Automation and suburbanization combined to cause sectoral decline. Sectoral decline is not a recent phenomenon in New York. Vernon and

Hoover found that between 1929 and 1939, and between 1947 and 1956, New York City lost ground with respect to its growing industries, while it held on to its declining ones. However, the problem has become more acute in recent years, thereby adversely and significantly affecting Puerto Ricans. A dramatic example can be seen in manufacturing. In 1960, manufacturing employed 60 percent of the Puerto Rican workforce. In the decade that followed, manufacturing jobs in the city decreased by 173,000. This loss was not offset by an increase in low-level service jobs, the other major area of Puerto Rican workforce concentration. Thus, as would be expected and as the Commission on Civil Rights of Puerto Ricans found, sectoral decline became an important contributory cause of high unemployment amongst Puerto Ricans.

Even in 1970, those sectors of decline were where the majority of Puerto Ricans were to be found, while those sectors of growth had few Puerto Ricans employed. Despite the decline in jobs in manufacturing, this area has continued to hold significant proportions of the Puerto Rican labor force. Even in 1968–1969, as the U.S. Commission on Civil Rights noted, Puerto Ricans in poor neighborhoods were still found in overwhelming numbers in manufacturing. In 1970, 60 percent of the manufacturing jobs paid less than was required to sustain a decent, minimum standard of living as determined by the Bureau of Labor Statistics.

## Blue-Collar Structural Unemployment

Sectoral decline combined with insufficient educational opportunities and retraining of blue-collar workers to produce blue-collar structural unemployment, which has been an almost chronic condition of the economy for about a decade. In simplest terms, the problem is an excess of blue-collar workers over blue-collar jobs and a scarcity of white-collar workers for excess white-collar jobs. The Regional Plan Association finds this to be one of the main problems of the regional economy. Puerto Ricans, again because of the labor force composition, have been and are bearing the brunt of this structural problem.

The trends in this area indicate a further deterioration of the situation. When you compare the labor force composition of Puerto Ricans (and blacks) against the present and projected job demand for blue- and white-collar jobs and service jobs, you see that blacks and Puerto Ricans do and will suffer the most from the problem of blue-collar structural unemployment. The unemployment could be diminished if more Puerto Ricans (and blacks) entered the white-collar rather than the blue-collar labor force. "However," as the Regional Plan Association states, "it appears that public schools in the region's older cities and manpower training programmes both tend to channel blacks and Puerto Ricans into blue collar work." Thus, it appears that New York's educational institutions and even its manpower agencies contribute to the problem.

## Trade Unions

The environment in which these trends have been occurring has been strongly affected by the unions. Formerly a vehicle of minority mobility, they now function to keep out minorities. Having battled the older entrenched ethnic groups for an occupational niche, the newer ethnic groups now use the unions as a means of securing their positions. Although data on unions are very difficult to come by, it is fairly clear that with the exception of low-level jobs in garment factories and food services, most skilled or craft unions are closed to Puerto Ricans. Thus, many Puerto Ricans' benefits and pay raises may be inferior to those of other workers doing the same job. (This may account, to some extent, for the income discrepancies by occupation noted previously for Puerto Ricans, blacks, and whites.) The result of union blockages has been the growth of freelance, nonunionized, and therefore lower paid, Puerto Rican plumbers, painters, plasterers, electricians, etc.

The net effect of the unions' role on the economy may turn out to be a negative one, for the unions have functioned to limit the supply of semiskilled and skilled labor in order to have a better bargaining position on wage demands. This tactic, however, may have hampered growth and possibly expansion of the economy; the growth of other lower-skilled, but complementary, job openings may also have been hampered in this way. (For example, the prohibitively high labor costs of construction were a definite factor in curtailing housing construction during the 1960s.) The net effect has been higher wages and benefits for union members, but fewer jobs. These few jobs did not go to unknown, unconnected, colored Puerto Ricans.

## Racial and Ethnic Prejudice

Also influencing the effects of these trends on Puerto Ricans were racial barriers. Although ethnic differences often presented a barrier to previous immigrant groups, Puerto Ricans have had to contend with institutionalized racism, as well as institutionalized hostility to ethnic differences. For although, officially, only 9 percent of Puerto Ricans are categorized as black (according to census self-classification), a much larger proportion appears racially nonwhite to Americans and will thus experience racial discrimination. Thus, racism is an important factor affecting the labor market for Puerto Ricans and accounts significantly for the severe distortions in resource allocation to which Puerto Ricans have been subject.

The more "objective" economic factors which have adversely influenced the economic integration of Puerto Ricans into New York City were automation, suburbanization, sectoral decline, and restrictive union policies, factors which were not present to any significant degree during the migrations of previous immigrant groups. Yet these factors have typified the regional New York economy (and to some extent the U.S. economy) in the last decades. When Puerto Ricans and southern blacks were arriving in great numbers, these factors interacted with each other and with racial and ethnic prejudice to create an economic environment inimical to Puerto Rican economic integration.

## Inadequate Educational Opportunities

Although it must be admitted that there are educational differentials between Puerto Ricans, blacks, and whites in New York City, these are not sufficient by themselves to explain the occupational patterning, income differentials by occupation, and the extremely high unemployment rates to which Puerto Ricans are subject. This is to say nothing of the causes of these educational differentials, such as the inferior schooling Puerto Ricans receive in the New York City schools, and received as a result of U.S. imperialistic educational policies in Puerto Rico.

Furthermore, if we compare the educational attainments of the New York City population in 1970, we see that although there are differences between ethnic groups, they are not as great as the above figures on income and occupation would lead us to expect. For example, close to 53 percent of the white population in New York

City twenty-five years and over are not high school graduates, compared to 80 percent of Puerto Ricans within this age group. Does this justify a median income about two times as large?

## Government Employment as a Last Resort

Wilhelm notes that the government has assumed an increasingly larger role as an employer of blacks. Because of this, black unemployment has been kept from increasing too dramatically. Government, however, has not intervened in the same way with respect to the Puerto Rican community, for in 1970 only 12 percent of Puerto Ricans were employed by government, compared to 23 percent of blacks, while local government employed only 7 percent of Puerto Ricans as compared with 15 percent of blacks. Thus, government has not served as an employer of last resort to Puerto Ricans.

A recent extensive survey of municipal government was so appalled at the high underrepresentation of Puerto Ricans in New York City government that it specifically recommended that, "Utmost priority should be given by the Department of Personnel and all agencies to recruiting members of the Puerto Rican community." No other ethnic group was so "honored."

## Summary

In summary, though Mayor Wagner went to San Juan to tell Puerto Ricans that the mainland needed migrants to fill jobs, Puerto Ricans were to meet the sad realities of job placement in New York. This job market had a decreasing demand, for low-skilled jobs were being eliminated by automation, others were protected by unions, others were moving to the suburbs, while suburbanites were taking many jobs in the city. Thus, Puerto Ricans moved into the only jobs available: low-wage work in the service sector (as waiters, kitchen help, porters, and hospital workers), and in light manufacturing (as sewing machine operators). In short, the jobs nobody else wanted. These tended to be low paying and the sectors in which they were found tended to be declining or unstable.

Not only were jobs few, low paying, and often insecure, but once a job was secured mobility was also bad. Where could you go from being a sewing machine operator? Perhaps to the post of supervisor, earning $10 more a week. Similarly, in the food trades the ladder to success started with dishwasher and usually ended with waiter. The few chef positions available were usually reserved for people who had more to offer in the way of "public relations"—as, for example, French chefs did. Most jobs were deadend jobs.

## MIGRATION DIVIDENDS TO THE ECONOMY

Despite the depressed position of Puerto Ricans in the New York economy, Puerto Ricans were and are crucial to its proper functioning. Even though the jobs do not pay much, they are important. Someone has to serve the table and wash the dishes of the white-collar workers. It is in this context that we must see the exploited, yet crucial, position of Puerto Ricans. The textile industry provides one example of the crucial role Puerto Ricans played in an industry vital to New York's economy.

New York accounts for 70 percent of all dollar sales of clothing in the United States at the wholesale level. Garment manufacturers produce and sell more than $7 billion in apparel each year. Although the total number of garment firms has declined over the years, the total dollar volume of business has risen. As with industrialization in farming, the remaining firms are larger and financially stronger.

Some scholars contend that but for the Puerto Rican migration, New York City would not have been able to hold on to this very important industry. Puerto Ricans have, in a sense, provided a "positive tipping point." Without this source of cheap labor many more firms would have left the city; those that stayed would have had to reduce their production. In this sense, New York's claim to be the garment capital of the world rests upon Puerto Rican shoulders.

The Harvard study of the New York metropolitan region took note of this role in the 1950s:

> The rate of Puerto Rican migration to New York is one of the factors that determine how long and how successfully the New York metropolitan region will retain industries which are under competitive pressure from other areas. To the extent that some of these industries have hung on in the area, they have depended on recently arrived Puerto Rican workers, who have entered the job market of the New York area at the rate of about 13,000 each year.

Puerto Rican migration was not at a consistently high level in the 1960s, and this may affect the numbers entering the job market. However, the rate of second-generation entry into the job market and the rate of non-Puerto Rican migration to the suburbs may compensate for decreased Puerto Rican migration. Thus, Puerto Ricans may retain their role as "tippers" who enable or encourage firms to stay or to grow. Low wages for Puerto Ricans continue and thus provide a main incentive in this respect.

Although figures are not available for the hotel and restaurant industry, it would seem that a similar phenomenon has occurred, and is occurring, there. If anything, the role of "tippers" would be accentuated because Puerto Ricans make up a greater percentage of employees in this field. To some extent, the growing numbers of blacks and Puerto Ricans in the health and hospitals services might be seen to be a forthcoming, and parallel, phenomenon. In this case, however, government intervenes sufficiently to ensure that blacks and Puerto Ricans are recruited into these occupations. These services can be seen to be almost public utilities that do not have the option of leaving the city, but of growing or deteriorating.

Although at present unresearched, Puerto Rican migration has also undoubtedly had a large role in moving previous immigrant groups up the economic ladder. Twenty-five years ago garment workers were predominantly Jewish and Italian; now Puerto Ricans and other new immigrants have taken their place. Although mortality accounts for a large part of the decline of Jewish and Italian employees, their children are seldom found as workers in the garment trades. Nor are they usually to be found in similar low-paying occupations. The question, of course, is whether a larger proportion of them would have had to take these low-paying jobs despite probable increased education and language skills. This question remains unanswered. But the fact remains that Puerto Ricans took these jobs and that the sons of previous immigrant groups in the garment trades took better jobs and perhaps became owners and managers in expanded firms. Whatever the causes, the ethnic queuing occurred.

The significance of the manufacturing industries to the welfare of the city cannot be overemphasized. There is a renewed awareness of the importance of the garment industry as the largest employer in the city. (The garment industry employs more people than any other type of manufacturing, providing a total annual payroll of $1.5 billion.) And as important as manufacturing is to the city, Puerto Ricans are to manufacturing. Despite the imposed marginality of the Puerto Rican community in decision-making, if there were an exodus of Puerto Ricans, the city would be in serious straits. Puerto Ricans provide the unacknowledged, but indispensable, role of perhaps all previous immigrant groups and blacks—that of workers supporting the base of the economic system. Although the number of Puerto Rican workers is not sufficient to allow us to speak of their being the major part of the workforce, their placement and concentration make for a strategically very significant position.

## WELFARE: THE ECONOMY'S RESPONSE

Given the low incomes, high unemployment, and insecure jobs held by Puerto Ricans, we would expect to see an extremely high rate of welfare recipients among the Puerto Rican population in New York. In fact, it is not as high as might be expected given the parameters of Puerto Rican poverty. In 1970, 30 percent of Puerto Rican families in New York were on welfare; that is, fully 70 percent were completely self-supporting. Of those families eligible for welfare, that is, with incomes less than poverty level, only 56 percent were on welfare. But the whole issue must be seen within a wider context in order to grasp the full significance of the role the economy has played in placing Puerto Ricans on welfare.

Soon after the large migration of Puerto Ricans to New York, there began to be heard the thesis that Puerto Ricans migrate to New York in order to go on welfare. In other words, the thesis was that welfare in New York was the Puerto Ricans' response to adverse economic conditions in Puerto Rico. This was coupled with claims of astronomically high rates of public assistance to Puerto Ricans. Both these points have been effectively rebutted by Valdivieso, who shows that there has been a significant time lag between migration and welfare assistance. During the 1950s when the great bulk of the Puerto Rican migrants arrived and qualified for public assistance payments, there was a very low rise in such payments. In the 1960s, when welfare rolls expanded, the proportion of Puerto Ricans on welfare rose. Factors other than ethnic propensity must account for this rise: Puerto Ricans did not migrate to get on welfare. It was not a pull factor.

Welfare can be seen to be a contracting economy's response to structural and sectoral unemployment. In addition to taking up the slack in the economy, it also provides jobs for clerical and higher skilled workers—the welfare establishment—while it cools out what may otherwise be an unbearable and explosive situation for the unemployed. At the same time, it tends to subsidize the low-wage industrial sector and the landlord class, which is a direct beneficiary of welfare rent payments. Given the fears associated with color in this country, it is not surprising that welfare has come to be used as an economic policy. That is to say, to some extent individuals are encouraged by the system to apply for welfare; this is done as a means of handling the more difficult structural economic problems.

The system encourages this through the economic factors already noted, for example, unemployment, low incomes, low-status jobs. But it also encourages it directly through the liberalization of welfare policy. Note, for example, those measures that were instituted between 1960 and 1970 when the welfare rolls swelled: doing away with "need" or proof of eligibility, investigator visits, and the man-in-the-home clause; rising rates of support; and support for drug addicts. The fact that welfare funds are mainly federal (50 percent) and state (25 percent) gives added incentive for the city government to cope with its economic problems in this way.

In this period of economic contraction, Puerto Ricans, as the poorest of the poor, have been shunted into welfare—but not more than in proportion to income. Their resistance has been substantial, however, for 70 percent have managed to sustain their families without welfare on extremely low wages, and much higher percentages managed to do so prior to 1960. But for increasing proportions, the only way to survive is welfare. It is in the dilution of alternatives that the system forces Puerto Ricans into welfare.

# Wampum to Pictures of Presidents

GERALD VIZENOR

The traditional style of ceremonial consumption and the ways in which tribal people made use of natural resources was in great contrast to the ambitions of white people who accumulated wealth and competed for political power.

Harold Hickerson in his book *The Chippewa and Their Neighbors* writes that the industrial and ideological systems of tribal people were "geared to the simple needs of small communities whose members exploited a rather difficult environment without using artificial means to produce animal or plant food." The exploitations of several thousand tribal people, who used little more than they needed from day to day, is less obvious an exploitation of natural resources than the waste left by large corporations.

The fur trade interposed the first anomalous economic burr on the traditional survival rhythms of woodland life and the equipoise of tribal spirits. Tribal people from the mountains, plains and waterways of the woodland, transcended or ignored their religious beliefs and family totems by killing millions of animals for peltry. Muskrat, beaver, marten, fisher, the sacred otter, mink, wolverine, fox, bear, moose, raccoon, and other animal pelts were exchanged for intoxicants, material goods, services, and sundries. Tribal people volunteered, they were not forced, to participate in this exploitation of natural resources.

But the personal reminiscence of tribal people is often in sharp contrast to the voices of exploitation around them in the woodland. Nodinens, for example, an old tribal woman, gave this information about her life to Frances Densmore almost fifty years ago: "When I was young everything was very systematic. We worked day and night and made the best use of the materials we had. My father kept count of the days on a stick. . . . He cut a big notch for the first day of a new moon and a small notch for each of the other days."

The American Fur Company was one of the first large private corporations operating in tribal country more than a century ago, before reservations were established. When the frivolous market for beaver felt hats, and other pelts, waned in favor of silks and other materials, the big fur companies with all their overloads of the trade, partners, interpreters, clerks, guides, canoemen, and tribal hunters at various woodland trading posts, diversified their business operations and capital investments into mining, timber, transportation, banking, manufacturing and land. Little of the enormous wealth accumulated from the fur trade was ever returned to the area for economic development. The wealth was used to build huge corporations, powerful banking institutions in urban centers, and national political organizations to favor the future accumulation of wealth.

Following their first commercial transactions as laborers and low cost factors in the fur trade, tribal people, except those who had intermarried and were canting to assimilation, were left to the spiritual spasms of cultural reunions on segregated enclaves.

The low cost of labor and available natural resources are still the fundamental reasons why private corporations locate on reservations. But since the fur trade, with the exception of timber and mineral and natural gas resources, commercial interests in reservations have been minimal. It has been what tribal people have in terms of natural resources, rather than who they are as human beings, that attracts businesses from the economies of the white world.

In his report, *Industrial Development on Indian Reservations in the Upper Midwest,* James Murray points out that notwithstanding attractive business incentives, private firms are not moving to reservations in large numbers, and those which do fail at a higher rate than the national average of business failures.

"One of the disappointing aspects of the effort to industrialize the reservations has been the rather large numbers of newly established firms which have failed or shut down after relatively short periods of operating on reservations," writes Murray, an economics professor. . . .

Poor management is the most frequent cause of business failures—reservation locations are no exception. In a ten year summary of business failure on reservations across the country, inexperienced management was the reason most often given for failure. In the ninth federal reserve district, lack of developed markets and undercapitalization were other reasons given for business failure on reservations.

"In a private enterprise economy, management, rather than creditors, material suppliers, laborers," Murray writes, "receives with its right to make decisions, the primary responsibility for the outcome of those decisions. To attribute business failures to bad management, therefore, is not very helpful to those who are attempting to reduce the rate of these failures.

Also, in the process of locating on the reservations, firms have had the advantage of feasibility studies, employment assistance, and other services provided by federal agencies. . . . This causes many people to wonder why the record of failure is as bad as or worse than the national average.

The first corporations which were attracted to locate on reservations, Murray continues,

are often firms which would probably not start at all, or would not locate on reservations, except for the added promotional effort on the part of development specialists and political bodies at all levels of government.

Many of the firms which have failed appear to have been firms which would not have been initiated if they had to rely on normal channels for credit, and would have had to bear the full cost of training their work force, constructing a building, and determining the marketability of their product.

In the struggle to create employment opportunities on the reservation, both tribal officials and government agencies may overlook certain facts which would suggest problems for the firm. This may be encouraged by the fact that they are evaluated in terms of the success they achieve in producing jobs in a short period of time rather than in terms of the permanence of those jobs.

One of the most perplexing realities of paraeconomic survival on reservations is the constant paternalistic, and in some cases socialistic, efforts of federal and tribal governments to create and control jobs on reservations rather than inspiring capitalistic profit making enter-

prises, which would benefit tribal organizations and individuals. The challenge is how to increase jobs and profits and reduce paternalism at the same time.

Leon Cook, who has several years of experience in tribal economic development, argues that tribal people have "internalized colonial attitudes of creating jobs rather than being motivated by profits which is the rule in the real world . . . people should go into business to make money." He is critical of the fact that so many tribal development organizations are non-profit corporations.

Exceptions to the development of paraeconomic tribal enterprises include commercial fishing and logging operations, oil and mineral leases, and several construction companies. The Minnesota Chippewa Tribal Construction Company is an outstanding example of a tribal government diminishing the need to depend on contractors in the white world. The profit corporation was established two years ago by the Minnesota Chippewa Tribe—a federation of six reservation tribal governments. Where contracts for work on six state reservations were offered to competing white contractors in the past, the work is now done by tribal people working for a profit making, tribal owned and managed corporation.

Most reservations do not have an independent functioning economic system through which social and political experiences are shared by those living in the communities. Most of the money earned in wages on reservations is spent in the consumption of goods and services in white communities off the reservations. With private and tribal enterprises controlling most reservation employment there are too few employers and not enough tribal people in small businesses offering their goods and services to people living on the reservation.

Elected tribal politicians who measure economic development by the number of jobs available must spend much of their time relating to white people and government officials who represent interests in the dominant economic system. Depending on federal programs as solutions to social and economic problems on reservations only perpetuates paraeconomics. Paternalistic programs spawn dependencies and limit personal expectations and aspirations for economic growth.

A decrease in reservation unemployment—underemployment and unemployment are serious problems on reservations—puts more money in the hands of individuals, but when most of that earned money will be spent off reservations it does little to reduce dominancies on the dependent economic system. Few communities are able to function without benefits from the dominant economic system, but interdependence on goods and services will diminish paraeconomics and strengthen social tolerances and sensitivities. Poor white people living in rural areas near reservations have shared the interdependent realities of unemployment and social problems in the past, but tribal people as a group have been excluded from the profits of white economic systems of the present.

Tribal people will continue to survive in a paraeconomic system without the independent and interdependent development of enterprises owned and operated for profit by tribal people living on reservations.

William Lawrence, law school graduate and former industrial development specialist for the Red Lake Reservation, proposed an impressive and ambitious development plan for the reservation, ranging from private enterprises offering goods and services, tribal owned businesses, such as a liquor store, golf course, airport, motel, and water and power associations. His economic development philosophy was to increase the number of reservation employers and encourage individuals and independent corporations of tribal people to establish enterprises on the reservation. His ideal was to have tribal people earning and spending—exchanging goods and services and sharing economic risks—on the reservation as a way of reducing dependencies on off-reservation businesses and government institutions. His was a long range plan that may never be realized because of cultural attitudes and tribal politics.

The political power of elected reservation leaders has increased in proportion to the number of jobs tribal governments create and control through private corporations or tribal enterprises operating on reservations. On several reservations, political discussions and government decisions are made in tribal languages, while the language of proposals for economic development originate from the values of the dominant society. These are political realities which limit economic change from the perspective of modern theorists.

Few reservations have a tribal civil service system to protect workers from political influences and abuses. Such a system would be too expensive for a small tribal government to maintain, but on a regional or state basis the idea is worth consideration.

"As a consequence of their experiences," Murray points out, tribal people "are often inclined to view political activity as more important than business acumen in achieving social and economic objectives. . . ."

Perhaps one reason so few private firms are inspired to locate on reservations is the unskilled labor available. Tribal politics may be another reason. In the dominant economic market, workers are paid well above minimum wage rates because they are productive and because of collective labor union organization. Murray emphasizes that there is a common misconception that "high wage industries have a difficult time competing in international markets.

> The opposite is in fact the case. Our high wage industries are also those where labor is the most productive but wages do not reflect the full potential of that productivity because of the ready availability of labor from industries with low productivity. Thus the industries with highest productivity are likely to have the greatest advantage of labor unit costs. It is the low-wage, low productivity industries which are threatened by foreign competition. . . .

If the firms are labor intensive with no methods of mechanization it would be difficult to increase the productivity of the laborers to compensate for a higher minimum wage. "In such firms, productivity differences depend largely upon differences in human qualities," Murray continues.

"While individuals can differ greatly in their ability to perform certain physical tasks, large groups of individuals seldom display the same degree of disparity. That is, in any community one can find certain people" who can work more quickly and efficiently than others.

> But, except for cultural or environmental differences relating to these activities, you can probably find a similar percentage of talents in almost any area in the world. It is, therefore, extremely difficult for any community to become substantially more productive than others in labor intensive activities, and even more difficult to maintain this advantage over time.
>
> In exploiting the pool of unskilled labor, it would seem wiser to pursue opportunities to perform custom work which is labor intensive rather than standardized work. . . .

The Brunswick Corporation operating on the Fort Totten Reservation and the MDS-Atron Corporation located at Belcourt on the Turtle Mountain Reservation, both in North Dakota, are successful examples of firms employing tribal people to perform customized work. Brunswick has a contract with a tribal development corporation and federal agencies for the customized manufacture of camouflage netting for military use. The operation has not only provided more than two hundred new jobs on the reservation but profits have also been realized by the tribal development corporation.

The MDS-Atron electronics operation at Belcourt has grown in the past three years to about fifty employees, most of whom are tribal people classified as electrical assemblers trained on the job in core memory stringing, hand soldering, and miniature wiring. The plant is located in a building owned by the tribal government.

John Miller, who is director of manufacturing and responsible for the operation, has pointed out that the apparent unwillingness of corporations to offer contracts to reservation businesses is not by design, but ratherg a problem in the systematic methods of purchasing from subcontractors. Habits and associations are difficult to change. Miller repeats the success of customized operations, but points out that operations on reservations also need diversification in production. Other experienced observers agree, and stress diversified production as a means of providing real economic choices which can be supported with education and training.

There are many other successful customized production facilities located on other reservations. For example, the electrical components operations on the Fort Berthold Reservation, the jewel bearing manufacturing plant on the Turtle Mountain Reservation, electronics operations on the Rosebud Reservation and the Mille Lac Reservation. There are also numerous customized wood products manufacturing operations on several reservations.

In his report, James Murray questions the extent to which reservation industrial development provides a satisfactory solution to the economic problems of tribal people. "In spite of the very encouraging activities of many reservations, the present rate of industrialization will not provide the employment opportunities required to significantly reduce the rate of unemployment among the rapidly growing Indian population. After ten years of activity by the staff of the Bureau of Indian Affairs and other agencies, coupled with the various incentives, about one thousand jobs have been created in the five state area of the upper midwest. . . ."

In the next decade the tribal population in this area may increase by more than twenty percent. "During that time approximately three thousand additional jobs will be needed," Murray predicts, "assuming that the same percentage of the Indian people remain on the reservation as have in the past.

With new resources, greater interest and experience on the part of tribal leaders, and, hopefully, the passage of legislation to assist in financing the effort, the industrialization program should be much more successful in the next ten years than in the past ten. However, even if it is twice as successful, it will provide only about ten or fifteen percent of the positions needed to really solve the problem, and there will be several thousand more unemployed Indian people living in poverty than there are now.

Since his report five years ago there have been dramatic changes in the potential for economic development, but no dramatic decrease in unemployment on reservations. Various federal service programs have increased the number of jobs on reservations and a few new plants have opened, but when federal programs are concluded, so will be most of the jobs. Reservation tribal life is still a paraeconomic survival experience.

In the past five years the number of tribal owned businesses has increased and several tribal governments are now contracting for the administration of federal programs in education and public services, which are all promising halfsteps toward reservation economic independence or at least interdependence. There has also been important litigation in federal courts favoring tribal jurisdiction over natural resources—such as tribal jurisdiction over hunting and fishing within treaty boundaries on the Leech Lake Reservation.

The most significant potential changes have been the organization of the American Indian National Bank and passage of the Indian Financing Act, which will make more money available to tribal governments and individual reservation enterprises.

Bernard Granum, who identifies himself as a resource economist for the Bureau of Indian Affairs, is optimistic that new sources of credit financing will relieve capitalization and industrial expansion problems on reservations. He believes in one national economic system.

"This nation can tolerate diversities in religion and in many other areas of life," said Granum, who remarked that he knows of no differences between the economic aspirations of tribal people and white people. "But we can tolerate only one economic system, and that is the world of work . . . in that system you either fit in or you are counted out."

"We all have the same economic system . . . it functions the same way, even though the objects have changed from wampum to pictures of the presidents."

# Racial Domination and Class Conflict in Capitalist Agriculture: The Oxnard Sugar Beet Workers' Strike of 1903

TOMÁS ALMAGUER

In February 1903 over 1,200 Mexican and Japanese farm workers organized the Japanese-Mexican Labor Association (JMLA) in the southern California community of Oxnard. The JMLA was the first major agricultural workers' union in the state comprised of different minority workers and the first to strike successfully against capitalist interests. In addition to being significant to labor history, the Oxnard strike also has sociological importance. The strike raises issues such as the historical interplay between class and racial stratification, the importance of these factors in labor organizing, and variations in Anglo-American racial attitudes at the time. Emerging as one of the many "boom towns" in California at the turn of the century, Oxnard owed its existence to the passage of the 1897 Dingley Tariff Bill, which imposed a heavy duty on imported sugar, and the introduction of the sugar beet industry to Ventura County. The construction of an immense sugar beet factory in Ventura County by Henry, James, and Robert Oxnard, prominent sugar refiners from New York, drew hundreds into the area and led to the founding of the new community. The sugar beet factory quickly became a major processing center for the emerging U.S. sugar beet industry, refining nearly 200,000 tons of beets and employing 700 people by 1903.

The developing Ventura County sugar beet industry had an important social impact on the new community. One major repercussion was the racial segregation of Oxnard into clearly discernible white and non-white social worlds. The tremendous influx of numerous agricultural workers quickly led to the development of segregated minority enclaves on the east side of town. The Mexican section of Oxnard, referred to as "Sonoratown," was settled by Mexican workers who migrated into the area seeking employment. Arriving in the early 1900s, the Mexican population was viewed by the Anglo population with disdain. The local newspaper, for example, disparagingly reported on the Mexican community's odd "feasting," "game playing," and "peculiar customs." Mexicans were seen as a "queer" people who could be tolerated so long as they kept to themselves.

Also segregated on the east side of town, adjacent to the Mexican colonia, was the "Chinatown" section of Oxnard. This segregated ethnic enclave was even more despised by the local Anglo population than "Sonoratown." Chinatown was described in the Oxnard *Courier* as consisting of numerous "measley, low, stinking and dirty huts with all kinds of pitfalls and dark alleys where murder can be committed in broad daylight without detection." Despite widespread anti-Oriental sentiment in the local community, the Asian population grew to an estimated 1,000 to 1,500 people in less than a decade after the founding of Oxnard.

Ventura County residents greatly disapproved of the impact that the minority population of Oxnard had on the social character of the county. Popular opinion blamed the minority population for all the detested vices (such as gambling, liquor, drugs, and prostitution) existing in Oxnard. One prominent Anglo pioneer described Oxnard at the time as a "very disreputable town," primarily inhabited by "riff raff" and "Mexicans." Corroborating this description, one visitor of Oxnard in 1901

From *Labor History*, vol. 25, no. 3 (summer, 1989), pp. 325–50. Reprinted with permission from *Labor History*. Footnotes have been deleted.

described the community as a "characteristic boom town," with "many saloons" and numerous "Mexicans and others loitering around."

Thus, two very different social worlds emerged in Oxnard during its early years. On the east side of town were the Mexican and Chinese enclaves, whose presence contributed to Oxnard reputedly having a "damning influence on her neighbors." The Anglo residents on the west side of town, in contrast, were comprised of "upstanding" German and Irish farmers and several Jewish families. "While the east side of town was a rip-roaring slum," according to one local historian, "the west side was listening to lecture courses, hearing WCTU [Women's Christian Temperance Union] speakers, having gay times at the skating rink in the opera house, [and] putting on minstrel shows . . ."

Underlying the segregated social worlds existing in Oxnard was the organization of the community along distinct racial and class lines. Along the class axis there existed a small class of large-scale entrepreneurs (such as the Oxnard brothers and the major growers); an intermediate stratum of farmers and independent merchants operating small-scale concerns; and a large working class comprised of skilled and unskilled wage workers tied to the local agricultural economy.

Closely parallelling this class structure was a racial stratification system that divided Oxnard into white and non-white spheres. The most obvious outward feature of this racial stratification was the residential segregation of the community. Also important, however, was the organization of the local labor market along racial lines. Anglo-Americans, for example, in the main comprised the upper class stratum of large-scale entrepreneurs and major agriculturalists. The 1900 federal manuscript census for Ventura County shows that nearly 95% of all farmers in the county were Anglo-American. In addition, white men completely monopolized the middle strata of the local class structure and held the best jobs in the low white-collar, skilled, and unskilled labor stratum. At the Oxnard sugar beet factory, for example, only Anglo-American men were employed as permanent staff. All of the major department heads, foremen, supervisors, office, and maintenance staff were white men. The only exception to this were the few white women employed as secretaries and stenographers.

The minority population in Oxnard, in contrast, were overwhelmingly employed as unskilled laborers and were the primary source of contracted farm labor in the area. Nearly 50%

of the Mexican and Japanese population and over 65% of the Chinese in the county were farm laborers in 1900. Another 18 to 33% of these groups were unskilled laborers in the same year.

Only a small segment of the minority population in the county were in the middle strata of the local occupational structure. The most important segment of this strata in Oxnard were the minority labor contractors. The existing racial and class stratification system in the county placed these contractors in a unique position. On the one hand, the class position of contractors resulted in their having class interests that conflicted with those of their working class compatriots. These contractors, for example, received a sizeable portion of the wages earned by those working under their supervision and thus benefitted directly from the exploitative contract labor system. At the same time, however, ties of ethnic solidarity led some labor contractors to protect their workers from abuses at the hands of unscrupulous farmers. In return for securing employment and receiving a portion of their workers' wages, labor contractors actively bargained to secure an equitable wage for their laborers and insure that they toiled under fair working conditions.

The existence of a racial-class stratification system that was not completely symmetrical had important consequences on the contending forces involved in the 1903 Oxnard strike. While racial status and class position were closely related, there did exist some fluidity in the stratification system. The particular location of minority labor contractors in the local class structure played a key role in the 1903 strike.

The development of the sugar beet industry in Ventura County led to a precipitous increase in the demand for seasonal farm laborers in Oxnard. Initially, sugar beet farmers in Oxnard relied upon Mexican and Chinese contracted laborers. The decline in the local Chinese population and the utilization of Mexicans in other sectors of agriculture, however, led to the recruitment of Japanese farm laborers to fill this labor shortage. Japanese farm laborers were first employed in the Oxnard sugar beet industry in 1899. By 1902 there were nine Japanese labor contractors meeting nearly all the seasonal need for farm laborers in the area.

In the spring of 1902, however, a number of prominent Jewish businessmen and bankers in Oxnard organized a new contracting company, the Western Agricultural Contracting Company (WACC). Among the first directors and principal organizers of the company were the presidents of the Bank of Oxnard and Bank of A. Levy, and two of the most important merchants in Oxnard. The major sugar refiner in the county, the American Beet Sugar Company, also played an instrumental role in supporting the formation of the WACC.

The initial purpose in forming the WACC was to provide local farmers with an alternative to the Japanese labor contractors in the area. Anglo farmers and the American Beet Sugar Company feared that these contractors would use their control of the local labor market to press for wage increases and improvements in working conditions. Under the leadership of Japanese contractors, Japanese farm laborers had already engaged in work slowdowns and strikes to secure concessions from Anglo farmers elsewhere in the state. Thus, Anglo businessmen formed the WACC in order to end reliance on Japanese labor contractors, stabilize the local sugar beet industry, reduce labor costs to local farmers, and provide a profitable return to investors. Since the businessmen and bankers behind the WACC already worked closely with local beet farmers, they easily secured contracts with them and quickly became the major suppliers of contracted labor in the area.

Undermining the position of Japanese labor contractors and gaining control of approximately 90% of the contracting business by February 1903, the WACC forced all minority labor contractors to subcontract through their company or go out of business. Through this arrangement, minority contractors and their employees were both forced to work on terms dictated by the WACC. The commission formerly received by minority contractors was reduced severely through this subcontracting arrangement and they could no longer negotiate wages directly with local farmers. The minority farm laborers employed on this basis also were affected negatively. In addition to paying a percentage of their wages to the minority contractor who directly supervised them, they also paid a fee to the WACC for its role in arranging employment. Furthermore, the WACC routinely required minority workers to accept store orders from its company-owned stores instead of cash payment for wages. Overcharging for merchandise at these stores was common.

To facilitate its operation, the WACC established two different divisions to supervise the recruitment and assignment of minority laborers. All the labor contractors and farm laborers employed by the WACC worked through these two major departments. The so-called "Jap department," located in the Chinatown section of Oxnard, was under the supervision of Inosuke Inose. Inose had formerly worked for the American Beet Sugar Company and had been one of the Japanese labor contractors in the area. Inose's association with the ABSC led to his selection as the head of the Japanese department. In addition to serving as department supervisor, Inose also managed the WACC's Japanese-American Mercantile Store. Supervising the WACC's Mexican department was Albert Espinosa. Little is known about Espinosa other than his being an experienced beet worker who had won the confidence of the WACC's directors.

Most of the Japanese farm laborers and labor contractors working in Oxnard were extremely dissatisfied with having to subcontract through the WACC. Mexican farm laborers in the area and the other numerous minority laborers recruited from other parts of the state also expressed displeasure with the new system. In direct response, a large group of disgruntled Japanese laborers and contractors organized a grievance meeting in Oxnard during the first week of February 1903. At this meeting a group of sixty Japanese contracted laborers recruited from San Francisco by Inosuke Inose complained bitterly about the operation of the WACC's Japanese department. The workers claimed that working conditions and wages promised by the WACC and Inose had not been meet. Instead of paying each worker a ten-hour-day's wage of $1.50, Inose gave them a piecework rate returning them considerably less. The workers thinned beets at $3.75 per acre instead of the prevailing piecework rate of $5.00 to $6.00 per acre.

The grievances of these disgruntled workers provided the key impetus for forming a union comprised of Japanese and Mexican farm workers and contractors in Oxnard. At a subsequent meeting held on February 11, 1903, approximately 800 Japanese and Mexican workers organized the Japanese-Mexican Labor Association, electing as officers Kosaburo Baba (president), Y. Yamaguchi (secretary of the Japanese branch), and J.M. Lizarras (secretary of the Mexican branch). Among the charter members of the JMLA were approximately 500 Japanese and 200 Mexican workers. The decision to form this union and challenge the WACC marked the first time the two minority groups successfully joined forces to organize an agricultural workers' union in the state. This was no minor achievement, as the JMLA's membership had to overcome formidable cultural and linguistic barriers. At their meetings, for example, all discussions were carried-out in both Spanish and Japanese, with English serving as a common medium of communication.

Although the JMLA was primarily a farm workers' union, it actually was composed of three distinct groups: labor contractors, contracted laborers, and boarding students who were only temporary workers. Japanese labor contractors and, to a lesser extent, boarding students provided the leadership for the new union. Kosaburo Baba, the union's president, was one of the labor contractors displaced by the WACC. It is also likely that J.M. Lizarras, the JMLA's Mexican secretary, was a labor contractor. The Japanese secretary of the union, Y. Yamaguchi, is identified in one Japanese-language source as a boarding student recruited from San Francisco.

Although it cannot be determined with certainty, it is likely that some of the Japanese leaders of the union, particularly the boarding students, were influenced by the Japanese Socialist Movement. This movement flourished in Japan after the Sino-Janapese War of 1894–95 and had a following among some of the Issei population who immigrated to California after that date. It is known, for example, that by 1904 there existed two Socialist groups among the Issei in California: one based in San Francisco and the other in Oakland. Originally organized as "discussion-study societies" these groups were led by prominent socialists such as Katayama Sen, who helped organize the short-lived San Francisco Japanese Socialist Party in February 1904.

The major purpose of the Japanese-Mexican Labor Association was to end the WACC's monopoly of the contract labor system in Oxnard. By eliminating the WACC's control, the JMLA sought to negotiate directly with local farmers and to secure better wages. Since the formation of the WACC, the prevailing rate of $5.00 to $6.00 per acre of beets thinned had been reduced to as low as $2.50 per acre. The new union wanted to return to the "old prices" paid for seasonal labor. By eliminating the WACC from the contracting business, the JMLA also sought to end the policy of enforced patronage. One of the WACC's company stores—the Japanese-American Mercantile Store—routinely overcharged for items by more than 60%. Japanese contracted laborers patronizing the store, for example, paid $1.20 for a $0.75 pair of work overalls.

In order to secure their demands the JMLA membership agreed to cease working through the WACC and their subcontractors. This decision was tantamount to call for a strike. In striking the JMLA threatened seriously the success of the local sugar beet crop because its profitability rested on the immediate completion of the thinning operation. This labor-intensive process required that workers carefully space beet seedlings and allow only the strongest beet plants to remain. Unlike the harvest, where timeliness was not as crucial, beet thinning required immediate attention in order to ensure a high-yield crop.

Although the JMLA was largely concerned with wages and the policy of enforced patronage, there is evidence that the leadership of the union saw their struggle in broad class terms. The reforms demanded by the union struck at the heart of the existing relationship between major capitalist interests in the county. Chief among these was that between the businessmen and bankers who owned the WACC, the American Beet Sugar Company, and the major sugar beet farmers in the area. All these special interests were benefitting from the exploitative use of the minority farm laborers working through the WACC. Although Anglos were primarily guilty of exploiting Japanese and Mexican laborers, individuals such as Inosuke Inose and those minority contractors still subcontracting through the WACC were also seen as adversaries. Thus, the JMLA did not simply define their struggle in racial terms. Eloquent testimony of the JMLA's position is captured vividly in one news release issued by the Japanese and Mexican secretaries of the union. In putting forth the union's demands, Y. Yamaguchi and J.M. Lizarras wrote:

> Many of us have families, were born in the country, and are lawfully seeking to protect the only property that we have—our labor. It is just as necessary for the welfare of the valley that we get a decent living wage, as it is that the machines in the great sugar factory be properly oiled—if the machines stop, the wealth of the valley stops, and likewise if the laborers are not given a decent wage, they too, must stop work and the whole people of this country suffer with them.

Reacting to the JMLA with hostility and mistrust, the Oxnard *Courier* posed the issue of the union's demands as "simply a question of whether the Japanese-Mexican laboring classes will control labor or whether it will be managed by conservative businessmen." There was no particular reason for local farmers to prefer dealing with the JMLA, the *Courier*'s editor asserted, when there existed "reliable American contractors" who could provide labor at lower costs. Furthermore, the editor continued, "if an organization of the ignorant, and for the most part alien, contract labor is allowed to over-power an American company, the farmers will find themselves in a state of dependence on irresponsible contractors." To support this claim, the editor noted that it was primarily a small number of Japanese and Mexican contractors who were "the real inspiration of the union."

In another editorial, the *Courier* contended that only a union "in the hands of intelligent white men" could provide the "enlightened management" needed to run such an organization and to provide the "mental and moral uplifting and material advancement" of the Japanese and Mexican laborers in Oxnard. The JMLA would not succeed, therefore, because it was essentially a minority union "in the hands of people whose experience has been only to obey a master rather than think and manage for themselves. . . ."

Reacting to the organization of the JMLA, the American Beet Sugar Company made clear that it would do everything in its power to insure that the new union did not disrupt the smooth operation of the sugar beet industry in Oxnard. It immediately informed the union that the company was fully in support of the WACC. In outlining the company's position, the manager of the American Beet Sugar Company, Colonel Driffil, stated to the union:

> I have heard that you have a scale of prices which is detrimental to the interests of the farmers, and the interests of the farmers are our interests, because if you raise the price of labor to the farmers and they see that they cannot raise beets at a profit, we will have to take steps to drive you out of the country and secure help from the outside—even if we have to spend $100,000 in doing so.

The only segment of the local Anglo population expressing any support for the JMLA were a few merchants in Oxnard. Their support of the minority union, however, was not based on humanitarian concerns. Instead, self-interest was the motivating factor. These merchants were anxious to see the WACC's enforced patronage policy ended so minority workers could freely patronize their businesses.

By the first week in March, the JMLA had successfully recruited a membership exceeding 1,200 workers or over 90% of the total beet workforce in the county. The JMLA's recruitment drive resulted in the WACC losing nearly all of the laborers it had formerly contracted. The growing strength of the JMLA greatly alarmed beet farmers in the area, for nothing

like the new union had been organized in Ventura County or, for that matter, anywhere else in southern California.

One of the first public displays of the JMLA's strength was exhibited at a mass demonstration and parade held in Oxnard on March 6, 1903. Describing the event, the Oxnard *Courier* reported that "dusky skinned Japanese and Mexicans marched through the streets headed by one or two contractors and beet laborers four abreast and several hundred strong." Although impressed by their numbers, the *Courier* described the JMLA's membership as "a silent grim band of fellows, most of them young and belonging to the lower class of Japanese and Mexicans."

Unwilling to allow this exhibition of strength to go unchallenged, the WACC initiated an effort to undercut the solidarity of the JMLA and regain its position as the major supplier of contracted labor in Oxnard. During the second and third week of March, the WACC helped form an alternative, minority-led union. In supporting the organization of the "Independent Agricultural Labor Union (IALU), the WACC sought to undercut the organizational successes of the JMLA and use the IALU to help regain its former dominance. The WACC believed it wiser to support a non-threatening, conservative union than face complete ruination at the hands of the JMLA.

Inosuke Inose of the WACC and "some of the most influential and best-educated of the Japanese residents of Oxnard" were among the initial board of directors of the IALU. The IALU described itself as a union striving "to secure and maintain harmonious relations between employers and employees of agricultural labor. . . ." Seeing this as its primary purpose, the IALU sought to defend its members from "any person or organization" preventing them to work "for wages and for such persons as shall be mutually satisfactory." Thus, the IALU's purpose was not to eliminate the abusive treatment of minority laborers but to help regain the stability of the sugar beet industry in the area.

Immediately after its formation, the IALU began working in conjuction with the WACC to meet the pressing labor needs of local farmers. These efforts were, of course, seen by the JMLA as a strikebreaking tactic. Describing the ensuing tension, one county newspaper reported that: "Oxnard is up against labor turmoil, and bloodspots are gathering on the face of the moon as it hovers over the sugartown. The Japanese-Mexican labor union has inspired an enmity and opposition that threatens to terminate in riot and bloodshed." This proved to be prophetic, as an outburst of violence occurred a few days after the IALU was organized.

Occurring on March 23, 1903 in the China-town section of Oxnard the violent confrontation was triggered when members of the JMLA attempted to place their union banner on a wagon loaded with IALU strikebreakers being taken to a ranch of a local farmer. The union's insignia consisted of a white banner with a red rising sun and pair of clasped hands. Superimposed over this insignia were the letters "J.M.L.A."

One newspaper described the ensuring confrontation in the following way: "[A] fusillade of shots was fired from all directions. They seemed to come from every window and door in Chinatown. The streets were filled with people, and the wonder is that only five persons were shot." When the shooting subsided, two Mexican and two Japanese members of the JMLA lay wounded from the erupting gunfire. Manuel Ramirez was shot in the leg and two Japanese workers were struck, one in the arm and the other in the face. Another Mexican, Luis Vasquez was dead, shot in the back.

Responsibility for the violent confrontation was placed on the JMLA. The Los Angeles *Times*, for example, reported that "agitation-crazed striking Mexicans and Japanese" had attacked "independent workmen" and precipitated a "pitched battle" in which dozens had been wounded and "thousands gone wild." The *Times* charged that "loud-mouthed and lawless union agitators" had directly triggered the violence. More specifically, it was the "trouble-making" Mexican leadership of the JMLA that had inflamed the "ignorant peons" into action and that "most of the firing was done by Mexicans." Even the Japanese laborers, seen as being "inclined to be peaceable," were "excited by their leaders" and fell victim to their exhortations "a good deal like sheep."

Although more restrained than the *Times*, the Oxnard *Courier* also blamed the union for precipitating the confrontation. The local weekly summed up the situation in the following way:

Naturally the riot and its causes have been a topic of general conversation on the streets [of Oxnard]. In most cases the union adherents are blamed for resorting to illegal and forceful methods to prevent men who are willing from working for the Western Agricultural Contracting Company. It is this that is primarily responsible for the riot. The attempt to

place a union label where it was not wanted is at the root of the disturbance, and in reality the union has only itself to blame for the riot. . . .

There was scarcely a newspaper account of the "riot" in Oxnard that did not blame the union for igniting the outburst. The only weekly that did not directly balme the JMLA was the Ventura *Independent.* This newspaper's editor, S. Goodman, argued that:

The root of the evil lies in the fact that ten men for every single job were shipped into the sugar beet territory [of Ventura County], bringing together a restless irresponsible element, only lacking in leadership to make all kinds of trouble. . . .

In the riot of Monday last, the Contracting Company is a measure at fault. Had someone of authority in the employment of the company, possessing a cool head, superintended the sending out of laborers, the restless element could have been subdued and all trouble averted.

Outraged over the biased coverage of the March 23rd confrontation the JMLA issued its own public statement. It was subsequently published in only two newspapers: the Los Angeles *Herald* and the Oxnard *Courier.* The newspaper that the JMLA was principally responding to, the Los Angeles *Times,* refused to publish the following release:

Owing to the many false statements printed in the Los Angeles *Times* about our organization, and the murderous assaults made upon the union men last Monday afternoon, we ask that the following statement of facts be printed, in justice to the thirteen hundred men whom the Japanese-Mexican Labor Association represents.

In the first place, we assert, and are ready to prove, that Monday afternoon and at all times during the shooting, the Union men are unarmed, while the nonunion men sent out by the Western Agricultural Contracting Company were prepared for a bloody fight with arms purchased, in many cases, recently from hardware stores in this town. As proof of the fact that the union men were not guilty of violence, we point to the fact that the authorities have not arrested a single union man— the only man actually put under bonds, or arrested, being deputy Constable Charles Arnold. Our union has always been law abiding and has in its ranks at least nine-tenths of all the beet thinners in this section, who have not asked for a raise in wages, but only that the wages be not lowered, as was demanded by the beet growers . . .

We assert that if the police authorities had done their duty, many arrests would have been made among the occupants of the company's house, from which the fatal volleys of bullets came. In view of the fact that many disorderly men have recently been induced to come to Oxnard by the Western Agricultural Contracting Company, and that they took part in the assaults of Monday afternoon, we demand that the police no longer neglect their duty, but arrest those persons who plainly participated in the fatal shooting.

Shortly after the shooting, Charles Arnold was arrested for the murder of Vasquez, and a coroner's inquest held to determine his guilt or innocence. The conflicting testimony of 50 eyewitnesses was heard at the inquest. A number of witnesses testified that Arnold did not shoot Vasquez and, in fact, that they had not even seen him raise a gun. One witness testified that an examination of Arnold's weapons after the shooting showed that they were fully loaded and had not been fired.

Testifying against Arnold were a number of Mexican witnesses claiming to have seen Arnold fire at JMLA members. Among these witnesses was Manuel Ramirez, a victim of the shooting, who testified that it was a Japanese strikebreaker in the WACC wagon who had shot him in the leg. Despite the evidence presented to the all male Anglo jury, it soon became apparent to JMLA members that Arnold would be cleared. At the close of the second day of hearings, for example, the county coroner notified the jury that another round of testimony was needed so that more Japanese witnesses could be heard. Angered by this request, the jury protested further continuation and stated that they were "prepared to render a verdict without further evidence." After a brief adjournment, the inquest reconvened and Arnold was cleared of any complicity in the death of Luis Vasquez.

Outraged at what they believed to be a gross miscarriage of justice, members of the JMLA stepped up their efforts to win the strike. Following the March 23rd confrontation, the union took the offensive and escalated militant organizing activities. In one incident, the Oxnard *Courier* reported that "a gang of 50 Mexicans, many of them masked, visited a contracting company camp on Chas. Donlon's ranch, cut the guy ropes of the tent and made the crew of some 18 men desert and come to town." A similar incident occurred at a labor camp on another local farmer's property near Oxnard.

Soon thereafter, Andres Garcia, the foreman on Charles Arnold's ranch, was fired upon and nearly killed by an unknown assailant. One county newspaper speculated that the assailant mistook Garcia for Arnold, the man originally charged with Luis Vasquez's murder. Since being cleared of the charge, Arnold had openly expressed opposition to the JMLA and hired nonunion laborers to work on his ranch.

In response to further strikebreaking efforts, the JMLA organized laborers being brought to Oxnard and succeeded in winning them over to the union's side. In doing so, the union stationed men at the nearby Montalvo railroad depot and met the newly recruited laborers as they arrived in the county. In one incident reported by the Ventura *Free Press,* a local rancher attempted to circumvent JMLA organizers by personally meeting incoming laborers and scurrying them off to his ranch. Before arriving at his ranch, however, the farmer was intercepted by a group of JMLA members who unloaded the strikebreakers and convinced them to join the union. In discussing the success of the JMLA in organizing potential strikebreakers, one county newspaper summarily noted that "by the time these men reached Oxnard they were on the side of the union and against the Western Agricultural Contracting Company."

The success of the JMLA in maintaining their strike led to a clearcut union victory. In the aftermath of the violent confrontation in Chinatown, representatives of local farmers, the WACC, and the JMLA met at the latter's headquarters in Oxnard to negotiate a strike settlement. Representing the farmers were Colonel Driffill (manager of the American Beet Sugar Company's Oxnard factory), T.H. Rice, P.S. Carr, Charles Donlon, and L. S. Rose. The WACC representative was the company's president, George E. Herz. The JMLA negotiating team was led by J. M. Lizarras, Kosaburo Baba, Y. Yamaguchi, J. Espinosa, and their counsel, W. E. Shepherd. Also representing the union were Fred C. Wheeler and John Murray, socialist union organizers affiliated with the Los Angeles County Council of Labor, the California State Federation of Labor, and the AFL.

J. M. Lizarras forcefully presented the JMLA's demands at the initial meeting. Insisting that the union wanted to bargain directly with local farmers, Lizarras threatened that the union would take all of their members out of the county, thereby ensuring the loss of the entire beet crop, if their demands were not met.

John Murray chastised farmers at this meeting for not quickly coming to terms with the JMLA. He impressed upon them that they should be thankful that the union was not striking for more than it was demanding. Fred Wheeler also addressed the assembly. In restating the JMLA's demands, he pointed out to local farmers that "you have the beets and we have the labor and want to work directly with you. We are members of the American Federation of Labor and are here to stay. It is bread and butter to us and we will deal directly with farmers." As will be seen, Wheeler's statement, giving farmers the impression that the JMLA was affiliated with the AFL, was premature.

The first sign of JMLA winning their strike occurred when the WACC partially acceded to the JMLA's demand to negotiate contracts directly with local farmers. The WACC offered the JMLA the right to provide labor on 2,000 of the 7,000 acres of farm land it had under contract. In return, the WACC requested that the JMLA order its men back to work and agree not to unionize men working for the WACC on the remaining farm land. This offer was flatly rejected by JMLA negotiators, who insisted that they would not end their strike until the WACC's monopoly was broken and all farmers agreed to contract directly with them. At one point in the negotiations the JMLA mockingly offered a proposal whereby each party would receive the right to provide labor to local farmers in proportion to the number of men they represented. Spokespersons for the JMLA noted that they represented 1,300 men while the WACC had only sixty men under contract. The union's strong showing at this initial session led one local county newspaper to report that the JMLA "showed a strong front, clearly demonstrating to the ranchers that they controlled the labor necessary to do their work, and without their services beet crops must perish."

On the second day of negotiations, Lizarras and Yamaguchi met with representatives of local farmers and the WACC at the American Beet Sugar Company factory in Oxnard. During this session the union firmly stood by its demand and gained the first important concession in the negotiations. It was an agreement from the farmer's committee to establish a minimum wage scale of $5.00, and a high of $6.00, per acre for the thinning of beets by union laborers. This was nearly double what the WACC was paying laborers before the strike.

On March 30, 1903, the tumultuous Oxnard sugar beet worker's strike ended with the JMLA winning a major victory. The agreement reached included a provision forcing the WACC to cancel all existing contracts with local sugar beet growers. The only exception to this was the 1,800 acre Patterson ranch, which was owned by the same family that operated the American Beet Sugar Company. This ranch remained the only

farm that the WACC would continue to provide labor. Thus, the final settlement meant that the WACC relinquished the right to provide labor to farmers owning over 5,000 acres of county farm land.

The success of the Oxnard Strike of 1903 raised a number of important issues for the labor movement. For years, trade unions were opposed to organizing minorities in industry and were even less interested in organizing agricultural workers. The JMLA's victory, however, forced the union movement to confront the issue of including agricultural workers in their ranks. It also forced white unions to clearly articulate their position on the organization of Japanese and Mexican workers.

The issue of admitting Mexicans and Japanese workers to the trade union movement became an important issue in both northern and southern California after the JMLA victory. In reporting local union discussion on whether or not to organize Asian workers in Oakland, the Oakland *Tribune,* for example, noted that the "recent strike of about 1,000 Japs and Mexicans at Oxnard against starvation wages and hard-treatment has brought the matter to the front."

The official attitude of organized labor toward the JMLA was, from the very beginning, mixed and often contradictory. Certain local councils, for example, supported the JMLA and further organizing of Japanese and Mexican workers. This tendency, led by prominent union socialists, also supported organizing all agricultural workers and including farm labor unions in the AFL. Most union councils and high-ranking AFL officials were, on the other hand, opposed to any formal affiliation with the JMLA. This position was based, in part, on organized labor's anti-Asian sentiment and its general opposition to organizing agricultural laborers.

Despite union opposition to minority labor and agricultural worker's unions, Fred C. Wheeler and John Murray convinced the Los Angeles County Council of Labor (LACCL) to adopt a resolution favoring the unionization of all unskilled laborers regardless of race or nationality. Shortly after the March 23rd confrontation in Oxnard, the LACCL unanimously adopted a resolution supporting the JMLA. This resolution, the San Francisco *Examiner* noted, represented "the first time that a labor council had put itself on record as in any way favoring Asiatic labor."

Although the LACCL's resolution supported organizing minority workers already in the United States, it also reaffirmed the local's staunch opposition to further Asian immigration. Thus, an important element of self-interest played a role in the LACCL's decision to support the JMLA. The LACCL's resolution expressed the contradictory views of the radical elements of the trade union movement concerning the organization of Japanese workers. Behind its public support of the JMLA, the LACCL acknowledged that Japanese and Mexican workers could successfully organize on their own and, therefore it was in the interest of the trade union movement to include them in their ranks. Additionally, if left unorganized, these racial minority workers could become strikebreakers and pose a serious threat to the white labor movement in southern California.

That self-interest played a key role in the passage of this resolution was later acknowledged by P.B. Preble, secretary of the Oakland Federated Trades Council and a high-ranking member of the AFL. In a candid interview with the Oakland *Tribune,* Preble discussed the LACCL resolution in the following terms:

> This is one of the most important resolutions ever brought to the attention of the [AFL] Executive Council. It virtually breaks the ice on the question of forming Orientals into unions so keeping them from 'scabbing' on the white people. . . .
>
> Down there [southern California] the white workingmen have been plumb up against it from Japs and Mexicans who were being imported wholesale. . . . Down there, the Union has succeeded in putting this important company out of business, and the men are now selling their labor at the Union scale, without any cutting by middle men being done.

The message was clear. The success of the JMLA forced the white trade union movement to either include or specifically exclude Mexican and Japanese workers from their ranks. In Preble's words, it became an issue only "when the forces of circumstances demands it."

While left elements in the trade union movement supported the JMLA, labor's principal organization—the AFL—was essentially hostile. Although the AFL convention of 1894 formally declared that "working people must unite to organize irrespective of creed, color, sex, nationality or politics," the reaction of the Federation leadership to the JMLA belied this stated purpose. Following the JMLA victory in March 1903, J. M. Lizarras—Secretary of the Mexican branch of the union—petitioned the AFL Executive Council for a charter making the JMLA the first agricultural laborers' union to be admitted into the AFL.

Upon receiving the JMLA's petition, which was submitted under the name of Sugar Beet and Farm Laborers' Union of Oxnard, Samuel Gompers granted the union a charter but stipulated a prohibition on Asian membership. In his letter notifying Lizarras of his decision, Gompers emphasized that:

> It is . . . understood that in issuing this charter to your union, will under no circumstance accept membership of any Chinese or Japanese. The laws of our country prohibit Chinese workmen or laborers from entering the United States, and propositions for the extension of the exclusion laws to the Japanese have been made on several occasions.

Evidence suggests that the San Francisco Council of Labor contacted Gompers and expressed their vehement opposition to the JMLA's request for a charter. Although the LACCL publicly supported the JMLA, the prevailing union movement's opposition to Asian labor, which Gompers shared, undoubtedly influenced this decision.

Left elements in the AFL reacted bitterly to Gompers' decision. In discussing the AFL's refusal to grant the requested charter, the *American Labor Union Journal* from Chicago charged that Gompers had "violated the express principles of the A.F. of L." and that it would "be impossible, so long as this ruling is sustained, to organize wage workers of California . . . for there are between forty and fifty thousand Japanese in this state, and nothing can be effectively done without their cooperation." Despite the objections of a few locals and councils, there is little evidence to suggest that most unions expressed anything but tacit approval of Gompers' decision.

Gompers' refusal to grant on AFL charter allowing Japanese membership was vehemently denounced by the Mexican branch of the JMLA. Outraged at Gomper's action, the Mexican membership of the union directed Lizarras to write Gompers what is undoubtedly the strongest testimony of the solidarity reached between the Mexican and Japanese farm workers of Oxnard. On June 8, 1903, Lizarras returned the issued charter to Samuel Gompers with the following letter:

> Your letter . . . in which you say the admission with us of the Japanese Sugar Beet and Farm Laborers into the American Federation of Labor can not be considered, is received. We beg to say in reply that our Japanese brother here were the first to recognize the importance of cooperating and uniting in demanding a fair wage scale . . .
>
> They were not only just with us, but they were generous when one of our men was murdered by

hired assassins of the oppressor of labor, they gave expression to their sympathy in a very substantial form. In the past we have counseled, fought and lived on very short rations with our Japanese brothers, and toiled with them in the fields, and they have been uniformly kind and considerate. We would be false to them and to ourselves and to the cause of unionism if we now accepted privileges for ourselves which are not accorded to them. We are going to stand by men who stood by us in the long, hard fight which ended in a victory over the enemy. We therefore respectfully petition the A.F. of L. to grant us a charter under which we can unite all the sugar beet and field laborers in Oxnard, without regard to their color or race. We will refuse any other kind of charter, except one which will wipe out race prejudices and recognize our fellow workers as being as good as ourselves. I am ordered by the Mexican union to write this letter to you and they fully approve its words.

In refusing to join the AFL without the Japanese branch of the union, the JMLA ultimately closed the door to any hopes of continuing its union activities in Oxnard. The AFL decision not to admit all members of the JMLA undoubtedly contributed to the union eventually passing out of existence. A systematic review of newspaper accounts of labor activities in Ventura County through 1910 failed to uncover further mention of the JMLA after its success in April 1903. No other evidence could be found concerning further JMLA activities or the exact date that the union ceased to exist. What appears to have happened is that the union continued operating for a few years and eventually disbanded. By 1906 there existed further discontent on the part of sugar beet workers in Oxnard, but no mention is made of the JMLA.

For years after the Oxnard strike, AFL hostility towards organizing Japanese workers and farm laborers persisted. Not until 1910 did the AFL Executive Council attempt to organize farm workers as an element of the Federation. These efforts, however, accomplished very little. According to one authority, the AFL's activities after 1910 were explicitly "designed to favor white workers at the expense of Orientals." Finally, during the war years, the Federation's efforts to organize farm laborers were abandoned altogether.

Beyond its significance for labor history, the Oxnard sugar beet workers' strike also has sociological importance. The strike, for example, provides us with important clues into the nature of class and race relations in California at the turn of the century. As in other parts of the state, the capitalist economy emerging in

Oxnard gave birth to a class structure in which racial divisions closely paralleled class divisions. The overrepresentation of Mexican and Japanese as contracted farm laborers and unskilled workers, and of Anglo-Americans as farmers and businessmen in Oxnard reveals the important convergence of racial and class stratification lines during this period. The class structure in Oxnard was not, however, a static one that approximated a caste system. Instead, a modicum of fluidity existed and some minorities successfully made inroads into the middle strata of the local class structure. Among the most important members of this stratum in Oxnard were the numerous minority labor contractors who served an intermediary function in the procurement of farm labor. Labor contractors were both the benefactors and exploiters of the men who worked under their direction. The peculiar position of these contractors in the minority community undoubtedly contributed to their playing a leadership role in the formation of the JMLA.

In the final analysis, it was the displacement of these minority contractors by local Anglo elites that led to the unification of minority contractors and farm laborers in a common cause. An alliance based on ethnic solidarity and common, short-term interests provided the impetus in forming the JMLA and overcoming the existing differences in the class position of minority labor contractors and farm laborers. Whether the JMLA merely wanted to return to the state in which minority contractors provided labor for local farmers or whether they truly sought to operate as a traditional union can not be determined with certainty. The paucity of available information on the JMLA after the strike makes it impossible to know the extent to which the JMLA actually functioned as a union or if it merely became an instrument used by minority contractors to regain their dominance of the local market. Regardless of the motives of the various elements in the JMLA or which of many forms the union took after the strike, it appears that local agribusiness elites ultimately regained the upper hand and made it impossible for the JMLA to continue to function. Whether internal divisions between farm workers and labor contractors within the JMLA played a role in its demise is not known. In any event, the unique class alliance and bonds of ethnic solidarity that underlied the JMLA proved to be short-lived.

The experience of the JMLA with organized labor at the time also clearly reveals differences in the racial attitudes of Anglo-Americans.

Mexicans and Japanese workers were not perceived as posing the same threat to the white working class. Differences between these two groups in racial and political-legal status, religion, language, and previous competition with white labor, shaped the way that the AFL reacted to the JMLA's petition for a Federation charter. Gompers' attitude toward the Japanese branch of the JMLA clearly illustrated that white racism at the time was not a monolithic structure that affected all minority groups in precisely the same way. Instead, important differences existed in the way Anglo Americans viewed and discriminated against different minority groups.

Anglo-American attitudes toward the Japanese were essentially an extension of their earlier view of the Chinese. Like the Chinese, the Japanese were seen as a direct threat to the jobs, wages, and working conditions of white labor. Furthermore, the non-white, alien status of the Japanese also contributed to their being seen as a threat to the preservation of the white race and American cultural standards and ideals.

Mexican workers, on the other hand, were not perceived at the time as posing the same threat to white labor. A number of factors account for this important difference. Foremost among these was the legal status of Mexicans as U.S. citizens and their racial status as a "white" population. The Treaty of Guadalupe Hidalgo in 1848 had extended all U.S. citizenship rights to Mexicans and socially defined them as "free white persons." Also important in mitigating Anglo racism toward Mexicans was the latters' perceived assimilability. Unlike Asians, who were viewed as uncivilized "pagan idolators," Mexicans were viewed as a Christian population

possessing a culture that was not as completely foreign as that of the Asian groups. In addition, economic factors tempered anti-Mexican sentiment at this time. The late entry of Mexicans into the capitalist labor market in California resulted in their not openly competing with Anglo workers for jobs. Additionally, Mexicans were concentrated largely in the rural backwaters of southern California, away from the urban manufacturing centers where white working class opposition to minority laborers emerged first. Finally, the Mexican population was relatively small. There were, for example, fewer Mexicans than Japanese in California at the time of the Oxnard strike. All of these factors contributed directly to the existing differences in Anglo attitudes toward the Mexican and Japanese population.

The Oxnard strike vividly captured these differences in racial attitudes. Anglo reaction toward these two groups in Oxnard and Samuel Gompers reaction to the JMLA request for an AFL charter provide clear examples of this. In both cases, reaction to the Japanese was more vehement and hostile than that toward the Mexican. Further Mexican immigration and direct competition with Anglos in later years would, however, lead to an anti-Mexican sentiment that was just as intensely racist as that against the Japanese in 1903. Thus, racism must be viewed in historical terms as a form of group domination that is shaped by the interaction of social, political, economic and demographic factors. It was the unique interplay of these factors in California at the turn of the century that accounts for the different reaction of Anglos to the Japanese and Mexican membership of the JMLA.

# A Theory of Ethnic Antagonism:
# The Split Labor Market

EDNA BONACICH

Societies vary considerably in their degree of ethnic and racial antagonism. Such territories as Brazil, Mexico, and Hawaii are generally acknowledged to be relatively low on this dimension; while South Africa, Australia, and the United States are considered especially high. Literally hundreds of variables have been adduced to account for these differences, ranging from religions of dominant groups, to whether the groups who migrate are dominant or subordinate, to degrees of difference in skin color, to an irreducible "tradition" of ethnocentrism. While some writers have attempted to synthesize or systematize some subset of these, one is generally struck by the absence of a developed theory accounting for variations in ethnic antagonism.

One approach to this problem is to consider an apparent anomaly, namely that ethnic antagonism has taken two major, seemingly antithetical forms: exclusion movements, and so-called caste systems. An example of the former is the "white Australia" policy; while South Africa's color bar illustrates the latter. The United States has shown both forms, with a racial caste system in the South and exclusion of Asian and "new" immigrants from the Pacific and eastern seaboards respectively. Apart from manifesting antagonism between ethnic elements, exclusion and caste seem to have little in common. In the one, an effort is made to prevent an ethnically different group from being part of the society. In the other, an ethnically different group is essential to the society: it is an exploited class supporting the entire edifice. The deep south felt it could not survive without its black people; the Pacific coast could not survive with its Japanese. This puzzle may be used as a touchstone for solving the general problem of ethnic

antagonism, for to be adequate a theory must be able to explain it.

The theory presented here is, in part, a synthesis of some of the ideas used by Oliver Cox to explain the Japanese-white conflict on the U.S. Pacific coast, and by Marvin Harris to analyze the difference between Brazil and the deep south in rigidity of the "color line." It stresses the role of a certain kind of economic competition in the development of ethnic antagonism. Economic factors have, of course, not gone unnoticed, though until recently sociological literature has tended to point them out briefly, then move on to more "irrational" factors. A resurgence of Marxian analysis has thrust economic considerations to the fore, but I shall argue that even this approach cannot adequately deal with the problem posed by exclusion movements and caste systems. In addition, both Marxist and non-Marxist writers assume that racial and cultural differences in themselves prompt the development of ethnic antagonism. This theory challenges that assumption, suggesting that economic processes are more fundamental.

No effort is made to prove the accuracy of the following model. Such proof depends on a lengthier exposition. Historical illustrations are presented to support it.

## ETHNIC ANTAGONISM

"Ethnic" rather than "racial" antagonism was selected as the dependent variable because the former is seen to subsume the latter. Both terms refer to groups defined socially as sharing a common ancestry in which membership is there-

From Edna Bonacich, "A Theory of Ethnic Antagonism: The Split Labor Market," *American Sociological Review* 37, no. 5 (October 1972): pp. 547–59. Copyright © 1972 by the American Sociological Association. Reprinted by permission of the American Sociological Association. Footnotes have been deleted.

fore inherited or ascribed, whether or not members are currently physically or culturally distinctive. The difference between race and ethnicity lies in the size of the locale from which a group stems, races generally coming from continents, and ethnicities from national subsections of continents. In the past the term "race" has been used to refer to both levels, but general usage today has reversed this practice. Ethnicity has become the generic term.

Another reason for choosing this term is that exclusion attempts and caste-like arrangements are found among national groupings within a racial category. For example, in 1924 whites (Europeans) attempted to exclude whites of different national backgrounds from the United States by setting up stringent immigration quotas.

The term "antagonism" is intended to encompass all levels of intergroup conflict, including ideologies and beliefs (such as racism and prejudice), behaviors (such as discrimination, lynchings, riots), and institutions (such as laws perpetuating segregation). Exclusion movements and caste systems may be seen as the culmination of many pronouncements, actions, and enactments, and are continuously supported by more of the same. "Antagonism" was chosen over terms like prejudice and discrimination because it carries fewer moralistic and theoretical assumptions. For example, both of these terms see conflict as emanating primarily from one side: the dominant group. Antagonism allows for the possibility that conflict is mutual; i.e. a product of interaction.

## THE SPLIT LABOR MARKET

The central hypothesis is that ethnic antagonism first germinates in a labor market split along ethnic lines. To be split, a labor market must contain at least two groups of workers whose price of labor differs for the same work, or would differ if they did the same work. The concept "price of labor" refers to labor's total cost to the employer, including not only wages, but the cost of recruitment, transportation, room and board, education, health care (if the employer must bear these), and the costs of labor unrest. The degree of worker "freedom" does not interfere with this calculus; the cost of a slave can be estimated in the same monetary units as that of a wage earner, from his purchase price, living expenses, policing requirements, and so on.

The price of a group of workers can be roughly calculated in advance and comparisons made even though two groups are not engaged in the same activity at the same time. Thus in 1841 in the colony of New South Wales, the Legislative Council's Committee on Immigration estimated the relative costs of recruiting three groups of laborers to become shepherds. Table 1 shows their findings. The estimate of free white labor, for example, was based on what it would take to attract these men from competing activities.

## FACTORS AFFECTING THE INITIAL PRICE OF LABOR

Labor markets that are split by the entrance of a new group develop a dynamic which may in turn affect the price of labor. One must therefore distinguish initial from later price determinants. The initial factors can be divided into two broad categories: resources and motives.

Table 1. Estimated Cost of Three Types of Labor to Be Shepherds in New South Wales, 1841

|  | Free Man (White) | | | Prisoner (White) | | | Coolie (Indian) | | |
|---|---|---|---|---|---|---|---|---|---|
|  | £ | s. | d. | £ | s. | d. | £ | s. | d. |
| Rations | 16 | 18 | 0 | 13 | 14 | 4 | 9 | 6 | 4 |
| Clothing | — | — | — | 3 | 3 | 0 | 1 | 1 | 8 |
| Wages | 25 | 0 | 0 | — | — | — | 6 | 0 | 0 |
| Passage from India | — | — | — | — | — | — | 2 | 0 | 0 |
| Total per Annum | 41 | 18 | 0 | 16 | 17 | 4 | 18 | 8 | 0 |

## Resources

Three types of resources are important price determinants. These are:

*Level of Living, or Economic Resources.* The ethnic groups forming the labor market in a contact situation derive from different economic systems, either abroad or within a conquered territory. For members of an ethnic group to be drawn into moving, they must at least raise their wage level. In general, the poorer the economy of the recruits, the less the inducement needed for them to enter the new labor market. Crushing poverty may drive them to sell their labor relatively cheaply. For example, Lind describes the effect of the living level on the wage scale received by immigrant workers to Hawaii:

> In every case [of labor importations] the superior opportunities for gaining a livelihood have been broadcast in regions of surplus manpower, transportation facilities have been provided, and finally a monetary return larger than that already received has been offered to the prospective laborer. The monetary inducement has varied considerably, chiefly according to the plane of living of the population being recruited, and the cheapest available labor markets have, of course, been most extensively drawn upon.

Workers need not accept the original wage agreement for long after they have immigrated, since other opportunities may exist; for instance, there may be ample, cheap land available for individual farming. One capitalist device for keeping wages low at least for a time is to bind immigrants to contracts before they leave the old economy. The Indian indenture system, for example, rested on such an arrangement.

*Information.* Immigrants may be pushed into signing contracts out of ignorance. They may agree to a specific wage in their homeland not knowing the prevailing wage in the new country, or having been beguiled by a false account of life and opportunity there. Williams, for example, describes some of the false promises made to draw British and Germans as workers to West Indian sugar plantations before the advent of African slavery. Chinese labor to Australia was similarly "obtained under 'false and specious pretences.' "

The possibilities for defrauding a population lacking access to the truth are obvious. In general, the more people know about conditions obtaining in the labor market to which they are moving, the better they can protect themselves against disadvantageous wage agreements.

*Political Resources.* By political resources I mean the benefits to a group of organizing. Organization can exist at the level of labor, or it can occur at higher levels, for example, in a government that protects them. These levels are generally related in that a strong government can help organize its immigrants. There are exceptions, however: strong emigrant governments tend not to extend protection to their deported convicts or political exiles; and some highly organized groups, like the Jews in the United States, have not received protection from the old country.

Governments vary in the degree to which they protect their emigrants. Japan kept close watch over the fate of her nationals who migrated to Hawaii and the Pacific coast; and the British colonial government in India tried to guard against abuses of the indenture system (for example, by refusing to permit Natal to import Indian workers for their sugar plantations until satisfactory terms had been agreed to). In contrast Mexican migrant workers to the United States have received little protection from their government, and African states were unable to intervene on behalf of slaves brought to America. Often the indigenous populations of colonized territories have been politically weak following conquest. Thus African nations in South Africa have been unable to protect their migrant workers in the cities.

In general, the weaker a group politically, the more vulnerable it is to the use of force, hence to an unfavorable wage bargain (or to no wage bargain at all, as with slavery). The price of a labor group varies inversely with the amount of force that can be used against it, which in turn depends on its political resources.

## Motives

Two motives affect the price of labor, both related to the worker's intention of not remaining permanently in the labor force. Temporary workers tend to cost less than permanent workers for two reasons. First, they are more willing to put up with undesirable work conditions since these need not be endured forever. If they are migrants, this tolerance may extend to the general standard of living. Often migrant temporary workers are males who have left the comforts of home behind and whose employers need not bear the cost of housing and educating their families. Even when families accompany them, such workers tend to be willing to accept a lower standard of living since it is only short term.

Second, temporary workers avoid involvement in lengthy labor disputes. Since they will be in the labor market a short while, their main concern is immediate employment. They may be willing to undercut wage standards if need be to get a job, and are therefore ripe candidates for strikebreaking. Permanent workers also stand to lose from lengthy conflict, but they hope for benefits to their progeny. If temporary workers are from elsewhere, they have no such interest in future business-labor relations. Altogether, temporary workers have little reason to join the organizations and unions of a permanent work force, and tend not to do so.

*Fixed or Supplementary Income Goal.* Some temporary workers enter the market either to supplement family income, or to work toward a specific purchase. The worker's standard of living does not, therefore, depend on his earnings on the job in question, since his central source of employment or income lies elsewhere. Examples of this phenomenon are to be found throughout Africa:

> . . . the characteristic feature of the labor market in most of Africa has always been the massive circulation of Africans between their villages and paid employment outside. In some places villagers engage in wage-earning seasonally. More commonly today they work for continuous though short-term periods of roughly one to three years, after which they return to the villages. . . . the African villager, the potential migrant into paid employment, has a relatively low, clearly-defined and rigid income goal; he wants money to pay head and hut taxes, to make marriage payments required of prospective bridegrooms, or to purchase some specific consumer durable (a bicycle, a rifle, a sewing machine, a given quantity of clothing or textiles, etc.).

Such a motive produces the "backward-sloping labor supply function" characteristic of many native peoples in colonized territories. In addition to the general depressing effects on wages of being temporary, this motive leads to a fairly rapid turnover in personnel, making organization more difficult and hindering the development of valuable skills which could be used for bargaining. If wages were to rise, workers would reach their desired income and withdraw more quickly from the market, thereby lessening their chances of developing

the political resources necessary to raise their wages further.

*Fortune Seeking.* Many groups, commonly called sojourners, migrate long distances to seek their fortune, with the ultimate intention of improving their position in their homeland. Such was the case with Japanese immigrants in the west coast and Italian immigrants on the east. Such workers stay longer in the labor market, and can develop political resources. However, since they are temporary they have little incentive to join the organizations of the settled population. Instead they tend to create competing organizations composed of people who will play a part in their future in the homeland, i.e. members of the same ethnic group.

Sojourner laborers have at least three features which affect the price of labor: lower wages, longer hours, and convenience to the employer. The Japanese show all three. Millis cites the U.S. Immigration Commission on the question of relative wages:

> The Japanese have usually worked for a lower wage than the members of any other race save the Chinese and the Mexican. In the salmon canneries the Chinese have been paid higher wages than the Japanese engaged in the same occupations. In the lumber industry, all races, including the East Indian, have been paid higher wages than the Japanese doing the same kind of work. As section hands and laborers in railway shops they have been paid as much or more than the Mexicans, but as a rule less than the white men of many races.

And so on. The lower wage level of Japanese workers reflects both a lower standard of living, and a desire to get a foothold in the labor market. As Iwata puts it: "Their willingness to accept even lower wages than laborers of other races enabled the Japanese to secure employment readily."

Millis describes a basket factory in Florin, California, where Japanese workers had displaced white female workers because the latter were unwilling to work more than ten hours a day or on weekends. The Japanese, anxious to return to Japan as quickly as possible, were willing to work twelve to fourteen hours per day and on weekends, thereby saving their employers the costs of a special overtime work force.

The Japanese immigrants developed political resources through a high degree of community organization. This could be used for the convenience of the employer, by solving his recruitment problems, seeing that work got done, and providing workers with board and lodging. In the case of seasonal labor, the Japanese community could provide for members during the off-season by various boarding arrangements and clubs, and by transporting labor to areas of demand. These conveniences saved the employer money.

As the reader may have noted, I have omitted a factor usually considered vital in determining the price of labor, i.e. differences in skills. I would contend, however, that this does not in itself lead to that difference in price for the same work which distinguishes a split labor market. While a skilled worker may be able to get a higher paying job, an unskilled laborer of another ethnicity may be trained to fill that job for the same wage. Skills are only indirectly important in that they can be used to develop political resources, which in turn may lead to a difference in wage level for the same work.

## PRICE OF LABOR AND ETHNICITY

Ethnic differences need not always produce a price differential. Thus, if several ethnic groups who are approximately equal in resources and/or goals enter the same economic system, a split labor market will not develop. Alternatively, in a two-group contact system, if one ethnic group occupies the position of a business elite and has no members in the labor force (or in a class that could easily be pushed into the labor force, e.g. low-capital farmers) then regardless of the other group's price, the labor market will not be split. This statement is a generalization of the point made by Harris that the critical difference in race relations between the deep south and Brazil was that the former had a white yeomanry in direct competition with ex-slaves, while the Portuguese only occupied the role of a business elite (plantation owners).

Conversely, a split labor force does not only stem from ethnic differences. For example, prison and female labor have often been cheaper than free male labor in western societies. Prison labor has been cheap because prisoners lack political resources, while women often labor for supplementary incomes.

That initial price discrepancies in labor should ever fall along ethnic lines is a function of two forces. First, the original wage agreement arrived at between business and new labor often takes place in the labor group's point of origin. This is more obviously a feature of immigrant labor, but also occurs within a territory when conquered peoples enter their

conquerors' economy. In other words, the wage agreement is often concluded within a national context, these nationalities coming to comprise the ethnic elements of the new labor market. One would thus expect the initial wages of co-nationals to be similar.

Second, nations or peoples that have lived relatively separately from one another are likely to have developed different employment motives and levels of resources (wealth, organization, communication channels). In other words, the factors that affect the price of labor are likely to differ grossly between nations, even though there may be considerable variation within each nation, and overlap between nations. Color differences in the initial price of labor only seem to be a factor because resources have historically been roughly correlated with color around the world. When color and resources are not correlated in the "expected" way, then I would predict that price follows resources and motives rather than color.

In sum, the prejudices of business do not determine the price of labor, darker skinned or culturally different persons being paid less because of them. Rather, business tries to pay as little as possible for labor, regardless of ethnicity, and is held in check by the resources and motives of labor groups. Since these often vary by ethnicity, it is common to find ethnically split labor markets.

## THE DYNAMICS OF SPLIT LABOR MARKETS

In split labor markets, conflict develops between three key classes: business, higher paid labor, and cheaper labor. The chief interests of these classes are as follows:

### Business or Employers

This class aims at having as cheap and docile a labor force as possible to compete effectively with other businesses. If labor costs are too high (owing to such price determinants as unions), employers may turn to cheaper sources, importing overseas groups or using indigenous conquered populations. In the colony of Queensland in Australia, for example, it was believed that cotton farming would be the most suitable economic enterprise:

> However, such plantations (being too large) could not be worked, much less cleared, by their owners;

neither could the work be done by European laborers because sufficient numbers of these were not available—while even had there been an adequate supply, the high rates of wages would have been prohibitive. This was a consideration which assumed vast importance when it was realized that cotton would have to be cultivated in Queensland at a considerably lower cost than in the United States in order to compensate for the heavier freights from Queensland—the more distant country from England. It seemed then that there was no possibility of successful competition with America unless the importation of some form of cheap labor was permitted.

Cheaper labor may be used to create a new industry having substantially lower labor costs than the rest of the labor market, as in Queensland. Or they may be used as strike-breakers or replacements to undercut a labor force trying to improve its bargaining position with business. If cheap labor is unavailable, business may turn to mechanization, or try to relocate firms in areas of the world where the price of labor is lower.

## Higher Paid Labor

This class is very threatened by the introduction of cheaper labor into the market, fearing that it will either force them to leave the territory or reduce them to its level. If the labor market is split ethnically, the class antagonism takes the form of ethnic antagonism. It is my contention that, while much rhetoric of ethnic antagonism concentrates on ethnicity and race, it really in large measure (though probably not entirely) expresses this class conflict.

The group comprising higher paid labor may have two components. First, it may include current employees demanding a greater share of the profits or trying to maintain their position in the face of possible cuts. A second element is the small, independent entrepreneur, like the subsistence farmer or individual miner. The introduction of cheaper labor into these peoples' line can undermine their position, since the employer of cheap labor can produce at lower cost. The independent operator is then driven into the labor market. The following sequence occurs in many colonies: settlement by farmers who work their own land, the introduction of intensive farming using cheaper labor, a rise in land value and a consequent displacement of independent farmers. The displaced class may move on (as occurred in much of the West Indies when African slave labor was

introduced to raise sugar), but if it remains, it comes to play the role of higher paid labor.

The presence of cheaper labor in areas of the economy where higher paid labor is not currently employed is also threatening to the latter, since the former attracts older industries. The importance of potential competition cannot be overstressed. Oftentimes writers assert the irrationality of ethnic antagonism when direct economic competition is not yet in evidence owing to few competitors having entered the labor market, or to competitors having concentrated in a few industries. Thus Daniels belittles the role of trade unions in the Asiatic Exclusion League by describing one of the major contributors as "an organization whose members, like most trade unionists in California, were never faced with job competition from Japanese." It does not take direct competition for members of a higher priced labor group to see the possible threat to their well-being, and to try to prevent its materializing. If they have reason to believe many more low-priced workers are likely to follow an initial "insignificant trickle," or if they see a large concentration of cheaper labor in a few industries which could easily be used to undercut them in their own, they will attempt to forestall undercutting.

Lest you think this fear misguided, take note that, when business could override the interests of more expensive labor, the latter have indeed been displaced or undercut. In British Guiana the local labor force, composed mainly of African ex-slaves, called a series of strikes in 1842 and 1847 against planters' attempts to reduce their wages. Plantation owners responded by using public funds to import over 50,000 cheaper East Indian indentured workers. A similar situation obtained in Mississippi, where Chinese were brought in to undercut freed blacks. Loewen describes the thinking of the white landowners: "the 'Chinaman' would not only himself supply a cheaper and less troublesome work force but in addition his presence as a threatening alternative would intimidate the Negro into resuming his former docile behavior." Such displacement has occurred not only to non-white more expensive labor, but, as the effects of slavery in the West Indies show, to whites by white capitalists.

## Cheaper Labor

The employer uses this class partly to undermine the position of more expensive labor, through strikebreaking and undercutting. The forces that make the cheaper group cost less permit this to occur. In other words, either they lack the resources to resist an offer or use of force by business, or they seek a quick return to another economic and social base.

With the possible exception of sojourners, cheaper labor does not intentionally undermine more expensive labor; it is paradoxically its weakness that makes it so threatening, for business can more thoroughly control it. Cox makes this point in analyzing why Pacific coast white and Asian workers could not unite in a coalition against business:

> . . . the first generation of Asiatic workers is ordinarily very much under the control of labor contractors and employers, hence it is easier for the employer to frustrate any plans for their organization. Clearly this cultural bar helped antagonize white workers against the Asiatics. The latter were conceived of as being in alliance with the employer. It would probably have taken two or three generations before, say, the East Indian low-caste worker on the Coast became sufficiently Americanized to adjust easily to the policies and aims of organized labor.

Ethnic antagonism is specifically produced by the competition that arises from a price differential. An oversupply of equal-priced labor does not produce such antagonism, though it too threatens people with the loss of their job. However, hiring practices will not necessarily fall along ethnic lines, there being no advantage to the employer in hiring workers of one or another ethnicity. All workingmen are on the same footing, competing for scarce jobs. When one ethnic group is decidedly cheaper than another (i.e. when the labor market is split) the higher paid worker faces more than the loss of his job; he faces the possibility that the wage standard in all jobs will be undermined by cheaper labor.

## VICTORY FOR MORE EXPENSIVE LABOR

If an expensive labor group is strong enough (strength generally depending on the same factors that influence price), they may be able to resist being displaced. Both exclusion and caste systems represent such victories for higher paid labor.

### Exclusion

Exclusion movements generally occur when the majority of a cheaper labor group resides outside a given territory but desires to enter it (often at the request of business groups). The exclusion movement tries to prevent the physical presence of cheaper labor in the employment area, thereby preserving a non-split, higher priced labor market.

There are many examples of exclusion attempts around the world. In Australia, for instance, a group of white workers was able to prevent capitalists from importing cheaper labor from India, China, Japan and the Pacific Islands. Attempts at importation were met with strikes, boycotts, petitions and deputations. Ultimately, organized white labor pressed for strong exclusion measures, and vigilantly ensured their enforcement. As Yarwood puts it: "A comparison of the records of various governments during our period [1896–1923] leaves no doubt as to the special role of the Labour Party as the guardian of the ports." In other words, a white Australia policy (i.e. the exclusion of Asian and Polynesian immigrants) appears to have sprung from a conflict of interests between employers who wanted to import cheap labor, and a labor force sufficiently organized to ward off such a move.

California's treatment of Chinese and Japanese labor is another example of exclusion. A socialist, Cameron H. King, Jr., articulates the threatened labor group's position:

> Unskilled labor has felt this competition [from the Japanese] for some time being compelled to relinquish job after job to the low standard of living it could not endure. The unskilled laborers are largely unorganized and voiceless. But as the tide rises it is reaching the skilled laborers and the small merchants. These are neither unorganized nor voiceless, and viewing the menace to their livelihood they loudly demand protection of their material interests. We of the Pacific Coast certainly know that exclusion is an effective solution. In the seventh decade of the nineteenth century the problem arose of the immigration of Chinese laborers. The Republican and Democratic parties failed to give heed to the necessities of the situation and the Workingman's party arose and swept the state with the cry of "The Chinese must go." Then the two old parties woke up and have since realized that to hold the labor vote they must stand for Asiatic exclusion.

King wrote this around the time of the Gentlemen's Agreement, an arrangement of the U.S. and Japanese governments to prevent further immigration of Japanese labor to the Pacific Coast. The Agreement was aimed specifically at labor and not other Japanese immigrants, suggesting that economic and not racial factors were at issue.

Exclusion movements clearly serve the interests of higher paid labor. Its standards are protected, while the capitalist class is deprived of cheaper labor.

## Caste

If cheaper labor is present in the market, and cannot be excluded, then higher paid labor will resort to a caste arrangement, which depends on exclusiveness rather than exclusion. Caste is essentially an aristocracy of labor (a term borrowed from Lenin), in which higher paid labor deals with the undercutting potential of cheaper labor by excluding them from certain types of work. The higher paid group controls certain jobs exclusively and gets paid at one scale of wages, while the cheaper group is restricted to another set of jobs and is paid at a lower scale. The labor market split is submerged because the differentially priced workers ideally never occupy the same position.

Ethnically distinct cheaper groups (as opposed to women, for example, who face a caste arrangement in many Western societies) may reside in a territory for two reasons: either they were indigenous or they were imported early in capitalist-labor relations, when the higher paid group could not prevent the move. Two outstanding examples of labor aristocracies based on ethnicity are South Africa, where cheaper labor was primarily indigenous, and the U.S. south, where they were imported as slaves.

Unlike exclusion movements, caste systems retain the underlying reality of a price differential, for if a member of the subordinate group were to occupy the same position as a member of the stronger labor group he would be paid less. Hence, caste systems tend to become rigid and vigilant, developing an elaborate battery of laws, customs and beliefs aimed to prevent undercutting. The victory has three facets. First, the higher paid group tries to ensure its power in relation to business by monopolizing the acquisition of certain essential skills, thereby ensuring the effectiveness of strike action, or by controlling such important resources as purchasing power. Second, it tries to prevent the immediate use of cheaper labor as undercutters and strikebreakers by denying them access to general education thereby making their training as quick replacements more difficult, or by ensuring through such devices as "influx control" that the cheaper group will retain a base in their traditional economies. The latter move ensures a backward-sloping labor

supply function undesirable to business. Third, it tries to weaken the cheaper group politically, to prevent their pushing for those resources that would make them useful as undercutters. In other words, the solution to the devastating potential of weak, cheap labor is, paradoxically, to weaken them further, until it is no longer in business's immediate interest to use them as replacements.

South Africa is perhaps the most extreme modern example of an ethnic caste system. A split labor market first appeared there in the mining industry. With the discovery of diamonds in 1869, a white working class emerged. At first individual whites did the searching, but, as with the displacement of small farms by plantations, they were displaced by consolidated, high-capital operations, and became employees of the latter. It was this class together with imported skilled miners from Cornwall (lured to Africa by high wages) which fought the capitalists over the use of African labor. Africans were cheaper because they came to the mines with a fixed income goal (e.g. the price of a rifle) and did not view the mines as their main source of livelihood. By contrast, European workers remained in the mines and developed organizations to further their interests.

Clearly, it would have been to the advantage of businessmen, once they knew the skills involved, to train Africans to replace the white miners at a fraction of the cost; but this did not happen. The mining companies accepted a labor aristocracy, not out of ethnic solidarity with the white workers but:

> (as was to be the case throughout the later history of mining) they had little or no choice because of the collective strength of the white miners. . . . The pattern which was to emerge was that of the Europeans showing every sign of preparedness to use their collective strength to ensure their exclusive supremacy in the labour market. Gradually the concept of trade unionism, and, for that matter, of socialism, became accepted in the minds of the European artisans as the means of maintaining their own position against non-white inroads.

The final showdown between mine owners and white workers occurred in the 1920's when the owners tried to substitute cheaper non-white labor for white labor in certain semi-skilled occupations. This move precipitated the "Rand Revolt," a general strike of white workers on the Witwatersrand, countered by the calling in of troops and the declaration of martial law. The result was a coalition between Afrikaner nationalists (predominantly workers and small-scale farmers being pushed off the land by larger, British owned farms) and the English-speaking Labor Party. The Revolt "showed the lengths to which white labour was prepared to go to defend its privileged position. From that time on, mine managements have never directly challenged the colour-bar in the mining industry."

The legislative history of much of South Africa (and of the post-bellum deep south) consists in attempts by higher price white labor to ward off undercutting by cheaper groups, and to entrench its exclusive control of certain jobs.

This interpretation of caste contrasts with the Marxist argument that the capitalist class purposefully plays off one segment of the working class against the other. Business, I would contend, rather than desiring to protect a segment of the working class supports a liberal or laissez faire ideology that would permit all workers to compete freely in an open market. Such open competition would displace higher paid labor. Only under duress does business yield to labor aristocracy, a point made in *Deep South,* a book written when the depression had caused the displacement of white tenant farmers and industrial workers by blacks:

> The economic interests of these groups [employers] would also demand that cheaper colored labor should be employed in the "white collar" jobs in business offices, governmental offices, stores, and banks. In this field, however, the interests of the employer group conflict not only with those of the lower economic group of whites but also with those of the more literate and aggressive middle group of whites. A white store which employed colored clerks, for example, would be boycotted by both these groups. The taboo upon the employment of colored workers in such fields is the result of the political and purchasing power of the white middle and lower groups.

In sum, exclusion and caste are similar reactions to a split labor market. They represent victories for higher paid labor. The victory of exclusion is more complete in that cheaper labor is less available to business. For this reason I would hypothesize that a higher paid group prefers exclusion to caste, even though exclusion means they have to do the dirty work. Evidence for this comes from Australia where, in early attempts to import Asian labor, business tried to buy off white labor's opposition by offering to form them into a class of "mechanics" and foremen over the "coolies." The offer was heartily rejected in favor of exclusion. Apartheid in South Africa can be seen as an attempt to move from caste to the exclusion of the African work force.

Most of our examples have contained a white capitalist class, a higher paid white labor group, and a cheaper, non-white labor group. Conditions in Europe and around the world, and not skin color, yield such models. White capitalists would gladly dispense with and undercut their white working-class brethren if they could, and have done so whenever they had the opportunity. In the words of one agitator for excluding Chinese from the U.S. Pacific coast: "I have seen men . . . American born, who certainly would, if I may use a strong expression, employ devils from Hell if the devils would work for 25 cents less than a white man."

In addition, cases have occurred of white workers playing the role of cheap labor, and facing the same kind of ethnic antagonism as non-white workers. Consider the riots against Italian strikebreakers in the coal fields of Pennsylvania in 1874. In the words of one writer: "Unions resented the apparently inexhaustible cheap and relatively docile labor supply which was streaming from Europe obviously for the benefit of their employers."

Even when no ethnic differences exist, split labor markets may produce ethnic-like antagonism. Carey McWilliams describes an instance:

> During the depression years, "Old Stock"—that is, white, Protestant, anglo-Saxon Americans, from Oklahoma, Arkansas, and Texas—were roundly denounced in California as "interlopers." The same charges were made against them that were made against the Japanese: they were "dirty"; they had "enormous families"; they engaged in unfair competition; they threatened to "invade" the state and to "undermine" its institutions. During these turgid years (1930–1938) California attempted *to exclude,* by various extra-legal devices, those yeoman farmers just as it had excluded the Chinese and Japanese. "Okies" were "inferior" and "immoral." There was much family discord when Okie girl met California boy, and vice versa. . . . The prejudice against the Okies was obviously not "race" prejudice; yet it functioned in much the same manner.

## CONCLUSION

Obviously, this type of three-way conflict is not the only important factor in ethnic relations. But it does help explain some puzzles, including, of course, the exclusion-caste anomaly. For example, Philip Mason develops a typology of race relations and finds that it relates to numerical proportions without being able to explain the dynamic behind this correlation. Table 2 presents a modified version of his chart. My theory can explain these relationships. Paternalism arises in situations where the cleavage between business and labor corresponds to an ethnic difference. A small business elite rules a large group of workers who entered the labor market at approximately the same price or strength. No split labor market existed, hence no ethnic caste system arises. The higher proportion of the dominant ethnicity under "Domination" means that part of the dominant group must be working class. A labor element that shares ethnicity with people who have sufficient resources to become the business elite

is generally likely to come from a fairly wealthy country and have resources of its own. Such systems are likely to develop split labor markets. Finally, competition has under it societies whose cheaper labor groups have not been a major threat because the indigenous population available as cheap labor has been small and/or exclusion has effectively kept business groups from importing cheap labor in large numbers.

This theory helps elucidate other observations. One is the underlying similarity in the situation of blacks and women. Another is the history of political sympathy between California and the South. And a third is the conservatism of the American white working class, or what Daniels and Kitano consider to be an "essential paradox of American life: [that] movements for economic democracy have usually been violently opposed to a thorough-going ethnic democracy." Without having to resort to psychological constructs like "authoritarianism," this theory is able to explain the apparent paradox.

In sum, in comparing those countries with the most ethnic antagonism with those having the least, it is evident that the difference does not lie in the fact that the former are Protestant and the latter Catholic: Protestants are found in all three of Mason's types, and Hawaii is a Protestant dominated territory. It does not lie in whether the dominant or subordinate group moves: South Africa and the deep south show opposite patterns of movement. It is evident that some of the most antagonistic territories have been British colonies, but not all British colonies have had this attribute. The characteristic that those British colonies and other societies high on ethnic antagonism share is that they all have a powerful white, or more generally higher paid working class.

Table 2. Numerical Proportion of Dominant to Subordinate Ethnic Groups

| | Category | |
|---|---|---|
| Domination | Paternalism | Competition |
| | Situations | |
| South Africa (1960) 1–4 | Nigeria (1952) 1–2000 | Britain (1968) 50–1 |
| U.S. South (1960) 4–1 | Nyasaland (1966) 1–570 | U.S. North (1960) 15–1 |
| Rhodesia (1960) 1–16 | Tanganyika 1–450 | New Zealand 13–1 |
| | Uganda 1–650 | |

# Colonized and Immigrant Minorities

ROBERT BLAUNER

During the late 1960s a new movement emerged on the Pacific Coast. Beginning at San Francisco State College and spreading across the bay to Berkeley and other campuses, black, Chicano, Asian, and Native American student organizations formed alliances and pressed for ethnic studies curricula and for greater control over the programs that concerned them. Rejecting the implicit condescension in the label "minority students" and the negative afterthought of "nonwhite," these coalitions proclaimed themselves a "Third World Movement." Later, in the East and Middle West, the third world umbrella was spread over other alliances, primarily those urging unity of Puerto Ricans and blacks. In radical circles the term has become the dominant metaphor referring to the nation's racially oppressed people.

As the term *third world* has been increasingly applied to people of color in the United States, a question has disturbed many observers. Is the third world idea essentially a rhetorical expression of the aspirations and political ideology of the young militants in the black, brown, red, and yellow power movements, or does the concept reflect actual sociological realities? Posed this way, the question may be drawn too sharply; neither possibility excludes the other. Life is complex, so we might expect some truth in both positions. Furthermore, social relationships are not static. The rhetoric and ideology of social movements, if they succeed in altering the ways in which groups define their situations, can significantly shape and change social reality. Ultimately, the validity of the third world perspective will be tested in social and political practice. The future is open.

Still, we cannot evade the question, to what extent—in its application to domestic race relations—is the third world idea grounded in firm historical and contemporary actualities? To assess this issue we need to examine the assump-

tions upon which the concept rests. There are three that seem to me central. The first assumption is that racial groups in America are, and have been, colonized peoples; therefore their social realities cannot be understood in the framework of immigration and assimilation that is applied to European ethnic groups. The second assumption is that the racial minorities share a common situation of oppression, from which a potential political unity is inferred. The final assumption is that there is a historical connection between the third world abroad and the third world within. In placing American realities within the framework of international colonialism, similarities in patterns of racial domination and exploitation are stressed and a common political fate is implied—at least for the long run. I begin by looking at the first assumption since it sets the stage for my main task, a comparison and contrast between immigrant and third world experience. I return to the other points at the end of the essay.

The fundamental issue is historical. People of color have never been an integral part of the Anglo-American political community and culture because they did not enter the dominant society in the same way as did the European ethnics. The third world notion points to *a basic distinction between immigration and colonization as the two major processes through which new population groups are incorporated into a nation.* Immigrant groups enter a new territory or society voluntarily, though they may be pushed out of their old country by dire economic or political oppression. Colonized groups become part of a new society through force or violence; they are conquered, enslaved, or pressured into movement. Thus, the third world formulation is a bold attack on the myth that America is the land of the free, or, more specifically, a nation whose population has been built up through successive waves of immigration. The third world perspective returns us to the origins of the American experience, reminding us that this nation owes its very existence to colonialism, and that along with settlers and immigrants there have always been conquered Indians and black slaves, and later defeated Mexicans—that is, colonial subjects—on the national soil. Such a reminder is not pleasant to a society that represses those aspects of its history that do not fit the collective self-image of democracy for all men.

The idea that third world people are colonial subjects is gaining in acceptance today; at the same time it is not at all convincing to those who do not recognize a fundamental similarity between American race relations and Europe's historic domination of Asia and Africa. (I discuss how U.S. colonialism differs from the traditional or classical versions toward the end of the essay.) Yet the experience of people of color in this country does include a number of circumstances that are universal to the colonial situation, and these are the very circumstances that differentiate third world realities from those of the European immigrants. The first condition, already touched upon, is that of a forced entry into the larger society or metropolitan domain. The second is subjection to various forms of unfree labor that greatly restrict the physical and social mobility of the group and its participation in the political arena. The third is a cultural policy of the colonizer that constrains, transforms, or destroys original values, orientations, and ways of life. These three points organize the comparison of colonized and immigrant minorities that follows.

## GROUP ENTRY AND FREEDOM OF MOVEMENT

Colonialism and immigration are the two major means by which heterogeneous or plural societies, with ethnically diverse populations, develop. In the case of colonialism, metropolitan nations incorporate new territories or peoples through processes that are essentially involuntary, such as war, conquest, capture, and other forms of force or manipulation. Through immigration, new peoples or ethnic groups enter a host society more or less freely. These are ideal-types, the polar ends of a continuum; many historical cases fall in between. In the case of America's racial minorities, some groups clearly fit the criterion for colonial entry; others exemplify mixed types.

Native Americans, Chicanos, and blacks are the third world groups whose entry was unequivocally forced and whose subsequent histories best fit the colonial model. Critics of the colonial interpretation usually focus on the black experience, emphasizing how it has differed from those of traditional colonialism. Rather than being conquered and controlled in their native land, African people were captured, transported, and enslaved in the Southern states and other regions of the Western hemisphere. Whether oppression takes place at home in the oppressed's native land or in the heart of the colonizer's mother country, colonization remains colonization. However, the term *internal colonialism* is useful for emphasizing the differences in setting and in the consequences that arise from it. The conquest and virtual elimination of the original Americans, a process that took three hundred years to complete, is an example of classical colonialism, no different in essential features from Europe's imperial control over Asia, Africa, and Latin America. The same is true of the conquest of the Mexican Southwest and the annexation of its Spanish-speaking population.

Other third world groups have undergone an experience that can be seen as part colonial and part immigrant. Puerto Rico has been a colony exploited by the mainland, while, at the same time, the islanders have had relative freedom to move back and forth and to work and settle in the States. Of the Asian-American groups, the situation of the Filipinos has been the most colonial. The islands were colonies of Spain and the United States, and the male population was recruited for agricultural serfdom both in Hawaii and in the States. In the more recent period, however, movement to the States has been largely voluntary.

In the case of the Chinese, we do not have sufficient historical evidence to be able to assess the balance between free and involuntary entry in the nineteenth century. The majority came to work in the mines and fields for an extended period of debt servitude; many individuals were "shanghaied" or pressed into service; many others evidently signed up voluntarily for serflike labor. A similar pattern held for the Japanese who came toward the end of the century, except that the voluntary element in the Japanese entry appears to have been considerably more significant. Thus, for the two largest Asian groups, we have an original entry into American society that might be termed semicolonial, followed in the twentieth century by immigration. Yet the exclusion of Asian immigrants and the restriction acts that followed were unique blows, which marked off the status of the Chinese and Japanese in America, limiting their numbers and potential power. For this reason it is misleading to equate the Asian experience with the European immigrant pattern. Despite the fact that some individuals and families have been able to immigrate freely, the status and size of these ethnic groups have been rigidly controlled.

There is a somewhat parallel ambiguity in the twentieth-century movement from Mexico, which has contributed a majority of the present Mexican-American group. Although the migration of individuals and families in search of work and better living conditions has been largely voluntary, classifying this process as immigration misses the point that the Southwest is historically and culturally a Mexican, Spanish-speaking region. Moreover, from the perspective of conquest that many Mexicans have retained, the movement has been to a land that is still seen as their own. Perhaps the entry of other Latin Americans approaches more nearly the immigrant model; however, in their case, too, there is a colonial element, arising from the Yankee neocolonial domination of much of South and Central America; for this reason, along with that of racism in the States, many young Latinos are third world oriented.

Thus the relation between third world groups and a colonial-type entry into American society is impressive, though not perfect or precise. Differences between people of color and Europeans are shown most clearly in the ways the groups first entered. The colonized became ethnic minorities *en bloc,* collectively, through conquest, slavery, annexation, or a racial labor policy. The European immigrant peoples became ethnic groups and minorities within the United States by the essentially voluntary movements of individuals and families. Even when, later on, some third world peoples were able to immigrate, the circumstances of the earlier entry affected their situation and the attitudes of the dominant culture toward them.

The essentially voluntary entry of the immigrants was a function of their status in the labor market. The European groups were responding to the industrial needs of a free capitalist market. Economic development in other societies with labor shortages—for example, Australia, Brazil, and Argentina—meant that many people could at least envision alternative destinations for their emigration. Though the Irish were colonized at home, and poverty, potato famine, and other disasters made their exodus

more of a flight than that of other Europeans, they still had some choice of where to flee. Thus, people of Irish descent are found today in the West Indies, Oceania, and other former British colonies. Germans and Italians moved in large numbers to South America; Eastern Europeans emigrated to Canada as well as to the United States.

Because the Europeans moved on their own, they had a degree of autonomy that was denied those whose entry followed upon conquest, capture, or involuntary labor contracts. They expected to move freely within the society to the extent that they acquired the economic and cultural means. Though they faced great hardships and even prejudice and discrimination on a scale that must have been disillusioning, the Irish, Italians, Jews, and other groups had the advantage of European ancestry and white skins. When living in New York became too difficult, Jewish families moved on to Chicago. Irish trapped in Boston could get land and farm in the Midwest, or search for gold in California. It is obvious that parallel alternatives were not available to the early generations of Afro-Americans, Asians, and Mexican-Americans, because they were not part of the free labor force. Furthermore, limitations on physical mobility followed from the purely racial aspect of their oppression.

Thus, the entrance of the European into the American order involved a degree of choice and self-direction that was for the most part denied people of color. Voluntary immigration made it more likely that individual Europeans and entire ethnic groups would identify with America and see the host culture as a positive opportunity rather than an alien and dominating value system. It is my assessment that this element of choice, though it can be overestimated and romanticized, must have been crucial in influencing the different careers and perspectives of immigrants and colonized in America, because choice is a necessary condition for commitment to any group, from social club to national society.

Sociologists interpreting race relations in the United States have rarely faced the full implications of these differences. The *immigrant model* became the main focus of analysis, and the experiences of all groups were viewed through its lens. It suited the cultural mythology to see everyone in America as an original immigrant, a later immigrant, a quasi-immigrant or a potential immigrant. Though the black situation long posed problems for this framework, recent developments have made it possible for scholars and ordinary citizens alike to force Afro-American realities into this comfortable schema. Migration from rural South to urban North became an analog of European immigration, blacks became the latest newcomers to the cities, facing parallel problems of assimilation. In the no-nonsense language of Irving Kristol, "The Negro Today Is Like the Immigrant of Yesterday."

## THE COLONIAL LABOR PRINCIPLE IN THE UNITED STATES

European immigrants and third world people have faced some similar conditions, of course. The overwhelming majority of both groups were poor, and their early generations worked primarily as unskilled laborers. The question of how, where, and why newcomers worked in the United States is central, for the differences in the labor systems that introduced people of color and immigrants to America may be the fundamental reason why their histories have followed disparate paths.

The labor forces that built up the Western hemisphere were structured on the principle of race and color. The European conquest of the Native Americans and the introduction of plantation slavery were crucial beginning points for the emergence of a worldwide colonial order. These "New World" events established the pattern for labor practices in the colonial regimes of Asia, Africa, and Oceania during the centuries that followed. The key equation was the association of free labor with people of white European stock and the association of unfree labor with non-Western people of color, a correlation that did not develop all at once; it took time for it to become a more or less fixed pattern.

North American colonists made several attempts to force Indians into dependent labor relationships, including slavery. But the native North American tribes, many of which were mobile hunters and warrior peoples, resisted agricultural peonage and directly fought the theft of their lands. In addition, the relative sparsity of Indian populations north of the Rio Grande limited their potential utility for colonial labor requirements. Therefore Native American peoples were either massacred or pushed out of the areas of European settlement and enterprise. South of the Rio Grande, where the majority of Native Americans lived in more fixed agricultural societies, they were too nu-

merous to be killed off or pushed aside, though they suffered drastic losses through disease and massacre. In most of Spanish America, the white man wanted both the land and the labor of the Indian. Agricultural peonage was established and entire communities were subjugated economically and politically. Either directly or indirectly, the Indian worked for the white man.

In the Caribbean region (which may be considered to include the American South), neither Indian nor white labor was available in sufficient supply to meet the demands of large-scale plantation agriculture. African slaves were imported to the West Indies, Brazil, and the colonies that were to become the United States to labor in those industries that promised to produce the greatest profit: indigo, sugar, coffee, and cotton. Whereas many lower-class Britishers submitted to debt servitude in the 1600s, by 1700 slavery had crystallized into a condition thought of as natural and appropriate only to people of African descent. White men, even if from lowly origins and serflike pasts, were able to own land and property, and to sell their labor in the free market. Though there were always anomalous exceptions, such as free and even slave-owning Negroes, people of color within the Americas had become essentially a class of unfree laborers. Afro-Americans were overwhelmingly bondsmen; Native Americans were serfs and peons in most of the continent.

Colonial conquest and control has been the cutting edge of Western capitalism in its expansion and penetration throughout the world. Yet capitalism and free labor as Western institutions were not developed for people of color; they were reserved for white people and white societies. In the colonies European powers organized other systems of work that were noncapitalist and unfree: slavery, serfdom, peonage. Forced labor in a myriad of forms became the province of the colonized and "native" peoples. European whites managed these forced labor systems and dominated the segments of the economy based on free labor. This has been the general situation in the Western hemisphere (including the United States) for more than three out of the four centuries of European settlement. It was the pattern in the more classical colonial societies also. But from the point of view of labor, the colonial dynamic developed more completely within the United States. Only here emerged a correlation between color and work status that was almost perfect. In Asia and Africa, as well as in much of Central and South America, many if not most of the indigenous peoples remained formally free in their daily work, engaging in traditional subsistence economies rather than working in the plantations, fields, and mines established by European capital. The economies of these areas came within the orbit of imperial control, yet they helped maintain communities and group life and thus countered the uprooting tendencies and the cultural and psychic penetration of colonialism. Because such traditional forms of social existence were viable and preferred, labor could only be moved into the arenas of Western enterprise through some form of coercion. Although the association of color and labor status was not perfect in the classical colonial regimes, as a general rule the racial principle kept white Europeans from becoming slaves, coolies, or peons.

Emancipation in the United States was followed by a period of rapid industrialization in the last third of the nineteenth century. The Civil War and its temporary resolution of sectional division greatly stimulated the economy. With industrialization there was an historic opportunity to transform the nation's racial labor principle. Low as were the condition and income of the factory laborer, his status was that of a free worker. The manpower needs in the new factories and mines of the East and Middle West could have been met by the proletarianization of the freedmen along with some immigration from Europe. But the resurgent Southern ruling class blocked the political and economic democratization movements of Reconstruction, and the mass of blacks became sharecroppers and tenant farmers, agricultural serfs little removed from formal slavery. American captains of industry and the native white proletariat preferred to employ despised, unlettered European peasants rather than the emancipated Negro population of the South, or for that matter than the many poor white Southern farmers whose labor mobility was also blocked as the entire region became a semi-colony of the North.

The nineteenth century was the time of "manifest destiny," the ideology that justified Anglo expansionism in its sweep to the Pacific. The Texan War of 1836 was followed by the full-scale imperialist conquest of 1846–1848 through which Mexico lost half its territory. By 1900 Anglo-Americans had assumed economic as well as political dominance over most of the Southwest. As white colonists and speculators gained control (often illegally) over the land and livelihood of the independent Hispano farming and ranching villages, a new pool of dependent labor was produced to work the fields and build the railroads of the region. Leonard Pitt sums up the seizure of California in terms applicable to the whole Southwest:

> In the final analysis the Californios were the victims of an imperial conquest. . . . The United States, which had long coveted California for its trade potential and strategic location, finally provoked a war to bring about the desired ownership. At the conclusion of fighting, it arranged to "purchase" the territory outright, and set about to colonize, by throwing open the gates to all comers. Yankee settlers then swept in by the tens of thousands, and in a manner of months and years overturned the old institutional framework, expropriated the land, imposed a new body of law, a new language, a new economy, and a new culture, and in the process exploited the labor of the local population whenever necessary. To certain members of the old ruling class these settlers awarded a token and symbolic prestige, at least temporarily; yet with that status went very little genuine authority. In the long run Americans simply pushed aside the earlier ruling elite as being irrelevant.

Later, the United States' economic hegemony over a semicolonial Mexico and the upheavals that followed the 1910 revolution brought additional mass migrations of brown workers to the croplands of the region. The Mexicans and Mexican-Americans who created the rich agricultural industries of the Southwest were as a rule bound to contractors, owners, and officials in a status little above peonage. Beginning in the 1850s, shipments of Chinese workmen—who had sold themselves or had been forced into debt servitude—were imported to build railroads and to mine gold and other metals. Later other colonized Asian populations, Filipinos and East Indians, were used as gang laborers for Western farm factories. Among the third world groups that contributed to this labor stream, only the Japanese came from a nation that had successfully resisted Western domination. This may be one important reason why the Japanese entry into American life and much of the group's subsequent development show some striking parallels to the European immigration pattern. But the racial labor principle confined this Asian people too; they were viewed as fit only for subservient field employment. When they began to buy land, set up businesses, and enter occupations "reserved" for whites, the outcry led to immigration restriction and to exclusion acts.

A tenet central to Marxian theory is that work and systems of labor are crucial in shaping larger social forces and relations. The orthodox Marxist criticism of capitalism, however, often obscures the significant patterns of labor status. Since, by definition, capitalism is a system of wage slavery and the proletariat are "wage slaves," the varied degrees of freedom within industry and among the working class have not been given enough theoretical attention. Max Weber's treatment of capitalism, though based essentially on Marx's framework, is useful for its emphasis on the unique status of the free mobile proletariat in contrast to the status of those traditional forms of labor more bound to particular masters and work situations. Weber saw "formally free" labor as an essential condition for modern capitalism. Of course, freedom of labor is always a relative matter, and formal freedoms are often limited by informed constraint and the absence of choice. For this reason, the different labor situations of third world and European newcomers to American capitalism cannot be seen as polar opposites. Many European groups entered as contract laborers, and an ethnic stratification (as well as a racial one) prevailed in industry. Particular immigrant groups dominated certain industries and occupations: the Irish built the canal system that linked the East with the Great Lakes in the early nineteenth century; Italians were concentrated in road building and other construction; Slavs and East Europeans made up a large segment of the labor force in steel and heavy metals; the garment trades was for many years a Jewish enclave. Yet this ethnic stratification had different consequences than the racial labor principle had, since the white immigrants worked within the wage system whereas the third world groups tended to be clustered in precapitalist employment sectors.

The differences in labor placement for third world and immigrant can be further broken down. Like European overseas colonialism, America has used African, Asian, Mexican, and, to a lesser degree, Indian workers for the cheapest labor, concentrating people of color in the most unskilled jobs, the least advanced sectors of the economy, and the most industrially backward regions of the nation. In an historical sense, people of color provided much of the hard labor (and the technical skills) that built up the agricultural base and the mineral-transport-communication infrastructure necessary for industrialization and modernization, whereas the Europeans worked primarily within the industrialized, modern sectors. The initial position of European ethnics, while low, was therefore strategic for movement up the eco-

nomic and social pyramid. The placement of nonwhite groups, however, imposed barrier upon barrier on such mobility, freezing them for long periods of time in the least favorable segments of the economy.

## Rural versus Urban

European immigrants were clustered in the cities, whereas the colonized minorities were predominantly agricultural laborers in rural areas. In the United States, family farming and corporate agriculture have been primarily white industries. Some immigrants, notably German, Scandinavian, Italian, and Portuguese, have prospered through farming. But most immigrant groups did not contribute to the most exploited sector of our industrial economy, that with the lowest status: agricultural labor. Curiously, the white rural proletariat of the South and West was chiefly native born.

## Industry: Exclusion from Manufacturing

The rate of occupational mobility was by no means the same for all ethnics. Among the early immigrants, the stigmatized Irish occupied a quasi-colonial status, and their ascent into a predominantly middle-class position took at least a generation longer than that of the Germans. Among later immigrants, Jews, Greeks, and Armenians—urban people in Europe—have achieved higher social and economic status than Italians and Poles, most of whom were peasants in the old country. But despite these differences, the immigrants as a whole had a key advantage over third world Americans. As unskilled laborers, they worked within manufacturing enterprises or close to centers of industry. Therefore they had a foot in the most dynamic centers of the economy and could, with time, rise to semiskilled and skilled positions.

Except for a handful of industrial slaves and free Negroes, Afro-Americans did not gain substantial entry into manufacturing industry until World War I, and the stereotype has long existed that Asians and Indians were not fit for factory work. For the most part then, third world groups have been relegated to labor in preindustrial sectors of the nonagricultural economy. Chinese and Mexicans, for example, were used extensively in mining and building railroads, industries that were essential to the early development of a national capitalist economy, but which were primarily prerequisites of industrial development rather than industries with any dynamic future.

## Geography: Concentration in Peripheral Regions

Even geographically the Europeans were in more fortunate positions. The dynamic and modern centers of the nation have been the Northeast and the Midwest, the predominant areas of white immigration. The third world groups were located away from these centers: Africans in the South, Mexicans in their own Southwest, Asians on the Pacific Coast, the Indians pushed relentlessly "across the frontier" toward the margins of the society. Thus Irish, Italians, and Jews went directly to the Northern cities and its unskilled labor market, whereas Afro-Americans had to take two extra "giant steps," rather than the immigrants' one, before their large-scale arrival in the same place in the present century: the emancipation from slavery and migration from the underdeveloped semicolonial Southern region. Another result of colonized entry and labor placement is that the racial groups had to go through major historical dislocations within this country before they could arrive at the point in the economy where the immigrants began! When finally they did arrive in Northern cities, that economy had changed to their disadvantage. Technological trends in industry had drastically reduced the number of unskilled jobs available for people with little formal education.

## Racial Discrimination

To these "structural" factors must be added the factor of racial discrimination. The argument that Jews, Italians, and Irish also faced prejudice in hiring misses the point. Herman Bloch's historical study of Afro-Americans in New York provides clear evidence that immigrant groups benefited from racism. When blacks began to consolidate in skilled and unskilled jobs that yielded relatively decent wages and some security, Germans, Irish, and Italians came along to usurp occupation after occupation, forcing blacks out and down into the least skilled, marginal reaches of the economy. Although the European immigrant was only struggling to better his lot, the irony is that his relative success helped to block the upward economic mobility of Northern blacks. Without

such a combination of immigration and white racism, the Harlems and the South Chicagos might have become solid working-class and middle-class communities with the economic and social resources to absorb and aid the incoming masses of Southerners, much as European ethnic groups have been able to do for their newcomers. The mobility of Asians, Mexicans, and Indians has been contained by similar discrimination and expulsion from hard-won occupational bases.

Our look at the labor situation of the colonized and the immigrant minorities calls into question the popular sociological idea that there is no fundamental difference in condition and history between the nonwhite poor today and the ethnic poor of past generations. This dangerous myth is used by the children of the immigrants to rationalize racial oppression and to oppose the demands of third world people for special group recognition and economic policies—thus the folk beliefs that all Americans "started at the bottom" and most have been able to "work themselves up through their own efforts." But the racial labor principle has meant, in effect, that "the bottom" has by no means been the same for all groups. In addition, the cultural experiences of third world and immigrant groups have diverged in America, a matter I take up in the next section.

## CULTURE AND SOCIAL ORGANIZATION

Labor status and the quality of entry had their most significant impact on the cultural dynamics of minority people. Every new group that entered America experienced cultural conflict, the degree depending on the newcomers' distance from the Western European, Anglo-Saxon Protestant norm. Since the cultures of people of color in America, as much as they differed from one another, were non-European and non-Western, their encounters with dominant institutions have resulted in a more intense conflict of ethos and world view than was the case for the various Western elements that fed into the American nation. The divergent situations of colonization and immigration were fateful in determining the ability of minorities to develop group integrity and autonomous community life in the face of WASP ethnocentrism and cultural hegemony.

Voluntary immigration and free labor status made it possible for European minorities to establish new social relationships and cultural forms after a period of adjustment to the American scene. One feature of the modern labor relationship is the separation of the place of work from the place of residence or community. European ethnics were exploited on the job, but in the urban ghettos where they lived they had the insulation and freedom to carry on many aspects of their old country cultures—to speak their languages, establish their religions and build institutions such as schools, newspapers, welfare societies, and political organizations. In fact, because they had been oppressed in Europe—by such imperial powers as England, Tsarist Russia, and the Hapsburg Monarchy—the Irish, Poles, Jews, and other East Europeans actually had more autonomy in the New World for their cultural and political development. In the case of the Italians, many of their immigrant institutions had no counterpart in Italy, and a sense of nationality, overriding parochial and regional identities, developed only in the United States.

But there were pressures toward assimilation; the norm of "Anglo-conformity" has been a dynamic of domination central to American life. The early immigrants were predominantly from Western Europe. Therefore, their institutions were close to the dominant pattern, and assimilation for them did not involve great conflict. Among later newcomers from Eastern and Southern Europe, however, the disparity in values and institutions made the goal of cultural pluralism attractive for a time; to many of the first generation, America's assimilation dynamic must have appeared oppressive. The majority of their children, on the other hand, apparently welcomed Americanization, for with the passage of time many, if not most, European ethnics have merged into the larger society, and the distinctive Euro-American communities have taken on more and more of the characteristics of the dominant culture.

The cultural experience of third world people in America has been different. The labor systems through which people of color became Americans tended to destroy or weaken their cultures and communal ties. Regrouping and new institutional forms developed, but in situations with extremely limited possibilities. The transformation of group life that is central to the colonial cultural dynamic took place most completely on the plantation. Slavery in the United States appears to have gone the farthest in eliminating African social and cultural forms; the plantation system provided the most restricted context for the development of new kinds of group integrity.

In New York City, Jews were able to reconstruct their East European family system, with its distinctive sex roles and interlocking sets of religious rituals and customs. Some of these patterns broke down or changed in response, primarily, to economic conditions, but the changes took time and occurred within a community of fellow ethnics with considerable cultural autonomy. The family systems of West Africans, however, could not be reconstructed under plantation slavery, since in this labor system the "community" of workers was subordinated to the imperatives of the production process. Africans of the same ethnic group could not gather together because their assignment to plantations and subsequent movements were controlled by slaveholders who endeavored to eliminate any basis for group solidarity. Even assimilation to American kinship forms was denied as an alternative, since masters freely broke up families when it suited their economic or other interests. In the nonplantation context, the disruption of culture and suppression of the regrouping dynamic was less extreme. But systems of debt servitude and semifree agricultural labor had similar, if less drastic, effects. The first generations of Chinese in the United States were recruited for gang labor; they therefore entered without women and children. Had they been free immigrants, most of whom also were male initially, the group composition would have normalized in time with the arrival of wives and families. But as bonded laborers without even the legal rights of immigrants, the Chinese were powerless to fight the exclusion acts of the late nineteenth century, which left predominantly male communities in America's Chinatowns for many decades. In such a skewed social structure, leading features of Chinese culture could not be reconstructed. A similar male-predominant group emerged among mainland Filipinos. In the twentieth century the migrant work situation of Mexican-American farm laborers has operated against stable community life and the building of new institutional forms in politics and education. However, Mexican culture as a whole has retained considerable strength in the southwest because Chicanos have remained close to their original territory, language, and religion.

Yet the colonial attack on culture is more than a matter of economic factors such as labor recruitment and special exploitation. The colonial situation differs from the class situation of capitalism precisely in the importance of culture as an instrument of domination. Colonialism depends on conquest, control, and the imposition of new institutions and ways of thought. Culture and social organization are important as vessels of a people's autonomy and integrity; when cultures are whole and vigorous, conquest, penetration, and certain modes of control are more readily resisted. Therefore, imperial regimes attempt, consciously or unwittingly, either to destroy the cultures of colonized people or, when it is more convenient, to exploit them for the purposes of more efficient control and economic profit. As Mina Caulfield has put it, imperialism exploits the cultures of the colonized as much as it does their labor. Among America's third world groups, Africans, Indians, and Mexicans are all conquered peoples whose cultures have been in various degrees destroyed, exploited, and controlled. One key function of racism, defined here as the assumption of the superiority of white Westerners and their cultures and the concomitant denial of the humanity of people of color, is that it "legitimates" cultural oppression in the colonial situation.

The present-day inclination to equate racism against third-world groups with the ethnic prejudice and persecution that immigrant groups have experienced is mistaken. Compare, for example, intolerance and discrimination in the sphere of religion. European Jews who followed their orthodox religion were mocked and scorned, but they never lost the freedom to worship in their own way. Bigotry certainly contributed to the Americanization of contemporary Judaism, but the Jewish religious transformation has been a slow and predominantly voluntary adaptation to the group's social and economic mobility. In contrast, the U.S. policy against Native American religion in the nineteenth century was one of all-out attack; the goal was cultural genocide. Various tribal rituals and beliefs were legally proscribed and new religious movements were met by military force and physical extermination. The largest twentieth-century movement, the Native American Church, was outlawed for years because of its peyote ceremony. Other third world groups experienced similar, if perhaps less concerted, attacks on their cultural institutions. In the decade following the conquest, California prohibited bullfights and severely restricted other popular Mexican sports. In the same state various aspects of Chinese culture, dress, pigtails, and traditional forms of recreation were outlawed. Although it was tolerated in Brazil and the Caribbean, the use of the drum, the instrument that was the central means of communication among African peoples, was successfully repressed in the North American slave states.

American capitalism has been partially successful in absorbing third world groups into its economic system and culture. Because of the colonial experience and the prevalence of racism, this integration has been much less complete than in the case of the ethnic groups. The white ethnics who entered the class system at its lowest point were exploited, but not colonized. Because their group realities were not systematically violated in the course of immigration, adaptation, and integration, the white newcomers could become Americans more or less at their own pace and on their own terms. They have moved up, though slowly in the case of some groups, into working-class and middle-class positions. Their cultural dynamic has moved from an initial stage of group consciousness and ethnic pluralism to a present strategy of individual mobility and assimilation. The immigrants have become part of the white majority, partaking of the racial privilege in a colonizing society; their assimilation into the dominant culture is now relatively complete, even though ethnic identity is by no means dead among them. In the postwar period it has asserted itself in a third-generation reaction to "overassimilation" and more recently as a response to third world movements. But the ethnic groups have basically accepted the overall culture's rules of "making it" within the system, including the norms of racial oppression that benefit them directly or indirectly.

The situation and outlook of the racial minorities are more ambiguous. From the moment of their entry into the Anglo-American system, the third world peoples have been oppressed as groups, and their group realities have been under continuing attack. Unfree and semifree labor relations as well as the undermining of non-Western cultures have deprived the colonized of the autonomy to regroup their social forms according to their own needs and rhythms. During certain periods in the past, individual assimilation into the dominant society was seen as both a political and a personal solution to this dilemma. As an individual answer it has soured for many facing the continuing power of racism at all levels of the society. As a collective strategy, assimilation is compromised by the recognition that thus far only a minority have been able to improve their lot in this way, as well as by the feeling that it weakens group integrity and denies their cultural heritage. At the same time the vast majority of third world people in America "want in." Since the racial colonialism of the United States is embedded in a context of industrial capitalism, the colonized must look to the economy, division of labor, and politics of the larger society for their individual and group aspirations. Both integration into the division of labor and the class system of American capitalism as well as the "separatist" culture building and nationalist politics of third world groups reflect the complex realities of a colonial capitalist society.

The colonial interpretation of American race relations helps illuminate the present-day shift in emphasis toward cultural pluralism and ethnic nationalism on the part of an increasing segment of third world people. The building of social solidarity and group culture is an attempt to complete the long historical project that colonial domination made so critical and so problematic. It involves a deemphasis on individual mobility and assimilation, since these approaches cannot speak to the condition of the most economically oppressed, nor fundamentally affect the realities of colonization. Such issues require group action and political struggle. Collective consciousness is growing among third world people, and their efforts to advance economically have a political character that challenges longstanding patterns of racial and cultural subordination.

## CONCLUSION: THE THIRD WORLD PERSPECTIVE

Let us return to the basic assumptions of the third world perspective and examine the idea that a common oppression has created the conditions for effective unity among the constituent racial groups. The third world ideology attempts to promote the consciousness of such common circumstances by emphasizing that the similarities in situation among America's people of color are the essential matter, the differences less relevant. I would like to suggest some problems in this position.

Each third world people has undergone distinctive, indeed cataclysmic, experiences on the American continent that separate its history from the others, as well as from whites. Only Native Americans waged a 300-year war against white encroachment; only they were subject to genocide and removal. Only Chicanos were severed from an ongoing modern nation; only they remained concentrated in the area of their original land base, close to Mexico. Only blacks

went through a 250-year period of slavery. The Chinese were the first people whose presence was interdicted by exclusion acts. The Japanese were the one group declared an internal enemy and rounded up in concentration camps. Though the notion of colonized minorities points to a similarity of situation, it should not imply that black, red, yellow, and brown Americans are all in the same bag. Colonization has taken different forms in the histories of the individual groups. Each people is strikingly heterogeneous, and the variables of time, place, and manner have affected the forms of colonialism, the character of racial domination, and the responses of the group.

Because the colonized groups have been concentrated in different regions, geographical isolation has heretofore limited the possibilities of cooperation. When they have inhabited the same area, competition for jobs has fed ethnic antagonisms. Today, as relatively powerless groups, the racial minorities often find themselves fighting one another for the modicum of political power and material resources involved in antipoverty, model-cities, and educational reform projects. Differences in culture and political style exacerbate these conflicts.

The third world movement will have to deal with the situational differences that are obstacles to coalition and coordinated politics. One of these is the great variation in size between the populous black and Chicano groups and the much smaller Indian and Asian minorities. Numbers affect potential political power as well as an ethnic group's visibility and the possibilities of an assimilative strategy. Economic differentiation may be accelerating both between and within third world groups. The racial minorities are not all poor. The Japanese and, to a lesser extent, the Chinese have moved toward middle-class status. The black middle class is also growing. The ultimate barrier to effective third world alliance is the pervasive racism of the society, which affects people of color as well as whites, furthering division between all groups in America. Colonialism brings into its orbit a variety of groups, which it oppresses and exploits in differing degrees and fashions; the result is a complex structure of racial and ethnic division.

The final assumption of the third world idea remains to be considered. The new perspective represents more than a negation of the immigrant analogy. By its very language the concept assumes an essential connection between the colonized people within the United States and the peoples of Africa, Asia, and Latin America, with respect to whom the idea of *le tiers monde* originated. The communities of color in America share essential conditions with third world nations abroad; economic underdevelopment, a heritage of colonialism and neocolonialism, and a lack of real political autonomy and power.

This insistence on viewing American race relations from an international perspective is an important corrective in the parochial and ahistorical outlook of our national consciousness. The economic, social, and political subordination of third world groups in America is a microcosm of the position of all peoples of color in the world order of stratification. This is neither an accident nor the result of some essential racial genius. Racial domination in the United States is part of a world historical drama in which the culture, economic system, and political power of the white West has spread throughout virtually the entire globe. The expansion of the West, particularly Europe's domination over non-Western people of color, was the major theme in the almost five hundred years that followed the onset of "The Age of Discovery." The European conquest of Native American peoples, leading to the white settlement of the Western hemisphere and the African slave trade, was one of the leading historical events that ushered in the age of colonialism. Colonial subjugation and racial domination began much earlier and have lasted much longer in North America than in Asia and Africa, the continents usually thought of as colonial prototypes. The oppression of racial colonies within our national borders cannot be understood without considering worldwide patterns of white European hegemony.

The present movement goes further than simply drawing historical and contemporary parallels between the third world within and the third world external to the United States. The new ideology implies that the fate of colonized Americans is tied up with that of the colonial and former colonial peoples of the world. There is at least impressionistic evidence to support this idea. If one looks at the place of the various racial minorities in America's stratified economic and social order, one finds a rough correlation between relative internal status and the international position of the original fatherland. According to most indicators of income, education, and occupation, Native Americans are at the bottom. The Indians alone lack an independent nation, a center of power in the world community to which they might look for political aid and psychic identification. At the other pole, Japanese-Americans are the most successful non-white group by conventional criteria, and Japan has been the most economically developed and politicially potent non-Western nation during most of the twentieth century. The transformation of African societies from colonial dependency to independent statehood, with new authority and prestige in the international arena, has had an undoubted impact on Afro-Americans in the United States; it has contributed both to civil rights movements and to a developing black consciousness.

What is not clear is whether an international strategy can in itself be the principle of third world liberation within this country. Since the oppression, the struggle, and the survival of the colonized groups have taken place within our society, it is to be expected that their people will orient their daily lives and their political aspirations to the domestic scene. The racial minorities have been able to wrest some material advantages from American capitalism and empire at the same time that they have been denied real citizenship in the society. Average levels of income, education, and health for the third world in the United States are far above their counterparts overseas; this gap will affect the possibility of internationalism. Besides which, group alliances that transcend national borders have been difficult to sustain in the modern era because of the power of nationalism.

Thus, the situation of the colonized minorities in the United States is by no means identical with that of Algerians, Kenyans, Indonesians, and other nations who suffered under white European rule. Though there are many parallels in cultural and political developments, the differences in land, economy, population composition, and power relations make it impossible to transport wholesale sociopolitical analyses or strategies of liberation from one context to another. The colonial analogy has gained great vogue recently among militant nationalists—partly because it is largely valid, partly because its rhetoric so aggressively condemns white America, past and present. Yet it may be that the comparison with English, French, and Dutch overseas rule lets our nation off too easily! In many ways the special versions of colonialism practiced against Americans of color have been more pernicious in quality and more profound in consequences than the European overseas varieties.

In traditional colonialism, the colonized "natives" have usually been the majority of the population, and their culture, while less prestigious than that of the white Europeans, still pervaded the landscape. Members of the third world within the United States are individually and collectively outnumbered by whites, and Anglo-American cultural imperatives dominate the society—although this has been less true historically in the Southwest where the Mexican-American population has never been a true cultural minority. The oppressed masses of Asia and Africa had the relative "advantage" of being colonized in their own land. In the United States, the more total cultural domination, the alienation of most third world people from a land base, and the numerical minority factor have weakened the group integrity of the colonized and their possibilities for cultural and political self-determination.

Many critics of the third world perspective seize on these differences to question the value of viewing America's racial dynamics within the colonial framework. But all the differences demonstrate is that colonialisms vary greatly in structure and that political power and group liberation are more problematic in our society than in the overseas situation. The fact that we have no historical models for decolonization in the American context does not alter the objective realities. Decolonization is an insistent and irreversible project of the third world groups, although its contents and forms are at present unclear and will be worked out only in the course of an extended period of political and social conflict.

# PART IV
# Gender

Studies of race and ethnicity often overlook gender, and studies of women often neglect race and ethnicity. Yet it is often noted that women and racial minorities occupy subordinate places in society: both earn lower average incomes than white men and are underrepresented in high-level occupations. But how valid is the analogy between women and racial minorities? Or do women constitute a special case?

Statistically it can be shown that women, like racial minorities, are located in a low stratum of income. Women, regardless of race, earn less than men generally. (See Table 1.) While black, Hispanic, and Chinese men earn less than white men, women generally receive less than their male counterparts. In fact, the incomes of women of different racial groups tend to converge. Black and white women, for example, earned respectively only 40 percent and 36.7 percent of white male income.

A pattern of shared characteristics based on gender can also be seen in terms of occupations. (See Table 2.) Women—white, black, and Hispanic—are concentrated in clerical and service occupations or in the secondary and low-paid segment of the labor market.

But what does it mean for both women and racial minorities to share similar income and occupational levels vis-à-vis white men? To compare the two groups, Thomas Sowell argues, is to compare apples and oranges. Women, unlike racial minorities, are not victims of discrimination. Sowell quickly dismisses the claim that "a woman is paid just 59 percent of what a man receives *for doing the same work.*" Actually, women who remain single earn 91 percent of the income of their male counterparts in the twenty-five to sixty-four age bracket. Thus, when these similar groups of women and men are compared, Sowell contends, they have equal incomes.

But, Sowell acknowledges, women as a group are behind men in incomes and occupations. The reason for this, however, is not discrimination. Rather, Sowell argues, it is "because most women become wives and mothers." Married women living with their husbands earn 25 percent of the yearly income of married men living with their wives. Women have a different career trajectory from men: "The very choice of occupation, and of education for an occupation, is dominated by the likelihood of a career interruption for a woman, due to marriage and motherhood."

Sowell emphasizes the importance of "choice": women choose to specialize in fields that they can leave and reenter some years later without large losses of knowledge and obsolescence of skills. As an editor, teacher, or librarian, a woman could have an employment interruption for six years and resume work again in the same occupation. But as a tax attorney or an aeronautical engineer, she could not take such a break in work, for the occupation would have changed substantially in such a period of time. Consequently,

Table 1. Per Person Mean Incomes of Full-Time Employed Men and Women, 25 to 55 years, by Race in California, 1980

| Race | Gender | Mean income | % of white male income |
|------|--------|-------------|------------------------|
| White | Male | $20,599 | 100 |
| White | Female | 7,569 | 36.7 |
| Black | Male | 12,617 | 61.3 |
| Black | Female | 8,233 | 40 |
| Hispanic | Male | 11,794 | 57.3 |
| Hispanic | Female | 5,406 | 26.2 |
| Chinese | Male | 17,233 | 83.7 |
| Chinese | Female | 8,275 | 40.2 |

From research based on 1980 Census by Larry Shinagawa and Gary Kawaguchi, University of California, Berkeley, 1985.

women choose occupations that allow employment interruptions. Women move in and out of employment more frequently than men: "The average white male remains continuously employed 77 percent longer than the average white female. Nor can this be readily attributed to employer bias against women. Women voluntarily quit more often than men."

Thus, women and racial minorities may occupy similar strata in terms of income and employment, but they do so for entirely different reasons. For women it is a matter of choice, states Sowell, while for blacks and other racial minorities it is due to discrimination. Another difference between the two groups, he adds, is based on class: "When the husband is affluent, the wife is not poor, even if her income is only 25 percent of his—or even zero percent of his." In other words, the low incomes of women and racial minorities cannot be compared, for married women share the incomes and the class of their husbands.

While Sowell's analysis is a helpful reminder of the class heterogeneity of women, it is saying in effect that women married to middle-class and wealthy men are extensions of their husbands socially and economically. But women in this situation may find such a view of them degrading, for it denies them autonomy and their needs for employment. It also dismisses the inequities women experience in the labor market. Sowell's emphasis on choice shrouds the sexual stratification of the occupational structure. Women, it can be argued, are located in certain kinds of jobs because of gender segregation in employment. And they also find themselves receiving low pay, even in skilled occupations. Many so-called female jobs actually require considerable knowledge, but they do not pay as well as comparable and even less comparable jobs held mainly by men. Male janitors, for example, often earn more than female secretaries and even more than female receptionists—skilled office workers usually assigned important responsibilities. In San Francisco, a general laborer receives about $5,000 more in wages annually than a nurse, and a city truck driver $8,000 more than a secretary. "There's a belief," a secretary complained, "that if you're a woman, you're not the primary supporter in the family, but many single women with children are working as . . . secretaries."

The convergence of low incomes and occupations for women of different races can indicate discrimination based on gender. Elizabeth McTaggart Almquist, for example, argues:

Table 2.  Occupational Distribution of Employed White, Black, and Hispanic-Origin Women and Men, 1982

| Occupational group | Percentage of women | Percentage of men |
|---|---|---|
| White (37,615,000 women; 50,287,000 men) | | |
| Professional-technical workers | 18.0 | 17.0 |
| Managerial-administrative, except farm, workers | 8.0 | 15.6 |
| Salespeople | 7.4 | 6.8 |
| Clerical workers | 35.1 | 6.1 |
| Craft workers | 2.1 | 20.8 |
| Operatives, excluding transport workers | 8.2 | 9.5 |
| Transport workers | 0.7 | 5.2 |
| Nonfarm laborers | 6.5 | 1.2 |
| Private household workers | 1.9 | (a) |
| All other service workers | 16.3 | 8.3 |
| Farmworkers | 1.2 | 4.1 |
| Black and other (5,641,000 women; 5,983,000 men) | | |
| Professional-technical workers | 15.7 | 12.7 |
| Managerial-administrative, except farm, workers | 3.9 | 7.4 |
| Salespeople | 3.3 | 2.9 |
| Clerical workers | 29.7 | 8.4 |
| Craft workers | 1.5 | 15.9 |
| Operatives, excluding transport workers | 13.5 | 13.5 |
| Transport workers | 0.7 | 7.6 |
| Nonfarm laborers | 1.5 | 11.8 |
| Private household workers | 5.4 | 0.2 |
| All other service workers | 24.4 | 16.9 |
| Farmworkers | 0.6 | 2.7 |
| Hispanic-origin (2,047,000 women; 3,111,000 men) | | |
| Professional-technical workers | 9.5 | 7.9 |
| Managerial-administrative, except farm, workers | 4.9 | 7.9 |
| Salespeople | 5.1 | 3.7 |
| Clerical workers | 32.8 | 6.9 |
| Craft workers | 2.4 | 20.3 |
| Operatives, excluding transport workers | 19.6 | 17.4 |
| Transport workers | 0.05 | 6.7 |
| Nonfarm laborers | 1.5 | 11.0 |
| Private household workers | 4.0 | 0.01 |
| All other service workers | 18.1 | 13.2 |
| Farmworkers | 1.6 | 4.9 |

*Note:*  Data are for persons 16 years of age and over.
[a]Less than 1 percent.
*Source:*  For whites and blacks and others, *Employment and Earnings* (January 1983), vol. 30, no. 1, table 22, p. 157. For Hispanic-origin, unpublished data from the 1982 annual averages made available by the Bureau of Labor Statistics. From Elizabeth McTaggart Almquist, "Race and Ethnicity in the Lives of Minority Women," in Jo Freedman, ed., *Women: A Feminist Perspective* (Palo Alto, Ca., 1984).

It seems clear that minority women have small paychecks more because they are women than because they are minorities. Two matters are paramount. First, the occupational pattern of minority women is the strongest predictor of their wages, and in this respect they resemble Anglo women. Second, to the extent that discrimination can be measured, explicit discrimination (e.g. unequal pay for equal work) also is based more on sex than on ethnicity.

Where Sowell claims women choose certain occupations due to considerations of marriage and motherhood, Almquist contends they are crowded into low-status and low-paid occupations because of gender discrimination.

But race may require more consideration than both Sowell and Almquist give it. In 1982, the poverty rates of persons fifteen years and older were: black female, 35.8 percent; black male, 23.8 percent; white female, 12.0 percent; and white male, 8.8 percent. Thus, Pamela Sparr points out, "although women have a higher incidence of poverty than men within each race, this generalization does not hold across races. Black men, for example, face higher poverty rates than white women. Hypothetically, if a black woman changes her race, she would have a better statistical chance of escaping poverty than if she were to change her gender."

The widening difference between white women and black women is underscored by the fact that in 1982 85 percent of white women lived in households with male earners, and 46 percent of black families were headed by women. Furthermore, the majority of women in some poverty categories such as "Aid to Families with Dependent Children" are minority women. The "feminization of poverty," some observers have noted, should be retermed the "racial feminization of poverty."

This difference has led Phyllis Marynick Palmer to ask: What does it mean to be "white and middle-class, as well as female, in a society with women who are nonwhite and, therefore, not middle-class"? As she addresses this question in "White Women/Black Women: The Dualism of Female Identity and Experience in the United States," Palmer focuses on the cultural imagery and the class differences dividing white and black women. Palmer's analysis raises a political question. Is it possible to forge an alliance between the "mainstream women's movement" and black women?

Can Chicanas be involved in such an alliance? This is one of the questions Alma M. Garcia addresses in "The Development of Chicana Feminist Discourse." In her view, Chicanas shared experiences with other women of color. Like them, they found themselves struggling to gain equality not only in the larger society but also within male-dominated nationalist movements in the Chicano community. Garcia confronts the issue directly: Are cultural nationalism and feminism incompatible?

But "where are all the Asian American women?" asks Esther Ngan-Ling Chow in her essay on "The Feminist Movement." Contrary to the stereotype, Chow argues, Asian American women have not been passive; they have simply tended to be more actively involved in women's groups of their respective ethnic communities rather than in the white feminist movement. But as activists, Asian American women face a dilemma between adherence to "Asian values" versus acceptance of "American values."

According to Chow, one American value is independence, and Paula Gunn Allen questions the "feminist practice" of rejecting tradition. In "Who Is Your Mother? Red Roots of White Feminism," she observes how "Indians think it is important to remember, while Americans believe it is important to forget." But what needs to be remembered? Here, Allen contends, history can be revealing as well as liberating.

History can also show that white women have not been a homogeneous group in terms of class and ethnicity. In "Sweatshops and Picket Lines," Elizabeth Ewen examines the experiences of European immigrant women, especially Italians and Jews. They worked in the garment factories of New York's Lower East Side and militantly struggled to improve their working conditions and lives in America.

Today, many of these garment workers are Puerto Rican women. In "Puertorriqueñas in the United States: The Impact of Double Discrimination," Lourdes Miranda King analyzes the ways Puerto Rican women are caught between two main forces: economic subordination and cultural racism. Commenting on the effects of the latter, King observes: "I am always saddened when I see Puerto Rican women with hair dyed flaming red or yellow."

Finally, Bonnie Thornton Dill brings together many of our themes in her essay on "Race, Class, and Gender: Prospects for an All-Inclusive Sisterhood." Racially, Dill and Palmer stand on different shores. They both underscore the differences between white and black women and seek to develop political strategies for a more "inclusive" women's movement. While presenting the voices of black women and allowing them to tell us what it means to be black, female, and workers, Dill also responds to Palmer's question about the possibility of alliances. Dill's essay provokes one to wonder about the sources of division and unity among all women.

# White Women/Black Women: The Dualism of Female Identity and Experience

PHYLLIS MARYNICK PALMER

Black women still remain largely invisible in American history (though with some recent improvement), and in popular conceptions of the nation's past. Yet the actions of one black woman, Sojourner Truth, have become familiar to almost everybody, a standard exhibit in modern liberal historiography. White feminists who may know almost nothing else of black women's history are moved by Truth's famous query, "A'n't I a woman?" They take her portrait of herself as one who "ploughed, and planted, and gathered into barns" as compelling proof of the falsity of the notion that women are frail, dependent, and parasitic. They do not, we may notice, use Sojourner Truth's battle cry to show that *black* women are not feeble: no one in America has ever doubted that black women toil and sweat. Rather they have used Sojourner Truth's hardiness and that of other black women as proof of white women's possibilities for, and performance of, productive work. Truth's experiences do replicate those of many white women, women who worked in mills, factories, stockyards, and on farms. Why, then, have not white feminists chosen one of these working-class women—such as Sarah Bagley, who led the textile workers of Lowell, Massachusetts, in the 1840s—to represent the productiveness of all women? Why a black figure?

In a way the answer is simple. Women such as Sojourner Truth embody and display strength, directness, integrity, fire. They are not "ladies" in the genteel connotations of the word: they are "womanly," without affectation or false reticence, and so ideally admirable in the eyes of women today. The current use of Truth as an image of heroism builds upon her role for white women at the 1851 convention, who were intimidated by pontifical male speakers (most of them clergy) and upset by hecklers among the audience. Sojourner Truth came to the rescue. As Frances Gage said of the speech that quieted the skeptics and drowned criticism in applause, "She had *taken us up in her strong arms* and carried us safely over the slough of difficulty[,] turning the whole tide in our favor."

The characterization of Sojourner in this account is fierce and yet maternal, a leader and yet a servant and "mammy." The image of white women being cradled in a black woman's arms has, we may suppose, exerted a lasting appeal—not only in nineteenth-century America, accustomed to black women as servant and slaves, but also to a more modern audience that still sees black women as those who, laboring in hospitals and laundries, challenge the stereotypes of female incapacity. It is black women rather than white women who popularly symbolize courageous, industrious womanhood. In both centuries, too, white society realizes, consciously or not, that black women have long been America's most oppressed group. As the section with the lowest income, lowest rate of completion of college education, highest proportion of adolescent pregnancy, and greatest likelihood of relying on Aid to Families with Dependent Children (AFDC) payments for subsistence, black women are for many white women the quintessential victims of sexist oppression.

This is obviously not the entire story. In the past quarter-century, athletes such as Wilma Rudolf and Althea Gibson did much to dispel the notion of women's sports being refined to the point of anemia. In politics, Fannie Lou Hamer, Shirley Chisholm, Barbara Jordan, and others have challenged the idea that women merely hold public offices as inheritances from

From Phyllis Marynick Palmer, "White Women/Black Women: The Dualism of Female Identity and Experience in the United States," *Feminist Studies* 9, no. 1 (1983): 151–70. Reprinted by permission of the publisher. Footnotes have been deleted.

deceased husbands or fathers. In these two traditionally male fields, athletics and politics, black women have provided a standard of the seriousness and competence with which women can work in arenas traditionally closed to them.

At the same time that feminists have lauded some black women's heroism and lamented the social mistreatment of others, white women have not, paradoxically, sought out or attracted large numbers of black women to the women's movement. This is especially curious for two reasons: first, a larger percentage of black women than white support the formal goals of the women's movement; and second, salient characteristics of black and white women's lives—level and kind of employment, single-parenting, and rising divorce and separation rates—are converging. Despite the similarities in demands for economic justice and for assistance as single parents, white feminists have not emphasized those issues, such as reform of the welfare system, increase in AFDC payments, improvements in job-training programs, and development of work-related child care, that might win black women to work in coalition with white-dominated organizations. Scholar-activists have done little research and writing on service, a traditionally black-occupied field. And housing, a primary concern for single female heads of household, is just emerging as an issue for the modern women's movement. Why? Why the disjunction between white women's embracing black women as images of strength and pathos and ignoring the realistic needs and interests of these same black women?

Most white women, and I include myself, have written and acted as if they have staked out the common feminist ground, and that divergence from this is a diversionary "special interest." White academics, in particular, have formulated theories grounded in notions of universal female powerlessness in relation to men, and of women's deprivation relative to men's satisfaction. Often treating race and class as secondary factors in social organization, feminist theorists write from experiences in which race and class are not felt as oppressive elements in their lives. It is this theorizing from white, middle-class experience that contributes to the ethnocentrism often observed in white feminist writings.

Having theorized from a position in which race and class are unimportant because they are unexperienced elements in their oppression, white feminists then engage in practical political work on issues that do not seem so compelling to black women. Most notably, white feminist

perspective has led theory and action to focus on the sexist behavior and preconceptions of men and to view *all* men as equivalent oppressors. This position has led to chastising black women for their unwillingness to talk about sexism in black society, a reality that does need to be discussed, but not in the same terms as are pertinent to white women. Black women rightly reply that it is difficult to pay attention to black men's sexism when white feminist theory and practice do not take account of a more historically accurate statement about American society, which is that white males, particularly those with class privileges, are the prime beneficiaries of sexism *and* racism. Similarly, the emphasis on sexism enables white women to deny their own history of racism and the benefits that white women have gained at the expense of black women.

A second paradox, then, infuses the women's movement and its relation to black women—that black women are used as symbols at the same time as they are criticized for their failure to support the movement. Both of these paradoxes—of a symbolization that *does not* entail political coalition but *does* result in chastisement—can be better understood through thinking more carefully about the ways in which we, as members of a white-dominant society and as white feminists, have symbolized black and white women and what the power of these symbols is. To examine these paradoxes, I shall reiterate and elaborate on points made by some black feminists, who have written about white women's insensitivity, by looking at the historical uses of images applied to black women and considering how these serve white women's interests. I will then summarize some of the material differences that underlie, but are nevertheless obscured by, the symbols attached to black and white women. Finally, I shall point out areas of theoretical inquiry and political activity that have not been fully developed because issues of race and class have been largely excluded from debates within the women's movement.

Anthropologists, from whom most of the thinking about symbols has come, do not agree about the process by which symbols form, or the causal links between symbols and human behavior. They do agree that symbols are mental images that pervade thinking, thus connecting formal, informal, and unconscious thought, and that underlie social organization by unifying discrete institutions, thoughts, and actions. Symbols give significance and order to any particular society's behavior; they provide emotional attachment to its formal ideas.

American historians have, in recent years, used various theories of symbols and the social process of symbolization to describe how America came to be a slave-holding country, and a racist one, with images that persisted long after slavery was legally abolished. Because the ideology of slavery was so antithetical to the formal ideals of individual freedom in the society, the notion of a more complex system of thought, which connected formally irreconcilable ideas in some unconscious or unexamined way, became a prevailing one for writers about slavery and racism. Historians had to explain, as Winthrop Jordan put it, why or how a man such as Thomas Jefferson could both hate slavery and yet live with it. Jefferson reconciled the contradiction, as Jordan shows, by thinking that the Negro was inferior, and "thinking" this in such a fashion that rational proofs could not make him believe otherwise.

Jefferson's fears about blacks had two parts, and, as Jordan argues, two partial explanations within the context of his society's overall organization. First, black men who, white men chronically feared, would rise up to overthrow slavery, were believed to be sexually as well as politically aggressive. Their sexuality could be controlled and punished even when they had not mounted an insurrection. Black women, on the other hand, were to be feared because, like white women, they were potential sexual enticers who could overthrow reason and social order. But unlike white women, black women were slaves, so that white men could enjoy sexual intercourse free of the fear that an overriding emotional attachment or sexual demands would follow.

While the symbols attached to black women and men held benefits for a society directed by white men, white women's share in the creation and maintenance of these beliefs (and their supporting institutions) is not so easy to explain. It has also not been so obvious what effect such a system had on white women. Some historians, such as Anne Firor Scott, have written about the pathetic white wife, bound to a man who found sensual pleasure with his slaves while his wife disguised the existence of the children of these unions, emphasizing the frustrated powerlessness of the white wife. Presumably, however, the wife received enough benefits—material and psychological—to remain a participant. What benefits did white women receive from a system that pictured black men as threatening satyrs and black women as sirens?

Part of the answer to this question comes from the content of the symbols attached to women: what choices were available to white women for perceiving and presenting themselves? The cultural imagery for European women, at least since classical Greece, had been a dualism: virgin or whore, or, after the spread of Christian symbolism, madonna or magdalen. The variation that began to appear at the end of the eighteenth century identified particular personality traits with particular classes or races of women. To separate the dual identity that had been contained in all women and to equate particular characteristics with particular groups of women was, one Victorian historian has implied, a major innovation of the nineteenth century, in keeping with its general trend towards specialization. Leonore Davidoff argues that overlaying the mental split between good and bad aspects of women onto socially distinct groups of women occurs in the nineteenth century, because of the material splitting of household tasks. The mistress no longer did heavy labor; all dirty, arduous physical labor was now performed by the domestic, whose stigmatizing labor accorded with her inferior character and her working-class status.

Although Americans did not have Victoria as their queen, they were Victorians in their economy, industry, and culture. The United States accepted and emulated the English belief in the dual nature of womanhood, and similarly assigned aspects of this nature to particular classes of women. While some working-class immigrant women, notably the Irish, were depicted as slovenly and rowdy, in America the symbolic roles of English domestic servants were carried by black women, or by those white working-class women who had sunk to the desperation of prostitution.

The symbolic division created in the nineteenth century was between the "good" women, who were pure, clean, sexually repressed, and physically fragile, and the "bad" women, who were dirty, licentious, physically strong, and knowledgeable about the evil done in the world. Good women were wives, mothers, spinsters—women dependent on men and sexually unchallenging. Bad women were whores, laborers, single mothers—women who earned their own bread and were politically and socially powerless. The dual symbolism of good/bad was usually connected with race and class, but it could be used to chastise any woman moving out of her assigned place. Thus, when middle-class white women sought to be politically active, they were ridiculed as "mannish" or discredited with the epithet of sexual licentiousness: "free lovers."

Because of the historic link between black and slave labor and between blacks and post–Civil War economic need, black women were the most likely of all women to be laborers, and to have the physical mobility and exposure required by working away from their own homes. In such a situation, the symbolic processes of splitting and distortion, of fastening the characteristics of "bad" women on black women, and then inflating these, could easily occur. Black women, even more than other women forced to labor outside their homes, came to symbolize sexuality, prowess, mysterious power (mysterious, certainly, since it was so at odds with their actual economic, political, and social deprivation); they came to embody the "myth of the superwoman."

Faced with the increasingly rigid cultural duality of images of womanhood (feelings which they also shared), white women whose class allowed it formed their identities around "good" womanhood; they accepted their difference from black women and the sterile superiority of their identities. White women's identity was an often laudable, but also self-limiting one. On the one hand, it entailed a mission of social improvement; on the other, it depended on maintaining the lines dividing white from black women. White women could accept their responsibility for injustice (indeed, welcome it as part of their moral mission) more easily than they could reorganize their identities to feel a sisterhood with black women. White women who organized the Association of Southern Women for the Prevention of Lynching in 1930, for instance, protested that they would no longer be a symbol used to terrorize black men; they could not, however, see themselves as allies or coworkers with black women. Alternatively, black women who established their own women's clubs and joined some of the newly formed white women's organizations during the 1880s and 1890s saw a common women's mission to work for self-education and social improvement, but they had an additional purpose to defend black women against the everyday charge of sexual immorality. Conventional white women could not free themselves from the feeling that they were better than black women; nor could they work with black women to overcome the stigma black women experienced.

Why did white women accept such limitations? As black women have observed, white women accepted their much-valued sexual probity, their physical fragility, their unchallenging

prettiness, in return for "this kind of angel feeling," as Fannie Lou Hamer said in the 1960s, the feeling that "you were untouchable . . ." and "*more* because you was a woman, and especially a white woman." Or, as Doris Davenport put it less gently in 1981:

A few of us . . . perceive white wimmin as very oppressed, and ironically, invisible. . . .

If *some* of us can do this, it would seem that some white feminists could too. Instead, they cling to their myth of being privileged, powerful, and less oppressed (or equally oppressed, whichever it is fashionable or convenient to be at the time) than black wimmin. Why? Because that is all they have. That is, they have defined, or re-defined themselves and they don't intend to let anything or anybody interfere. Somewhere deep down (denied and almost killed) in the psyche of racist white feminists there is some perception of their real position: powerless, spineless, and invisible.

The problem for white women, as both Hamer and Davenport point out, is that their privilege is not power, and it is based on accepting the image of goodness, which is powerlessness. As Lillian Smith, a Southern white woman who refused such privilege, put it, "They [white women] had no defense against blandishment," in a "region that still pays nice rewards to simple-mindedness in females."

While the rewards paid to women are tangible, as I shall indicate in the next section, the material rewards are becoming less secure than the psychological ones. At this point, the mental ones are increasingly self-defeating. As more and more women work outside the home and expect wages comparable to the compensation paid to men, unexamined ideas that prettiness and proper behavior bring rewards create two results. The first is that men can ignore that women are workers *just like men,* especially since women don't seem to treat their work with the same aggressive self-importance. The second is that women undermine their own efforts by continuing to hope that they will fulfill the girlhood fantasy of being carried off and cared for by appearing helpless and fragile. Both of these notions have been discredited in formal thought and government reports, but neither has been given much critical attention. Indeed, much of the message of popular culture is that virtue is still rewarded with lifelong devotion and support.

In such a world white women have little encouragement to give up the feelings of angelic purity derived partially from the accident of their skin color. There are contradictory psychological rewards for identifying with black women who symbolize strength, but whose social and economic positions are relatively unprotected: the result, so the unconscious says, of their not being good women. Such women may be praised and patronized, but they are not to be emulated.

The cultural imagery dividing black and white women has justified material differences in their lives, which give some reality to fantastical beliefs. Historically, black and white women *have* had different experiences as workers and as contributors to family incomes. Black women have been essential providers much more often than have white women, first as slaves and later as wage-earning domestics, washers and ironers, building maintenance workers, and practical nurses. Even when married, black women continued to work for wages outside the home at higher rates than white women did, supplementing the low wages generally paid to black males. True, there have been noticeable changes in black women's occupations and earnings during the past decade. But the basic importance of the black wife's income has not declined. In middle-income groups, black women work longer hours and more regularly than do white women to achieve the same total family income. Indeed, the major improvements made in black family income relative to white family income during the 1970s were due to the rise in black women's wages relative to white women's, so that black, full-time women workers now have a median income that is 90 percent of the median of full-time white women workers. The increase in black female wages has disguised the failure of black men's incomes to rise above 71 percent of white men's for annual full-time work.

Although the necessity for two income earners has been growing in white families, and rising numbers of white women participate at least part-time in the labor force, white women's chances of relying on the income of a second, higher-paid earner are still considerably greater than are the prospects available to black women. Two factors are important in explaining this fact. First, white male income earners are substantially better paid than are black, and they work slightly more regularly at full-time, year-round jobs. In 1981, 65.2 percent of white males sixteen years and older worked fifty to fifty-two weeks; 58.8 percent of black males were so employed. Black men in families, then, are less likely to find full-time, year-round employment at jobs that pay what white men's jobs pay.

Second, and more strikingly, black women more often have sole responsibility for earning income and supporting a household than do white women. In 1981, almost 42 percent of black households were headed by women; almost 12 percent of white households were. Although the proportion of husband-wife families among all families is declining, among whites as well as among blacks, the proportion is still quite high among whites (85 percent in March 1981) whereas the proportion of black husband-wife families has declined from 66 percent in March 1971 to 54 percent in March 1981. While the same factors—divorce and separation—are affecting both black and white families, they affect blacks disproportionately. The number of divorces for blacks rose from 92 per 1,000 in March 1971 to 233 per 1,000 in March 1981, while the comparable increase for whites was from 48 to 100 per 1,000. More spectacularly, the rate of separations per 1,000 black families rose from 172 in March 1971 to 225 in March 1981 compared with a rise for white families of 21 to 29 per 1,000.

Black women are more likely than white women to be the single support of their households, not only because separations and divorces are more common among blacks, but also because there are many fewer black males of marriageable age than black females in the same age cohorts (fifteen to forty-four). The 1980 Census data indicate that so long as patterns of racially segregated marriages hold, most white women will have a man to marry. According to the 1980 Census of Population, white males in the age range fifteen to forty-four outnumbered white females by about 137,000 out of a total population of 86 million. In fact, white males outnumber white females in all cohorts between fifteen and thirty. In the smaller adult black population of 12.5 million, black women outnumber black men in the fifteen-to-forty-four age range by 680,000. A census undercount of about 9.8 percent for black males age fifteen to forty-four makes these figures slightly less dramatic, although the undercount covers only 70 percent of the imbalance. Why black males are absent is a troubling problem, which may be partially accounted for by much higher rates of death due to homicide among blacks than among whites—39.7 per 100,000 versus 5.8 per 100,000 in 1974. Another factor is the lower male to female ratio at birth: 102:100 among blacks and 106:100 among whites. The 1980 figures are only the most recent indication, however, of a lack of available adult men to share household life. And as Jacquelyne Jackson suggests in "But Where Are The Men?" they have not been present for decades. The black male-to-female ratio has declined during the twentieth century—from a ratio of 98.6 in 1900 to 90.8 in 1970.

When white women claim that they are discriminated against in wages and demonstrate their common plight with black women by pointing to the evidence that all women earn less than black and white men, black women disagree with the conclusion that the major social oppression is sexism. As one black feminist has noted, "the class hierarchy as seen from the poor black woman's position is one of white male in power, followed by white female, then by black male and lastly the black female." While this ranking may not be accurate for white women living on their own incomes (an experience that increasing numbers of white women have at least temporarily), it is true for *most* white women, whose material well-being is assured by the fact that they live with the highest income earners: white men. Thus it is a fallacy when white women claim that they are only slightly better off than black women. Most white women do not *in reality* live on what they earn; they have access to the resources of white male income earners, whose incomes contribute substantially to the actual standard of living for the household or family.

White women are correct in asserting that all female incomes remain low compared with all male incomes, and any woman living as a sole income earner is likely to be precariously perched just above the poverty line. Black women are correct in asserting that the expectation of living on a single female income is much less pervasive or probable for white women. Because of the accident of class position derived from association through daughterhood, wifehood, or sisterhood with various male relations, many white women have assumed that political and legal rights, and protection for women within the family, were universally preeminent goals. Especially in the middle class, they have tacitly accepted degrees of economic dependence and have been unwilling to violate social forms, or to risk economic loss, by demanding that they be separately responsible for their economic support and separately accountable for their wage earnings. At the simplest level, many married middle-class white women have a choice about whether or not to work full-time for wages. They generally do not *have* to earn an equal or major portion of the income that provides their food, clothing, or

shelter. They can choose to engage in political activity, or to find jobs that enable them to perform household chores and to care for preschool children, or to be at home when children return from school. Increasing numbers of married white women with husbands in middle-income brackets are entering the labor market, particularly on a part-time basis, and contributing to family income (on the average, all working wives earn about 27 percent of family income). However, married white middle-class women do not usually have the primary responsibility (and authority) that is derived from earning incomes equivalent to their husbands'. Even in middle-class households where the wife is a full-time income earner, her income is substantially less than her husband's. Ironically, the higher the household income, the less important may be the wife's wages. As Carolyn Shaw Bell has shown, the lower the family's overall earnings, the more significant is the percentage brought in by wives' employment: a reminder that female income is most essential in those families where female incomes are usually the lowest. (A corollary may be that women are more powerful in those families that have less power in society.)

For working-class families, a wife's income may be more essential than in a middle-class family, and yet the income itself so low that working-class women are more aware of their continued need for their husbands' paychecks. So working-class women seem to have recognized their vulnerability on both counts, and they have begun the work of organizing women to demand higher wages in the female sectors and to demand work in higher-paid, working-class male occupations, such as mine workers. The low wages available to white working-class women, however, may have made them more reluctant, like black women fortunate to be living with a male income earner, to join a middle-class women's movement that seems more concerned with redistributing power within the family than challenging the powerlessness of women (and men) outside the home.

The essential fact—that for most women, economic well-being means attachment to a male wage earner—might have led middle-class white women to join efforts with white working-class and with black women to increase their ability to earn income and to end the economic dependency that provides a material basis for male dominance. But white middle-class women have the greatest dependence on male income, in the sense that their households' incomes are highest because of it. Because their derived income is greatest, they have the least incentive to challenge their economic dependence and to advocate the economic self-reliance of all women. In the long run, as divorce and separation statistics indicate, such women do not have a protected and guaranteed position; it is in their long-term interest to consider what their situations might be as single women. But to do so, to consider seriously the problems raised by lesbians, by single black women and by working women who live with working-class white and black men, is to question the organization of a society in which "their" men fare the best.

The necessity to rethink theory so that it incorporates race and class into a coherent comprehension of the life circumstances of varieties of women becomes evident when we are confronted with specific political decisions. In the most recent Congress, several bills were introduced to remedy the "marriage penalty" in the tax system, a system that taxed singles at a lower rate than married couples filing joint returns. This was considered a feminist issue, because it raised the question of how wives' income was to be treated in relation to husbands', and the income of married couples in relation to unmarried ones. There was little discussion, however, of what a feminist goal in changing tax laws would be. Is the goal to encourage the wives of well-paid men to work by not taxing their income as the add-on that raises the family's rate? Is it to reward the family where two earners make almost the same amount, as opposed to the household where the husband earns twice what the wife earns? Is it to support marriage by allowing married couples with joint incomes to pay lower taxes than unmarried couples with joint incomes? Or, should the tax system support all cohabitation by heterosexual couples, thus penalizing single-sex partnerships in relation to heterosexual and/or married ones? All these goals could be advanced by tax legislation.

There has been a paucity of theorizing on other salient issues. Although white women's groups have made some political efforts around policies on employment, wages, welfare payments, and non-traditional job training, their principal energies have gone into causes that might be considered of primary interest to women living in male-dominated households: interests of middle-class women who have not earned their own incomes. Aside from issues of sexual control such as battering, rape, and abortion, which need to be reexamined in light of their impact on women of different races and classes, national women's groups have put much effort into strengthening legislation and enforcement to protect women within families and to ease the consequences of the breakdown of family structures. In national legislation, the guarantee of entitlements to retirement income for divorced and married homemakers has been a major concern. The same desire to protect homemakers has sparked the effort to assure wives' entitlement to private pension income, and to require that husbands inform wives when survivors' benefits are *not* chosen as an option in their pension plans. Even in the area of employment, where women have striven to improve the enforcement of Title VII and equal employment opportunity regulations, some of the most successful efforts have focused on displaced homemakers and their special training and employment needs as a largely white middle-class population who have been disappointed in their dependency on husbands' incomes.

Two vital systems not adequately addressed by either the white liberal or socialist wings of the women's movement are welfare and employment programs. Welfare is a central though difficult topic for feminists to consider. The payment of welfare benefits by the state poses the dilemma that these are then determined by white males who control the state machinery; but payments to mothers also allow arguments about what is fair maintenance to be fought out in the political arena and not in the private household. At the least, we must develop a theory that allows for necessary social dependency, but does not tie dependency to powerlessness. Equally, we need a feminist analysis of employment policy. Should all adults have paid employment, as has been true for many families, especially black ones, and, if so, how will household and consumer chores, and the care of dependent children, the sick and aged, be accommodated? Will the white middle-class women's movement raise the issue of full employment for all adults and not just job equity for those women who "choose" to work?

Welfare, full employment, childcare, and housing seem to be the essential concerns of black women and of working-class women of all races. But they are precisely the theoretical questions and political issues that arouse emotion, because they point to a world in which women live separate from, or as economic equals with, men: the world inhabited by many black women, lesbians, and poor (often old) white women. They return us to the question of why the mainstream women's movement has not allied with black women—why white women have marriage and motherhood as the universal women's issues and the problems of black, lesbian, and single women as special interests.

The speculation provided by my analysis is that white women will not be able to make common cause with black women until they escape the still-powerful identifications of "good" and "bad" women that have been such a pervasive influence in this country. As Fannie Lou Hamer observed in the 1960s, "You [white women] thought you was *more* because you was a woman, and especially a white woman, you had this kind of angel feeling that you were untouchable. . . . But coming to the realization of the thing, her freedom is shackled in chains to mine, and she realizes for the first time that she is not free until I am free." Indeed, white women will not be free of the fear of their own economic self-reliance and psychological independence until they work with black women to raise the status of women who symbolized and displayed female strength, and suffered its burdens.

# The Development of Chicana
# Feminist Discourse

ALMA M. GARCIA

Between 1970 and 1980, a Chicana feminist movement developed in the United States that addressed the specific issues that affected Chicanas as women of color. The growth of the Chicana feminist movement can be traced in the speeches, essays, letters, and articles published in Chicano and Chicana newspapers, journals, newsletters, and other printed materials.

During the sixties, American society witnessed the development of the Chicano movement, a social movement characterized by a politics of protest. The Chicano movement focused on a wide range of issues: social justice, equality, educational reforms, and political and economic self-determination for Chicano communities in the United States. Various struggles evolved within this movement: the United Farmworkers unionization efforts, the New Mexico Land Grant movement, the Colorado-based Crusade for Justice, the Chicano student movement, and the Raza Unida Party.

Chicanas participated actively in each of these struggles. By the end of the sixties, Chicanas began to assess the rewards and limits of their participation. The 1970s witnessed the development of Chicana feminists whose activities, organizations, and writings can be analyzed in terms of a feminist movement by women of color in American society. Chicana feminists outlined a cluster of ideas that crystallized into an emergent Chicana feminist debate. In the same way that Chicano males were reinterpreting the historical and contemporary experience of Chicanos in the United States, Chicanas began to investigate the forces shaping their own experiences as women of color.

The Chicana feminist movement emerged primarily as a result of the dynamics within the Chicano movement. In the 1960s and 1970s, the American political scene witnessed far-reaching social protest movements whose political courses often paralleled and at times exerted influence over each other. The development of feminist movements have been explained by the participation of women in larger social movements. Macias, for example, links the early development of the Mexican feminist movement to the participation of women in the Mexican Revolution. Similarly, Freeman's analysis of the white feminist movement points out that many white feminists who were active in the early years of its development had previously been involved in the new left and civil rights movements. It was in these movements that white feminists experienced the constraints of male domination. Black feminists have similarly traced the development of a Black feminist movement during the 1960s and 1970s to their experiences with sexism in the larger Black movement. In this way, then, the origins of Chicana feminism parallel those of other feminist movements.

## ORIGINS OF CHICANA FEMINISM

Rowbotham argues that women may develop a feminist consciousness as a result of their experiences with sexism in revolutionary struggles or mass social movements. To the extent that such movements are male dominated, women are likely to develop a feminist consciousness. Chicana feminists began the search for a "room of their own" by assessing their participation within the Chicano movement. Their feminist consciousness emerged from a struggle for equality with Chicano men and

From *Gender & Society,* Vol. 3, no. 2 (June, 1989) pp. 217–38. © 1989 Sociologists for Women in Society. Reprinted with permission from Sage Publications, Inc. Footnotes have been deleted.

from a reassessment of the role of the family as a means of resistance to oppressive societal conditions.

Historically, as well as during the 1960s and 1970s, the Chicano family represented a source of cultural and political resistance to the various types of discrimination experienced in American society. At the cultural level, the Chicano movement emphasized the need to safeguard the value of family loyalty. At the political level, the Chicano movement used the family as a strategic organizational tool for protest activities.

Dramatic changes in the structure of Chicano families occurred as they participated in the Chicano movement. Specifically, women began to question their traditional female roles. Thus, a Chicana feminist movement originated from the nationalist Chicano struggle. Rowbotham refers to such a feminist movement as "a colony within a colony." But as the Chicano movement developed during the 1970s, Chicana feminists began to draw their own political agenda and raised a series of questions to assess their role within the Chicano movement. They entered into a dialogue with each other that explicitly reflected their struggles to secure a room of their own within the Chicano movement.

## DEFINING FEMINISM FOR WOMEN OF COLOR

A central question of feminist discourse is the definition of feminism. The lack of consensus reflects different political ideologies and divergent social-class bases. In the United States, Chicana feminists shared the task of defining their ideology and movement with white, Black, and Asian American feminists. Like Black and Asian American feminists, Chicana feminists struggled to gain social equality and end sexist and racist oppression. Like them, Chicana feminists recognized that the nature of social inequality for women of color was multidimensional. Like Black and Asian American feminists, Chicana feminists struggled to gain equal status in the male-dominated nationalist movements and also in American society. To them, feminism represented a movement to end sexist oppression within a broader social protest movement. Again, like Black and Asian American feminists, Chicana feminists fought for social equality in the 1970s. They understood that their movement needed to go beyond women's rights and include the men of their group, who also faced racial subordination. Chicanas believed

that feminism involved more than an analysis of gender because, as women of color, they were affected by both race and class in their everyday lives. Thus, Chicana feminism, as a social movement to improve the position of Chicanas in American society, represented a struggle that was both nationalist and feminist.

Chicana, Black, and Asian American feminists were all confronted with the issue of engaging in a feminist struggle to end sexist oppression within a broader nationalist struggle to end racist oppression. All experienced male domination in their own communities as well as in the larger society. Ngan-Ling Chow identifies gender stereotypes of Asian American women and the patriarchal family structure as major sources of women's oppression. Cultural, political, and economic constraints have, according to Ngan-Ling Chow, limited the full development of a feminist consciousness and movement among Asian American women. The cross-pressures resulting from the demands of a nationalist and a feminist struggle led some Asian American women to organize feminist organizations that, however, continued to address broader issues affecting the Asian American community.

Black women were also faced with addressing feminist issues within a nationalist movement. According to Thornton Dill, Black women played a major historical role in Black resistance movements and, in addition, brought a feminist component to these movements. Black women have struggled with Black men in nationalist movements but have also recognized and fought against the sexism in such political movements in the Black community. Although they wrote and spoke as Black feminists, they did not organize separately from Black men.

Among the major ideological questions facing all three groups of feminists were the relationship between feminism and the ideology of cultural nationalism or racial pride, feminism and feminist baiting within the larger movements, and the relationship between their feminist movements and the white feminist movement.

## CHICANA FEMINISM AND CULTURAL NATIONALISM

Throughout the seventies and in the eighties, Chicana feminists have been forced to respond to the criticism that cultural nationalism and feminism are irreconcilable. In the first issue of the newspaper, *Hijas de Cuauhtemoc,* Anna Nieto Gomez stated that a major issue facing Chicanas active in the Chicana movement was the need to organize to improve their status as women within the larger social movement. Francisca Flores, another leading Chicana feminist, stated:

[Chicanas] can no longer remain in a subservient role or as auxiliary forces in the [Chicano] movement. They must be included in the front line of communication, leadership and organizational responsibility. . . . The issue of equality, freedom and self-determination of the Chicana—like the right of self-determination, equality, and liberation of the Mexican [Chicano] community—is not negotiable. Anyone opposing the right of women to organize into their own form of organization has no place in the leadership of the movement.

Supporting this position, Bernice Rincon argued that a Chicana feminist movement that sought equality and justice for Chicanas would strengthen the Chicano movement. Yet in the process, Chicana feminists challenged traditional gender roles because they limited their participation and acceptance within the Chicano movement.

Throughout the seventies, Chicana feminists viewed the struggle against sexism within the Chicano movement and the struggle against racism in the larger society as integral parts of Chicana feminism. As Nieto Gomez said:

Chicana feminism is in various stages of development. However, in general, Chicana feminism is the recognition that women are oppressed as a group and are exploited as part of *la Raza* people. It is a direction to be responsible to identify and act upon the issues and needs of Chicana women. Chicana feminists are involved in understanding the nature of women's oppression.

Cultural nationalism represented a major ideological component of the Chicano movement. Its emphasis on Chicano cultural pride and cultural survival within an Anglo-dominated society gave significant political direction to the Chicano movement. One source of ideological disagreement between Chicana feminism and this cultural nationalist ideology was cultural survival. Many Chicana feminists believed that a focus on cultural survival did not acknowledge the need to alter male-female relations within Chicano communities. For example, Chicana feminists criticized the notion of the "ideal Chicana" that glorified Chicanas as strong, long-suffering women who had endured and kept Chicano culture and the family intact. To Chicana feminists, this concept represented an obstacle to the redefinition of gender roles. Nieto stated:

Some Chicanas are praised as they emulate the sanctified example set by [the Virgin] Mary. The woman *par excellence* is mother and wife. She is to love and support her husband and to nurture and teach her children. Thus, may she gain fulfillment as a woman. For a Chicana bent upon fulfillment of her personhood, this restricted perspective of her role as a woman is not only inadequate but crippling.

Chicana feminists were also skeptical about the cultural nationalist interpretation of machismo. Such an interpretation viewed machismo as an ideological tool used by the dominant Anglo society to justify the inequalities experienced by Chicanos. According to this interpretation, the relationship between Chicanos and the larger society was that of an internal colony dominated and exploited by the capitalist economy. Machismo, like other cultural traits, was blamed by Anglos for blocking Chicanos from succeeding in American society. In reality, the economic structure and colony-like exploitation were to blame.

Some Chicana feminists agreed with this analysis of machismo, claiming that a mutually reinforcing relationship existed between internal colonialism and the development of the myth of machismo. According to Sosa Riddell, machismo was a myth "propagated by subjugators and colonizers, which created damaging stereotypes of Mexican/Chicano males." As a type of social control imposed by the dominant society on Chicanos, the myth of machismo distorted gender relations within Chicano communities, creating stereotypes of Chicanas as passive and docile women. At this level in the feminist discourse, machismo was seen as an Anglo myth that kept both Chicano and Chicanas in a subordinate status. As Nieto concluded:

Although the term "machismo" is correctly denounced by all because it stereotypes the Latin man . . . it does a great disservice to both men and women. Chicano and Chicana alike must be free to seek their own individual fulfillment.

While some Chicana feminists criticized the myth of machismo used by the dominant society to legitimate racial inequality, others moved beyond this level of analysis to distinguish between the machismo that oppressed both men and women and the sexism in Chicano communities in general, and the Chicano movement in particular, that oppressed Chicana women. According to Vidal, the origins of a Chicana feminist consciousness were prompted by the sexist attitudes and behavior of Chicano males, which constituted a "serious obstacle to women anxious to play a role in the struggle for Chicana liberation."

Furthermore, many Chicana feminists disagreed with the cultural nationalist view that machismo could be a positive value within a Chicano cultural value system. They challenged the view that machismo was a source of masculine pride for Chicanos and therefore a defense mechanism against the dominant society's racism. Although Chicana feminists recognized that Chicanos faced discrimination from the dominant society, they adamantly disagreed with those who believed that machismo was a form of cultural resistance to such discrimination. Chicana feminists called for changes in the ideologies responsible for distorting relations between women and men. One such change was to modify the cultural nationalist position that viewed machismo as a source of cultural pride.

Chicana feminists called for a focus on the universal aspects of sexism that shape gender relations in both Anglo and Chicano culture. While they acknowledged the economic exploitation of all Chicanos, Chicana feminists outlined the double exploitation experienced by Chicanas. Sosa Riddell concluded: "It was when Chicanas began to seek work outside of the family groups that sexism became a key factor of oppression along with racism." Francisca Flores summarized some of the consequences of sexism:

It is not surprising that more and more Chicanas are forced to go to work in order to supplement the family income. The children are farmed out to a relative to baby-sit with them, and since these women are employed in the lower income jobs, the extra pressure placed on them can become unbearable.

Thus, while the Chicano movement was addressing the issue of racial oppression facing all Chicanos, Chicana feminists argued that it lacked an analysis of sexism. Similarly, Black and Asian American women stressed the interconnectedness of race and gender oppression. Hooks analyzes racism and sexism in terms of their "intersecting, complementary nature." She also emphasizes that one struggle should not take priority over the other. White criticizes Black men whose nationalism limited discussions of Black women's experiences with sexist oppression. The writings of other Black Feminists criticized a Black cultural nationalist ideology that overlooked the consequences of sexist oppression. Many Asian American women were also critical of the Asian American movement whose focus on racism ignored the impact of sexism on the daily lives of women. The participation of Asian American women in various community struggles increased their encounters with sexism. As a result, some Asian American women developed a feminist consciousness and organized as women around feminist issues.

## CHICANA FEMINISM AND FEMINIST BAITING

The systematic analysis by Chicana feminists of the impact of racism and sexism on Chicanas in American society and, above all, within the Chicano movement was often misunderstood as a threat to the political unity of the Chicano movement. As Marta Cotera, a leading voice of Chicana feminism, pointed out:

The aggregate cultural values we [Chicanas] share can also work to our benefit if we choose to scrutinize our cultural traditions, isolate the positive attributes and interpret them for the benefit of women. It's unreal that *Hispanas* have been browbeaten for so long about our so-called conservative (meaning reactionary) culture. It's also unreal that we have let men interpret culture only as those practices and attitudes that determine who does the dishes around the house. We as women also have the right to interpret and define the philosophical and religious traditions beneficial to us within our culture, and which we have inherited as our tradition. To do this, we must become both conversant with our history and philosophical evolution, and analytical about the institutional and behavioral manifestations of the same.

Such Chicana feminists were attacked for developing a "divisive ideology"—a feminist ideology that was frequently viewed as a threat to the Chicano movement as a whole. As Chicana feminists examined their roles as women activists within the Chicano movement, an ideological split developed. One group active in the Chicano movement saw themselves as "loyalists" who believed that the Chicano movement did not have to deal with sexual inequities since Chicano men as well as Chicano women experienced racial oppression. According to Nieto Gomez, who was not a loyalist, their view was that if men oppress women, it is not the men's fault but rather that of the system.

Even if such a problem existed, and they did not believe that it did, the loyalists maintained that such a matter would best be resolved internally within the Chicano movement. They denounced the formation of a separate Chicana feminist movement on the grounds that it was a politically dangerous strategy, perhaps Anglo inspired. Such a movement would undermine the unity of the Chicano movement by raising an issue that was not seen as a central one. Loyalists viewed racism as the most important issue within the Chicano movement. Nieto Gomez quotes one such loyalist:

I am concerned with the direction that the Chicanas are taking in the movement. The words such as liberation, sexism, male chauvinism, etc., were prevalent. The terms mentioned above plus the theme of individualism is a concept of the Anglo society; terms prevalent in the Anglo women's movement. The *familia* has always been our strength in our culture. But it seems evident . . . that you [Chicana feminists] are not concerned with the *familia,* but are influenced by the Anglo woman's movement.

Chicana feminists were also accused of undermining the values associated with Chicano culture. Loyalists saw the Chicana feminist movement as an "anti-family, anti-cultural, and anti-man and therefore an anti-Chicano movement." Feminism was, above all, believed to be an individualistic search for identity that detracted from the Chicano movement's "real" issues, such as racism. Nieto Gomez quotes a loyalist as stating:

And since when does a Chicana need identity? If you are a real Chicana then no one regardless of the degrees needs to tell you about it. The only ones who need identity are the *vendidas,* the *falsas,* and the opportunists.

The ideological conflicts between Chicana feminists and loyalists persisted throughout the seventies. Disagreements between these two groups became exacerbated during various Chicana conferences. At times, such confrontations served to increase Chicana feminist activity that challenged the loyalists' attacks, yet these attacks also served to suppress feminist activities.

Chicana feminist lesbians experienced even stronger attacks from those who viewed feminism as a divisive ideology. In a political climate that already viewed feminist ideology with suspicion, lesbianism as a sexual lifestyle and political ideology came under even more attack. Clearly, a cultural nationalist ideology that perpetuated such stereotypical images of Chicanas as "good wives and good mothers" found it difficult to accept a Chicana feminist lesbian movement.

Cherríe Moraga's writings during the 1970s reflect the struggles of Chicana feminist lesbians who, together with other Chicana feminists, were finding the sexism evident within the Chicano movement intolerable. Just as Chicana feminists analyzed their life circumstances as members of an ethnic minority and as women, Chicana feminist lesbians addressed themselves to the oppression they experienced as lesbians. As Moraga stated:

My lesbianism is the avenue through which I have learned the most about silence and oppression. . . . In this country, lesbianism is a poverty— as is being brown, as is being a woman, as is being just plain poor. The danger lies in ranking the oppressions. The danger lies in failing to acknowledge the specificity of the oppression.

Chicana, Black, and Asian American feminists experienced similar cross-pressures of feminist-baiting and lesbian-baiting attacks. As they organized around feminist struggles, these women of color encountered criticism from both male and female cultural nationalists who often viewed feminism as little more than an "anti-male" ideology. Lesbianism was identified as an extreme derivation of feminism. A direct connection was frequently made that viewed feminism and lesbianism as synonymous. Feminists were labeled lesbians, and lesbians as feminists. Attacks against feminists—Chicanas, Blacks, and Asian Americans—derived from the existence of homophobia within each of these communities. As lesbian women of color published their writings, attacks against them increased.

Responses to such attacks varied within and between the feminist movements of women of color. Some groups tried one strategy and later adopted another. Some lesbians pursued a separatist strategy within their own racial and ethnic communities. Others attempted to form lesbian coalitions across racial and ethnic lines. Both strategies represented a response to the marginalization of lesbians produced by recurrent waves of homophobic sentiments in Chicano, Black, and Asian American communities. A third response consisted of working within the broader nationalist movements in these communities and the feminist movements within them in order to challenge their heterosexual biases and resultant homophobia. As early as 1974, the "Black Feminist Statement" written by a Boston-based feminist group—the Combahee River Collective—stated: "We struggle together with Black men against racism, while we also struggle with Black men against sexism." Similarly, Moraga challenged the white feminist movement to examine its racist tendencies; the Chicano movement, its sexist tendencies; and both, their homophobic tendencies. In this way, Moraga argued that such movements to end oppression would begin to respect diversity within their own ranks.

Chicana feminists as well as Chicana feminist lesbians continued to be labeled *vendidas* or "sellouts." Chicana loyalists continued to view Chicana feminism as associated, not only with melting into white society, but more seriously, with dividing the Chicano movement. Similarly, many Chicano males were convinced that Chicana feminism was a divisive ideology incompatible with Chicano cultural nationalism. Nieto Gomez said that "[with] respect to [the] Chicana feminist, their credibility is reduced when they are associated with [feminism] and white women." She added that, as a result, Chicana feminists often faced harassment and ostracism within the Chicano movement. Similarly, Cotera stated that Chicanas "are suspected of assimilating into the feminist ideology of an alien [white] culture that actively seeks our cultural domination."

Chicana feminists responded quickly and often vehemently to such charges. Flores answered these antifeminist attacks in an editorial in which she argued that birth control, abortion, and sex education were not merely "white issues." In response to the accusation that feminists were responsible for the "betrayal of [Chicano] culture and heritage," Flores said, "Our culture hell"—a phrase that became a dramatic slogan of the Chicana feminist movement.

Chicana feminists' defense throughout the 1970s against those claiming that a feminist movement was divisive for the Chicano movement was to reassess their roles within the Chicano movement and to call for an end to male domination. Their challenges of traditional gender roles represented a means to achieve equality. In order to increase the participation of and opportunities for women in the Chicano movement, feminists agreed that both Chicanos and Chicanas had to address the issue of gender inequality. Furthermore, Chicana feminists argued that the resistance that they encountered reflected the existence of sexism on the part of Chicano males and the antifeminist attitudes of the Chicana loyalists. Nieto Gomez, reviewing the experiences of Chicana feminists in the Chicano movement, concluded that Chicanas "involved in discussing and applying the women's question have been ostracized, isolated and ignored." She argued that "in

organizations where cultural nationalism is extremely strong, Chicana feminists experience intense harassment and ostracism."

Black and Asian American women also faced severe criticism as they pursued feminist issues in their own communities. Indeed, as their participation in collective efforts to end racial oppression increased, so did their confrontations with sexism. Ngan-Ling Chow describes the various sources of such criticism directed at Asian American women:

> Asian American women are criticized for the possible consequences of their protests: weakening the male ego, dilution of effort and resources in Asian American communities, destruction of working relationships between Asian men and women, setbacks for the Asian American cause, co-optation into the larger society, and eventual loss of ethnic identity for Asian Americans as a whole. In short, affiliation with the feminist movement is perceived as a threat to solidarity within their own community.

Similar criticism was experienced by Black feminists.

## CHICANA FEMINISTS AND WHITE FEMINISTS

It is difficult to determine the extent to which Chicana feminists sympathized with the white feminist movement. A 1976 study at the University of San Diego that examined the attitudes of Chicanas regarding the white feminist movement found that the majority of Chicanas surveyed believed that the movement had affected their lives. In addition, they identified with such key issues as the right to legal abortions on demand and access to low-cost birth control. Nevertheless, the survey found that "even though the majority of Chicanas . . . could relate to certain issues of the women's movement, for the most part they saw it as being an elitist movement comprised of white middle-class women who [saw] the oppressor as the males of this country."

Nevertheless, some Chicana feminists considered the possibility of forming coalitions with white feminists as their attempts to work within the Chicano movement were suppressed. Since white feminists were themselves struggling against sexism, building coalitions with them was seen as an alternative strategy for Chicana feminists. Almost immediately, however, Chicana feminists recognized the problems involved in adopting this political strategy. As Longeaux y Vasquez acknowledged, "Some of our own Chicanas may be attracted to the white woman's liberation movement, but we really don't feel comfortable there. We want to be a Chicana *primero* [first]." For other Chicanas, the demands of white women were "irrelevant to the Chicana movement."

Several issues made such coalition building difficult. First, Chicana feminists criticized what they considered to be a cornerstone of white feminist thought, an emphasis on gender oppression to explain the life circumstances of women. Chicana feminists believed that the white feminist movement overlooked the effects of racial oppression experienced by Chicanas and other women of color. Thus, Del Castillo maintained that the Chicana feminist movement was "different primarily because we are [racially] oppressed people." In addition, Chicana feminists criticized white feminists who believed that a general women's movement would be able to overcome racial differences among women. Chicanas interpreted this as a failure by the white feminist movement to deal with the issue of racism. Without the incorporation of an analysis of racial oppression to explain the experiences of Chicanas as well as of other women of color, Chicana feminists believed that a coalition with white feminists would be highly unlikely. As Longeaux y Vasquez concluded: "We must have a clearer vision of our plight and certainly we cannot blame our men for the oppression of the women."

In the 1970s, Chicana feminists reconciled their demands for an end to sexism within the Chicano movement and their rejection of the saliency of gender oppression by separating the two issues. They clearly identified the struggle against sexism in the Chicano movement as a major issue, arguing that sexism prevented their full participation. They also argued that sexist behavior and ideology on the part of both Chicano males and Anglos represented the key to understanding women's oppression. However, they remained critical of an analysis of women's experiences that focused exclusively on gender oppression.

Chicana feminists adopted an analysis that began with race as a critical variable in interpreting the experiences of Chicano communities in the United States. They expanded this analysis by identifying gender as a variable interconnected with race in analyzing the specific daily life circumstances of Chicanas as women in Chicano communities. Chicana feminists did not view women's struggles as secondary to the nationalist movement but argued instead for an analysis of race and gender as multiple sources of oppression. Thus, Chicana feminism went beyond the limits of an exclusively racial theory of oppression that tended to overlook gender and also went beyond the limits of a theory of oppression based exclusively on gender that tended to overlook race.

A second factor preventing an alliance between Chicana feminists and white feminists was the middle-class orientation of white feminists. While some Chicana feminists recognized the legitimacy of the demands made by white feminists and even admitted sharing some of these demands, they argued that "it is not our business as Chicanas to identify with the white women's liberation movement as a home base for working for our people."

Throughout the 1970s, Chicana feminists viewed the white feminist movement as a middle-class movement. In contrast, Chicana feminists analyzed the Chicano movement in general as a working-class movement. They repeatedly made reference to such differences, and many Chicana feminists began their writings with a section that disassociated themselves from the "women's liberation movement." Chicana feminists as activists in the broader Chicano movement identified as major struggles the farmworkers movement, welfare rights, undocumented workers, and prison rights. Such issues were seen as far removed from the demands of the white feminist movement, and Chicana feminists could not get white feminist organizations to deal with them.

Similar concerns regarding the white feminist movement were raised by Black and Asian American feminists. Black feminists have documented the historical and contemporary schisms between Black feminists and white feminists, emphasizing the socioeconomic and political differences. More specifically, Black feminists have been critical of the white feminists who advocate a female solidarity that cuts across racial, ethnic, and social class lines. As Thornton Dill states:

> The cry "Sisterhood is powerful!" has engaged only a few segments of the female population in the United States. Black, Hispanic, Native American, and Asian American women of all classes, as well as many working-class women, have not readily identified themselves as sisters of the white middle-class women who have been in the forefront of the movement.

Like Black feminists, Asian American feminists have also had strong reservations regarding the white feminist movement. For many Asian

Americans, white feminism has primarily focused on gender as an analytical category and has thus lacked a systematic analysis of race and class.

White feminist organizations were also accused of being exclusionary, patronizing, or racist in their dealings with Chicanas and other women of color. Cotera states:

> Minority women could fill volumes with examples of put-down, put-ons, and out-and-out racism shown to them by the leadership in the [white feminist] movement. There are three major problem areas in the minority-majority relationship in the movement: (1) paternalism or materialism, (2) extremely limited opportunities for minority women . . . , (3) outright discrimination against minority women in the movement.

Although Chicana feminists continued to be critical of building coalitions with white feminists toward the end of the seventies, they acknowledged the diversity of ideologies within the white feminist movement. Chicana feminists sympathetic to radical socialist feminism because of its anticapitalist framework wrote of working-class oppression that cut across racial and ethnic lines. Their later writings discussed the possibility of joining with white working-class women, but strategies for forming such political coalitions were not made explicit.

Instead, Del Castillo and other Chicana feminists favored coalitions between Chicanas and other women of color while keeping their respective autonomous organizations. Such coalitions would recognize the inherent racial oppression of capitalism rather than universal gender oppression. When Longeaux y Vasquez stated that she was "Chicana *primero*," she was stressing the saliency of race over gender in explaining the oppression experienced by Chicanas. The word *Chicana* however, simultaneously expresses a woman's race and gender. Not until later—in the 1980s—would Chicana feminist ideology call for an analysis that stressed the interrelationship of race, class, and gender in explaining the conditions of Chicanas in American society, just as Black and Asian American feminists have done.

Chicana feminists continued to stress the importance of developing autonomous feminist organizations that would address the struggles of Chicanas as members of an ethnic minority and as women. Rather than attempt to overcome the obstacles to coalition building between Chicana feminists and white feminists, Chicanas called for autonomous feminist organizations for all women of color. Chicana feminists believed that sisterhood was indeed powerful but only to the extent that racial and class differences were understood and, above all, respected. As Nieto concludes:

> The Chicana must demand that dignity and respect within the women's rights movement which allows her to practice feminism within the context of her own culture. . . . Her approaches to feminism must be drawn from her own world.

## CHICANA FEMINISM: AN EVOLVING FUTURE

Chicana feminists, like Black, Asian American, and Native American feminists, experience specific life conditions that are distinct from those of white feminists. Such socioeconomic and cultural differences in Chicano communities directly shaped the development of Chicana feminism and the relationship between Chicana feminists and feminists of other racial and ethnic groups, including white feminists. Future dialogue among all feminists will require a mutual understanding of the existing differences as well as the similarities. Like other women of color, Chicana feminists must address issues that specifically affect them as women of color. In addition, Chicana feminists must address those issues that have particular impact on Chicano communities, such as poverty, limited opportunities for higher education, high school dropouts, health care, bilingual education, immigration reform, prison reform, welfare, and, most recently, United States policies in Central America.

At the academic level, an increasing number of Chicana feminists continue to join in a collective effort to carry on the feminist legacy inherited from the 1970s. In June 1982, a group of Chicana academics organized a national feminist organization called Mujeres Activas en Letras y Cambio Social (MALCS) in order to build a support network for Chicana professors, undergraduates, and graduate students. The organization's major goal is to fight against race, class, and gender oppression facing Chicanas in institutions of higher education. In addition, MALCS aims to bridge the gap between academic work and the Chicano community. MALCS has organized three Chicana/Latina summer research institutes at the University of California at Davis and publishes a working paper series.

During the 1982 conference of the National Association for Chicano Studies, a panel organized by Mujeres en Marcha, a feminist group from the University of California at Berkeley, discussed three major issues facing Chicana feminists in higher education in particular and the Chicano movement in general. Panelists outlined the issues as follows:

1. For a number of years, Chicanas have heard claims that a concern with issues specifically affecting Chicanas is merely a distraction/diversion from the liberation of Chicano people as a whole. What are the issues that arise when women are asked to separate their exploitation as women from the other forms of oppression that we experience?

2. Chicanas are confronted daily by the limitations of being a woman in this patriarchal society; the attempts to assert these issues around sexism are often met with resistance and scorn. What are some of the major difficulties in relations amongst ourselves? How are the relationships between women and men affected? How are the relationships of women to women and men to men affected? How do we overcome the constraints of sexism?

3. It is not uncommon that our interests as feminists are challenged on the basis that we are simply falling prey to the interests of white middle-class women. We challenge the notion that there is no room for a Chicana movement within our own community. We, as women of color, have a unique set of concerns that are separate from white women and from men of color.

While these issues could not be resolved at the conference, the panel succeeded in generating an ongoing discussion within the National Association for Chicano Studies (NACS). Two years later, in 1984, the national conference of NACS, held in Austin, Texas, adopted the theme "Voces de la Mujer" in response to demands from the Chicana Caucus. As a result, for the first time since its founding in 1972, the NACS national conference addressed the issue of women. Compared with past conferences, a large number of Chicanas participated by presenting their research and chairing and moderating panels. A plenary session addressed the problems of gender inequality in higher education and within NACS. At the national business meeting, the issue of sexism within NACS was again seriously debated as it continues to be one of the "unsettled issues" of concern to Chicana feminists. A significant outcome of this conference was the publication of the NACS 1984 conference proceedings, which marked the first time that the association's anthology was devoted completely to Chicanas and Mexicanas.

The decade of the 1980s has witnessed a rephrasing of the critical question concerning the nature of the oppression experienced by Chicanas and other women of color. Chicana feminists, like Black feminists, are asking what are the consequences of the intersection of race, class, and gender in the daily lives of women in American society, emphasizing the simultaneity of these critical variables for women of color. In their labor-force participation, wages, education, and poverty levels, Chicanas have made few gains in comparison to white men and women and Chicano men. To analyze these problems, Chicana feminists have investigated the structures of racism, capitalism, and patriarchy, especially as they are experienced by the majority of Chicanas. Clearly, such issues will need to be explicitly addressed by an evolving Chicana feminist movement, analytically and politically.

# The Feminist Movement:
# Where Are All the Asian American Women?

ESTHER NGAN-LING CHOW

From its inception the feminist movement in the United States has been predominantly white and middle class. Like blacks, Hispanics, and other women of color, Asian American women have not joined white women and, thus far, have not made a great impact on the movement. Since the late 1960s, Asian Americans have begun to organize themselves and build bonds with other women's groups to advocate for their civil rights as a racial minority and as women. Their relative lack of political activism stems from cultural, psychological, and social oppressions which historically discouraged them from organizing. This resulted in their apparent political invisibility and powerlessness.

## POLITICAL ORGANIZING OF ASIAN AMERICAN WOMEN: AN OVERVIEW

Following the civil rights movement in the 1950s, and the feminist movement in the 1960s, Asian American women began to organize formally and informally to address various sources of discontent and social inequities, and to work toward improving conditions for themselves and the Asian American communities. However, political organizing among Asian American women has been slow and limited in many respects. Their political invisibility is related partly to their small numbers in the U.S. population, a result of past restrictive U.S. immigration policies toward Asians. As of the 1980 census, Asian Americans comprise 1.6 percent (3.5 million) of the total U.S. population. Slightly over half of the Asian American population is female. In addition, ethnic diversity among Asian Americans and geographic dispersion make it difficult for them to organize

and be perceived as a significant group with political force.

To some extent, political participation may be a class privilege for women who have the luxury of time, money, and energy. Slightly more than half of the Asian women in the United States are immigrants and they are generally preoccupied with balancing responsibilities at home, in the workplace, and in the community. Like their white counterparts, well-to-do or better-educated Asian American women formed the early women's groups, such as church organizations, social service centers, and women's professional societies.

Few in number and with little institutionalized leadership, these groups have been traditional and conservative in nature, frequently serving as auxiliaries to male organizations that tend to support the male status quo. Only to a very limited extent have they functioned to advance the cause of women's liberation. While there have been efforts to organize Asian American women around specific issues and concerns (e.g., the unavailability or high cost of basic goods, preservation of history and poetry of the Angel Island Immigration Station, World War II internment camps), these attempts have generally lacked continuity and support, thus limiting the emergence of Asian American women as a formalized force. However, these initial efforts of organizing served as a forum where women acquired leadership skills and political experience helpful in future organizing.

The civil rights and feminist movements guide Asian American women in many ways. They help them to become aware of their doubly disadvantaged positions as members of a racial minority and as females, to learn about the structural sources of their deprivation and

From Asian Women United of California, *Making Waves: An Anthology of Writings by and about Asian American Women* (Boston: Beacon, 1989). Reprinted with permission from Beacon Press. Footnotes have been deleted.

social inequalities, and to acknowledge the need to resolve their unique problems.

Following the lead of blacks, many Asian American organizations were created to combat racism and to work toward unity with other racial minorities. The women who joined these organizations are mostly middle-class, U.S.-born, college-educated, professional, and relatively established, and many are strong and active participants. Many others are aware they occupy subservient positions and are relegated to traditional women's functions. They know this prevents them from developing their potential or from holding leadership positions, but their ethnic pride and loyalty frequently keep them from revolt.

More recently, Asian American women have recognized that some of these organizations have not been responsive to their particular needs and concerns. These members also protest that their intense involvement has not, and will not, result in equal participation and leadership development as long as the traditional sex-role relationship between Asian men and women remains unchanged. Despite their efforts at sensitizing Asian men about their attitudes toward, and treatment of, women, some Asian women have opted for a separate organization to deal with their specific issues and problems and to maximize their participation.

Since the late 1960s, several Asian American women's groups have been established in local communities across the country. These include women's courses sponsored by college-level Asian American studies programs, community education programs, social service programs, women's unions, physical and mental health projects, and political interest groups. Many of these groups were short-lived because they lacked funding, leadership, grassroots support, membership, or strong networking. Susie Ling and Sucheta Mazumdar recently pointed out that a lack of momentum and direction also plagued many of the organizations.

Contrary to the common belief about the passivity of Asian American women, they tend to be more actively involved in women's groups of their respective ethnic backgrounds and in Asian groups than in white feminist organizations. Many of them (e.g., National Organization of Pan Asian Women, Asian American Women United, Vietnamese Women's Association, Filipino American Women Network, and Cambodian Women for Progress, Inc.) are organized at the regional level and are in the process of expanding their influence and building networks from the grassroots level to a

national one. For example, the Organization of Chinese American Women is nationally based, with over one thousand members throughout the United States. And the National Network of Asian and Pacific Women consists of many regional groups working to build a visible political force.

Like their white counterparts, the Asian women participants in the feminist movement are not homogeneous, but can be classified into two main types: the radical group and women's rights support group. Many participants in the radical group joined the civil rights movement in the 1960s. Subscribing to radical politics, some of these Asian women organized small study groups. They did research to analyze the circumstances and events causing the subordinate position of women, explored new ways of thinking to alter or revolutionize the social conditions of Asian American women, and sought collective action to end all forms of oppression, including sexism.

The second group, the women's rights support group, consists of those who have gained confidence, leadership skills, and experience through women's groups within the Asian communities and have become active in various women's organizations of the larger society. Some of its members witnessed or suffered from gender oppression within the Asian American communities and the society at large and then sought to organize women's groups with this and other specific women's concerns as their top priorities.

The radical group and women's rights support group differ more in their ideological positions than in their strategies and actions. The goals of the women's rights group are to combat sexism and racism, to achieve social equality and justice in society, and to increase the social participation of women at all levels. The goal of the radical group is to build a classless society, for its members believe that once the class struggle is over, sexism and racism will be resolved. While the women's rights groups subscribes to a reform ideology attempting to make more limited and gradual change within the social system, the radical group adheres to a radical ideology advocating large-scale revolutionary change that would eliminate structural barriers based on gender, race, class, and culture and lead to social equality and human liberation.

In other words, the women's rights group maintains a certain commitment to the basic structure of the system viewing it as either essentially just or at least acceptable. Hence, their efforts are aimed at making specific improvements within the system. The radical group is, however, critical of the American system, which they see as never intending to include Asian Americans, nonwhites, or even the majority of working-class Americans. Building a class movement and/or supporting the civil rights movement are primary concerns for some members of this group rather than actively joining the feminist movement in the larger society.

However, different as their political ideologies are, the two groups share many common tactics and strategies, such as consciousness-raising, education and training, peaceful demonstration and rallies, establishment of counter-institutions for women, active lobbying and negotiation for policy changes, and other program interventions.

## BARRIERS TO POLITICAL ACTIVISM

In order to become and remain politically active, Asian American women must overcome many barriers at various levels: in individuals, in racial relations, in the cultural system, in the class structure, in gender-role stratification, and in the legal-political system. These constitute the main sources of multiple oppression faced by this group of minority women and can be classified into two major types: internal and external barriers.

The former refers to those factors that are specifically inherent to Asian American women as a group, including psychological constraints, cultural restrictions, and patriarchy and structural impediments. The latter refers to those elements existing primarily in American society at large that have kept them from full involvement in the women's liberation movement, including legal-political barriers, racial insensitivity and unreceptivity, and class cleavage. External barriers are more invidious and harder for Asian American women to overcome than internal ones. These two types of barrier may be dialectical in nature, providing stability as well as contradiction in the life experience of many Asian American women.

## INTERNAL BARRIERS

### Psychological Constraints

Because of their dual status, Asian American women derive their identification and self-esteem from both ethnicity and gender. Although Asian American women may benefit from and contribute significantly to the feminist movement, joining such a movement seems to be a double bind for them because it pits ethnic identity against gender identity. It could also lead to absorption or cooptation into the larger society, resulting in an eventual loss of ethnic identity. In any case, Asian American women must deal with this identity crisis. The key issue here is how to balance one's ethnic and sexual or gender identification in order to develop a healthy self-concept.

Research has indicated that gender-role stereotypes are psychologically and socially detrimental to the personality and achievement of women. And Asian American women suffer from racial stereotypes as well. All stereotypes, whether positive or negative, serve as self-fulfilling prophecies when contending with them gradually leads to internalizing them as part of an illusionary reality. Being perceived generally as subservient, obedient, passive, hard working, and exotic, Asian American women themselves become convinced that they should behave in accordance with these stereotyped expectations. But if they act accordingly, they are then criticized for doing so, becoming victims of the stereotypes imposed by others. For Asian American women to develop their political potential, they must develop a positive self-concept and maintain psychological well-being.

### Cultural Restrictions

Although certain Asian values emphasizing education, achievement, and diligence account for the high level of aspiration and success of some Asian American women, other values hinder active political participation. Such cultural limitation is further compounded by the adjustment to American culture, which is often in conflict and contradiction with their ethnic one.

Four cultural dilemmas frequently face Asian American women: (1) obedience vs. independence; (2) collective (or familial) vs. individual interest; (3) fatalism vs. change; and (4) self-control vs. self-expression or spontaneity. On the one hand, adherence to Asian values, that is, obedience, familial interest, fatalism, and self-control, tends to foster submissiveness, passivity, pessimism, timidity, inhibition, and adaptiveness, which are not necessarily conducive to political activism. On the other hand, acceptance of the American values of independence, individualism, mastery of one's environment through change, and self-expression generates self-interest, aggressiveness, initiative, and expressive spontaneity. All these traits tend to encourage political activism, but at the same time are incompatible with the family upbringing of most Asian American women. The key problem here is how to maintain a bicultural existence by selecting appropriate elements of both cultural worlds to make the best adaptation according to the demands of social circumstances.

Among Asian Americans, apathy and avoidance are common reactions to unpleasant and stressful situations, particularly when others are trying to involve them in political activity. Because one of the major reasons Asians immigrate to this country is to seek political refuge and escape the political purges and turmoils of their homelands, this avoidance is not surprising. For example, generally and historically women in China have been socialized to be politically apathetic and now as immigrants are still discouraged from participating in organizations that challenge the status quo.

Unfamiliarity with the language is another factor that hinders the acculturation and political participation of Asian immigrant women. This barrier limits the extent to which Asian American women can express themselves, reduces their ability to make demands, restricts their access to many types of information, curtails the flow and scope of communication with others, and eventually limits the development of political efficacy in America. Although the English proficiency level of many Asian American women of foreign birth is generally adequate for functioning well in the workplace and in social circles, language remains a handicap for some. These women tend to prefer speaking in their native tongue, feel inhibited from engaging in open dialogue with others in English, and subsequently increase their political powerlessness and decrease their ability to influence others. The American-born are better able to overcome this communication difficulty and thereby can participate readily in the larger society. However, their physical features still remind others of their foreign backgrounds, thus presumably limiting full acceptance by others in the larger society. The integration of Asian American women of diverse backgrounds and generations into both the Asian American communities and the larger feminist movement remains key for their future political activism.

## Patriarchy and Structural Impediments

As long as patriarchy persists, the social institutions that encompass Asian American women will continue to perpetuate the devaluation and subjugation of women. School, family, workplace, and other social institutions within and outside the Asian communities all reinforce this gender-role conditioning. The education system has frequently failed to provide women with knowledge of their legal rights. The doctrine of three obediences for a Chinese woman to her father, husband, and son well illustrates her subservient roles. The male is still perceived as major breadwinner and the woman as homemaker. For many employed Asian American women, managing multiple roles is a significant problem. Those with young children are more likely than their white counterparts to stay at home. Overburdened with family and work, and without much support and cooperation from their spouses and sometimes from other family members, Asian American women find political participation beyond their own ethnic group difficult, if not impossible.

Although many Asian American women do engage in political organizing within ethnic communities, their activity in white feminist organizations is often perceived by their male partners and even their female peers as a move toward separatism. They are warned that the consequences of separation will threaten the male ego, damage working relationships between Asian men and women, and dilute efforts and resources for the Asian American cause. All these forces have impeded Asian American women from more active participation in the larger feminist movement.

## EXTERNAL BARRIERS

### Legal-Political Barriers

Historically, structural receptivity to Asian Americans, men and women alike, has been low in the United States. Legal and political barriers deeply rooted in the social system can be documented from the first immigration of Asians to this country. For example, fourteen pieces of legislation were written by state and federal governments to discriminate against the Chinese in America and to strip them of their rights as lawful members of society. The economic exploitation and deprivation that frequently go hand in hand with legal exclusion under political dominance are strongly evident in the century-old history of Asian Americans.

To prevent Asian Americans from forming a strong coalition and political force, U.S. immigration policies emphasized the importance of cheap labor and discouraged the formation of family unity by setting up restrictive quotas for women and children of Asian laborers. The virtual absence of Asian women until the 1950s and the enforcement of antimiscegenation laws made it difficult for these laborers to find mates in this country. As a result, bachelor communities consisting mainly of single males became characteristic of many Asian ethnic groups.

Although many of these discriminatory laws have been revoked, the community still bears the long-term effects of cultural, socioeconomic, and political exploitation and oppression. Institutional discrimination and deprivation continue, but in new forms, such as the Immigration Reform and Control Act of 1986, which disproportionately affects people of color, including Asians, and exclusion elsewhere of Asian Americans as minorities entitled to special services and opportunities. As long as Asian Americans are not treated as full citizens of this country, their political participation and contribution will remain limited.

## Racial Insensitivity and Unreceptivity

Along with other women of color, some Asian American women criticize the role that white women, in partnership with white men, play in defending and perpetuating racism. The capitalist patriarchy has differential effects on white women and Asian American women. While white women experience sexism, Asian American women suffer from both racism and sexism. For example, sexual stereotypes compounded with racial stereotypes continue to degrade the self-image of Asian American women. White supremacy and male dominance, both individually and in combination, have detrimental effects on the political functioning of Asian American women. For this reason, white women are seen as partly responsible for perpetuating racial prejudice and discriminatory practices.

More specifically, Asian American women who are committed to fighting both sexism and racism feel that white feminists are not aware of or sympathetic to the differences in concerns and priorities of Asian American women. Although Asian American women share many common issues and concerns with white feminists, many tend to place a higher priority on eradicating

racism than sexism. They prefer to join groups that advocate improved conditions for people of their own ethnic background rather than groups oriented toward women's issues only. They advocate for multiculturally sensitive programs, not ones just aimed at reforming gender inequality. For instance, they prefer multilingual childcare programs and counseling services that bridge communication gaps and promote cultural understanding.

Some white feminists may accept Asian American women and other women of color as an integral part of the movement in the abstract. But entrance into the predominantly white feminist organizations has not been extended to include them in actuality. The open-door policy allows Asian American women as members, but closed attitudes limit their efforts to work on issues and problems concerning Asian American women, to build coalitions, and to influence decision making. Without understanding the history and culture of Asian American women, some white feminists are impatient with the relatively low level of consciousness and apparent slow progress made by Asian American women in organizing. Their token presence indicates the superficial nature of the invitation to join. The same frustrations of voicelessness, namelessness, and powerlessness run parallel to the experience of white women trying to break into a male-dominated system, the "old-boy" network. While white feminists belong to the center of the movement, Asian American women and women of color remain on its margin.

## Class Cleavage

In addition to racial insensitivity, the typical middle- and upper-class composition of the feminist movement repels many Asian American women who feel more concern about working-class women. The economic class structure has unfortunately created social barriers between working-class women and middle- or upper-class women. While affluent white women, because of their class entitlement, have more resources, extra time, and the personal energy for political organizing, working-class Asian American women struggle to survive and have little time to question the economic structure. They may not therefore fully understand how the class structure of America limits their aspirations and achievements. Furthermore, greater acceptance of traditional sex-typed ideology by Asian American women and their perception of the feminist movement as alien, radical, and irrelevant to their needs also account for their lack of participation. As a result, it is difficult for them to relate their own economic issues to other women's concerns and place them in a larger sociopolitical context.

Class cleavage exists not only in the larger feminist movement, but also among Asian American women as well. While Asian American working-class women tend to see economic survival as a primary concern, those with high levels of education, social status, and income tend to be more concerned with job advancement, professional licensing requirements, and career development. Regardless of occupational levels, the immigrant status of Asian American women and their families does not enable them to adapt easily to current demands and requirements of the American labor market. Many experience tremendous status and financial losses as the result of immigration.

Ethnicity, however, cuts across all the class sectors, and provides a form of identification and social bonding among Asian American women from different classes. Limited efforts, such as providing tutoring, social, legal, and health services, women's shelters, counseling, job-training programs, and outreach, are helping bridge the gap between class groups. Class barriers are thus much easier to overcome among Asian American women than between the white feminists and Asian American women from working-class backgrounds.

## IMPLICATIONS AND CONCLUSION

Asian American women confront problems on multiple fronts. Thus no social movement that addresses only one of the problem areas can adequately resolve their multiple oppressions sexually, racially, legally, economically, and culturally. The feminist movement is not an exception to this, for the specific concerns of Asian American women are often not those of white feminists. Without recognizing these multiple oppressions, political participation in the larger movement will be incompatible with the definition, goals, and interests of the Asian American cause. In this case, the concept of feminism needs to be broadly defined to address the interconnectedness of sex, gender, race, class, and culture so that its defining character and meaning are grounded in the experience of various kinds of women, including Asian American women. Broadening feminism implies that sisterhood is inclusive regardless of one's race, class background, national origin, sexual preference, physical condition, and life-style. Then strategies of collective action are needed to address the specific needs of Asian American women, to overcome the barriers that block their political participation, and to strengthen their relationship with others in the feminist movement as well as human liberation as a whole.

If Asian American women participate in the larger feminist movement, they can benefit from as well as contribute to it. By and large, the movement has provided an impetus for the organizing and political activism of Asian American women. For some, working with white feminists has inspired critical examination of their subordinate status and limited role. They have been prompted to develop themselves fully as contributing members of the family, their ethnic community, and society, thus raising their level of consciousness. Through support from the movement, a number of Asian American women have established their own organizations and have gained skills in language, assertiveness, leadership, coalition building, and negotiation. Thus they are now able to communicate effectively with others and to build strong networks with groups of white women and women of color in the larger society.

In return, Asian American women can also contribute to the movement in unique ways. The presence of Asian American women and other women of color in feminist organizations and activities has sensitized white women to their ethnocentric view, broadened their concerns, and challenged the existing social structure that has persistently defined and perpetuated sexist and racist values. As advocates for the civil rights, social equality, and human liberation of all people, Asian American women have shown support for feminist issues by participating in political activities (e.g., marches in support of the Equal Rights Amendment), forming coalitions with feminists on common issues (e.g., voter registration projects in the 1984 and 1988 elections), sharing resources for important causes, and providing leaders as representatives to women's meetings. They have also enlightened women in the larger movement concerning the uniqueness of their social and cultural backgrounds, the experience of the combined effects of sexism and racism, and the pressing needs of working-class women.

The increased involvement of Asian American women in the feminist movement will enhance the Asian American cause by broadening the perspective of their political struggle; by identifying more resources, channels, and opportunities existing in the larger society; and by gaining support through the formation of networks with diverse groups. Asian American women involved in both Asian American activism and the larger feminist movement have played an important role in decreasing sex and racial discrimination, in providing leadership and role models for others to emulate, and in paving the way for Asian American political visibility and efficacy in the society at large. As Rita Elway remarks, "Asian and Pacific women in elective office have, for the most part, introduced more community people to the political process; they have responded to a broader range of concerns both inside and outside of the community; they have advocated for civil rights on behalf of all ethnic minorities and women."

Therefore, it is important that Asian American women should increase their political participation in the Asian American community as well as in society at large. Although some Asian American women have been actively involved in their communities, their accomplishments are not less than those of white feminists in the larger society. Because the origins of many of the barriers encountered by Asian American women are beyond their control and are deeply embedded in the social structure, collective efforts are needed to solve these structural problems. Asian American women should join forces with others to increase their political clout and to work for lasting social change. Thus political activism is the first step toward becoming visible, eradicating the stereotype of passivity, and challenging the condition of namelessness. Political participation is also necessary to help overcome voicelessness as Asian American women, to gain power in making demands on their own behalf, and to address the pressing needs and problems of disadvantaged people. It is through political participation that Asian American women will be able to establish networks with other women's groups and to empower themselves in the struggle for equality, justice, and liberation for all people.

To effect their political course of action Asian American women must develop strategies and programs to overcome internal and external barriers. When developing appropriate courses of action, the differences in their historical pasts, the uniqueness of their subculture, and structural arrangements within the Asian American communities and in the larger society must be taken into account. What has successfully advanced the cause of other women's groups cannot be simply imposed on Asian American women.

Five major suggestions are outlined here. First, strategies targeted to overcome psychological barriers may include consciousness-raising techniques to deal directly with identity crises and conflicting loyalties resulting from the double status as women and as members of a racial minority group. Asian American women might develop a transcendent type of gender consciousness that encompasses concern for all forms of multiple oppression. Education is one of the necessary ingredients for increasing political awareness and the power of Asian American women. The women need to develop leadership and organizational skills in order to become active in the political arena. They may identify outstanding women leaders as role models to emulate. Networking and coalition building would provide them mutual support and contact with other women's groups. Programs designed to overcome language difficulties and to improve communication skills and image management are also needed. The goal is to develop a healthy self-concept, positive in outlook, assertive in behavior, and androgynous in style.

Second, self-awareness and cultural programs aimed toward cultural pluralism may be designed to educate Asian American women. They can learn what past conditions and ineffectual activities have led to their current plight. These programs will assist them in seeking cultural resolutions by combining the parts of the Asian and American cultures that are compatible with one another and most appropriate given the demands of current social circumstances. By exposing Asian American women to a wide range of life options, they will learn to demand self-determination, to explore ways of self-expression, and to seek strategies for self-empowerment. They will realize that they can change the course of their life by their own actions.

Third, the role of males in the life struggle of Asian American women is a critical but unanswered question to be explored. As long as patriarchy persists, male dominance will exist inside and outside Asian American communities. While some Asian American women are willing to work with men in partnership for happiness and success, others may opt for independence from males politically and/or sexually. The issue here is that freedom of choice must be available to women if they are to be totally liberated. Whatever choices Asian

American women make, others, whoever they are, have to accept these women's definition of gender relationship and respect their choice of self-determination.

Fourth, white feminists and Asian American women should work to build a foundation for feminist solidarity and deal together with racism and classism. White feminists must first critically examine their attitudes and behavior toward women of color and different classes. They need to demonstrate consistency in attitudes and behavior when relating to Asian American women. They need to show sensitivity toward Asians and place the eradication of racism and classism as the top priority in the larger feminist movement. They should take responsibility for educating the general public about cultural and ethnic differences and join Asian American women in protesting and stopping actions that reinforce racism and classism.

Finally, Asian American women must unite with other women of color who, for the most part, share similar life circumstances, experience multiple oppression, and struggle for common goals. Unless the whole social structure is uprooted, many institutional barriers in law, housing, education, employment, economics, and politics that are deeply embedded in the system will remain unchanged. Only when different groups work effectively and strategically together as a political force will all women achieve a new political consciousness and gain collective strength, to supersede the race, gender, sexual, class, and cultural differences that now divide them.

# Who Is Your Mother?
# Red Roots of White Feminism

PAULA GUNN ALLEN

At Laguna Pueblo in New Mexico, "Who is your mother?" is an important question. At Laguna, one of several of the ancient Keres gynocratic societies of the region, your mother's identity is the key to your own identity. Among the Keres, every individual has a place within the universe—human and nonhuman—and that place is defined by clan membership. In turn, clan membership is dependent on matrilineal descent. Of course, your mother is not only that woman whose womb formed and released you—the term refers in every individual case to an entire generation of women whose psychic, and consequently physical, "shape" made the psychic existence of the following generation possible. But naming your own mother (or her equivalent) enables people to place you precisely within the universal web of your life, in each of its dimensions: cultural, spiritual, personal, and historical.

Among the Keres, "context" and "matrix" are equivalent terms, and both refer to approximately the same thing as knowing your derivation and place. Failure to know your mother, that is, your position and its attendant traditions, history, and place in the scheme of things, is failure to remember your significance, your reality, your right relationship to earth and society. It is the same as being lost—isolated, abandoned, self-estranged, and alienated from your own life. This importance of tradition in the life of every member of the community is not confined to Keres Indians; all American Indian Nations place great value on traditionalism.

The Native American sense of the importance of continuity with one's cultural origins runs counter to contemporary American ideas: in many instances, the immigrants to America have been eager to cast off cultural ties, often seeing their antecedents as backward, restrictive, even shameful. Rejection of tradition constitutes one of the major features of American life, an attitude that reaches far back into American colonial history and that now is validated by virtually every cultural institution in the country. Feminist practice, at least in the cultural artifacts the community values most, follows this cultural trend as well.

The American idea that the best and the brightest should willingly reject and repudiate their origins leads to an allied idea—that history, like everything in the past, is of little value and should be forgotten as quickly as possible. This all too often causes us to reinvent the wheel continually. We find ourselves discovering our collective pasts over and over, having to retake ground already covered by women in the preceding decades and centuries. The Native American view, which highly values maintenance of traditional customs, values, and perspectives, might result in slower societal change and in quite a bit less social upheaval, but it has the advantage of providing a solid sense of identity and lowered levels of psychological and interpersonal conflict.

Contemporary Indian communities value individual members who are deeply connected to the traditional ways of their people, even after centuries of concerted and brutal effort on the part of the American government, the churches, and the corporate system to break the connections between individuals and their tribal world. In fact, in the view of the traditionals, rejection of one's culture—one's traditions, language, people—is the result of colonial oppression and is hardly to be applauded. They believe that the roots of oppression are to be found in the loss of tradition and memory because that loss is always accompanied by a loss of a positive sense of self. In short, Indians think it is important to remem-

From Paula Gunn Allen, *The Sacred Hoop* (Boston: Beacon Press, 1986), pp. 209–21. © 1986, 1992 by Paula Gunn Allen. Reprinted with permission from Beacon Press. Footnotes have been deleted.

ber, while Americans believe it is important to forget.

The traditional Indians' view can have a significant impact if it is expanded to mean that the sources of social, political, and philosophical thought in the Americas not only should be recognized and honored by Native Americans but should be embraced by American society. If American society judiciously modeled the traditions of the various Native Nations, the place of women in society would become central, the distribution of goods and power would be egalitarian, the elderly would be respected, honored, and protected as a primary social and cultural resource, the ideals of physical beauty would be considerably enlarged (to include "fat," strong-featured women, gray-haired, and wrinkled individuals, and others who in contemporary American culture are viewed as "ugly"). Additionally, the destruction of the biota, the life sphere, and the natural resources of the planet would be curtailed, and the spiritual naure of human and nonhuman life would beome a primary organizing principle of human society. And if the traditional tribal systems that are emulated included pacifist ones, war would cease to be a major method of human problem solving.

## RE-MEMBERING CONNECTIONS AND HISTORIES

The belief that rejection of tradition and of history is a useful response to life is reflected in America's amazing loss of memory concerning its origins in the matrix and context of Native America. American does not seem to remember that it derived its wealth, its values, its food, much of its medicine, and a large part of its "dream" from Native America. It is ignorant of the genesis of its culture in this Native American land, and that ignorance helps to perpetuate the longstanding European and Middle Eastern monotheistic, hierarchical, patriarchal cultures' oppression of women, gays, and lesbians, people of color, working class, unemployed people, and the elderly. Hardly anyone in America speculates that the constitutional system of government might be as much a product of American Indian ideas and practices as of colonial American and Anglo-European revolutionary fervor.

Even though Indians are officially and informally ignored as intellectual movers and shapers in the United States, Britain, and Europe, they are peoples with ancient tenure on this soil. During the ages when tribal societies existed in the Americas largely untouched by patriarchal oppression, they developed elaborate systems of thought that included science, philosophy, and government based on a belief in the central importance of female energies, autonomy of individuals, cooperation, human dignity, human freedom, and egalitarian distribution of status, goods, and services. Respect for others, reverence of life, and, as a by-product, pacifism as a way of life; importance of kinship ties in the customary ordering of social interaction; a sense of the sacredness and mystery of existence; balance and harmony in relationships both sacred and secular were all features of life among the tribal confederacies and nations. And in those that lived by the largest number of these principles, gynarchy was the norm rather than the exception. Those systems are as yet unmatched in any contemporary industrial, agrarian, or postindustrial society on earth. . . .

There are many female gods recognized and honored by the tribes and Nations. Femaleness was highly valued, both respected and feared, and all social institutions reflected this attitude. Even modern sayings, such as the Cheyenne statement that a people is not conquered until the hearts of the women are on the ground, express the Indians' understanding that without the power of woman the people will not live, but with it, they will endure and prosper.

Indians did not confine this belief in the central importance of female energy to matters of worship. Among many of the tribes (perhaps as many as 70 percent of them in North America alone), this belief was reflected in all of their social institutions. The Iroquois Constitution or White Roots of Peace, also called the Great Law of the Iroquois, codified the Matrons' decision-making and economic power:

The lineal descent of the people of the Five Fires [the Iroquois Nations] shall run in the female line. Women shall be considered the progenitors of the Nation. They shall own the land and the soil. Men and women shall follow the status of their mothers. (Article 44)

The women heirs of the chieftainship titles of the League shall be called Oiner or Otinner [Noble] for all time to come. (Article 45)

If a disobedient chief persists in his disobedience after three warnings [by his female relatives, by his male relatives, and by one of his fellow council members, in that order], the matter shall go to the council of War Chiefs. The Chiefs shall then take away the title of the erring chief *by order of the women in whom the title is vested*. When the chief is deposed, the women shall notify the chiefs of the League . . . and the chiefs of the League shall sanction the act. The women will then select another of their sons as a candidate and the chiefs shall elect him. (Article 19) (Emphasis mine)

The Matrons held so much policy-making power traditionally that once, when their position was threatened, they demanded its return, and consequently the power of women was fundamental in shaping the Iroquois Confederation sometime in the sixteenth or early seventeenth century. It was women

> who fought what may have been the first successful feminist rebellion in the New World. The year was 1600, or thereabouts, when these tribal feminists decided that they had had enough of unregulated warfare by their men. Lysistratas among the Indian women proclaimed a boycott on lovemaking and childbearing. Until the men conceded to them the power to decide upon war and peace, there would be no more warriors. Since the men believed that the women alone knew the secret of childbirth, the rebellion was instantly successful.
>
> In the Constitution of Deganawidah the founder of the Iroquois Confederation of Nations had said: "He caused the body of our mother, the woman, to be of great worth and honor. He purposed that she shall be endowed and entrusted with the birth and upbringing of men, and that she shall have the care of all that is planted by which life is sustained and supported and the power to breathe is fortified: *and moreover that the warriors shall be her assistants.*"
>
> The footnote of history was curiously supplied when Susan B. Anthony began her "Votes for Women" movement two and a half centuries later. Unknowingly the feminists chose to hold their founding convention of latter-day suffragettes in the town of Seneca [Falls], New York. The site was just a stone's throw from the old council house where the Iroquois women had plotted their feminist rebellion. (Emphasis mine)

Beliefs, attitudes, and laws such as these became part of the vision of American feminists and of other human liberation movements around the world. Yet feminists too often believe that no one has ever experienced the kind of society that empowered women and made that empowerment the basis of its rules of civilization. The price the feminist community must pay because it is not aware of the recent presence of gynarchical societies on this continent is unnecessary confusion, division, and much lost time.

## THE ROOT OF OPPRESSION IS LOSS OF MEMORY

An odd thing occurs in the minds of Americans when Indian civilization is mentioned: little or nothing. As I write this, I am aware of how far removed my version of the roots of American feminism must seem to those steeped in either mainstream or radical versions of feminism's history. I am keenly aware of the lack of image Americans have about our continent's recent past. I am intensely conscious of popular notions of Indian women as beasts of burden, squaws, traitors, or, at best, vanished denizens of a long-lost wilderness. How odd, then, must my contention seem that the gynocratic tribes of the American continent provided the basis for all the dreams of liberation that characterize the modern world.

We as feminists must be aware of our history on this continent. We need to recognize that the same forces that devastated the gynarchies of Britain and the Continent also devastated the ancient African civilizations, and we must know that those same materialistic, antispiritual forces are presently engaged in wiping out the same gynarchical values, along with the peoples who adhere to them, in Latin America. I am convinced that those wars were and continue to be about the imposition of patriarchal civilization over the holistic, pacifist, and spirit-based gynarchies they supplant. To that end the wars of imperial conquest have not been solely or even mostly waged over the land and its resources, but they have been fought within the bodies, minds, and hearts of the people of the earth for dominion over them. I think this is the reason traditionals say we must remember our origins, our cultures, our histories, our mothers and grandmothers, for without that memory, which implies continuance rather than nostalgia, we are doomed to engulfment by a paradigm that is fundamentally inimical to the vitality, autonomy, and self-empowerment essential for satisfying, high-quality life.

The vision that impels feminists to action was the vision of the Grandmothers' society, the society that was captured in the words of the sixteenth-century explorer Peter Martyr nearly five hundred years ago. It is the same vision repeated over and over by radical thinkers of Europe and America, from François Villon to John Locke, from William Shakespeare to Thomas Jefferson, from Karl Marx to Friedrich Engels, from Benito Juarez to Martin Luther King, from Elizabeth Cady Stanton to Judy Grahn, from Harriet Tubman to Audre Lorde, from Emma Goldman to Bella Abzug, from Malinalli to Cherrie Moraga, and from Iyatiku to me. That vision as Martyr told it is of a country where there are "no soldiers, no gendarmes or police, no nobles, kings, regents, prefects, or judges, no prisons, no lawsuits . . . All are equal and free," or so Friedrich Engels recounts Martyr's words.

Columbus wrote:

> Nor have I been able to learn whether they [the inhabitants of the islands he visited on his first journey to the New World] held personal property, for it seemed to me that whatever one had, they all took shares of . . . They are so ingenuous and free with all they have, that no one would believe it who has not seen it; of anything that they possess, if it be asked of them, they never say no; on the contrary, they invite you to share it and show as much love as if their hearts went with it.

At least that's how the Native Caribbean people acted when the whites first came among them; American Indians are the despair of social workers, bosses, and missionaries even now because of their deeply ingrained tendency to spend all they have, mostly on others. In any case, as the historian William Brandon notes,

> the Indian *seemed* free, to European eyes, gloriously free, to the European soul shaped by centuries of toil and tyranny, and this impression operated profoundly on the process of history and the development of America. Something in the peculiar character of the Indian world gave an impression of classlessness, or propertylessness, and that in turn to an impression, as H. H. Bancroft put it, of "humanity unrestrained . . . in the exercise of liberty absolute."

## A FEMINIST HEROINE

Early in the women's suffrage movement, Eva Emery Dye, an Oregon suffragette, went looking for a heroine to embody her vision of feminism. She wanted a historical figure whose life would symbolize the strengthened power of women. She found Sacagawea (or Sacajawea) buried in the journals of Lewis and Clark. The Shoshoni teenager had traveled with the Lewis and Clark expedition, carrying her infant son, and on a small number of occasions acted as translator.

Dye declared that Sacagawea, whose name is thought to mean Bird Woman, had been the guide to the historic expedition, and through Dye's work Sacagawea became enshrined in American memory as a moving force and friend of the whites, leading them in the settlement of western North America.

But Native American roots of white feminism reach back beyond Sacagawea. The earliest white women on this continent were well acquainted with tribal women. They were neighbors to a number of tribes and often shared food, information, child care, and health care. Of course little is made of these encounters in official histories of colonial America, the period from the Revolution to the Civil War, or on the ever-moving frontier. Nor, to my knowledge, has either the significance or incidence of intermarriage between Indian and white or between Indian and Black been explored. By and large, the study of Indian-white relations has been focused on government and treaty relations, warfare, missionization, and education. It has been almost entirely documented in terms of formal white Christian patriarchal impacts and assaults on Native Americans, though they are not often characterized as assaults but as "civilizing the savages." Particularly in organs of popular culture and miseducation, the focus has been on what whites imagine to be degradation of Indian women ("squaws"), their equally imagined love of white government and white conquest ("princesses"), and the horrifyingly misleading, fanciful tales of "bloodthirsty, backward primitives" assaulting white Christian settlers who were looking for life, liberty, and happiness in their chosen land.

But, regardless of official versions of relations between Indians and whites or other segments of the American population, the fact remains that great numbers of apparently "white" or "Black" Americans carry notable degrees of Indian blood. With that blood has come the culture of the Indian, informing the lifestyles, attitudes, and value of their descendents. Somewhere along the line—and often quite recently—an Indian woman was giving birth to and raising the children of a family both officially and informally designated as white or Black—not Indian. In view of this, it should be evident that one of the major enterprises of Indian women in America has been the transfer of Indian values and culture to as large and influential a segment of American immigrant populations as possible. Their success in this endeavor is amply demonstrated in the Indian values and social styles that increasingly characterize American life. Among these must be included "permissive" childrearing practices, for as noted in an earlier chapter ("When Women Throw Down Bundles"), imprisoning, torturing, caning, strapping, starving, or verbally abusing children was considered outrageous behavior. Native Americans did not believe that physical or psychological abuse of children would result in their edification. They did not believe that children are born in sin, are congenitally predisposed to evil, or that a good parent who wishes the child to gain salvation, achieve success, or earn the respect of her or his fellows can be helped to those ends by physical or emotional torture.

The early Americans saw the strongly protective attitude of the Indian people as a mark of their "savagery"—as they saw the Indian's habit of bathing frequently, their sexual openness, their liking for scant clothing, their raucous laughter at most things, their suspicion and derision of authoritarian structures, their quick pride, their genuine courtesy, their willingness to share what they had with others less fortunate than they, their egalitarianism, their ability to act as if various lifestyles were a normal part of living, and their granting that women were of equal or, in individual cases, of greater value than men.

Yet the very qualities that marked Indian life in the sixteenth century have, over the centuries since contact between the two worlds occurred, come to mark much of contemporary American life. And those qualities, which I believe have passed into white culture from Indian culture, are the very ones that fundamentalists, immigrants from Europe, the Middle East, and Asia often find the most reprehensible. Third- and fourth-generation Americans indulge in growing nudity, informality in social relations, egalitarianism, and the rearing of women who value autonomy, strength, freedom, and personal dignity—and who are often derided by European, Asian, and Middle Eastern men for those qualities. Contemporary Americans value leisure almost as much as tribal people do. They find themselves increasingly unable to accept child abuse as a reasonable way to nurture. They bathe more than any other industrial people on earth—much to the scorn of their white cousins across the Atlantic, and they sometimes enjoy a good laugh even at their own expense (though they still have a less developed sense of the ridiculous than one might wish).

Contemporary Americans find themselves more and more likely to adopt a "live and let live" attitude in matters of personal sexual and social styles. Two-thirds of their diet and a large share of their medications and medical treatments mirror or are directly derived from Native American sources. Indianization is not a simple concept, to be sure, and it is one that Americans often find themselves resisting; but it is a process that has taken place, regardless of American resistance to recognizing the source of many if not most of American's vaunted freedoms in our personal, family, social, and political arenas.

This is not to say that Americans have become Indian in every attitude, value, or social institution. Unfortunately, Americans have a way to go in learning how to live in the world in ways that improve the quality of life for each individual while doing minimal damage to the biota, but they have adapted certain basic qualities of perception and certain attitudes that are moving them in that direction.

## AN INDIAN-FOCUSED VERSION
## OF AMERICAN HISTORY

American colonial ideas of self-government came as much from the colonists' observations of tribal governments as from their Protestant or Greco-Roman heritage. Neither Greece nor Rome had the kind of pluralistic democracy as that concept has been understood in the United States since Andrew Jackson, but the tribes, particularly the gynarchical tribal confederacies, did. It is true that the *oligarchic* form of government that colonial Americans established was originally based on Greco-Roman systems in a number of important ways, such as its restriction of citizenship to propertied white males over twenty-one years of age, but it was never a form that Americans as a whole have been entirely comfortable with. Politics and government in the United States during the Federalist period also reflected the English common law system as it had evolved under patriarchal feudalism and monarchy—hence the United States' retention of slavery and restriction of citizenship to propertied white males.

The Federalists did make one notable change in the feudal system from which their political system derived on its Anglo side. They rejected blooded aristocracy and monarchy. This idea came from the Protestant Revolt to be sure, but it was at least reinforced by colonial America's proximity to American Indian nonfeudal confederacies and their concourse with those confederacies over the two hundred years of the colonial era. It was this proximity and concourse that enabled the revolutionary theorists to "dream up" a system in which all local polities would contribute to and be protected by a central governing body responsible for implementing policies that bore on the common interest of all. It should also be noted that the Reformation followed Columbus's contact with the Americas and that his and Martyr's reports concerning Native Americans' free and easy egalitarianism were in circulation by the time the Reformation took hold.

The Iroquois federal system, like that of several in the vicinity of the American colonies, is remarkably similar to the organization of the federal system of the United States. It was made up of local, "state," and federal bodies composed of executive, legislative, and judicial branches. The Council of Matrons was the executive: it instituted and determined general policy. The village, tribal (several villages), and Confederate councils determined and implemented policies when they did not conflict with the broader Council's decisions or with theological precepts that ultimately determined policy at all levels. The judicial was composed of the men's councils and the Matron's council, who sat together to make decisions. Because the matrons were the ceremonial center of the system, they were also the prime policymakers.

Obviously, there are major differences between the structure of the contemporary American government and that of the Iroquois. Two of those differences were and are crucial to the process of just government. The Iroquois system is spirit-based, while that of the United States is secular, and the Iroquois Clan Matrons formed the executive. The female executive function was directly tied to the ritual nature of the Iroquois politic, for the executive was lodged in the hands of the Matrons of particular clans across village, tribe, and national lines. The executive office was hereditary, and only sons of eligible clans could serve, at the behest of the Matrons of their clans, on the councils at the three levels. Certain daughters inherited the office of Clan Matron through their clan affiliations. No one could impeach or disempower a Matron, though her violation of certain laws could result in her ineligibility for the Matron's council. For example, a woman who married *and took her husband's name* could not hold the title Matron.

American ideas of social justice came into sharp focus through the commentaries of Iroquois observers who traveled in France in the colonial period. These observers expressed horror at the great gap between the lifestyles of the wealthy and the poor, remarking to the French philosopher Montaigne, who would heavily influence the radical communities of Europe, England, and America, that "they had noticed that in Europe there seemed to be two moities, consisting of the rich 'full gorged' with wealth, and the poor, starving 'and bare with need and povertie.' The Indian tourists not only marveled at the division, but marveled that the

poor endured 'such an injustice, and that they took not the others by the throte, or set fire on their house.' " It must be noted that the urban poor eventually did just that in the French Revolution. The writings of Montaigne and of those he influenced provided the theoretical framework and the vision that propelled the struggle for liberty, justice, and equality on the Continent and later throughout the British empire.

The feminist idea of power as it ideally accrues to women stems from tribal sources. The central importance of the clan Matrons in the formulation and determination of domestic and foreign policy as well as in their primary role in the ritual and ceremonial life of their respective Nations was the single most important attribute of the Iroquois, as of the Cherokee and Muskogee, who traditionally inhabited the southern Atlantic region. The latter peoples were removed to what is now Oklahoma during the Jackson administration, but prior to the American Revolution they had regular and frequent communication with and impact on both the British colonizers and later the American people, including the African peoples brought here as slaves.

Ethnographer Lewis Henry Morgan wrote an account of Iroquoian matriarchal culture, published in 1877, that heavily influenced Marx and the development of communism, particularly lending it the idea of the liberation of women from patriarchal dominance. The early socialists in Europe, especially in Russia, saw women's liberation as a central aspect of the socialist revolution. Indeed, the basic ideas of socialism, the egalitarian distribution of goods and power, the peaceful ordering of society, and the right of every member of society to participate in the work and benefits of that society, are ideas that pervade American Indian political thought and action. And it is through various channels—the informal but deeply effective Indianization of Europeans, and christianizing Africans, the social and political theory of the confederacies feuding and then intertwining with European dreams of liberty and justice, and, more recently, the work of Morgan and the writings of Marx and Engels—that the age-old gynarchical systems of egalitarian government found their way into contemporary feminist theory.

When Eva Emery Dye discovered Sacagawea and honored her as the guiding spirit of American womanhood, she may have been wrong in bare historical fact, but she was quite accurate in terms of deeper truth. The statues that have been erected depicting Sacagawea as a Matron in her prime signify an understanding in the American mind, however unconscious, that the source of just government, of right ordering of social relationships, the dream of "liberty and justice for all" can be gained only by following the Indian Matrons' guidance. For, as Dr. Anna Howard Shaw said of Sacagawea at the National American Woman's Suffrage Association in 1905:

Forerunner of civilization, great leader of men, patient and motherly woman, we bow our hearts to do you honor! . . . May we the daughters of an alien race . . . learn the lessons of calm endurance, of patient persistence and unfaltering courage exemplified in your life, in our efforts to lead men through the Pass of justice, which goes over the mountains of prejudice and conservatism to the broad land of the perfect freedom of a true republic; one in which men and women together shall in perfect equality solve the problems of a nation that knows no caste, no race, no sex in opportunity, in responsibility or in justice! May 'the eternal womanly' ever lead us on!

# Sweat Shops and Picket Lines:
# European Immigrant Women

ELIZABETH EWEN

*Hail the waist makers of 1909*
*Making their stand on the picket line*

*Breaking the power of those who reign*
*Pointing the way and smashing the chain*

*In the black winter of 1909*
*When we froze and bled on the picket line*
*We showed the world that women could fight*
*And we rose and we won with women's might.*

The factory, that outer world through which new immigrants were introduced to American industry, separated the experience of daughters from the homebound history of their mothers. While the home had encompassed the mothers' labor, concerns, and vision of womanhood for generations, the experience of being "factory girls" provided a different, wider, world view for their daughters. Social theorists and social workers often interpreted this as a sign of a developing modern consciousness. In *The New Basis of Civilization,* a book based on a series of lectures given at the New York School of Social Work in 1905 and reprinted eight times, Simon Patten argued that modern industry aroused and cultivated the economic instincts of working-class family life, and noted two different responses on the part of women: resistance and adaptation. He identified resistance with the mother:

> The woman in the shelter is slow to leave the base on which a multiplicity of home industries long since established her. She often lags behind the man in a slough of confusion and dejection for the old idealism of which she is the center [and which] had not yet been penetrated and broken by the imperative necessities that readjusted men to modern production. Women feel that their times are out of joint because they are not yet coordinated with the industrial civilization which is penetrating their home and sifting through their activities.

The weapon in industry's arsenal against the mother was factory work. Patten argued that the decisive break with the past would come as women entered production:

> The woman who in her girlhood learned to be punctual at her factory bench, impressed her acquired quality upon her family and is proud to be named by her tenement neighbors as the most particular woman in the house. Thrilling with pride in the appearance of people for whom she is responsible, and in objects she now possesses, she has a delight—new to her class—in precision, simplicity of form and in order. Her desire is to add to the number of her things, and because of the rapid cheapening of commodities this primary aesthetic longing is among the first to be gratified.

Factory work, in this analysis, was a primary means for internalizing habits and practices necessary for bringing women into the industrial world, and the factory girl was in the vanguard of this movement: by absorbing industrial discipline at work, she would transform her home life with the public display of newly acquired habits and consumer values.

If this was the social worker's image of the factory girl, the reality of work and the understanding of that work were quite different. Factory managers may have attempted to impose discipline on the workers, but the women did not immediately accept the new order. If going to work separated mothers and daughters, the reason for going in the first place was intimately connected to the home, and if work was an educational experience, it was an education in exploitation.

The Lower East Side was the most industrialized neighborhood in the city. It housed many small garment shops and factories, as well as a host of other kinds of light industry. Women found jobs through kinship and community

From Elizabeth Ewen, *Immigrant Women in the Land of Dollars* (New York: Monthly Review Press, 1985), pp. 242–62. © 1985 by Elizabeth Ewen. Reprinted with permission from Monthly Review Foundation. Footnotes have been deleted.

networks. A study of Italian women in industry reported: "Of 874 who told of how they had secured their first position in New York City, 685, or over three-fourths, had found their first job through some friend or relative." Factory work required little training, and a recommendation from a friend or relative was enough for most employers.

During this period, the manufacturers were replacing artisan labor with factory workers and there was a growing division of labor; one worker rarely put together a whole garment from start to finish. One manufacturer explained the system: "Coats go through forty-odd processes in the making. There is no such thing as a tailor in ready-made business now." If this created jobs for unskilled workers, it also meant that the "prime requisite for success is not any special skill, but speed, and this comes with practice after the worker has been shown how to do the work." The need for training was greatly reduced: " 'The forelady showed me once,' usually summarized how a girl learned the work and practice did the rest. Speed, with accuracy, was the only qualification necessary for the slight advancement possible."

Some Italian women had been trained as artisan clothesmakers, and came from a tradition of craft and pride of work. These women were often critical of the organization of the clothing industry in New York:

"Your work is all right provided it is done quickly enough" was the criticism frequently made. "They only do cheap work in this country. Everything must be done in a hurry. In Italy it would take six months to do a pillow and here it was done in three or four hours. Cheap work!" A finisher on dresses complained that she had to learn the trade all over again when she came here because in Italy there was more handsewing, and no subdivision of processes. If one worked fast there, people would say that the work was badly done and everyone was taught to do as beautiful sewing as possible.

Adriana Valenti, still imbued with a craft sense, took a job making men's cuffs but "got tired of doing cuffs all day. I says no, I don't want this. I'll never learn how to do things." Her next job, making skirts, she liked better "because I made it complete, at least I learned to sew for myself."

Rosina Giuliani was known in her town in Italy for her expert millinery skills. When she came to the United States, she landed a job as the forelady of a hat factory, where she made $25 a week. Her daughter talked about the use that was made of her skill:

Mama always knew how to make beautiful hats. When she first came here, they used to tease her in the factory. Rosina, Rosina, you're the fastest in the shop, they used to say. Mama became a forelady because she showed the boss how to make her beautiful hats. He used her skill and made her a forelady. Mama taught Papa how to make hats. They tried to go into business themselves, but failed because they never had enough money to get started. That's why they ended up in the factory for most of their lives.

In Eastern Europe, the industrial process was farther advanced than in Italy, but there was still a mixture of artisanal craft, apprenticeship systems, and machine work. Judith Weissman, for example, got her training in the garment industry from her father, who designed and cut garments that young girls would baste and male apprentices would finish on a sewing machine. He had five people working in his shop, which was also his home. People came to his house, ordered their clothes, and he gave each garment special attention. Wealthy Gentiles sent a wagon for him, and he would load the sewing machine on the wagon and make their clothing in their homes. His apprentices, according to custom, received board but no pay.

Yetta Bursky learned to be a dressmaker in Galicia. As an apprentice, she made patterns. She then became the "supporter of the family" with her dressmaking. By the time she was sixteen, she had started her own shop:

When I was sixteen I made a bunch of dresses for a woman and I delivered them. I expected about $15 but she gave me $1.50. She was an aristocrat, but money she didn't believe in paying. I burst into tears, went home and told my mother, "I'm going to America." I had to make money to help the family. I did that, but I ended up in the factory making waists by machines.

Bella Feiner trained as a dressmaker in Poland, beginning as an apprentice when she was twelve years old. In the United States, however, she was an operator. She summed up the feelings of other artisan dressmakers when she said, "When I came here, I knew more than I know now. I knew how to make a whole dress."

The seasonal nature of certain light industries and the consequent yearly periods of slack time meant that women shifted from one job to another, often working in several different kinds of industry over one year:

During the course of two years, sixteen-year-old Maria Viviana had tried her hand in eight such different industries as the making of aprons, straw hats, dresses, shirtwaists, gloves, underwear, dresses and silk embroidery. "I have worked in every trade in New York City," exclaimed Emilia, a girl of twenty, as she told of her working on women's neckwear, hats, pins, children's cloaks. . . . Another girl had run the gamut of the trades, from packing candy to spooling thread. "I have worked in lots of places. You see, I have been working for ten years."

The conditions of work provided an education in the excesses of discipline. A twelve- to fourteen-hour day was common. Workers were often cheated out of their full wages—clocks were slowed down during working hours or sped up at lunchtime. Workers were charged for needles, thread, mistakes, and even electrical power (if there was any). They were fined for being late, talking, singing, and taking too much time in the bathroom. The sanitary conditions were deplorable, the working conditions unsafe; floors collapsed in small lofts incapable of carrying the weight of machines and people, the doors were locked when work began, and shop fires were common. The speed of the work was intense. Maria Ganz's first work experience was instructive. She got a job putting small pearl buttons on cards at a wage of $2.50 a week:

> If a girl came in even a few minutes late, the lost time was charged against her pay. We were not permitted to talk to each other. Sometimes, some girl, unable to endure the silence any longer, would begin humming a tune which would be taken up by others near her. Marks, the foreman, would question us until he had learned who began the singing. The he would deduct three hours from her pay. If any girl objected to this treatment she was told to look for work elsewhere. It was my first real job and I was afraid of losing it, so I tried to keep silent. But for a lively girl like me to keep her mouth shut for eleven hours is torture; it almost drove me wild.

Agnes Santucci, in describing her first job, gave a similar account:

> The machine used to go, keep agoing, keep agoing. I was so unhappy to stay there all day, no go out like it was a prison. I couldn't speak English. I used to stay at the machine all day without seeing anybody. The forelady used to be back and forth, back and forth, look this way, look the other way. Do your work, do your work. An Italian girl fell asleep at the machine and she was fired.

Grace Grimaldi described her work life in a blouse-making factory as a kind of slavery:

> Between the years 1914 and 1918, it was a slavery really. You couldn't open your mouth. God forbid you came five minutes late or they'd actually throw you out of the place. You couldn't talk. . . . You

couldn't even go to the bathroom. We were treated like slaves. I worked for Scher Brothers—a place people of my generation never forgot. He was a real slavedriver. He used to pick people from the boat and use them for slavery. But people had to earn. So when you want to earn your own, you take anything.

Ida Shapiro's first job was equally typical: "You didn't have a little water to drink, you didn't have nothing. Everything was dirty. The bosses could fire girls for any reason they liked. The boss fired women who fought back, women who were smart. Getting on those American clothes every morning always made me five to ten minutes late. You had to punch a clock you know. I got fired."

Bessie Gitlin's first real disappointment in life came from her first job in New York: "I came here, my god was I disappointed. It was the first time in my life in a shop where you couldn't just leave, but I got over it. After all, I was responsible for bringing over my sister. But I was very unhappy."

Deductions were made for time lost opening bundles or learning new styles:

> The bosses would count the stitches. I would try to make my bosses understand, it's not only the stitches to make the garment, but the labor. When you open a bundle, time goes by. We were supposed to make so much an hour. And it takes about five minutes—you have to write out your ticket . . . and every time you open a bundle you lose five minutes which equals two hours by the end of the week. You have to turn it, you have to study the garment. We always have new styles. We have to have new styles, makes people buy, this gives us work . . . but the bosses would feel by giving the workers less they had more in their pocket.

Shirley Levy explained how this system worked in her shop: "In my shop, we worked on the same style, because you could produce more. You don't have to look at the sample. First week on a style you might make $9. Second week $10. But even when we produced more than that, the boss gave us the same amount. No matter how much we produced on the same sample we never got ourselves higher than $9."

One of the evils of the needle trades was the subcontracting system, whereby a factory owner would give out jobs to several men who would then hire young women to work for them—all in the owners' factory. Shirley Levy went to work in a ladies' waist factory that used the subcontracting system:

> My friend got me a job in a waist factory. The factory was very large, about two hundred work-

ers. The factory was owned by five brothers, they had a very good income. The rates the workers got were indescribable. Most of us were under twenty and came from small towns and we didn't know a trade or anything. They gave the men four or five machines, and he'd take on four or five immigrant girls and anybody with a little intelligence could learn how to run the machines in an hour or so. The men that hired the girls would pay a small wage—$2 or $3 a week. The boss would give the man the work, he would give it to the girls, he made his money by the piece.

Sonia Farkas worked with three women who had come over on the boat with her. She wanted to go to school, but her family could not afford it, and at fourteen she went to work. She got a job as a finisher because she knew how to sew:

It was a big shop, it has three floors and five hundred people. All the three of us got jobs as finishers. In those years the operator would take a finisher and one finisher would work for two or three operators. They would pay me. They would get the money from the boss and we would get it from them. The boss exploited us that way. That's how it used to be.

There were two ways of being paid: by the piece or by the hour. Most women seemed to have preferred piece work. Bessie Polski worked in a shirtwaist factory that employed Jewish and Italian women. She identified being paid at the end of the week—"week work"—with slavery: "We were week workers. We were like slaves. You couldn't pick your head up. You couldn't talk. We used to go to the bathroom. The forelady used to go after us, we shouldn't stay too long. We hardly had a chance to wash our hands."

Andriana Valenti also preferred piece work: "When I was a piece worker, I would sing. I would fool around, say jokes, laugh, talk to the girls. With time work, I would put my head down and I would work . . . and it seemed to me the day would never pass."

With piece work there was more room for socializing, and the work itself seemed more human. Yetta Bursky put it this way: "I admired the operators on piece work. They were sitting and talking and were jolly, having fun. I became a piece work operator as soon as I could." And Katy Bluestone explained how socializing and work could go hand in hand: "We were six to eight girls and we talked and enjoyed ourselves. It was piece work so it was our own time. We used to sing and talk. The boss never minded if the work was good and fast."

But piece work also had its problems. Fania Horvitz reported: "In piece work you can socialize because it's your own time. But I preferred week work to piece work. In piece work you rush yourself to death." Another woman explained the advantages of week work: "You don't have to rush. You don't have to be jealous—this one gets a bigger bundle—you get a smaller one and believe me there were plenty of arguments like that—'oh, Sarah got a bundle twice as large as mine'—like that."

The work was debilitating mentally and physically; a combination of monotonous work, constant supervision, and long hours led to feelings of isolation, frustration, and depression. Industrial accidents were frequent, as were such health problems as tuberculosis, pneumonia, backaches, and general physical deterioration. In addition, the women suffered sexual abuse by the bosses and male workers in the shop. One woman recalled how she was afraid of her boss: "He tried to hug me and I was so ashamed because I didn't know what to say or do. No man had ever kissed me except my father before. Finally, I told my father and he wouldn't let me go back." The bosses often expected sexual favors from the women and would hold back wages if they were refused. Cutters—always men—who taught the women how to work the machines often made "fresh remarks" and were sexually insulting. Some bosses would even require that their female workers wear makeup in an effort to hide their pale faces and make them more alluring.

It was also difficult for Jewish women who did not work in all-Jewish shops to keep up dietary and religious practices. Garment worker Lillie Tamarakin worked in one such shop:

It was filled with machine operators, mostly single Italian women, they thought I was German. When it came to the Jewish holidays, I took off and they were surprised. During Passover, I couldn't eat *hometz* [food not prepared for Passover], so I ran all the way home for lunch and then came back. God knows how I did it.

Saturday was the Sabbath for Jews, and working the usual half-day was often a problem for many Jewish women. Bella Feiner was fired several times because her mother would not allow her to break the Sabbath taboo on work: "I lost many jobs. My mother didn't let me go to work. I had to work a half day on Saturday and my mother objected because it was the Sabbath—so they used to fire me for that." Doria Shatsky described herself as a "Sabbath observer" and said she never "worked a half day Saturday. If I was fired, I found another job."

Despite the exploitative conditions, there was camaraderie among the women that helped to relieve the situation. Women helped each other with their work in times of accident or distress, told jokes, laughed, sang, and tried to slow down the pace of the work itself. They talked about men, marriage, the social conditions of the job, the neighborhood, and their families. One woman recalled how one day she hummed an old Russian love song, only to see the young woman working the next machine break into tears. Hearing the song brought back the memory of her love, who had died in a pogrom. Then, at her request, all of the women began to sing the song to ease the pain of her memory.

During slack times, when there was not enough work to go around, the women also helped each other out. Yetta Adelman described how she shared: "When I worked on samples and the other girls didn't have work, I divided my money with them because we had to make the same thing. Because if they didn't call me in, I would have to be out too. So we shared."

Shop forewomen had reputations like supers, good or bad depending on the degree of solidarity they showed with the workers. To Bella Cohen the "forewomen were like everybody else. We were all workers." Lenore Kosloff, herself a forewoman, demonstrated her solidarity by socializing with the other women and repairing their mistakes: "I socialized with the other girls in the shop. They were in the same station as I was. I stayed at work and repaired mistakes the operators had made. I spent my lunch hours fixing up mistakes. I didn't want them to lose money. In my position I could act as a mediator."

Lillie Tamarakin noted that there was a clear distinction between the bosses, the male workers, and the women workers. The bosses kept their distance, the male cutters made sexual comments, but the women got along well together. When she left the shop to get married, the women workers "showered" her with gifts. Getting married was a big event in the factory and the women would pool what little surplus cash they had to give each other presents. Maria Ganz ran into the wife of one wedding couple, the Eckstoffs, who had to return to factory work because they had used up their wedding money and pawned their furniture. The wife had only kept a few pieces, along with a set of four framed pictures—"The

pictures were a wedding present from the employees of the shop where the bride was employed at the time of the marriage."

Ida Shapiro was working in a ladies' waist shop that employed fifty Jewish and Italian women when she got married: "They gave me a surprise party in the shop when I got married. The machines even were decorated. The girls gave me a crystal candlestick and flowers. I had a big wedding and everyone in the shop came. The Italian girls came too." Bella Cohen also worked with Italian and Jewish women, and had a similar experience: "Whenever a girl got married the workers made a collection. Everyone chipped in. I didn't tell them but they found out and came to my apartment and gave me a beautiful roll of Irish linen. I was overwhelmed."

Industrial accidents were frequent and fellow workers took care of each other, even when the boss took that time out of their pay. For example, Lillie Tamarakin had an accident at work: "I once got my finger caught and badly mangled in the machine and I had to be taken to the hospital. One of the machine operators, a young girl, took me. But she was an hourly worker so they didn't pay her for the time she spent taking me. I felt terrible."

While they worked, the women stole time for themselves by daydreaming and singing. Dreams of marriage, of freedom from work, and songs of love allowed the young women to create visions of another life for themselves as they sat locked up in the factory. Adriana Valenti described her daydreams:

> I'd make up stories in my mind while I'm working. I'd say, "What kind of a person's going to wear this dress. Is she in good health, is she a good person? Where is she going to go? . . . Will she just throw this dress aside [laughs] . . . because on each ticket you put your name or number so you know who made it. Like you're creating something and someone is going to enjoy it. And then I'd think— what kind of a person? Is she going to be careful? Is she going to keep it well? It's not mine. I only made it and got paid for it.

In her daydream, Adriana Valenti was able to establish a more direct relationship between the creator/producer and the consumer/enjoyer than was possible in reality. Her reverie pierced the exploitative nature of the work to grasp the real meaning of work as creation and of consumption as pleasure.

Bella Feiner's daydreams were more romantic:

> All of us young people were sitting and dreaming in the shops. Well it's only for a season or two. I'll

be doing this, I'll be doing that. I'll get married. An aunt will be able to take care of me. We used to even sing songs—Yiddish naturally . . . singing the dream songs, the love songs and this is how we dreamed away our youth and go out gay and happy and what not. We enjoyed it, our young life with all its problems.

Another woman explained why she used to sing to herself all day:

You know what I used to do. I used to sing the whole day when I worked with the machine. So the boss used to say, "Oh Irene's really working." You know, I sing that I want to forget that I'm working the whole day by the machine. There were about twenty-five girls there. They all said, "Irene, oh look how happy she is all the time!" I used to sing Hungarian all the time. I told them I used to sing the whole day there with the machine to forget that I had to work there. I used to sing love songs.

But the women never forgot the exploitation, and, infused with old-world radical traditions and new-world ideas of freedom, they took part in creating a militant, organized labor movement on the Lower East Side, electrifying a stagnant American labor movement. For the first time, new immigrants took center stage in the history of organized labor in the United States.

The Lower East Side had long had a thriving radical culture that stimulated the organization of labor unions and the more general fight against industrial exploitation. Given new fuel by the influx of Russian Jews following the abortive Russian revolution of 1905, the movement to transform social conditions on the Lower East Side grew rapidly. Women garment workers formed the vanguard of this movement.

Adriana Valenti had learned about the power of collective action from her father. When she was a child, he had told her of the fear that would come from isolation and of how the people of his village would stick together in the face of the landowners' demands. As she put it, "So that's what I always remembered, that's why I love the union, because unity, strength, power, you're together, you're not alone." When she went to work she found that it was hard for the European people to stand up to the boss because they were so grateful to be earning a little money, but "I was the youngest there. And I would tell them, let's ask for more money, let's stick together." Since she had the support of her mother and no family of her own, she wasn't afraid to be fired: "I was a fighter. I always fought. I didn't worry because if I didn't work, I didn't have to pay board— whatever I earned I took it to my mother."

Many of the Jewish women who came to the United States had been politically active at home. Rachel Cohen argued that the "girls who were the organizers were the ones who had been socialists in the old country and who had never worked in shops before." Although her family was opposed to her organizing in the shops, her father's greatest moment in life had been the Russian Revolution, when he knelt down in prayer, saying "Thank God, I lived to see the Czar overthrown."

Sonia Farkas had been active in the revolutionary movement in Kiev when she was young. She had gone to meetings, done undercover work, and participated in the general strikes:

We had a general strike once where everything stopped. The cars and everything. It was like you make a revolution. It was 1905. A lot of people were beaten up and arrested but we had it for one day. But we had quite a nice revolution that day. It didn't last long because the police weren't with us. I couldn't understand when I came to the U.S. why we couldn't make a revolution in the U.S.

On the Lower East Side she became a union organizer:

I went to look for a union because I worked in a non-union shop. They threw down sixty pressers. The pressers wanted a union so the boss threw them out. I saw that and started to cry. I went to look for a union. Where can I get a union so they could come and organize a strike. I knew what movement meant and I knew what a union was. I found one on East Broadway. In 1906 the union was very small. So when I came to the union, I said that I want to organize the shop. He says, "Where are you working?" I told him. He said, "It's five hundred people in that shop and we don't have five hundred members. How can you take on a shop like that?" So he laughed at me. I started to bang on the table and crying, "I want a union." They had to take me from that job and put me in a union shop. A small shop. They had a couple, but very few.

Yetta Bursky's father had been arrested during a strike in a factory in Poland and her mother had not known if she would ever see him again. Yetta grew up in the midst of pogroms and the mass slaughter of Jews, at a time when it was dangerous for more than a few people to gather together in the same house. Her parents and their friends used to take out marriage permits and then hold political meetings instead. She came to the United States when she was twelve, got work in the garment industry, and became "a fighter":

I got a job in a waist factory. It was the rottenest boss I ever worked for. I refused to work on a particular garment and I convinced the others not to also and I got into trouble. But we made a stoppage. Oh, I loved it. If the boss didn't do the right thing, a stoppage. See, in the beginning the boss could do anything he wanted. The boss used women and paid them less than men. He hated me. He used to say, "If she wouldn't be a woman, I'd cut her into pieces." But we could make a stoppage.

She also hated the forewoman, but felt that the union could deal with her demands: "She was a little runt. You have to take this from her. With the union, you make a stoppage. She has to stop it. Before the union she liked us but we don't have to stand for this. As long as we have the union, the hell with them." Sometimes the women in the shop were more courageous than the union's business agents: "The boss once maltreated a male worker. The union business agent encouraged us to go back to work before the incident was settled, but we refused to until the man was given an apology. I forced the boss to apologize." Yetta took part in many strikes and walked many picket lines. Following Polish custom, she used to follow the scabs home from work and harass them. She always carried her lunch when picketing in order to convince the police that she was a good worker—she thought this gave her a kind of tactical protection. She was once arrested for pinching a scab but she was not afraid. Eventually she became a union organizer. She would get a job for a few weeks and organize until she was fired. As she herself summed up her own history, "Kids like me made the union."

Adriana Valenti got a job in a shop where thirty-five operators worked for practically nothing, and became angry thinking of what this meant for the women's families. Although she knew it was wrong she shut the power off in the shop. The wife of the owner came after her with an umbrella, poked her in the stomach, and ordered her to get out, but, as she ironically put it, "We got out, but we took the girls with us."

When Judith Weissman was working in an underwear factory, she met an older woman who had been educated in radical politics in Europe and was the chairperson of the union; although she came from a religious family, all of her children were socialists. Judith admired the woman and "followed her around." She carried an umbrella to protect herself from the goons who attacked her during the many strikes the union called. The police would arrest her, but she would show the judge a book of U.S. history and be freed. On one occasion, all of the pickets were locked up, including Judith, who did not get home until one o'clock in the morning. Although her mother was crying, thinking her daughter dead, Judith "loved it."

Bessie Polski went to work in a big factory that had 120 machines. The operators, Jewish and Italian women, told their union local that they wanted a piece-work system and better working conditions. When their demands were rejected, they went on strike. The bosses brought in scabs and called in the police, but "the police didn't club the scabs, they clubbed the strikers. You know how police are. The bosses used to look through the windows and they had the pleasure of it." Bessie Polski and an Italian woman were arrested for using a "female weapon" against a scab—a hat pin. The Italian woman decided to act hysterical, and cried and carried on until she was released the next day. Bessie was taken to night court, where "no nice girls go." The judge told her that he "sympathized very much with the girls, they were fighting for their rights. But you have to have respect for an officer and not spit in his face." She said she had not spit in the officer's face, "it was not in my nature I should spit on somebody," but she got locked up for three days anyway. The union finally won the strike, and Bessie argued that "we made the union, all those European boys and girls, we made the union. Otherwise, there still wouldn't be a union."

Shirley Levy worked in a factory run by five brothers. A union representative came to organize the shop:

> The five brothers nearly broke his head and threw him down the stairs. So it was like a fortress— couldn't organize the place. My friend and I decided that we would try to go out and find a job in a union factory. So we did. And it was all the difference in the world. The first week I earned $16. I helped maintain the shop. The boss was very annoyed at me because I fought for good prices and pulled all kinds of tricks.

Grace Grimaldi became involved in union activities because she worked for a slave driver. Joining the union was an important step for her:

> I was praying for someone to come and help us change the working conditions. I was always for the union. It really helped change the slavery conditions of the workers. It was really for the workers. My father was afraid to let me go to the picket line. I used to do behind-the-scenes work in the office. But the women who went out to the picket line—you've got to be a fighter. It's in you. Some people are more fighters than others so they take the front. For twenty years, things were very bad. Only those who were here before 1930 can understand the difference between 1910 and 1930.

Her husband was also active in the union—they were a union family. She described her husband as a "fighting idealist" who "sold his mind and body to the ideals of the cause." Even when raising a family inhibited her full-time participation, Grace Grimaldi always supported the union's work.

The strike was the key weapon in the union's battle, and two mass strikes—the shirtwaist strike of 1909 and the cloakmakers' strike of 1910—revolutionized the labor movement, both in New York City and across the nation. The shirtwaist strike of 1909, which became known as the "uprising of the 30,000," was not only the first large-scale protest in a new and rapidly growing industry but was the largest strike of women workers in the United States up to that point.

Responding to the growth of the national market—production in 1909 was worth about $50 million retail—the shirtwaist industry was in the process of changing from domestic manufacture to factory production. Most of the shops were medium sized, but some were large, employing over one hundred workers in one shop.

In 1909 a series of local strikes culminated in a strike in the two biggest shirtwaist factories, the Leierson and Triangle Shirtwaist shops. Striking pickets were met by the combined force of scabs, police, and thugs hired by management. The women began to feel that a general strike was the only effective weapon against the police power of the employers. The middle-class members of the recently organized Women's Trade Union League came to picket in solidarity with the striking women and were also arrested by the police. This brought the strike new publicity, as well as support from progressive elements across the city.

A leaflet calling for a general meeting of all workers in the shirtwaist trade printed in Italian, Yiddish, and English was distributed across the Lower East Side. The meeting was held at Cooper Union and illustrated dramatically the potentially explosive alliance between new forms of rank-and-file militancy and old-world traditions of community and solidarity. The speakers were moderate and uninspired until Clara Lemlish, a striker from the Leierson shop, spoke up—in Yiddish: "I am a working girl. One of those who are on strike against intolerable conditions. I am tired of listening to speakers who talk in general terms. What we are here for is to decide whether we shall or shall not strike. I offer a resolution that a general strike be declared—now." The speech electrified the audience and cries of support and

enthusiasm swept the hall. A second was called for, people jumped to their feet, and the chairman called for the taking of the old Jewish oath: "Two thousand hands were raised in the air with the prayer: 'If I turn traitor to the cause I now pledge, may this hand wither from the arm I now raise.' " Thus a general strike, the newest weapon against industry, was cemented by an oath of solidarity emanating from a communal past.

As the general strike began there were over fifteen thousand shirtwaist makers on the picket lines. The strike itself was held together by the women. As Louis Levine wrote:

> In fact, though the principal union officials were men and the direction of the strike was in the hands of men, the women played a preponderant role in carrying it through. It was mainly women who did the picketing, who were arrested and fined, who ran the risk of assault and who suffered ill treatment from the police and the courts.

One sympathetic social worker, in *Survey* magazine shortly afterward, described the spirit of the strike:

> Into the forefront of this great motion picture comes the figure of one girl after another as her services are needed. With extraordinary simplicity and eloquence she will tell before any kind of audience, without false shame and without self-glorification, the conditions of her work, her wages and the pinching poverty of her home and the homes of her comrades. Then she withdraws into the background to undertake quietly the danger and humiliation of picket duty or to become a nameless sandwich girl selling papers on the street, no longer the center of attention but the butt of the most unspeakable abuse.

One judge expressed the outrage of official society at the idea of women on strike. While sentencing one woman striker, Judge Olmstead told her pointblank: "You are on strike against God and Nature, whose firm law is that man shall earn his bread by the sweat of his brow. You are on strike against God." The activities of the women strikers were perceived as a blow against a civilization that demanded submission and docility on the part of its women.

The Progressive coalition that formed around the strike demanded a different definition of civilization and Americanization. Made up of the families of the strikers, socialist organizations on the Lower East Side, Progressive social workers, and the middle-class Women's Trade Union League, the coalition represented the interests of trade unions, suffragettes, and socialists, all of whom wanted a different kind of country. Unionists demanded higher wages and better working conditions because they believed that true Americanization occurred when workers stood up for their rights and demanded the reappropriation of the profits of their labor. Suffragists demanded the vote because they believed that the rights of women extended beyond the home to include an active participation in the affairs of civil society. Socialists (and varieties of anarchists) demanded the redistribution of the wealth created by industrial capitalism to the workers who had produced it in the first place. This vision of Americanism was voiced by Elizabeth Gurley Flynn during a strike at the textile mills in Lawrence, Massachusetts, in 1912:

> We talked of "Solidarity," a beautiful word in all languages. Stick together!—Workers unite! One for all and all for one! An injury to one is injury to all! The workers are all one family! It was internationalism. It was also real Americanism— the first they had heard. "One nation indivisible with liberty and justice for all." They hadn't found it here, but they were willingly fighting to create it.

The coalition was unified in a series of public meetings. At one, where the stage was set up like a rally for woman suffrage, "flags of blue on both side walls carried the words in white 'Votes for Women,'" the *New York Times* reported that 'socialism, unionism, women's suffrage and what seemed to be something like anarchism was poured into the ears of fully 8,000 people who gathered.' "

Nevertheless, ethnic barriers did not fall all at once, and there were some uncomfortable moments during the shirtwaist strike. Since the strike was organized primarily by the Jewish labor movement, its leaders were not always sympathetic to the Italian women, who found it more difficult to join the strike than did their Jewish sisters. Some Italian families were unwilling to allow their daughters to go on picket duty or to be involved in strike activities that took them out of the house. A common divisive tactic on the part of the bosses was to deliberately seat Jewish workers next to Italian workers. Language barriers and ethnic contempt made the situation worse. Yet this was the first time that Jewish and Italian women had worked together in an organized fashion, and in time the problems were somewhat overcome. Through the work of the Italian organizers of the Italian branch of the Socialist Party, anarchist societies, women's mutual-benefit societies, and individual contacts, increasing numbers of Italian women joined the strike and became active in the union.

After three grueling months the strike ended, with some gains and some losses. The employers agreed to shorter hours and the abolition of charges for needles but refused to recognize the union or to employ only union help. But even this partial success inspired the workers in the men's clothing industry to strike in 1912, when about 115,000 people went out on strike, including 10,000 Italian women finishers. The bosses attempted to buy the women off with promises of higher pay, but failed. One woman had been out six weeks when she was interviewed by Louise Odencrantz. She stayed on strike because, she said, "I will not betray my *patria.*"

In both strikes there was a tension between male trade union officials and women workers. The male officials often made policy decisions that were to the women's detriment. During the shirtwaist strike, for example, the male negotiators won on wage and hour demands but compromised on health and safety issues— issues on which the owners refused to budge. A year later the Triangle Waist Company went up in flames. On the day of the fire there were about eight hundred workers in the plant, and all the doors were locked—company policy in order to keep track of the women. One hundred and forty-six people died and hundreds more were injured. One reporter who covered the scene wrote: "I looked upon the dead bodies and I remembered these girls were the shirtwaist makers. I remembered their great strike of last year in which the same girls had demanded more sanitary conditions and more safety precautions in the shops. Their dead bodies were the answer."

In the 1912 strike, the male union leadership agreed to a settlement that set different standards of pay for male and female workers. In the famous "Protocols of the Dress and Waist Trade of 1913," the first labor agreement to use outside arbitrators, the lowest paid male earned more than the highest paid female, and the highest paid jobs were reserved for men only. These conditions made it difficult for women to remain in the industry, and showed the extent to which the industry and the union were intent on maintaining the sexual division of labor. The male-dominated trade union movement, by accepting a pay scale based on the sexual division of labor, in effect agreed that the principles of the family economy should be replaced by the more "Americanized" idea of a wage-earning father who was the sole support of the family.

In a larger sense, however, the shirtwaist

strike was a real victory for the women. It lifted the work of immigrant women out of obscurity and into public consciousness, and helped demonstrate the power of organized resistance. It was a living example of the American radical tradition—of spontaneous activism, solidarity, and the promise inherent in American ideals of democratic action.

In addition, the activity of the women and their emergence as a public force created new alliances in the community. The previously middle-class suffrage movement was bolstered by the power of women workers who were challenging the prevailing ideology of a woman's place, and in 1917 the referendum on women's suffrage was carried by 100,000 votes in New York City alone. Mary Simkhovitch thought that it passed because of

> the plain fact that though indeed the women's place is in the home, in our neighborhood it is also largely in the factory, workshop, the store and office, [and] that fathers and brothers and sons have long been convinced of the inevitability of this great political change. In the case of the Italians in our district, the fact that their women are beginning to work so largely in factories was the dominant reason for the change in attitude about suffrage. "My daughter she works, she must vote like me." It is indeed obvious.

The collective activity of immigrant women also demonstrated that the atomization inherent in American society could be confronted with the dignity and collectivity of labor. The union was often described as a family—a collective family that could provide for the needs and the well-being of the community itself.

Rebecca Markowitz expressed her understanding of the intimate connection between home and workplace: "If industry is sick—nobody makes any money. It's like housekeeping. If you don't have the money, you can't be a good housekeeper. In order to make good meals and take care of your family, you need the what with. That's why we needed the union." Bella Feiner articulated the same thought in a more political way: "Poor people didn't have anything. We had to seek ways of bettering our lives. The union was the way of meeting our economic and political needs. We had to deal with the present and the future."

Most women felt that the union had made a big difference in the shops. Fabbia Orzo re-ported that conditions improved after the union came in: "Quite a lot of improvement came after the union came in. Before the union came in, the hours were 48 a week at most of the shops. There were no breaks except for lunch. After, the hours were down to forty, then down to thirty-six. We got better pay." Bella Feiner expressed the same sentiment: "When the union came, it was wonderful. Before we had to work so long that I used to faint many times when I came home from work. I enjoyed working but we didn't get nothing before the union. After, it was a pleasure."

The union did, however, create class cleavages within the community. Garment manufacturers who prided themselves on their radical past in Eastern Europe were threatened by union activists in the United States. Fanny Rosen recalled: "My boss was a so-called liberal. He called himself a liberal and became a millionaire. He had been a student radical who fled Russia in the Revolution of 1905. He believed that strikes were legitimate but when it came to bargaining, he bargained like all the rest and kept informers in his shop."

Becky Brier summed up the feeling about bosses when she said, "You never liked a boss. He always lived better than the rest. He had a nicer home, even automobiles and vacations. He got that by paying us starvation wages. So, you never liked a boss."

The response of the clothing manufacturers to union organizing was twofold: some compromised their need for profit to meet the demands of the workers, while others began to move their factories and shops out of the city. By 1921 union organizers were facing the realities of the "runaway shop." As one official survey of the region noted: "The clothing manufacturer who announced to an investigator his intention to move his plant from New York to some town where he could tell 'those damned Bolsheviks to go to hell' undoubtedly voiced the sentiments of many exasperated fellow employers."

Ultimately trade union activity created an alternative to Americanization for immigrant women—and particularly for their daughters. If the Americanization movement assumed that it could change the immigrant working class, the trade unions offered a way for them to change America.

# Puertorriqueñas in the United States:
# The Impact of Double Discrimination

LOURDES MIRANDA KING

The Puerto Rican woman is too often pictured as a passive female, bending first to the will of her father, then of her husband—an obscure figure shuffling to the needs of her children and the men in her family.

This image has become an excuse to justify excluding her from full participation in the life of the United States. It reinforces the Anglo American stereotype of the Latin woman as childlike, pampered, and irresponsible.

The view supports the notion that Puerto Rican women deserve their subordinate status. After all, are not many of them employed in service occupations and as unskilled labor? That must mean they are suited only for demeaning work and is proof enough that they belong in that category. If one adds the prevalent assumption that Puerto Rican women are all alike, the stereotype is complete.

In many ways, the image of the Puerto Rican woman is similar to that of Puerto Rican men. That image is embellished by the perception of Latin men as indolent skirtchasers, in addition to being irresponsible and undependable. They, too, are at the bottom of the occupational ladder—which serves, in turn, to justify their exclusion and discrimination.

The adoption of the terms *macho* and *machismo* from Spanish to describe the supreme male chauvinist reflects the Latin male stereotype. Is it a coincidence that earlier the English borrowed *Don Juan,* the stereotype of the great lover?

Surely, other cultures have created words and literary figures to portray the traits of lovers, "banty-roosters," and authoritative males. If such spontaneous labels faithfully reflect life, as has been pointed out, then the selection of words from one culture for the popular language of

another must reflect deep-rooted value judgments and cultural assumptions.

Official statistics show the disastrous results brought about by false assumptions. The overall situation of Puerto Ricans in the United States attests to the low esteem in which they are held. By any standards, Puerto Ricans are a severely deprived ethnic group.

## A PROFILE

In 1972, Puerto Ricans had lower median incomes ($6,210 for a family of four), higher unemployment rates (9.6 percent in New York), and lower educational attainment (8 median years of schooling) than any other group in the United States, including blacks. Puerto Rican men are concentrated in the lower paying occupations, such as operatives, laborers, and service workers. Of all Puerto Rican families, 27.9 percent have incomes below $5,000; 12 percent have incomes below $2,000.

As did others before them, Puerto Ricans came to the mainland United States in search of work and improved economic opportunities. They arrived by plane in massive numbers during the late 1940s, mostly as unskilled workers entering a specialized economy.

Unlike previous immigrants, however, Puerto Ricans are American citizens. They all retained a nostalgic hope of returning to Puerto Rico—a new type of non-European immigrant.

On arrival, Puerto Ricans encountered numerous problems—their scanty knowledge of English, differences in customs, experience in a racially mixed society which ill prepared

From Lourdes Miranda King, "Puertorriqueñas in the United States: The Impact of Double Discrimination," *Civil Rights Digest* 6, no. 3 (Spring 1974): 20–26. Reprinted by permission of the publisher.

them for confronting racial inequities. All these factors conspired to sour the "American dream."

Today, even such fundamental facts as our numbers within the population are unclear. The 1.4 million count of the 1970 Census understated the true total, especially in New York. There, 200,000 Puerto Ricans remained uncounted, according to the Center for Social Research of the City University of New York.

Although approximately 60 percent of the Puerto Rican population in the United States is concentrated in New York City, that is not the only place where Puerto Ricans live. Substantial numbers are dispersed throughout the country—in New Jersey, Pennsylvania, Connecticut, Florida, Massachusetts, Illinois, Ohio, Indiana, Wisconsin, and as far west as California and Hawaii.

It is within this context that one must view the status of the Puerto Rican woman in the United States. Her situation is intertwined with that of the Puerto Rican male in American society. Both question their sense of worth, both feel the impact of discrimination as members of a minority. As a young woman told me, "Our men don't have equal rights or equal pay. We are all fighting for the same thing; both male and female are oppressed."

How Puerto Rican men are treated when they try to enter the so-called "mainstream of society" greatly influences Puerto Rican women. If, as has been the case, the Puerto Rican man is defeated or does not fare well, the woman bears the brunt of this treatment.

## THE PUERTO RICAN WOMAN

The Puerto Rican woman becomes a part of the cycle of failure. She drops out of school at an early age or enters the labor force at the lowest level, in the hope that her earnings will help lift her family out of poverty. Or her family unit may disintegrate through separation or divorce, leaving her the sole provider and head of household.

The Puerto Rican woman in the United States fits the historical pattern of the immigrant woman who worked alongside her man, sharing the burden of work and responsibilities. Unlike any other woman who has preceded her, however, she is a member of a group in continuous flux, moving between the United States and Puerto Rico for varying lengths of time throughout her life.

Studies have shown that women predominate among the return migrants to Puerto Rico. Some are single young women who have lost their jobs; others are older women whose children have left home. A still larger group is composed of women who have returned after a marital break-up.

It is not unusual to find women working in the United States whose children are cared for by grandmothers or other relatives in Puerto Rico, or to find wives and children living in Puerto Rico while their husbands find work in the mainland, or to find working wives in Puerto Rico "pioneering the resettlement" of husband and children—different patterns, yet with the same divisive effect on families. The woman is thrust into the role of sole supporter, creating the new immigrant woman and incidentally destroying the myth of the passive female.

As has been the case in other minority groups, the woman frequently has had more access to the larger Anglo-American society than has the Puerto Rican man. I have often heard, "When we came to the United States, my mother was able to get a job first while my father was still looking."

For many reasons, Puerto Rican women found employment more readily. Sexist attitudes permitted hiring a woman for a lower wage than a Puerto Rican man. Either they were seen as less of a threat in the white male hierarchy, or the available opportunities were so-called "women's jobs"—that is, unskilled.

In many communities with a concentration of Puerto Ricans, the pattern of employment was reversed and women had a lower unemployment rate. As late as 1969, according to the study, *Poverty Area Profiles: The New York Puerto Rican:* "Whereas normally the jobless rate for women is higher than for men, among Puerto Rican workers the pattern was reversed. Adult men 25–54 had a rate of nearly 8 percent, compared with less than 4 percent for women in this age group."

The Census Bureau attempted to explain this difference:

> Puerto Rican men in their prime, no matter what their employment status, are as firmly attached to the labor force as men in their prime generally, while Puerto Rican women tend more readily than women generally to withdraw from the labor force upon being laid off, or to re-enter it only when recalled or when accepting a new job. The short average duration of unemployment among these women in part reflects these unusual patterns of labor force entry and exit, and makes for low jobless rates.

Later data and trends belie this simplistic and confusing explanation. The low rate of unemployment is more likely caused by "dropping out" of a labor force which does not offer useful work—considering women's supreme difficulties in finding a job and their childbearing and child rearing functions. The harm was done, however, and a generation of Puerto Ricans were led to believe that Puerto Rican women were better off than their men.

## THE MYTH OF SUCCESS

In spite of a current 10 percent unemployment rate for Puerto Rican women in New York (the highest unemployment of any group in that city) and the decrease during the past decade in the level of Puerto Rican female participation in the job market from 38 to 28 percent (which runs against the national trend), the myth of female success was firmly entrenched among the Puerto Rican communities on the mainland. The belief prevailed that any attempt at upgrading the status of Puerto Rican women would of necessity take jobs away from the men, downgrading the Puerto Rican man and the Puerto Rican family.

As one woman told me, "We have so many bread and butter issues and such few human resources that we have to establish priorities and my main interest is toward Puerto Rican issues, regardless of sex." She added, however, "as long as the women's movement is fighting for those things which we as a minority group are fighting for—such as equal rights, the end to poverty, and expansion of child care centers—we are with them."

The aversion toward focusing on the status of the Puerto Rican woman has been detrimental to both males and females. It blatantly ignores the economic facts. The Women's Bureau of the U.S. Department of Labor has found that: "There were 19.2 million married women (husband present) in the labor force in March 1972; the number of unemployed men was 3.1 million. If all the married women stayed home and unemployed men were placed in their jobs, there would be 16.1 million unfilled jobs."

History has shown that gains in income by the productivity of a new group do not come at the expense of existing groups.

Many of the Puerto Rican community leaders who have swallowed the myth of female success are women. They have been made to feel guilty about their leadership role in relation to Puerto Rican men, even though more than half of the Puerto Rican population is composed of women. I was horrified—and mortified—when a prominent Puerto Rican woman leader was telling me about her tribulations in locating a young male to serve as president of a Puerto Rican youth leadership group.

"The most promising candidate, and the one most likely to be elected, was a young woman," she said. "I quickly had to come up with a boy to back for president. . . . There are just too many women leaders in the Puerto Rican community already." Although clearly not the most qualified, the boy was elected president.

The Puerto Rican woman in the United States then is caught between two forces. On the one hand, she is entrapped within the bleak economic and political powerlessness affecting the Puerto Rican population in general. On the other hand, she suffers from the socialization of sex roles which causes her to have guilt feelings about the fulfillment of her potential and its expression in a society which looks down its aquiline Anglo nose at her and her people. Above it all, the statistics verify that her situation is worse than even she might be willing to admit.

## SOME COMPARISONS

The Puerto Rican woman in the mainland United States feels the impact of double discrimination as a woman and as a Puerto Rican—often as a woman, a black, and a Puerto Rican. The Puerto Rican man has a median income of $5,613 a year; the Puerto Rican woman earns $2,784 a year. Of all Puerto Rican males, 12 percent have incomes below $2,000, compared to 34 percent of all Puerto Rican women. The men complete 9.3 years of school, while women finish 8.8 years.

Unemployment among Puerto Rican women is a whopping 17.8 percent—the highest rate among any Spanish origin group, and almost three times higher than the national average. The Puerto Rican male unemployment rate, although high, is 8.8 percent.

The Puerto Rican woman is often prevented from working by the number of small children in the family who need her care and attention, for the Puerto Rican population in the mainland United States is extremely young. The median age is 18 years. Of all Puerto Rican families, 76 percent have children under 18, and of all Puerto Ricans living in this country, 28.7 percent are under 10 years old.

This situation is further aggravated by the greater family responsibilities and income needs of larger families. Over half of these families have more than five members in the family.

Lack of child care facilities specifically geared to the language and cultural needs of the Puerto Rican child (bilingual child care centers, since Spanish is the language spoken in 73 percent of Puerto Rican homes) often force the mother either to stay at home, or to ship her children off to a willing relative in Puerto Rico.

If she does brave that obstacle, she starts her day earlier than the average worker in order to dress and feed her children before taking them to be cared for in someone's home. In any case, knowing that her children are being raised by another person often a thousand miles away under less than adequate conditions, or that they are roaming the streets alone after school, becomes a source of further worry and stress.

For 105,000 Puerto Rican families in the United States, female employment and earnings are vital. Those families (29 percent of the total number of Puerto Rican families) are headed by Puerto Rican women. Yet official figures show that only 12.7 percent of those Puerto Rican women were able to work full-time all year, compared to 80.3 percent of white and 73.5 percent of black female heads of households who worked at full-time jobs. Only 23.6 percent of such Puerto Rican women worked part of the year.

We all know that a part-time job is not enough to support a family above the poverty level. Should it astound us, then, to find that a shocking 65 percent of the Puerto Rican families headed by women were living in poverty in 1971? This is much higher than the 27 percent of all white female-headed families and 54 percent of all black female-headed families living at the poverty level.

Among the migrants returning to Puerto Rico, more than one-fifth were women heads of households. José Hernandez, in *Return Migration to Puerto Rico,* found that 42.8 percent of the female heads of household were married women whose spouses were absent. He concludes: "It is clear that this category contained many survivors of family breakage at the 'launching stage.' . . ."

When she is able to work, the Puerto Rican woman faces serious disadvantages. She lacks sufficient education and training to command a decent salary, thus compounding her housing, health, and overall problems further. Lack of full command of English is yet another obstacle.

And always present are the subtle pressures of finding her values as a Puerto Rican threatened and misunderstood. Since her livelihood depends on it, she has to prove herself constantly—among men and women—in the larger society, straining to conform.

I am always saddened when I see Puerto Rican women with hair dyed flaming red or yellow. Is it not the ideal of beauty to be a long-limbed slim-hipped blonde? As the Anglo woman chases a male-determined standard of beauty, the Puerto Rican woman pursues that same standard established by cultures other than her own. She can't stretch herself, but she can always color her hair.

## THE WOMEN'S MOVEMENT

The Puerto Rican woman, both in Puerto Rico and in the United States, must examine the issues surrounding the women's movement. Today, the participation of Puerto Rican women in the women's movement in the United States has been limited to a small core of middle class professional women and, to a lesser degree, working class women who have always had to struggle for survival. Others active in the movement have been completely "assimilated" into the American middle class structure, sometimes rejecting that which is unique about our culture. However, a small group of Puerto Rican women with clearly defined priorities have chosen to work through the women's movement as part and parcel of the advancement of all Puerto Ricans.

Unfortunately, the women's rights movement has barely started to reach the ordinary middle class woman who, through the "success" of some man, has vicariously achieved "success" as defined by our society, and has built her life around her family, her house, and the incessant acquisition of material goods—never realizing that she is but a man away from poverty.

For all Puerto Rican women, the movement must concentrate on education concerning the issues involved and the true distinction between the women's rights movement and the negative image of "women's liberation" created by the media. Although we have been mistakenly led to believe that radical feminists advocate doing so, Puerto Rican women are not going to divorce themselves from their cultural heritage or be alienated from their men.

The Puerto Rican woman's views on the

qualities of womanhood, her strong family ties, and her respect for the family as an institution will accept a movement which asserts, but not one which divides. If the movement appeals to the basic issue of human rights for both men and women, to the values inherent in the freedom of men and women from sexism in their relationships, to the fact that a woman with freedom of choice also frees the man to decide what he wants to do with his life—if it appeals to the real issues involved and not the image—then Puerto Rican women will support it.

It has been basic misundertanding of the movement as anti-male, anti-family, and somehow sexually promiscuous which has made it difficult for more Puerto Rican women—as well as Anglo American women, I might add—to embrace the cause of feminism.

# Race, Class, and Gender:
# Prospects for an All-Inclusive Sisterhood

BONNIE THORTON DILL

The concept of sisterhood has been an important unifying force in the contemporary women's movement. By stressing the similarities of women's secondary social and economic positions in all societies and in the family, this concept has been a binding force in the struggle against male chauvinism and patriarchy. However, as we review the past decade, it becomes apparent that the cry "Sisterhood is powerful!" has engaged only a few segments of the female population in the United States. Black, Hispanic, Native American, and Asian American women of all classes, as well as many working-class women, have not readily identified themselves as sisters of the white middle-class women who have been in the forefront of the movement.

This essay examines the applications of the concept of sisterhood and some of the reasons for the limited participation of racially and ethnically distinct women in the women's movement, with particular reference to the experience and consciousness of Afro-American women. The first section presents a critique of sisterhood as a binding force for all women and examines the limitations of the concept for both theory and practice when applied to women who are neither white nor middle class. In the second section, the importance of women's perception of themselves and their place in society is explored as a way of understanding the differences and similarities between black and white women. Data from two studies, one of college-educated black women and the other of black female household workers, are presented to illuminate both the ways in which the structures of race, gender, and class intersect in the lives of black women and the women's perceptions of the impact of these structures on their lives. This essay concludes with a discussion of the prospects for sisterhood and suggests

political strategies that may provide a first step toward a more inclusive women's movement.

## THE LIMITATIONS OF SISTERHOOD

In a recent article, historian Elizabeth Fox-Genovese provided a political critique of the concept of sisterhood. Her analysis identifies some of the current limitations of this concept as a rallying point for women across the boundaries of race and class. Sisterhood is generally understood as a nurturant, supportive feeling of attachment and loyalty to other women which grows out of a shared experience of oppression. A term reminiscent of familial relationships, it tends to focus upon the particular nurturant and reproductive roles of women and, more recently, upon commonalities of personal experience. Fox-Genovese suggests that sisterhood has taken two different political directions. In one, women have been treated as unique, and sisterhood was used as a basis for seeking to maintain a separation between the competitive values of the world of men (the public-political sphere) and the nurturant values of the world of women (the private-domestic sphere). A second, more recent and progressive expression of the concept views sisterhood as an element of the feminist movement which serves as a means for political and economic action based upon the shared needs and experiences of women. Both conceptualizations of sisterhood have limitations in encompassing the racial and class differences among women. These limitations have important implications for the prospects of an all-inclusive sisterhood.

Fox-Genovese argues that the former conceptualization, which she labels bourgeois individu-

From Bonnie Thornton Dill, "Race, Class, and Gender: Prospects for an All-Inclusive Sisterhood." *Feminist Studies* 9, no. 1 (Spring 1983): 131–48. Reprinted by permission of the publisher. Footnotes have been deleted.

alism, resulted in "the passage of a few middle class women into the public sphere," but sharpened the class and racial divisions between them and lower-class minority women. In the latter conceptualization, called the politics of personal experience, sisterhood is restricted by the experiential differences that result from the racial and class divisions of society.

> Sisterhood has helped us, as it helped so many of our predecessors, to forge ourselves as political beings. Sisterhood has mobilized our loyalty to each other and hence to ourselves. It has given form to a dream of genuine equality for women. But without a broader politics directed toward the kind of social transformation that will provide social justice for all human beings, it will, in a poignant irony, result in our dropping each other by the wayside as we compete with rising desperation for crumbs.

These two notions of sisterhood, as expressed in the current women's movement, offer some insights into the alienation many black women have expressed about the movement itself.

The bourgeois individualistic theme present in the contemporary women's movement led many black women to express the belief that the movement existed merely to satisfy needs for personal self-fulfillment on the part of white middle-class women. The emphasis on participation in the paid labor force and escape from the confines of the home seemed foreign to many black women. After all, as a group they had had higher rates of paid labor force participation than their white counterparts for centuries, and many would have readily accepted what they saw as the "luxury" of being a housewife. At the same time, they expressed concern that white women's gains would be made at the expense of blacks and/or that having achieved their personal goals, these so-called sisters would ignore or abandon the cause of racial discrimination. Finally, and perhaps most important, the experiences of racial oppression made black women strongly aware of their group identity and consequently more suspicious of women who, initially at least, defined much of their feminism in personal and individualistic terms.

Angela Davis, in "Reflections on the Black Woman's Role in the Community of Slaves," stresses the importance of group identity for black women. "Under the impact of racism the black woman has been continually constrained to inject herself into the desperate struggle for existence. . . . As a result, black women have made significant contributions to struggles against racism and the dehumanizing exploitation of a wrongly organized society. In fact, it

would appear that the intense levels of resistance historically maintained by black people and thus the historical function of the black liberation struggle as harbinger of change throughout the society are due in part to the greater objective equality between the black man and the black woman." The sense of being part of a collective movement toward liberation has been a continuing theme in the autobiographies of contemporary black women.

> Ideas and experiences vary, but Shirley Chisholm, Gwendolyn Brooks, Angela Davis and other black women who wrote autobiographies during the seventies offer similar . . . visions of the black woman's role in the struggle for black liberation. The idea of collective liberation . . . says that society is not a protective arena in which an individual black can work out her own destiny and gain a share of America's benefits by her own efforts. . . . Accordingly, survival, not to mention freedom, is dependent on the values and actions of the groups as a whole, and if indeed one succeeds or triumphs it is due less to individual talent than to the group's belief in and adherence to the idea that freedom from oppression must be acted out and shared by all.

Sisterhood is not new to black women. It has been institutionalized in churches. In many black churches, for example, membership in the church entitles one to address the women as "sisters" and the men as "brothers." Becoming a sister is an important rite of passage which permits young women full participation in certain church rituals and women's clubs where these nurturant relationships among women are reinforced. Sisterhood was also a basis for organization in the club movements that began in the late 1800s. Finally, it is clearly exemplified in black extended family groupings that frequently place great importance on female kinship ties. Research on kinship patterns among urban blacks identifies the nurturant and supportive feelings existing among female kin as a key element in family stability and survival.

While black women have fostered and encouraged sisterhood, we have not used it as the anvil to forge our political identities. This contrasts sharply with the experiences of many middle-class white women who have participated in the current women's movement. The political identities of Afro-American women have largely been formed around issues of race. National organizations of black women, many of which were first organized on the heels of the nineteenth century movement for women's rights, "were (and still are) decidedly feminist in the values expressed in their literature and in many of the concerns which they addressed, yet they also always focused upon issues which resulted from the racial oppression affecting *all* black people." This commitment to the improvement of the race has often led black women to see feminist issues quite differently from their white sisters. And, racial animosity and mistrust have too often undermined the potential for coalition between black and white women since the women's suffrage campaigns.

Many contemporary white feminists would like to believe that relations between black and white women in the early stages of the women's movement were characterized by the beliefs and actions of Susan B. Anthony, Angelina Grimke, and some others. The historical record suggests however, that these women were more exceptional than normative. Rosalyn Terborg-Penn argues that "discrimination against Afro-American women reformers was the rule rather than the exception within the woman's rights movement from the 1830's to 1920." Although it is beyond the scope of this essay to provide a detailed discussion of the incidents that created mistrust and ill-feeling between black and white women, the historical record provides an important legacy that still haunts us.

The movement's early emphasis upon the oppression of women within the institution of marriage and the family, and upon educational and professional discrimination, reflected the concerns of middle-class white women. During that period, black women were engaged in a struggle for survival and a fight for freedom. Among their immediate concerns were lynching and economic viability. Working-class white women were concerned about labor conditions, the length of the working day, wages, and so forth. The statements of early women's rights groups do not reflect these concerns, and "as a rigorous consummation of the consciousness of white middle-class women's dilemma, the [Seneca Falls] Declaration all but ignored the predicament of white working-class women, as it ignored the condition of black women in the South and North alike."

Political expediency drove white feminists to accept principles that were directly opposed to the survival and well-being of blacks in order to seek to achieve more limited advances for women. "Besides the color bar which existed in many white women's organizations, black women were infuriated by white women's accommodation to the principle of lynch law in order to gain support in the South and the attacks of well-known feminists against anti-lynching crusader, Ida Wells Barnett."

The failure of the suffrage movement to sustain its commitment to the democratic ideal of enfranchisement for all citizens is one of the most frequently cited instances of white women's fragile commitment to racial equality. "After the Civil War, the suffrage movement was deeply impaired by the split over the issue of whether black males should receive the vote before white and black women . . . in the heated pressures over whether black men or white and black women should be enfranchised first, a classist, racist, and even xenophobic rhetoric crept in." The historical and continued abandonment of universalistic principles in order to benefit a privileged few on the part of white women is, I think, one of the reasons why black women today have been reluctant to see themselves as part of a sisterhood that does not extend beyond racial boundaries. Even for those black women who are unaware of the specific history, there is the recognition that under pressure from the white men with whom they live and upon whom they are economically dependent, many white women will abandon their "sisters of color" in favor of self-preservation. The feeling that the movement would benefit white women and abandon blacks, or benefit whites at the expense of blacks, is a recurrent theme. Terborg-Penn concludes, "The black feminist movement in the United States during the mid 1970's is a continuation of a trend that began over 150 years ago. Institutionalized discrimination against black women by white women has traditionally led to the development of racially separate groups that address themselves to race determined problems as well as the common plight of women in America."

Historically, as well as currently, black women have felt called upon to choose between their commitments to feminism and to the struggle against racial injustice. Clearly they are victims of both forms of oppression and are most in need of encouragement and support in waging battles on both fronts. However, insistence on such a choice continues largely as a result of the tendency of groups of blacks and groups of women to battle over the dubious distinction of being the "most" oppressed. The insistence of radical feminists upon the historical priority, universality, and overriding importance of patriarchy in effect necessitates acceptance of a concept of sisterhood that places one's womanhood over and above one's race. At the same time, blacks are accustomed to labeling discriminatory treatment as racism and therefore may tend to view sexism only within the bounds of the black community rather than see it as a systemic pattern. On the one hand, the choice between identifying as black or female is a product of the "patriarchal strategy of divide-and-conquer" and, therefore, a false choice. Yet, the historical success of this strategy and the continued importance of class, patriarchal, and racial divisions, perpetuate such choices both within our consciousness and within the concrete realities of our daily lives.

Race, of course, is only one of the factors that differentiate women. It is the most salient in discussions of black and white women, but it is perhaps no more important, even in discussions of race and gender, than is the factor of class. Inclusion of the concept of class permits a broader perspective on the similarities and differences between black and white women than does a purely racial analysis. Marxist feminism has focused primarily upon the relationship between class exploitation and patriarchy. While this literature has yielded several useful frameworks for beginning to examine the dialectics of gender and class, the role of race, though acknowledged, is not explicated.

Just as the gender-class literature tends to omit race, the race-class literature gives little attention to women. Recently, this area of inquiry has been dominated by a debate over the relative importance of race or class in explaining the historical and contemporary status of blacks in this country. A number of scholars writing on this issue have argued that the racial division of labor in the United States began as a form of class exploitation which was shrouded in an ideology of racial inferiority. Through the course of U.S. history, racial structures began to take on a life of their own and cannot now be considered merely reflections of class structure. A theoretical understanding of the current conditions of blacks in this country must therefore take account of both race and class factors. It is not my intention to enter into this debate, but instead to point out that any serious study of black women must be informed by this growing theoretical discussion. Analysis of the interaction of race, gender, and class falls squarely between these two developing bodies of theoretical literature.

Black women experience class, race, and sex exploitation simultaneously, yet these structures must be separated analytically so that we may better understand the ways in which they shape and differentiate women's lives. Davis, in her previously cited article, provides one of the best analyses to date of the intersection of gender, race, and class under a plantation economy. One of the reasons this analysis is so important is that she presents a model that can be expanded to other historical periods. However, we must be careful not to take the particular historical reality which she illuminated and read it into the present as if the experiences of black women followed some sort of linear progression out of slavery. Instead, we must look carefully at the lives of black women throughout history in order to define the peculiar interactions of race, class, and gender at particular historical moments.

In answer to the question: Where do black women fit into the current analytical frameworks for race and class and gender and class? I would ask: How might these frameworks be revised if they took full account of black women's position in the home, family, and marketplace at various historical moments? In other words, the analysis of the interaction of race, gender, and class must not be stretched to fit the procrustean bed of any other burgeoning set of theories. It is my contention that it must begin with an analysis of the ways in which black people have been used in the process of capital accumulation in the United States. Within the contexts of class exploitation and racial oppression, women's lives and work are most clearly illuminated. Davis's article illustrates this. Increasingly, new research is being presented which grapples with the complex interconnectedness of these three issues in the lives of black women and other women of color.

## PERCEPTIONS OF SELF IN SOCIETY

For black women and other women of color an examination of the ways in which racial oppression, class exploitation, and patriarchy intersect in their lives must be studied in relation to their perceptions of the impact these structures have upon them. Through studying the lives of particular women and searching for patterns in the ways in which they describe themselves and their relationship to society, we will gain important insights into the differences and similarities between black and white women.

The structures of race and class generate important economic, ideological, and experiential cleavages among women. These lead to differences in perception of self and their place in society. At the same time, commonalities of class or gender may cut across racial lines providing the conditions for shared understanding. Studying these interactions through an examination of women's self perceptions is complicated by the fact that most people view their lives as a whole and do not explain their daily experiences or world view in terms of the differential effects of their racial group, class position, or gender. Thus, we must examine on an analytical level the ways in which the structure of class, race, and gender intersect in any woman's or group of women's lives in order to grasp the concrete set of social relations that influence their behavior. At the same time, we must study individual and group perceptions, descriptions, and conceptualizations of their lives so that we may understand the ways in which different women perceive the same and different sets of social structural constraints.

Concretely, and from a research perspective, this suggests the importance of looking at both the structures which shape womens lives and their self-presentations. This would provide us, not only with a means of gaining insight into the ways in which racial, class, and gender oppression are viewed, but also with a means of generating conceptual categories that will aid us in extending our knowledge of their situation. At the same time, this new knowledge will broaden and even reform our conceptualization of women's situations.

For example, how would our notions of mothering, and particularly mother-daughter relationships, be revised if we considered the particular experiences and perceptions of black women on this topic? Gloria I. Joseph argues for, and presents a distinctive approach to the study of black mother-daughter relationships, asserting that

> to engage in a discussion of black mothers and daughters which focused on specific psychological mechanisms operating between the two, the dynamics of the crucial bond, and explanations for the explicit role of patriarchy, without also including the important relevancy of racial oppression . . . would necessitate forcing black mother/daughter relationships into pigeonholes designed for understanding white models.
>
> In discussing black mothers and daughters, it is more realistic, useful and intellectually astute to speak in terms of their roles, positions, and functions within the black society and that society's relationship to the broader (white) society in America.

Unfortunately, there have been very few attempts in the social sciences to systematically investigate the relationship between social structure and self perceptions of black women. The profiles of black women that have been appear-

ing in magazines like *Essence,* the historical studies of black women, fiction and poetry by and about black women, and some recent sociological and anthropological studies provide important data for beginning such an analysis. However, the question of how black women perceive themselves with regard to the structures of race, gender, and class is still open for systematic investigation.

Elizabeth Higginbotham, in a study of black women who graduated from college between 1968 and 1970, explored the impact of class origins upon strategies for educational attainment. She found that class differences within the black community led not only to different sets of educational experiences, but also to different personal priorities and views of the black experience. According to Higginbotham, the black women from middle-class backgrounds who participated in her study had access to better schools and more positive schooling experiences than did their working-class sisters. Because their parents did not have the economic resources to purchase the better educational opportunities offered in an integrated suburb or a private school, the working-class women credited their parents' willingness to struggle within the public school system as a key component in their own educational achievement. Social class also affected college selections and experience. Working-class women were primarily concerned with finances in selecting a college and spent most of their time adjusting to the work load and the new middle-class environment once they had arrived. Middle-class women, on the other hand, were freer to select a college that would meet their personal, as well as their academic, needs and abilities. Once there, they were better able to balance their work and social lives and to think about integrating future careers and family lives.

Among her sample, Higginbotham found that a larger proportion of women from working-class backgrounds were single. She explained this finding in terms of class differences in socialization and mobility strategies. She found that the parents of women from working-class backgrounds stressed educational achievement over and above other personal goals. These women never viewed marriage as a means of mobility and focused primarily upon education, postponing interest in, and decisions about, marriage. In contrast, women from middle-class backgrounds were expected to marry and were encouraged to integrate family and educational goals throughout their schooling.

My own research on household workers demonstrates the ways in which class origins, racial discrimination, and social conceptions of women and women's work came together during the first half of the twentieth century to limit work options and affect family roles and the self perceptions of one group of Afro-American women born between 1896 and 1915. Most of them were born in the South and migrated North between 1922 and 1955. Like the majority of black working women of this period, they worked as household workers in private homes. (During the first half of the twentieth century, labor force participation rates of black women ranged from about 37 percent to 50 percent. Approximately 60 percent of black women workers were employed in private household work up until 1960.)

The women who participated in this study came from working-class families. Their fathers were laborers and farmers, their mothers were housewives or did paid domestic work of some kind (cooking, cleaning, taking in washing, and so forth). As a result, the women not only had limited opportunities for education, but also often began working when they were quite young to help support their families. Jewell Prieleau (names are pseudonyms used to protect the identity of the subjects), one of eight children, described her entrance into work as follows: "When I was eight years old, I decided I wanted a job and I just got up early in the morning and I would go from house to house and ring doorbells and ask for jobs and I would get it. I think I really wanted to work because in a big family like that, they was able to feed you, but you had to earn your shoes. They couldn't buy shoes although shoes was very cheap at that time. I would rather my mother give it to the younger children and I would earn my way."

Queenie Watkins lived with her mother, aunt, and five cousins and began working in grammar school. She described her childhood jobs in detail.

When I went to grammar school, the white ladies used to come down and say "Do you have a girl who can wash dishes?" That was how I got the job with the doctor and his wife. I would go up there at six o'clock in the morning and wash the breakfast dishes and bring in scuttles of coal to burn on the fireplace. I would go back in the afternoon and take the little girl down on the sidewalk and if there were any leaves to be raked on the yard, I'd rake the leaves up and burn them and sweep the sidewalk. I swept off the front porch and washed it off with the hose and washed dishes again—for one dollar a week.

While class position limited the economic resources and educational opportunities of most of these women, racial discrimination constricted work options for black women in such a way as to seriously undercut the benefits of education. The comments of the following women are reflective of the feelings expressed by many of those in this sample:

When I came out of school, the black man naturally had very few chances of doing certain things and even persons that I know myself who had finished four years of college were doing the same type of work because they couldn't get any other kind of work in New York.

In my home in Virginia, education, I don't think was stressed. The best you could do was be a school teacher. It wasn't something people impressed upon you you could get. I had an aunt and cousin who were trained nurses and the best they could do was nursing somebody at home or something. They couldn't get a job in a hospital. I didn't pay education any mind really until I came to New York. I'd gotten to a certain stage in domestic work in the country and I didn't see the need for it.

Years ago there was no such thing as a black typist. I remember girls who were taking typing when I was going to school. They were never able to get a job at it. In my day and time you could have been the greatest typist in the world but you would never have gotten a job. There was no such thing as getting a job as a bank teller. The blacks weren't even sweeping the banks.

For black women in the United States, their high concentration in household work was a result of racial discrimination and a direct carryover from slavery. Black women were in essence "a permanent service caste in nineteenth and twentieth century America." Arnold Anderson and Mary Jean Bowman argue that the distinguishing feature of domestic service in the United States is that "the frequency of servants is correlated with the availability of Negroes in local populations." By the time most of the women in this sample entered the occupation a racial caste pattern was firmly established. The occupation was dominated by foreign-born white women in the North, and black freedwomen in the South, a pattern which was modified somewhat as southern blacks migrated north. Nevertheless, most research indicates that black women fared far worse than their white immigrant sisters, even in the North. "It is commonly asserted that the immigrant woman has been the northern substitute for the Negro servant. In 1930, when one can separate white servants by nativity, about twice as large a percentage of foreign as of native women were domestics. . . . As against this 2:1 ratio between immigrants and natives, the ratio of Negro to white servants ranged upward from 10:1 to 50:1. The immigrant was not the northerner's Negro."

Two major differences distinguished the experiences of black domestics from that of their immigrant sisters. First, black women had few other employment options. Second, black household workers were older and more likely to be married. Thus, while private household work cross-culturally, and for white women in the United States, was often used as a stepping-stone to other working-class occupations, or as a way station before marriage, for black American women it was neither. This pattern did not begin to change substantially until World War II.

Table 1 indicates that between 1900 and 1940 the percentage of black women in domestic service actually increased, relative to the percentage of immigrant women which decreased. The data support the contention that black women were even more confined to the occupation than their immigrant sisters. At the turn of the century, large numbers of immigrants entered domestic service. Their children, however, were much less likely to become household workers. Similarly, many black women entered domestic service at that time, but their children tended to remain in the occupation. It was the daughters and granddaughters of the women who participated in this study that were among the first generation of black women to benefit from the relaxation of racial restrictions which began to occur after World War II.

Finally, black women were household workers because they were women. Private household work is women's work. It is a working-class occupation, has low social status, low pay, and few guaranteed fringe benefits. Like the

housewife who employs her, the private household worker's low social status and pay is tied to the work itself, to her class, gender, and the complex interaction of the three within the family. In other words, housework, both paid and unpaid, is structured around the particular place of women in the family. It is considered unskilled labor because it requires no training, degrees, or licenses, and because it has traditionally been assumed that any woman could or should be able to do housework.

The women themselves had a very clear sense that the social inequities which relegated them and many of their peers to household service labor were based upon their race, class, and gender. Yet different women, depending upon their jobs, family situations, and overall outlooks on life, handled this knowledge in different ways. One woman described the relationship between her family and her employer's as follows: "Well for *their* children, I imagine they wanted them to become like they were, educators or something that-like [sic]. But what they had in for my children, they say in me that I wasn't able to make all of that mark but raised my children in the best method I could. Because I wouldn't have the means to put *my* children through like they could for their children." When asked what she liked most about her work, she answered, "Well what I like most about it, the things that I weren't able to go to school to do for my children. I could kinda pattern from the families that I worked for, so that I could give my children the best of my abilities." A second woman expressed much more anger and bitterness about the social differences which distinguished her life from that of her female employer. "They don't know nothing about a hard life. The only hard life will come if they getting a divorce or going through a problem with their children.

Table 1. Percentage of Females of Each Nativity in U.S. Labor Force Who Were Servants, by Decades, 1900–1940

|  | 1900 | 1910 | 1920 | 1930 | 1940 |
|---|---|---|---|---|---|
| Native white | 22.3 | 15.0 | 9.6 | 10.4 | 11.0 |
| Foreign-born white | 42.5 | 34.0 | 23.8 | 26.8 | |
| Negro | 41.9 | 39.5 | 44.4 | 54.9 | 54.4 |
| Other | 24.8 | 22.9 | 22.9 | 19.4 | 16.0 |
| Total | 30.5 | 24.0 | 17.9 | 19.8 | 17.2 |
| (N, in thousands) | (1,439) | (1,761) | (1,386) | (1,906) | (1,931) |
| (Percent of all domestic servants) | (95.4) | (94.4) | (93.3) | (94.1) | (92.0) |

*Source:* George J. Stigler, *Domestic Servants in the United States: 1900–1940,* Occasional Paper no. 24 (New York: National Bureau of Economic Research, 1946), p.7.

But their husband has to provide for them because they're not soft. And if they leave and they separate for any reason or [are] divorced, they have to put the money down. But we have no luck like that. We have to leave our children; sometime leave the children alone. There's times when I have asked winos to look after my children. It was just a terrible life and I really thank God that the children grow up to be nice." Yet while she acknowledged her position as an oppressed person, she used her knowledge of the anomalies in her employers' lives—particularly the woman and her female friends—to aid her in maintaining her sense of self-respect and determination and to overcome feelings of despair and immobilization. When asked if she would like to switch places with her employers, she replied, "I don't think I would want to change, but I would like to live differently. I would like to have my own nice little apartment with my husband and have my grandchildren for dinner and my daughter and just live comfortable. But I would always want to work. . . . But, if I was to change life with them, I would like to have just a little bit of they money, that's all." While the women who participated in this study adopted different personal styles of coping with these inequities, they were all clearly aware that being black, poor, and female placed them at the bottom of the social structure, and they used the resources at their disposal to make the best of what they recognized as a bad situation.

Contemporary scholarship on women of color suggests that the barriers to an all-inclusive sisterhood are deeply rooted in the histories of oppression and exploitation that blacks and other groups encountered upon incorporation into the American political economy. These histories affect the social positions of these groups today, and racial ethnic women in every social class express anger and distress about the forms of discrimination and insensitivity which they encounter in their interactions with white feminists. Audre Lorde has argued that the inability of women to confront anger is one of the important forces dividing women of color from white women in the feminist movement. She cites several examples from her own experience which resonate loudly with the experiences of most women of color who have been engaged in the women's movement.

After fifteen years of a women's movement which professes to address the life concerns and possible futures of all women, I still hear, on campus after campus, "How can we address the issues of racism? No women of color attended." Or, on the other side of that statement, "We have no one in our department equipped to teach their work." In other words, racism is a black women's problem, a problem of women of color, and only we can discuss it.

White women are beginning to examine their relationships to black women, yet often I hear you wanting only to deal with the little colored children across the roads of childhood, the beloved nurse-maid, the occasional second-grade classmate. . . . You avoid the childhood assumptions formed by the raucous laughter at Rastus and Oatmeal . . . the indelible and dehumanizing portraits of Amos and Andy and your daddy's humorous bedtime stories.

Bell Hooks points to both the racial and class myopia of white feminists as a major barrier to sisterhood.

When white women's liberationists emphasized work as a path to liberation, they did not concentrate their attention on those women who are most exploited in the American labor force. Had they emphasized the plight of working class women, attention would have shifted away from the college-educated suburban housewife who wanted entrance into the middle and upper class work force. Had attention been focused on women who were already working and who were exploited as cheap surplus labor in American society, it would have de-romanticized the middle class white woman's quest for "meaningful" employment. While it does not in any way diminish the importance of women resisting sexist oppression by entering the labor force, work has not been a liberating force for masses of American women.

As a beginning point for understanding the potential linkages and barriers to an all-inclusive sisterhood, Lorde concludes that "the strength of women lies in recognizing differences between us as creative, and in standing to those distortions which we inherited without blame but which are now ours to alter. The angers of women can transform differences through insight into power. For anger between peers births change, not destruction, and the discomfort and sense of loss it often causes is not fatal, but a sign of growth."

## PROSPECTS FOR AN ALL-INCLUSIVE SISTERHOOD

Given the differences in experiences among black women, the differences between black and white women, between working-class and middle-class women, between all of us, what then are the prospects for sisterhood? While this article has sought to emphasize the need to study and explicate these differences, it is based upon the assumption that the knowledge we gain in this process will also help enlighten us as to our similarities. Thus, I would argue for the abandonment of the concept of sisterhood as a global construct based on unexamined assumptions about our similarities, and I would substitute a more pluralistic approach that recognizes and accepts the objective differences between women. Such an approach requires that we concentrate our political energies on building coalitions around particular issues of shared interest. Through joint work on specific issues, we may come to a better understanding of one another's needs and perceptions and begin to overcome some of the suspicions and mistrust that continue to haunt us. The limitations of a sisterhood based on bourgeois individualism or on the politics of personal experience presently pose a very real threat to combined political action.

For example, in the field of household employment, interest in the needs of a growing number of middle-class women to participate in the work force and thus find adequate assistance with their domestic duties (a form of bourgeois individualism) could all too easily become support for a proposal such as the one made by writer Anne Colamosca in a recent article in the *New Republic*. She proposed solving the problems of a limited supply of household help with a government training program for unemployed alien women to help them become "good household workers." While this may help middle-class women pursue their careers, it will do so while continuing to maintain and exploit a poorly paid, unprotected, lower class and will leave the problem of domestic responsibility virtually unaddressed for the majority of mothers in the work force who cannot afford to hire personal household help. A socialist feminist perspective requires an examination of the exploitation inherent in household labor as it is currently organized for both the paid and unpaid worker. The question is, what can we do to upgrade the status of domestic labor for ALL women, to facilitate the adjustment and productivity of immigrant women, and to insure that those who choose to engage in paid private household work do so because it represents a potentially interesting, viable and economically rewarding option for them?

At the same time, the women's movement may need to move beyond a limited focus on "women's issues" to ally with groups of women and men who are addressing other aspects of race and class oppression. One example is school desegregation, an issue which is engaging the time and energies of many urban black women today. The struggles over school desegregation are rapidly moving beyond the issues of busing and racial balance. In many large cities, where school districts are between 60 percent and 85 percent black, Hispanic, or Third World, racial balance is becoming less of a concern. Instead, questions are being raised about the overall quality of the educational experiences low-income children of all racial and ethnic groups are receiving in the public schools. This is an issue of vital concern to many racially and ethnically distinct women because they see their children's future ability to survive in this society as largely dependent upon the current direction of public education. In what ways should feminists involve themselves in this issue? First, by recognizing that feminist questions are only one group of questions among many others that are being raised about public education. To the extent that blacks, Hispanics, Native Americans, and Asian Americans are miseducated, so are women. Feminist activists must work to expand their conceptualization of the problem beyond the narrow confines of sexism. For example, efforts to develop and include nonsexist literature in the school curriculum are important. Yet this work cannot exist in a vacuum, ignoring the fact that schoolchildren *observe* a gender-based division of labor in which authority and responsibility are held primarily by men while women are concentrated in nurturant roles; or that schools with middle-class students have more funds, better facilities, and better teachers than schools serving working-class populations. The problems of education must be addressed as structural ones. We must examine not only the kinds of discrimination that occurs within institutions, but also the ways in which discrimination becomes a fundamental part of the institution's organization and implementation of its overall purpose. Such an analysis would make the linkages between different forms of structural inequality, like sexism and racism, more readily apparent.

While analytically we must carefully examine the structures that differentiate us, politically we must fight the segmentation of oppression into categories such as "racial issues," "feminist issues," and "class issues." This is, of course, a task of almost overwhelming magnitude, and yet it seems to me the only viable way to avoid the errors of the past and to move forward to make sisterhood a meaningful feminist concept for all women, across the boundaries of race and class. For it is through first seeking to understand struggles that are not particularly shaped by one's own immediate personal priorities that we will begin to experience and understand the needs and priorities of our sisters—be they black, brown, white, poor, or rich. When we have reached a point where the differences between us ENRICH our political and social action rather than divide it, we will have gone beyond the personal and will, in fact, be "political enough."

# PART V

# Public Policy

The task is not only to understand the world, a philosopher once observed, but also to transform it. So, finally, we must ask ourselves: How should the prospects for American society—current public policies as well as proposed programs and strategies for the future—be assessed? To address this question, both politicians and pundits have focused much of their attention on two groups: Asian Americans and blacks.

During the 1980s, Asian Americans found themselves increasingly congratulated for their successful entry into the mainstream of society. *Newsweek* proclaimed Asian Americans a "Model Minority" as it reported that they enjoyed the nation's highest median family income: $22,075 a year compared with $20,840 for whites. In a speech to a group of Asian and Pacific Island Americans, President Ronald Reagan declared that they represented the immigrants' search for the American dream, a vision of hope and new opportunity symbolized by the Statue of Liberty. "Asian and Pacific Americans," he said, "have helped preserve that dream by living up to the bedrock values that make us a good and worthy people," values such as "fiscal responsibility" and "hard work." Praising them for their economic achievement, Reagan then added: "It's no wonder that the median income of Asian and Pacific American families is much higher than the total American average."

This celebration of Asian American "success" has led William Raspberry of the *Washington Post* to ask: If Asian Americans can make it, why can't blacks? Blacks can, Raspberry has contended. What they must do is stop blaming "racism" for their plight, and start imitating law-abiding, hard working, and self-reliant Asian Americans. Noting that "in fact" West Coast Asian Americans have "outstripped" whites in income, Raspberry has exhorted his fellow blacks to view the successful Asian American minority as a "model."

But what are the facts in this case? How do we evaluate the claims of Reagan, Raspberry, and other celebrators of Asian American "success"? Data from the 1980 Census, can help us determine what the facts may be in this case.

If we take median household incomes for California, we find that Asian Americans earned $20,790 in 1979, compared to $19,552 for whites and $12,534 for blacks. But does this "in fact" mean that Asian Americans have "outstripped" whites? These income figures mean very little unless they are analyzed in relation to the number of workers per household. Here we find that Asian Americans had 1.70 workers per household, compared with only 1.28 for whites and 1.20 for blacks. Thus, Asian Americans actually earned only $12,229 per worker, while whites received $15,275. In other words, Asian American income per household worker was only 80 percent of white income. The income gap is even wider in urban areas, where most Asian Americans reside. In San Francisco and Oakland, Asian American earnings reached only 71 percent of white income, merely seven percentage points above black income. Asian Americans still have not achieved the equality, much less the superiority of income touted by Reagan and Raspberry.

But should Asian Americans be used as a model for blacks? Not only does this advice, in effect, pit the two groups against each other; it also overlooks important sociological differences between them.

Forty-six percent of black families have a female head of household (no husband present), compared to only 11 percent of Asian American families (15 percent for whites). Sixty-four percent of all female-headed black families are below the poverty line, and currently over half of all black children are born to single women. The difference in family sociology between blacks and Asian Americans, due mainly to each group's particular location in the economy and its social or class composition rather than simply its cultural values or degree of dependency on welfare, affects a group's ability to use education as a strategy for social mobility. Children raised by a single female parent tend not only to have less parental attention and support but also less economic resources due to the feminization of poverty or the low incomes of families headed by women. Thus, they are less likely to be able to take full advantage of education than their counterparts in families with two parents.

Furthermore, Asian Americans have increasingly become an immigrant population, and large numbers of recent Chinese, Filipino, and Korean immigrants have carried both skills and capital with them to the United States. For example, in 1973, 65 percent of the Korean immigrants had been professionals, technicians, and managers in their home country. Thus, many recent Asian immigrants have resources—education, employable skills, and finances—which underclass blacks do not have.

These differences in social and economic composition between Asian Americans and blacks—only two of several differences—warn us that strategies for one group may not be applicable for another group. They also show that education and individual effort alone may not be sufficient for racial minorities to achieve income equality.

What all of this suggests is the need for scholars and journalists to be more restrained in asking blacks to copy Asian Americans and shun government intervention and structural economic changes in favor of conservative strategies of self-help and ethnic enterprise. They also need to check out their information more carefully before exalting Asian Americans as a model minority and challenging blacks to emulate them. But why are blacks being urged to be like Asian Americans?

Historically, Asians in this country have been used as examples for blacks. Shortly after the Civil War, white planters in Louisiana and Mississippi imported several hundred Chinese contract laborers and pitted them against former black slaves. Describing the Chinese workers as "reliable, industrious and patient," they thought the new laborers would serve as good examples for the black freedmen. Pleased that his twenty-five Chinese laborers had outproduced the same number of blacks within a month, planter Thomas J. Shaffer hoped that the newly imported workers could be used to "regulate" the "detestable system of black labor." A Southern governor explained the reason for introducing Chinese labor into the land of Dixie: "Undoubtedly the underlying motive for this effort to bring in Chinese laborers was to punish the negro for having abandoned the control of his old master, and to regulate the conditions of his employment and the scale of wages to be paid him."

A century later, amid the smoke and ashes of black urban revolts in Watts, Newark, and other cities, the Asian American model continued to give instructions to blacks. A few months after the 1965 Watts explosion, with cries of "Burn, baby, burn" still reverberating across America, the *New York Times* published an article by sociologist William Peterson entitled "Success Story—Japanese American Style." In December, *U.S. News & World Report* followed with an article on Chinese Americans, "Success Story of One Minority Group in the U.S." Asian Americans were making it, and they were doing it through working hard rather than rioting. This adulation of Asian Americans in the media was capped in 1971 by a *Newsweek* essay, "Success Story: Outwhiting the Whites." In its conclusion, *Newsweek* quoted George Kobayashi. A Nisei, or second-generation Japanese American who had been interned in detention camps during World War II, Kobayashi had worked hard to become the owner of a profitable appliance store and a new split-level home in California. "If a black family moved in next door, I wouldn't like it," he said. "I've just moved in here and it would drive property values down. It's always the same story. You maintain a good neighborhood and they just seem to let the whole place fall apart. If they want to get ahead, they have to work—just like the Nisei did."

The message *Newsweek* conveyed through Kobayashi foreshadowed the way the Asian American model would serve a new need in the eighties—one based on the changing place of blacks in the American economy. Blacks have historically been an integral part of the American work force, as slave laborers in the South in the nineteenth century and as industrial workers in Northern cities in the twentieth century. During the last two decades, however, black labor has been decreasing in importance as America developed into a service and high-technology economy, and also as America deindustrialized and relocated much of its production in Third World countries. Within this new economic context, we find an unprecedented high rate of black unemployment and the formation of a "black underclass."

In earlier decades, such as the 1920s, the rate of white unemployment actually exceeded that of blacks. But beginning in the 1980s, we have had a different situation, where blacks proportionately are unemployed two times more than whites, and the unemployment rate for black teenagers is nearly three times that for white teenagers. Today, due to structural changes in the economy, blacks in large numbers are not only unemployed but unemployable. Either they lack the clerical and high-technology skills necessary for employment or they live in economically depressed inner cities and in regions of the country, such as the area of smokestack industries, where the economy is contracting.

For blacks who may be permanently outside the regular workforce, the Asian American model functions in effect as a mechanism for social control rather than labor control, a way to instruct blacks in how they should behave as members of society. This "soft" way of setting standards of law-abiding and acceptable social behavior telegraphs to underclass blacks that they should not depend on welfare and should not riot or engage in militant activity or try to survive by stealing or robbing.

But if they do steal or rob, they would then be disciplined by the "hard" mechanisms of social control—the prison or possibly even the direct method of Bernhard Goetz. After shooting four black teenagers on a New York subway train in 1984, Goetz insisted his action was justifiable, claiming they were would-be muggers. Suddenly he found himself riding a tremendous wave of congratulations. This popular support for Goetz's vigilante violence reflected pervasive fears of what many perceived to be a new disorderly underclass—young, largely black, and increasingly menacing to citizens who feel vulnerable in public places like parks, streets, and subways. Graffiti scrawled on the walls of the New York subway may have said it all: "Goetz rules niggers."

The coexistence of the Asian American model minority, the black underclass, and Bernhard Goetz may not be a coincidence. They may be profoundly connected. But the Asian American model minority fulfills an even larger need. Intellectually, it helps to explain "losing ground"—why the situation of blacks has deteriorated during the last two decades of expanded government social services and programs for them—in terms of the government and individual choices rather than the structural nature of racism and black unemployment. According to this new analysis, the interventionist federal state, operating on the misguided "elite wisdom" of the sixties, not only failed to help blacks but it made matters worse. Welfare programs rendered it "rational" for many blacks to choose dependency and thus contributed to the development of the black underclass. What is needed, then, is the "scrapping" of the entire federal welfare system and the restoration of what neoconservative intellectual Charles Murray calls a "white popular wisdom"—the work ethic and individual responsibility, values representing not coincidentally the bedrock of Asian American "success."

Psychologically and politically, the Asian American model minority allows America to reaffirm itself as a fair and just society at a moment when it is finding the problem of race increasingly bewildering and when it is withdrawing from the commitments of the Civil Rights era. The image of "successful" Asian Americans, reclaiming the belief that individuals should be responsible for their own welfare, makes it possible for pundits and politicians to say reassuringly: "After all—the war on poverty, civil rights legislation, affirmative action—none of them was really necessary. Look at the Asian Americans! They did it on their own, believing in the principles of hard work and self-reliance that this society has always held dear. All must be right in America."

In this final section, we will find William Raspberry's essay "Beyond Racism," as well as Thomas Sowell's "We've More Than Our Quota of Quotas." While Raspberry tells his fellow blacks what they must do to succeed, Sowell warns blacks not to depend on affirmative action. Scoffing at quotas, he calls the claim of "discrimination" based on measuring the statistical "representation" of a minority group "the great mindless idea of our time." Laws, Sowell insists, should be color blind.

But color-blind laws can actually perpetuate color divisions in society. Massachusetts Institute of Technology economist Lester Thurow explains why affirmative action is necessary to achieve equality and offers a defense of the federal government policy in "Affirmative Action in a Zero-Sum Society." "We are a society that professes belief in 'equal opportunity' for individuals," he says, "but how could you tell whether equal opportunity does or does not exist?" In view of the reality of racial inequality, Thurow argues, a concern for groups is "unavoidable." Otherwise, the current effects of past discrimination can "linger forever."

Similarly, Ronald Takaki supports affirmative action in his essay "To Count or Not to Count by Race and Gender?" Criticizing the "culture of meritocracy," he makes a distinction between inequality due to employer "taste" and inequality due to structural conditions. He also reminds us of the fact that throughout American history there had always been affirmative action for white men. Finally, Takaki provides data showing that affirmative action policies and programs have made a difference in the employment of racial minorities and women.

But William Julius Wilson, in "The Black Community: Race and Class," doubts that affirmative action reaches and helps the people who need it most—underclass blacks. The problem of inequality for large numbers of blacks is based on class rather than race. Rather than defending affirmative action against the assaults of the Bakkes of America, Wilson contends, we should be pressing for economic reforms such as full employment.

The existence of the black underclass has stirred a debate over welfare. This issue is sharply joined in the exchange between Charles Murray (" 'White Popular Wisdom': Losing Ground") and Ronald Takaki ("A Dream Deferred: The Crisis of 'Losing Ground.' ")

But the crisis also includes Hispanics. Among Hispanics, Puerto Ricans have often been overlooked. Yet, as Marta Tienda shows, they have been experiencing extreme unemployment and poverty. Why? This is the question she addresses in "Puerto Ricans and the Underclass Debate." But the issue of economic distress among Hispanics is related to a larger context. By the year 2000, there will be more than 21 million new workers. A majority of them will be workers of color, and, among them, most will be Hispanic. The significance of this demographic pattern can be seen in California. There the number of Hispanics entering the workforce will increase, while Anglos will continue to constitute a large majority of the elderly. "What does all this portend for the future work force?" ask David Hayes-Bautista and his co-authors in "The Burden of Support: Young Latinos in an Aging Society." They note that in 1980, working-age Anglos had an educational level of 13.5 years, while Hispanics, with a high school dropout rate of 60 percent, lagged behind with only 10.4 years. Is the largely Anglo population of today, Hayes-Bautista questions, willing to commit a sufficient portion of its economic pie to an investment in Hispanic youth?

# Beyond Racism

## WILLIAM RASPBERRY

I annoyed a few people a week or so ago when I proposed that blacks, "just for the hell of it," should pretend that racism explains very little of their plight and, on that basis, look for other explanations of the problems that confront them.

The idea was to shift the debate from the easy fingering of culprits to the far trickier problem of finding solutions. But since I don't like to annoy anyone needlessly, I thought I might just turn my little game on its head. Let us assume that racism is a critical impediment to black progress. Let us assume that, by devoting all our efforts and resources to its removal, we are finally able to lay racism to rest.

Then what? Obviously we'd have to do something else. Simply removing racism would put most of black America in exactly the same situation that low-income whites are in today. In other words, the end of racism wouldn't solve black problems; it would only make the solutions possible.

So, assuming success in the elimination of racism, the immediate question would be: What is the next step in order to turn this new opportunity into practical gain? There are a thousand answers to that question, many of them worthy of serious national debate. But I have another question: Why don't we just move directly to the next step right now? And what might some of those next steps be?

For some, the next step might consist of helping people to overcome the deleterious effects of past racism: cultural, attitudinal, educational and otherwise. For others, it might be to help the jobless find work, perhaps by fashioning tax programs and other incentives for the private sector to hire more of the hard-core unemployed; perhaps by rewarding employers who give enthusiastic youngsters a chance to show what they can do, even if their potential doesn't reveal itself in written tests. For still others, it might be to prepare young blacks to take advantage of the post-racism opportunities: by encouraging them to take their education seriously, by remodeling their behavior, by postponing short-term pleasure in the interests of longer-term goals.

For some, the logical next step might be to address the black economic situation. Blacks might, for instance, be encouraged to pool their resources to launch their entrepreneurially minded brothers and sisters into businesses that would make it possible to retain some of the considerable economic muscle of the black community *in* the black community, thereby creating both wealth and jobs.

Or they might, more conservatively, consider enhancing black economic leverage by concentrating their capital—including the Sunday-morning collections of black churches—in specific institutions, perhaps black-owned institutions, which could then be the source of business and mortgage loans for blacks.

The possibilities of "next steps" are subject only to the limits of imagination. The point is: Why not take those next steps now, without waiting for the problematical demise of racism?

The model I have in mind is that of West Coast Asian-Americans, who, if they had waited for the end of anti-Oriental prejudice, might still be living in poverty, rather than outstripping white Americans in education and income, as they in fact are. They still suffer from race prejudice, but they suffer in relative comfort.

Unfortunately, the current model seems closer to that of the Indian reservation, with the emphasis on the level of funding of, and the degree of sympathy manifested by, the Bureau of Indian Affairs.

The truth—far easier to see on the reservations than in the ghettos—is that even if you could ensure that every Indian on the reservation were given the most nutritional food, warm clothing freely supplied and permanent, centrally heated and cooled housing, the result would be not salvation but cultural, spiritual and economic genocide.

# We've More Than Our Quota of Quotas

THOMAS SOWELL

When certain ideas take hold in fashionable circles, many individuals and institutions rush toward these ideas, like lemmings rushing to the sea. The great mindless idea of our time is that all groups would be equally "represented" everywhere if it were not for discrimination or other sins of "society."

A flood of words and mountains of statistics have poured out, applying this principle. But the principle itself remains almost totally unexamined.

Are statistical "imbalances" or "underrepresentation" of groups so rare that we can say discrimination must be involved whenever such things appear? On the contrary, few groups of any kind are evenly represented anywhere, and lopsided percentages are commonplace.

Even at this late date in history, you would have to move the homes of 52 percent of all Americans of Southern European ancestry if you wanted them to be spread evenly among Americans of Northern European ancestry. Are we now going to start busing Greeks into Irish neighborhoods?

Women are just over half of the population, but commit only about one-fourth of the murders or suicides. Are women going to have to step up their rate of carnage, in the name of equality?

One-fourth of all American hockey players come from one state (Minnesota). Is it really surprising that each of the 50 states (including California and Florida) doesn't provide its 2 percent of hockey players?

Half of all Mexican-American women get married in their teens, while only 10 percent of Japanese-American women get married that young. Every group has its own values and priorities, and these affect all sorts of economic and social results. That is why human beings are not randomly distributed anywhere.

Television stations keep elaborate statistics on who watches what programs, because the composition of audiences is very different from one show to the next—and advertisers want to know whom they are talking to. Voting patterns, child-rearing practices, alcohol consumption, and all sorts of other voluntarily chosen activities vary enormously by education, location, religion and numerous other factors. It can't be discrimination, because each person makes his own decisions for himself. We are not random in our behavior because we come from different backgrounds.

Everyone knows that there has been discrimination against some racial and ethnic groups, and that it has still not been completely stamped out. We don't need pseudo-science claiming that one can measure discrimination by statistical "representation."

Even an ideally non-discriminating society would not have an even distribution of ethnic groups in jobs, colleges, or other places. Racial and ethnic groups are very different from one another in many ways: age, fertility, regional distribution, and many other variables. Polish-Americans are a decade older than Chinese-Americans, who in turn are almost a decade older than Mexican-Americans. Age makes a big difference in income, so different ethnic groups would be earning different pay even if everything else was the same between them, and even if no employers ever had a speck of prejudice.

Income differences between age brackets are even greater than income differences between blacks and whites. So are income differences among the states.

One of the driving ideas behind the school integration crusade of the past quarter of a century is that black youngsters performed poorly because they were in segregated schools. It was a reasonable theory and a humane desire to help. What was unreasonable was turning this belief

From Thomas Sowell, "We've More Than Our Quota of Quotas," *Los Angeles Herald Examiner*, July 4, 1979. Reprinted by permission of the publisher.

into gospel, and the gospel into law. What was inhumane was disrupting children's lives over an unproven idea in vogue with the anointed.

Disparities in school performance have existed as long as there have been statistics and different groups of people. Even when all the groups were white, when all lived in the same neighborhoods, and all sat next to each other in school, different ethnic groups did not perform the same. Back before World War I, a study in New York City showed that German and Jewish school children graduated from high school at a rate more than 100 times that for Irish or Italian children. Similar results were found in various other cities around the country.

Mental test scores, which are now supposed to be "racially biased," showed disparities among various groups of white children that are as great as those between blacks and whites today. Some of the low-I.Q. ethnic groups of the past now have average or even above-average I.Q.s, so these scores are not fixed in concrete. But neither are they purely a matter of discrimination.

There must be some better way to advance disadvantaged groups than by tearing the country apart over wholly unsubstantiated theories about statistical "representation" in schools, jobs and other activities. Polls show minorities themselves reject such theories.

# Affirmative Action in a Zero-Sum Society

## LESTER THUROW

In our society the whole issue of group justice is often seen as illegitimate. Individual blacks may have been unfairly treated, but blacks have not been treated unfairly as a group. Consequently, remedies must come at the individual level (a case-by-case fight against discrimination or remedial education programs for individuals) and not at a group level. Affirmative action or quotas programs that create group preferences are fought on the ground that they are unfair even if everyone agrees that many or all members of the group to be helped have suffered from unfair treatment in the past.

Our economic theory is based upon the same tradition. Western economics is at its heart an economics of the individual. Individuals organize voluntary economic associations (the firm), but individuals earn and allocate income. Group welfare is, if anything, only the algebraic summation of the individual welfare of the members of the group. There are no involuntary groups. Individuals join groups only when groups raise individual welfare. No one assigns someone to a group to which he or she does not wish to belong. Race and sex are not economic variables from this perspective.

At the same time, our age is an age of group consciousness. Economic minorities argue that group parity is a fundamental component of economic justice and that an optimum distribution of income consists of more than an optimum distribution of income across individuals. In doing so, they are not advocating something new but extending to themselves old doctrines that are invoked to help farmers and many other industries. While there is plenty of precedent for helping groups in our economy, a faster rate of growth may call for ending help to different industrial groups. Should the same principles be used to resist instituting aid for other social groups? Is the correct economic strategy to resist group welfare measures and group redistribution programs wherever possible? Or do groups have a role to play in economic justice?

We are a society that professes belief in "equal opportunity" for individuals, but how could you tell whether equal opportunity does or does not exist? In a deterministic world we could tell whether equal opportunity existed by seeing whether each individual reached a level of economic performance consistent with his or her inputs (talents, efforts, human capital). Individuals could be identified as receiving less than equal treatment.

But the real world is highly random and not deterministic. Since everyone is subject to a variety of good and bad random shocks, no one can tell whether any individual has been unfairly treated by looking at his or her income. Individuals may have participated in the same economic lottery, but in the end, someone lost and someone won. My low income and your high income do not prove that I was unfairly treated relative to you. You were lucky and I was unlucky. But I was not unfairly treated, and I did not suffer from discrimination or some systematic denial of equal opportunities.

Since those variables that we normally think of as the deterministic variables—education, skills, age, and so forth—only explain 20 to 30 percent of the variance in individual earnings, our economy is one where the stochastic shocks (or unknown factors) are very large relative to the deterministic (or known) part of the system. And the larger the stochastic portion of the system relative to the deterministic portion of the system, the less possible it is to identify individuals who have been unfairly treated. In the economic area, no one can say that any individual has been subject to systematic discrimination as opposed to random bad luck. This is a judgment that can only be made at the level of the group.

This can be seen in the standard economic tests for the existence of discrimination. Earnings data are collected for different groups of individuals, and a statistical equation is estimated to show the relationship between earnings and the normal human capital factors (work effort, skills, education) for each of the groups. These equations are then examined to see if they are significantly different. If they are, the different groups do not participate in the same economic lottery.

Using economic analysis it is impossible to determine whether any individual has suffered from the denial of equal opportunity. Within any group—no matter how privileged—there will be individuals who have been denied equal opportunities and suffered from discrimination, but they have not been subject to a systematic denial of opportunities. Society may be concerned, but it is completely incapable of doing anything about random discrimination. It is simply one type of random good or bad luck that affects us all. A Polish American may feel aggrieved and may have been denied equal opportunities, but Polish Americans do not suffer from systematic denials of equal opportunity since their earnings functions do not meet the necessary tests. Conversely, within any group—no matter how underprivileged—there will be individuals who have not suffered from a systematic denial of opportunities.

All society can do is to test whether the economic lottery played by whites is or is not statistically equivalent to the economic lottery played by blacks. It cannot tell whether any individual, black or white, has been equally treated. Discrimination affects individuals, but it can only be identified at the level of the group. As a result, it is not possible for society to determine whether it is or is not an equal opportunity society without collecting and analyzing economic data on groups.

But the measurement problem also creates a remedy problem. If it is impossible to identify individual discrimination, upon whom should the remedies for systematic discrimination be focused? The inability to identify anything except group discrimination creates an inability to focus remedies on anything other than the group. We can attempt to create an economy where everyone participates in the same economic lottery, but we cannot create an economy where each individual is treated equally. If you believe current earnings functions, 70 to 80 percent of the variance in individual earnings are caused by factors that are out from under the control of even perfect government economic policies. The economy will treat different individuals unequally no matter what we do. Only groups can be treated equally.

Groups, rather than individuals, are also going to enter into our decisions because we need groups to make efficient decisions. At the same time, what is "efficient" for the economy is always "unfair" to some individuals. The problem is how to balance the gains from efficiency against the losses from unfairness.

Suppose that you were the dean of a medical school charged with the task of maximizing the number of M.D.'s produced for some given budget. In the process of carrying out this mandate, you noticed that 99 percent of all male admissions completed medical school, and that 99 percent of all male graduates go on to become lifetime doctors, but that the corresponding percentages for women were each 96 percent. As a consequence, each male admission represents .99 lifetime doctors and each female admission represents .96 lifetime doctors. Seeking to be efficient and obey your mandate to maximize the number of practicing doctors, you establish a "male only" admissions policy.

In this case, the dean of the medical school is practicing statistical discrimination. He is treating each group fairly, based on the objective characteristics of the group, but he is unfairly treating 96 percent of all women because they would, in fact, have gone on to become practicing doctors. His problem is that he has no technique for identifying which 4 percent of all women will fail to become practicing doctors, and therefore he expands a very small difference in objective characteristics (a one percentage point difference in each of the two probabilities) into a zero-one decision rule that excludes all women. Is the dean acting fairly or unfairly, efficiently or inefficiently?

To be efficient is to be unfair to individuals. Where is the balance to be drawn? Wherever the balance is drawn, groups become important since it is efficient for employers to open or close opportunities to individuals based on the groups to which employers assign them. But since employers will of necessity use groups, government must become involved in the question as to what consitutes a legitimate group or an illegitimate group. The option of prohibiting all decisions based on group characteristics simply isn't possible since the efficiency price would be too high.

A controversy of just this type recently arose in Massachusetts over automobile insurance rates. In the past, these rates have been set based on the age, sex, and geographic location of the driver and the associated accident data. The insurance commissioner of the state shifted to a system that rates drivers based upon the number of years they have had a license, their accident record, and their arrest record. Different individuals will pay very different insurance premiums under the two systems. Which is the right set of groups?

Ideally, group data could only be used for making economic decisions where all members of the group had the same characteristics. Fair treatment for the group would be a fair treatment of each individual member of the group. Unfortunately, this situation almost never exists. Homogeneous groups do not exist. A trade-off must be made between efficiency and justice. Since employers are only interested in efficiency, they will make the trade-off in favor of efficiency and in favor of unfair individual treatment unless they are restrained from using certain group classifications. As a result, the state is forced to establish categories of illegitimate groups. Our social desires for individual justice, at least to some extent, take precedence over our social desires for efficiency.

Since we have both a desire for efficiency and a desire for individual justice, we have a dilemma. Individuals have to be judged based on group data, yet all systems of grouping will result in the unfair treatment of some individuals. Thus we must establish some standard as to how large differences in mean characteristics have to be before a particular set of groups is legitimate. Most of us would be unwilling to let the dean of our medical school exclude women on the basis of a 3 percent difference in objective probabilities, but what would our judgments be if the objective differences were fifty percentage points or ninety percentage points? At what point would we be willing to exclude women? Yet if we did this at any point, we would be unfairly treating some individual female. But if we did not exclude them, we would be wasting a larger and larger fraction of our resources.

What this illustrates, however, is that every society has to have a theory of legitimate and illegitimate groups and a theory of when individuals can be judged on group data and when they cannot be judged on group data. A concern for groups is unavoidable.

On first thought, mobility (or the lack of mobility) would seem to be an easy way to determine what groupings are legitimate. If it is easy for an individual to leave any group, then individuals in that group cannot claim to be unfairly treated. The value of the group must exceed the costs of the group or they would not belong. They may receive less measurable income by being a member of the group, but their psychic income from being a member of the group must at least counterbalance the lower measurable income. It is precisely this argument that lies at the heart of the recommendation that government should not have special programs to raise the money incomes of farmers. Farmers may have lower incomes than urban dwellers, but they could always cease to be farmers and become urban dwellers. Therefore, farmers cannot be unfairly treated regardless of the relative income of farmers and regardless of the sources of this relative difference.

While this argument may sound reasonable to those of us who are not farmers, it is equally applicable to regions or religions. Technically it is just as easy, if not easier and less costly, to move from one region to another or from one religion to another. Yet most of us would not be willing to argue that one must change his or her religion to achieve economic parity. Why? What is the difference between changing one's occupation and one's religion? Individuals can certainly be just as psychologically committed to a particular occupation as they are to a particular religion.

If one looks at our social programs, society certainly cannot claim to focus consistently on individuals as opposed to groups. Affirmative action for economic minorities may be on the defensive, but we are in an age when industrial and regional programs are expanding rapidly. The same people who oppose special programs for blacks support special programs for textiles. Imagine the furor that would arise if we started a program for blacks similar to that now in place for farmers. It would be denounced as "un-American" from every rooftop. Given that our society clearly is not willing to be consistent and use an individual focus when it comes to politically popular groups, it is easy to see why the insistence on an individual focus for minorities can be viewed as simply a more sophisticated version of discrimination. Those who got ahead in the economic race stay ahead for a very long time even after discrimination has ceased to be actively practiced.

While we undoubtedly are not willing to use mobility as the sole test of whether a group is illegitimate—almost no one would be willing to force individuals to change their religion to secure equal economic treatment—it is still the basic ingredient. We need to be most concerned about discrimination against groups where individuals cannot easily leave the group in question. In the case of industrial groups, this means that society should focus on improving the ease of exit for individuals rather than aiding the group as it is now constituted. When ease of exit is high, we can concentrate on efficiency, knowing that it will not lead to much unfairness. When the ease of exit is low, the reverse is true.

In the end we have a problem. Various groups are demanding parity in their income position and there is little reason to believe that these demands will disappear in the future. Few are willing to stand up and publicly defend the idea that blacks, Hispanics, and women should permanently earn less than white males. There are many who object to every conceivable remedy, but this only exacerbates the tension without either solving the problem or causing it to go away.

Nor will the normal actions of the economy cause the problem to fade away with time. A simple look at what has been happening can force anyone to abandon the comfortable "do-nothing" hypothesis. The essence of any minority group's position can be captured with the answer to three questions: (1) Relative to the majority group, what is the probability of the minority's finding employment? (2) For those who are employed, what are the earnings opportunities relative to the majority? (3) Are minority group members making a break-through into the high-income jobs of the economy? In each case, it is necessary to look not just at current data, but at the group's economic history. Where has it been, where is it going, how fast is it going, and how fast is it progressing?

In terms of ethnic origin, there are three economic minorities in the United States—blacks, Hispanics, and American Indians. Of the almost 100 million other Americans who list themselves in the census as having an ethnic origin, all have incomes above those of Americans who list no ethnic origin. The highest family incomes are recorded by Russian-Americans, followed by Polish-Americans and Italian-Americans. "Ethnic" Americans sometimes talk as if they were economically deprived, but they are actually perched at the top of the economic ladder. Females constitute the other major economic minority. Many of them may live in families with high incomes, but when it comes to earnings opportunities, they do not participate in the same economic ball game as men.

If you examine the employment position of blacks, there has been no improvement and perhaps a slight deterioration. Black unemployment has been exactly twice that of whites in each decade since World War II. And the 1970s are no exception to that rule. Whatever their successes and failures, equal opportunity programs have not succeeded in opening the economy to greater employment for blacks. Given this thirty-year history, there is nothing that would lead anyone to predict improvements in the near future. To change the pattern there would need to be a major restructuring of existing labor markets.

Viewed in terms of participation rates, there has been a slight deterioration in black employment. In 1954, 59 percent of all whites and 67 percent of all blacks participated in the labor force. By 1978 white participation rates had risen to 64 percent and black participation rates had fallen to 63 percent. This change came about through rapidly rising white female participation rates and falling participation rates for old and young blacks. In the sixteen to twenty-one age category, black participation rates are now fifteen percentage points below that for whites.

At the same time, there has been some improvement in the relative earnings for those who work full-time, full-year. In 1955 both black males and females earned 56 percent of their white counterparts. By 1977 this had risen to 69 percent for males and 93 percent for females. While black females made good progress in catching up with white females, this has to be viewed in a context where white females are slipping slightly relative to white males. If black males were to continue their relative progress at the pace of the last twenty years—five percentage points every ten years—it would take black males another sixty years to catch up with white males.

While the greatest income gains have been made among young blacks and one can find particular subcategories that have reached parity (intact college-educated, two-earner families living in the Northeast), there still is a large earnings gap among the young. Black males twenty-five to thirty-four years of age earned 71 percent of what their white counterparts earned in 1977. Among full-time, full-year workers, the same percentage stood at 77 percent. Young black males are ahead of older black males, but they have not reached parity. As with black females in general, young black females do better than males. Females twenty-five to thirty-four years of age earned 101 percent of whites, and full-time, full-year black females earned 93 percent of what whites earned.

Using the top 5 percent of all jobs (based on earnings) as the definition of a "good job," blacks hold 2 percent of these jobs while whites hold 98 percent. Since blacks constitute 12 percent of the labor force they are obviously underrepresented in this category. Relative to their population, whites are almost seven times as likely to hold a job at the top of the economy than blacks. At the same time, this represents an improvement in the position of blacks relative to 1960. Probabilities of holding a top job have almost doubled.

Separate data on Hispanics only started at the end of the 1960s and are not as extensive as that available for blacks, but during the 1970s Hispanics seemed to have fared slightly better than blacks in the labor market. Where their family income was once lower than that of blacks, it is now higher. This is probably due to the fact that Hispanics are much more heavily concentrated in the sunbelt, with its rapidly expanding job opportunities.

Instead of having unemployment twice that of whites, unemployment is only 45 percent higher. Labor force participation rates are rising even more rapidly than those for whites. In terms of relative earnings, full-time, full-year males earn 71 percent of what whites earn, and females have reached 86 percent of parity. While there are substantial differences in family income among different Hispanic groups, earnings are very similar among the major groups. In 1976 Cuban-Americans, Mexican-Americans, and Puerto Ricans were all within $200 of each other in terms of personal income, for those with income.

In terms of the best jobs, Hispanics hold 1 percent of these jobs but constitute 4 percent of the labor force. Relative to their population, whites are three times as likely to be in the top 5 percent of the job distribution as Hispanics. In terms of breaking into the good jobs of the economy, Hispanics are far ahead of blacks.

American Indians are the smallest and poorest of America's ethnic groups. They are poorly described and tracked by all U.S. statistical agencies. Despite the existence of the Bureau of Indian Affairs, only the roughest estimate for their economic status is available. In terms of family income, reservation Indians probably have an income about one-third that of whites. Where nonreservation Indians stand no one knows.

Female workers hold the dubious distinction of having made the least progress in the labor market. In 1939 full-time, full-year women earned 61 percent of what men earned. In 1977

they earned 57 percent as much. Since black women have gained relative to black men, white women have fallen even more in relation to white men over this forty-year period. Adult female unemployment rose from 9 percent higher than men in 1960 to 43 percent higher in 1978. From 1939 to 1977 the percentage of the top jobs held by females has fallen from 5.5 percent to 4 percent although women rose from 25 percent to 41 percent of the labor force. Relative to their population, a man was seventeen times as likely as a woman to hold a job at the top of the economy in 1977.

With the exception of breaking into the top jobs in the economy, much of this decline can be attributed to rapidly rising female participation rates. With more women in the labor force, there is simply more competition leading to lower wages and more unemployment. At the same time, the results indicate that the structure of the economy has not changed, and women have not broken through into a world of equal opportunity. In such a world they would compete with men and not just with each other.

At the bottom of the labor force stand the young—our modern lumpen proletariat. In 1978, 49 percent of all unemployment was concentrated among sixteen- to twenty-four-year-olds. Unemployment rates were three times that of the rest of the population. Among male full-time, full-year workers, relative earnings stood at 40 percent for fourteen- to nineteen-year-olds and 65 percent for twenty- to twenty-four-year-olds. Among females the same percentages were 64 and 104. In terms of holding the top jobs, sixteen- to twenty-four-year-olds held 0.5 percent although they constituted 24 percent of the labor force.

While low earnings can be dismissed on the grounds that the group is acquiring skills and will in the future earn higher incomes, the unemployment is not so easy to dismiss. Unemployed young people or young people who have dropped out of both school and the work force represent individuals who are not acquiring skills and good work habits. What this portends for the distribution of earnings in the future is hard to say since we have never before had a period where so much of the unemployment of our society is concentrated among the young and especially among young minorities. Certainly it is hard to think that it will do anything except make the distribution of earnings more unequal in the future.

While it is convenient to the position that if we were just to eliminate discrimination and create an equal opportunity world, minority group problems would take care of themselves, this position is untenable in both practice and theory. Imagine a race with two groups of runners of equal ability. Individuals differ in their running ability, but the average speed of the two groups is identical. Imagine that a handicapper gives each individual in one of the groups a heavy weight to carry. Some of those with weights would still run faster than some of those without weights, but on average, the handicapped group would fall farther and farther behind the group without the handicap.

Now suppose that someone waves a magic wand and all of the weights vanish. Equal opportunity has been created. If the two groups are equal in their running ability, the gap between those who never carried weights and those who used to carry weights will cease to expand, but those who suffered the earlier discrimination will never catch up. If the economic baton can be handed on from generation to generation, the current effects of past discrimination can linger forever.

If a fair race is one where everyone has an equal chance to win, the race is not fair even though it is now run with fair rules. To have a fair race, it is necessary to (1) stop the race and start over, (2) force those who did not have to carry weights to carry them until the race has equalized, or (3) provide extra aid to those who were handicapped in the past until they catch up.

While these are the only three choices, none of them is a consensus choice in a democracy. Stopping the race and starting over would involve a wholesale redistribution of physical and human wealth. This only happens in real revolutions, if ever. This leaves us with the choice of handicapping those who benefitted from the previous handicaps or giving special privileges to those who were previously handicapped. Discrimination against someone unfortunately always means discrimination in favor of someone else. The person gaining from discrimination may not be the discriminator, but she or he will have to pay part of the price of eliminating discrimination. This is true regardless of which technique is chosen to eliminate the current effects of past discrimination.

An individualistic ethic is acceptable if society has never violated this individualistic ethic in the past, but it is unacceptable if society has not, in fact, lived up to its individualistic ethic in the past. To shift from a system of group discrimination to a system of individual performance is to perpetuate the effects of past discrimination into the present and the future. The need to practice discrimination (positive or negative) to eliminate the effects of past discrimination is one of the unfortunate costs of past discrimination. To end discrimination is not to create "equal opportunity."

The problem of group demands cannot be left to the economy to solve. Major elements of the problem are not being solved at all and where progress is being made it is so slow that economic minorities would have to be patient for many more years. Yet any government program to aid economic minorities must hurt economic majorities. This is the most direct of all of our zero-sum conflicts. If women and minorities have more of the best jobs, white males must have fewer. Here the gains and losses are precisely one for one.

# To Count or Not to Count by Race and Gender?

RONALD TAKAKI

Affirmative action is at a crossroads. Recently its critics in the academy and in Washington have demanded the removal of government regulations requiring employers to utilize numerical goals for the hiring of racial minorities and women. To count or not to count—that is the question. How we answer it depends largely on how we perceive the problem of inequality in American society.

"Counting by race is a form of racism," Attorney General Edwin Meese declared in a recent speech. Advocating the abolition of requirements for numerical goals, he argued that an affirmative action program "that prefers one person over another because o race, gender or national origin is unfair." Government policy, he insisted, should be "colorblind."

In his attack on affirmative action, Meese echoed the complaints of neoconservative intellectuals like Nathan Glazer, Thomas Sowell, and Charles Murray. Their view can be described as the culture of meritocracy—the belief that men and women should be treated as individuals and be judged (rewarded or punished) on the basis of merit or lack of it. The function of government, according to their perspective, should be a limited one: it should only prohibit discrimination. The problem of inequality, then, would be solved in the marketplace, where racial minorities and women who have merit would be able to find employment and advance themselves.

But would such an integration of the work force actually occur? Meese's perception of inequality is based on the notion of "taste" discrimination. In other words, employers as individuals prefer to hire white men for certain jobs. Hence, once the government prohibits such "taste" discrimination, women and minorities would have equal opportunity.

Meese's criticism of affirmative action completely overlooks an all-important historical fact: throughout American history, there had always been affirmative action for white men.

Educational and employment opportunities had always been reserved for white men; white men did not compete in an open field with racial minorities and women. And many of them are beneficiaries of this history of exclusion based on race and gender, and pass their economic and social advantages on to white men in the next generation. Thus, the very status quo represents inequality in society, and merely to prohibit discrimination is in effect to deny equality of opportunity to racial minorities and women.

Moreover, Meese's understanding of the problem of inequality is dated. It fails to recognize the enormous transformation of the economy in recent decades and how this change has affected the employment of racial minorities and women. Racial inequality is no longer simply dependent on individual employer "taste." Rather, it is largely reinforced by social conditions and economic structures. Living in slums and attending inadequate inner-city schools preclude the possibility of equal opportunity for many people. Occupational stratification based on training and education also limits their employment possibilities. Millions of racial minorities and women are excluded from the higher strata of employment because they do not have the requisite knowledge, skills, and credentials. Employers do not have to discriminate against them in order to avoid hiring them. Structural patterns of employment and education reproduce in the present configurations of inequality that were formed in the past.

Affirmative action as a public policy and a strategy for social change seeks to address inequality as a structural problem. It generates pressures to educate, recruit, train, and employ racial minorities and women across occupational strata in order to assure them equality of opportunity. But to do this effectively requires counting by race and gender. Otherwise the government would have no way to monitor and measure the efforts of employers to train and hire racial minorities and women.

Large American corporations have recently indicated their intention to retain affirmative action programs. "We will continue goals and timetables no matter what the government does," said John L. Hulck, chairman of Merck. Whether or not they actually do so, should the government no longer require numerical goals and timetables, remains to be seen. After nearly twenty years of affirmative action, corporations recognize the importance of counting. William S. McEwen, director of equal opportunity affairs at Monsanto and chairman of the National Association of Manufacturers' human resources committee, acknowledged, "Setting goals and timetables for minority and female participation is simply a way of measuring progress."

It is a way of measuring progress and also lack of progress. For example, in 1973 AT&T entered into a six-year consent decree with the Equal Employment Opportunity Commission to correct its prior discriminatory employment practices. By 1978, minorities in management at AT&T had jumped from 4.6 percent to 10.0 percent, and women in craft from 2.8 percent to 10.1 percent. Similarly, IBM established an equal opportunity department in 1968 to comply with affirmative action requirements. Between 1971 and 1980, the number of black managers at IBM increased from 429 to 1,596, Hispanics from 83 to 436, and women from 471 to 2,350. Between 1974 and 1980, according to a study by the Office of Federal Contract Compliance Programs, among some 77,000 companies with 20 million employees, companies with government contracts and therefore affirmative action plans, increased minority employment 20 percent and female employment 15 percent. But companies without affirmative action plans had smaller increases of only 12 and 2 percent for each respective group. Here, clearly, counting or not counting made a difference.

# The Black Community:
# Race and Class

WILLIAM JULIUS WILSON

Civil rights supporters are puzzled by recent developments in the black community. Despite the passage of antidiscrimination legislation and the creation of affirmative action programs, they sense that conditions are getting worse not better for the vast majority of black Americans. This perception emerges because of the constant flow of pessimistic reports concerning the sharp rise in black unemployment, the substantial decline of blacks in the labor force, the steady drop in the black-white family income ratio, the consistent increase in the percentage of blacks on the welfare roles, the remarkable growth of single-parent households, and the persistent problems of black crime and black victims of crime. The perception is reinforced by the almost uniform cry among black leaders that not only are conditions deteriorating, but white Americans have abandoned the cause of blacks as well. In the face of these developments, there are noticeable signs that demoralization has set in among many blacks who have come to believe that "nothing really works" and among many whites who are otherwise committed to social reform.

However, a careful review of the issues makes it immediately clear that significant variations in the black experience tend not to be noted or appreciated and that the differing effect of policy programs on different segments of the black population are usually not specified. In this essay, these issues are examined within the context of a broader framework of macroeconomic and political change. In the process I hope to focus on a series of mounting problems that are not receiving serious attention, but that have profound implications for the structure of the black community and for the future of race relations in America.

## CHANGING DEFINITIONS OF THE PROBLEM

In the mid-1960s, a series of insightful articles were written by black and white intellectuals that raised questions about the direction and goals of the black protest movement. Basically, the authors of these articles made it clear that from 1955 to 1965, the chief objectives of the Civil Rights movement were to integrate public accommodations and to eliminate black disfranchisement. These were matters of constitutional rights and basic human dignity, matters that affected blacks and other minorities exclusively and therefore could be defined and addressed simply as problems of civil rights. However, these authors noted that despite the spectacular victories in the area of civil rights, by the latter half of the 1960s, a more complex and fundamental set of problems had yet to be attacked—problems of jobs, education, and housing that affected not only blacks, but other minorities and whites as well.

A consistent theme running throughout these articles is that in the period from 1955 to 1965, all blacks, regardless of their station in life, were concerned about the banning of discrimination in public accommodations and in voting. As Bayard Rustin observed, "Ralph Bunch was as likely to be refused service in a restaurant or a hotel as any illiterate sharecropper. This common bond prevented the latent class differences and resentments from being openly expressed." However, it did not take long to realize that the group that had profited the most from the civil rights legislation up to 1965 were middle-class blacks—blacks who had competitive resources such as steady incomes, educa-

From William Julius Wilson, "The Black Community in the 1980s: Questions of Race, Class, and Public Policy," *American Academy of Political and Social Science Annals* 454 (March 1981): 26–41. Reprinted by permission of the author and the American Academy of Political and Social Science. Footnotes and tables have been deleted.

tion, and special talents. As Kenneth Clark argued in 1967, "The masses of Negroes are now starkly aware of the fact that recent civil rights victories benefited a very small percentage of middle-class Negroes while their predicament remained the same or worsened."

What these observers were telling us in the mid-1960s is that a close examination of ghetto black discontent, most dramatically revealed in the riots of that period, revealed issues that transcended the creation and implementation of civil rights laws. "To the segregation by race," Bayard Rustin observed in 1967, "was now added segregation by class, and all the problems created by segregation and poverty—inadequate schooling, substandard and overcrowded housing, lack of access to jobs and job training, narcotics and crime—were greatly aggravated." In short, for ghetto blacks the issue of human rights is far more important than the issue of civil rights. The late Martin Luther King, Jr., recognized this point in 1968 when shortly before his death he asked, "What good is it to be allowed to eat in a restaurant if you can't afford a hamburger?" It would not be unfair to suggest that he was probably influenced by the thoughts of Bayard Rustin who, four years earlier in his now classic article "From Protest to Politics," phrased the matter in much the same way: "What is the value of winning access to public accommodations for those who lack money to use them?"

Thus the removal of artificial racial barriers would not enable poor blacks to compete equally with other groups in society for valued resources because of an accumulation of disadvantages flowing from previous periods of prejudice and discrimination, disadvantages that have been passed on from generation to generation. Basic structural changes in our modern industrial economy have compounded the problems of poor blacks because education and training have become more important for entry into the more desirable and higher-paying jobs and because the increased reliance on labor-saving devices has contributed to a surplus of untrained black workers. In short, once the movement faced these more fundamental issues, argued Rustin in 1964, "it was compelled to expand its version beyond race relations to economic relations, including the role of education in society."

During the same period in which problems of structural inequality were being raised, scholars such as Kenneth Clark and Lee Rainwater were also raising important issues about the experiences of inequality. Both scholars sensitively examined the cumulative effects of chronic subordination and racial isolation on life and behavior in the urban ghettos. As Kenneth Clark put it, "The symptoms of lower-class society affect the dark ghettos of America—low aspirations, poor education, family instability, illegitimacy, unemployment, crime, drug addiction, and alcoholism, frequent illness and early death." And whether the focus was on the social and psychological dimensions of the ghetto, as in the case of Clark's study, or on the analysis of ghetto family patterns, as in the case of Rainwater's study, facts of ghetto life "that are usually forgotten or ignored in polite discussions" were vividly described and carefully analyzed.

Indeed, what was both unique and important about Clark and Rainwater's studies was that their discussions of the experiences of inequality were inextricably tied to their discussions of the structure of inequality. Thus in reading their works one received a clear understanding of how the economic and social situations into which so many poor blacks are born produce modes of adaptation and the creation of subcultural patterns that take the form of a "self perpetuating pathology." In other words, and in sharp contrast to approaches that simply "blame the victim" or which use a "culture of poverty" thesis to explain group disadvantages, the works of Clark and Rainwater not only presented a sensitive portrayal of the destructive features of ghetto life, they also provided a comprehensive analysis of the deleterious structural conditions that produce these features.

However, arguments stressing economic relations in determining the structure of inequality and in significantly influencing the experiences of inequality began to compete with a new definition, description, and explanation of the black condition. This new approach, proclaimed as the "black perspective," revealed an ideological shift from interracialism to racial solidarity. It first gained currency among militant black spokesmen in the late 1960s and became a theme in the writings of young black academics and intellectuals by the early 1970s. Although the "black perspective" represented a variety of views and arguments on issues of race, the trumpeting of racial pride and self-affirmation was common to all the writings and speeches on the subject. Thus interracial cooperation and integration were being challenged by the ideology of racial solidarity; and the rhetoric of black militancy, symbolized by the cry of "Black Power," gradually moved from expressions of selective to generalized hostility toward whites.

The complex factors associated with this shift in emphasis cannot be reviewed in full detail in a short essay, but I would like to point out that the declining support for interracialism and the rising emphasis on black solidarity in the late 1960s was typical of a pattern that had been repeated throughout the history of dominant-subordinate group relations in multiethnic societies. Perhaps Robert Merton comes closest to providing the theoretical explanation for this shift when he states that "when a once powerless collectivity acquires a socially validated sense of growing power, its members experience an intensified need for self-affirmation. Under such conditions, collective self-glorification, found in some measure among all groups, becomes a predictable and intensified counterresponse to long standing belittlement from without." Few would deny the fact that the black liberation movement in the late sixties and early seventies was marked by an avowed effort to minimize effects of subordinate status through a strong emphasis on black pride, black identity, and black cultural heritage. And in this atmosphere of race chauvinism a series of studies written by scholars proclaiming a "black perspective" appeared.

The arguments set forth in these studies made it clear that a substantial and fundamental shift in both the tone and focus of race relations scholarship was occurring. Consistent with the emphasis on black glorification and the quest for self-affirmation, arguments maintaining that some aspects of ghetto life were pathological (in the sense that the logical outcome of racial isolation and class subordination is that individuals are forced to adapt to the realities of the ghetto community and are therefore seriously impaired in their ability to function in any other community) were categorically rejected in favor of those emphasizing black community strengths. And arguments proclaiming the deterioration of the poor black family were dismissed in favor of those extolling the "virtues" and "strengths" of black families. Thus behavior described as pathological by some scholars was reinterpreted as functional by the black perspective proponents—functional in that blacks were displaying the ability to survive and flourish in a ghetto milieu. Ghetto families were described as resilient and were seen as creatively adapting to an oppressive racist society. The net effect of these revisionist studies, designed to "liberate" the social sciences from the influence of "racism," is that black achievement was emphasized at the expense of devoting sufficient and warranted attention to the

consequences and ramifications of oppression, including the psychological damage emanating from chronic subordination.

Also consistent with the dominant focus on racial solidarity in the writings of the black perspective proponents was an emphasis on "we" versus "they" and "black" versus "white." Since the emphasis was solely on race, little attention was paid to the internal differences within the black community. Moreover, since the problems were defined in racial terms, very little discussion was devoted to problems with the economy and the need for economic reform. This is why Orlando Patterson was led to proclaim in a later analysis that black ethnicity had become "a form of mystification, diverting attention from the correct kinds of solutions to the terrible economic condition of the group" thereby making it difficult for blacks to see "how their fate is inextricably tied up with the structure of the American economy."

Meanwhile, during this period of black glorification, significant developments were occurring in the black community that were related both to changes in the economy and in the laws and policies of the state. These changes prompted some writers to revive the arguments postulating the centrality of economic relations, to once again stress the deteriorating conditions of life in the ghetto and their behavioral consequences, and to return to the discussion of public policy that involves matters of both race and economic class position. In the next three sections, I shall attempt to document some of these developments.

## INTERNAL CHANGES IN THE BLACK COMMUNITY SINCE 1960

Although the black population is often regarded as a monolithic socio-economic group by social scientists and social commentators alike, since the end of World War II, and especially since 1960, blacks have become increasingly differentiated along occupational lines. The proportion of employed black workers from 1960 to 1978 increased 10.7 percent and 9.6 percent in professional and technical positions and in clerical jobs, respectively, and decreased 13.4 percent and 5.0 percent in service workers and laborer jobs and in farm worker jobs, respectively.

However, these occupational changes only partly demonstrate the nature of internal change within the black population. The major problem is that occupational data on employed workers, which reveal substantial progress in the movement of black workers from lower-paying to higher-paying positions, fail to capture the relative decline in the economic position of poor blacks during the last decade—a growing number of whom are either unemployed, underemployed, or outside the labor force altogether. Thus in order to more completely describe the range of experiences in the black community, I should like to conceptualize a black class structure that includes a middle class represented by white-collar workers and skilled blue-collar workers, a working class represented by semiskilled operatives, and a lower class represented by unskilled laborers and service workers. Within the lower class is an underclass population, a heterogeneous grouping at the very bottom of the economic class hierarchy. This underclass population includes those lower-class workers whose income falls below the poverty level, the long-term unemployed, discouraged workers who have dropped out of the labor market, and the more or less permanent welfare recipients.

Although the underclass constitutes the more impoverished segment of the lower class, I shall attempt to show that even full-time "lower-class" workers increasingly face structural barriers in advanced industrial society that trap them in menial, dead-end jobs. Nonetheless, the concept of "underclass" depicts a reality that is not fully captured in using the more general designation of "lower class." For example, unlike other families in the black community, the head of the household in underclass families is almost invariably a woman. The distinctive characteristics of the underclass are also reflected in the large number of unattached adult males who have no fixed address, who live mainly on the streets, and who roam from one place of shelter to another.

## PROBLEMS OF EMPLOYMENT AND UNEMPLOYMENT

The question of what happens to individuals who are trapped in depressed areas and are therefore denied access to the normal channels of economic opportunity and mobility takes on even greater meaning for the black poor today than in previous years. Poor black Americans, heavily concentrated in inner cities, have experienced a worsening of their economic position on the basis of nearly all the major labor-market indicators. The unemployment rates for both black men and black women from 1955 to 1978 have increased more rapidly at all age levels than those of comparable whites, with black teenage unemployment showing the sharpest increase—from 13.4 percent in 1955 to 34.4 percent in 1978 for men, and from 19.2 percent in 1955 to 38.4 percent in 1978 for women. The unemployment rates of blacks age 20 to 24 also reached very high proportions in 1978—20 percent for men and 21.3 percent for women—extending a trend of increasing joblessness that began in the mid-1960s. The significant rise in unemployment for younger blacks stands in sharp contrast to the slight change in the rate of unemployment for blacks 25 years old and over. Still, even the older blacks had unemployment rates above those of their white counterparts.

The severe problems of joblessness for black teenagers and young adults are also seen in the data on changes in the male civilian labor-force participation rates. The percentage of black males who were in the labor force fell from 45.6 in 1960 to 30.8 in 1977 for those 16 and 17 years old, from 71.2 to 57.8 for those 18 and 19, and from 90.4 to 78.2 for those 20 to 24. Even blacks 25 to 34 years old experienced a decline in labor-force participation; however, the drop was not nearly as steep as that recorded by younger blacks—from 96.2 percent to 90.4 percent. Whereas black males are dropping out of the labor force in significant numbers, white males have either maintained or slightly increased their rate of participation since 1960—from 46.0 to 53.8 for those 16 and 17 years old, from 69.0 to 65.8 for those 18 and 19, from 87.8 to 86.8 for those 20 to 24, and from 97.7 to 96.0 for those 25 to 34.

But even unemployment rates and labor-force participation rates do not reveal the real depth of joblessness among younger blacks. If we consider the ratio of the employed civilian population to the total civilian noninstitutional population, that is, the employment population ratio, we find that less than 30 percent of all black male teenagers and only 62 percent of all black young adult males 20 to 24 years old were employed in 1978. In short, the problem of joblessness for young black men has reached catastrophic proportions.

Finally, the bleak employment picture for young blacks is further demonstrated by the data on work experience in any given year. Whereas the proportion of white male teenagers 16 to 19 years old and young adults 20 to 24 years old with work experience has changed very little from 1966 to 1977 and the proportion of white female teenagers and young adults with work experience has increased, the proportion of young blacks with work experience has decreased from 67.3 to 47.2 percent for black male teenagers, from 90.1 to 76.7 percent for young adult black males, from 48.9 to 37.5 percent for black female teenagers, and from 67.2 to 63.6 percent for young adult black females.

Thus the combined indicators of unemployment, labor-force participation, employment-population ratios, and work experience reveal a disturbing picture of black joblessness, especially among younger blacks. If the evidence presented in recent longitudinal research is correct, then black youth joblessness will have a long-term harmful effect on their chances in the labor market. For all these reasons, a significant segment of the black population is in danger of being permanently locked out of the mainstream of the American occupational systems. It cannot be overemphasized that the increasing black youth joblessness is a problem primarily experienced by lower-income blacks; for example, 67 percent of unemployed black teenagers living at home in 1977 were from families with incomes of less than $10,000. And among those unemployed teenagers living at home and not enrolled in school, 75 percent were from families with less than $10,000 incomes and 41 percent were from families with less than $5000 income.

The high incidence of joblessness among blacks as a group is partly related to the fact that they constitute a disproportionate percentage of workers employed in the lowest-paying jobs, such as service work and unskilled labor—jobs that have a high turnover and are susceptible to unemployment. Nonetheless, this fact alone cannot account for the rapid deterioration of the position of poor blacks in the labor market; nor can their employment problems be adequately explained in terms of racial discrimination. These issues will be further clarified by considering the effect of basic shifts in the economy on the life chances of lower-class blacks. But first let me pay special attention to changes that are occurring in poor black families, changes that have accompanied their worsening economic plight and that could have long-term effects on their future employment prospects.

## THE ECONOMIC CRISIS AND THE POOR BLACK FAMILY

In 1969, black median family income was 61 percent that of whites; by 1976 it had dropped

to 59 percent; by 1977 to 57 percent; and by 1978, it had risen slightly to 59 percent, but was still below the ratio of 1969. However, it should be pointed out that the ratio of black to white median family income in male-headed homes was 72 percent in 1969, rose to 80 percent in 1976, declined to 75 percent in 1977, then climbed back up to 80 percent in 1978.

What should be underlined, therefore, is that the overall relative decline in black family income since 1969 has been accompanied by the sharp increase in female-headed homes during this period—from 28 percent in 1969, to 37 percent in 1976, to 39 percent in 1977, and finally to a staggering 40 percent in 1978. And when we take into account the fact that the median income of black male-headed families ($15,678) in 1978 was $9690 more than the median income of black female-headed families, it becomes clear why the recorded black-to-white family income ratio has declined in recent years. By 1978, the proportion of all poor black families headed by women had reached 74 percent.

The class-related features of black female-headed households cannot be overemphasized. I have already stated that what is distinctive about underclass black families is that the head of the household is almost invariably a woman. The powerful connection between class background and the structure of the black family can be further revealed. Whereas 80.3 percent of all black families with incomes of less than $4000 and 63.8 percent with incomes between $4000 and $6999 were headed by women in 1978, only 15.3 percent of those with incomes between $16,000 and $24,999 and 7.7 percent with incomes of $25,000 and more were headed by women. In metropolitan areas the differences in the proportion of black families with female heads was even greater, with extremes of 85.1 percent for those whose incomes were below $4000 and 7.6 percent for those whose incomes were $25,000 and more. Although the factor of race is clearly associated with the difference in the makeup of black and white families, the relationship between type of family and level of income is much stronger among blacks than among whites.

Reflecting the rise in black female-headed families, the proportion of black children living with both parents has decreased sharply from 64 percent in 1970, to 56 percent in 1974, and finally, to 48.5 percent in 1978. An extremely high percentage of the black children who do not live with both parents are impoverished. More specifically, 41.2 percent of all black children under 18 years old and 42.5 percent of all black children under 6 years old were living in families whose incomes were below the poverty level in 1978. Even more startling, 32.1 percent of all black children under 18 years old and 33.6 percent of all black children under 6 years old were living in female-headed families whose incomes were below the poverty level. Finally, if we focus on black families below the poverty level, 78 percent of all poor black children under 18 years old and 79 percent of all poor black children under 6 years old lived in female-headed homes in 1978.

Thus the problem for female-headed families is not simply the absence of fathers. The problem is that an overwhelming number of these families are impoverished. Given the fact that most of these families are more or less permanent recipients of welfare, unless a program of economic reform is introduced, the odds are extremely high that the children in these families will be permanently trapped in the underclass.

The findings in this section and the ones presented in the previous sections have profound implications for both the future of race relations in this country and for the internal structure of the black community. They also raise serious questions about existing policy programs that have been designed to address matters of racial inequality.

In the next section, I should like to take a critical look at these programs and suggest why they have not sufficiently addressed the problems and experiences of underclass blacks. In the process I hope to show that the problems of poor blacks are closely related to changes in the modern American economy.

## ISSUES OF RACE, CLASS, AND PUBLIC POLICY

Since World War II, political changes in the government and structural changes in the economy have both contributed to a gradual and continuous process of deracialization in the economic sector—in other words, a process in which racial distinctions gradually lose their importance in determining individual mobility in the United States. The expansion of the economy, on the one hand, facilitated the movement of blacks from southern rural areas to the industrial centers of the nation and created job opportunities leading to greater occupational differentiation within the black community. On the

other hand, the state, instead of reinforcing the racial barriers that were created during previous periods, has, in recent years, promoted racial equality. Partly in response to the pressure of increased black political resources—resources that were a result of the growing concentration of blacks in large industrial cities—and partly in response to the pressures of black protest movements—pressures which in many ways were a manifestation of greater black political strength—the state has consistently intervened in behalf of blacks with the enactment and enforcement of antidiscrimination legislation. In short, a combination of economic and political changes created greater economic mobility opportunities for a substantial element of the black population.

The curious paradox, however, is that whereas economic growth since World War II enabled many blacks to experience occupational mobility, recent structural shifts in the economy have diminished mobility opportunities for others. And whereas antidiscrimination legislation has removed many racial barriers, not all blacks are in a position to benefit from them. Indeed the position of the black underclass has actually deteriorated during the very period in which the most sweeping antidiscrimination legislation and programs have been enacted and implemented. The net effect is a growing bifurcation between the "haves" and "have nots" in the black community.

Thus while poor blacks are recording rising levels of employment, declining labor-force participation rates, sharp drops in employment-population ratios, and decreasing proportions with work experience, the number of blacks in professional and managerial positions climbed to more than 1.8 million by the second quarter of 1980, over two and a half times the number in 1965 (728,000). Moreover, whereas prior to the late 1960s, the ratio of black income to white income actually decreased as educational attainment increased, today the reverse seems to be the case, especially for younger black males. In 1978, 25- to 29-year-old black males who graduated from high school earned on the average only 79 percent as much as their white counterparts—$9995 for blacks and $12,678 for whites—whereas those who graduated from college actually earned on the average more than comparable whites—$15,217 for blacks and $14,013 for whites.

The failure to recognize these profound differences in the black experience, differences based on economic class position, often leads to policies that do not address the specific needs and concerns of those blacks who are the most disadvantaged. For example, it has been argued in many quarters, and with rising insistence, that there should be a more vigorous enforcement of affirmative action programs to reverse the decline in the black-white family income ratio. However, as I have attempted to show, the recent relative decline in black family income is largely due to the growth of female-headed families, an overwhelming percentage of whom are impoverished. And, as I shall argue in more detail, affirmative action programs, which have helped to enhance the economic position of the more trained and educated blacks, are not really designed to address the unique economic problem of poor blacks. Indeed, even if all racial discrimination in labor-market practices were eliminated, unless there were a serious attempt to address the problems of structural barriers to decent jobs, the economic position of poor blacks would not improve significantly. I shall elaborate briefly on this argument.

People who argue that current racial bias is the major cause of the deteriorating plight of the black poor not only have a difficult time explaining the simultaneous economic progress of more privileged blacks, but they also fail or in some cases refuse to recognize how the fate of poor blacks is inextricably connected with the structure and functioning of the modern American economy. The net effect is that policy programs are recommended that do not confront the fundamental causes of poverty—underemployment and unemployment. In other words, policies that do not take into account the changing characteristics of the national economy—including its rate of growth and the nature of its variable demand for labor; the factors that affect industrial employment, such as profit rates, technology, and unionization; and patterns of institutional and individual migration that are a result of industrial transformation and shifts—will not effectively handle the economic dislocation of poor blacks.

It cannot be overemphasized that poor blacks are particularly vulnerable to structural economic changes beyond racial considerations such as the shift from goods-producing to service-producing industries, the increasing segmentation of the labor market, the growing use of industrial technology, and the relocation of industries out of the central city. All of these changes have profoundly altered the character of the labor market in central cities. As John D. Kasarda has put it:

The central cities have become increasing specialized in jobs that have high educational prerequisites just at the time that their resident populations are increasingly composed of those with poor educational backgrounds. As a result, inner-city unemployment rates are more than twice the national average and even higher among inner-city residents who have traditionally found employment in blue-collar industries that have migrated to suburban locations.

The extent to which white-collar jobs are replacing blue-collar positions in central cities is illustrated in the data on the number of jobs in five selected occupational categories in 18 older northern cities. Whereas the professional, technical, and clerical employment increased by 291,055 positions from 1960 to 1970, blue-collar employment—craftsmen, operatives, and laborers—decreased by 749,774 positions. And the overwhelming majority of the jobs lost were the higher-paying blue-collar positions: craftsmen and operatives. There is also some indication that the blue-collar jobs decline in large northern cities has accelerated. During the decade of the 1970s, Chicago lost more than 200,000 jobs, mostly in manufacturing. New York City lost 600,000 jobs during the 1970s despite the fact that the number of white-collar, professional, managerial, and clerical jobs increased in Manhattan.

In considering these job shifts, it should be emphasized that roughly 60 percent of the unemployed blacks in the United States reside in the central city, mostly within the cities' low-income areas. Conversely, there is much more dispersion among unemployed whites, as approximately 40 percent live in suburban areas and an additional 30 percent reside in non-metropolitan areas. Furthermore, the proportion of black men employed as laborers and service workers—occupational categories with a higher than average jobless ratio—is twice that of white workers employed in these jobs. In the final analysis, the lack of economic opportunity for lower-class blacks means that they are forced to remain in economically depressed ghettos and their children are forced to attend inferior ghetto schools. This gives rise to a vicious circle as ghetto isolation and inferior opportunities in education reinforce their disadvantaged position in the labor market and contribute to the growing gap in the economic resources of the haves and have nots in the black community.

Given these basic economic realities, it is instructive to examine race-oriented policies and programs such as affirmative action. Of all the programs created to improve the economic position of blacks, none has received as much attention as affirmative action. However, whereas affirmative action programs have contributed to the recent occupational mobility of trained and educated blacks, they are not designed to break down color-blind barriers created by the shift from goods-producing to service-producing industries, the relocation of industries, the segmentation of the labor market, and the growth of technology and automation.

Furthermore, affirmative action programs are irrelevant to the problem of labor surplus in low-wage industries. Many of the dead-end and low-paying jobs in these industries do not generate racial competition between black and white workers because they are not in high demand and are now identified as "minority jobs." Because fewer black and white workers are willing to accept an economic arrangement that consigns them to dead-end, menial, and poorly paid jobs, low-wage service and manufacturing industries have increasingly used immigrant labor, including illegal aliens or undocumented workers from Mexico and other Latin American countries, to control labor problems and keep wages depressed.

If race-oriented policies are not designed to deal with the deteriorating economic condition of poor blacks, then more attention has to focus on programs of economic reform. Everything from growing unemployment to the growth of female-headed families can be traced to economic dislocation. As Lee Rainwater observed 14 years ago, unemployed men are more likely to abandon their families than are employed men. Indeed, the female-headed pattern in the ghetto symbolizes the poverty-stricken nature of the underclass. To repeat, the main problem is that the lower-class black family is in the throes of an economic depression and the rising percentage of female-headed families is one of the symptoms, not the cause, of that problem.

However, if a program of economic reform is to be meaningful, it has to be directed at improving the job prospects of both poor black men and poor black women. And considering the fact that most poor black families are now headed by women, it would even be advisable to include the creation of publicly financed day-care centers in this reform program so that women can avail themselves of job opportunities if and when they develop.

In suggesting the need for economic reform, I am fully aware that it will be more successful if it can generate conditions that guarantee sustained full employment. I am also aware of the difficulty entailed in trying to create such conditions. Unlike several other capitalist democracies, the United States does not have a system of central government planning to further economic growth, establish long-range industrial policy, and outline labor-market projections and to design land use, regional distribution of resources, and educational development. Accordingly, the government response to economic fluctuations is much more likely to be determined by short-term political considerations, to reflect the interests of the more powerful and organized groups in society, and therefore to underrepresent the interests of the poor and the unemployed.

Moreover, even many of those committed to social reform have yet to recognize that current discrimination is not as central to the plight of the black poor as is the problem of economic dislocation. We only need to consider the fact that in the latter half of the 1970s, articulate black and white supporters of equal rights expressed far more concern and devoted far more attention to the *Bakke* case than to the Humphrey Hawkins full-employment bill. If the nation is to avert serious domestic problems in the future, a shift in emphasis will soon have to occur. And a first step in that direction is to recognize what the problem is and where it is concentrated.

# "White Popular Wisdom": Losing Ground

CHARLES MURRAY

As the *Sturm und Drang* of the 1960s faded and we settled into the 1970s, the realization gradually spread that things were getting worse, not better, for blacks and poor people in this country. It was seldom put in just that way. The lower poverty percentages were insistently credited to the reforms. Each court decision affirming the constitutionality of steps to equalize outcome was seen as a victory for civil rights. But few could avoid recognizing that the inner cities were more violent and ravaged than ever before. It was difficult to take much satisfaction in the poverty statistics—which by the early 1970s had stopped looking better anyway— when pictures of the devastated South Bronx kept getting into the newspapers. It was difficult to take much satisfaction in the legal edifice of black rights when black teenage unemployment was approaching 40 percent.

For most of the 1970s, mainstream politicians, academicians, journalists, and bureaucrats remained stuck in a mindset. The War on Poverty had become a domestic Vietnam in which they were committed to a way of thinking about poor people and race and social policy that did not seem to be working as it was supposed to. But, not unlike Lyndon Johnson with the Vietnam War, they saw no choice but to sweat it out. The budgets for the CETAs and entitlements and social-action programs continued to grow by inertia.

There had been an alternative set of ideas all along, of course. If during the 1960s and 1970s there was an elite wisdom that shaped the direction of social policy, there was also a popular wisdom about why things were falling apart.

This popular wisdom, which is as prevalent today as it was then, is just that—the views to be heard in most discussions in most blue-collar bars or country-club lounges in most parts of the United States. It is the inarticulate constellation of worries and suspicions that helped account for

Ronald Reagan's victory in 1980. It is perhaps more precisely called a white popular wisdom, but some of its major themes are also voiced quietly by a conservative black working class.

The popular wisdom is characterized by hostility toward welfare (it makes people lazy), toward lenient judges (they encourage crime), and toward socially conscious schools (too busy busing kids to teach them how to read). The popular wisdom disapproves of favoritism for blacks and of too many written-in rights for minorities of all sorts. It says that the government is meddling far too much in things that are none of its business.

The hostility one hears in the *vox populi* may account for the reluctance of many intellectuals to consider whether this view might not be right. To listen carefully to the popular wisdom is also to hear a good deal of mean-spirited (often racist) invective. Acknowledging the merits of its insights is seen as approving of the invective as well. And one might add that to the minds of many professional social analysts, the explanations of the popular wisdom are too *simple,* too unsubtle, to be true.

By the end of the 1970s, however, a synthesis of wisdoms was underway. Too much of what we saw going on around us confirmed too many of the popular view's premises to be ignored. Stripped of the prejudices and the bombast, these, as I see them, are three core premises of the popular wisdom that need to be taken into account:

- Premise #1: People respond to incentives and disincentives. Sticks and carrots work.
- Premise #2: People are not inherently hard working or moral. In the absence of countervailing influences, people will avoid work and be amoral.
- Premise #3: People must be held responsible for their actions. Whether they *are* responsible in some ultimate philosophical or bio-

chemical sense cannot be the issue if society is to function.

The thesis here is that social policy since 1964 has ignored these premises and that it has thereby created much of the mess we are in.


## A PROPOSAL FOR PUBLIC WELFARE

I begin with the proposition that it is within our resources to do enormous good for some people quickly. We have available to us a program that would convert a large proportion of the younger generation of hardcore unemployed into steady workers making a living wage. The same program would drastically reduce births to single teenage girls. It would reverse the trendline in the breakup of poor families. It would measurably increase the upward socioeconomic mobility of poor families. These improvements would affect some millions of persons.

All these are results that have eluded the efforts of the social programs installed since 1965, yet, from everything we know, there is no real question about whether they would occur under the program I propose. A wide variety of persuasive evidence from our own culture and around the world, from experimental data and longitudinal studies, from theory and practice, suggests that the program would achieve such results.

The proposed program, our final and most ambitious thought experiment, consists of scrapping the entire federal welfare and income-support structure for working-aged persons, including AFDC, Medicaid, Food Stamps, Unemployment Insurance, Worker's Compensation, subsidized housing, disability insurance, and the rest. It would leave the working-aged person with no recourse whatsoever except the job market, family members, friends, and public or private locally funded services. It is the Alexandrian solution: cut the knot, for there is no way to untie it.

It is difficult to examine such a proposal dispassionately. Those who dislike paying for welfare are for it without thinking. Others reflexively imagine bread lines and people starving in the streets. But as a means of gaining fresh perspective on the problem of effective reform, let us consider what this hypothetical society might look like.

A large majority of the population is unaffected. A surprising number of the huge American middle and working classes go from birth to grave without using any social welfare benefits until they receive their first Social Security check. Another portion of the population is technically affected, but the change in income is so small or so sporadic that it makes no difference in quality of life. A third group comprises people who have to make new arrangements and behave in different ways. Sons and daughters who fail to find work continue to live with their parents or relatives or friends. Teenaged mothers have to rely on support from their parents or the father of the child and perhaps work as well. People laid off from work have to use their own savings or borrow from others to make do until the next job is found. All these changes involve great disruption in expectations and accustomed roles.

Along with the disruptions go other changes in behavior. Some parents do not want their young adult children continuing to live off their income, and become quite insistent about their children learning skills and getting jobs. This attitude is most prevalent among single mothers who have to depend most critically on the earning power of their offspring.

Parents tend to become upset at the prospect of a daughter's bringing home a baby that must be entirely supported on an already inadequate income. Some become so upset that they spend considerable parental energy avoiding such an eventuality. Potential fathers of such babies find themselves under more pressure not to cause such a problem, or to help with its solution if it occurs.

Adolescents who were not job-ready find they are job-ready after all. It turns out that they can work for low wages and accept the discipline of the workplace if the alternative is grim enough. After a few years, many—not all, but many—find that they have acquired salable skills, or that they are at the right place at the right time, or otherwise find that the original entry-level job has gradually been transformed into a secure job paying a decent wage. A few—not a lot, but a few—find that the process leads to affluence.

Perhaps the most rightful, deserved benefit goes to the much larger population of low-income families who have been doing things right all along and have been punished for it: the young man who has taken responsibility for his wife and child even though his friends with the same choice have called him a fool; the single mother who has worked full time and forfeited her right to welfare for very little extra money; the parents who have set an example for their children even as the rules of the game have taught their children that the example is outmoded. For these millions of people, the instantaneous result is that no one makes fun of them any longer. The longer-term result will be that they regain the status that is properly theirs. They will not only be the bedrock upon which the community is founded (which they always have been), they will be recognized as such. The process whereby they regain their position is not magical, but a matter of logic. When it becomes highly dysfunctional for a person to be dependent, status will accrue to being independent, and in fairly short order. Noneconomic rewards will once again reinforce the economic rewards of being a good parent and provider.

The prospective advantages are real and extremely plausible. In fact, if a government program of the traditional sort (one that would "do" something rather than simply get out of the way) could *as plausibly* promise these advantages, its passage would be a foregone conclusion. Congress, yearning for programs that are not retreads of failures, would be prepared to spend billions. Negative side-effects (as long as they were the traditionally acceptable negative side-effects) would be brushed aside as trivial in return for the benefits. For let me be quite clear: I am not suggesting that we dismantle income support for the working-aged to balance the budget or punish welfare cheats. I am hypothesizing, with the advantage of powerful collateral evidence, that the lives of large numbers of poor people would be radically changed for the better.

There is, however, a fourth segment of the population yet to be considered, those who are pauperized by the withdrawal of government supports and unable to make alternate arrangements: the teenaged mother who has no one to turn to; the incapacitated or the inept who are thrown out of the house; those to whom economic conditions have brought long periods in which there is no work to be had; those with illnesses not covered by insurance. What of these situations?

The first resort is the network of local services. Poor communities in our hypothetical society are still dotted with storefront health clinics, emergency relief agencies, employment services, legal services. They depend for support on local taxes or local philanthropy, and the local taxpayers and philanthropists tend to scrutinize them rather closely. But, by the same token, they also receive considerably more resources than they formerly did. The disman-

tling of the federal services has poured tens of billions of dollars back into the private economy. Some of that money no doubt has been spent on Mercedes and summer homes on the Cape. But some has been spent on capital investments that generate new jobs. And some has been spent on increased local services to the poor, voluntarily or as decreed by the municipality. In many cities, the coverage provided by this network of agencies is more generous, more humane, more wisely distributed, and more effective in its results than the services formerly subsidized by the federal government.

But we must expect that a large number of people will fall between the cracks. How might we go about trying to retain the advantages of a zero-level welfare system and still address the residual needs?

As we think about the nature of the population still in need, it becomes apparent that their basic problem in the vast majority of cases is the lack of a job, and this problem is temporary. What they need is something to tide them over while finding a new place in the economy. So our first step is to re-install the Unemployment Insurance program in more or less its previous form. Properly administered, unemployment insurance makes sense. Even if it is restored with all the defects of current practice, the negative effects of Unemployment Insurance *alone* are relatively minor. Our objective is not to wipe out chicanery or to construct a theoretically unblemished system, but to meet legitimate human needs without doing more harm than good. Unemployment Insurance is one of the least harmful ways of contributing to such ends. Thus the system has been amended to take care of the victims of short-term swings in the economy.

Who is left? We are now down to the hardest of the hard core of the welfare-dependent. They have no jobs. They have been unable to find jobs (or have not tried to find jobs) for a longer period of time than the unemployment benefits cover. They have no families who will help. They have no friends who will help. For some reason, they cannot get help from local services or private charities except for the soup kitchen and a bed in the Salvation Army hall.

What will be the size of this population? We have never tried a zero-level federal welfare system under conditions of late-twentieth-century national wealth, so we cannot do more than speculate. But we may speculate. Let us ask of whom the population might consist and how they might fare.

For any category of "needy" we may name,

we find ourselves driven to one of two lines of thought. Either the person is in a category that is going to be at the top of the list of services that localities vote for themselves, and at the top of the list of private services, or the person is in a category where help really is not all that essential or desirable. The burden of the conclusion is not that every single person will be taken care of, but that the extent of resources to deal with needs is likely to be very great—not based on wishful thinking, but on extrapolations from reality.

To illustrate, let us consider the plight of the stereotypical welfare mother—never married, no skills, small children, no steady help from a man. It is safe to say that, now as in the 1950s, there is no one who has less sympathy from the white middle class, which is to be the source of most of the money for the private and local services we envision. Yet this same white middle class is a soft touch for people trying to make it on their own, and a soft touch for "deserving" needy mothers—AFDC was one of the most widely popular of the New Deal welfare measures, intended as it was for widows with small children. Thus we may envision two quite different scenarios.

In one scenario, the woman is presenting the local or private service with this proposition: "Help me find a job and day-care for my children, and I will take care of the rest." In effect, she puts herself into the same category as the widow and the deserted wife—identifies herself as one of the most obviously deserving of the deserving poor. Welfare mothers who want to get into the labor force are likely to find a wide range of help. In the other scenario, she asks for an outright and indefinite cash grant—in effect, a private or local version of AFDC—so that she can stay with the children and not hold a job. In the latter case, it is very easy to imagine situations in which she will not be able to find a local service or a private philanthropy to provide the help she seeks. The question we must now ask is: What's so bad about that? If children were always better off being with their mother all day and if, by the act of giving birth, a mother acquired the inalienable right to be with the child, then her situation would be unjust to her and injurious to her children. Neither assertion can be defended, however—especially not in the 1980s, when more mothers of all classes work away from the home than ever before, and even more especially not in view of the empirical record for the children growing up under the current welfare system.

Why should the mother be exempted by the system from the pressures that must affect everyone else's decision to work?

As we survey these prospects, important questions remain unresolved. The first of these is why, if federal social transfers are treacherous, should locally mandated transfers be less so? Why should a municipality be permitted to legislate its own AFDC or Food Stamp program if their results are so inherently bad?

Part of the answer lies in conceptions of freedom. I have deliberately avoided raising them—the discussion is about how to help the disadvantaged, not about how to help the advantaged cut their taxes, to which arguments for personal freedom somehow always get diverted. Nonetheless, the point is valid: Local or even state systems leave much more room than a federal system for everyone, donors and recipients alike, to exercise freedom of choice about the kind of system they live under. Laws are more easily made and changed, and people who find them unacceptable have much more latitude in going somewhere more to their liking.

But the freedom of choice argument, while legitimate, is not necessary. We may put the advantages of local systems in terms of the Law of Imperfect Selection. A federal system must inherently employ very crude, inaccurate rules for deciding who gets what kind of help. At the opposite extreme—a neighbor helping a neighbor, a family member helping another family member—the law loses its validity nearly altogether. Very fine-grained judgments based on personal knowledge are being made about specific people and changing situations. In neighborhoods and small cities, the procedures can still bring much individualized information to bear on decisions. Even systems in large cities and states can do much better than a national system; a decaying industrial city in the Northeast and a booming sunbelt city of the same size can and probably should adopt much different rules about who gets what and how much.

A final and equally powerful argument for not impeding local systems is diversity. We know much more in the 1980s than we knew in the 1960s about what does not work. We have a lot to learn about what *does* work. Localities have been a rich source of experiments. Marva Collins in Chicago gives us an example of how a school can bring inner-city students up to national norms. Sister Falaka Fattah in Philadelphia shows us how homeless youths can be rescued from the streets. There are numberless such lessons waiting to be learned from the diversity of local efforts. By all means, let a hundred flowers bloom, and if the federal government can play a useful role in lending a hand and spreading the word of successes, so much the better.

The ultimate unresolved question about our proposal to abolish income maintenance for the working-aged is how many people will fall through the cracks. In whatever detail we try to foresee the consequences, the objection may always be raised: We cannot be *sure* that everyone will be taken care of in the degree to which we would wish. But this observation by no means settles the question. If one may point in objection to the child now fed by Food Stamps who would go hungry, one may also point with satisfaction to the child who would have an entirely different and better future. Hungry children should be fed; there is no argument about that. It is no less urgent that children be allowed to grow up in a system free of the forces that encourage them to remain poor and dependent. If a strategy reasonably promises to remove those forces, after so many attempts to "help the poor" have failed, it is worth thinking about.

But that rationale is too vague. Let me step outside the persona I have employed and put the issue in terms of one last intensely personal hypothetical example. Let us suppose that you, a parent, could know that tomorrow your own child would be made an orphan. You have a choice. You may put your child with an extremely poor family, so poor that your child will be badly clothed and will indeed sometimes be hungry. But you also know that the parents have worked hard all their lives, will make sure your child goes to school and studies, and will teach your child that independence is a primary value. Or you may put your child with a family with parents who have never worked, who will be incapable of overseeing your child's education—but who have plenty of food and good clothes, provided by others. If the choice about where one would put one's own child is as clear to you as it is to me, on what grounds does one justify support of a system that, indirectly but without doubt, makes the other choice for other children? The answer that "What we really want is a world where that choice is not forced upon us" is no answer. We have tried to have it that way. We failed. Everything we know about why we failed tells us that more of the same will not make the dilemma go away.

## THE IDEAL OF OPPORTUNITY

Billions for equal opportunity, not one cent for equal outcome—such is the slogan to inscribe on the banner of whatever cause my proposals constitute. Their common theme is to make it possible to get as far as one can go on one's merit, hardly a new ideal in American thought.

The ideal itself has never lapsed. What did lapse was the recognition that practical merit exists. Some people are better than others. They deserve more of society's rewards, of which money is only one small part. A principal function of social policy is to make sure they have the opportunity to reap those rewards. Government cannot identify the worthy, but it can protect a society in which the worthy can identify themselves.

I am proposing triage of a sort, triage by self-selection. In triage on the battlefield, the doctor makes the decision—this one gets treatment, that one waits, the other one is made comfortable while waiting to die. In our social triage, the decision is left up to the patient. The patient always has the right to say "I can do X" and get a chance to prove it. Society always has the right to hold him to that pledge. The patient always has the right to fail. Society always has the right to let him.

There is in this stance no lack of compassion but a presumption of respect. People—all people, black or white, rich or poor—may be unequally responsible for what has happened to them in the past, but all are equally responsible for what they do next. Just as in an idealized educational system in which a student can come back a third, fourth, or fifth time to a course, in an idealized society a person can fail repeatedly and always be qualified for another chance—to try again, to try something easier, to try something different. The options are always open. Opportunity is endless. There is no punishment for failure, only a total absence of rewards. Society—or our idealized society—should be preoccupied with making sure that achievement is rewarded.

There is no shortage of people to be rewarded. Go into any inner-city school and you will find students of extraordinary talent, kept from knowing how good they are by rules we imposed in the name of fairness. Go into any poor community, and you will find people of extraordinary imagination and perseverance, energy and pride, making tortured accommodations to the strange world we created in the name of generosity. The success stories of past generations of poor in this country are waiting to be repeated.

There is no shortage of institutions to provide the rewards. Our schools know how to educate students who want to be educated. Our industries know how to find productive people and reward them. Our police know how to protect people who are ready to cooperate in their own protection. Our system of justice knows how to protect the rights of individuals who know what their rights are. Our philanthropic institutions know how to multiply the effectiveness of people who are already trying to help themselves. In short, American society is very good at reinforcing the investment of an individual in himself. For the affluent and for the middleclass, these mechanisms continue to work about as well as they ever have, and we enjoy their benefits. Not so for the poor. American government, in its recent social policy, has been ineffectual in trying to stage-manage their decision to invest, and it has been unintentionally punitive toward those who would make the decision on their own. It is time to get out of their way.

# A Dream Deferred:
# The Crisis of "Losing Ground"

RONALD TAKAKI

Why, Charles Murray asks in *Losing Ground,* has the situation for the poor and blacks deteriorated during the last thirty years, during a time of expanded government social programs and an increasingly interventionist state? Murray's answer is clear and forthright: they are worse off today because of the social policies of the federal government. The federal welfare program has rendered it "rational" for the poor to choose welfare. The very programs intended to alleviate poverty have instead contributed to the formation of a new dependent and growing welfare class. Thus, concludes Murray, what is needed is the "scrapping" of the entire federal welfare system—Aid to Families with Dependent Children (AFDC), Food Stamps, Medicaid, Unemployment Insurance, and even Disability Insurance. To do so would be to heed what Murray calls "white popular wisdom."

Described as the bible for President Ronald Reagan's social policies, Murray's book presents the neoconservative case against welfare as well as the latest neoconservative explanation of contemporary racial inequality. But how substantial and sound is Murray's book as scholarship? And why have blacks "lost ground" in the seventies and eighties?

The increase in the numbers of AFDC families was due, no doubt, to the expansion of eligibility requirements in the late sixties. But the increase also reflected the convergence of several different developments.

One of them was demographic. Between 1960 and 1980, the baby boom of post–World War II entered young adulthood. During these years, the total population of the United States increased by a quarter, but the eighteen-to-twenty-four-year-old group nearly doubled in number. In other words, there were simply more adults in the early childbearing age in the sixties and seventies.

A second development was the divorce revolution. Divorce rates doubled in the sixties and continued to soar in the seventies as no-fault divorce was instituted in forty-eight states. The rate of divorced women per 1,000 married women rose from 9.2 percent in 1960 to 14.9 percent in 1970 to 22.6 percent ten years later. Millions of newly divorced women discovered they were "but one man removed from poverty." They found themselves facing the "feminization of poverty"—financially responsible for their children and also crowded into low-wage sales and clerical occupations or unemployed. One study showed that 14 percent of the divorced women surveyed joined AFDC rolls within the first year after their divorce.

But how do we assess Murray's explanation for the great increase in AFDC families?

At the heart of Murray's book is a parable about Phyllis and Harold. This parable constitutes the hinge of his thesis; his argument swings on it. Phyllis and Harold are dramatis personae, and we are asked to imagine them in order to understand the members of this new welfare class.

In 1960, Phyllis and Harold are a young unmarried couple. Phyllis becomes pregnant and finds that welfare will not provide sufficient support for the three of them. So, setting up a household with Harold, even with his minimum-wage income, is "by far the most sensible choice." In 1970, Phyllis and Harold or a couple with the same names find themselves in a similar situation but they have more options available to them. Phyllis decides to depend on AFDC rather than Harold to support herself and her child. She does so, Murray answers, because the welfare system has made it "rational" for her to choose AFDC. According to Murray's calculations, Phyllis's AFDC cash payments plus food stamps and Medicaid total more than Harold's earnings.

But the questions we need to ask here are: What factor made her decision to go on welfare a rational one? Was it the high welfare payment available to Phyllis, or was it the low wages available to Harold? Had Harold's wages been higher than welfare, Phyllis would have "rationally" chosen to set up a household with Harold. In other words, welfare operated within a larger economic context. What the parable of Phyllis and Harold actually shows is that it was the economic system—the labor market and its low wages, not the welfare system alone—which rendered it rational for Phyllis to choose welfare.

But the choice for Phyllis may not be between AFDC and Harold's wages. Harold may be unemployed. If we examine unemployment, we will find that it climbed steeply during the seventies—from 2.8 million in 1968 to 7.6 million in 1980 or an increase of nearly 5 million workers. Meanwhile, AFDC families grew from 1.5 million to 3.8 million, or a little over 2 million families. Significantly, unemployment rose faster and in greater numbers than AFDC families. What this suggests is that families were being pushed onto welfare rolls by unemployment, not simply pulled there by welfare benefits.

But how do we explain the fact that in 1970— the year Phyllis got pregnant—most families below the poverty line were not on AFDC, and many of them were families with children? Why weren't these poor people acting "rationally"? If AFDC were such a good deal, why were these families not on welfare?

To answer such questions, we have to return to the parable of Phyllis and Harold and ask where Murray got his high figures for welfare payments. Murray's text simply tells us that the calculations are based on a "typical Northern state." But why take a Northern state, we must question, and compare it to minimum-wage income which was national? If we check Murray's footnote, we will find that Murray's typical Northern state is Pennsylvania. How typical is Pennsylvania in terms of all the states? According to the *Social Security Bulletin Annual Supplement* for 1970, forty-three out of fifty states had average monthly AFDC payments below that of Pennsylvania. Furthermore, 75 percent of all AFDC recipients received less than recipients living in Pennsylvania. In short, Pennsylvania is not a typical state, and by choosing it Murray biases his AFDC calculations upward.

Actually, welfare payments are not as high as Murray claims they are. In 1979, for example, the average monthly AFDC standard of need for a mother and child was only $246.71, while a minimum-wage job paid $502.66 per month.

This explains why there are heads of poor families with children who work, even for low wages, rather than collect AFDC. This also explains why 90 percent of AFDC families are headed by single female parents, over half of them with children under six years of age. These women cannot work or cannot find work. And if they do find work, they discover they are usually not paid enough to cover child-care and living expenses. Hence they have no choice but AFDC to survive.

While poor should not be equated with black (in 1983 whites constituted 68 percent of all poor and blacks 28 percent), blacks are represented on AFDC rolls in disproportionate numbers. Only 12 percent of the total population, they constitute 43 percent of all AFDC families. Unlike white families, black families have increasingly become headed by single female parents. In 1960, 8 percent of white families were headed by women, rising to 12 percent in 1980. During this time, the percentage of black female-headed families nearly doubled, from 22 percent to 40 percent. Why are so many AFDC families black, and why are nearly all of them headed by single women?

Here the feminization of poverty and racial discrimination have combined with other factors to push black mothers onto AFDC. To understand one of these factors, we have to look at what has happened to black men. The majority of black mothers on AFDC are young, under thirty years old. If we examine black men, aged twenty to twenty-four, in 1980, we will find them:

| | |
|---|---|
| Unemployed | 22.2% |
| Intermittently employed | 19.8 |
| Involuntarily employed part-time | 7.1 |
| Working for marginal jobs | 18.3 |
| Working full-time with below-poverty wages | 5.0 |
| Total | 72.4% |

Statistically it is impossible for even a third of all black women in this age group to be married to employed black men earning above poverty incomes. (For white men aged twenty to twenty-four, in terms of unemployment and underemployment, the rate is only 36.6 percent.)

The crisis of "losing ground" is not simply dependency on welfare; it is the feminization of poverty, unemployment, and low wages. These three problems became increasingly severe in the seventies and eighties due to enormous economic changes and developments.

During the last twenty years, the American economy has been relocated internally in a significant way as corporations moved their plants and offices from the central cities to the suburbs. If we examine the metropolitan population by race in terms of residence, we find that 71 percent of blacks live in central cities whereas 66 percent of whites live in suburbs. This racial pattern of residency means that whether you are employed is determined to a large extent by where you live. Chicago illustrates the dynamic interaction among the relocation of production, unemployment, and welfare. During the 1960s, Chicago lost 229,000 jobs and gained 290,000 welfare recipients, while its suburbs gained 500,000 jobs. Trapped in inner cities, blacks have found themselves geographically isolated from the places of employment.

The movement of jobs from the city to the suburbs is only part of the picture. Plant shutdowns in the eastern and midwestern regions of the country reflected the movement of production to the U.S. Southwest and also overseas. The "deindustrialization of America" has had a severe impact on minority workers. In Illinois, for example, minorities represented 20 percent of the workers in 2,380 firms shut down between 1975 and 1978, which were surveyed by the Illinois Advisory Committee to the U.S. Civil Rights Commission. Statewide minorities constituted only 14 percent of the work force. Thus, minorities suffered a disproportionate share of the burden created by plant closings. Corporations have been relocating much of their production outside the United States, developing low-wage industrial work forces in Mexico, Taiwan, Korea, and other Third World countries. Some 22 million jobs were lost between 1969 and 1976 due to plant closings and out-migrations of production. Consequently the need for domestic industrial labor has diminished, and unemployment has soared. A study, completed in 1986 by the Congressional Office of Technology Assessment, found that 11.5 million workers lost jobs because of plant shutdowns or relocations from 1979 to 1984, and that only 60 percent of them got new jobs in that period. Of the displaced black workers, only 42 percent of those who had held their previous jobs at least three years were able to find new employment.

Furthermore, the economy has been transformed from a manufacturing to a service economy, and this shift has altered the gender composition of the work force. In the last fifteen years, more than 70 percent of all new jobs have been in low-wage sales and service employment. The expanding area of employment has been in the so-called female clerical and secretarial occupations. Two-thirds of the jobs created in the last ten years were filled by women.

These macroeconomic developments, rather than the growth of the welfare state, help to explain why the American working class has been "losing ground" and why so many people are mired in poverty. They also reveal why the current crisis of black America is so profoundly destructive. Essential to the work force in the past, blacks in large numbers, especially men, have been rendered superfluous as workers in the present. In short, the structural context of the American economy helps to explain why the welfare class has swollen in such distressing numbers and why such a large proportion of the underclass is black.

What is the solution to the crisis of "losing ground"? Murray proposes the restoration of individualism, the "scrapping" of social welfare programs, and the forcing of poor people into the labor market. His is a Hobbesian solution. Murray emphasizes punishment: "Do not work, and we will make sure that your existence is so uncomfortable that any job will be preferable to it."

But Murray's solution will not work, for it addresses the symptoms of the problem rather than the sources of poverty, welfare dependency, and inequality located in the structure of the American economy. The key to the reduction of the welfare class and inequality in society is not to punish people for being poor. The solution is to move from a "zero-sum" society to an "increasing-sum" society. To do this requires us to slow down and reverse the "deindustrialization" of America, and to increase the numbers of jobs and the rewards for working, specifically to raise wages, to make it possible for people to subsist, even live decently, on what they earn.

Behind what Murray terms "white popular wisdom" is a philosophy, a culture of meritocracy. This perspective is widely shared in American society. Essentially, it is grounded on the belief that men and women should be defined as individuals and be responsible for themselves. They should be judged (rewarded or punished) on the basis of individual merit.

This culture of meritocracy springs out of much of America's history. Protestantism, carried here by the early English settlers, contained within it a belief in individual responsibility, and the American Revolution established a new polity based on the principle that its citizens should be self-governing. Authority, henceforth, would be located within the individual self. But this new government of individualism, while it offered freedom from external authority, also constituted an "iron cage." In this cage, the individual would rule himself or herself, elevating rationality and imposing self-control. In this cage, the individual would be autonomous, separated from community.

During the nineteenth century there emerged two other iron cages—the corporate iron cage and the demonic iron cage. The second iron cage represented what Max Weber described as the tremendous economic cosmos of modern bureaucratic corporate capitalism. It radically transformed nineteenth-century America from a wilderness, farms, and small towns into a new world of factories and cities. The third iron cage was America's violent expansionism westward—this country's movement across Indian lands, its war against Mexico, and its thrust toward empire in Asia, culminating in the Spanish-American War and the annexation of the Philippines.

In the twentieth century, the three iron cages seem to have come together, constituting what can be called a fourth iron cage. We still do not clearly see or understand fully this latest cage. The tremendous economic cosmos has expanded beyond Weber's wildest imagination. Corporations owning each other not only dominate America but have global reach, with industrial work forces located all over the world. Corporations owning each other produce not only services and goods but also information for our society. Corporations owning each other design triggering devices for nuclear warheads and also give us our news. In this fourth iron cage, American workers find themselves struggling to find work in what has become an international labor market, competing with low-wage workers in Taiwan and Korea, forced into low-paying jobs here, or into unemployment, or into welfare.

Our very belief of individualism and our very culture of meritocracy render remote the possibility of freeing ourselves from this fourth iron cage. They only isolate us from each other. Our "habits of the heart" of individualism have led to a concentration of the self and a fragmentized society. And within this fourth iron cage, we find a certain irony: meritocracy itself, proclaiming the ideal of equality of opportunity, is denying its possibility for many Americans.

But, if we look again at America's history, we can find other habits of the heart—of community, social responsibility, and a collective spirit. We find them in Bacon's Rebellion of 1676, when the poor of Virginia or the "giddy multitude"—black slaves and white indentured servants—joined together in revolt against the planter class. We also find them in the Populist movement of the 1890s, when black and white farmers struggled together against the railroads and the banks; the New Deal and the Congress of Industrial Organizations of the 1930s; and the civil rights movement of the sixties. These habits of the heart of community expressed a vision of a collective polity and called for the government to intervene, to act for the community.

Today, we seem to need to recover and to practice, more than ever before, the habits of the heart of community. Otherwise we will continue to find our dreams deferred. And we ask, as did the black poet Langston Hughes:

> *What happens to a dream deferred?*
> *Does it dry up*
> *Like a raisin in the sun . . .*
> *Or does it explode?*

Like F. Scott Fitzgerald's Dutch sailors over three centuries ago, many Americans still gaze upon this land as the "fresh, green breast of the new world," as a place of possibilities for all. Yet we find our dreams deferred, carried, like "boats against the current," back "ceaselessly into the past."

# Puerto Ricans and the Underclass Debate

MARTA TIENDA

Despite the appreciable drop in poverty since 1960, recent empirical work on the economic status of minorities has documented persisting and in some instances widening differentials in poverty and economic well-being according to race and national origin. Among Hispanics, between 1970 and 1985 Puerto Ricans experienced a sharp deterioration in economic well-being while Mexicans experienced modest, and Cubans substantial, improvement in economic status.

A few indicators illustrate the extent to which economic disparities between the three major Hispanic populations have widened. Puerto Rican family income declined by 7.4 percent in real terms during the 1970s and by an additional 18.0 percent between 1979 and 1984. Mexican and Cuban real family incomes increased during the 1970s, then fell after 1980; but the decline for neither group approached the magnitude experienced by Puerto Ricans. Unlike that of Puerto Ricans, black real family income rose gradually during the 1970s, then fell 14.0 percent following the recession of the early 1980s. While real family incomes of all population groups—minority and non-minority alike—fell between 1979 and 1984, the decline was steepest among minorities, Puerto Ricans in particular.

Equally disturbing are findings that family income concentration has increased for Puerto Ricans since 1970. The share of Puerto Rican families with income below one-quarter of the median income of whites rose from 11 percent in 1960 to 15 percent in 1970, 26 percent in 1980, and 33 percent in 1985. A similar pattern was not discerned among Mexicans or Cubans, indicating that Puerto Ricans are diverging from other Hispanics. William Julius Wilson and others claim that black family incomes have become bifurcated, with increasing shares of families concentrated at the upper and lower tails of the income distribution. So severe has the decline in Puerto Rican economic status been that this minority group has fared worse than blacks in the 1980s, a reversal of the situation prevailing during the 1960s. This generalization obtains whether based on national data or those for New York City, which houses the single largest concentration of Puerto Ricans.

Although the reasons for the measured increases in racial and economic inequality are not well understood, there is a growing consensus that three interrelated sets of circumstances are involved: (1) uneven changes in family composition and labor market position according to race and national origin; (2) a heavier toll of cyclical downturns on the job prospects of minority workers; and (3) the persisting significance of race in allocating social position. By themselves, these factors do not explain why some minority groups, such as blacks and Puerto Ricans, have lost more economic ground than others, such as Cubans, Mexicans, or Native Americans, nor do they enable us to predict the future course or magnitude of inequality.

Signs of economic distress among Puerto Ricans have fostered considerable speculation that Puerto Ricans have become part of the urban underclass, but the available evidence is more suggestive than conclusive. Answering this question in the affirmative requires, at a minimum, longitudinal data showing that extreme economic deprivation is both chronic and concentrated among a segment of the Puerto Rican population; that chronic deprivation is accompanied by labor market detachment; and that both conditions are sustained by social and spatial isolation from mainstream institutions and activities. Although inadequate for demonstrating the coincidence of these three conditions for Puerto Ricans, repeated

From THE ANNALS of the American Academy of Political and Social Science, v. 501 (Jan. 1989), pp. 105–119. Reprinted by permission.

cross-sectional census surveys can shed some light on the emerging debate about whether and to what extent the deteriorating economic status of Puerto Rican families is accompanied by one form of social dislocation, namely, labor market detachment.

One objective is to examine the labor market position of Puerto Rican men in comparison with that of Mexicans and Cubans. A second objective is to document the influence of structural factors, namely, ethnic labor market concentration and ethnic job queues, on Puerto Ricans' earnings. The working hypothesis guiding the analysis is that structural factors—to wit, rapidly falling employment opportunities in jobs where Puerto Ricans traditionally have worked, and the concentration of Puerto Ricans in areas experiencing severe economic dislocation—are major factors accounting for the impoverishment of this minority group.

The following section sets forth theoretical issues bearing on the significance of national origin in producing and maintaining labor market inequality. The next sections compare the labor market standing of Mexican, Puerto Rican, and Cuban men from 1970 to 1985, emphasizing the uniqueness of the Puerto Rican labor force withdrawal process both in timing and magnitude, and then assess the economic consequences of ethnic job queues and ethnic labor market concentration on earnings. The concluding section discusses these empirical findings in light of growing speculation that Puerto Ricans are becoming part of the urban underclass.

## THEORETICAL CONSIDERATIONS

Evidence from cross-sectional data suggests that the declining economic status of Puerto Ricans can be traced both to poor economic performance and to the low stocks of human capital possessed by Puerto Rican workers. Although a substantial literature documents the importance of education for labor market success, the low educational achievement of Mexicans challenges the completeness of the human-capital explanations. Mexicans have not experienced declines in labor market standing and economic well-being comparable to those of Puerto Ricans, even though their educational levels are similar.

That a steep increase in poverty was not experienced by all Hispanic groups raises questions about the salience of structural factors in

restricting these effects to Puerto Ricans. My case is that the weakened labor market position of Puerto Ricans and their consequent impoverishment have roots in their placement at the bottom of an ethnic hiring queue coupled with residential concentration in a region that experienced severe economic decline and industrial restructuring after 1970. Each of these ideas is elaborated in the following pages.

## ETHNIC HIRING QUEUES

The significance of ethnicity for the labor market stratification of minority workers depends not only on local employment conditions but also on how individual ethnic traits circumscribe choices, how ethnic traits are evaluated in the marketplace, and how ethnic traits are used to organize the labor market. If national origin is used as a criterion to define and maintain job queues, then the economic costs and benefits of residential concentration will derive not only from opportunities to interact with members of like ethnicity but also from the role of national origin in channeling minority workers to particular categories of jobs.

The viability of ethnic hiring queues, however, is related to patterns of ethnic geographical concentration. Stanley Lieberson, who succinctly summarized the ecological foundations of racial or ethnic occupational differentiation, claimed that a discriminatory hiring queue results when employers activate their prejudices and preferentially hire workers on the basis of ethnic traits rather than market skills. Two aspects of Lieberson's queuing premises have direct implications for the ensuing analyses. One is that the job configuration of groups will vary in accordance with their share of the labor force in a given labor market. Second, because of the existence of ethnic hiring queues, shifts in unemployment will be highest for the group or groups at the bottom of the queue in the event of a wave of unemployment. This interpretation appears to be consistent with the Puerto Rican experience after the mid-1970s.

Lieberson's argument has considerable appeal for explaining the growing economic inequality among Hispanic workers. For example, Mexicans have been preferred workers in agricultural jobs at least since the mid-1800s. While the incomes of agricultural workers are low compared with those in other low-skilled jobs, when evaluated against the alternative of unemployment or nonparticipation in the labor force, agricultural work is preferable because it at least ensures some earnings. Puerto Ricans, unlike Mexicans, never have been preferred laborers for specific jobs, with the possible exception of women in garment and textile industries. Unionization initially protected textile and garment workers, but the massive industrial restructuring in the Northeast, which has resulted in the elimination of many unskilled and unionized jobs, has dimmed the employment prospects of all Puerto Ricans, including youths and mature men.

Viewed in this way, the declining economic status of Puerto Ricans may have resulted partly from the rapid decline in the types of jobs in which they were disproportionately concentrated and partly from a loss in relative earning power owing to low stocks of human capital in a market whose demand for labor increased in some sectors while it decreased in others. That Cuban men did not have a similar experience, despite their disproportionate representation in two of the same labor markets as Puerto Ricans—in New York and New Jersey—suggests either that Cubans are ranked higher in an employment queue or that Cuban workers displaced by the employment-restructuring processes were more successful finding alternative employment by moving from New York and New Jersey to Miami.

## LABOR MARKET CONCENTRATION

The burgeoning literature on structural aspects of labor market outcomes has identified both positive and negative effects of ethnic residential concentration on employment outcomes. For present purposes it suffices to note that positive effects of minority labor market concentration are consistent with an overflow or power thesis: the former would derive from the spillover of minorities into higher-status jobs and/or the reorganization of labor markets along ethnic lines, while the latter would stem from greater political leverage of minority groups as a function of increasing group size. Negative effects would be consistent with the discrimination and subordination theses, whereby minorities are systematically excluded from jobs or relegated to the least desirable jobs. This process would be accentuated by the demarcation of hiring queues along ethnic lines.

These ideas concerning how ethnic density and ethnic typing of jobs influence employment outcomes suggest two working hypotheses.

First, I hypothesize that the unequal labor market experiences of Mexican, Puerto Rican, and Cuban men during the 1970s reflect their unequal placement in a hiring queue, with Cubans at the top of the Hispanic queue and Puerto Ricans at the bottom. Second, the disadvantaged labor market status of Puerto Ricans results partly from the unequal benefits of minority labor market concentration reaped by each group. These ideas will be empirically evaluated here, after a brief review of the extent of labor market detachment experienced by Puerto Ricans since 1970.

## LABOR MARKET DETACHMENT IN COMPARATIVE PERSPECTIVE

Failure to participate in the labor market, along with social isolation and persisting deprivation, is a defining feature of the urban underclass. Although national data on chronicity of poverty and labor force nonparticipation do not exist for Puerto Ricans, annual Current Population Survey data permit an initial foray into questions of labor market detachment and withdrawal. For this purpose, Hispanic men were classified into three categories based on their employment status at the time of, and five years prior to, the 1975, 1980, and 1985 Current Population Surveys: the stable active category consists of persons, including the unemployed, who were in the labor force at both points in time; persons who were in the labor force at the beginning of the five-year period but not at the end, or vice versa, are classified in the unstable active category; the stable inactive category includes persons who were out of the labor force, and not looking for work, at both the beginning and the end of the period.

While less than ideal for evaluating the hypothesis of labor market detachment because these cross-sectional data do not represent the continuous employment history of the same individuals over the entire time span, results summarized in Table 1—first row for each panel—clearly show a steeper rise in labor market instability and incomplete withdrawal from the work force among Puerto Ricans. Whereas the category of stable inactive was virtually nonexistent prior to the onset of economic decline in the mid-1970s, the share of unstable employment rose between 1970 and 1985, a period characterized by slow growth and two major recessions.

The share of men experiencing unstable

Table 1 Selected Characteristics of Adult Hispanic Men Aged 25–64 by Labor Force Experience (Means or percentages)

| | Period and Work Experience Category* | | | | | | | | |
| | 1970–75 | | | 1975–80 | | | 1980–85 | | |
| | Stable active | Unstable active | Stable inactive | Stable active | Unstable active | Stable inactive | Stable active | Unstable active | Stable inactive |
|---|---|---|---|---|---|---|---|---|---|
| Mexicans | | | | | | | | | |
| Category total (percentage) | 91.0% | 9.1% | 0.0% | 91.5% | 7.8% | 0.8% | 89.8% | 9.0% | 1.1% |
| Education (years) | 8.5 | 7.4 | NA | 9.3 | 8.6 | 7.1 | 9.5 | 7.6 | 8.2 |
| (s.d.)† | (4.5) | (4.1) | — | (4.5) | (4.7) | (4.9) | (4.3) | (4.6) | (3.4) |
| Family income (1974 dollars) | $8,015 | $5,935 | — | $8,890 | $5,601 | $4,849 | $8,031 | $5,579 | $4,484 |
| (s.d)† | (4,947) | (4,411) | — | (5,602) | (5,188) | (3,266) | (5,650) | (4,522) | (3,438) |
| Poverty rate (percentage) | 15.5% | 27.5% | — | 9.9% | 38.3% | 34.5% | 17.7% | 39.5% | 44.1% |
| [N]‡ | [652] | [67] | [0] | [1773] | [157] | [18] | [1814] | [176] | [24] |
| Puerto Ricans | | | | | | | | | |
| Category total (percentage) | 86.8% | 13.2% | 0.0% | 84.3% | 13.4% | 2.2% | 74.8% | 19.3% | 5.9% |
| Education (years) | 9.2 | 5.3 | NA | 10.1 | 7.5 | 5.1 | 10.8 | 6.9 | 8.0 |
| (s.d.)† | (3.6) | (3.2) | — | (3.7) | (3.8) | (5.5) | (3.5) | (4.4) | (4.3) |
| Family income (1979 dollars) | $7,752 | $4,750 | — | $8,453 | $4,343 | $4,425 | $7,908 | $3,956 | $4,293 |
| (s.d.)† | (4,287) | (3,721) | — | (5,280) | (5,951) | (2,360) | (5,107) | (3,574) | (4,715) |
| Poverty rate (percentage) | 11.6% | 49.4% | — | 11.1% | 65.1% | 34.1% | 12.2% | 49.2% | 46.7% |
| [N]‡ | [152] | [24] | [0] | [287] | [49] | [9] | [320] | [69] | [22] |
| Cubans | | | | | | | | | |
| Category total (percentage) | 95.8% | 4.2% | 0.0% | 95.7% | 4.3% | 0.0% | 90.0% | 6.8% | 3.2% |
| Education (years) | 11.1 | 8.2 | NA | 11.2 | 10.5 | — | 11.3 | 8.8 | 10.9 |
| (s.d.)† | (4.0) | (3.7) | — | (3.6) | (4.6) | — | (3.9) | (4.0) | (3.9) |
| Family income (1984 dollars) | $9,565 | $4,280 | — | $10,199 | $8,283 | — | $10,499 | $3,656 | $8,152 |
| (s.d.)† | (5,427) | (2,581) | — | (5,963) | (5,553) | — | (7,829) | (3,383) | (4,732) |
| Poverty rate (percentage) | 5.5% | 22.3% | — | 6.4% | 8.3% | — | 5.3% | 51.2% | 0.0% |
| [N]‡ | [114] | [5] | [0] | [199] | [9] | [0] | [227] | [14] | [7] |

Note: Unless otherwise indicated, the figures in this table are weighted to approximate population parameters.
*Stable active: in labor force at beginning and end of interval; unstable active: changed labor force status during interval; stable inactive: out of labor force at beginning and end of interval.
†Standard deviation.
‡Unweighted sample size.
Source: Current Population Survey, standardized files, 1975, 1980, 1985.

employment hovered around 8 to 9 percent among Mexicans and 4 to 7 percent among Cubans. For Puerto Ricans it was not only considerably higher than that for either Mexicans or Cubans throughout the period but also rose more steeply between the 1975–80 and the 1980–85 intervals, from 13 to 19 percentage points. An increase in unstable employment experiences is significant because it appears to be a precursor to complete withdrawal. By 1985, the share of chronic detachment among Puerto Ricans had reached nearly 6 percent, compared to 1 percent for Mexicans and 3 percent for Cubans.

The notable rise in Cuban labor market instability and withdrawal during the 1980–85 interval partly reflects the presence of a large segment of low-skilled immigrants whose labor market integration process was more difficult than that of earlier Cuban immigrants. A similar period-immigration-effect cannot be claimed for Puerto Ricans, yet among them labor market withdrawal was even more pronounced. Moreover, the lower levels of market withdrawal and detachment among Mexicans, who also have become increasingly diversified by a high influx of immigrants since 1970, challenge any simplistic explanations that international migration or, in the case of Puerto Ricans, circular migration—between island and mainland—was largely responsible for the observed instability and withdrawal.

Table 1 also provides information about social and economic characteristics of the men according to employment-experience categories. Although the sample characteristics are weighted to approximate those of the total population, the small sample sizes warrant cautious comparisons between some categories, particularly for Cubans. Nevertheless, the contrasts between Mexicans and Puerto Ricans are striking and instructive.

That labor market position is directly associated with economic well-being is clearly apparent in the poverty and income data, which show substantially higher poverty risks for men whose labor market experience was characterized by instability or inactivity. Of course, stable employment does not always preclude poverty, because a share of the poor are full-time, year-round workers whose poverty status derives from low wages, but the incidence of poverty for the stable active experience category is considerably less than for workers in the other two categories.

While real family incomes declined for most groups between 1980 and 1985, they did so differentially according to employment category and national origin. Cuban men illustrate one pattern: essentially, stably employed men did not experience a decrease in real family incomes throughout the period, although the rate of growth slowed during the early 1980s, from roughly 6.6 percent for the 1975–80 period to 2.9 percent for the 1980–85 interval.

In sharp contrast to the Cuban experience, family incomes of Mexicans and Puerto Ricans who were stably employed during the 1975–80 period rose roughly 11 and 9 percent in real terms, while the family incomes of men unstably employed—unstable active—fell by 5.6

percent and 8.6 percent, respectively. During the 1980–85 interval, among Mexicans real incomes of those stably employed fell 9.7 percent, incomes of the unstably employed were virtually constant, and those of chronically inactive men dropped substantially, by 7.5 percent. Puerto Ricans fared somewhat worse in the 1980s: family incomes fell 6.4 percent among men stably employed, 9.0 percent among those unstably employed, and 3.0 percent among those who were out of the labor force continuously. Thus the declining economic status of Puerto Ricans appears to be rooted in two factors: the rising shares of prime-age men with unstable employment and chronic inactivity, and sharper declines in the incomes of those with unstable labor market experiences. The latter may contribute to the withdrawal process, as chronically low earnings and unstable work lead to total discouragement and alienation from the market.

Arguments about the importance of education for labor market success also find some support in the tabulations reported in Table 1. For all groups, labor force withdrawal and detachment were associated with lower stocks of education. The average educational attainment of Mexican and Puerto Rican men was roughly similar at the beginning of the period, 8.4 and 8.6 years, respectively, but over time, as the average schooling stocks for these groups rose, differentials within experience categories increased, favoring Puerto Ricans over Mexicans among those stably employed, and Mexicans over Puerto Ricans among those unstably employed or chronically out of the labor force. If human capital were the major determinant of labor market withdrawal and detachment, then the shares of Mexicans with unstable and inactive work trajectories would be greater than those of similarly classified Puerto Ricans. In fact, just the opposite occurred. This justifies a search for structural explanations, which is the topic of the following section.

## JOB QUEUES AND DECLINING LABOR MARKET OPPORTUNITIES

The theoretical and substantive issues raised earlier focus on how residence in ethnic labor markets—that is, whether individual workers reside in labor markets with high levels of ethnic concentration—and ethnic job segmentation—whether jobs were ethnic typed, Anglo typed, or not ethnically differentiated—

operate to stratify the annual earnings of Hispanic-origin men. The data used for this part of the analysis are from the 5 percent sample of the Public Use Microdata Samples of the 1980 census.

My arguments about the influence of ethnic concentration and ethnic segmentation of jobs in shaping the economic opportunities and outcomes for Hispanic workers integrate two structural attributes of labor markets—the ethnic segmentation of jobs and the ethnic composition of markets—and assess their influence on logged annual earnings. I evaluate these premises by regressing the log of annual earnings of Mexicans, Puerto Ricans, and Cubans on measures of ethnic labor market concentration and incumbency in an ethnic job queue.

Table 2 reports descriptive statistics for samples of Mexican, Puerto Rican, and Cuban men who worked during the year prior to the 1980 census. The rank ordering of the groups according to average annual earnings shows Cubans well above Mexicans—23 percent higher—and Puerto Ricans—30 percent higher—while a

Table 2  Demographic and Labor Market Characteristics of Hispanic Men Aged 25–64, 1980

|  | Mexicans | Puerto Ricans | Cubans |
|---|---|---|---|
| Dependent variable |  |  |  |
| Annual earnings (logged) | 9.23 | 9.18 | 9.43 |
| (s.d.) | (.89) | (.87) | (.82) |
| Annual mean earnings | $13,342 | $12,587 | $16,368 |
|  | (9,414) | (8,647) | (13,069) |
| Individual characteristics |  |  |  |
| Education (percentage) |  |  |  |
| Did not complete high school | 62.3% | 59.9% | 41.2% |
| High school graduate | 33.3% | 36.1% | 40.9% |
| Some college | 4.4% | 4.0% | 17.9% |
| Age (years) | 39.3 | 39.5 | 46.1 |
| (s.d.) | (10.6) | (10.1) | (10.0) |
| Good English (percentage) | 78.0% | 82.7% | 63.6% |
| Foreign born (percentage) | 36.3% | 77.3% | 93.3% |
| Work disabled (percentage) | 5.0% | 5.8% | 3.5% |
| Weeks worked | 46.2 | 46.7 | 48.1 |
| (s.d.) | (11.0) | (10.8) | (9.2) |
| Average hours worked weekly | 41.7 | 40.0 | 42.6 |
| (s.d.) | (10.2) | (10.0) | (11.1) |
| Household head (percentage) | 85.2% | 79.6% | 89.6% |
| Married (percentage) | 81.3% | 71.7% | 81.8% |
| Market characteristics |  |  |  |
| Ethnic job queue (percentage) |  |  |  |
| Ethnic typed | 13.0% | 18.0% | 13.0% |
| Anglo typed | 4.3% | 6.6% | 14.4% |
| Nontyped | 82.7% | 75.4% | 72.6% |
| Concentrated area (percentage) | 85.9% | 83.2% | 84.4% |
| Area wage rate | $7.21 | $7.88 | $7.37 |
|  | (0.97) | (0.72) | (0.61) |
| Area unemployment rate | 6.19 | 6.69 | 5.66 |
|  | (1.98) | (1.23) | (1.30) |
| [N] | [5,726] | [5,908] | [3,895] |

Note: The sample includes approximately half of the men aged 25–64 who self-reported their race or national origin as Mexican, Puerto Rican, or Cuban. Restricting the lower end of the age distribution to 25 rather than 16 ensured that most respondents had completed school at the time of the census, hence school enrollment would not limit labor force participation. Additional restrictions on the sample excluded individuals who met the following conditions: (1) never worked, or were out of the labor force continuously during the five years prior to the census; (2) were enrolled in school or in the military in either 1975 or 1980; or (3) resided outside the United States in 1975. In this table, standard deviations appear in parentheses; they are descriptive statistics based on a sample with nonzero earnings in 1979.

*Source:* Public Use Microdata Samples, A-File, 1980.

difference of less than 6 percent separates the latter two groups. Equally striking are the educational gaps according to national origin. Beyond the average schooling differentials reported in Table 1, these data show appreciable discrepancies in the credentials held by Hispanic men. At one extreme, roughly two-thirds of Mexican and Puerto Rican adult men had completed less than 12 years of formal schooling; at the other extreme, about 4 percent had attended college, in contrast with 18 percent of Cuban men. Mexicans and Puerto Ricans thus appear quite similar in terms of human-capital characteristics as well as hours and weeks of labor supply. Only in English proficiency do Cubans appear to be disadvantaged relative to Mexicans and Puerto Ricans, reflecting the shorter immigration history of the Cuban population. The national-origin groups also differ in terms of their family status: among men aged 25–65, Puerto Ricans were less likely to be married and to be household heads than either Mexicans or Cubans.

My argument about the influence of structural factors in explaining the weakened labor market position of Puerto Ricans finds some support in the summary market characteristics. Puerto Ricans' residential configuration afforded them the highest unemployment rates and the highest average wage rates. Cubans, on the other hand, resided in labor markets with relatively lower unemployment—a difference of nearly one percentage point, on average, compared to Puerto Ricans—while the unemployment rates where Mexicans resided were between the Puerto Rican and Cuban extremes.

Space restrictions preclude a full discussion of the implications of market conditions for the labor supply decisions of Hispanic men. Suffice it to note that, in a separate analysis, area unemployment rates exerted a significant negative effect, and average area wage rates a significant positive effect, on the labor force decisions of Puerto Ricans, while for Cubans and Mexicans these effects were essentially zero. This appears to indicate that the labor market behavior of Puerto Ricans is more sensitive to labor market conditions than that of either Cubans or Mexicans, but why this is so is less obvious. Moreover, among those individuals who do secure employment, uneven placement in the job queue further weakens their labor market position, leaving them vulnerable to economic cycles and ethnic prejudices.

Support for this proposition is found in Table 2, which shows that Puerto Ricans were more likely to work in ethnic-typed jobs than either Mexicans or Cubans, and in Table 3, which shows that Puerto Rican incumbents of ethnic-typed jobs were penalized 17 percent relative to their statistically equivalent counterparts engaged in nontyped jobs. For Mexicans, the earnings penalty for incumbency in ethnic-typed jobs was somewhat lower, roughly 12 percent, while incumbency in Anglo-typed jobs sustained economic rewards 19 percent above those received by incumbents of nontyped jobs. These effects are net of individual productivity characteristics—for example, education, English proficiency, disability status, age, and the conditional probability of being in the wage sample. Puerto Ricans, however, did not reap additional earnings bonuses from incumbency in Anglo-typed jobs.

Equally interesting are the earnings consequences of labor market conditions. Whereas both Mexicans and Cubans gained significant financial rewards from residence in high-wage areas—13 percent and 3 percent, respectively—no such benefit accrued to Puerto Ricans. Moreover, residence in labor markets with high concentrations of the respective nationality groups translated into an economic liability for each group, but less for Puerto Ricans than for either Mexicans or Cubans. This suggests that residential concentration does not increase the ability of these groups to protect ethnic workers via political leverage derived from group size, nor does group concentration result in massive spillover into high-status and well-paying jobs. That Mexicans and Cubans were more residentially concentrated than Puerto Ricans in 1980 partly explains why the effects of concentration were more pronounced for them, but it is also conceivable that discrimination has intensified because of the loss of low-skilled jobs in New York City coupled with the growing presence of Dominican and Colombian immigrants willing to work in jobs that offer low wages and poor working conditions.

Substantively, the findings in Table 3 suggest that the process of channeling Puerto Ricans into so-called Puerto Rican jobs, coupled with the absence of earnings bonuses for securing nontyped jobs, reinforces the low earnings of Puerto Ricans who do manage to secure employment. But, as the analyses in Table 1 show, since 1975 increasing shares of adult Puerto Rican men have not secured jobs, and residence in high-concentration areas has not improved the chances of employment for Hispanics, irrespective of national origin.

Table 3 Effects of Ethnic Job Queues on Earnings of Hispanic Men Aged 25–64, 1980 (Metric coefficients)

| | Mexicans | Puerto Ricans | Cubans |
|---|---|---|---|
| Ethnic job queue | | | |
| Ethnic typed | − .116* | − .170* | − .257* |
| | (.029) | (.025) | (.033) |
| Anglo typed | .193* | .067 | .112* |
| | (.048) | (.039) | (.031) |
| Labor market | | | |
| Area wage | .126* | .016 | .035* |
| | (.010) | (.014) | (.018) |
| Concentrated area | − .172* | − .079* | − .180* |
| | (.029) | (.027) | (.031) |
| Education | | | |
| High school graduate | − .253* | − .068 | − .238* |
| | (.050) | (.064) | (.037) |
| Did not complete high school | − .412* | − .183* | − .283* |
| | (.052) | (.070) | (.045) |
| Age | .042* | .032* | .025* |
| | (.008) | (.008) | (.010) |
| Age$^2$ | − .0004* | − .0003* | − .0002 |
| | (.0001) | (.0001) | (.0001) |
| Good English | .185* | .126* | .206* |
| | (.027) | (.026) | (.026) |
| Foreign born | − .029 | − .080* | − .070* |
| | (.024) | (.024) | (.044) |
| Work disabled | − .135* | − .192* | − .200* |
| | (.045) | (.042) | (.060) |
| Lambda[a] | .120* | .096* | .083* |
| | (.015) | (.014) | (.016) |
| Constant | 5.552 | 6.330 | 6.708 |
| $R^2$ | .334 | .300 | .336 |
| [N] | [5,726] | [5,908] | [3,895] |

Note: Effects of ethnic job queues are adjusted for the effects of weeks worked and usual hours worked. Standard errors are in parentheses. The sample includes approximately half of the men aged 25–64 who self-reported their race or national origin as Mexican, Puerto Rican, or Cuban. Restricting the lower end of the age distribution to 25 rather than 16 ensured that most respondents had completed school at the time of the census, hence school enrollment would not limit labor force participation. Additional restrictions on the sample excluded individuals who met the following conditions: (1) never worked, or were out of the labor force continuously during the five years prior to the census; (2) were enrolled in school or in the military in either 1975 or 1980; or (3) resided outside the United States in 1975.
[a]Inverse of Mills ratio to correct for self-selection into the wage sample.
*Significant at the 95 percent level.
Source: Public Use Microdata Samples, A-File, 1980.

## DISCUSSION

During the 1960s and 1970s it was common-place to attribute the existence of racial and economic inequality to discrimination and to direct policy initiatives aiming toward equal employment opportunity and affirmative action. The experience of the 1980s, however, has reaffirmed that a healthy economy is a necessary, albeit insufficient, condition for reducing inequality. The economic experiences of Puerto Ricans provide stark testimony concerning the deleterious consequence of economic decline.

Although discrimination may still be a major factor accounting for the disadvantaged economic status of Puerto Ricans, it does not address the issue of why the economic status of Cubans and especially Mexicans has not followed suit. While not denying the importance of prejudice in maintaining socioeconomic inequality along racial and ethnic lines, a structural interpretation is consistent with the uneven regional effects of economic growth and decline that occurred during the late 1970s and early 1980s. But a simple Rustbelt-Sunbelt dichotomy set against the backdrop of major recessions also is inadequate to explain the impoverishment of Puerto Ricans; their increasing labor market instability and withdrawal (Table 1) can only partly be understood in these terms.

Additional and equally important insights into the declining economic status of Puerto Ricans obtain from the results showing that the existence of ethnic labor market divisions also places constraints on the earnings frontiers of Hispanic workers, and Puerto Ricans in particular. This is evident in results (Table 3) showing strong negative penalties for incumbency in Puerto Rican jobs, and no additional compensation or bonus for the small share of Puerto Ricans who manage to secure Anglo-typed jobs. Yet these results also raise many questions about the economic significance of ethnic job queues, which appear to operate differently for Mexicans and Cubans. While both groups benefit financially from incumbency in Anglo-typed jobs, the share of each group able to secure these better-paying jobs differs (Table 2). Moreover, both groups are penalized for incumbency in ethnic-typed jobs, Cubans more so than Mexicans.

On balance, the empirical results presented are more suggestive than conclusive as to the importance of structural factors in explaining the declining economic status of Puerto Ricans. While the evidence of labor force withdrawal has aroused speculation about the emergence of an underclass among Hispanics, largely concentrated among Puerto Ricans, the absence of longitudinal data prevents examination of the duration of labor market detachment.

My results place the Puerto Rican experience in a comparative perspective and emphasize the promise of a structural interpretation of labor force withdrawal. While evidence of growing labor market instability and withdrawal is consistent with one of the premises of the persisting poverty syndrome, further scrutiny of the concentration of labor market withdrawal and social isolation is needed before concluding that Puerto Ricans have become part of the urban underclass. Priority issues worth investigating include establishing whether increased labor market competition from immigrants—Dominicans and Colombians in particular—has exacerbated the economic problems of Puerto Ricans and the extent to which industrial restructuring has been responsible for the labor market withdrawal of Puerto Rican men. Beyond these structurally focused lines of inquiry, additional study of labor market trajectories is essential to determine whether the patterns of nonparticipation based on repeated cross sections represent the accumulation of chronic spells and permanent withdrawal among a segment of the total population, or whether the observed increase in nonparticipation among Puerto Ricans reflects the increasing prevalence of short spells of nonparticipation among the total population. Until these questions are satisfactorily answered, discussions about the development of a Puerto Rican urban underclass will be largely speculative.

# The Burden of Support:
# Young Latinos in an Aging Society

DAVID E. HAYES-BAUTISTA, WERNER O. SCHINK, AND JORGE CHAPA

## CALIFORNIA IN 2030:
## THE WORST-CASE SCENARIO

In the same way that a physical model of a bridge provides a testing ground for different combinations of design and materials, a scenario allows us to model society in the future. We offer here some grounded speculation about the future of society, given two very important trends occurring simultaneously: the aging of the well-educated, Anglo Baby Boom generation; and the growth of the much younger, less-educated Latino population. The worst-case scenario below is designed to be extreme.

### The Scenario

By 1995 the growth of the Latino population in California was viewed with growing concern by the Anglo population. Spreading out from such areas of concentration as East Los Angeles, East San Jose, South San Diego, central Orange County, and the Mission District of San Francisco, Latino communities began to overflow into and then absorb many previously Anglo areas. Residential suburbs "turned" almost overnight, as Anglo homeowners left in a near-panic, hoping to sell their houses before a general property devaluation set in. New suburbs were pushed farther away from the city cores, requiring both the conversion of agricultural land and virgin desert to residential use and the development of increasingly elaborate systems to provide transportation and water to these areas far removed from the decaying cores.

Meanwhile, the graying of the Anglo population continued, with the number of elderly climbing steadily but slowly after 1985 until 2010, when the Baby Boom generation began to turn 65. Thereafter, the number of elderly increased rapidly. The pool of Social Security recipients nearly doubled between 1990 and 2020. The Medicare program saw a tremendous increase in its beneficiaries. Much of the attention in health care shifted to providing expensive services to these people. Hospitals that catered to the elderly sprang up, eager to take advantage of the fact that their illnesses were chronic, needing attention over a long period of time. Indeed, the medical-care industry was in a growth mode from 1995 until about 2015, expanding services and structures on the projected volume of business the growth of the elderly population would bring.

By 1995 most Californians had become aware that Latinos were the single largest group enrolled in public schools. This had two effects. First, it accelerated the "white flight" away from public schools and into private schools. And second, since fewer and fewer Anglo children were being born, a trend that had started at least a decade earlier, educational issues had long since ceased being a priority for the Anglo population. Bond issues to replace decaying, and at times dangerous, facilities were routinely defeated, and there was an increasing clamor from the electorate to reduce overall expenditures in education. If there were few Anglo children of school age and if most of those were enrolled in private schools, so the argument went, why should the Anglo population be taxed for services that it was not using? Beginning in 1995 revenues for schools began to be cut drastically. After 2010 they were cut still

From David E. Hayes-Bautista, Werner O. Schink, and Jorge Chapa, *The Burden of Support* (Stanford: Stanford University Press, 1988), pp. 1–9; 144–50. Reprinted with the permission of the publishers, Stanford University Press. © 1988 by the Board of Trustees of the Leland Stanford Junior University.

more drastically, as the state began to develop programs to make up for the deficiencies in the federal Social Security and Medicare systems and private pension plans.

Indeed, the aging Anglo population was beginning to feel somewhat smug about its ability to provide for itself. As a generational consciousness took hold after the year 2000, the Baby Boomers' voting rates increased markedly, even beyond what was normally expected for the consistently diligent voters in the 45–65 age category. Realizing that federal benefits were spotty and unreliable, the Baby Boom electorate began to construct state programs to benefit the elderly. Soci-Cal Security was voted in by referendum. Building on the federal Social Security program, Soci-Cal expanded coverage to include people who had never paid Social Security taxes and people whose private pension plans did not provide comprehensive benefits. Virtually everyone over 65 was to be covered by the program. Benefits were expanded beyond the federal level, to provide complete 65-to-death income-maintenance and medical benefits.

Because of the number of beneficiaries involved, Soci-Cal became the largest single item in the state's budget. Although exact figures were never established, economists estimated that it consumed between 35 percent and 50 percent of the state's annual revenues. Despite occasional grumblings by younger voters about the amount of money Soci-Cal required, the virtually rock-solid voting bloc of people 55 and over made any contraction in coverage an act of political suicide. Indeed, as new needs were discovered, additions were made to the program to cover particular groups or conditions that had not been foreseen by those who drafted the referendum. The voting bloc of elderly was considered a model of generational politics, and political scientists from around the country came to study the organization of an interest group that had brought about the passage of what was now considered to be the national model.

Funding for the Soci-Cal program came both from an expanded state tax base and from cuts in programs that had been targeted for younger groups. After all, the reasoning went, since there were fewer younger people around, there should be less demand for those sorts of services. Among the worst-hit victims were the state's institutions of higher learning. In an effort to keep the funding level for the Soci-Cal program up, several campuses of the University of California system, the state college and university system, and the community college system were closed and auctioned off. The combination of salary savings and capital infusion from the sale of buildings and property to a consortium of offshore businessmen helped balance the state budget for a while.

Meanwhile, trouble had long been brewing on the border. Finally, in 1997, Mexico's ruling party lost its grip on the country. In the space of a few days, overburdened by the nation's foreign debt commitments, some of the top leaders, sensing the failure of the political compromises that had held the country together since 1917, looted the treasuries and bank accounts of the various federal agencies in their charge and fled the country, leaving a bankrupt government. Not only was the foreign debt no longer serviced; the government was simply unable to pay for its own continuation. A succession of military coups followed. Each military government was weaker and shorter-lived than its predecessor. Fearing a recurrence of the revolution that shook Mexico in 1910–17, the wealthy families moved out of the country, shutting down their factories and businesses and leaving caretakers to guard their estates until such time as law and order could be reestablished.

With the Mexican economy at a standstill and the government for all practical purposes nonexistent, the population faced two alternatives: stay in a politically unstable country with no prospects of a restoration of order and no prospects of employment, or move northward to the United States, where there was at least stability. So in a period of 10 years over 10 million Mexicans left the country and followed the route northward that had been blazed by the farmworkers recruited by U.S. agents during the heyday of the bracero program (1943–64). Approximately half, or about five million, found their way to California, another two million went to Texas, and the rest were dispersed across the country.

Technically, of course, these people were not political refugees, and since they had entered illegally, were not eligible to receive any social benefits such as education or health services. At the same time the presence of such a large supply of unskilled but very cheap labor was not lost on astute businessmen, who found in California an ideal climate for the development of assembly plants: political stability, low wages, almost no unionization, and proximity to markets.

To the public at large and specifically the Anglo population, however, this influx of Latinos was an unwelcome development. The passage of strict immigration controls at the federal level after Mexico's collapse had made the non-Latino population feel safe for a while. The implementation of a computerized system for on-the-spot checking of identity cards had also helped to allay people's fears. The qualms of civil libertarians were eased when the decision was made to check the cards of everyone, not just Latin-looking people, at checkpoints that were to be arranged at randomly chosen times and locations. But neither measure stemmed the flow of immigrants. Many agencies, especially those providing social services, instituted their own residency checks. Schools seemed to be a particularly good point for such checks, allowing administrators to screen ineligible children out of the shrinking school system.

Despite all this, the Latino population continued to grow. Most of the petty and violent crime was laid at the door of the Latinos. And even though criminologists pointed out how the ethnic correlation was a function of age, with Latino youths filling most of the slots in the historically high-crime 15–25 bracket, and not a matter of inherent criminality, this argument was lost on an older generation that increasingly began to see itself as the target of ethnically related crime.

Visible police protection was demanded, and when not provided by public entities, privately retained security forces filled the gap. In urban areas the remaining elderly Anglos adopted all sorts of security measures, huddling behind high, tamper-proof fences, with gate guards, canine patrols, entry and exit checks, and thick grills on windows to protect them. Gradually, similar measures were adopted in the suburban residential areas. Though such precautions were not all that necessary in the suburbs, they made the residents feel safe and secure, by keeping the darker, younger population at bay.

And that population persisted in being different. Despite laws mandating the use of English on job sites and in schools, Spanish was still to be heard everywhere on the streets. Many municipalities had passed ordinances outlawing the celebration of any holidays other than "American" holidays, such as the Fourth of July. A measure that puzzled many people outside the state was the declaration passed by local initiative in San Diego County that "American culture" was to be the only culture allowable. There was so much confusion regarding the definition of American culture that the law was considered unenforceable. Nonetheless, the very fact that it was voted in demonstrated that there was much public sentiment to

maintain some bulwark against the influence of "non-American" elements.

Between 2000 and 2015 the Anglo population began to feel more comfortable and secure: programs benefiting the Baby Boom generation were growing, and the influence of the Latino population was seemingly being held to a minimum (at least behind the security walls). But pressures were building that would soon threaten the Anglos' tranquility.

Because of the massive funding shifts to the Baby Boom elderly, the younger generation was finding itself increasingly at a disadvantage. To begin with, the school system had deteriorated so badly that by the year 2000 the educational achievement of students had begun to decline. Native-born Latinos were the most severely injured of all groups: each year fewer and fewer of them finished high school or entered into the shrunken university system. Most of the children of the foreign-born Latinos, without benefit of documents, were barred from the classroom, and did not even achieve the primary-school level their parents had attained in Mexico and other parts of Latin America.

The employment patterns of Latinos were weighted toward the areas needing unskilled labor. Because of the massive waves of immigrants, California had become a repository of unskilled labor, and a labor surplus kept wages low. This had encouraged the construction of assembly plants for products developed and partially manufactured elsewhere. Large corporations from both the east coast and the Orient had discovered the advantage of having assembly plants in California rather than in Mexico and other politically or economically unstable countries. Because of the decline in educational and research activities, California had long since ceased to be the center of high technology research and development. Indeed, most of the activities requiring a highly educated work force, such as product design, had shifted away from the state by the mid-1990s. The high cost of land and the high taxes imposed by the state to fund its old-age security programs helped to push the remaining industries out.

No longer a leader in the Pacific Rim economy, California was now content with exporting primary foodstuffs. In fact, so vicious was the downward spiral in the California economy that the state began to look a little like an underdeveloped country—exporting primary products for a relatively cheap price and importing consumer goods for a fairly high price. The only local industry left that was totally in the hands of Californians was light industry, which manufactured some articles for local consumption. The sheer size of the economy was impressive, but sharp-eyed economists and investors had noted the shift in activities at its base, and investment capital no longer flowed from the Pacific Rim into California, except into small projects that could take advantage of the seemingly inexhaustible supply of cheap labor.

Few Anglos were personally touched by this shift in the state's economic base. Because of the overabundance of cheap labor, it had become customary for almost all non-Latinos to have at least one Latino servant. Many of the elderly Baby Boomers were able to hire two or three people to keep house, as well as to provide the care and attention they needed in their old age.

The younger population, a large portion of which was now Latino, felt itself caught in a squeeze. Elderly benefit contributions alone accounted for nearly 40 percent of the payroll taxes. Federal income tax rates were also quite high, to cover both the increasing cost of additional benefits programs for the elderly and the continuing cost of expensive military systems. On top of all this the state income tax took nearly another 20 percent, most of it destined for California's elderly benefits package, Soci-Cal Security. The younger workers saw huge amounts of their paychecks eaten up to fund programs for the elderly with little in the way of benefits returned to them. Never mind the failing school system for their children—capital expenditures for roads, water systems, and public buildings and spaces had dwindled to almost nothing. Not only were old structures falling into disrepair; new services were usually not available in the areas of heaviest Latino population growth. By the turn of the century it had become common to see unpaved roads in the Latino sections of towns and to find hoses and electrical lines snaking along the ground, sometimes for miles, to provide water and electricity in areas where no other form of service was available.

The older, native-born Latinos chafed under the burden, feeling a resentment that their children were not able to enjoy public benefits that the Baby Boomers had enjoyed while they were growing up: free, good education at all levels; public health services such as the old polio vaccine campaigns; paved roads; public parks and lands. A drive into a Latino town after the year 2000 was likened by some to a drive through a typical town in underdeveloped parts of Latin America: the dust, the hunger, the throngs of unemployed, the stench of burning garbage, the listless, apathetic, defeated look of people in the streets.

The Californians who had been born in the state between 1970 and 1990 were the most frustrated. Most of their parents were safely in the Baby Boom generation, and from them they had heard of how good the life in the state had once been. Consequently, they had been raised with certain aspirations. But now, however hard they worked, they found themselves quite unable to fulfill those aspirations. Between taxes to support the elderly and the high cost of housing, there seemed to be little money left over to support their families on, let alone to satisfy their own desire for consumer goods.

Although many of these workers had managed to find some marginally secure positions in government or industry, they felt increasingly threatened by the constant contraction of programs and the economy. The only growth area seemed to be in providing services to the elderly.

This generation of workers had grown up before residential and school segregation had become so marked, and thus the Latinos had contacts with their non-Latino peers. A breakaway group from the nearly defunct Democratic Party, composed of Latino and non-Latino post-Baby Boomers, began to meet to see how they might create better opportunities for themselves and their children. Gradually, it became clear to this breakaway group that, as the number of elderly continued to swell, their own situation would become still more precarious. Various economic analysts among them argued persuasively that if the services to the elderly were curtailed sharply, by perhaps as much as 70 percent, that income could be used to rebuild the state's infrastructure and invite the outside investment needed to revive the California economy. Recognizing that such a decision was fraught with political dangers, and that no legislator would dare suggest cuts of this magnitude, given the voting power of the elderly, the group decided only an initiative would do. They also recognized that its passage could be accomplished only by appealing to the younger members of the voting-age population, a group that was nearly 50 percent Latino. This would have the effect of making a racial issue out of a generational one, but they saw no alternative.

The ensuing campaign was a partial success; it succeeded in dividing the electorate along generational lines, but the initiative itself failed. In the aftermath, the older generation vowed not to let its security be so threatened again, and activities that could be perceived as political were sharply curtailed. Social meetings and parties by Latinos were routinely broken up, and under the monolingual laws already in effect, Spanish-language radio, television, newspaper, and book-publishing activities were outlawed.

These harsh measures backfired badly. The younger Latinos responded by calling mass demonstrations; violence broke out at many of them when the frightened older generation tried to halt them. Clandestine presses rolled in the Latino barrios, churning out literature designed to incite the younger generation to rebel, to refuse to pay its taxes or cooperate in any other way. Strikes broke out in assembly plants, security walls were set afire and toppled, the sale of guns, and their price, soared in the elderly areas. The younger Latinos painted the elderly as parasites, who had enjoyed all the benefits of society when those benefits were free and now blithely continued to tax the workers to maintain their style of living, without a thought to the damage it was doing to them. The elderly painted the younger Latinos as parasites, as foreigners who were soaking up benefits that should go to the elderly, as non-Americans who were threatening to dilute American culture, as crime-ridden, disease-ridden, and lawless.

The year following the failure of the initiative saw upheaval after upheaval, charge and countercharge. Then both sides retreated temporarily to their strongholds, the elderly behind their security-patrolled villages, the younger Latinos to their unlit, unpaved barrios. Each side prepared for a last assault on the other, either a physical assault or a political assault that would remove the problem permanently.

Civil revolt was only months away.

We began with a worst-case scenario, our conception of the current trends and tendencies. We will end it with a presentation of the policy window and the best-case scenario that may result from the implementation of appropriate policies. Once again we emphasize that demographic trends are not destiny. Rather, the future is very much what we make of it.

## CALIFORNIA IN 2030:
## THE BEST-CASE SCENARIO

In the preceding chapters we pointed to a number of policy areas to be dealt with.

Urgency is imperative. In our estimation, there is a narrow policy window of about 15 to 20 years available on all of them: to wait until the year 2010 to become concerned about the health, education, and income-earning capacity of Latinos and other minorities will not do. Significant lead time is needed to achieve changes in the level of preparation of human resources. The social needs of the elderly will require attention as they arise in the near to midrange future: they cannot be postponed. But neither can the needs of the Latinos in our midst today, for as we hope we have demonstrated, the future of the one group is indisputably bound to the future of the other.

In the daily political framework, 15 years is a long time—a legislator can stand for reelection seven times. The electorate and politicians are often accused of looking no farther than the next election. The fulfillment of the intergenerational compact in the future will require the forging of an interethnic compact in the present. This will require that Latino and non-Latino politicians be identified, prepared, and involved in a 30-year policy process.

To provide an idea of the best that might happen as a result of such an effort, we offer now a best-case scenario. Like the worst-case scenario, it is extreme. But we remain optimistic.

### The Scenario

By 1995 the growth of the Latino population in California was viewed with growing concern by the Anglo population. Spreading out from such areas of concentration as East Los Angeles, East San Jose, South San Diego, central Orange County, and the Mission District of San Francisco, Latino communities began to overflow into and then absorb many previously Anglo areas. Residential suburbs "turned" almost overnight, as Anglo homeowners left in a near-panic, hoping to sell their houses before a general property devaluation set in. New suburbs were pushed farther away from the city cores, requiring both the conversion of agricultural land and virgin desert to residential use and the development of increasingly elaborate systems to provide transportation and water to these areas far removed from the decaying cores.

The vast majority of these "urban refugees" were Baby Boomers. Life had been good to this generation. Hitting a vigorous mid-life stride, the Boomers were riding the crest of a wave of economic well-being. Their education was paying off, their income was high, and because they had few children, their discretionary spending was at an all-time high.

But just beneath the surface of a seemingly wealthy and thriving California were serious structural problems that threatened its stability. While the Latino population was growing, its participation in the state's economic, political, and cultural life was not welcomed. The passage of English-only laws was nearly a decade behind, but Spanish was still to be heard on the streets. The continuing linkages between the Latino population and Mexico and other Latin American countries was seen as a potential threat to societal cohesion. Latino emphasis on family life was seen as a quaint but functionless relic that impeded economic mobility.

Much of the growth in the Latino population was due to an unraveling situation in Mexico. The high foreign debt forced Mexico to spend upwards of $25 billion per year in debt service alone. This massive expenditure drained the country, making investment in business and human resources nearly impossible. While each year over a million persons entered the job market, virtually no new jobs were being created. The quality of life had been steadily deteriorating since the 1980's. Inflation raged at over 300 percent a year and the economy was unable to provide even the basic necessities of life for over half the country's population. Political stability was very much in question. United States television programs and movies pointed out to Mexicans, on a daily basis, the widening gap in living standards between the two countries.

Things were not completely well within the state of California either. The job market had become segmented, so that there were few positions in the higher paying, professional levels: the growth was in the poorly paid services sector. Anglos predominated in the upper segment, Latinos in the lower. Manufacturing in the state was in a weak position. Because of sporadic enforcement of the Simpson-Rodino immigration act of 1986, manufacturers were sometimes able to operate with a full labor force, but periodic sweeps and subsequent employer fines had made production difficult to budget and schedule. California's competitive position in the Pacific Rim economy was softening. Agricultural and raw forest and mineral products accounted for an increasingly large proportion of the total value of export goods, while sophisticated consumer goods continued to flood in from other Rim countries. Labor economists pointed out that the decline in educational expenditures

in the 1970s and 1980s was now being reflected in a noticeable decline in the education level of the labor force. In short, the California economy seemed to be positioned for a long, slow, downwards slide. This condition led to an awakening and a transformation in society.

Thanks to the Affirmative Action programs of the 1970s and 1980s, there was a group of educators, physicians, dentists, attorneys, administrators, artists, scientists, clinical workers, researchers, planners, and businesspeople to give the state something that had been nearly totally lacking during the heyday of the Chicano movement in the 1960s—a critical mass of well-educated Latinos with a good understanding of their relation to their communities and their state. Drawing upon the experience of the veterans and the bases of community organization laid down in the 1960s and 1970s, these new Latino leaders were able to tap into a wellspring of symbolism and emotion that lurked just beneath the surface of many Latino communities. These leaders inspired Latino parents and youth to reach into themselves to strive for excellence and the highest levels of performance. Meanwhile, the Anglo Baby Boomers found their political voice in leaders who were able to rekindle the generational enthusiasm that, 30 years earlier, had led to a decade of selfless public service in such organizations as the Peace Corps and VISTA.

These two currents of interest—of the young Latinos and the aging Baby Boomers—converged in the development of a policy framework aimed at preserving the intergenerational compact through the development of an interethnic compact. The changing demographics of the state, leading to an age-ethnic stratified society, was becoming apparent to this group of leaders. But rather than see the growth of the Latino population as a problem, they came to see it as a solution to the problem of support for the aging Baby Boomers. Although some called it merely enlightened self-interest, both sets of leaders realized that an investment in the younger Latino population was the best guarantee of support for the elderly in the near future. Some even dared to call this policy a human rights policy—all members of society should have a chance to maximize their participation, irrespective of age or ethnicity.

The first major investment that had to be made was in the education of the younger, largely Latino population. Boosting educational achievement became a priority policy for the state. Probably the most important event in this effort was the emergence of a Latino intellectual tradition. The critical mass of Latino professionals provided a seedbed for the generation of excitement about exploring the intellectual tradition of Mexico and Latin America. Not only did the artists and humanists draw upon the old Latin American tradition, they helped to create the new Latino tradition. This new tradition served as a magnet, drawing out Latino youth and providing them with new horizons.

This new spirit was built upon by the policy makers. A new policy in bilingual education was adopted, mandating that graduating high school seniors be fluent in a major Pacific Basin foreign language. The public schools were open to all, regardless of legal status. The political commitment to quality education attracted Anglo students back into the public schools. Latino participation in higher education was not limited to the arts and humanities, and enrollment in math and science classes began to rise. The new attention to education helped to bring about the renewal of adult education, designed to raise the achievement level of former dropouts and immigrant parents, so that they could function better in the economy.

Side by side with this effort came an equally great investment in health. The coalition of Latino and Anglo leaders realized that the rapidly aging Baby Boomers would soon, by their sheer numbers, draw policy attention to their massive health care needs. The health needs of the younger, generally Latino population had to be served as well. A state-underwritten health insurance and services program called Soci-Cal was developed, providing for balanced services over a person's lifetime. In this way, the Latino needs for maternal and child health would balance the Anglo need for geriatrics. A major component of the plan was extensive health education and preventive health care.

The policy of investing in the state's future was not lost on business leaders. Confidence in the economy's future rose following the increase in expenditures for research at the university level. Basic business investment began to be made, halting a downward trend. The resulting increase in business activity brought about an expansion in the economy, which in turn necessitated a larger, better prepared workforce. At the national level, spot shortages of labor around the country helped to create a climate in which a new immigration law was to be written. The prospect of a common market embracing Mexico, the United States, and Central America formed the basis for this new effort. This increased investment in Mexico and Central America created more jobs and boosted employment in that region. More people were enjoying greater income, and gradually the standard of living began to rise. Fertility dropped, and life expectancy increased. Emigration to the United States slowed.

California's improved business outlook was noted in many areas. Research and development spending improved, requiring ever more highly trained scientists and administrators. Increasingly, many of these were Latinos. Through quality education and comprehensive adult training programs, the wage gap between Anglos and Latinos closed.

Continuing a trend, Latino educational achievement continued to rise, until by 2030 it equaled Anglo achievement. The universities blossomed with new intellectual vigor, and California remained the academic center of the Pacific Basin region. Arts and sciences flourished, and did so bilingually. Latinos became fully represented in the sciences. Most important of all, a new intellectual tradition was becoming formalized.

The state health insurance program was expanded to cover income support, housing, social services, and death benefits for retiring California workers. The cost of this program was large, but the rising California economy was able to carry the expense. The younger, now highly productive, Latinos willingly shouldered the burden of support, for they felt that all inhabitants of the state were linked together regardless of age, gender, or ethnicity.

Their support was the result of a continuing societal commitment to Latino health and education. Public spending for education was seen as the key to generating sufficient economic growth to carry the Soci-Cal program in the future. The trajectory for rising Latino educational achievement had been discovered and merely required continuing attention.

After the year 2030, California society faced the future confidently. It was universally recognized all over the world as the model for twenty-first century society. Its economy and culture reflected a happy fusion of elements from Western Europe, Latin America, Asia, and Africa, leading to a new language, new social values, and even new forms of political dialogue. As that new decade began, California was the lead state for the other 49, and the lead society for other Pacific Rim societies. The future looked bright indeed.

# PART VI
# Prospects

Suddenly, on April 29, 1992, the reality of racial tension rudely woke America like a firebell in the night. Immediately after four Los Angeles police officers were found not guilty of brutality against Rodney King, rage exploded in Los Angeles. Race relations reached a new nadir. During the nightmarish rampage, scores of people were killed, over two thousand injured, twelve thousand arrested, and almost a billion dollars of property destroyed. The live televised images mesmerized America. The rioting and the murderous melee on the streets resembled the fighting in Beirut and the West Bank. The thousands of fires burning out of control and the dark smoke filling the skies brought back images of the burning oil fields of Kuwait during Desert Storm. Entire sections of Los Angeles looked like a bombed city.

"Is this America?" many shocked people asked. "I don't feel like I'm in America anymore," said Denisse Bustamente as she watched the police protecting the firefighters. "I feel like I am far away." Indeed, Americans have been witnessing ethnic strife erupting around the world—the rise of Neo-Nazism and the murder of Turks in Germany, the ugly "ethnic cleansing" in Bosnia, the terrible and bloody clashes between Muslims and Hindus in India. Is the situation here different, we have been nervously wondering, or do ethnic conflicts elsewhere represent a prologue for America? What is the nature of malevolence? Is there a deep, perhaps primordial, need for group identity rooted in hatred for the other? Is ethnic pluralism possible for America? But answers have been limited. Television reports have been little more than thirty-second sound bites. Newspaper articles have been mostly superficial descriptions of racial antagonisms and the current urban malaise. What is lacking is historical context; consequently, we are left feeling bewildered.

"It took a brutal beating, an unexpected jury verdict, and the sudden rampage of rioting, looting, and indiscriminate violence to bring this crisis [of urban America] back to the forefront," *Business Week* reported. "Racism surely explains some of the carnage in Los Angeles. But the day-to-day living conditions with which many of America's urban poor must contend is an equally compelling story—a tale of economic injustice." This usually conservative magazine pointed out that "the poverty rate, which fell as low as 11% in the 1970s, moved higher in the Reagan years and jumped during the last couple of years. Last year, an estimated 36 million people—or about 14.7% of the total population—were living in poverty."

South Central Los Angeles has come to symbolize the plight of poor blacks trapped in inner cities. "South Central Los Angeles is a Third World country," declared Krashaun Scott, a former member of the Los Angeles Crips gang. "There's a south central in every city, in every state." Describing the desperate conditions in his community, he continued,

"What we got is inadequate housing and inferior education. I wish someone would tell me the difference between Guatemala and south central." This comparison graphically illustrated the squalor and poverty present within one of America's wealthiest and most modern cities. Like a Third World country, South Central Los Angeles is also extremely volatile. A gang member known as Bone explained that the recent violence was "not a riot—it was a class struggle. When Rodney King asked, 'Can we get along?' it ain't just about Rodney King. He was the lighter and it blew up."

What exploded was anguish born of despair. "What happens to a dream deferred?" asked Langston Hughes in Harlem during the 1920s.

> *Does it dry up*
> *Like a raisin in the sun?*
> *. . . Or does it explode?*

But what happens when there are no dreams? Plants and factories have been moving out of central Los Angeles into the suburbs as well as across the border into Mexico and even overseas to countries like South Korea. Factories, which had employed many of the parents of these young blacks, are now boarded up, like tombs. In terms of manufacturing jobs, South Central Los Angeles has become a wasteland. Many young black men and women nervously peer down the corridor of their futures and see no possibility of full-time employment paying above minimum wages, or any jobs at all. The unemployment rate in this area is 50 percent—higher than the national rate during the Great Depression.

"Once again, young blacks are taking to the streets to express their outrage at perceived injustice," *Newsweek* reported, "and once again, whites are fearful that The Fire Next Time will consume them." But this time, the magazine noticed, the situation was different from the earlier riot: the recent conflict was not just between blacks and whites. "The nation is rapidly moving toward a multiethnic future," *Newsweek* reported, "in which Asians, Hispanics, Caribbean islanders, and many other immigrant groups compose a diverse and changing social mosaic that cannot be described by the old vocabulary of race relations in America." The terms "black" and "white," *Newsweek* concluded, no longer "depict the American social reality."

At the street level, black community organizer Ted Watkins observed: "This riot was deeper, and more dangerous [than the 1965 uprising]. More ethnic groups were involved." Watkins had witnessed the Watts rebellion, an expression of black fury; since then, he had watched the influx of Hispanics and Koreans into South Central Los Angeles. Beyond this awareness was another lesson: the need for all of us to become listeners. "A riot," Martin Luther King, Jr., had asserted, "is the language of the unheard." As Americans watched the live television coverage of the violence and destruction in Los Angeles, the cry of the ghetto could be heard everywhere. "I think good will come of [the riot]," stated Janet Harris, a chaplain at Central Juvenile Hall. "People need to take off their rose-colored glasses," she added, "and take a hard look at what they've been doing. They've been living in invisible cages. And they've shut out that world. And maybe the world came crashing in on them and now people will be moved to do something."

The racial conflagration in Los Angeles violently highlighted America's economic problems. Racial antagonisms in Los Angeles and cities across the country are being fueled by a declining economy and rising general unemployment. One of the major causes for our economic downturn has been the recent deescalation of the U.S.-Soviet conflict: our economy has become so dependent on federal military spending that budget cuts for defense contractors have led to massive layoffs, especially in the weapons-producing states such as Massachusetts, Texas, and California. This economic crisis has been fanning the fires of racism in American society: Asian Americans have been bashed for the "invasion" of Japanese cars, Hispanics accused of taking jobs away from "Americans," and blacks attacked for their dependency on welfare and the special privileges of affirmative action.

Still, there are new prospects for change and progress. The end of the Cold War has given us the opportunity to shift our resources from nuclear weapons development to the production of consumer goods, which could help revitalize the American economy, making it more competitive with Japan and Germany. "It's as though America just won the lottery," the *New York Times* editorialized exuberantly in March 1990. "With Communism collapsing, the United States, having defended the free world for half a century, now stands to save a fortune. Defense spending could drop by $20 billion next year and $150 billion a year before the decade ends." This tremendous resource can now be directed into the consumer-goods economy. What is needed, proposed Ann Markusen of Rutgers University, is "an independent Office of Economic Conversion, designed to be self-liquidating by the year 2000 and accountable to the President."

In the wake of the Cold War's end, the United States is perched on the threshold of a new era of economic expansion. To meet the research needs of the military over the last half century, the government has educated and supported an impressive array of brilliant engineers and scientists. "These wizards of the cold war comprise the greatest force of scientific and engineering talent ever assembled," observed journalist William J. Broad in 1992. "Over the decades this army of government, academic and industry experts made the breakthroughs that gave the West its dazzling military edge." Released from military R&D, they now have the opportunity to give the United States an economic edge in the consumers goods market. Under the guidance of a comprehensive national industrial strategy, giant American corporations like Rockwell International, Grumman, Northrup, Martin Marietta, and Lockheed could now start designing and producing "smart" consumer goods rather than "smart" bombs. A growing demand for labor in a revitalized economy, combined with the rebuilding of the manufacturing base in inner cities as well as education and job training programs funded by the "peace dividend," could help to bring minority workers into the mainstream economy without making white laborers feel threatened. These needed economic changes face formidable difficulties, however. The tremendous federal debt incurred under President Reagan could dissipate the dividend generated by military budget reductions. Automation and the suburbanization of production could continue to shut out workers, especially minority laborers. The labor market has been internationalized, and American corporations could continue to relocate their production facilities in low-wage countries like Indonesia and Mexico, rendering millions of American workers superfluous. Nonetheless, the decomposition of the Soviet Union and the end of its military threat have given us new options for economic development.

"Please, we can get along here," pleaded Rodney King, calling for calm during the days of rage in Los Angeles. "We all can get along. I mean, we're all stuck here for a while. Let's try to work it out." But the question is: how do we work it out?

Shortly after the 1992 explosion, social critic Richard Rodriguez reflected in his essay, "Horizontal City": "The Rodney King riots were appropriately multiracial in this multicultural capital of America. We cannot settle for black and white conclusions when one of the most important conflicts the riots revealed was the tension between Koreans and African Americans." Out of the Los Angeles conflict came a sense of connectedness. "Here was a race riot that had no border," Rodriguez wrote, "a race riot without nationality. And, for the first time, everyone in the city realized—if only in fear—that they were related to one another."

But how do they learn about their relationship to one another? Should Americans be identified in terms of different ethnic and racial groups? What should we learn about ourselves in our schools and colleges? These are the questions debated by Molefi Kete Asante, Diane Ravitch, Arthur Schlesinger, Jr., and Ronald Takaki. Students will see that all four scholars share a deep concern for America's future. As young people today approach the twenty-first century, they are certainly wondering: Who are we as Americans? How should we define ourselves not only in terms of our specific ethnic and racial communities but also to our nation? Can we all get along? Can we work it out? These are some of the complex and difficult questions we need to address as we ponder the meaning of our society composed of peoples "from different shores."

# Horizontal City

## RICHARD RODRIGUEZ

Los Angeles has broken apart. People shake their heads, wring their hands; they say L.A. has fractured. But what Los Angeles gave America for decades was precisely a notion of a city of separate lives.

Here was a place of individual houses, individual lawns, behind good Protestant fences. Los Angeles became a verb. A threat, a joke, a protest against the notion of a city anchored by a center of spires. People elsewhere in America mocked Los Angeles for having no center, but the point of Los Angeles was democratic. The horizontal city that was nowhere the city was everywhere a city. Los Angeles gave metropolitan stature to the suburban; it reconciled individuality (separate houses) with a large civic ideal.

But then the palm trees burned. And now, after the Rodney King riots, everything seems changed about the city.

Twenty-five years ago, after the riots in Watts and Detroit and Newark, the collective wisdom of institutional America was bound up and presented to the nation as the Kerner Report. Its most famous conclusion was that America was dividing into two nations, one black, the other white. If that conclusion seems a bit simplistic from the distance of two decades and from multicultural California, it remains, nonetheless, an important idea for many white liberals. I notice, for example, in my neighborhood bookstore the widely reviewed book by Andrew Hacker with this antique title—"Two Nations: Black and White, Separate, Hostile, Unequal." In the aftermath of the Rodney King riots, African American newspaper columnists and activists speak of "black rage." But in the Los Angeles of 1992 it is crucial to remember that the majority of looters who were arrested have turned out to be Hispanic.

The Rodney King riots were appropriately multiracial in this multicultural capital of America. We cannot settle for black and white

conclusions when one of the most important conflicts the riots revealed was the tension between Koreans and African Americans.

To say that Los Angeles has complicated our sense of racial relations should not, I think, deny black Americans their special place on the American stage. For a long time, as a Hispanic, I have been disturbed by the tendency of various civil rights movements to describe their plight by analogy to black Americans. In the 1960s, there was that hideous example of racial slumming, a college best-seller called "The Student as Nigger." In the years since, I have heard white middle-class feminists and Hispanics and senior citizens (Gray Panthers) and homosexuals, and many others, compare their suffering to that of blacks. My fear is that multiculturalism is going to trivialize further the distinct predicament of black Americans—most especially the plight of the young black male. It is my belief that there are two stories in American history that are singular and of such extraordinary magnitude that they should never be casually compared to the experiences of other Americans. One is the story of the American Indian; the other is the story of the black slave.

Black Americans have been generous, at least publicly, if also privately bemused, at the spectacle of so many Americans jumping onto the black civil rights movement for their own political benefit. Black leaders, with the notable exception of the Reverend Jesse Jackson, seem extraordinarily provincial in how they envision America. Listen to the major black civil rights leaders and you will hear mainly references to white and black America. A black leadership might yet emerge in L.A. different from any other in America.

In Los Angeles, African Americans must live within a new kind of national complexity, alongside Russian Jews, Syrians, Mexicans, Armenians and Vietnamese.

From San Francisco *Chronicle*, May 24, 1992. © 1992 by Richard Rodriguez, Pacific News Service. Reprinted with permission.

In this most famous horizontal city, solutions will need to be horizontal in coming weeks. Peace will come as people from different neighborhoods negotiate with one another. Peace will not be dispensed from a mythical center. The key to saving Los Angeles will come immediately from a Korean-black dialogue.

A few years ago, L.A. officially celebrated its multiculturalism with a festival. Peter Sellars, the festival organizer, brought to the city troops of Indonesian dancers and Salvadoran craftsmen and Chinese acrobats. I remember watching Sellars on TV explaining to Bill Moyers the diversity of L.A. Was I the only person watching who found it odd that the multicultural city was being defined by a white man?

Multiculturalism has, thus far, been a feel-good term that has trivialized the very reality it trumpets. There are politicians and academics and think-tank types in L.A. who go on and on about multiculturalism, but they usually settle for improbable terms like "Asian" and "Hispanic," lumping together diverse populations. Thus does the white Hispanic TV producer get categorized with a Guatemalan immigrant just arrived and the third-generation tattooed Chicano who runs with the Crips street gang.

There is true diversity in the multicultural city, but often those who talk about it most are the least prepared to make room for it. The academics at UCLA or the futurist magazine editors or the city hall types and all those famous leaders in those "100 most important people in L.A." articles do not determine the variety of L.A. L.A. has no center!

But neither is L.A. simply a collection of separate neighborhoods. The fact is that people, living alongside one another, driving the same freeways, watching the same TV, are bound to influence one another. In the midst of the chaos, the city was melting. Black rage led Hispanics to loot their own mini-mall, which in turn encouraged white teenagers to loot the sporting goods store on Melrose.

The most pessimistic conclusion one hears now, after the riots, is that the city has fractured. But when was this city anything but a city constructed on separateness? In fact, Los Angeles learned something very important and contrary during the darkest hours of fire and smoke. The idea came within terror: The riot in South Central was spreading; it couldn't be contained. Soon there were flames blocks away and then miles away.

Here was a race riot that had no border, a race riot without nationality. And, for the first time, everyone in the city realized—if only in fear—that they were related to one another. And not simply was Westwood related in danger to Watts, the effect of L.A. in flames was looting in Atlanta and Las Vegas and San Francisco and Toronto and even Rio.

The irony is this. L.A. was constructed for most of this century as a place, a paradoxical city, of separateness. This was its optimism and the source of its youthful indifference. Now the city has lost its childish innocence with the realization that lives are related. From this knowledge, this idea born in the middle of the night, fed by flames, from this knowledge of tragedy, L.A. may find its redeeming maturity.

# The Afrocentric Idea

MOLEFI KETE ASANTE

We are all implicated in the positions we hold about society, culture, and education. Although the implications may take quite different forms in some fields and with some scholars, such as the consequences and our methods and inquiry on our systems of values, we are nevertheless captives of the positions we take, that is, if we take those positions honestly.

In a recent article in *The American Scholar* (Summer 1990), Diane Ravitch reveals the tensions between scholarship and ideological perspectives in an exceedingly clear manner. The position taken in her article "Multiculturalism: E Pluribus Plures" accurately demonstrates the thesis that those of us who write are implicated in what we choose to write. This is not a profound announcement since most fields of inquiry recognize that a researcher's presence must be accounted for in research or a historian's relationship to data must be examined in seeking to establish the validity of conclusions. This is not to say that the judgment will be invalid because of the intimacy of the scholar with the information but rather that in accounting for the scholar's or researcher's presence we are likely to know better how to assess the information presented. Just as a researcher may be considered an intrusive presence in an experiment, the biases of a scholar may be just as intrusive in interpreting data or making analysis. The fact that a writer seeks to establish a persona of a non-interested observer means that such a writer wants the reader to assume that an unbiased position is being taken on a subject. However, we know that as soon as a writer states a proposition, the writer is implicated and such implication holds minor or extreme consequences.

The remarkable advantage of stating aims and objectives prior to delivering an argument is that the reader knows precisely to what the author is driving. Unfortunately, too many writers on education either do not know the point they are making or lose sight of their point in the making. Such regrettably is the case with Diane Ravitch's article on multicultural education.

Among writers who have written on educational matters in the last few years, Professor Ravitch of Columbia University's Teacher's College is considered highly quotable and therefore, in the context of American educational policy, influential. This is precisely why her views on multiculturalism must not remain unchallenged. Many of the positions taken by Professor Ravitch are similar to the positions taken against the Freedmen's Bureau's establishment of black schools in the South during the 1860s. Then, the white conservative education policymakers felt that it was necessary to control the content of education so that the recently freed Africans would not become self-assured. An analysis of Ravitch's arguments will reveal what Martin Bernal calls in *Black Athena* "the neo-Aryan" model of history. Her version of multiculturalism is not multiculturalism at all, but rather a new form of Eurocentric hegemonism.

People tend to do the best they can with the information at their disposal. The problem in most cases where intellectual distortions arise is ignorance rather than malice. Unlike in the political arena where oratory goes a long way, in education, sooner or later the truth must come out. The proof of the theory is in the practice. What we have seen in the past twenty-five years is the gradual dismantling of the educational kingdom built to accompany the era of white supremacy. What is being contested is the speed of its dismantling. In many ways, the South African regime is a good parallel to what is going on in American education. No longer can the structure of knowledge which supported white hegemony

From Molefi Kete Asante and Diane Ravitch, "Multiculturalism: An Exchange," THE AMERICAN SCHOLAR (Spring 1991). Reprinted with permission.

be defended; whites must take their place, not above or below, but alongside the rest of humanity. This is a significantly different reality than we have experienced in American education and there are several reasons for this turn of events.

The first reason is the accelerating explosion in the world of knowledge about cultures, histories, and events seldom mentioned in American education. Names of individuals and their achievements, views of historiography and alternatives to European perspectives have proliferated due to international interaction, trade, and computer technology. People from other cultures, particularly non-Western people, have added new elements into the educational equation. A second reason is the rather recent intellectual liberation of large numbers of African-descended scholars. While there have always been African scholars in every era, the European hegemony, since the 1480s, in knowledge about the world, including Africa, was fairly complete. The domination of information, the naming of things, the propagation of concepts, and the dissemination of interpretations were, and still are in most cases in the West, a Eurocentric hegemony. During the twentieth century, African scholars led by W. E. B. DuBois began to break from the intellectual shackles of Europe and make independent inquiries into history, science, origins, and Europe itself. For the first time in five hundred years, a cadre of scholars, trained in the West, but largely liberated from the hegemonic European thinking began to expose numerous distortions, often elevated to "truth" in the works of Eurocentric authors. A third reason for the current assault on the misinformation spread by white hegemonic thinkers is the conceptual inadequacy of simply valorizing Europe. Few whites have ever examined their culture critically. Those who have done so have often been severely criticized by their peers: the cases of Sidney Willhelm, Joe Feagin, Michael Bradley, and Basil Davidson are well known.

As part of the Eurocentric tradition, there seems to be silence on questions of hegemony, that is, the inability to admit the mutual conspiracy between race doctrine and educational doctrine in America. Professor Ravitch and others would maintain the facade of reasonableness even in the face of arguments demonstrating the irrationality of both white supremacist ideas on race and white hegemonic ideas in education. They are corollary and both are untenable on genetic and intellectual grounds.

## EUROCENTRIC HEGEMONISM

Let us examine the argument of the defenders of the Eurocentric hegemony in education more closely. The status quo always finds its best defense in territoriality. Thus, it is one of the first weapons used by the defenders of the white hegemonic education. Soon after my book *The Afrocentric Idea* was published, I was interviewed on "The Today Show" along with Herb London, the New York University professor/politician who is one of the founders of the National Association of Professors. When I suggested the possibility of schools weaving information about other cultures into the fabric of the teaching-learning process, Professor London interrupted that "there is not enough *time* in the school year for what Asante wants." Of course there is, if there is enough for the Eurocentric information, there is enough time for cultural information from other groups. Professor Ravitch uses the same argument. Her strategy is to cast serious examinations of the curriculum as pressure groups, much like creationists in biology. Of course, the issue is neither irrational nor sensational; it is preeminently a question of racial dominance, the maintenance of which, in any form, I oppose. On the contrary, the status quo defenders, like the South African Boers, believe that it is possible to defend what is fundamentally anti-intellectual and immoral: the dominance and hegemony of the Eurocentric view of reality on a multicultural society. There is space for Eurocentrism in a multicultural enterprise so long as it does not parade as universal. No one wants to banish the Eurocentric view. It is a valid view of reality where it does not force its way. Afrocentricity does not seek to replace Eurocentricity in its arrogant disregard for other cultures.

## THE PRINCIPAL CONTRADICTIONS

A considerable number of white educators and some blacks have paraded in single file and sometimes in concert to take aim at multiculturalism. In her article Professor Ravitch attempts to defend the indefensible. Believing, I suspect, that the best defense of the status quo is to attack, she attacks diversity, and those that support it, with gusto, painting straw fellows along the way. Her claim to support multiculturalism is revealed to be nothing more than an attempt to apologize for white cultural supremacy in the curriculum by using the same logic as white racial supremacists used in trying to defend white racism in previous years. She assumes falsely that there is little to say about the rest of the world, particularly about Africa and African Americans. Indeed, she is willing to assert, as Herbert London has claimed, that the school systems do not have enough time to teach all that Afrocentrists believe ought to be taught. Nevertheless, she assumes that all that is not taught about the European experience is valid and necessary. There are some serious flaws in her line of reasoning. I shall attempt to locate the major flaws and ferret them out.

Lip service is paid to the evolution of American education from the days of racial segregation to the present when "new social historians" routinely incorporate the experiences of other than white males. Nowhere does Professor Ravitch demonstrate an appreciation for the role played by the African American community in overcoming the harshest elements of racial segregation in the educational system. Consequently, she is unable to understand that more fundamental than eliminating racial segregation has to be the removal of racist thinking, assumptions, symbols, and materials in the curriculum.

However, there is no indication that Professor Ravitch is willing to grant an audience to this reasoning because she plods deeper into the same quagmire by attempting to conceptualize multiculturalism, a simple concept in educational jargon. She posits a *pluralist* multiculturalism—a redundancy—then suggests a *particularistic* multiculturalism—an oxymoron—in order to beat a dead horse. The ideas are nonstarters because they have no reality in fact. I wrote the first book in this country on transracial communication and edited the first handbook on intercultural communication, and I am unaware of the categories Professor Ravitch seeks to forge. She claims that the pluralist multiculturalist believes in pluralism and the particularistic multiculturalist believes in particularism. Well, multiculturalism in education is almost self-defining. It is simply the idea that the educational experience should reflect the diverse cultural heritage of our system of knowledge. I have contended that such is not the case and cannot be the case until teachers know more about the African American, Native American, Latino, and Asian experiences. This position obviously excites Professor Ravitch to the point that she feels obliged to make a case for "mainstream Americans."

## THE MYTH OF MAINSTREAM

The idea of "mainstream American" is nothing more than an additional myth meant to maintain Eurocentric hegemony. When Professor Ravitch speaks of mainstream, she does not have Spike Lee, Aretha Franklin, or John Coltrane in mind. Bluntly put, "mainstream" is a code word for "white." When a dean of a college says to a faculty member, as one recently said, "You ought to publish in mainstream journals," the dean is not meaning *Journal of Black Studies* or *Black Scholar.* As a participant in the racist system of education, the dean is merely carrying out the traditional function of enlarging the white hegemony over scholarship. Thus, when the status quo defenders use terms like "mainstream," they normally mean "white." In fact, one merely has to substitute the words "white controlled" to get at the real meaning behind the code.

## MISUNDERSTANDING MULTICULTURALISM

Misunderstanding the African American struggle for education in the United States, Professor Ravitch thinks that the call to multiculturalism is a matter of anecdotal references to outstanding individuals or descriptions of civil rights. But neither acknowledgment of achievements per se, nor descriptive accounts of the African experience adequately conveys the aims of the Afrocentric restructuring, as we shall see. From the establishment of widespread public education to the current emphasis on massaging the curriculum toward an organic and systemic recognition of cultural pluralism, the African American concept of nationhood has been always central. In terms of Afrocentricity, it is the same. We do not seek segments or modules in the classroom but rather the infusion of African American studies in every segment and in every module. The difference is between "incorporating the experiences" and "infusing the curriculum with an entirely new life." The real unity of the curriculum comes from infusion, not from including African Americans in what Ravitch would like to remain a white contextual hegemony she calls mainstream. No true mainstream can ever exist until there is knowledge, understanding, and acceptance of the role Africans have played in American history. One reason the issue is debated by white scholars such as Ravitch is because they do not believe there is substantial or significant African information to infuse. Thus, ignorance becomes the reason for the strenuous denials of space for the cultural infusion. If she knew or believed that it was possible to have missed something, she would not argue against it. What is at issue is her own educational background. Does she know classical Africa? Did she take courses in African American studies from qualified professors? Those who know do not question the importance of Afrocentric or Latino infusion into the educational process.

## THE MISUSE OF SELF-ESTEEM

Professor Ravitch's main critique of the Afrocentric, Latinocentric, or Americentric (Native American) project is that it seeks to raise "self-esteem and self-respect" among Africans, Latinos, and Native Americans. It is important to understand that this is not only a self-serving argument, but a false argument. In the first place, I know of no Afrocentric curriculum planner—Asa Hilliard, Wade Nobles, Leonard Jeffries, Don McNeely being the principal ones—who insists that the primary aim is to raise self-esteem. The argument is a false lead to nowhere because the curriculum planners I am familiar with insist that the fundamental objective is to provide *accurate* information. A secondary effect of accuracy and truth might be the adjustment of attitudes by both black and white students. In several surveys of college students, research has demonstrated that new information changes attitudes in both African American and white students. Whites are not so apt to take a superior attitude when they are aware of the achievements of other cultures. They do not lose their self-esteem, they adjust their views. On the other hand, African Americans who are often as ignorant as whites about African achievements adjust their attitudes about themselves once they are exposed to new information. There is no great secret in this type of transformation. Ravitch, writing from the point of view of those whose cultural knowledge is reinforced every hour, not just in the curriculum, but in every media, smugly contends that she cannot see the value of self-esteem. Since truth and accuracy will yield by-products of attitude adjustments, the Afrocentrists have always argued for the accurate representation of information.

Afrocentricity does not seek an ethnocentric

curriculum. Unfortunately, Diane Ravitch chose to ignore two books that explain my views on this subject, *The Afrocentric Idea* (1987) and *Kemet, Afrocentricity and Knowledge* (1990) and instead quotes from *Afrocentricity* (1980), which was not about education but about personal and social transformation. Had she read the later works she would have understood that Afrocentricity is not an ethnocentric view in two senses. In the first place, it does not valorize the African view while downgrading others. In this sense, it is unlike the Eurocentric view, which is an ethnocentric view because it valorizes itself and parades as universal. It becomes racist when the rules, customs, and/or authority of law or force dictate it as the proper view. This is what often happens in school curricula. In the second place, as to method, Afrocentricity is not a naive racial theory. It is a systematic approach to presenting the African as subject rather than object. Even Ravitch might be taught the Afrocentric Method!

## AMERICAN CULTURE

There is no common American culture as is claimed by the defenders of the status quo. There is a hegemonic culture to be sure, pushed as if it were a common culture. Perhaps Ravitch is confusing concepts here. There is common American *society,* which is quite different from a common American culture. Certain cultural characteristics are shared by those within the society but the meaning of *multicultural* is "many cultures." To believe in multicultural education is to assume that there are many cultures. The reason Ravitch finds confusion is because the only way she can reconcile the "many cultures" is to insist on many "little" cultures under the hegemony of the "big" white culture. Thus, what she means by multiculturalism is precisely what I criticized in *The Afrocentric Idea,* the acceptance of other cultures within a Eurocentric framework.

In the end, the neat separation of pluralist multiculturalists and particularistic multiculturalists breaks down because it is a false, straw separation developed primarily for the sake of argument and not for clarity. The real division on the question of multiculturalism is between those who truly seek to maintain a Eurocentric hegemony over the curriculum and those who truly believe in cultural pluralism without hierarchy. Ravitch defends the former position.

Professor Ravitch's ideological position is

implicated in her mis-reading of several scholars' works. When Professor John Stanfield writes that modes of social knowledge such as theology, science, and magic are different, not inferior or superior, Ravitch asks, "If Professor Stanfield broke his leg, would he go to a theologian, a doctor, or a magician?" clearly she does not understand the simple statement Stanfield is making. He is not writing about *uses* of knowledge, but about *ranking* of knowledge. To confuse the point by providing an answer for a question never raised is the key rhetorical strategy in Ravitch's case. Thus, she implies that because Professor George Ghevarughese Joseph argues that mathematics was developed in Egypt, Babylonia, Mesopotamia, and India long before it came to Europe, he seeks to replace modern math with "ancient ethnic mathematics." This is a deliberate misunderstanding of the professor's point: mathematics in its modern form owes debts to Africans and Asians.

Another attempt to befuddle issues is Ravitch's gratuitous comment that Koreans "do not study ancient mathematics" and yet they have high scores. There are probably several variables for the Koreans making the highest scores "in mathematics on international assessments." Surely one element would have to be the linkage of Korean traditions in mathematics to present mathematical problems. Koreans do not study European theorists prior to their own; indeed they are taught to honor and respect the ancestral mathematicians. This is true for Indians, Chinese, and Japanese. In African traditions, the *European* slave trade broke the linkage, and the work of scholars such as Ahmed Baba and Hypathia remains unknown to the African American and thus does not take its place in the family of world mathematics.

Before Professor Ravitch ends her assault on ethnic cultures, she fires a volley against the Haudenosaunee political system of Native Americans. As a New Yorker, she does not like the fact that the state's curriculum guide lists the Haudenosaunee Confederation as an inspiration for the United States Constitution along-side the Enlightenment. She says readers "might wonder what it is." Bluntly put, a proper education would acquaint students with the Haudenosaunee Confederation, and in that case Professor Ravitch's readers would know the Haudenosaunee as a part of the conceptual discussion that went into the development of the American political systems. Only a commitment to white hegemony would lead a writer to assume that whites could not obtain political ideas from others.

Finally, she raises a "controversy" that is no longer a controversy among reputable scholars: Who were the Egyptians? Most scholars accept a simple answer: They were Africans. The question of whether or not they were black was initially raised by Eurocentric scholars in the nineteenth century seeking to explain the testimony of the ancient Greeks, particularly Herodotus and Diodorus Siculus, who said that Egyptians were "Black with woolly hair." White hegemonic studies that sought to maintain the false notion of white racial supremacy during the nineteenth century fabricated the idea of a European or an Asian Egyptian to deny Africa its classical past and to continue the Aryan myth. It is shocking to see Professor Ravitch raise this issue in the 1990s. It is neither a controversial issue nor should it be to those familiar with the evidence.

The debate over the curriculum is really over a vision of the future of the United States. Keepers of the status quo, such as Professor Ravitch, want to maintain a "white framework" for multiculturalism because they have no faith in cultural pluralism without hierarchy. A common culture does not exist, but this nation is on the path toward it. Granting all the difficulties we face in attaining this common culture, we are more likely to reach it when we allow the full participation of all ethnic groups in a quest for a usable curriculum. In the end, we will find that such a curriculum, like inspiration, will not come from this or that individual model but from integrity and accuracy.

# Cultural Pluralism

## DIANE RAVITCH

In responding to Professor Asante's critique of my article, "Multiculturalism: E Pluribus Plures," I had continually to reread what I had written, because I did not recognize my article from his description. His repeated allegations of racism and "neo-Aryanism" are not supported by quotations from the text, because nothing in my article validates his outrageous charges either directly or by inference. His statements associating my views with those who opposed the education of black children after the Civil War and with white South Africans are simply mud-slinging. He acknowledges in passing that my view of multiculturalism is shared by some black educators, but this anomaly does not cause him to pause in his scurrilous allegations of racism.

In the article, I described the major changes that have occurred in the school curriculum over the past generation. I stated that the teaching of American history had long ignored the historical experiences of minority groups and women, and that recent scholarship had made it possible, indeed necessary, to forge historical narratives that *accurately* represent the diverse nature of our society. The resulting effort to weave together the different strands of our historical experience, I argued, provides a more *accurate* portrait of the American people than the flawed historical account that it replaced. Children in school now learn, I wrote, "that cultural pluralism is one of the norms of a free society; that differences among groups are a national resource rather than a problem to be solved. Indeed, the unique feature of the United States is that its common culture has been formed by the interaction of its *subsidiary* cultures. It is a culture that has been influenced over time by immigrants, American Indians, Africans (slave and free) and by their descendants. American music, art, literature, language, food, clothing, sports, holidays, and customs all show the effects of the commingling of diverse cultures in one nation. Paradoxical though it may seem, the United States has a common culture that is multicultural."

I then went on to argue that demands for diversification of the curriculum had in some instances been pressed to the extremes of ethnocentrism; that some educators want not a portrait of the nation that shows how different groups have shaped our history, but immersion of children in the ancestral exploits of their own race or ethnic group. In trying to explain the bifurcation of the multicultural movement, I struggled to find the right nomenclature for the two competing strains of thought, and I used the terms *pluralistic* and *particularistic*. Professor Asante is right that I should not have called one of them "pluralistic multiculturalism" and the other "particularistic multiculturalism." While pluralism *is* multicultural, particularism is not. Pluralism and particularism are opposite in spirit and method. The demands for ethnocentrism associated with the Afrocentric movement should not be seen as an extreme form of multiculturalism, but as a *rejection* of multiculturalism. Afrocentrism and other kinds of ethnocentrism might better be described as racial fundamentalism. What has confused the matter is the fact that Afrocentrists present their program in public forums as "multicultural," in order to shield from public view their assertions of racial superiority and racial purity, which promote not the racial understanding that our society so desperately needs, but racial antagonism.

Professor Asante and others in the Afrocentric movement like Leonard Jeffries, Jr., Wade Nobles, and Asa Hilliard are inconsistent about whether Afrocentrism is for descendants of Africans only, or for everyone. Their literature sometimes claims that everyone—not only blacks—must learn that all the achievements of

From Molefi Kete Asante and Diane Ravitch, "Multiculturalism: An Exchange," THE AMERICAN SCHOLAR (Spring 1991). Reprinted with permission.

civilization originated in Africa; but at other times, Afrocentrists appear to endorse the idea that each racial group should study its own peculiar history (which I call "*multiple-centrisms*"). The former version of Afrocentrism veers toward racism, with its specious claims about the superiority of those whose skin is darkened by melanin and its attacks on whites as the "ice people." The latter, the "multiple-centrisms" approach, is in its way even more dangerous, because it is insidious. The "multiple-centrisms" position is superficially appealing, because on the surface it gives something to everyone: African Americans may be Afrocentric, Asian Americans may be Asiacentric, Native Americans may be Native Americentric, and Latinos may be Latino-centric, while those who are of European descent must be taught to feel guilt and shame for the alleged misdeeds of their ancestors. This "multiple-centrisms" model is now a hot educational trend, emanating from Portland, Oregon, where the local office of multicultural education has prepared Afrocentric curricular materials and plans to develop similar materials for Asian Americans, Latino Americans, Native Americans, and Pacific Islanders. This was also the organizing principle of Commissioner Thomas Sobol's "task force on minorities" in New York State, whose misnamed "Curriculum of Inclusion" called not for inclusion of minority cultures into a pluralistic mainstream but for "multiple-centrisms."

The "multiple-centrisms" approach is deeply flawed. It confuses race with culture, as though everyone with the same skin color has the same culture and history. It ignores the fact that within every major racial group, there are many different cultural groups, and within each major racial group, there exist serious ethnic and cultural tensions. Furthermore, the "multiple-centrisms" approach denies the *synchretistic* nature of all cultures and civilizations that mingle, and the multiple ways in which they change one another. Neither world history nor American history is the story of five racial groups; such a concept leads to false history and to racial stereotyping. This gross oversimplification of history and culture could be taken seriously only in a society where educators are themselves either intimidated or uneducated.

Professor Asante relentlessly argues against positions that I did not take and attributes to me things that I did not write. For example, Professor Asante quotes Herbert London of New York University to the effect that there is "not enough time in the school year" to teach black history and proceeds to say that I "use the same argument." He does not quote me because he cannot find support for his statement in my article. In fact, I do believe in the importance of teaching black history, drawing on the work of such respected scholars of African American history as John Hope Franklin, Eric Foner, Eugene Genovese, Gary Nash, Leon Litwack, Winthrop Jordan, and Nathan Huggins. It is not possible to teach the history of the United States accurately without teaching black history.

Professor Asante willfully misconstrues a reference that I made to "mainstream Americans." The context was as follows: I wrote about how American history textbooks had for generations ignored race, ethnicity, and religion, and how "the main narrative paid little attention to minority groups and women. With the ethnic revival of the 1960s, this approach to the teaching of history came under fire, because the history of national leaders—virtually all of whom were white, Anglo-Saxon, and male—ignored the place in American history of those who were none of the above. The traditional history of elites had been complemented by an assimilationist view of American society, which presumed that everyone in the American melting pot would eventually lose or abandon those ethnic characteristics that distinguished them from mainstream Americans. The ethnic revival demonstrated that many groups did not want to be assimilated or melted." Professor Asante distorts this to claim that I felt "obliged to make a case for 'mainstream Americans.' " I nowhere made a case for the mainstream, nor did I describe who was included or excluded in this putative "mainstream." I wrote: "The pluralist approach to multiculturalism promotes a broader interpretation of the common American culture and seeks due recognition for the ways that the nation's many racial, ethnic, and cultural groups have transformed the national culture. The pluralists say, in effect, 'American culture belongs to us, all of us; the U.S. is us, and we remake it in every generation.' " By this description, Spike Lee and Aretha Franklin are very much part of the common culture and the American mainstream. So are Duke Ellington, Count Basie, Bill Cosby, Eddie Murphy, Oprah Winfrey, William Raspberry, Carl Lewis, Marion Barry, Malcolm X, Jackie Robinson, Leontyne Price, Langston Hughes, James Weldon Johnson, Countee Cullen, Alice Walker, Martin Luther King, Jr., Frederick Douglass, Jesse Jackson, Henry Gates, Derrick Bell, Jr., and Kenneth B. Clark. As for publishing in "mainstream" journals, Professor Asante misunderstands the dean. She (or he) does not mean that one must publish in a *white* journal; she means that one gains credibility in the academic world by publishing in a journal that has clear standards of scholarship, where false charges of racism, character assassination, and out-of-context quotations are not permissible.

Professor Asante asserts that the ethnocentric curriculum does not claim to raise the self-esteem of students of the same racial or ethnic group. This is not correct. Professor Wade Nobles, whom he cites, runs a state-funded program in California called the HAWK Federation Youth Development and Training Program which aims to immerse young black males in African and African American culture; its purpose, according to the program's brochure, is to address "simultaneously the problems of substance abuse prevention [*sic*], gang violence, academic failure and low aspirations and poor self-esteem." The New York State task force report, "A Curriculum of Inclusion," whose chief consultant was Professor Leonard Jeffries, Jr., repeatedly asserts the relationship between the curriculum and the self-esteem of students. The report claims that a rewriting of the curriculum will promote "higher self-esteem and self-respect" among children from racial minorities "while children from European cultures will have a less arrogant perspective of being part of the group that has 'done it all.' "

After stating that the leaders of the Afrocentric movement do not rest their case on building self-esteem, but rather on truth, Professor Asante then claims that Korean students do well in mathematics because "they are taught to honor and respect the ancestral mathematicians. This is true for Indians, Chinese, and Japanese." Here is the full-blown ethnocentric premise: You can do well if you are taught that your ancestors did it before you. Professor Asante offers no evidence for his statements about Asian children, because none exists. According to Professor Harold Stevenson of the University of Michigan, who has conducted extensive cross-cultural studies of mathematics education in the United States, Japan, and China, children in Japan and China do not study "the ancestral mathematicians." They study mathematics; they learn to solve problems.

Of course, everyone needs to know that they, and people like them, are respected as equals in the society they live in. But to assume that self-esteem is built on reverence for one's ancestors is highly questionable. If this were true, the highest academic achievement in the Western world would be recorded by children of Greek and Italian ancestry, since they are the descendants of ancient Greece and Rome; but this is not the case either in the United States or in international assessments. In fact, according to a recent article in the *New York Times,* Italian-American students—the lineal descendants of Cicero and Julius Caesar—have the lowest achievement and the highest dropout rate of any white ethnic group in the New York City schools.

Nor is it clear that self-esteem (in the sense of feeling good about yourself) is a reliable indicator of academic achievement. In the most recent international assessment of mathematics, Korean children had the highest achievement and American children had the lowest achievement. When the students were asked whether they were good in mathematics, the Koreans had the lowest score, and the Americans had the highest score. In other words, the Americans had the highest self-esteem and the lowest achievement; the Koreans had the lowest self-esteem and the highest achievement. Why did Korean students fare so well? Consider the research report that accompanied the assessment results: "Korea's success can be partially attributed to the nation's and parents' strong interest in education, reflected in a 220-day school year. While there is virtually no adult illiteracy in the country, only 13 percent of Korea's parents have completed some post-secondary education. They nonetheless see education as the hope for their children and grandchildren. Everyone recognizes that Korea's job market is very demanding and that the scientific and technological areas carry high prestige." Another contributing factor to Korean success is a national curriculum that is two-to-three years more advanced than the mathematics that American children study. Presumably, what Korean children learn is not that they are the greatest, but that those who care about them expect them to work hard and to study, and that if they do, they will succeed.

Professor Asante's appeal to the instructional power of ethnocentrism ignores the fact that Asian children in the United States outperform children of all other racial and ethnic groups in mathematics; the SAT mathematics scores of Asian students are far above those of other groups. Asian American children study mathematics in the same classrooms, using the same textbooks as their classmates; they do not study their "ancestral mathematicians." But, according to numerous studies, Asian children do more homework, take school more seriously, and study harder than children of other groups. The enormous success of Asian American students in American schools and universities suggests that their hard work pays off in academic achievement.

One of Professor Asante's most remarkable statements is: "Few whites have ever examined their culture critically." As I survey my own bookshelf, I see the works of scores of critics of American culture, of European culture, and of white racism. I see books by John Dewey, Gunnar Myrdal, and Karl Marx, among many others; I see the works of feminists, liberals, conservatives, radicals, Marxists, and other critics. Professor Asante is under the misapprehension that everything written about Europe or the United States by white scholars is celebratory, perhaps because he believes that every writer is irredeemably ethnocentric.

The purpose of historical study is not to glorify one's ancestors, nor anyone else's ancestors, but to understand what happened in the past and to see events in all their complexity. The fascination of historical study is that what we know about the past changes as scholars present new interpretations supported by evidence. The problem with the ethnocentric approach is that it proposes to teach children the greatness of their ancestors, based on claims that have not been validated by reputable scholars. So, in the Afrocentric curriculum, children are taught that the ancient Egyptians were responsible for the origins of mathematics, science, philosophy, religion, art, architecture, and medicine. No other civilization made any noteworthy contribution to any field, though all learned at the feet of the ancient Egyptians. The ancient Egyptians are shown as the most perfect civilization in all history. They did not enslave the Hebrews; indeed, unlike other ancient civilizations, they held no slaves at all. They were unrelated to today's Arab population, which allegedly did not arrive in Egypt until the seventh or eighth century. Such assertions ought to be reviewed by qualified, reputable scholars before they are taught in compulsory public schools. Nor is the relationship of African American children to the ancient Egyptians altogether clear, since the Africans who were brought in chains to the Western hemisphere were not from Egypt, but from West Africa.

The issue here is not the color of the ancient Egyptians; nor is it a matter of debate that Egypt is on the African continent or that it was a great civilization. What does matter is the claim that a single ancient civilization was responsible for every significant advance in the history of humankind. No civilization can claim credit for every idea, discovery, and forward movement in the history of humankind. Every great civilization grows by exchanging ideas, art, and technology with other civilizations.

Professor Asante is generously willing to permit "Eurocentrism" to survive "so long as it does not parade as universal." But there are elements in every civilization that have universal resonance, and every serious study of world history demonstrates the movement of ideas, art, and technology across national boundaries and across oceans and continents. Those ideas, those artistic achievements, and those technological advances that are most successful do become truly universal. Aspects of American popular culture, some amalgam of jeans, Coca-Cola, jazz and rock, has become part of the universal culture, as mediated by television and Hollywood. It is not only the West that has produced ideas, art, and technology that are universal; the educated person learns about universal features in all great civilizations. Picasso and other great modern artists freely acknowledged their debt to African art. Whether one is in Tokyo, Paris, Buenos Aires, New York, or any other great cosmopolitan center, the multiple influences of Europe, Asia, Africa, the United States, and Latin America are everywhere apparent.

This is why, for example, in California, the recently adopted history curriculum for the state requires all children to study three years of world history. All children will learn about the art, ideas, religions, and culture of the world's great civilizations. For the first time in American history, American public school children will study not only ancient Greece and Rome, but also the African kingdoms of Mali and Ghana, the Aztecs, Mayans, and Incas, and the ancient civilizations of China and India.

But they also study those elements of the Western democratic ideology that have become universal over time and that provide a standard for human rights activists on every continent today. This is not just a political system based on the consent of the governed (a revolutionary concept in world history), but a philosophy that promotes the ideas of individualism, choice, personal responsibility, the pursuit of happiness, and belief in progress. In the spring of 1989, Chinese students in Tiananmen Square carried signs that quoted Patrick Henry and Thomas Jefferson. In the fall of 1989, Czechoslovakian students sang "We shall overcome" and quoted Martin Luther King, Jr. In the fall of 1990, Gibson Kamau Kuria, a Kenyan human rights lawyer and dissident, went into exile in the United States. Kamau Kuria resisted the undemocratic actions of the Kenyan government and appealed to the democratic standards contained in the Universal Declaration of Human Rights.

Some of Professor Asante's complaints about Eurocentrism in the United States are built upon legitimate grievances against the racism that excluded knowledge of black history and achievements from the curriculum of schools and universities for most of our nation's history. I, too, would banish the Eurocentrism found in the textbooks of earlier generations, because their monocultural perspective led to wild inaccuracies and pervasive bias. If, however, Asante's scorn for Eurocentrism is a reflexive aversion to everything European or white, then his own view leads to wild inaccuracies and pervasive bias. Europe has a unique place in the history of the United States for a variety of reasons. Europe is significant for Americans because our governmental institutions were created by men of British descent who had been educated in the ideas of the European Enlightenment; they argued their ideas extensively in print, so the sources of their beliefs are not a secret. Europe is important, too, because the language that most Americans speak is English, and throughout American history, there have been close cultural, commercial, and political ties with European nations. And, not least, Europe is important to America as the source of seminal political ideas, including democracy, socialism, capitalism, and Marxism.

Europe, of course, is not the whole story, not of the United States and not of the world. We Americans—coming as we do from every part of the globe—have been significantly influenced, and continue to be influenced, by people who do not trace their origins to Europe. Our openness to ideas and people from all over the world makes our society dynamic. What is most exciting about American culture is that it is a blending of elements of Europe, Africa, Latin America, and Asia. Whether or not we have a melting pot, we do have a cultural mosaic or at the very least a multitextured tapestry of cultures. Whatever our differences, we are all Americans.

Behind this exchange between Professor Asante and me is a disagreement about the meaning of truth and how it is ascertained. The Afrocentrists alternately say that they want to teach the Truth, the lost, stolen, or hidden truths about the origins of all things; or they say that "truth" is defined by who is in power. Take your choice: either there is absolute Truth or all "truth" is a function of power. I make a different choice. I reject the absolute truths of the fundamentalists, and I reject the relativistic idea that truth depends on power alone. I claim that what we know must be constantly tested, challenged, and reexamined, and that decisions about knowledge must be based on evidence and subject to revision. Reason and intelligence, not skin color and emotion, must be the ultimate arbiters of disputes over fact.

Professor Asante suggests that we disagree about our vision of the future of the United States. He is right. I fear that Afrocentrism intends to replace the discredited white supremacy of the past with an equally disreputable theory of African supremacy. The theory of white supremacy was wrong and socially disastrous; so is the theory of black supremacy. I fear that the theory of "multiple -centrisms" will promote social fragmentation and ethnocentrism, rather than racial understanding and amity. I think we will all lose if we jettison the notion of the common good and learn to identify only with those people who look just like ourselves. The ethnocentrists believe that children should learn to "think with their blood," as the saying goes. This is the way to unending racial antagonism, as well as disintegration of the sense of mutuality on which social progress depends.

# The Return to the Melting Pot

ARTHUR SCHLESINGER, JR.

"What then is the American, this new man?" a French immigrant asked two centuries ago. Hector St. John de Crevecoeur gave the classic answer to his own question. "He is an American, who, leaving behind him all his ancient prejudices and manners, receives new ones from the new mode of life he has embraced, the new government he obeys, and the new rank he holds. . . . Here individuals of all nations are melted into a new race of man."

The conception of America as a transforming nation, banishing old identities and creating a new one, prevailed through most of American history. It was famously reformulated by Israel Zangwill, an English writer of Russian Jewish origin, when he called America "God's crucible, the great melting pot where all the faces of Europe are melting and re-forming." Most people who came to America expected to become Americans. They wanted to escape a horrid past and to embrace a hopeful future. Their goals were deliverance and assimilation.

Thus Crevecoeur wrote his "Letters from an American Farmer" in his acquired English, not in his native French. Thus immigrants reared in other tongues urged their children to learn English as speedily as possible. German immigrants tried for a moment to gain status for their language, but the effort got nowhere. The dominant culture was Anglo-Saxon and, with modification and enrichment, remained Anglo-Saxon.

## REPUDIATION OF THE MELTING POT

The melting pot was one of those metaphors that turned out only to be partly true, and recent years have seen an astonishing repudiation of the whole conception. Many Americans today righteously reject the historic goal of "a new race of man." The contemporary ideal is not assimilation but ethnicity. The escape from origins has given way to the search for "roots." "Ancient prejudices and manners"—the old-time religion, the old-time diet—have made a surprising comeback.

These developments portend a new turn in American life. Instead of a transformative nation with a new and distinctive identity, America increasingly sees itself as preservative of old identities. We used to say e pluribus unum. Now we glorify pluribus and belittle unum. The melting pot yields to the Tower of Babel.

The new turn has had marked impact on the universities. Very little agitates academia more these days than the demands of passionate minorities for revision of the curriculum: in history, the denunciation of Western civilization courses as cultural imperialism; in literature, the denunciation of the "canon," the list of essential books, as an instrumentality of the existing power structure.

A recent report by the New York State Commissioner of Education's task force on "Minorities: Equity and Excellence" luridly describes "African Americans, Asian Americans, Puerto Ricans/Latinos and Native Americans" as "victims of an intellectual and educational oppression." The "systematic bias toward European culture and its derivatives," the report claims, has "a terribly damaging effect on the psyche of young people of African, Asian, Latino and Native American descent"— a doubtful assertion for which no proof is vouch safed.

Of course teachers of history and literature should give due recognition to women, black Americans, Indians, Hispanics and other groups who were subordinated and ignored in the high noon of male Anglo-Saxon dominance. In recent years they have begun belatedly to do so. But the *cult of ethnicity*, pressed too far, exacts costs— as, for example, the current pressure to teach history and literature not as intellectual challenges but as psychological therapy.

There is nothing new, of course, about the yearnings of excluded groups for affirmations of their own historical and cultural dignity. When Irish-Americans were thought beyond the pale, their spokesmen responded much as spokesmen for blacks, Hispanics and others respond today. Professor John V. Kelleher, for many years Harvard's distinguished Irish scholar, once recalled his first exposure to Irish-American history—"turgid little essays on the fact that the Continental Army was 76% Irish, or that many of George Washington's closest friends were nuns and priests, or that Lincoln got the major ideas for the Second Inaugural Address from the Hon. Francis P. Mageghegan of Alpaca, New York, a pioneer manufacturer of cast-iron rosary beads." John Kelleher called this "the there's-always-an-Irishman-at-the-bottom-of-it-doing-the-real-work approach to American history."

Fortunately most Irish-Americans disregarded their spokesmen and absorbed the American tradition. About 1930, Kelleher said, those "turgid little essays began to vanish from Irish-American papers." He added, "I wonder whose is the major component in the Continental Army these days?" The answer, one fears, is getting to be black, Jews and Hispanics.

There is often artificiality about the attempts to use history to minister to psychological needs. When I encounter black insistence on inserting Africa into mainstream curricula, I recall the 1956 presidential campaign. Adlai Stevenson, for whom I was working, had a weak record on civil rights in America but was a champion of African nationalism. I suggested to a group of sympathetic black leaders that maybe if Stevenson talked to black audiences about Africa, he could make up for his deficiencies on civil rights. My friends laughed and said that American blacks couldn't care less about Africa. That is no longer the case; but one can't escape the feeling that present emotions are more manufactured than organic.

Let us by all means teach women's history, black history, Hispanic history. But let us teach them *as history,* not as a means *of promoting group self-esteem.* I don't often agree with Gore Vidal, but I liked his remark the other day: "What I hate is good citizenship history. That has wrecked every history book. Now we're getting 'The Hispanics are warm and joyous and have brought such wonder into our lives,' you know, and before them the Jews, and before them the blacks. And the women. I mean, cut it out!"

Novelists, moralists, politicians, fabulators can go beyond the historical evidence to tell inspiring stories. But historians are custodians of professional standards. Their objective is critical analysis, accuracy and objectivity, not making people feel better about themselves.

Heaven knows how dismally historians fall short of their ideals; how sadly our interpretations are dominated and distorted by unconscious preconceptions; how obsessions of race and nation blind us to our own bias. All historians may in one way or another mythologize history. But the answer to bad history is not "good citizenship history"—more bad history written from a different viewpoint. The answer to bad history is better history.

The ideological assault in English departments on the "canon" as an instrument of political oppression implies the existence of a monolithic body of work designed to enforce the "hegemony" of a class or race or sex. In fact, most great literature and much good history are deeply subversive in their impact on orthodoxies. Consider the American canon: Emerson, Whitman, Melville, Hawthorne, Thoreau, Mark Twain, Henry Adams, William and Henry James, Holmes, Dreiser, Faulkner. Lackeys of the ruling class? Agents of American imperialism?

Let us by all means learn about other continents and other cultures. But, lamentable as some may think it, we inherit an American experience, as America inherits a European experience. To deny the essentially European origins of American culture is to falsify history.

We should take pride in our distinctive inheritance as other nations take pride in their distinctive inheritances. Certainly there is no need for Western civilization, the source of the ideas of individual freedom and political democracy to which most of the world now aspires, to apologize to cultures based on despotism, superstition, tribalism and fanaticism. Let us abjure what Bertrand Russell called the fallacy of "the superior virtue of the oppressed."

Of course we must teach the Western democratic tradition in its true proportions—not as a fixed, final and complacent orthodoxy, intolerant of deviation and dissent, but as an ever-evolving creed fulfilling its ideals through debate, self-criticism, protest, disrespect and irreverence, a tradition in which all groups have rights of heterodoxy and opportunities for self-assertion. It is a tradition that has empowered people of all nations and races. Little can have a more "terribly damaging effect on the psyche" than for educators to tell young blacks and Hispanics and Asians that it is not for them.

## ONE STEP AT A TIME

Belief in one's own culture does not mean disdain for other cultures. But one step at a time: No culture can hope to ingest other cultures all at once, certainly not before it ingests its own. After we have mastered our own culture, we can explore the world.

If we repudiate the quite marvelous inheritance that history has bestowed on us, we invite the fragmentation of our own culture into a quarrelsome spatter of enclaves, ghettos and tribes. The bonds of cohesion in our society are sufficiently fragile, or so it seems to me, that it makes no sense to strain them by encouraging and exalting cultural and linguistic apartheid. The rejection of the melting pot points the republic in the direction of incoherence and chaos.

In the 21st century, if present trends hold, non-whites in the U.S. will begin to outnumber whites. This will bring inevitable changes in the national ethos but not, one must hope, at the expense of national cohesion. Let the new Americans forswear the cult of ghettoization and agree with Crevecoeur, as with most immigrants in the two centuries since, that in America "individuals of all nations are melted into a new race of man."

# At the End of the Century:
# The "Culture Wars" in the U.S.

RONALD TAKAKI

As we approach the twenty-first century, we are offered two meditations on the meaning of this transition to what might be either a new order or new chaos in the world. What we are witnessing, claims Francis Fukuyama, is the "end of history." Liberal democracy, he trumpets, remains "the only coherent" political ideology. Capitalism with its "free market" has succeeded in producing new levels of material prosperity in the industrially developed countries and also many Third World countries. Traditional identities of tribe and ethnicity are being replaced by rational forms of social organization based on efficiency and natural rights. John Lukacs is not so sanguine, however. "The twentieth century is now over," he observes. "It was a short century. It lasted seventy-five years—from 1914 to 1989." Its end is being accompanied by explosions of "tribalisms" throughout the world. Both Fukuyama and Lukacs compel us to examine the United States at the conclusion of the century.

As Americans experience the end of the twentieth century, many of them have been anxiously wondering about the future. The sound and fury of the 1992 Los Angeles conflagration over the Rodney King issue highlighted the reality of race and its multiracial dimensions—the presence not only of African Americans but also Hispanics and Asian Americans. Old and traditional dichotomies such as whites versus blacks now seem dated; race relations theories such as assimilationism and internal colonialism now seem punctured. What seems to be left are pained and confused observations. Is Los Angeles, many pundits and politicians worry, prologue for America?

Ironically, this crisis is occurring at the very moment of what Fukuyama celebrates as the triumph of liberal democracy and capitalism led by the United States. As the Cold War concluded, Americans found the age of their nation's global economic ascendancy coming to an end. Measured against world production, the U.S. economy was in relative decline. The trade deficit ballooned, and the U.S. was transformed from the world's largest creditor to its largest debtor country. As a "great power," according to historian Paul Kennedy, the United States had begun to "fall." Complex and multidimensional, the current crisis represents what Lukacs terms the end of the "American Century."

Within the context of these racial tensions and economic problems have emerged the "culture wars." More than ever before, as whites approach the time when they will become a minority, many of them are perplexed about America's national identity and future as one people. Susan Falludi has brilliantly written about the backlash against women. She points out that there has been underway an aggressive campaign against feminism. Seeking to return women to the home and family, the intellectuals and leaders of this backlash have been asking: What does it mean to be a man?

A parallel backlash aimed at people of color has also been underway: What does it mean to be white? This was the question Pat Buchanan was actually addressing when he urged his fellow Americans at the 1992 Republican Convention to take back "our culture," "our cities," "our country." For Americans of color watching Buchanan on television, "we" did not include them.

Buchanan's speech shocked many viewers, but he was only bringing into the political arena the "culture wars" already erupting on many college campuses. The movement for cultural pluralism has been exposing racism and challenging hierarchical class structures. No wonder conservative foundations have been financing projects to promote their own political agenda on campuses across the country, and the National Association of Scholars has been attacking the movement for cultural pluralism by smearing it with the brush called "political correctness." Under the banner of intellectual freedom, Eurocentric conservatives have been imposing their own intellectual orthodoxy by denouncing those who disagree with them as "the new barbarians."

Author of *The Closing of the American Mind,* Allan Bloom has emerged as a leader of a conservative backlash against cultural diversity. In his view, students entering the university are "uncivilized," and the faculty have the responsibility to "civilize" them. Bloom claims he knows what their "hungers" are and "what they can digest." Noting the "large black presence" in major universities, he laments the "one failure" in race relations—black students have proven to be "indigestible." They do not "melt as have *all* other groups." The problem, he contends, is that "blacks have become blacks": they have become "ethnic." This separatism has been reinforced by an academic permissiveness that has befouled the curriculum with "Black Studies" along with "Learn Another Culture." The only solution, Bloom insists, is "the good old Great Books approach."

Similarly, E. D. Hirsch worries that America is becoming a "Tower of Babel," and that this multiplicity of cultures is threatening to tear our social fabric. He, too, longs for a more cohesive culture and a more homogeneous America: "If we *had* to make a choice between the *one* and the *many,* most Americans would choose the principle of unity, since we cannot function as a nation without it." The way to correct this fragmentization, Hirsch proposes, is to acculturate "disadvantaged children." What do they need to know? "Only by accumulating shared symbols, and the shared information that symbols represent," Hirsch answers, "can we learn to communicate effectively with one another in our national community." Though he concedes the value of multicultural education, he quickly dismisses it by insisting that it "should not be allowed to supplant or interfere with our schools' responsibility to ensure our children's mastery of American literate culture." In *Cultural Literacy: What Every American Needs to Know,* Hirsch offers a long list of terms that excludes much of the history of minority groups.

Recently, Arthur Schlesinger has joined the backlash against multiculturalism. In *The Disuniting of America,* this old-time liberal historian denounces what he calls "the cult of ethnicity"—the shift from assimilation to group identity, from integration to separatism. The issue at stake, he argues, is the teaching of "*bad* history under whatever ethnic banner." After acknowledging that American history has long been written in the "interests of white Anglo-Saxon Protestant males," he describes the enslavement of Africans, the seizure of Indian lands, and the exploitation of Chinese railroad workers. But his discussion on racial oppression is perfunctory and parsimonious, and he devotes most of his attention to a defense of traditional history. "Anglocentric domination of schoolbooks was based in part on unassailable facts," Schlesinger declares. "For better or worse, American history has been shaped more than anything else by British tradition and culture." Like Bloom, Schlesinger utilizes the metaphor of eating. "To deny the essentially European origins of American culture is to falsify history," he explains. "Belief in one's own culture does not require disdain for other cultures. But one step at a time: no culture can hope to ingest other cultures all at once, certainly not before it ingests its own." Defensively claiming to be an inclusionist historian, Schlesinger presents his own credentials : "As for me, I was for a time a member of the executive council of the *Journal of Negro History.* . . . I have been a lifelong advocate of civil rights."

What happens when people of color define their civil rights in terms of cultural pluralism and group identities? They become targets of Schlesinger's scorn. This "exaggeration" of ethnic differences, he warns, only "drives ever deeper the awful wedges between races," leading to an "endgame" of self-pity and self-ghettoization. The culprits responsible for this divisiveness are the "multicultural zealots," especially the Afrocentrists. Schlesinger castigates them as campus bullies, distorting history and creating myths about the contributions of Africans.

What Schlesinger refuses to admit or is unable to see clearly is how he himself is culpable of historical distortion: his own omissions in *The Age of Jackson* have ignored what James Madison had described then as "the black rose within our bosom" and "the red on our borders." Both groups have been entirely left out of Schlesinger's study: they do not have headings in the index. Moreover, there is no mention of two marker events—the Nat Turner insurrection and Indian Removal, which Andrew Jackson himself would have been surprised to find omitted from a history of his era. Unfortunately, Schlesinger fails to meet even his own standards of scholarship: "The historian's goals are accuracy, analysis, and objectivity in the reconstruction of the past."

Behind Schlesinger's cant against multiculturalism is fear. What will happen to our national ideal of "*e pluribus unum*?" he worries. Will the "center" hold, or will the Melting Pot yield to the Tower of Babel? For answers, he looks abroad. "Today," he observes, "the nationalist fever encircles the globe." Angry and violent "tribalism" is exploding in India, the former Soviet Union, Indonesia, Guyana, and other countries across the world. "The ethnic upsurge in America, far from being unique, partakes of the global fever." Like Bloom, Schlesinger prescribes individualism as the cure. "Most Americans," he argues, "continue to see themselves primarily as individuals and only secondarily and trivially as adherents of a group." The dividing of society into "fixed ethnicities nourishes a culture of victimization and a contagion of inflammable sensitivities." This danger threatens the "brittle bonds of national identity that hold this diverse and fractious society together." The Balkan present, Schlesinger warns, may be America's prologue.

But Schlesinger's very attack indicates that the cultural terrain is being contested. Many Americans of color have been challenging traditional and dominant notions regarding nationality. They have been asking: How should America and Americans be defined? Whose history is it? One focus of their struggle has been education, and they have been demanding a more inclusive, culturally pluralistic curriculum. Institutions of learning have been responding to their pressures. In 1990, the Task Force on Minorities for New York emphasized the importance of a culturally diverse education. "Essentially," the *New York Times* commented, "the issue is how to deal with both dimensions of the nation's motto: 'E pluribus unum'—'Out of many, one.' " Universities from New Hampshire to Berkeley have established American cultural diversity graduation requirements. "Every student needs to know," explained University of Wisconsin's chancellor Donna Shalala, "much more about the origins and history of the particular cultures which, as Americans, we will encounter during our lives." Even the University of Minnesota, located in a state that is 98 percent white, requires its students to take ethnic studies courses. Asked why multiculturalism is so important, Dean Fred Lukermann answered: As a national university, Minnesota has to offer a national curriculum—one that includes all of the peoples of America. He added that after graduation many students move to cities like Chicago and

Los Angeles and thus need to know about racial diversity.

Many writers and intellectuals of color have been in the forefront of this struggle for cultural pluralism. They have been insisting on telling stories about their communities. By writing about the people on Mango Street, Sandra Cisneros explained, "the ghost does not ache so much." The place no longer holds her with "both arms. She sets me free." Indeed, stories may not be as innocent or simple as they seem to be. Native-American novelist Leslie Marmon Silko cautioned:

> I will tell you something about stories . . .
> They aren't just entertainment.
> Don't be fooled.

An understanding of our multicultural selves must spring from critical awareness. "To finally recognize our own invisibility," declares Asian-American activist Mitsuye Yamada, "is to finally be on the path toward visibility." To become visible is for Americans to see themselves and each other in a different mirror of history. As Audre Lorde pointed out,

> It is a waste of time hating a mirror
> or its reflection
> instead of stopping the hand
> that makes glass with distortions.

But, as the twentieth century ends, most Americans still see their past as through a glass darkly. "The whole point of history," observes Arthur C. Danto, "is *not* to know about actions as witnesses might, but as historians do, in connection with later events and as parts of temporal wholes." But historians have not enabled Americans to comprehend their past in terms of the whole. Consequently, Americans are still unable to understand how they, representing an immense diversity of peoples, are connected to a larger narrative of the United States.

While the primary reason for this ignorance remains the hegemony of a Eurocentric culture, the failure also reflects some shortcomings of the cultural pluralists themselves. In their critique of domination, they frequently focus exclusively on culture and hence overlook the material basis of racial inequality. Hence, they do not help different groups pitted against each other understand the economic context of their subordination and exploitation. Furthermore, the analysis of the cultural pluralists is sometimes so abstract and their writings so elusive in language that they render their critical scholarship remote from the very communities they are seeking to help empower. What this body of writings often offers is a debate over scholarly representations of other scholarly representations of the original representations.

Ironically, the challenging of racial hierarchy can sometimes end up serving it. For example, the deconstructing of colonial ideology contains the study of people of color as the "Other." Thus the critique of domination becomes complicit in the "Othering" of racially oppressed groups. Here, again, reference to feminist scholarship can be helpful. Feminist criticism calls attention to the "Tootsie trope"—the failure of a scholarly study to allow its feminist intentions to alter its male-centered focus of analysis. A similar "Orientalist trope" continues to center Western culture by exclusively examining the West and its manufacture of the "Oriental Other." The members of the stereotyped groups remain faceless and voiceless; their subordination is reinforced, albeit inadvertently. Thus, "Orientals" remain "Orientalized."

This very action of representing is freighted with responsibility, for multicultural scholarship, like the traditional body of knowledge it seeks to oppose, has been engaged in meaning-making through representation. The critical issue is not only whose history is to be told but also who should be doing the telling? One problem here is the reality that the scholars in the universities are predominantly *not* members of the oppressed racial groups they are studying and representing. This might account for the continued marginalization of the "Other" as object rather than subject; it also contributes unintentionally to the reproduction of the exclusion of racial diversity within the academy. The "Others" cannot represent themselves; hence, they must be represented.

But regardless of who does the telling, much of what is presented as multicultural scholarship also tends to fragmentize American society by separately studying specific groups such as African Americans or Hispanics. Inter-group relationships become invisible, and the big picture is missing. This decontextualizing only reinforces the bewilderment already separating racially and ethnically diverse Americans from one another. We are left with shards of a shattered mirror of our diversity. The very search for the voices of people has sometimes reinforced this fragmentization by focusing on specific texts of individuals, which are examined in isolation from larger social and economic contexts. All of this shattering only burdens

socially concerned intellectuals in carrying out their task of not only comprehending but also transforming the world.

At a deeper level is a lack of new theoretical work capable of analyzing a multiracial reality. Cultural pluralist scholars continue to operate largely within the river banks of two major theories—the assimilationist theory seeking to explain race relations in terms of the incorporation of minorities into the white mainstream versus the internal colonialist theory contending that peoples of color in the U.S. represent colonized groups. Both paradigms assume the existence of a racial hierarchy in terms of white and black, or white and people of color. But they become woefully inadequate to explain tensions between different groups of color such as the antagonism between African Americans and Korean Americans. Crucial to any effort to address this need for new theory and new multicultural analysis is the re-visioning of history. Scholars need to approach the past from a broad and comparative perspective in order to comprehend the dynamic, dialectical process in which different groups came together from different shores to create a new society in North America.

This need for an understanding of the making and meaning of a multicultural United States is especially crucial at this moment. Contrary to Fukuyama, we have not reached the end of history. In order for democracy to emerge in a country, Fukuyama notes, its citizens must share a strong sense of national unity and accept one another's rights. This made democracy possible in Britain, France, and the United States. Thus democracy is linked to national identity. Actually, in the United States, rights and nationality have not been extended to all groups. Liberal democracy and capitalism must still address the continuing economic and racial inequality in America itself. The American ideal of human rights and dignity still remains for many citizens of color a dream deferred; the material abundance of the "free market" continues to be enjoyed by a privileged group. Fukuyama argues that the problem of racial inequality is not "insoluble on the basis of liberal principles." But his optimism does not resonate reassurance to a society witnessing escalating racial tensions and conflicts. Indeed, Fukuyama's very celebratory insistence that history has ended only shrouds the explosive reality Lukacs describes as tribalism—identities and interests based on ethnicity.